CULTURGRAMS:

The Nations around Us

Developed by the
David M. Kennedy Center
for International Studies

Brigham Young University

Volume II

Africa, Asia, and Oceania

About the Culturgram Series...

This book (Volume II) includes *Culturgrams* for Africa, Asia, and Oceania.

A related volume (Volume I) includes *Culturgrams* for the Americas and Europe.

These bound volumes of *Culturgrams* may be ordered from Garrett Park Press, PO Box 190B, Garrett Park, MD 20896; phone (301) 946–2553, or from Brigham Young University, Kennedy Center Publications, PO Box 24538, Provo, UT 84602; phone (800) 528–6279 or (801) 378–6528. The price is $35.00 per volume for education/nonprofit groups; $52.50 retail for profit-making organizations.

Because the reproduction of the *Culturgrams* in this volume is strictly prohibited, copies should be ordered from the David M. Kennedy Center for International Studies. *Culturgrams* are currently available as a complete set (both bound and loose-leaf), as area and language sets, and individually. To order, contact Kennedy Center Publications at the address above.

Library of Congress Cataloging-in-Publication Data

Culturgrams : the nations around us /
developed by the David M. Kennedy Center for International Studies, Brigham Young University. 2 v. : maps : 28 cm.

ISBN 0-912048-86-7 (set)

Contents: v. 1. The Americas and Europe — v. 2. Africa, Asia, and Oceania.

1. Manners and customs. 2. Intercultural communication. I. David M. Kennedy Center for International Studies.

GT150.C85 1993
390—dc20   93-29643

© 1995 by Brigham Young University. All rights reserved.

David M. Kennedy Center for International Studies,
Grant P. Skabelund, Managing Editor; Susan M. Sims, Editor; Lisa M. Ralph, Associate Editor.

ISBN 0-912048-86-7 (for set)   0-912048-87-5 (for Volume II)

Library of Congress Card 93-29643 (for set)

Contents

Foreword

For years the best known introduction of many Americans to many foreign countries has come by way of the four-page *Culturgrams* prepared and distributed by the David M. Kennedy Center for International Studies at Brigham Young University in Provo, Utah. Many thousands of these simple, straightforward handouts have been distributed to Americans in all levels of our society and by all types of organizations. Certainly more Americans, in my experience, are already familiar with them than know about other similar materials which are on the market.

Culturgrams are particularly useful because they put so much emphasis on the unique values, customs and cultural assumptions of the people they are describing. One can find the population statistics or the square mileage of the country from many other standard sources, but the "people maps" are much more difficult to locate. As far as I am concerned, this is why *Culturgrams* remain at the top of the list in people's minds, and this is what justifies their continuing success as the most widely distributed publications explaining the customs and traditions of the world's peoples.

With a high concern for accuracy and the current validity of the data they contain, the Kennedy Center's publications division keeps the reports up to date and continues to add more countries to their expanding coverage.

Their inclusion, now, in two bound volumes (*Culturgrams: The Nations around Us*, Volumes I and II) that give us access to the complete set, serves a different but complementary function—to place a wealth of information about more than 140 countries in a single repository, so that those who need to have handy access to such data will be able to keep the book within reach of their desk.

I sincerely hope that new editions of *Culturgrams: The Nations around Us* will continue to be forthcoming well into the 21st century.

L. Robert Kohls
Scholar in Residence
Institute for Intercultural Leadership

Introduction

In 1974, President Spencer W. Kimball of the Church of Jesus Christ of Latter-day Saints issued a challenge to Mormons to build more effective bridges of understanding and friendship with people all over the world. Brigham Young University contributed to the effort by inviting people from about 50 countries to share what they thought was the essential information about their country and its people. These interviews laid the foundation for the *Culturgrams*, which were first published by BYU's language and Intercultural Research Center and were transferred in 1981 to the David M. Kennedy Center for International Studies.

There are 143 *Culturgrams* in the 1995–96 edition. Included for the first time in this edition is a glossary for some of the concepts used throughout the *Culturgrams*. Each four-page *Culturgram* introduces the reader to the daily customs and lifestyle of a society, as well as to its political and economic structure. Each text represents the efforts of individuals from all over the world who have had experience living and working in each particular country. Kennedy Center Publications requests and receives input from scholars within each target culture, academics in the United States and Europe, volunteers from such organizations as the Peace Corps and the International Red Cross, expatriate diplomats and business people, educators, and many others.

This approach allows the Center to take advantage of a wide variety of perspectives and professional backgrounds to bring our readers a unique look at daily culture around the globe. It also means that *Culturgrams* contain information that is based as much on opinion as on fact, although a wide variety of perspectives are consulted. *Culturgrams* do not focus on statistical data. Other resources present statistics for each country, but none tell a reader about people on a personal level. Our goal is to bring the people of a culture into the reader's view, thus encouraging understanding and appreciation between people of different nationalities.

Each new *Culturgram* is written by someone who meets certain residence, educational, and professional criteria. Each draft is reviewed by a panel of individuals with similar qualifications, but usually different backgrounds. This panel is asked to correct errors, comment on accuracy, and generally help us know whether the expressed opinions and facts form a fair and broad description of the culture. A *Culturgram* cannot contain everything about a culture or about each ethnic group in a particular country, but it does endeavor to paint a broad picture about life for the majority of people in a country. All project participants are asked to be as fair and current as possible. Once a new *Culturgram* has been published (after six to twelve months of work), it is reviewed annually by our professional staff of editors trained in international studies. When necessary, information is updated and the text revised to keep abreast of current events. This helps ensure that each *Culturgram* text is an up-to-date source of information about people's lives, their society, and their culture.

The list of contributors to and supporters of *Culturgrams* is long and irretrievable. We thank the hundreds of individuals who have contributed their valuable expertise to make the *Culturgrams* a beneficial intercultural learning tool. We also acknowledge the support of the current university leadership.

Culturgrams meet the needs of a wide variety of individuals. Students, teachers, resource librarians, international student advisors, business travelers, health care workers, government and military personnel, tourists, missionaries, international development workers, and many others benefit from *Culturgrams*. With your purchase of *Culturgrams*, you join the millions who have come to count on the accurate, up-to-date information that continues to build bridges of understanding between Earth's peoples. Enjoy.

Grant Skabelund
Managing Editor

CULTURGRAM ™ '96

Aa Glossary Zz

The following is a list of some common concepts found in Culturgrams. *These are not definitions; they are explanations of how the terms are used in the series, what significance they hold in regard to understanding the culture, and often how they are calculated. For explanations of international organizations (United Nations, European Union, and so forth), please refer to reference sources in a library.*

Cash Crops

A cash crop is an agricultural product that is grown for sale, not for the farmer's consumption. It is often a crop (coffee, cotton, sugarcane, rice and other grains) that requires manufacturing or processing. It may also be a crop (oranges, potatoes, bananas) that can be consumed upon harvest but is cultivated primarily to be sold. Cash crops are most effectively produced on a large scale, but they can be grown on small plots of land. When grown on a large scale, the crops are more likely to be exported than consumed locally, although small growers in developing countries may sell to a local buyer who then sells larger quantities domestically and abroad. The economies of many countries depend heavily on the sale of cash crops.

Diversified Economy

An economy is considered diversified if its stability relies on a variety of industries rather than one or two commodities. For example, oil-rich countries that rely almost solely on the petroleum industry for their income are vulnerable to changes in the price of oil on the world market. When the price drops significantly, the countries are suddenly unable to pay debts or finance social development projects. The same is true for countries that rely on agricultural products such as coffee or on minerals such as copper for their income. Countries whose economies are based not only on agricultural products but also on manufacturing, services, technology, and so forth are better able to withstand global price changes. Thus, the more diversified a country's economic base, the better.

What is a *Culturgram*?

Each four-page *Culturgram* is designed to introduce readers to the daily customs and lifestyles, as well as the political and economic structure, of a nation. *Culturgrams* represent the contributions of individuals worldwide who have experienced living and working in each country. BYU's David M. Kennedy Center for International Studies requests and receives input from scholars within each target culture, U.S. and European academics, volunteers from organizations such as the Peace Corps and International Red Cross, expatriate diplomats and businesspeople, educators, and others.

This approach allows us to draw from a wide variety of perspectives and professional backgrounds in bringing our readers a unique look at culture. It also means that *Culturgrams* contain information based as much on opinion as on fact; however, we consult a wide variety of perspectives before publishing any information. A *Culturgram* cannot describe every ethnic group or cultural aspect of a given country, but it does paint a broad picture about life for the majority of people there.

Culturgrams do not focus on statistical data. A number of other fine resources present national statistics, but none really informs readers about people on a personal level. Our goal is to give readers an accurate view of a culture in order to encourage understanding and appreciation between people of different nationalities.

Each new *Culturgram* is written by someone who meets certain residency, educational, and professional criteria.

Drafts are reviewed by panels of individuals with similar qualifications but differing backgrounds. Panels are asked to correct errors and generally comment on whether the expressed opinions and facts form a broad, fair description of the culture. All project participants are asked to be as fair and up-to-date as possible.

Once a new *Culturgram* has been published (after six to twelve months of work), it is reviewed periodically by qualified reviewers and annually by our professional staff of editors trained in international relations. When necessary, the editors revise and update the text to reflect current events. This helps ensure that each text is a timely source of information about people's lives, their society, and the cultural environment in which they live.

Extended Family

As used in *Culturgrams*, this term refers to a family unit that includes parents, their children, and one or more relatives. The relatives most often include grandparents and sometimes cousins, aunts, and uncles. Some extended family units are organized with older parents, their married sons (occasionally daughters) and their families, and all unmarried sons and daughters. Extended families may share a single household or live in a compound that includes living structures for each nuclear unit, in which case families share work and other responsibilities. When a *Culturgram* states the extended family is the basic unit of society, it means the average household is comprised of the extended family.

Foreign Language Phrases

Most *Culturgrams* contain phrases and words in the target culture's official or common language. In general, a *Culturgram* does not provide a pronunciation guide for these phrases due to limited space. Also, including pronunciation and a translation tends to interrupt the flow of the text. A *Culturgram* is not designed to teach foreign languages. Rather, the phrases contained in a *Culturgram* are there to facilitate the description of how people interact with one another. Their translation often provides insights about the culture, but pronunciation is not necessary to gain that insight. In the few cases where pronunciation hints are provided, they are necessary for English-speakers to properly pronounce a word not otherwise expressed in English. For instance, the country Lesotho is not pronounced as it would seem. Instead of saying "le-SEW-tho," one should say "le-SUE-too."

Free and Compulsory Education

Most countries provide free education to their citizens, meaning a public school system open to all children who fall into certain age groups is operated by the government. It does not necessarily mean there are no costs involved in attending school. Students may be required to wear uniforms (which must be purchased), might live far from the nearest school (and parents must pay for transportation), or may need to supply their own paper, pencils, and other basic items. In addition, having a child in school can cost a rural family one laborer on the family farm. This can become such a burden to poorer families that free education is still not accessible to them.

Compulsory education refers to the fact that the law requires children to attend school for a certain number of years. In many countries this rule is seldom enforced. Therefore, it may reflect the government's target for how long children should remain in school to obtain a basic education, rather than how long they are actually required to attend. Compulsory education usually encompasses six to nine years, and optional schooling usually continues for three or more years.

Gross Domestic Product (GDP) Per Capita

This economic statistic refers to the value of all goods and services produced annually in an economy per person.

Naturally, not every person produces goods and services, but the total is averaged for the entire population. If the term is expressed as "gross national product" (GNP), it is essentially the same statistic except for the addition of income earned abroad, minus the income earned in the country by noncitizens. This is significant when part of the population works in other countries and sends back money to their families. It is also significant for countries that have substantial investments abroad. For most countries, the two statistics, GDP and GNP, are almost interchangeable.

In the past, GDP was calculated in terms of the U.S. dollar after conversion from the local currency at official exchange rates. This caused accuracy problems because of artificially set exchange rates and because a dollar may not buy the same amount of goods in the United States as it does in another country. Social scientists have recently developed the concept of Purchasing Power Parity (PPP), a measurement that tries to account for the inconsistencies of the past. When GDP is figured in terms of PPP, an *international dollar* not affected by exchange rates is used. Likewise, PPP attempts to express the relative ability of a person to purchase goods with the local currency. Therefore, measured with PPP, $500 will buy essentially the same things in the United States as it will in Brazil or Japan. For many countries, PPP data does not yet exist and only estimates are available for others. Most *Culturgrams* use the PPP with GDP, as expressed with the phrase "real gross domestic product." When the word "real" is absent, only the GDP has been calculated. The real GDPs in the *Culturgrams* are usually taken from the *Human Development Report 1994* (New York: Oxford University Press for the United Nations Development Program, 1994). In cases when the real GDP is low (below $1,000, for example), one can assume that people have very little disposable income. But one should also remember that rural families may grow their own food and, therefore, need less disposable income to meet basic needs. In other cases, such a low figure indicates people may indeed be without food, shelter, clothing, or other necessities.

Human Development Index

Originating with the United Nations Development Program, the Human Development Index (HDI) attempts to address the inability of income or GDP indicators to accurately describe living conditions for the average person. For example, if a country has a GDP of $10,000, it may really mean that a few wealthy individuals earn far more than that and most other people earn far less. Also, the statistic does not reflect the value of those dollars in the local economy, and a low income might not necessarily mean a socially poor existence, since governments can often provide, at least initially, a better or more promising life through social programs.

HDI combines different data that, together, more accurately reflect whether the average person enjoys access to basic elements that help one enjoy life. For example, one's *access* to schooling, health care, and purchasing power (income) are all considered for this index, since such access has proven vital to a person's ability to participate fully in the community and take advantage of economic opportunities. People who are sick (and cannot get well), illiterate, or living on limited funds are often locked into an existence that provides little hope for the future. But in countries where health and education are adequately available, people have a greater chance of improving their purchasing power and, ultimately, their lives. *Culturgrams* have adopted HDI as a way to gauge whether the average person has access to the benefits of a modern, prosperous global community.

Income Distribution

This phrase is generally used in connection with the gap between what the poorest people in a country earn and what the richest earn. If income distribution is highly unequal, a small wealthy class generally controls the economy (and often the government) and owns most property. The much larger poor class is often landless, which is significant since the people are probably farmers who must rent property and receive only a small share of the benefits from their own labor. An unequal, but not highly unequal, income distribution often indicates that a middle class is beginning to grow. When the distribution is fairly equal, as is the case in a minority of countries, it is due mostly to a large and prosperous middle class. However, it can also indicate the presence of a broad poor class and absence of a wealthy elite. Generally, having a highly unequal income distribution means the economy is unhealthy, whereas the existence of a strong middle (consumer) class is good for an economy.

Infant Mortality Rate

This statistic is expressed as the number of children per 1,000 live births who die before their first birthday. It is an important indicator for the overall health of a population, since infants who die at this age are usually subject to preventable diseases or birth defects related to the mother's health. Those who die at birth often do so because of a lack of prenatal care and medical attention at birth. People who have access to health care, clean water, nutritious food, and education are more likely to have a low infant mortality rate than people who lack such access. Industrialized countries generally have a low rate (below 10 per 1,000), while developing countries usually have a higher rate (averaging more than 30). The poorest countries may have rates higher than 100.

Life Expectancy

This measurement refers to how long a person can expect to live from birth if mortality patterns remain unchanged. Someone born today may be expected to live 80 years if living in some European countries but only 58 years if living in parts of Africa. However, since mortality patterns do change throughout a person's lifetime, the statistic is really a better reflection of how long an adult who is currently living can expect to live. So a person who is 50 today can expect to live until 80 in some countries or only a few more years in others. Women live longer than men in most countries, and people in industrialized countries live longer than those in developing countries. People in countries with high pollution have lower rates of life expectancy.

Culturgrams usually express this statistic as a range of years, which most often corresponds to an average for women at the longer-living end and men at the shorter-living end. This statistic, like infant mortality, helps the reader understand the overall health of a population and whether the people have access to nutritious food, clean water, health care, and proper sanitation.

Literacy Rate

Most countries and international organizations define literacy in terms of those older than 15 years of age who can read and write. Sometimes that only means they can read and write their names or perform other basic tasks. In a few cases, literacy is defined as having attended school, even if only for a short time. Most educational experts agree that current definitions fall short of actually measuring whether the population is literate, since being able to write one's name does not mean one can read a newspaper or understand a bus schedule or work instructions.

Literacy may also be defined in terms of an official language not spoken on a daily basis by a majority of the population, which can make the definition even more irrelevant. However, since world organizations cannot agree on how to measure literacy, and since collecting such data is difficult, the current definitions remain in force. Researchers try to add to the statistic by also looking at such things as how many years of schooling the average person completes, whether the labor force is skilled or unskilled, and so forth. In *Culturgrams*, we usually list the official literacy rate or an expert estimate, and we often add other information as appropriate.

Nuclear Family

As used in *Culturgrams*, this term refers to a family unit that includes one or two parents and their children. The nuclear family usually lives in a single-family dwelling. When a *Culturgram* states the nuclear family is the basic social unit, it means the average household is composed of a nuclear family.

Population and Population Growth Rate

The population listed for each country in the *Culturgram* series is an estimate for the year previous to publication (i.e., 1994 population for text published in 1995). The estimate is based on the actual population at the last census multiplied by an annual growth rate. The estimate may seem to conflict with other sources, since other sources often only print the population as of the latest census (whenever it may have been taken) or an estimate made in a base year (i.e., 1990). *Culturgram* estimates are in keeping with figures in

U.S. government publications, but they are sometimes modified by information from the government of the target culture. Each population estimate is revised on an annual basis; it is rounded to the nearest 100,000 or 10,000, depending on the size of the population.

The population growth rate is an estimate, rounded to the nearest 10th of a percent, based on the previous year's difference between births and deaths and the net number of migrants leaving or entering the country. The growth rate may change substantially in a single year if there is a large influx of immigrants, a massive emigration, a natural disaster, or an epidemic. Growth rates tend to be low in industrialized countries because families are small, averaging one or two children. Growth rates are generally high in developing countries, especially in areas where subsistence farming is the primary economic activity. These cultures require large families to help farm the land, but they often have a high infant mortality rate; many children are conceived to ensure that enough will survive into adulthood. In small nations, the growth rate may be low due to emigration, as people must go elsewhere to find work.

Staple Food

Staple foods are those foods that supply the majority of the average person's calories and nutrition. A culture's primary staple food is usually starchy, such as cassava (manioc), corn, rice, millet, or wheat. Staple foods also include the meats, fruits, and vegetables eaten in large quantities or on a frequent basis.

Subsistence Farming

Subsistence farming refers to farming as the main source of a family's livelihood. That is, a family will grow its own food, raise its own livestock, build its own home, and often make its own clothing. Members of such a family generally do not earn a wage by working at a job, but they are usually not entirely without a cash income. Family members might sell surplus produce or livestock, or make crafts or other items (blankets, baskets, etc.), in order to buy items they cannot provide for themselves. These usually include such items as sugar, cooking oil, clothing, rice or another staple food, and so forth. Subsistence farmers may also set aside part of their land to grow cash crops in order to earn money. Subsistence farmers generally do not grow an abundance of anything. They often live on small owned or rented plots of land, and they seldom enjoy the luxuries of running water or electricity.

Underemployment

Underemployment refers to the case when workers are not officially unemployed but are not able to either find enough work in their profession or are working in jobs below their skill level. For example, if a country's universities graduate many people in engineering or other professional fields, but the economy is not diversified or well developed, those people may find themselves unemployed, working in jobs that do not take advantage of their skills, or only working part-time in their fields. In the latter case, they may return to farming or local retailing. In too many cases, the most educated people simply emigrate to another country to find work, resulting in what is called a "brain drain."

Government unemployment figures do not usually include underemployment; it must be estimated. However, when unemployment is high (more than 10 percent), one can usually assume that underemployment affects at least as many or more workers. This condition reflects an economy that is not growing, and it can lead to social unrest. High underemployment (more than 40 percent) often leads to political turmoil and violence. Employing and paying people according to their skill level helps secure social stability and encourage economic growth.

Western/Western-style

This term usually refers to the dress and eating customs, culture, and traditions of Western Europe, the United States, and Canada. This culture is often referred to as Western because of its common ancient (primarily Greek and Roman) philosophical, legal, political, and social heritage. The term Western can also refer to cultures that have a Judeo-Christian value system and religious orientation.

Metric Conversions

Celsius	Fahrenheit	Kilometers	Miles	Meters	Inches/Feet
0°	32°	1	.62	1mm	.039"
4°	39°	10	6.2	50mm	1.95"
8°	46°	50	31	100mm	3.9"
12°	54°	100	62	1m	39.37"
16°	61°	250	155	50m	164'
20°	68°	500	311	100m	328'
24°	75°	750	465	500m	1,640'
28°	82°	1,000	621	1,000m	3,280'
32°	90°	2,000	1,242	1,609m	5,280'
36°	97°	3,000	1,860	5,000m	16,400'
40°	104°	5,000	3,100	10,000m	22,960'

A *Culturgram* is a product of native commentary and original, expert analysis. Statistics are estimates and information is presented as a matter of opinion. While the editors strive for accuracy and detail, this document should not be considered strictly factual. It is a general introduction to culture, an initial step in building bridges of understanding between peoples. It may not apply to all peoples of the nation. You should therefore consult other sources for more information.

CULTURGRAM™ '96

Islamic State of
Afghanistan

Boundary representations not necessarily authoritative.

BACKGROUND

Land and Climate

Afghanistan is located in central Asia. With an area of 251,773 square miles (652,090 square kilometers), it is a bit smaller than Texas. It is a landlocked country of rugged mountains, the highest of which reaches 24,550 feet. The most important mountain range is the Hindu Kush, which extends about 600 miles from the far northeast to the southwest, effectively bisecting the country. North of the Hindu Kush, the Turkestan Plains run down to the Amu River on the northern border. After broadening into the Hazarajat central plateau, the mountains disappear into western deserts like the Registan. Afghanistan relies on four major river systems (Amu Darya, Kabul, Helmand, Harī Rūd) for water.

The climate varies according to elevation and location. For instance, Kābul (at 6,000 feet) has cold winters and nice summers; Jalālābād (1,800 feet) has a subtropical climate; and Kandahār (3,500 feet) is mild year-round.

History

Located along the famous Silk Road, Afghanistan has been the "Crossroads of Asia" since ancient times and, as such, has always been subject to invasion. Emperors and conquerors (Greeks, Persians, Central Asians, Indians, and others) throughout history have attempted to control or pacify the region's inhabitants, always finding them fiercely independent and formidable military opponents.

Islam was introduced in the seventh century and flourished in the Ghaznavid Empire (977–1186). Great destruction occurred in the 13th century with the Mongol invasions of Genghis Khan. His Turko-Mongol descendent, Tamerlane, established the Timurid Dynasty (1370–1506), famed for its arts and architecture. The Moghul Dynasty (1526–1707) rose to control eastern Afghanistan and the Indian subcontinent, while the Persian Safavid Dynasty (1501–1732) held western Afghanistan.

Afghanistan's modern roots are in the Durrani Dynasty founded in 1747 by Ahmed Shah Durrani. Members of his Pashtun sub-tribe basically ruled Afghanistan until 1978. During the 19th century, Afghanistan was caught in the "Great Game" between the expansionist Russian Empire in Central Asia and the rival British Empire in India. The British fought two wars in Afghanistan during this period (1838–42 and 1879–80) and retained nominal control over Afghan foreign policy until the Third Anglo-Afghan War produced full independence in 1919. Internal unification had occurred during the rule of the "Iron Amir," Abdur Rahman Khan (1880–1901).

Cold War politics after World War II subjected Afghanistan to U.S. and Soviet competition. Five years after the monarchy was overthrown in 1973, a Soviet-backed internal coup prompted popular rebellion. The Communist government received Soviet aid in the form of an invasion in 1979. The resulting Soviet-Afghan War produced widespread destruction throughout Afghanistan, killed 1.5 million people, and drove over six million refugees into Pakistan and Iran. When Soviet troops withdrew in 1989, civil war continued between the communist government led by President Najibullah and Muslim *mujahideen* (holy warriors) from several political parties. When Najibullah's regime collapsed in April 1992, so did the uneasy alliance between the various parties that had defeated it. Fighting therefore continues between several major armed factions for control of Kābul and other major cities.

PEOPLE

Population

Afghanistan's population is disputed but estimated to be about 17 million. Over 40 percent is younger than age 15. About 80 percent of the people live in rural areas. Kābul is the capital and traditionally the largest city, with perhaps 1.5 million residents before 1992. Fighting has reduced its numbers to fewer than 500,000. Other major cities are Kandahār, Herāt, Mazār-i-Sharīf, and Jalālābād.

Afghanistan has many ethnic groups. The largest is the Pashtun tribal society, which comprises 40 to 45 percent of the population and is divided into several major sub-tribes. Most Pashtuns live in the east and south. Most Tajiks (25 percent) live in the north, Uzbeks (6–9 percent) in the north-center, and the Hazara (9-19 percent) in the center. Smaller numbers of Baluchi, Brahui, Kirgiz, Nuristani, Qizilbash, and Turkmen together comprise 10 to 12 percent of the population. Many refugees who left the country during the 1980s have returned.

Language

Some 32 languages and dialects are spoken in Afghanistan. Dari (a form of Persian), the language of government and business, is spoken most widely and has several dialects. Pashto, spoken by Pashtuns, has two major variants and many dialects. Uzbeks speak Uzbeki and Turkmen speak Turkic languages. Smaller ethnic groups speak their own languages or a dialect of a major language. For instance, the Hazara speak a Dari dialect.

Religion

Islam is the religion of virtually all Afghans, but as a unifying force it has not overcome ethnic differences. About 84 percent of people are Sunni Muslims, while 15 percent (primarily Hazara and some Persian speakers) are *Shī'a* (Shiite) Muslims. There are small numbers of Sikhs and Hindus in the cities.

Founded by Muhammad of Arabia in 622, Islam is based on the belief in one God (*Allah*). Islam shares many biblical figures with Judaism and Christianity, but Muslims accept Muhammad as the last and greatest prophet. The *Qur'an* (Koran) is said to contain *Allah*'s will as revealed through the angel Gabriel to Muhammad. The war against the Soviets was considered a holy war waged by the *mujahideen*, and through it Islam's political power increased. Culturally, Islam dominates most people's lives from birth to death. Its influence on daily activities is often shared with such local behavior codes as *Pushtunwali* (code of the Pashtuns). Many Muslims pray five times daily and observe the dawn-to-dusk fast for the month of *Ramadan*.

General Attitudes

Afghans are typically friendly and hospitable, but they can also be stern and hard depending on their experience in the war. Although aware of themselves as Afghans, primary loyalty is usually to their family, kin group, clan, or tribe, through which they express their identity. Their various codes are often strict and inflexible, stressing honor and one's responsibility to fulfill expected roles. Personal disputes are not easily solved because of one's need to protect his or her honor. The honor of the family is also affected by personal behavior, so living the code properly is considered essential. Piety and stoicism are admired traits.

Rural Afghans value wealth as defined by land ownership or a large family. Urban residents are more likely to view wealth in terms of money or possessions, and education is highly valued. Nomadic people define wealth by the size of their herds.

People's outlook on life is influenced by a great faith that *Allah* controls everything and everything that happens is according to his will. This belief helps them accept a hard life, even if it somewhat dampens personal initiative.

Personal Appearance

Nearly all Afghans wear *Perahan tunban*, a long shirt that falls to the knees over baggy trousers pulled tight with a drawstring. Flat sandals, sneakers, boots, or dress shoes—all common footwear—are removed for prayers. Men may wear a dress coat or vest over the *Perahan tunban*, and women may wear a short jacket, long coat, or shawl. Given the harsh winters, most people cover their heads with a flat wool cap, a turban with *kolah* (turban cap) in a color and design distinctive to the wearer's ethnic area or place of origin, or the *qarakuli* cap made from the skin of the karakul sheep.

Women are rarely seen in public, but if they are, they wear a *chadiri* (head-to-toe covering) over their clothing; others wear a *chador* (shawl/veil). Jewelry made from gold and silver is common and often features lapis lazuli and garnet, two locally abundant semiprecious stones. Many people, especially children, wear a *tawiz* (amulet) to protect against evil.

CUSTOMS AND COURTESIES

Greetings

A handshake is common among men, who tend to be expressive in greeting friends and may pat backs during an embrace. Lengthy verbal greetings are often accompanied by placing the right hand over the heart. A man does not shake hands with or otherwise touch a woman in public, although he may greet her verbally in an indirect way. Women friends embrace each other and kiss three times on alternating cheeks. Women might also shake hands.

Greetings vary by region and ethnic group, but Arabic greetings are used and universally accepted. *Assalaam alaikum* (Peace be upon you) is replied to with *Waalaikum assalaam* (And peace also upon you). A common Dari greeting is *Khubus ti?* (How are you?) and the Pashto equivalent is *Sanga ye?* Good-bye is *Khoda hafiz*.

Titles are very important. In formal situations, an academic or professional title is a must. *Haji* (pilgrim) is reserved for those who have made a pilgrimage to Makkah (in Saudi Arabia). Socioeconomic status can also determine which title (like *Khan*, meaning "sir") to use. Some people are respectfully only referred to by title (e.g., *Haji Khan*). Usually, however, titles are combined with names. Parents are often called by a child's name, such as *Umm* (mother of) Muhammad or *Abu* (father of) Alam. Friends use given names and nicknames among themselves.

Gestures

Hands are not used much while speaking. Men often finger worry beads (*tasbe*) during conversation. Male friends link arms or hold hands while walking, but members of the opposite sex do not touch in public. To beckon a person, one motions downward with the palm of the hand facing down. To request divine assistance at the beginning or end of an activity (trip, meal, project), one holds both hands in front of the chest, palms up as if holding a book. Afghans typically sit with legs crossed, and it is impolite to let the soles of the feet face someone else. It is also impolite and considered unclean to use the left hand for passing items.

Visiting

Visiting between family, friends, and neighbors provides the mainstay of social life. However, it is common for women to spend their adult lives in *purdah*, which means they are not seen by males who are not close family members. Consequently, visiting is mostly segregated by gender. Homes often have a special room (*hujra*) where male guests are received by the male host. Females socialize elsewhere in the compound. Guests are served tea and, depending on the time of day, perhaps something to eat. Guests are expected to have at least three cups of hospitality tea. Any business discussions occur after refreshments. Guests do not bring gifts. The ability of an Afghan to generously receive guests is a sign of social status.

Eating

Rural Afghans commonly eat only breakfast and dinner, but some may have a light lunch. Most have snacks between meals. At meals, Afghans usually sit on the floor around a mat on which food is served in a communal dish. To eat, one uses the fingers of the right hand or a piece of *nan* (unleavened bread). The left hand is never used to serve oneself, as it is traditionally reserved for cleaning after using the toilet. One eats until satisfied, and leftover food is saved for later or the next day's breakfast. In many areas, belches are considered a sign of a satisfied diner. Families normally eat together, but if a male guest is present, females eat separately. Most Afghans don't eat at restaurants, but these sometimes have booths or a separate dining area for families so women may dine out.

LIFESTYLE

Family

Life is centered around the extended family, which provides the basis for most social, economic, and political interaction. The rural family may be quite large, with several generations living together in the same, adjoining, or nearby compounds. The most common dwelling of the settled population is a mud-brick structure of several rooms, surrounded by high mud walls that provide security from enemies, seclusion for women, and keep animals inside. Within the compound, the family is led by the senior male (father or grandfather). Household tasks are divided by gender, age, and experience. Women do all the cooking, washing, and cleaning. They may engage in light farming, but their lives are centered on the household. The wife of the senior male is the dominant female. Males work in the fields or family business and handle all contacts with the outside world, such as shopping in the market or dealing with local officials. In many cases, men even shop for personal items (clothing) for their wives so they do not have to threaten their modesty by leaving home. Only adult males participate in the *jirga* (village council) or other political events, but women are well informed about local happenings and are influential in shaping men's opinions.

Dating and Marriage

Dating is virtually nonexistent since the sexes are segregated at puberty. Teenage girls enter *purdah* and so have no contact with non-family males. Marriages are normally arranged, often with senior females playing a prominent role in the decision. Among urban or Westernized families, it may be permissible for the prospective bride and groom to meet or view each other and approve of or reject the union. Marriages between cousins are common and often preferred, as they strengthen family ties. Matchmakers engage in lengthy negotiations over the bride-price (paid by the groom's family to the bride's) and/or dowry (what the bride brings to the marriage).

Marriage and engagement rituals are numerous, varied, and complex. Traditionally, the ceremony itself occurs over a three-day period, with part of the festivities at the bride's family home and part at the groom's. Most activities occur with the sexes segregated, but all gather for the contract signing and *Qur'an* recitation. Divorce is simple (e.g., the man need only announce it in public three times) but rare. A man may have up to four wives, but he must provide for each equally; this generally limits most to one wife. Premarital and extramarital sex are strictly forbidden and may be grounds for severe punishment (including death) in tribal areas.

Diet

Afghan cuisine is influenced by the foods of South and Central Asia, China, and Iran. Perhaps the most common foods are the many types of *pilau* (rice mixed with meat and/or vegetables), *qorma* (vegetable sauce), *kebab* (skewered meat), *ashak* or *mantu* (pasta dishes), and *nan*. Tomatoes, spinach, potatoes, peas, carrots, cucumbers, and eggplant are popular. Yogurt and other dairy products are dietary staples. Sugarcane, pudding, a variety of fruits (fresh and dried), and nuts are eaten as desserts and snacks. *Chai* (tea), either green or black, is the most popular drink. Most Afghans cannot regularly afford meat, but they enjoy beef, mutton, chicken, and many types of game. An urban diet is usually more varied than a rural one, but shortages have been severe at times. Islamic law forbids the consumption of alcohol and pork, and most people comply. Local tobacco, hashish, and opium are smoked widely among men.

Recreation

Afghanistan's unique national sport is *buzkashi*, a precursor to polo, in which teams of horsemen compete to see who can carry the headless carcass of a calf from a circle to a spot a few hundred feet away, and return it to the circle. Any player in possession of the calf will suffer all manner of abuse to make him drop it, sometimes even from his own teammates who may want the game prolonged. Only truly superb horsemen are able to master the game. Afghans also enjoy soccer, volleyball, and wrestling. Television and radio play a limited role in people's lives. Most leisure activities occur in the evening and center around the family. Music is popular and is based on singing, drums, stringed instruments similar to lutes, and a clarinet-like instrument called a *surnai*.

Holidays

Secular holidays include Victory of the Muslim Nation (28 April), Remembrance Day (4 May), and Independence Day (18 August). Islamic holidays are more important and are scheduled according to the lunar calendar. They include the first day of *Ramadan*, the three-day feast at the end of *Ramadan* (called *Id al-Fitr*), *Nawrooz* (New Year's Day), *Id al-Adha* (Feast of Sacrifice honoring Abraham for his willingness to sacrifice his son), *Ashura* (a Shiite day to mark the martyrdom of Imam Husayn), and *Roze-Maulud* (the birthday of the Prophet Muhammad). During *Ramadan*, families and friends gather in the evening to eat and visit.

Commerce

Banking and government hours are 8:00 a.m. to 5:00 P.M., March–October, and 9:00 a.m. to 3:30 P.M. the rest of the year. During *Ramadan*, offices close at 2:00 P.M. each day. Larger urban *bazaars* (markets) are divided into many small shops that are grouped together by product in the same section of the bazaar. Prices may be fixed, but large purchases involve extensive haggling, preceded and accompanied by tea. Small stalls and open-air vendors service rural and other areas.

SOCIETY

Government

Officially an Islamic state since the fall of President Najibullah, Afghanistan is in disarray. The 1993 interim constitution allows for a president and leadership council to govern with a prime minister and cabinet, whose members are drawn from the 205-member Parliament. The Supreme Court functions under *shari'a* (Islamic law). An ongoing power struggle between President Burhanuddin Rabbani and former Prime Minister Gulbuddin Hekmatyar has caused widespread death and destruction in and around Kābul and has made their coalition government an impossibility.

Officially, the country has 31 provinces, but a pattern of regional autonomy has emerged during the fighting such that government authority outside Kābul is limited and control is constantly shifting between militias. Each of Afghanistan's several political parties are connected to a particular ethnic, family, religious, and/or linguistic group. Major figures in the battle for power include not only President Rabbani, but also his ally Ismael Khan and his rival Rashid Dostam. A movement of religious students, called *Taliban*, also controls territory. Hekmatyar has allies in the east, and *Shī'a* (Shiite) Muslims dominate around Hazarajat.

Rabbani has been president since 1992. Elections scheduled for 1994 were delayed due to continued violence and disagreements over election rules. Rabbani had agreed to step aside for new elections, but he changed his decision because of the *Taliban* challenge and successes by his own military forces.

Economy

The economy relies on agriculture, pastoralism, and mining, with the bulk of the labor force engaged in these activities. Agricultural products are mostly for domestic consumption. Major exports include natural gas and textiles. Afghan carpets are well-known. Major trading partners include the republics of the former Soviet Union. Disruption of the economy due to the war has led to an increase in high-profit opium/heroin production, making Afghanistan the second largest producer in the world. The government controls large industries, mining, and transportation, but private enterprises also function.

Prospects for development are limited by the continued power struggle and associated violence, which naturally restrict the amount of vital international aid and investment the country receives. Still, Afghanistan is in a geographical position important for regional trade, and might be able to capitalize on that in the future. Afghanistan's Human Development Index (0.208) ranks it 171st out of 173 countries; real gross domestic product per capita is about $700. Poverty affects more than half of the population and many families are unable to meet basic needs. Economic infrastructure is underdeveloped and in disrepair, and substantial efforts will be needed to build a viable economy. The currency is the *afghani* (AF).

Transportation and Communication

Afghanistan's one major road, the Ring Road, creates a large "U" as it runs south from Herāt to Kandahār , northeast to Kābul, and then north through the Salang Tunnel (at 11,100 feet in elevation) to Kundūz and on to Mazār-i-Sharīf. Paved roads run from these major cities to the nearest border towns, such as from Kābul through Jalālābād to the Khyber Pass on the Pakistani border. These roads have, however, been substantially damaged in the war and travel is difficult. Off-road travel is dangerous because of land mines. Many rural areas are essentially inaccessible to vehicles, so people walk, ride animals, or use horse-drawn carts. In cities and over major transit routes, buses and minibuses are used. Few people own private cars. There are no railroads, but a national airline offers limited service.

The government runs one television station, but service has been irregular during the fighting, and television sets are not widely available. Radio service is more reliable; most men listen regularly to BBC news broadcasts. Phones are limited but functioning, and postal service exists throughout the country.

Education

Although some urban schools operated during the war, disruptions and other factors kept attendance at about 15 percent. Total literacy is estimated at below 30 percent (14 percent for women). Many scholars and teachers fled or were killed during the war, and the curriculum was changed in the 1980s to reflect Communist ideology. Students also fled, were killed, or were themselves engaged in the war. Many were and still are needed as laborers at home. The Communist curriculum has been replaced, but enrollment and funding are still serious problems.

Health

Medical services are extremely limited. There is only one doctor for every 10,000 people. Hospitals are found only in some cities, and these are not well equipped. Rural areas completely lack modern medical care. Accordingly, the infant mortality rate is 162 per 1,000 and life expectancy is 43 years. Water is not safe and many diseases affect the population.

FOR THE TRAVELER

U.S. citizens need a passport and visa to travel to Afghanistan, but travel is not recommended. For recorded advisories, call the U.S. State Department at (202) 647–5225. Yellow fever immunizations are required for all travelers coming from infected areas. There are few operating hotels. Many archaeological sites have been destroyed or are off limits. For information, contact the Embassy of Afghanistan, 2341 Wyoming Avenue NW, Washington, DC 20008; phone (202) 234-3770.

A *Culturgram* is a product of native commentary and original, expert analysis. Statistics are estimates and information is presented as a matter of opinion. While the editors strive for accuracy and detail, this document should not be considered strictly factual. It is a general introduction to culture, an initial step in building bridges of understanding between peoples. It may not apply to all peoples of the nation. You should therefore consult other sources for more information.

Democratic and Popular Republic of
Algeria

Boundary representations not necessarily authoritative.

BACKGROUND

Land and Climate

Algeria, with an area of 919,590 square miles (2,381,740 square kilometers), is just over one-fourth the size of the continental United States, and is the world's tenth largest country. Located in northern Africa, it borders six African countries as well as the Mediterranean Sea. The capital city, Algiers, is on the coast. In fact, about 90 percent of the population inhabits the northern coastal region, which is called "the Tell." Central and southern Algeria form part of the vast Sahara, where only an occasional oasis capable of supporting life can be found. The Tell enjoys a mild Mediterranean climate and moderate rainfall, with a rainy season that extends from December to March. A hot, dusty wind called *Sirocco* is common during the summer. The Tell and the Sahara are separated by parallel mountain ranges: the Atlas Mountains and the Haut Plateau. The Kabylia coastal mountain range lies east of Algiers.

History

Algeria's earliest inhabitants were called Berbers, a nonindigenous collective term commonly used in modern history to describe these ancient peoples who still account for a significant minority of the population. The earliest important invaders were the Phoenicians, under whom the Carthaginian Empire in North Africa flourished (ca. 800–146 B.C.) until its

destruction by the Romans. The coastal region was held successively by the Romans and the Vandals until the Umayyad (Arab) invasion of the 600s A.D. The present coastal cities of Algiers, Oran, Constantine, and Annaba owe their development to the period of Arab conquest. The Umayyads introduced Islam to the Berbers, who, in the eighth century, regained control of the region and established their own Islamic empire. Several Berber empires flourished until the 13th century, when Bedouins immigrated to the area and local peoples adopted the Bedouin nomadic lifestyle.

From the early 1500s, the area was part of the Ottoman Empire, centered in Turkey. Algier's distance from the Ottomans allowed for significant local control and for European powers to establish relations with Algeria. During the Ottoman period, Barbary Coast pirates consistently attacked European ships, disrupting trade. The piracy was one reason why France invaded in 1830. Fighting lasted for several years, but Algeria eventually became a French-controlled territory and, ultimately, a department of the French Republic.

Algeria's present borders were established by France in 1902. Despite large-scale French colonization, a smoldering independence movement erupted into open warfare in 1954. After eight years of bitter fighting, Algeria was granted independence on 3 July 1962. Fearing for their lives, nearly one million French and other European colonists evacuated when the French army withdrew. During the 1960s and 1970s, Algeria went through a challenging period of adjustment and internal change before emerging as a firm socialist republic.

The National Liberation Front (FLN) was the republic's only political party until February 1989, when a new constitution allowing a multiparty system was approved. Reelected in 1988 for a five-year term, President Chadli Bendjedid promised political reforms demanded during and after riots that year.

The nation's first free elections (local and regional) were held in 1990 and full national elections were set for late 1991. The Islamic Salvation Front (FIS) gained surprising victories in the 1990 elections and made it clear it wanted Algeria to become an Islamic republic. To press the government toward quicker elections, Islamic fundamentalists staged strikes in 1991. Subsequent violence led Bendjedid to dismiss the government, postpone elections, and declare a state of emergency. Elections were eventually held in December 1991. Again, fundamentalists appeared to be heading for victory. To prevent the FIS from taking power, the military took control of the government and forced Bendjedid to resign. A High Security Council was formed that would eventually cancel all election results and (in 1992) ban the FIS. The Council's president was assassinated in June 1992, which led to an even heavier crackdown on fundamentalists. The High Security Council created the High Council of State, a five-member collective presidency, to govern. For two years, it presided over Algeria's slide into economic and political chaos. The group was replaced in January 1994 by a single president, General Lamin Zeroual, but the High Security Council remains in control of major government decisions.

Muslim militants increased their strength after 1992, forming a substantial guerrilla army and gaining control of urban enclaves and small cities. In areas where the FIS is in control, fundamentalist law is strictly enforced. The militants ordered all foreigners to leave in 1993 and began to kill foreign workers, government officials, intellectuals, and secularists. Most foreign nationals left the country over a period of months and international investment began to be withdrawn. Government forces participated in questionable law enforcement efforts, and order gave way to chaos. Factions formed on both sides and began fighting amongst themselves in addition to against their foes. Full civil war did not seem far away, but the government continued to look for ways to end the conflict. In 1995, Prime Minister Mokdad Sifi announced the government's intentions to hold multiparty presidential elections before the end of the year. But with the FIS still prohibited from the process, it is doubtful whether such efforts will be successful.

THE PEOPLE.

Population

Algeria's population of approximately 27.8 million is growing at an annual rate of 2.3 percent. Algeria has a very young population: 46 percent is under the age of 15 and 75 percent is under 25. Fifty-two percent of the people live in urban areas. The capital city of Algiers has nearly two million residents. About 16 percent of Algerians are native Berbers inhabiting the Kabylia mountainous region. The rest (about 83 percent) is of Arabic descent, with less than 1 percent having European heritage.

Language

Arabic is the official language of Algeria. French was the primary language of business before 1992, but is now only rarely used in the country. Various Berber dialects are spoken in Berber homes and in remote areas, but most Berbers also speak Arabic.

Religion

Islam is Algeria's state religion; 99 percent of the population is Sunni Muslim. However, Algeria is not an Islamic republic, so Muslim religious practices are not necessarily law in Algeria. Still, Islamic philosophy is deeply rooted in the minds, hearts, and behaviors of the people. Islamic scripture, the *Qur'an* (Koran), is considered the final and complete word of God. Muslims accept and revere all major Judeo-Christian prophets from Adam to Jesus, but they proclaim Muhammad to be the last and greatest emissary of *Allah* (God). The Islamic day of worship is Friday, a day for men to go to the mosque and hear a sermon. Women may also go to the mosque, but they pray in a different area than the men. Islam is a religion practiced every day through dress, dietary codes, praying, and constant references to *Allah*'s will. Muslims pray five times daily, always facing the holy city of Makkah, Saudi Arabia.

General Attitudes

Algerians are a formal and traditional people, yet they are quite expressive and individualistic. One is expected to speak one's mind, yet in an inoffensive manner. Although Algerians enjoy good conversation, being overly frank and direct in speech is considered impolite. Expressiveness, courtesy, individualism, and formality are key attributes of the Algerian character.

Algerian society is struggling with the issue of who should govern the country. While the FIS enjoyed broad support in 1991 and 1992, the more secular elements of society now reject their fundamentalist views. At the same time, many impoverished people support the FIS goals, as they espouse a more equal society without a wealthy elite. Whatever the future, most people seek an end to the fighting. The average Algerian simply wants a secure life with a decent income and peace for the future generation.

In this male-dominated society, sex roles are clearly defined. Nevertheless, some women do fill important positions in public and private professions. About 10 percent of the labor force is female.

Personal Appearance

Although Western clothing is common, especially in urban areas, traditional North African Muslim clothing is also prominent. In areas of FIS control, the majority of people wear some form of traditional attire, especially women. In public, it is proper to be dressed conservatively. Militants have demanded that women be veiled, and are willing to enforce their orders. Even in non-FIS areas, modest clothing is worn by all segments of society.

CUSTOMS AND COURTESIES

Greetings

In Algeria, as throughout the Arab world, hospitality is a cultural keynote. This is especially true in Algerian cities, where Arabic custom is blended with equally warm Gallic traditions. Greetings are genuinely cordial and open to friend and stranger alike; they are usually accompanied by a handshake and frequently an embrace (between members of the same sex). Anything less friendly in the way of a greeting is considered impolite. Although many specific greetings are used for various situations, there are a few that are appropriate for most cases. *Ahlan wa sahlan* (May your way be easy) is an Arabic phrase used to welcome someone. *Marhaban bikoum* (Hello to you) is another common Arabic greeting.

Strangers and acquaintances are addressed by title and family name, but friends and relatives use given names. In small gatherings, it is polite to greet each individual present. Elders are greeted first.

Gestures

Using the fingers to point at objects or people is considered impolite. Separate use of the left hand is avoided. When handing something to or receiving it from another person, one uses either both hands or the right hand only. Care is generally taken not to let the sole of the foot point at another person.

Visiting

Visiting, whether for business or pleasure, is a social occasion in Algeria. Guests are offered refreshments, and it is impolite to refuse them. Guests may ask for a substitute if they are not able to eat what is offered. Algerians visit family members and close friends often and without prior arrangement, but others are expected to make plans in advance. Invitations for strangers or acquaintances to visit private homes are an honor and should always be accepted.

During conversation, considerable time is first spent discussing such things as the weather, health, or the latest news. When the formalities of small talk are over, the conversation shifts smoothly and logically to the topics at hand. One is careful not to discuss members of the opposite sex or the host's family, unless the host himself suggests the topic. If the visit is strictly for social purposes, it is customary to bring the host a small gift—food (but not alcohol) is appropriate under most circumstances.

Eating

Although Algerians generally eat with utensils, some foods are still eaten with the hand, especially dishes prepared with rich sauces where bread is used as a scoop. When the hand is used, only the right hand should touch food. Algerians are complimented when guests leave a little food on their plates, as this is a sign of the host's ability to more than adequately provide for his guests.

LIFESTYLE

Family

The Algerian family is an important, private, and male-dominated entity, often including three or more generations (grandparents, married sons and their wives, and unmarried children) under the roof of a single home. There is, however, a definite trend in urban areas toward a smaller nuclear family unit. Mothers are expected to care for the children and household, while fathers are responsible for family income and discipline. Children are expected to honor their parents, obeying them in youth and taking care of them in their old age.

Dating and Marriage

Algerian youth meet openly at universities, public places, and on special occasions, but they do not date in the Western tradition. Marriage represents the linking not just of individuals, but of families. Consequently, matchmaking is often a family affair, and romantic love is seen as something that grows with time after marriage. Women generally marry in their early 20s, and men a few years later.

Diet

Native Algerian cuisine is found in great variety in both city and rural environments. Urban cuisine matches the best in the world and has a strong Gallic flavor. Popular are lamb and chicken dishes, stews, and pastas. *Couscous,* a pasta-like semolina cooked with lamb or chicken and vegetables, is perhaps the most popular Algerian dish. It is the chosen dish for special occasions and holidays. Muslims do not eat pork or drink alcoholic beverages.

Recreation

Recreation is largely a family activity and often takes place in the home. However, people also enjoy going to the beach, having picnics, and watching movies. Soccer is by far the most popular sport in Algeria.

Holidays

National holidays include New Year's Day, Labor Day (1 May), Revolution Day (19 June), Independence Day (5 July), and the Revolution Anniversary (1 November). Muslim holy days vary in date from year to year according to the Islamic calendar. Three Muslim celebrations are the most important in the Islamic world. The first is *Eid al-Fitr,* a three-day feast held at the end of the month of *Ramadan* (usually in the spring). Visiting friends and family, feasting, and worshipping are common. *Ramadan* is the month in which the *Qur'an* was revealed to Muhammad. During this month, Muslims do not eat, drink, or smoke from sunrise to sunset. In the evenings, they eat and visit with family and friends.

The second most important holy day is *Eid al-Adha* or Feast of the Sacrifice. It is held in conjunction with the pilgrimage to Makkah, Saudi Arabia, in June or July. It commemorates not only the pilgrimage but also the willingness of Abraham to sacrifice his son. The prophet Muhammad's birthday, celebrated in September or October, is the third most important Islamic holy day.

Commerce

Normal business hours are Saturday through Wednesday, 8:30 A.M. to noon, and 2:30 to 6:30 P.M. The Western (Gregorian) calendar is officially used in Algeria, but everyday activities of the people are regulated by the lunar-based Islamic calendar.

SOCIETY

Government

Before the High Security Council took power, executive authority was held by a president, prime minister, and cabinet. The National People's Assembly had 281 seats. The 1991–92 elections would have established the first multiparty assembly. The High Security Council maintains it will hold elections when the situation allows. The FIS favors establishing an Islamic republic, with secularism and Western culture banned. All citizens are members of one of 48 states (*wilayaat*), which assume duties of political and economic direction at the local level.

Economy

Algeria's exports include crude oil, other petroleum products, natural gas, and wine. With four major natural gas deposits, Algeria holds 3.4 percent of the world's total reserves. Agriculture employs about one-fourth of the labor force, but the country is not self-sufficient in food production. Nomadic herding is the primary economic activity in the sparsely populated desert regions.

Algeria's Human Development Index (0.553) ranks it 109th out of 173 nations. Real gross domestic product per capita is $2,870, a figure that reflects the country's petroleum wealth. Most people do not enjoy such a high income, and many have been impacted by the nation's 30 percent unemployment rate, the political strife, and the withdrawal of foreign companies. Inflation is well above 100 percent and food shortages are common.

The government has attempted to begin economic reform, but is now introducing austerity measures to try to control inflation and other problems. As the political situation deteriorates, economic progress will become more difficult. The currency is the Algerian *dinar* (DA).

Transportation and Communication

Most highways in Algeria are paved, but roads are less reliable in desert regions than in the Tell. Cars are a common form of transport. Taxis and buses are available in major cities. Five international airports link Algeria's major cities and the nation with other countries. As with transportation, communication systems in the north are very good, but they are less reliable in the south. Telephones are common in urban areas. There are several daily newspapers.

Education

Algeria's literacy rate is 57 percent. Schooling is free and compulsory to age 15. Education on all levels is conducted mainly in Arabic, a change from a generation ago when French was the primary language of instruction. Beginning at age six, students first attend nine years at a "fundamental" school. This school stresses not only basic skills, but also science and technology. Those who successfully complete a fundamental education (about 82 percent of all students) may go on to secondary school. Boys are more likely than girls to complete their education. The University of Algiers and other universities, including those in Oran and Constantine, provide a high level of instruction. They are supplemented by a variety of other higher education institutions.

Health

Algerians have access to more than 700 medical facilities. A national health plan (*Sécurité Sociale*) covers the needs of employed persons. All other people receive free care in hospitals, clinics, and mobile health facilities. Tap water is not potable and must be boiled. Disease, poverty, and malnutrition are still serious, but the health of Algerians is better than a decade ago. Life expectancy (currently between 66 and 68 years) is rising and the infant mortality rate (currently 52 per 1,000) is dropping. These improvements are partly the result of a special program that began in 1984 to combat child mortality.

FOR THE TRAVELER

The United States government issued a travel warning in 1995 that stated Americans are in severe danger if they visit Algeria. Muslim militants have killed many foreigners and have vowed to kill any seen in public. For updated travel warnings that may provide additional information, call the U.S. State Department at (202) 647–5225. Algeria requires U.S. travelers to have a valid passport and visa. No immunizations are required, but they may be recommended according to one's length of stay. Water should be boiled before use, even for brushing teeth, although water in major hotels is generally safe. Peel all fruit and cook vegetables before eating. For more information, contact the Consular Section of the Embassy of the Democratic and Popular Republic of Algeria, 2118 Kalaroma Road NW, Washington, DC 20008; phone (202) 265–2800.

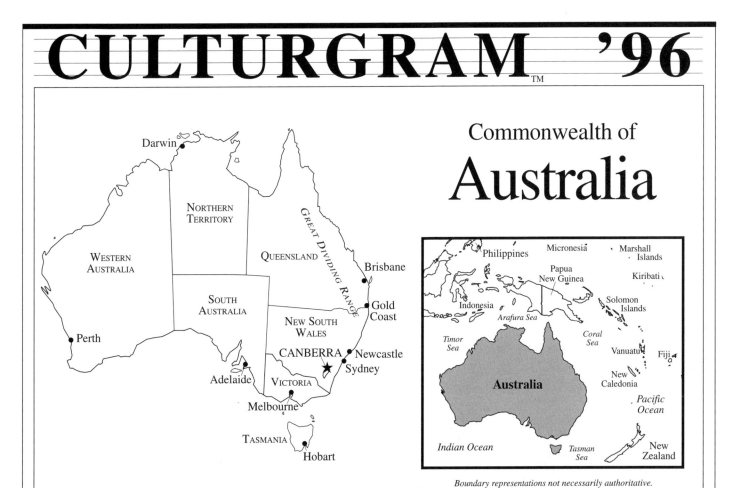

Commonwealth of
Australia

Boundary representations not necessarily authoritative.

BACKGROUND

Land and Climate

Australia is the sixth largest country in the world (2,967,892 square miles—7,686,850 square kilometers) and is only slightly smaller than the United States. It is the only country that occupies a complete continent. It is also the driest continent in the world. About one-third of the land is desert and another third is composed of poor-quality land. A long chain of mountains, the Great Dividing Range, runs along the Pacific coast. Fertile farmland lies between the coast and the Great Dividing Range. The western slopes and plains are important wheat-producing areas. Cattle stations reach the edge of the barren interior desert. Australia is known for its marsupials, including koalas, kangaroos, spiny anteaters, and the platypus. Summer is December through February and winter is June through August. The climate ranges from tropical in the north to temperate in the south.

History

The Aborigines were the only inhabitants when the Dutch explored parts of the continent in the 1620s. Most of Australia was left largely undisturbed until 1770, when Captain James Cook took formal possession of the eastern coast for Britain. The British arrived in 1788 and founded penal colonies in what became modern-day Sydney, Hobart, and Brisbane. Many of the early settlers of Australia were therefore convicts or soldiers. Free settlements were established in Melbourne, Adelaide, and Perth. With the discovery of gold in 1851, the number of free men immigrating to Australia increased rapidly. In 1868, the practice of transporting convicts to Australia ceased.

In 1901, the six colonies agreed to federate as the Commonwealth of Australia. The country has enjoyed stability and growth throughout the 20th century. Attempts in Western Australia to secede from the Commonwealth in the 1930s failed. Australia established close ties with the United States during World War II. Since that conflict, Australia has been active in global politics.

Robert Hawke became the prime minister in 1983 and was reelected in 1990. Due to the recession that began in the 1990s, Hawke's popularity declined and he was removed as head of the Labor party. Because the leader of the dominant political party is automatically prime minister, Hawke also lost that position. He was replaced in 1991 by Paul Keating. Parliamentary elections were held in March 1993, and Keating maintained his position as prime minister.

THE PEOPLE

Population

The population of Australia, about 18 million, is growing at a rate of 1.4 percent a year. While the overall population density rate is low, approximately 85 percent of the people live in urban areas, mostly in coastal cities. Sydney is the

OCEANIA

largest city with more than six million people. Nearly 40 percent of all Australians live in Sydney and Melbourne combined. Australia has a young population; about one-third of all Australians are under age 20.

At least 95 percent of the people are Caucasian. Sixty percent of these have an Anglo-Celtic heritage. Because of heavy immigration, Australia is a mosaic of many different nationalities, including Cambodian, Dutch, Estonian, French, German, Greek, Italian, Latvian, Lithuanian, Polish, Polynesian, Vietnamese, Yugoslavian, and other Asian and Latin American peoples. The Asian population has grown from 1 to 4 percent since 1975.

Aborigines (the original inhabitants of Australia) make up 1.5 percent of the population. Aborigines have their own very distinct culture. It was once nearly destroyed, but has now been recognized as an integral and important part of Australia's heritage. Large tracts of land (including one-third of the Northern Territory) have been granted to Aborigines, and efforts are being made to preserve their culture. Aborigines feel a spiritual link to the land. This relationship guides their entire lives as they care for and are cared for by the land. Aboriginal society is complex, but the family is its center. Rituals, ceremonies, and social responsibilities help the Aborigines maintain their link to each other and the land.

Language

English is the national language and is taught in all schools. Immigrant groups often continue to use their native languages at home. The Aborigines once had more than 250 languages, but only about 50 have survived in teachable form. There is now an effort to reverse a trend toward stressing English over Aboriginal languages. Aborigines have their own radio system that broadcasts in their languages, and more families are speaking traditional languages at home. In many Aborigine schools, Aborigine languages are used for instruction at first; English is introduced later.

Australian English uses many words and phrases that are expressions of the country's unique culture, such as *no worries, mate* (no problem, pal), *rubbish* (garbage), *over the road* (across the street), or *rubber* (eraser). The hood of a car is a *bonnet*, while the trunk is a *boot*. Colloquialisms and idioms also add to Australian English. For example, *spot on* means "right on." A *bingle* is a "fender-bender." To call something *dinky-di* is to call it "genuine," as in truly Australian. *Fairdinkum!* more generally mean something is true, good, or genuine. And to say someone or something is moving fast, one might use the phrase *like a possum up a gum tree*. Australians, or "Aussies" as they are often called, also shorten words for everyday conversation. Examples include *uni* (university), *kindi* (kindergarten), and *teli* (television). Because some Australian slang might be offensive to other English speakers, and vice-versa, visitors should use standard English.

Religion

Approximately 76 percent of the people are Christians, divided among the Anglicans (26 percent), the Catholics (26 percent), and other denominations (24 percent). Other religions and nonreligious parts of the population account for the remaining 24 percent. Generally, religion does not play a strong role in daily life.

General Attitudes

Australia is a clean country and people are expected to maintain its standards. In fact, there is a stiff fine for littering. Australians are amiable and easygoing about most things in life; clubs and social groups are popular. Many people frequent local pubs after work and on weekends. Being prompt is important. When conversing, Australians often gesture with their hands to emphasize and clarify. Australians are outgoing and relaxed in public; they are quite comfortable with expressing feelings openly.

Personal Appearance

Australians generally follow European and North American fashion trends. They tend to dress casually. However, this does not mean that dress is sloppy. For example, while short pants are common in the summer, tattered clothing is not acceptable. And people tend to dress up to go into the city or for social functions. Many people wear hats in the summer as protection from the sun. In winter, warmer clothing (sweaters, etc.) is necessary even in private homes, as most do not have central heating.

CUSTOMS AND COURTESIES

Greetings

Australians greet friends with a casual *G' Day* (Good Day) and a warm handshake. Close female friends might hug and kiss lightly on the right cheek. More formal greetings involve a simple *Hello, how are you?* People generally prefer to use first names, even with those they have just met. From a distance, a wave is acceptable, and for casual passerby greetings, the Australians may nod their head up and to the right instead of saying *Good Day* or *Hello*.

Gestures

Rules of basic etiquette are strongly adhered to in Australia. Winking at women is considered inappropriate. When yawning, one should cover the mouth and then excuse oneself. Most hand gestures are the same as in the United States, but a few typical American gestures may be considered offensive. For example, forming a "V" with the index and middle fingers, palm facing in, is vulgar. U.S. Americans often use the gesture to express the number two. Pointing at someone with the index finger is impolite. One preferably points with an open hand in the person's general direction. Sniffing several times when one has a cold is impolite. A person should blow his or her nose in private.

Visiting

Australians often entertain in the home and enjoy inviting others to dinner. Upon being invited by friends, Australians normally offer to bring something to the meal. The hosts can accept or decline the offer, depending on the event. Guests are greeted warmly at the door before being invited to enter a home.

Flowers or a bottle of wine are often brought to the hostess by guests invited for lunch or dinner. After dinner, the company sometimes "goes out" to a dance club, movie, or sports club.

One popular reason for getting together is the barbecue. It may be very informal, where guests bring their own meat and maybe another item, but it is just as common for hosts to provide all the food. Parties and card games are also popular activities.

Eating

The continental style of eating is generally used—the fork is held in the left hand and the knife remains in the right hand. In a private home, guests do not serve themselves from various dishes at the table but receive a plate already served. At a restaurant, a simple, polite hand gesture will attract the waiter's attention. Water is not served with a meal, unless asked for. Salads are usually served at the same time as the main course, not before. Persons who want a salad before the meal order it as an entrée. An entrée in Australia is not a main dish, but an appetizer. Placing utensils on the plate together indicates one is finished and wishes to have the dish cleared away. The bill is usually paid at the register after the meal. While tipping is not necessary, it is becoming more common in many restaurants due to the influence of tourists. If the service is good, a small tip is appreciated.

LIFESTYLE

Family

The average family has two or three children, although larger families are not uncommon. Society is family oriented, and Australian family life is similar to family life in the United States. As in other parts of the world, there are more and more single-parent homes and families where both father and mother work outside of the home. About 38 percent of the work force is comprised of women. Women are generally considered equal to men in Australia, with about the same amount of education, fairly equal wages, and important leadership positions in the private and public sectors. Teenagers are rather independent. Communities for senior citizens are funded by church, government, and community groups. Home ownership is valued highly and is part of the "Australian Dream." Despite usually high interest rates on home loans, about 70 percent of all Australians have their own homes.

Dating and Marriage

Australian dating habits are similar to those in the United States. Dating usually begins by age 15, perhaps beginning with small groups. Movies, dancing, and socializing are the most popular activities. The average age for a woman to marry is 23; it is 25 for men. Church weddings are still common. A growing number of couples also choose to live together before, or instead of, marriage. This is referred to as a *de facto marriage*.

Diet

Eating habits are similar to those in the United States. Fruits and vegetables are grown year-round. Take-out (*take-away*) and fast-food businesses are popular. All varieties of fish and meat are common. As in many countries, there is a trend toward eating lighter foods. Salads, seafood, and fresh vegetables are increasing in popularity. The main meal of the day is eaten in the evening; it is usually called *dinner*, but may also be called *tea* if it is a smaller meal. A snack before bedtime is called *supper*.

Recreation

Physical fitness and exercise are important to most Australians. Football (played by Australian rules, this game is different than American football), soccer, rugby, cricket, basketball, cycling, *bush walking* (hiking), tennis, lawn bowling, and swimming are enjoyed by people of all ages. Horse racing and golf are also popular. The Melbourne Cup horse race is a nationally televised event and interests many people. *Netball*, a game similar to basketball and played by girls, is popular all over the country. Girls learn *netball* as early as age five and play it throughout school. Australians consider sportsmanship to be important. Of all outdoor recreational activities, fishing is by far the most popular. It is also important for the economy and creates thousands of jobs.

Holidays

Australia Day (26 January) commemorates the arrival of the first European settlers to Australia. Other holidays are New Year's Day, Good Friday, Easter, Easter Monday, Anzac Day (or Veterans Memorial Day, 25 April), Queen Elizabeth's Birthday (second Monday in June), Christmas, and Boxing Day (26 December). Boxing Day comes from an old British tradition of boxing up unwanted items to give to the poor. It is now simply a day to visit friends and relatives and to "box up" exchange items for return to the store. Labor Day, bank holidays, and holidays for local horse races or cultural festivals vary from state to state. Ethnic festivals and local holidays provide an opportunity to celebrate cultural diversity. These are popular throughout Australia.

Commerce

Most Australians work 38 to 40 hours a week and some work overtime on weekends or in the evening. Nearly all salaried workers receive four weeks of paid vacation each year. Businesses are generally open Monday through Friday from 8:30 A.M. to 5:30 P.M., and from 9:00 A.M. to noon on Saturday. One evening a week, usually Thursday, shops stay open until 9:00 P.M. In large cities, these shops often remain open late on the weekends as well. Some shops are open on Sunday. Banking hours are generally from 9:30 A.M. to 4:00 P.M. on weekdays.

SOCIETY

Government

Australia is a federal parliamentary state, consisting of six federated states, the Australian Capital Territory around Canberra, and the Northern Territory. Each individual state enjoys much autonomy, although national law overrides any state laws that conflict with it. The federal Parliament consists of a 76-seat Senate and a 147-seat House of Representatives. All citizens age 18 and over are required to vote in federal and state elections. Those who do not vote may be fined. The next elections are in 1996. Keating's Labor Party is the governing party. With near-equal representation stands an opposition coalition composed of the Liberal Party and the National Party.

Although Australia is a sovereign nation, it is still a member of Britain's Commonwealth and officially recognizes Queen Elizabeth II as its monarch. A governor-general (William George Hayden) formally represents the queen. Prime Minister Paul Keating and others support converting Australia into a full republic and withdrawing from the Commonwealth, a move that would require a national referendum and constitutional change. Other political groups strongly oppose such a move, and the public has generally expressed the desire to maintain the status quo.

Economy

Australia has a strong economy, although its mineral and agricultural exports are sensitive to fluctuations in world market prices. These fluctuations restricted economic growth in the 1980s and were a factor in the 1990–92 recession. Australia exports many minerals, including iron ore, bauxite, diamonds, coal, silver, gold, and copper. Livestock is important in Australia, the world's leading exporter of wool and beef (much of which is exported to the United States). It also ranks high in sheep production. Australia is self-sufficient in food production.

Australia's manufacturing industry mainly supplies domestic demand, but a growing number of items are being exported to Asian and Pacific nations. There is also a large and diversified service sector. Tariff barriers that protect local manufacturing industries are being reduced dramatically to stimulate trade. Unemployment is about 10 percent. Inflation is less than 3 percent. The currency is the Australian dollar ($A).

Australia's Human Development Index (0.926) ranks it seventh out of 173 countries. Real gross domestic product per capita is $16,680, which has more than doubled in the last generation. These figures indicate most people earn a decent income and have access to the benefits of Australia's economic prosperity. Poverty does exist, and the poorest 40 percent of all households together earn less than 16 percent of the country's income. This indicates there is a fairly wide gap between the wealthy and the poor, but even the poor have access to social institutions that can help people rise above their conditions.

Transportation and Communication

The transportation system includes taxis, rental cars, interstate bus lines, railways, and an extensive airline system. The bus system is very good in metropolitan areas. On fixed routes, such as from the airport to a hotel, taxi drivers tell passengers the fare of the trip before they begin. Otherwise, meters are used. Sydney has a ferry system. There is also an overnight ferry service, the Able Tasman, from Victoria to Tasmania. Melbourne has an extensive *tram* (streetcar) system. Australia ranks fifth in the world in the number of automobiles per capita, with many families owning two cars. Because of their British heritage, Australians drive on the left side of the road. Nearly all Australian households have a telephone. There are three major communications network companies, as well as one national and several smaller companies. In recent years, the Australian film industry has seen great success at home and in the United States.

Education

Public education is administered by the state governments and financed by federal funds. Schooling is compulsory from ages six to fifteen (sixteen in Tasmania). Correspondence instruction, supplemented by two-way radio, reaches children in remote areas. Approximately one-fourth of all Australian children attend private schools. All states have universities, colleges, and institutes. The school year is divided into four terms of about ten weeks each; breaks occur in April, July, and October. Tasmania has three terms with breaks in June and September. The literacy rate is 99 percent. Most Australian adults have completed an average of 11 years of schooling; that is, most finish compulsory education and go on to finish high school as well. A significant portion of the population has had higher education.

Health

A national health care system, called Medicare, is financed by a 1.25 percent income tax. It covers all care provided by public hospital doctors. There is also a private health care system. Patients treated in public or private hospitals by private doctors pay for their care. About two-thirds of all hospitals are public. The infant mortality rate is 7 per 1,000; life expectancy averages 74 to 80 years.

FOR THE TRAVELER

A valid passport and visa are required of U.S. citizens traveling to Australia. Also, if one is traveling through nations known to be infected with yellow fever, one must have a certificate of vaccination to enter Australia. Otherwise, no vaccinations are required. A departure tax must be paid at the airport. Dual-voltage small appliances and plug adaptors are necessary to use electrical outlets. For a free copy of *Destination Australia* contact the Australian Tourist Commission, located at 2121 Avenue of the Stars, Los Angeles, CA 90067; phone (800) 333–0262. You may also wish to use the Aussie Help Line; phone (800) 333–0199. The Embassy of Australia is located at 1601 Massachusetts Avenue NW, Washington, DC 20036–2273; phone (202) 797–3000. Consulates, which offer the same services as embassies, are located in several major U.S. cities.

Printed on recycled paper

Azerbaijan

(Azerbaijani Republic)

Boundary representations not necessarily authoritative.

A
S
I
A

BACKGROUND

Land and Climate

Azerbaijan, a country slightly larger than the state of Maine, is situated south of Russia. It also borders Georgia, Armenia, and Iran. The province of Nakhichevan, which borders Iran, is cut off from the main part of Azerbaijan by Armenia. Mountains, including the Caucasus and Talysh ranges, and the Karabakh plateau dominate three sides of the country. Between the mountains are valleys and lowlands with rich flora and fauna. Azerbaijan also has a subtropical zone known for its exotic plants, including pomegranate, pistachio, persimmon, fig, olive, and saffron. The amount of saffron grown on plantations is enough for commercial processing.

The Caspian Sea forms Azerbaijan's eastern border. Enormous oil and natural gas reserves beneath the sea may bring great wealth to the country. The Caspian is also rich in biological life; it holds 90 percent of the world's sturgeons. Their habitat is threatened by oil extraction, which began in 1870 and was poorly managed for decades, but efforts are being made to clean up the environment. Two major rivers, the Kura and the Aras, cross the republic, and there are a number of smaller rivers, lakes, and springs.

Azerbaijan has a mild climate with more than 300 days of sunshine each year. Winters are short and cool, and summers are hot and sunny. Fall is very pleasant with warm days and cool nights.

History

The name of the country originates from the ancient Atrapatakan, mentioned by Strabo, the Greek historian, in the first century A.D. as the name of a country on Azerbaijan's present territory. Caucasian Albania, another ancient country unrelated to present-day Albania, also inhabited the territory. Both nations were well developed, had trade links with various countries, and had their own languages. Beginning in the seventh century, the area was dominated by Arabs. They introduced Islam, which replaced Zoroastrianism and Christianity as the major religion. Arabic was also introduced. While it did not replace existing languages, its script was used for the Azeri language until 1924.

Because of its geographical location at the juncture of Europe and Asia, the area was dominated either by Turkey or Iran (Persia) for much of its history. It was also ruled by the Mongols and the Russians. According to an 1828 treaty between Russia and Iran, northern Azerbaijan became part of Russia, while the south became part of Iran. The divided Azeris have since experienced different destinies. Present-day Iran has an Azeri population larger than that of Azerbaijan. During the Soviet era, it was difficult for relatives to visit one another across the border, but people are now able to maintain much closer ties.

Azerbaijan declared itself independent in 1918, but was suppressed by Russia's Red Army in 1920 and made part of the Soviet Union. In 1922, it was joined with Georgia and Armenia as the Trancaucasian Soviet Federal Socialist Republic. In 1936, it became a Soviet Socialist Republic, remaining so through the 1980s. A violent conflict with Armenia erupted in the late 1980s regarding the area of Nagorno-Karabakh, which is part of Azerbaijan but is mostly inhabited by Armenians. It became the subject of fierce fighting as the Armenians sought self-determination rights. A large refugee problem, battles over supply lines, and the Soviet Union's inability to stop the fighting caused great hardship in the country. In 1994, the UN Security Council demanded that Armenia withdraw from Azerbaijan, where it had seized up to 20 percent of the territory and displaced one million people. A ceasefire went into effect, but Armenian troops remained; progress seems uncertain.

As Soviet central authority began to weaken, Azerbaijan's Popular Front emerged in opposition to the local Communist party. But it was Azeri Communist leaders who declared independence in 1991, a few months before the Soviet Union dissolved. Still, Popular Front Chairman Abulfez Elchibey won the first contested elections in 1992 and became the country's president. Unfortunately major setbacks in the war for Nagorno-Karabakh and economic troubles weakened the Front's government. Elchibey called on a former Communist leader, Heydar Aliyev, to help stabilize the government. However, when a rebel militia moved on Baku in June 1993, Elchibey fled the capital. Aliyev was named interim president, and he named the rebel military commander as prime minister. Elchibey remained in the country and refused to resign. However, Aliyev sponsored elections in October 1993 and carried 97 percent of the vote. In late 1994, his prime minister seemed to mount a coup against him, seizing buildings and territory, but Aliyev's supporters and international pressure helped encourage more peaceful dialogue in a dispute over certain government officials.

THE PEOPLE
Population
Azeris descend from the early Caucasian Albanians and migrating Turks. The largest wave of Turks was the Seljuks, who came in the 11th century. Their numbers account for the region's adoption of the Turkish language and culture. The current population is about 7.6 million, of which 83 percent is Azeri. The rest includes Russians, Tatars, Talyshs, Georgians, Ukrainians, Armenians, Lezghians, Kurds, and others. The proportions of these groups is unknown due to the war. For instance, most Armenians have fled the country. Some minority groups, such as the Talyshs, settled in the region long ago, but others were attracted to the rich oil fields of Baku in the late 1800s. More than two million people live in Baku, a cosmopolitan city with many grand buildings and mosques.

Language
Azeri belongs to the Oghuz group of Turkish languages and is similar to modern Turkish. In the 1920s the Arabic script was changed to a Latin script, which was changed to a Cyrillic script in the 1930s. The Azeri script is now returning to the Latin alphabet. During the Soviet era, Russian and Azeri were official languages, with Russian dominating for government purposes. Today Azeri dominates for all purposes. Many Azeris can speak Russian, and many of the country's publications are in Russian. Government decrees are published in both Azeri and Russian.

Religion
Azerbaijan is traditionally an Islamic nation, but religious worship was outlawed during the Soviet era. This weakened devotion to Islam, as two generations grew up with little knowledge of it. Today, people can practice their religion freely, praying at home and attending mosque as they please. Jews and Armenian Christians also practice their respective religions. Still, society is more secularized than in neighboring countries.

Most people go to mosque for Friday prayers, as Friday is the Muslim day of worship. Men and women pray separately. Most Azeris are Shi'a Muslims (Shiites). They accept the *Qur'an* (Koran) as the word of *Allah* (God) revealed to Muhammad the Prophet. Shiites, in contrast to Sunni Muslims, also revere Fatima, Muhammad's daughter, her husband, Ali, and their sons, Hassan and Hussein. They believe Fatima's descendants, called *Imams* (holy men), disappeared but will reappear in the future to guide Muslims to their destiny.

General Attitudes
The attitude of Azeris as a nation has changed over the years. Conditioned to view themselves as Soviets after World War II, the people still felt separate from Russians. The nation experienced a revival of native literature and history in the 1970s that has provided the basis for Azeri feelings in today's political climate. A desire for national prosperity, love for the motherland, and pride in the native language and culture are strong and being fostered. Unfortunately, an initial optimism about Azerbaijan's future has been dampened by the long war with Armenia. On a daily basis the war does not touch most people's lives, but it does affect the nation's mood, its economic welfare, and its ability to develop and progress.

Personal Appearance
Men and women generally wear Western clothing. However, rural women sometimes wear traditional clothing that includes a long, pleated skirt, a long-sleeved blouse, and a *charshab*—a long piece of cloth wrapped loosely around the skirt. Young women cover their heads with light kerchiefs or an *orpack*, a small piece of cloth that wraps around the head and shoulders. Older men usually wear the traditional *papah,* a high, round lambskin hat.

CUSTOMS AND COURTESIES
Greetings
When greeting each other, men shake hands and say *Salem* (Peace). Women also say *Salem*, but they do not shake hands. Female friends or relatives might hug and kiss. Another common greeting is *Sagh ol* (Be well), which is also used at parting. If people are acquainted, the greeting is followed by *Nejasiniz?* (How are you?). One often asks about the health of the other's family.

People of the same age call each other by first names. It is common to use *hanum* (Miss or Mrs.) or *hala* (aunt) after the given name of a woman, and *ami* or *dayi* (uncle) after the man's given name. *Bey* (Mr.) is also used after a man's given name at social gatherings or work. Its use was banned in 1920 when Russia invaded, but it is again becoming a preferred way to address men.

Gestures
Shoes are removed before entering mosques. When an older person or woman enters a room, those present stand to greet him or her. It is impolite to cross one's legs, smoke, or chew gum in the presence of elders. It is impolite to speak

loudly to one's colleagues. The right hand is used in handshakes and other interactions; it is rude to use the left hand unless the right hand is busy. One may point at objects but not people with the index finger. Shaking it while it is vertical is used to reprimand or warn someone. The index finger is also use to attract a listener's attention. The "thumbs-up" gesture is used for "fine" or "okay." Rounding the finger to touch the thumb tip and form a circle is obscene.

Visiting

Visiting relatives or friends is popular in Azerbaijan. Hospitality is part of the culture. Friends and family visit without prior notice. Guests are often invited for a meal or for "tea." Tea is a mid-afternoon affair that includes pastries, fruit preserves (not jam), fruit, candy, and tea. At other times any guest will be offered tea and some sweets. Tea is served in *armudi stakan* (small, pear-shaped glasses). In rural areas it is customary to invite guests to have tea in the backyard in the spring and summer. People also visit in open-air tea houses. Men like to have tea in a *chaihana* (a light building or tent), especially in the summer along Baku's Caspian shore.

Visitors, especially those who have adopted Russian customs, often take gifts to their hosts, such as flowers, candy, or pastries. A wrapped present is not opened in the presence of the giver.

Eating

People usually eat three meals a day. For breakfast, tea with bread and butter, cheese, or marmalade is common. Dinner, eaten in the afternoon, includes a meat or vegetable soup, followed by *pilau* (pilaf), a meat dish, potatoes, or macaroni. For supper, people usually eat the same as for dinner without the soup. Vegetables and fresh herbs are eaten at both dinner and supper.

The fork is held in the left hand and the knife in the right for eating. In most traditional homes the cook prepares the plates in the kitchen for each person. In other homes, serving dishes are placed on the table. Guests do not serve themselves; they are served by others. Tea is usually served at the end of each meal.

In cities, women and men eat together at large social gatherings, but they eat separately in rural areas. Eating at restaurants is not common; it is generally reserved for special occasions. The host pays the entire bill and tip.

LIFESTYLE

Family

Azeris value family over the individual and family needs come first. Men are protective of women in the family. An Azeri would commonly swear by his mother (as opposed to Deity), because she is the most valuable person on earth. Parents feel a lifelong commitment to provide their children with financial support, even after marriage.

Rural Azeris tend to live in extended families. The father is the undisputed head of the family. Married sons and their families live with their parents until financially independent, and all members of the family are loyal to and dependent on the group. This tradition is less evident in cities, where nuclear families are somewhat more common. Rural parents usually build a house for their married sons, and urban parents might buy them apartments.

Unmarried adults generally live with their parents, regardless of age. Adult children are expected to care for their elderly parents. Relatives remain close, visiting each other often and gathering for special occasions. Grandparents help care for grandchildren when necessary.

Dating and Marriage

Dating in the Western sense is not common in Azerbaijan. If urban men and women go out, their relationship is expected to lead to marriage. Premarital sex is strongly discouraged. Urban Azeris choose their spouses, but rural Azeris are expected to follow their parents' wishes regarding a mate.

To become engaged, a man sends a formal proposal to the woman's parents through an older relative. Weddings are celebrated elaborately. A folk music group usually accompanies a groom and his relatives to the bride's house in several cars decorated with flowers and ribbons. The party moves inside the bride's home where the couple's parents and relatives dance. A special wedding melody is played as a signal for the bride to say good-bye to her parents and to join the groom. The bride's parents then give the couple their blessings. The actual wedding ceremony usually takes place at night. The bride is accompanied by friends and relatives carrying candles and a decorated mirror.

Diet

Azeris are proud of their cuisine, which they refer to as the "French cuisine of the East." The area's abundance of vegetables, fruits, and fragrant herbs and spices has inspired Azeri cooks to create distinctive national dishes. Cooks often use cilantro, dill, mint, saffron, ginger, garlic, cinnamon, pepper, and other flavors in their dishes. The most popular dish, *pilau,* is made of rice that has been steamed for a long time and is topped by a variety of foods. These toppings might include chicken, lamb, dried fruit, or milk. *Kebab* is grilled pieces of meat (lamb, chicken, or sturgeon) on a stick. *Piti* is a lamb broth with potatoes and peas cooked in clay pots in the oven. *Dovga* (yogurt, rice, and herbs) is often served after the main meal at celebrations. It is believed to improve digestion. Dinner ends with sherbet or tea, *mürebbe* (preserves), and pastries. The preserves are made from quince, figs, apricots, peaches, cherries, grapes, plums, strawberries, raspberries, walnuts, or mulberries.

Recreation

The most popular sports are wrestling and soccer. Azeri wrestlers compete internationally. Going to movies or theaters is common in the cities, and visiting is a favorite everywhere. For middle and upper class families, vacations (three to four weeks) are spent in summer houses that dot the Caspian seashore.

It is common during social gatherings to recite poems of native poets. Folk music is enjoyed and Azeris have many unique musical instruments. In rural areas it is common for members of larger families to perform as a folk group.

Holidays

Azerbaijan has replaced Soviet-era holidays with its own. For example, the Day of Commemoration (19 January) honors the victims of the 1990 Soviet invasion of Baku. Among the most favorite holidays is *Novrus Bairami*, the New Year celebration that occurs at the beginning of spring. For days before the holiday women gather in families to bake pastries. Then on New Year's Eve, families come together to eat *pilau* and have tea with pastries. Young people make fires in front of their homes and jump over them; they dance and play games. One can hear national melodies everywhere.

There are two Independence Day celebrations: one on 28 May to mark the 1918 declaration of independence and one on 18 October to mark freedom in 1991. Azeris also recognize various Muslim holidays, the most important being the feast to end the month of *Ramadan*. During that month, Muslims fast from sunrise to sunset and eat only in the evenings. Forty days later, *Kurban Bairami*, the holiday of sacrifice, commemorates the pilgrimage season and also Abraham's willingness to sacrifice his son.

Commerce

Offices are open weekdays from 8:00 or 9:00 A.M. to 5:00 or 6:00 P.M. Stores and shops are also open on Saturday, but they often close an hour each afternoon for dinner. Open-air markets offer fruits, vegetables, meats, herbs, eggs, and other dairy products. Prices at markets are not fixed, so one may bargain with the merchant.

SOCIETY

Government

Azerbaijan is a republic. The country's constitution allows for a president elected on a five-year term, a prime minister, and a national assembly, known as *Milli Majlis*. All citizens may vote at age 18. Despite the turmoil of its first years, the fledgling government generally seeks to create a democratic, stable country with all of its fundamental freedoms and rights. This effort will be a long process that will depend on the outcome of the war, relations with Russia and other neighbors, economic development, and stable transfers of executive authority. Prominent political parties include the president's New Azerbaijan Party and the Azerbaijan Popular Front (led by Elchibey), but many other parties exist.

Economy

The economy is based on the production of oil and natural gas. With its huge untapped Caspian oil reserves, Azerbaijan has great potential for economic development. Negotiations with Western oil firms are expected to bring Azerbaijan new technology and a greater ability to develop its industry. Russia is also participating in the negotiations. Once deals are finalized, the country will benefit from new jobs, foreign capital, and large revenues. A new pipeline is also being planned to deliver oil from the Caspian to the Mediterranean.

Oil-extraction-equipment manufacturing and the chemical industry are both important sectors of the economy that expect to be modernized with help from the West. Progress will likely be slow, as Azerbaijan's planned transition to a market economy has not been smooth or substantive.

In agriculture, the most important cash crops are cotton and tobacco. They provide employment in rural areas. Azerbaijan also exports fruits, vegetables, nuts, grapes, and saffron. Trade disruption due to the war, the Soviet Union's collapse, rising unemployment, and the refugee problem has led to decreased agricultural output and exports.

Azerbaijan's currency is the *manat*, although the Russian ruble is still in circulation. The country's Human Development Index (0.73) ranks it 71st out of 173 nations. Real gross domestic product per capita is $3,670. These figures may be artificially high, since output has been declining, inflation rising, and foreign investment lacking. Still, the educated workforce and natural resources show potential for a stronger economy once political issues are settled.

Transportation and Communication

Buses, a subway, trolleys, taxis, and suburban trains provide public transportation in Baku. Travel between cities is done mainly by train and bus. Most roads are paved, but urban roads are in better condition. In 1992, Azerbaijan's airlines began flying internationally.

A number of daily national newspapers and some regional and local papers are in circulation. Postal service is not effective at present because old postal connections were destroyed and new ones have not yet been fully established. Most urban homes have telephones, but most rural families do not. The entire communications system needs modernization.

Education

Education is provided free through the university level. The government spends more of its budget on education than on anything else except defense. The literacy rate is nearly 100 percent. Due to the lack of facilities, schools must operate in two shifts: morning and afternoon. Classes are held Monday through Saturday. Schools are not divided into levels. Children graduate from the same school they began attending at age six or seven. Eight years of attendance are mandatory and the final three are optional. Those who choose not to complete the full 11 years may attend trade schools to learn a profession. A number of colleges and universities are available; most are located in Baku.

Health

Medical care is provided free, but facilities are not well equipped. Rural areas especially lack clinics and equipment. Drugs and vaccines are in short supply. This has led to an increase of measles and diphtheria. Childhood immunization has become a government priority. There is a great need for drugs and other medical supplies due to the fighting.

The infant mortality rate is 34 per 1,000; life expectancy is between 67–74 years.

FOR THE TRAVELER

U.S. travelers need a valid passport and visa to enter Azerbaijan. Although a visa can be obtained on arrival, one must surrender a passport for at least a day to get it. Because registration at a hotel is impossible without a passport, get a visa in advance. Tourist travel is not recommended due to the instability. Credit cards are not accepted; only the local currency and U.S. dollars are taken. Travelers should drink boiled or bottled water. For travel or other information contact the Embassy of the Azerbaijani Republic, PO Box 28790, Washington, DC 20038–8790; phone (202) 842–0001.

Printed on recycled paper

State of
Bahrain

Boundary representations not necessarily authoritative.

BACKGROUND

Land and Climate

Bahrain consists of 33 islands, only three of which are inhabited. They are Al Bahrain, Al Muharraq, and Al Sitra. Manama, the capital, is located on the largest island, Al Bahrain. A causeway links that island to Al Muharraq, where the international airport is located. Many of the country's smaller islands are actually under water during high tides. The total land area of Bahrain is 240 square miles (620 square kilometers).

Bahrain is nestled on the western side of the Arabian (Persian) Gulf between Saudi Arabia and Qatar. It is connected to Saudi Arabia by a causeway. Generally flat, the country is dominated by desert terrain. However, it contains a number of natural springs that foster the growth of vegetation and abundant date palm trees. The climate is hot and humid. Summer months often see temperatures above 100°F (38°C). It is cooler between late December and February.

History

Owing to its strategic location in the Gulf and its natural springs, Bahrain has been the object of invaders' and traders' attention for thousands of years. The Romans, Greeks, Portuguese, British, and others ventured to Al Bahrain to conquer the island or trade with its inhabitants. For many years, people in the Gulf region buried their dead on the islands and there are some 175,000 burial mounds still visible. Many mounds have been excavated and some are up to 3,000 years old. The

Portuguese captured Bahrain in 1521 and ruled until 1602. After they were forced from the region, the islands were alternately controlled by different Arab and Persian groups until the Arab Utub tribe expelled the Persians in 1783. At that time, the current ruling Al Khalifa family (part of the Utub tribe) took control of Bahrain. Modern-day Iran (Persia) still maintains a claim to Bahrain and has renewed that claim as recently as 1993.

British influence and military domination in Bahrain began in the early 1800s, when Britain used force to establish a shipping and trading outpost that remained until 1971. At that time, Bahrain became a fully independent state headed by Emir Shaikh Issa bin Salman Al Khalifa. The emir had been the Bahraini monarch since 1961, but he became the sovereign leader at full independence. He was 38 years old and continues to hold the throne today.

In 1993, a *shura* council was formed by the emir and the prime minister, who appointed its citizen members. The council is to give greater voice to citizens. Although it will likely not criticize the Al Khalifa government, it does give some democratic opportunities to the people.

THE PEOPLE

Population

Bahrain's population of about 585,000 is growing at 2.9 percent annually. About one-fourth of all residents are expatriates from the Middle East, Asia, Europe, Africa, and North

America. The other 75 percent are Arabs. About 65 percent of the total population are Bahraini citizens. Non-Bahraini residents can become naturalized citizens by petitioning the emir, the prime minister, or the crown prince. Of the Arab population, most (70 percent) are *Shī'a* (Shiite) Muslims. The others, including the royal family, are Sunni Muslims. Bahrain, Iraq, and Iran are the only three countries in the Gulf region that have Shiite majorities.

Language

The official language of Bahrain is Arabic. English is also widely used, especially in business and banking circles. Farsi, a Persian dialect, is spoken by many Shiite Muslims, but it is not officially recognized. Many other languages are spoken by various expatriate groups. It is common for people living in Bahrain to be bilingual or multilingual.

Religion

The majority of people living in Bahrain are Muslims. *Islam* literally means "submission to the will of *Allah* (God)." A devout Muslim prays five times daily (prayer times shift by season according to sun position), and obeys the laws of the Muslim holy book, the *Qur'an* (Koran). These laws include avoiding alcohol, pork, and gambling. A Muslim fasts from sunrise to sunset during the month of *Ramadan* and must make a pilgrimage (*Hajj*) to the city of Makkah (Mecca) in Saudi Arabia at least once in a lifetime. The Sunni and Shiite Muslims have opposing traditions in Islam, especially in regards to the succession of the Prophet Muhammad; they also differ in their approach to certain teachings.

Religion is a central part of Bahraini culture. Work often stops during prayer times. Religion and government are deeply interwoven; it is *Shari'a* (the law of Islam) that establishes social order in connection with the civil law code.

Religious freedom is the policy in Bahrain and there are a number of Christian services available. Very few local Arabs would attend them or convert to Christianity because of the social pressure against it, but it is legal to do so.

General Attitudes

Bahrainis are proud of their country and its image as a nation of warm and friendly inhabitants. Bahrain's citizens are among the best educated in the Gulf. Most view their country as a key trading and banking center. As such, Bahrain is exposed to many foreign cultures and depends upon such interaction for its post-oil economic success. Bahrainis are also proud of their country's relatively low crime rate.

Although the population as a whole is familiar with the material ways of the West, Bahrainis remain dedicated to traditional values. The extended family remains the most important social institution. People fiercely defend their family's name and honor. After a death, relatives are close at hand to help with the grieving process. They also come to the aid of one another in times of need or financial hardship.

Personal Appearance

In villages, dress is traditional. Men wear a long, light robe (*thobe*) that reaches to the ankles. The head is covered by a light cloth headdress (*gutra*), clamped down by a heavy cloth ring (*ocal*). During warmer months the *thobe* is white. As temperatures get cooler, various colors are worn. The *gutra* is usually white, although it may also be white and red checked. The royal family and some of the very wealthy often adorn their attire with gold trim and wear an outer robe (*mishlah*) over the *thobe*. Women wear a full-length black robe (*ubaiya*) year-round. They wear a colorful dress underneath, but it cannot be seen in public. Some women also cover their hair with a scarf (*hijab*), and the most conservative cover their faces with a *burqa*, a veil that covers the bridge of the nose and cheeks. Both genders wear sandals on their feet.

In urban areas, the style of attire is generally a combination of traditional and Western dress. For example, some men may wear a sport coat over the *thobe* and choose shoes over sandals. Bahrainis tend to dress neatly; modesty is the norm. Both men and women use perfume.

CUSTOMS AND COURTESIES

Greetings

Personal greetings are important in Bahraini society. The most common way to say "Hello" is *Assalam alikum* (The peace of Allah be upon you). The usual reply is *Alikum essalam*, which has virtually the same meaning as *Assalam alikum*. The reply to *SabaHel khair* (Good morning) is *SabaHel nur*, and to *MasaEl khair* (Good evening), *MasaEl nur*. The people respond to "How are you?" (*Eshloanak* for a man; *Eshloanich* for a woman) with *Zain, al-Humdulillah* (Good, thanks be to *Allah*). "Good-bye" is *Ma'assalameh*.

Handshakes are common and may last the length of the conversation. This or a hand lightly grasping the person's arm shows friendliness. Good friends of the same sex sometimes kiss a number of times on the right and left cheeks. It is socially unacceptable for a man to greet a woman, unless the greeting is part of business protocol. Women, especially those from traditional rural families, look down in the presence of men.

It is customary to greet a member of the royal family by using the title *Shaikh* (for a man) or *Shaikha* (for a woman). For instance, Mohammed bin Rashid Al Khalifa would be addressed as Shaikh Mohammed or Shaikh Mohammed bin Rashid Al Khalifa. *Bin* means "son of."

Nicknames, formal and informal, are common. *Abu* means "father of" when it is used before the given name of the oldest son. For example, Abu Mohammed is the father of Mohammed. *Ibn* means "son of." So, Ibn Khuldoon is the son of Khuldoon. Informal nicknames used among friends are often adapted forms of a person's given name. Examples include Aboud for Abdulla, Hamoud for Mohammed, Fatoum for Fatima, Abbasi for Abbas, and Salmano for Salman.

Gestures

Most Bahrainis have become Westernized to the extent that using one's left hand to pass items or using fingers or hands to point is no longer considered rude. People beckon one another with all four fingers and the palm facing up. Waving with the palm down is used to assert authority over someone. Shaking a finger means "no." Bringing the tips of all fingers together facing up can mean "wait," "let me finish," impatience, or exasperation. The more the hand moves vertically, the more intense the message.

It is disrespectful to show others the soles of one's feet. Smoking is considered mature and many Bahrainis smoke, but it is rude to do so in the presence of elders. Many Bahrainis also chew gum or cardamom seeds.

Visiting

Bahrainis often invite relatives, friends and even foreigners into their homes. They visit immediate family almost daily, and visit cousins and other relatives usually every week. For more formal visits it is customary for guests to phone ahead and state the expected time of arrival. When visiting, a small gift is often brought for the hosts, such as sweets or flowers. Close friends and relatives might bring gifts such as perfume or clothing. Usually an invitation includes the offering of a large meal. Depending on the host's lifestyle, men and women might eat together at one table. But if the host is more traditional, men do not socialize with unmarried women who are not their daughters or sisters.

In traditional homes, a guest stays until the hosts bring out incense (*Bakhour*) and perfume for them. The incense is burned over a hot coal on a special stand (*mabkhara*). The incense and perfume are waved inward towards one's body and hair. After this ritual, a guest is expected to leave. To stay longer is impolite.

Eating

People eat while seated on an Arabic sofa that rests on the floor. Using their hands, everyone eats out of communal dishes. The names of the daily meals are *Iftar* or *Foutour* (breakfast), *Ghada* (lunch), and *Esha* (supper). Devout Muslims do not eat or drink with their left hand, but others will eat with either hand.

During a meal or even a light snack, guests are fed well. Bahraini hosts are pleased when guests enjoy the food and try all the dishes. Guests who are full must act quickly with polite firmness to refuse more food. If one hesitates, more food is served. It is polite in traditional settings to leave a small amount of food on one's plate. Typically a sweet tea is served with meals. Tea is also offered as the social drink for any occasion.

Bahrain has many fine restaurants and fast-food establishments. At better restaurants, the standard 10 percent service charge is usually not received by the servers. To personally reward a server, one must add a tip to the service charge. It is customary for the eldest man in a group to pay the restaurant bill and tip, especially on a family outing.

LIFESTYLE

Family

Extended family ties are a strong and dominant part of Bahraini culture. The father is the ultimate authority in the home. Children, especially daughters, do not lightly disobey their father's wishes. Married daughters often return to their parents' home before they give birth and stay for 40 days after the birth to receive care from their mothers and female relatives. The closeness of the family is also evident in the respectful and loving treatment given the elderly. Traditionally large families are growing smaller due to greater family planning, more women staying in school longer, and concerns for economic welfare.

Families typically live in free-standing, concrete dwellings. The home usually surrounds an open-air courtyard and has few windows. This protects the family's privacy. In older homes, wind towers provide air circulation and ventilation. Newer homes have air conditioners and electric ceiling fans.

Dating and Marriage

Dating is a controversial subject in Bahrain. Some young people are beginning to date with or without parental permission, but they do so mostly in secret to avoid embarrassing their families. This is because a girl is traditionally looked down upon if she goes out in the company of men other than family members. Society considers these women to be of lesser virtue, so parents worry that they will not be able to marry. Any woman who becomes pregnant out of wedlock faces difficult choices and must often bear the child in secret. Such children may be left to the care of the state, since single motherhood is not socially acceptable.

Some marriages are still arranged, while most marriages that are not arranged in the strict sense still have parental approval; few people marry without family authorization. In the past, women married in their early teens. This is increasingly rare and most marry in their late teens or early twenties.

Marriage celebrations usually last for three days, with separate festivities for men and women. On one night, the bride's hands and feet are decorated with henna, a brown plant dye that stays on the skin for days. The bride is also adorned with gold jewelry, including a *qobqob* (head piece). The bride's family pays for the henna day and the groom's family pays for the other two days.

A man is still allowed to have four wives if he provides equally for each wife. However, this is now typically practiced only among the older generations. Few young persons, even in the royal family, view polygamy as a desirable lifestyle.

Diet

Breakfast often consists of fresh *kobouz* (unleavened bread), scrambled eggs mixed with thin noodles and sprinkled with sugar, and cooked beans. Lunch usually consists of some type of spicy rice dish like *beryani* (rice with meat) or *machbous* (rice, meat, tomatoes, and lentils). Other popular dishes include *saloneh* (mixed vegetables) and *harees*, a traditional dish served during the month of *Ramadan*. *Harees* is a blend of wheat and meat cooked until mushy, with lard melted over the top. *Halwa*, a starch pudding mixed with crushed cardamom seeds, saffron, sugar, and fat, is traditionally served before *qahwa* (unsweetened coffee) to conclude the noon meal. The evening meal consists mainly of *bajella* (boiled beans), *kobouz*, an assortment of cheeses, and lots of sweet tea and milk. *Rottab* (dates) are served with every meal. Fish and seafood are also staples of the typical diet. Western influence on the diet is increasingly evident, especially in urban homes. Some Bahrainis now eat packaged breakfast cereals and fast food.

Recreation

The most popular sport is soccer. Basketball, volleyball, field hockey and cricket are also enjoyed. There are organized leagues for men, but women's leagues were dissolved in 1979 after the Iranian revolution. Currently, girls and women may only play sports in connection with school, but there is talk that organized leagues may again be established. Bahrainis and expatriates participate in a variety of recreational activities, including sailing, waterskiing, fishing, falconry, horse racing, desert camping, aerobics, softball, ice skating, horseback riding, tennis, and more. Renting videos is also popular.

Holidays

Religious holidays are celebrated according to the lunar *Hijri* calendar, which is shorter than the Western (Gregorian) year by about 11 days. Since dates are set according to the moon's phases, the Gregorian dates for holidays vary from year to year. The most important holidays include *Eid al Fitr*, a three-day feast at the end of the month of *Ramadan*; *Eid al Adha*, which commemorates Abraham's willingness to sacrifice his son and also marks the time for the *Hajj*; and the Prophet Muhammad's birthday. The Shiites celebrate *Assura*, a two-day holiday through which they express their beliefs. They parade in the streets, enacting the suffering of the martyr Hussain, the grandson of Muhammad. National Day is celebrated on 16 December. Many Bahrainis also celebrate New Year's on 1 January. The Christmas season is celebrated as the "festive season;" even though the religious significance of the holiday is minimal, it is not uncommon for Bahrainis to have Christmas trees and exchange gifts.

Commerce

Shops are typically open Saturday through Thursday from 8:00 A.M. to 1:00 P.M. They often close from 1:00 to 3:30 P.M. and then reopen until about 8:00 P.M. Business hours are gradually becoming longer. Certain stores are remaining open until midnight and some fast-food places are open 24 hours. Banking hours are normally from 8:00 A.M. to noon, Saturday through Thursday, and individual branches remain open three afternoons from 3:30 to 5:30 P.M.

When conducting business or shopping in Bahrain, people customarily exchange greetings and converse politely before getting down to details. Many messages important to the transaction are conveyed in the context of this conversation.

SOCIETY

Government

Bahrain is a traditional monarchy. The majority of key government positions are held by members of the Al Khalifa family. The emir is a respected leader and is generally well liked, as is the rest of the family. There is, however, some distrust in the Shiite community.

Bahrain employs the traditional Islamic administrative system of the *majlis*, which allows people to directly petition the emir. In practice, the few times available for citizens to meet with the emir reduce the interaction to greetings and other pleasantries rather than serious discussion. But it still gives people the unique chance to have valuable, direct contact with the monarch. The emir is said to have a remarkable ability to remember people from year to year and to take a genuine interest in what they have to say. All inquiries are met with an official reply, and such inquiries have often led to government action.

There is no legislature, but the appointed members of the *shura* council can be non-royal citizens. There are no political parties or elections.

Economy

Being an island nation with limited natural resources, Bahrain must rely on foreign trade to thrive economically. It has one of the world's largest oil refineries. Bahrain is also home to the world's largest aluminum smelter; the nation is trying to find its niche in the competitive world aluminum market. Bahrain pursues an ambition to be a regional banking center, despite heavy competition from Hong Kong and the United Arab Emirates. Progress in the industry was hampered in the 1980s because of the crash of oil prices.

Pearl diving was a prominent and honored occupation in the past, but the industry has been in serious decline since the introduction of cultured pearls harvested in other countries. Fishing, another traditional occupation, continues to be important to the domestic economy, but it is only a small portion of the export economy. The currency is the *dinar*.

Bahrain's Human Development Index (0.791) ranks it 58th out of 173 countries. Real gross domestic product per capita is $11,536. These figures reflect the country's oil wealth, but also the fact that the wealth has not yet provided the majority of people with economic prosperity.

Transportation and Communication

Bahrain's transportation network is modern, and most people own cars. Public buses are used mostly by poor expatriates. Bahrainis prefer taxis for public transportation.

Most homes have telephones. Cellular phones and mobile pagers have become a status symbol for men. Newspapers from around the world are available. Three local newspapers, which are subject to government control, have a wide readership. International programming is available in radio and television broadcasts.

Education

Bahrain is respected in the Gulf for its strong education system. Compulsory schooling exists for both boys and girls through the secondary level. Public schools are all single sex through grade 12, but most private schools are coeducational. Bahrain University admits both men and women. The overall literacy rate is 77 percent, but among the youth it approaches 100 percent.

Health

Health care is provided through a system of local clinics and a few major hospitals. Most services are available for free or at low cost to all residents. Private practices and facilities also exist. Bahrain's infant mortality rate is 19 per 1,000; the average life expectancy is 73 years. Nearly all children receive immunizations, and all women have access to prenatal care.

FOR THE TRAVELER

U.S. travelers need a valid passport and a visa to enter Bahrain. A three-to-seven-day transit visa can be obtained at the airport upon arrival, provided the traveler can prove he or she is in transit. Tourists will want to see the Grand Mosque, the Arad Fort, the burial mounds, the National Museum, the main *souq* near Bab Al Bahrain, and archaeological sites. A sea trip by wooden *dhow* is also interesting. Packaged tours are available, but one can also rent a car and set a personal itinerary. Dress conservatively and learn some Arabic. For more information, contact Bahrain's embassy, 3502 International Drive NW, Washington, DC 20008; phone (202) 342–0741.

People's Republic of
Bangladesh

Boundary representations not necessarily authoritative.

BACKGROUND

Land and Climate

With 55,599 square miles (144,000 square kilometers), Bangladesh is about the same size as Wisconsin. It is a fertile delta, except in the southeast and northeast, where it's hilly. Rivers and channels run throughout the country; the three largest rivers are the Ganga, Jamuna, and Meghna. Winter (October–March) is cool and mild; summer (March–June) is hot and humid. The monsoon season (June–October) brings most of Bangladesh's yearly rain; floods, tidal waves, and cyclones are common. In 1991, a cyclone took over 139,000 lives in the coastal area, destroying entire villages and flooding croplands. A better warning system prevented such a tragedy during storms in 1994.

History

In the 12th century, Muslims began to conquer Hindus in the area now known as Bangladesh. British rule came in the 18th century and the area was part of British India for nearly 200 years. When British rule ended in 1947, the area became part of the new nation of Pakistan and was called East Pakistan. While linked by religion, the two areas were separated culturally and geographically. East Pakistan did not feel it enjoyed equality with West Pakistan. Calls for autonomy peaked in 1971 and a nine-month civil war began in March. The war eventually involved India because it was flooded by refugees. After the stranded Pakistani army surrendered to Indian forces, Bangladesh became independent. Sheikh Mujibur Rahman, leader of the Awami League political party, became the first prime minister and is considered the father of the country. He was assassinated in a 1975 coup.

Following a shaky interim period, Ziaur Rahman governed from 1977 to 1981, when he was assassinated. Hussain Mohammed Ershad took control and governed until 1990 when public protests forced his resignation. A transitional government sponsored free national elections in 1991 and Begum Khaleda Zia, the widow of Ziaur Rahman, was elected to lead a new democracy. Challenged by natural disasters, regional problems, and a long-running insurgency in the southeast, Zia faced continual difficulty in stabilizing the country. While some progress was made, political opponents tried to force her from office. All opposition members of parliament resigned at the end of 1994 and called for a series of strikes in 1995 to force early elections under a neutral caretaker government. Zia refused to step down, but said she would leave office at least a month ahead of elections in 1996.

THE PEOPLE

Population

Bangladesh has more than 125 million people and is growing at about 2.3 percent annually. With a population density of more than 2,200 persons per square mile (870 per square kilometer), Bangladesh is one of the most densely populated countries in the world. Most people live in Bangladesh's thousands of small villages. Only about 16 percent live in cities.

Except for about 250,000 Biharis (Muslims who immigrated from Bihar, India) and some small groups in the southeast, Bangladeshis consider themselves a homogeneous people. They have an Indo-European heritage, with some Arab, Persian, and Turkish influence. The people of West Bengal in India are of the same ethnic group as the Bangladeshis, but they are mostly Hindus. To emphasize this difference, most people refer to themselves as Bangladeshis rather than Bangalis (the technical term for Bangla speakers).

Language

Bangla, the official language, is also spoken in India's West Bengal. Spoken Bangla has several distinct dialects, the strongest (most guttural) of which are spoken in the northeastern and southeastern districts of Bangladesh. Most Bangla dialects are soft and somewhat musical. People with a university education usually speak English. They incorporate various colloquialisms derived from Bangla into spoken English. The Biharis speak Urdu, an official language in Pakistan. Small groups along the southeast border speak their own languages.

Religion

Bangladesh has the second largest Muslim population in the world; more than 85 percent of the people are Muslim. Most Bangladeshis are Sunni Muslims. Muslims pray five times daily. The midday *Ju'mma* service on Friday is the most important prayer time. Muslims accept the *Qur'an* (Koran) as scripture, believing it was revealed by *Allah* to Muhammad through the angel Gabriel.

Hindus (13 percent) make up the other major religious group. Christians are few in number, but Christian churches are appreciated for their relief efforts and educational institutions.

Muslims do not drink alcohol or eat pork. Hindus do not eat beef. Muslims fast from sunrise to sundown during the month of *Ramzan* (*Ramadan*). Each evening the fast is broken with special snacks called *iftar*. It is polite for non-Muslims to avoid daytime public eating, drinking, or smoking during *Ramzan*. Bangladeshis stress cleanliness near holy books and places. Shoes are removed before entering mosques and temples.

General Attitudes

A calm and serious face is considered a sign of maturity. Therefore, while Bangladeshis might not smile in public, they are not being unfriendly. It is not customary to thank someone for a favor. Although the word *dhannabad* (thanks) exists, Bangladeshis avoid using it in everyday life. Instead, one returns the favor. *Dhannabad* is used, however, in formal situations. Bangladeshis value the group more than the individual, so family needs come first. Friendships are expected to be strong and durable. Society is male dominated. Men are protective of women in the family. Women are discouraged from being out alone after sunset. Except in the upper class, women generally have a low status in society, but there is a growing movement to promote women's rights. Women comprise just 7 percent of the labor force.

Social classes play an integral but diminishing role in Bangladesh. For example, class is often still an important factor when considering marriage. The way a woman is treated by her husband's family is often determined by her father's wealth; if he is poor, she may be treated poorly.

Bangladeshis are proud of their artistic tradition, which is much older than their young country. They appreciate poetry, music, and literature. Bangali poetry, known for its passion and emotion, reflects the character of the Bangladeshi people. Fatalism—reflected in the arts—plays an important role in people's lives. Many are happy to lead simple, modest lives without various material comforts.

Personal Appearance

Although many men wear Western clothing, especially in urban areas, women generally wear a traditional *saree*—a long piece of printed cloth wrapped around the body in a special way. Jewelry is important to a woman's wardrobe; it also serves as financial security. Women do not wear pants. Adults do not wear shorts. Some men wear white religious clothing called *pajama* (like a Western pajama bottom) and *panjabi* (like a pajama top, but extending to the knee). Men in rural villages often wear a *lungi* (a circular piece of cloth, knotted at the waist, that extends to the ankles) with a *genji* (a sleeveless vest).

CUSTOMS AND COURTESIES

Greetings

Muslim Bangladeshis greet each other with *Assalaa-mualaikum* (Peace be upon you) and respond with *Waalaikum assalaam* (And peace be upon you). Each person may raise the right hand to his forehead, palm curved and relaxed, in a salute-like gesture. Men might also shake hands and may embrace during religious festivals. One does not shake hands, kiss, or embrace a member of the opposite sex in public. A common Hindu greeting is *Adab* (Hello). At parting, a Muslim might say *Khoda hafiz* (May God be with you). *Ashi* (So long) is common for all groups.

In addressing people, Bangladeshis add different suffixes to names to show not only respect, but also closeness. For example, a man adds *bhabi* (wife of older brother) to the name of his friend's wife, even though they have no family ties. The terms "sister" and "brother" are used as commonly for friends and colleagues as for family members. Age difference is the key factor in determining how to address another person. A person of the same age is usually addressed by name, whereas an older person (regardless of how few years separate the two) may be addressed by name plus a family-related suffix (older brother, son of father's brother, older sister, etc.) or by the suffix alone. So, a young adult might address an older woman by adding *apa* (older sister) to her name or simply by calling her *apa*.

Gestures

Eye contact during conversation shows sincerity. However, to show respect to an older person or someone of higher social standing, one usually looks down and speaks only when spoken to. In general, it is impolite to cross one's legs or to smoke in the presence of elders, regardless of what the older person does. One does not point the bottom of the shoe or foot at a person because it is thought to lower that person's worth. Bangladeshis are also sensitive about one's foot touching books or other reading materials. Should a person accidently touch a book with a foot, the person apologizes by touching the book with the fingertips of the right hand, and then touching the chest and then the lips.

It is polite to point with the chin, but impolite to whistle or wink in public. Beckoning with the index finger is very rude. In general, it is impolite to beckon adults, but beckoning is done with the palm turned down and all fingers waving together. The American sign for "okay" (thumb and index finger touching to form a circle) is obscene. The thumbs-up gesture is a sign of rejection in Bangladesh.

Visiting

Bangladeshis visit each other often, usually in the late morning or late afternoon. Guests are offered tea (rarely coffee) and sometimes sweets. It is customary to decline the offer a few times but to eventually accept at least some tea. Guests visiting at mealtime are usually invited to eat.

For social occasions, most people avoid being the first or among the last to arrive. When people are invited to an event, but cannot go, they still say they will try to attend. Saying "No" may be interpreted as not valuing the host's friendship. The entire extended family is expected to be invited.

Because Bangladeshis are class-conscious, they avoid inviting people they think they cannot satisfactorily entertain. Also, people evade certain invitations, such as birthday parties, if they feel they cannot take a proper gift. No gifts are expected of dinner guests, but dinner invitations are usually reciprocated.

Eating

Bangladeshis generally do not use knives and forks at home, but spoons are used to eat sweets. Food is eaten with the right hand, which is washed before each meal. Because the left hand is used for sanitation, it is not used to pass objects or to eat. *Shu'ra* (a sauce) is often served with meals. For reasons of cleanliness, people don't let *shu'ra* touch above their knuckles when eating.

Bangladeshis do not converse much during a meal, especially at home. Food is not passed around the table; rather, plates are taken to a main dish for serving. Bones and other food wastes are placed on bone plates so they are separate from one's meal. On special occasions, children often eat first. Men and women eat separately at large social gatherings (such as weddings), but not for everyday meals.

At restaurants, the wealthiest person often pays for everyone's meal, particularly among relatives. It is, however, becoming more common among students to pay individually. Expensive restaurants have utensils, but ordinary restaurants often do not.

LIFESTYLE

Family

Due to economic necessity, extended families often share the same dwelling, but the nuclear family is becoming more popular with the younger generation. Children, especially sons, are expected to care for their elderly parents. Bangladesh has no social security system or nursing homes. Grandparents or older siblings are responsible for child care when the parents are away or working.

Dating and Marriage

Young people have fewer opportunities for social interaction with the opposite sex as they grow older. Dating is unknown. When men and women go out together, as do a small number of university students, the relationship is expected to lead to marriage. Sexual relations outside of marriage are strongly discouraged; self-restraint is considered an indicator of one's potential to build a strong marriage. Women often marry before they are 18, especially in rural areas. Men marry after they finish education or have some financial security.

Marriage is often arranged through a *ghatak* (matchmaker), who could be a relative or family friend. If a man and woman get to know each other on their own, the man sends a formal proposal to the woman's parents through an older relative. For weddings, both the bride and groom's houses are decorated with lights. Bamboo gates, decorated with colorful pieces of cloth, are placed at the entrance. The bride wears a *saree* and jewelry; the groom wears a *shirwani* (knee-length coat), a *pagri* (traditional cap), and *nagra* (flat shoes that curl upward in front). A Muslim groom pledges money for the bride's future if the marriage fails; it is recorded in the *ka'been* (marriage registry). Although divorce and polygamy are legal, both carry a negative stigma. While having more than one wife is increasingly rare, divorce is slowly becoming more common.

Diet

Rice is the main staple food. Because Bangladesh has many rivers, fish is cheaper and more available than meat. With a few exceptions (carrots, cucumbers, and tomatoes), vegetables are fried in oil. Spicy food is preferred. Popular spices include cumin, ginger, coriander, tumeric, and pepper. Food is often marinated in *shu'ra* (made from chopped onions and spices marinated in warm cooking oil). A good *shu'ra* is considered an index of fine cooking. Dessert is not usually eaten after meals, but sweets are eaten on special occasions. Two popular sweets (*rashogolla* and *kalojam*) are variations of dough boiled in syrup.

Recreation

The most popular sports are soccer, field hockey, cricket, table tennis, and badminton. Visiting friends and relatives is another form of recreation; in fact, it is expected because it reinforces the family support network. Televisions and video machines are becoming popular in cities. Movie theaters are plentiful. Hindu movies (often musicals) from India are favorites, and the youth enjoy movies from the United States. Dance and music performances are attended by the wealthy, but there are no discotheques in Bangladesh.

In villages, the most popular youth game is called *ha-dudu* or *kabaddi*, which is played on a square court. While holding his breath, one team's player enters the other side's area and tries to touch as many of the other players as possible before returning to his side. If he's successful, the other team loses the players he touched and his team gains an equal number of its own players back (from previous rounds). If, however, he's trapped by the opposite team while trying to tag its members and is forced to release his breath, he's out and the opposing team gains one of its members back. The first team to eliminate all players on the other side wins.

Holidays

Political and cultural holidays follow the Western calendar, but religious holidays follow the lunar calendar (so they are on different days each year). A third Bangla calendar determines seasons and the new year (*Pahela Baishak*). Political holidays include *Ekushe February* (21 February, honoring three students who died in a 1952 political protest), Independence Day (26 March, when independence was declared), Labor Day (1 May), and Victory Day (16 December, when independence was actually achieved). The most important religious (Muslim) holidays are *Eid-ul-Fitr* (at the end of *Ramzan*), *Eid-ul-Azha* (commemorating Abraham's willingness to sacrifice his son), and *Shab-i-Barat* (a special night for asking blessings). Some Hindu, Buddhist, and Christian feasts are also celebrated as national holidays.

The *Eid* holidays begin with prayer services and are marked by three days of feasting and visiting. It is common for children to bow and touch the feet of older people in the extended family to show respect. The older people then give the children gifts, usually money. It is also customary to exchange one-third of the meat sacrificed during *Eid-ul-Azha* as gifts (one-third is donated to the poor and one-third is kept). During *Shab-i-Barat*, neighbors exchange sweets.

Commerce

Weekdays are from Saturday to Thursday; offices are closed Friday. Small grocery and retail stores may stay open every day late into the night. Prices in stores are neither marked nor fixed, so bartering is common. Business people interact socially to build trust and a network of acquaintances. Problems are best solved privately by appealing to civility, honor, and goodwill, although legal channels are available.

SOCIETY

Government

In its early years, Bangladesh had a parliamentary system of government with a prime minister as chief executive. Mujib (the "ur," often part of a person's full name, is dropped if referring to the person by his popularly known name) changed the government to a presidential system, which both Ershad and Zia retained. A national referendum in September 1991 reestablished a parliamentary system. Mrs. Zia is the prime minister. The president is Abdur Rahman Biswas. The *Jatiya Sangsad* (parliament) has 300 elected seats. A person can run for and win more than one seat, so there are not always the same number of members as seats. An additional 30 seats are reserved for women. All citizens over age 18 may vote.

Economy

The economy is based on agriculture, which employs 60 percent of the labor force. Jute, a plant whose fiber is used to make carpets, is the main export. In fact, Bangladesh is the world's largest exporter of jute. Other important exports include tea, leather, and shrimp. The country imports many of its consumer goods and food. The textile industry is expanding. Wages sent home from Bangladeshis working in Middle Eastern countries have been an important source of income, but many Bangladeshis lost their jobs during the Gulf War. Extreme poverty, along with high unemployment (30 percent) and natural disasters, hinders economic growth.

Bangladesh's Human Development Index (0.309) ranks it 146th out of 173 countries. Real gross domestic product per capita is $1,160, which has increased somewhat in the last generation. These figures indicate most people either do not earn an income or do not earn enough to meet basic needs. Three-fourths of all people live in poverty. The currency is the *taka* (Tk).

Transportation and Communication

Traffic moves on the left. Roads are not extensive and most are not paved. The main forms of public transportation include buses (often crowded), *rickshaws*, and *babi-taxis* (three-wheeled motor scooters). For private transport, most people walk or ride bicycles. Because of the many rivers but few bridges, land transportation links are poorly developed. However, rivers are used to transport people and goods throughout the country. Railways are also important.

Telephones are available in urban areas. A person is billed for every call, even local ones. Bangladesh has a national television station and nine radio stations. There are a number of daily newspapers. Mail delivery is slow.

Education

Bangladesh's literacy rate is 35 percent (47 for men and 22 for women). Boys and girls attend separate schools. Fewer than one-fifth get a secondary education. Universities are coeducational. Approximately 3 percent of the people complete an education of ten years of school, two years of college (comparable to grades 12 and 13), and three or more years at a university.

Health

Bangladesh has a high infant mortality rate (107 per 1,000 births) due partly to malnutrition. The life expectancy for men and women averages 55 years; it's higher in urban areas than in rural areas. Sanitation is poor and water is not potable in most areas. Hospital care is free, but it's inadequate to meet people's needs. Private clinics provide better care, but only the wealthy can afford them. Services are limited in rural areas.

FOR THE TRAVELER

A passport, visa, and proof of onward passage are required for U.S. visitors to enter Bangladesh. Malaria and cholera are common, as are typhoid and hepatitis. Consult a doctor for recommended vaccinations. Avoid drinking water that has not been boiled; do not eat food from street vendors or poorly maintained restaurants. Wash and peel all fruits and vegetables. Be sure all meat is well cooked and served hot. For more information, contact the Embassy of Bangladesh, 2201 Wisconsin Avenue NW, Suite 300, Washington, DC 20007.

CULTURGRAM™ '96

Republic of
Benin

Boundary representations not necessarily authoritative.

BACKGROUND

Land and Climate

Benin is a small western African nation located between Togo and Nigeria. Covering 43,482 square miles (112,620 square kilometers), it is just smaller than Pennsylvania. From its coast on the Atlantic Ocean, Benin runs only 420 miles to the northern border. Rolling hills and plains dominate the landscape, but the Atacora Mountains provide variety in the north. Major rivers include the Ouéme, Zou, Pendjari, Mékrou, Alibori, Sota, and Niger. The capital is Porto-Novo.

Benin's north is generally higher in elevation and drier; rain falls between June and September. The hot season is October to April, with January temperatures reaching above 100°F (37°C). Between December and March, the harmattan (dry hot wind) blows from north to south. The lower-lying south experiences four seasons: a long rainy season March–July, followed by a short hot season until September; and a short rainy season to November, followed by a long hot season until March. Temperatures are cooler than in the north, but it is still hot (95°F or 35°C).

Deforestation has destroyed many southern forests, but ceiba, ebony, mahogany, and palm trees are still found. Elephants, lions, giraffes, antelopes, monkeys, boars, crocodiles, wildebeest, and snakes all inhabit Benin. Most snakes are poisonous, and the python is considered sacred.

History

The history of Benin (called Dahomey until 1975) cannot be separated from the history of the powerful Fon kingdom of Danhomê. It was known for its slave trade and production of palm oil, and for having an army of women (the Amazons). Other kingdoms were prominent at the same time as Danhomê, such as the Kingdom of Porto-Novo in the south and the northern kingdoms of Borgu, Nikki, Djougou, and Kouande. Danhomê expanded its northern frontier in the early 1800s to acquire more slaves from neighboring tribes. It also fiercely resisted French incursions beginning in 1857. In 1893, the French finally defeated King Gbehanzin, the hero of the resistance, and gradually spread their administrative control throughout the region. By 1904, Dahomey was fully integrated into French West Africa.

Independence came in 1960, but the first 12 years were marked by regional strife, trade union and student strikes, and six military coups. No one could unite the nation until Major Matthieu Kérékou seized power. He eventually (1974) adopted Marxism-Leninism as the official ideology, renamed the country the People's Republic of Benin, and governed with a strong hand until 1989.

When communism disintegrated in Europe, Kérékou sponsored a national conference in which it was decided that Benin would become a multiparty democracy. Kérékou headed a transitional government until a new constitution was written and elections could be held in 1991. Although the period was unstable due to strikes and opposition activities, national elections were held on schedule. Nicéphore Soglo defeated Kérékou to become president of the newly declared Republic of Benin. Beninese proudly point to this transition from a one-party state to a democracy as a model for other nations.

PEOPLE

Population

The population of 5.3 million grows annually at 3.3 percent. Benin's diversity of ethnic groups is the result of migrations, conquests, and the mixing of groups over time. The Fon is the largest single group with 47.1 percent of the population. Other larger groups include the Adja (12.2 percent), Bariba (9.7), and Yoruba or Aizo (5.1). In the north, a number of smaller groups form 5 percent of the population; these include the Dendi, Betamari, Berba, Kountemba, Ouama, and others. Southern and northern Beninese do not have the best relations, and northerners are often insultingly referred to as *Somba* by southerners. More recent immigrants to Benin include Togolese, Ghanaians, and Nigerians. Two-thirds of all people live in the south, particularly between Cotonou and Abomey. Cotonou alone claims 12 percent of the total population.

Language

French, the official language, is used in government and education. No indigenous language has been accepted as a national language, so French remains the unifying tongue. Still, many rural people have trouble speaking it. The Adja-Fon language group (Fon, Adja, Houéda, Popo, Mahi, Mina, Goun, etc.) dominates in the south and central regions. Yoruba is also widely spoken in these areas. Bariba and other languages are spoken in the north. To promote literacy, from 1975 to 1990 the government encouraged the use of major national languages in radio and television broadcasts. English, Spanish, German, and Russian are offered in secondary schools, and many Beninese can understand Nigerian Pidgin English.

Religion

Although Christianity has had a presence in Benin since the 17th century, indigenous belief systems permeate the country's culture. Most Beninese believe in a supreme God (*Mahu* among the Fon and *Olorun* or *Olodumare* among the Yoruba), and in a life after death. They attach great importance to worshipping ancestors who protect them against misfortune. Accordingly, death is regarded as an important family event and, in some cases, funeral rites are sophisticated. Divination is a central feature of local faith; people regularly consult an oracle about significant events they wish to undertake. People worship the supreme God through local divinities (*Voodoos* among the Fon and *Orisha* among the Yoruba). Most families have a fetish to which they pray and offer sacrifice in order to get help from these local gods.

Even Beninese who have adopted Christianity or Islam continue to practice fetish worship and other indigenous rites. They do not see the rules of organized religion as particularly binding or exclusive. Indeed, forms of Christianity that integrate African practices are developing quickly, and there is little religious conflict between groups. Twenty percent of Benin's population is Christian, mostly Catholic. Islam (15 percent) is practiced mostly in the north.

General Attitudes

Although attitudes and values differ between ethnic groups, some common traits are characteristic. For instance, few Beninese value privacy. Most wonder why anyone would actually want to be alone. They take life at a fairly casual pace and have a good sense of humor that allows them to laugh at life's trivial problems. Humor does not extend to sarcasm, however, which is viewed as insulting. The Beninese are proud of their heritage. Most value hard work and material success, but these come second to family priorities and friendship bonds. Although perhaps initially distrustful of individuals, Beninese are very hospitable. Once trust is established, relationships remain strong. Misconceptions between the north and south are partly due to the fact that northerners are more traditional and reserved than people in the south, who have greater exposure to Western ideas and education.

Personal Appearance

Cleanliness and neatness are extremely important. As much as possible, people mend all holes and iron out all wrinkles in their clothing. They wear the best they can afford and shower daily.

Beninese dress is conservative. Urban residents wear anything from Western shirts, trousers, and suits to local fashions. Men's casual clothing often consists of a pair of loose trousers and a long-sleeved shirt that can reach to the knees. Formal outfits consist of three embroidered pieces: trousers, a long shirt, and a top usually called a *boubou* or *agbada*. Imported fabrics are used in addition to locally produced material. Rural men often wear a cloth about the waist and a small *dashiti* top or short-sleeved shirt, or they may wrap the waist cloth up to cover the chest and one shoulder.

Rural and urban women often wear a *pagne* (wraparound skirt). This can be long or short depending on one's age and marital status. A loose *boumba* (blouse) completes the outfit. Women wear a long *boubou* on formal occasions.

CUSTOMS AND COURTESIES

Greetings

A proper greeting always precedes conversation. When joining or leaving a small group, each individual is greeted. Men usually shake right hands, with the oldest person initiating the handshake. Women only shake hands with men if the man initiates. To show special respect, particularly to an older person, one bows slightly and grasps the right elbow with the left hand during a handshake. In cities, young men snap fingers when they shake hands. Many urban relatives and friends tend to kiss three or four times alternately on the cheeks. Some rural people do this and add a kiss to the mouth.

The Fon ask *A fon dagbe a?* (Did you wake up well?), while the Yoruba say *E Karo* (Good morning). Similar expressions are used in other languages throughout Benin. When addressing others, people of the same age and status use first names or nicknames. Titles are reserved for official functions. It is disrespectful to call older people by their first names. Instead, one uses brother or sister (*Fofo* or *Dada* among the Fon) and uncle or aunt. If the eldest child is named Dossa, parents are often called Dossa's mother (*Dossanon*) or Dossa's father (*Dossato*).

Gestures

Everyday conversation is accompanied by many gestures and sounds. For instance, when women complain, they often hit the side of their thighs. Various verbal noises can express agreement or exasperation. It is considered offensive to beckon someone with the index finger; instead, all fingers of the right hand are waved with the palm facing down. Public displays of affection are unacceptable, but friends of the same gender often hold hands or touch when talking or walking. Using the left hand for gestures is unclean and considered bad luck.

Showing respect for elders is vital. One does not interrupt an older person in conversation, nor does one talk to him or her with hands in the pockets or while chewing gum or wearing a hat. Avoiding eye contact shows deference to elders. Among equals, eye contact can indicate frankness.

Visiting

Visiting friends and relatives is regarded as considerate, and it is not necessary to notify them in advance. Visitors are warmly welcomed and offered some water to drink. The host may take a sip before offering it to guests, and in rural areas guests often spill a bit on the earth to show respect for the dead.

If visitors arrive during a meal, hosts feel obligated to offer some food. Visitors should accept at least a bite, as it is rude not to taste the food, but they can politely decline to eat the entire meal. Visitors ask for permission to leave; when the host agrees, he walks them at least to the door and sometimes further. Reciprocity is an important part of relationships, so today's guest is expected to be tomorrow's host.

While most visiting takes place in the home, the marketplace is also a popular point of social contact. Every town or village has a market day once a week or so where people enjoy meeting to chat.

Eating

Eating habits depend on one's activities. Rural peasants eat anytime in the morning, often in the fields. They have lunch at home later in the afternoon and dinner at night. Wage earners may have one, two, or three meals, depending on their financial means. Urban dwellers often have breakfast between 7:00 and 10:00 A.M., lunch between 1:00 and 3:00 P.M., and dinner between 7:00 and 10:00 P.M. Spoons and other utensils may be used for some foods, but the hand is generally preferred, especially for okra, *eba* (see Diet), or pounded yam. At home, people eat from a common bowl (children share one and parents share another). The father is usually served first, and families eat together. In northern areas, however, when male guests are present, the wife eats separately.

LIFESTYLE

Family

The traditional family structure consists of an extended family living in a compound of separate houses surrounded by a wall or fence and having a common courtyard with a well, space for animals, and a cooking area. Such a family expects to work hard together to meet basic needs, and all members expect to share the fruits of labor. Tolerance and support are key elements to family interaction, and it is considered a curse to have bad relations within the family unit. While this structure is preferred and remains mostly intact in rural areas, it is undergoing profound change in cities, where nuclear families are more common and where the idea of working together has become less important. Because the desire is still strong to share in what others have accomplished, some conflicts have arisen and society is struggling to keep the system working.

Polygamy is legal and practiced across all ethnic groups and religions, but most families are monogamous. Northern men are more likely than southern men to have two wives. Women do much of the work in a family, but the father is its head. Nevertheless, women are respected for their role in raising children and for considerable success in agriculture and trade (retail and wholesale). Elderly women are highly regarded. Most families have more than two children and prefer to have at least one son to perpetuate the family name.

Dating and Marriage

While urban dating is becoming more of a casual affair, traditional dating is geared toward marriage. Depending on the area's customs, young people might socialize at local ceremonies, dance parties, dinners, or family functions like marriages or funerals.

Wedding traditions vary widely. Most Beninese attach a lot of importance to customary and religious marriages. Christians and Muslims mix their respective customs with local ways. A common practice is negotiating the bride-price. Elder women from the bride's family preside over a ceremony where they accept the groom's gifts and officially agree to the marriage, which is considered an alliance between two families. This bride-price, which legislation has sought to discourage, and the cost of a proper wedding can be so high that the wedding might be postponed for months or years until sufficient finances are available. In such cases, couples may live together and have children as if married.

Diet

The Beninese prefer hot and spicy foods. The basic daily meal is a spicy stew eaten with a stiff porridge made from corn flour (*wo, amiwo*) in the south, yam flour (*amala* or *loubo*) in Yoruba areas, or millet and sorghum flour in the north. Side dishes are pounded yam, fried or boiled yam and cassava, sweet potatoes, and fried bananas and *gari*, a kind of grits made from cassava. *Gari* is also eaten with any kind of stew or soup, or it is thinned and drunk like a porridge with sugar or milk. Boiled in water, *gari* is also served as a side dish (*eba*) eaten with stew. Beans are popular. Rice, which is mostly imported, is increasingly consumed. Beninese stews have many ingredients: vegetables and leaves, okra, peanuts, palm nut pulp, and so on.

The Beninese eat a variety of tropical fruits (bananas, mangos, oranges, papayas, avocados, tangerines, and pineapples) and snacks in the morning or late afternoon. Meat is saved for special occasions because it is so expensive; favorite types include chicken, goat, beef, and a special delicacy, *agouti* (sugarcane rat). The entire animal is eaten with no part being wasted. French cuisine is found in urban areas. Fresh seafood is plentiful in the south.

Recreation

Beninese enjoy getting together; visiting is a major form of recreation. Many social events are closely related to family or religious ceremonies. People also love soccer and other games like basketball, handball, and boxing. Wrestling is common in the north. Televisions are scarce, but people have access to one somewhere in the village, and large groups often get together to watch favorite programs or World Cup soccer. Only a few people can afford to go to a restaurant or on beach outings. The Beninese enjoy playing cards, checkers, or *adji* (a popular mathematical and probability game) outdoors. Traditional dancing to drums is popular.

Holidays

Official holidays are New Year's Day (1 January), Easter Monday, International Workers' Day (1 May), Independence Day (1 August), Christmas Day, *Odun Idi* (feast at the end of the holy Muslim month of *Ramadan*), and *Odun Lea* (Muslim Feast of Sacrifice). Rural people have local celebrations as well.

Commerce

Government offices are open weekdays 8:00 A.M. to noon and 3:00 to 6:30 P.M. Banks usually close by 4:00 P.M. Private businesses operate on their own schedules. Business should only be initiated after a greeting and social conversation. Shop prices are usually fixed, but bargaining is essential at open markets. Merchants respect a good bargainer and see the exchange as a game as well as a transaction. The most famous market, *Tokpa* or *Dantokpa* ("near the river"), is held every five days in Cotonou. Street hawkers informally sell their goods at crossroads. The first customer of the day is important because he or she brings either hard or good luck.

SOCIETY

Government

Benin is a multiparty democracy composed of six provinces. The president acts as chief of state and head of government and is directly elected for a five-year term. The National Assembly has 64 members, who are also freely elected. Every citizen may vote at age 18. More than 50 political parties are active in this young democracy, but only a handful have legislative representation. No one party has yet established dominance. Regionalism, a system of political clientelism based on ethnic origin that flourished prior to 1990, has not entirely disappeared, but President Nicéphore Soglo's government is working hard to unite the country.

Economy

Benin is one of the poorest countries in the world. Its Human Development Index (0.261) ranks it 156th out of 173 countries. Real gross domestic product per capita is about $1,500, but most wealth is concentrated in the hands of a few. Two-fifths of all people live in poverty, relying on subsistence farming for their livelihood. In fact, 90 percent of all agricultural output comes from small farms. Agriculture accounts for 35 percent of export earnings. Major crops include corn, cassava and other tubers, groundnuts, sorghum, and millet. Cotton is the chief export crop, but cash crops like coffee, cocoa, peanuts, and tobacco are also produced in small quantities. Industry employs only 2 percent of the workforce. Crude oil is the country's most important export. Remittances from Beninese working abroad are vital to the economy.

Benin imports far more than it exports, and a lot of illegal trade is conducted across Benin's borders, particularly with Nigeria. The current government is implementing reforms and encouraging foreign investment to stimulate growth. Some success has been noted and annual growth is about 3 percent. The currency is the *CFA franc*.

Transportation and Communication

Benin's few roads are mostly unpaved. Urban public transport hardly exists, although inexpensive taxis do operate in large cities. Taxi-motorcycles called *zemidjans* have quickly become a substitute for taxis in Porto-Novo and Cotonou. Many people also have their own motorcycles and some have cars. Driving is unsafe as traffic rules are minimal.

Private telephones are rare, but the number of public phones is increasing. Benin has one government-operated television station and broadcasts from neighboring countries can sometimes be received. Abundant newspapers enjoy a wide urban readership. Rural people receive news from private radio stations and through village meetings.

Education

In 1974, the government tried to replace its French-based educational system, but it failed for a number of reasons. While it allowed people to learn written local languages (most languages are oral) instead of French, facilities and materials were lacking. Since 1990, more private and Catholic schools have opened and the curriculum is reverting to the French model. Nevertheless, the challenges remain the same: to create a school system flexible enough to take into account changing national realities, to help reduce unemployment, and to absorb the vast majority of children under 15 who represent 40 percent of the total population. The drop-out rate is high. Reasons vary and often involve finances. Children are important members of the family labor pool and cannot be spared for many years of schooling, which begin at age six. Only about one in ten children gains a secondary education. Most students at all levels are boys. The literacy rate is 25 percent.

Benin has a university in Abomey-Calavi with a medical school. Other professional schools (for nursing, administration, and teaching) are also available.

Health

Benin has no national health care system. Public hospitals require payment for services, but they are cheaper than private clinics. Preventive medicine is not widely practiced. For instance, immunizations are not trusted, food taboos for pregnant women have caused malnutrition, and most people only seek medical attention when they get sick. Doctors are few, as most go abroad to practice. Many diseases afflicting Benin (yellow fever, influenza, river blindness, etc.) could be avoided if people would accept a more preventive approach. Indigenous (mostly herbal) medicines are more trusted, and the government is trying to integrate them with modern treatments. Training and modern equipment are badly needed. The infant mortality rate is 110 per 1,000; life expectancy is about 52 years.

FOR THE TRAVELER

A valid passport, visa, and proof of onward passage are required for U.S. citizens to enter Benin. The yellow fever and cholera vaccinations are mandatory. Malaria is common, so suppressants must be taken continuously. Eat only hot and well-cooked foods; wash and peel fruits and vegetables. Do not drink unboiled water. Beaches are clean and safe if guarded. For tourist information, contact the Embassy of Benin, 2737 Cathedral Avenue NW, Washington, DC 20008; phone (202) 232–6656.

CULTURGRAM '96 ™

Republic of
Botswana

Boundary representations not necessarily authoritative.

BACKGROUND

Land and Climate

Botswana, a landlocked country in southern Africa, covers 585,370 square miles (600,370 square kilometers). It is about the same size as France or Texas. About 80 percent of its territory (west of most cities) is covered by the Kgalagadi (Kalahari) Desert, which consists of savanna grasses and shrubs, but no water. Gently rolling hills form the eastern border. The Okavango Delta, the world's largest inland delta, is found in the north. Its wetlands, as well as the country's many national parks, harbor a wide variety of animals and plant life.

Reservoirs provide water for major urban areas, but most water comes from wells. Small dams catch rain runoff for cattle, which far outnumber the human population. Drought cycles are common to the region. Six years of drought ended in 1988, but rains since then have been late, light, or so quick that the earth has not been able to absorb enough water to support a full crop. Hence, drought conditions still exist in the 1990s.

Summer is from October to April, with temperatures often above 100°F (37°C). During winter (May to August), days are sunny and cool or warm. Temperatures may go below freezing at night in some areas.

History

Tswana ethnic groups began moving into eastern Botswana from the southeast in the early 1500s. They displaced and absorbed other peoples as they spread out to claim all land that had surface water or was suitable for grazing and agriculture. Various chiefdoms developed over the next several decades.

Ethnic disputes beginning in the mid-1700s left Tswana chiefdoms vulnerable to invasions by refugee armies from Zulu wars in Natal. These wars began in the early 1800s and caused great upheaval in southern Africa. Boer (white settlers) encroachment from 1852 onward led major Tswana chiefs, under the direction of Khama III, to seek protection from the British government. The British, eager to secure a labor supply for their South African mines and a route to newly discovered gold in Matabeleland (Zimbabwe), established the Bechuanaland Protectorate in 1885.

In the 20th century, unrest in the Rhodesias and apartheid in South Africa led various groups to form political parties and demand independence from Britain. The Bechuanaland Democratic Party (BDP) led the way to independence in 1966. The founders of the BDP, Sir Seretse Khama and Sir Ketumile Masire, were declared the president and vice president, respectively, of the new Republic of Botswana. Khama won three consecutive elections, but he died in 1980. Masire succeeded Khama and he was reelected in 1984, 1989, and 1994. Today the BDP (now the Botswana Democratic Party) leads one of the most stable democracies in Africa.

THE PEOPLE

Population

Botswana's population is about 1.35 million, with half younger than age 15. The population is growing by 3 percent a year. Descendants of the original Tswana peoples (Kwena, Ngwato, Ngwaketse, Kgatla, Tawana, Lete, Tlokwa, and Rolong) constitute about half of the total population. These groups essentially consider themselves one people because they descend from a common ancestor, but they tend to concentrate in different areas. The other half of the population is composed of the Kalanga, Kgalagadi, Birwa, Tswapong, Yei, Mbukushu, Subiya, Herero, and Khoesan groups. Whites, Indians, and other Asians compose small minorities.

More than 70 percent of the population lives in rural areas, a figure that was nearly 100 percent in 1960. There is a strong trend to move to urban areas. Gaborone, the capital, is one of the world's fastest growing cities. Most people live in the eastern part of the country, where the railroad is located, where soil supports agriculture, and where rainfall generally sustains life.

Language

Although English is the official language of government and secondary education, Setswana is the national language spoken by most people. Primary schooling is conducted in Setswana. But for many children, Setswana is a second language because each minority group speaks its own language. Tjikalanga (also called Ikalanga), for example, dominates in the northeast. Like Setswana, these other languages are Bantu tongues and are therefore related. In Bantu languages, the noun prefix is the key to grammatical connections. For example, the *mo* prefix refers to a person. Thus, a *Motswana* is a Tswana person. The plural of *mo* is *ba* (many). So *Batswana* means Tswana people (and citizens of Botswana, regardless of ethnicity). Non-Bantu tongues spoken in Botswana are known collectively as Khosesan (or Sarwa).

The only languages in print are English and Setswana, but that may change in the future as publishers endeavor to provide the Bible in every language in Africa. Ikalanga is a written language in Zimbabwe.

Religion

Religious freedom is protected under the constitution, but Christianity is accepted as an official religion in the sense that the school day and official functions begin with prayer. School children also sing Christian hymns before classes begin, but religious instruction is not compulsory. Christianity was introduced in the early 1800s by missionaries (David Livingstone and others) traveling from South Africa. This opened the interior of Africa to exploitation by European hunters and slave traders. Because Christianity was often viewed as a means to Western technology, education, and health care, missions were allowed by many chiefs. During his reign (1835–1923), Chief Khama III, who converted to Christianity in 1862, tried to abolish many traditional practices (polygamy, initiation ceremonies, passing widows to a deceased man's brother, rainmaking ceremonies, and other rites) that conflicted with Christian teachings. Some traditions have not entirely disappeared from village life.

Today, Catholics and Protestants comprise about one-fourth of the population. Many local churches combine traditional beliefs with those of Western Christianity. The largest of these is the Zion Christian Church; another major congregation is the Spiritual Healing Church. Many rural people (up to half) continue to follow indigenous beliefs exclusively.

General Attitudes

Society is founded on traditional law, with the community as the core of Tswana life and the chief as the symbol of unity. Traditionally, schools, roads, and health clinics were built through local organization. This practice of self-help, evident in such Setswana words as *ipelegeng* (carry yourselves), continues today, even though the government is now more responsible for infrastructure. Each individual is expected to benefit the community. The more a person does, the greater that person's status with the group. Anything that can benefit the group is valued, such as one's educational level, integrity, and generosity. Working family members are expected to support those without jobs, and people are expected to house traveling relatives for as long as necessary. Batswana also value the lack of conflict, evident in their friendly discussions at community meetings.

Personal Appearance

Western dress is common in most areas. Despite the heat, urban men wear business suits and ties and women wear dresses or a skirt and blouse. Some young urban women wear pants. Rural women often wear a wrap over their dresses to protect them from dirt. Mothers carry their babies on their backs in fabric slings. Older men wear overalls to protect their clothing. Men wear hats, except in the *kgotla* (meeting place), and married women cover their heads with a kerchief. Both sexes typically have short hair. Cleanliness and neatness are important throughout the country.

Church members wear uniforms to church that distinguish their denominations, and political party members display their party's colors through clothing. Women of the Herero ethnic group, which migrated from Namibia in 1904, wear the long bouffant-skirted costume introduced in Namibia by German missionary wives. The heavy, colorful dress may require up to ten yards of fabric. A matching headdress is arranged to indicate one's marital status.

CUSTOMS AND COURTESIES

Greetings

Greetings are important; to fail to greet someone is rude. Formal verbal greetings, accompanied by shaking the right hand while supporting one's elbow with the left hand, are used among Setswana acquaintances and when greeting an elder or one of higher social status. Elders and those approaching greet first. A common adult greeting is *Dumela Rra/Mma, O tsogile jang?* (Greetings sir/madam, how did you wake?). The response is *Ke tsogile sentle* (I awoke well). At social gatherings, people greet those they know and are introduced to others. The handshake is less of a grasp and more a matter of palms and fingertips touching. Informal greetings are used among children and peers. For instance, the Setswana reply to *O kae?* (How are you?) is *Ke teng* (literally, "I am here," meaning "fine"). *Tsamaya sentle* (Go well) is said to one departing and *Sala sentle* (Stay well) to one staying.

Greeting customs vary for other ethnic groups. For example, among the Kalanga the younger person always greets first. Young children greet elders by extending both hands or clapping; the elder responds by kissing both hands and saying *Wa muka?* (Are you well?).

Children may be named for some circumstance related to their birth and also given a pet name by which they are known at home. Students often give themselves nicknames for use at school. Traditionally, the father's first name became the child's surname. Now, the child takes the father's surname. Upon the birth of her first child, a woman is thereafter referred to as the mother of that child (e.g., *Mma Jamey* in Setswana or *Bakajamey* in Tjikalanga).

Gestures

Hands (palms and fingers) may be pressed together in front of one's chest before accepting a gift with both hands. Gifts are given with both hands or with the right hand supported by the left at the elbow. Batswana use a variety of gestures to suggest "no," "no thanks," or that something is all gone. One way is to rotate the wrist with fingers outstretched or pointing down. Hitchhikers rapidly wave their right hand with arm extended to hail a vehicle.

It is impolite to walk between two people in conversation. If passing through cannot be avoided, one bows below the level of the conversation and says *Intshwarele* (Excuse me). Respect for elders during conversation is best shown by looking down toward the ground rather than into their eyes. Public displays of affection are inappropriate.

Visiting

Relatives visit one another as often as they can. Because personal relationships are valued, unannounced visitors are welcomed into the home. Most visits cannot be arranged in advance due to a lack of telephones. Guests are offered water or tea to drink. Anyone who arrives at mealtime is expected to eat with the family. Guests who are not hungry are expected to try offered food and take some home. Urban relatives often bring staples and household goods as gifts, while people from the *lands* (fields) bring in-season crops. Acquaintances are not expected to bring gifts.

Much socializing takes place at the standpipe (where people get water), general stores, and church activities. Men socialize at local *chibuku* depots (bars selling sorghum beer).

Eating

Eating habits vary between urban and rural settings, but sharing is the common denominator. For most, family meals involve eating from common bowls or plates. Visitors receive separate plates. Children share a bowl among them. Utensils are used, but some foods are eaten with the hands. Everyone usually leaves a little food behind to indicate the meal has been filling. Guests often say *Ke itumetse* (I am pleased) to thank the hosts. Drinks are never shared; each person has a cup. Smelling the food before eating it implies something is wrong with it. Leftovers are kept for later or given to departing guests.

LIFESTYLE

Family

Batswana historically lived in large villages with their agricultural and grazing lands at a distance. With women at the *lands* and men at the cattle posts, families were apart much of the time. Then, during colonial times, many men began working in South African mines. Later, the youth moved to cities in search of work. Families remained tied through an extended family network. Today, although few men now work in South Africa, a continuous search for employment keeps families separate. For instance, married couples who are teachers might work across the country from one another. With men so often absent, women remain primarily responsible for the family, agriculture, and entrepreneurial pursuits.

Women head the majority of rural families, but they also receive help from extended family members nearby.

Dating and Marriage

Living away from home villages (for work or schooling) has dramatically changed the way young people interact. It was once rather restricted, but the youth now meet at discos and other sites. School competitions and youth clubs also provide socialization. Because of the expense and obligations involved in formal marriage, more than half of all couples live together rather than marrying. Those who do marry may choose rites under either civil or customary law. Customary ceremonies involve two days or more of eating, drinking, dancing, and speeches. When a couple becomes engaged, the two families begin negotiations regarding the *bogadi* (bride price), which the groom's family will give the bride's family sometime in the future. Civil weddings are sometimes followed by traditional celebrations.

Diet

Bogobe (porridge) made from *mabele* (sorghum), maize, or millet (in the northeast) is a staple food. It is served soft and often soured for breakfast and thick for the midday and evening meals. *Paleche* (white maize), although vulnerable to drought, is replacing sorghum as the primary grain. Many people have tea or *mageu* (a thick sorghum drink) instead of porridge for breakfast. Some enjoy *fat cakes* (deep-fried dough) with tea for breakfast or lunch. *Bogobe* is accompanied by relish to provide variety to a meal. A popular relish is made of onions, chicken stock, and tomato sauce. Various fruits and vegetables are eaten in season. *Phane* worms, a delicacy gathered from the *mophane* trees in the northeast, are dried in hot ashes and eaten. Goats and chickens are raised for meat. Cattle are slaughtered for special occasions such as weddings and funerals. Rice replaces *bogobe* at weddings.

Recreation

Batswana enjoy visiting, dancing, singing, and playing sports. Young men play soccer, often competing on village teams. Schools offer field sports (running, jumping, and discus throw) and ball sports (soccer, softball, volleyball, and netball) for all students. Schools also sponsor choirs and traditional dance groups that perform at public events. Traditional dancing is popular in villages, where women play drums to provide the dancers with rhythm. At public performances some dancers use loud whistles to direct movement. Ballroom dancing is popular in cities, especially among young professionals.

Holidays

Batswana celebrate the New Year (1–2 January), Easter (Friday–Monday), Ascension, President's Day (third weekend in July), Botswana Day (30 September–1 October), Christmas, and Boxing Day (26 December). Christmas is the most important holiday and people go to their home villages to be with extended family. Gifts are not exchanged, but family members usually receive new clothes. Boxing Day comes from the British tradition where service workers or the poor are given small boxed gifts on the day after Christmas. It is now a day to visit and relax. Batswana also go home for a four-day weekend on President's Day. On this weekend, government-sponsored programs begin with prayer and have traditional dancing, singing, speeches, and praise poems. Easter is a time for church and family.

Commerce

Formal greetings are exchanged before conducting any business. Hours generally extend from 8:00 or 9:00 A.M. until about 5:00 P.M., with many offices and shops closing for an hour at 1:00 P.M. Wholesale and retail businesses are important, as there are few factories and most goods are imported.

SOCIETY

Government

Botswana is a parliamentary republic. Each village is divided into *wards* (neighborhoods), each with a *headman* (an elder appointed by the village chief) and a *kgotla* (meeting place). Decisions at the ward and village levels are made in the *kgotla* through a consensus process in which all adult males discuss the issue. Women may also express opinions but they remain in the back of the meeting hall. The chief's *kgotla* is used to settle matters that cannot be determined at the ward level. Local councils are responsible for administrating schools, health facilities, and other matters.

Batswana are proud of their democratic heritage, which is also reflected at the national level. Members of the 40-seat National Assembly (parliament) are directly elected, and the majority party's leader takes office as president. A 15-member House of Chiefs, representing major ethnic groups, advises parliament on legislation pertaining to custom and tradition. The independent judiciary has two branches. Cases involving customary law are heard in the *kgotla* by local chiefs and headmen, while statutory cases are heard in Magistrate Court or the High Court. There is also an Appeals Court.

Botswana has never experienced a coup or been ruled by a dictator. This is partly due to five factors: Tswana cohesion and acceptance of other ethnic groups, Batswana are pastoralists and are not interested in dominating others, an internal democracy based on consensus, well-educated and strong leaders before and after independence, and a stable economy based on diamond mining. Both main opposition parties, the Botswana National Front (BNF) and the Botswana People's Party (BPP) favor national unity over divisive politics.

Economy

With strong annual growth rates since independence and large foreign reserves, Botswana has enjoyed a stable economy. Diamonds account for 80 percent of export revenue. When world diamond prices fall, as they did in the early 1990s, Botswana's economy can be severely strained. The government is trying to diversify the economy. Other exports include copper, nickel, and beef. The currency is the *pula* (rain). *Pula* is also used as a greeting or at the end of speeches to mean good wishes.

Despite relative stability, problems exist. Unemployment is high, reaching half of the younger Batswana. A shortage of skilled labor keeps industrial growth low, and land deterioration hampers agriculture. More than 60 percent of the nation's cattle, a measure of wealth, is owned by less than 10 percent of the population. Botswana's Human Development Index (0.670) ranks it 87th out of 173 countries. Real gross domestic product per capita is $4,690. Poverty affects about 43 percent of the population. Although improving, these figures reflect a wide gap between rich and poor, and they indicate that economic prosperity is enjoyed by a small percentage of people.

Transportation and Communication

A paved highway and a rail line parallel the eastern border, linking the major towns. The train is used for longer distances. Rural people often walk long distances or hitchhike. If given a ride, they pay bus fare to the driver. Some families use bicycles locally. A minority own cars, but more urban residents are buying them. Buses or *combies* (minibuses) run between towns and major villages.

Few people, even in towns, have telephones, but pay phones are located in post offices. Radio Botswana broadcasts in Setswana and English and the *Daily News* is sent free by the government to schools. Independent newspapers enjoy freedom of the press and wide circulation.

Education

Botswana has the highest elementary completion rate in Africa and a literacy rate of 74 percent. The abolition of school fees in 1987 marked the first step in providing primary and secondary schooling to all children. Construction then more than doubled the number of junior secondary classrooms. However, senior secondary schools are only located in large towns, meaning two-thirds of Junior Certificate (JC) holders cannot advance. But the government is implementing reforms. The Brigades (production units providing technical training) and other vocational programs accept some JC students. Senior secondary graduates qualify for higher education by earning the Cambridge Overseas School Certificate and performing a year of community service. There are six teacher-training colleges, a National Health Institute, the University of Botswana, a polytechnic institute, and an agricultural college.

Health

Clean water, infant immunization, and other factors combine to keep infant mortality relatively low (39 per 1,000). The average life expectancy is 63 years. Nurse-staffed primary care clinics are within reach of most people. Doctors practice in cities and larger towns. Traditional doctors prescribe herbal medicine and provide an important alternative to Western medicine. The most frequently diagnosed infections and diseases are related to poverty. Malnutrition is a problem. AIDS cases have increased dramatically over the last decade. Malaria, schistosomiasis, and sleeping sickness are found in the north.

FOR THE TRAVELER

U.S. citizens do not need a visa for stays of fewer than 90 days, but a passport is necessary. A visa is required for longer stays. With national parks and game reserves, there is ample opportunity for viewing wildlife. Islands of the Okavango Delta are accessible both by plane and *mokoro* (dugout canoe). A four-wheel-drive vehicle is necessary in remote areas. Take precautions against malaria and do not swim in freshwater ponds or lakes. You may also wish to contact the Embassy of the Republic of Botswana, 3400 International Drive NW, Suite 7M, Washington, DC 20008.

Kingdom of
Cambodia

Boundary representations not necessarily authoritative.

BACKGROUND

Land and Climate

Covering 69,900 square miles (181,040 square kilometers), Cambodia is just smaller than Oklahoma and is circular in shape. Its fertile soil is fed by the waters of the Tibetan-Himalayan glaciers, which flow to Cambodia by way of the Mekong River. There are mountains to the north and southwest. The center is basically flat, with a large lake, the *Tonlé Sap*, roughly in the middle. The lake swells to several times its surface area during the rainy season because excess water from the Mekong River is naturally diverted to it. More than 75 percent of the land was once covered with forests and woodlands. Today, due to rampant logging by foreign and local firms, less than 40 percent of Cambodia holds forests. The rapid deforestation threatens the fresh fish supply and other natural habitats, and has increased the severity of floods. Without regulation, the forests could be decimated by the end of the century. Cambodia's climate is tropical, and annual temperatures average between 80°and 100°F (26–38°C). The dry season is from December to April; the rainy season is from May to November.

History

The word *Kampuchea* (the term used by Cambodians to refer to their land) comes from the Kingdom of Kambuja, an empire established by Indian settlers over 1,800 years ago. From the ninth to the thirteenth centuries, the Khmer empire flourished and reigned over much of southeast Asia. The Angkor Wat (temple), built in the 12th century, is the largest religious building in the world and represents the glory of the Khmer empire. Today, it is the national symbol of Cambodia. The area known today as Cambodia was colonized by France in the 1860s and remained under French control (except during Japanese occupation in World War II) until 1953, when Cambodia was granted its independence. In 1970, the monarchy under Prince Norodom Sihanouk was overthrown. In 1975, the Khmer Rouge began a violent, forced restructuring of the entire society. During the Khmer Rouge's four-year rule, more than one million people were killed or died of starvation and disease. The educated and business classes were all but eliminated, and the economy was completely destroyed. Pol Pot, leader of the Khmer Rouge, wanted to return the country to an agrarian, communal society.

Vietnam invaded Cambodia in December 1978. The Vietnamese forced Pol Pot to flee and installed a government loyal to Vietnam with Heng Samrin as president. Hun Sen was later named prime minister. The invasion, while halting the genocide, was condemned by Western nations, who called for the withdrawal of Vietnamese troops. The Vietnamese remained and fought guerrillas opposed to the Hun Sen government until 1989, when they withdrew their troops. During Vietnam's occupation, the Hun Sen government was not recognized by the United Nations. Instead, a coalition of three guerrilla groups (Khmer Rouge, Khmer People's National Liberation Front, and supporters of Prince Sihanouk) was recognized as a government in exile (as the Coalition Government of Democratic Kampuchea). After Vietnam withdrew, Hun Sen continued to run the country and sought to implement reform. The United Nations urged the guerrilla groups to enter into peace talks with Hun Sen.

Little progress was made until 1990 when the United States and other nations withdrew their support for the guerrilla coalition. In August 1990, all four parties agreed to adopt a UN plan that created a Supreme National Council (SNC) as an interim government. The United Nations sent troops and other personnel to take over the country's administration and organize national elections. Prince Sihanouk returned to Cambodia as head of the SNC and was immediately accepted by most Cambodians as the only person capable of establishing peace. The United Nations began registering voters in 1992 for elections in May 1993. Violence between the government, Sihanouk's supporters, and the Khmer Rouge frequently threatened to halt the peace process. The Khmer Rouge eventually withdrew from the process and refused to participate in elections. It promised more violence, but this did not deter the United Nations or the country's 4.5 million eligible voters from preparing for elections.

The May elections were peaceful, free, and fair. But when the government saw it was losing to the Royalist opposition (loyal to Sihanouk), it threatened to reject election results. Sihanouk, who was not a formal candidate or party leader, stepped in to create a coalition government. After several attempts, he forged an agreement in June 1993 that created a copresidency between his son, Prince Ranariddh, and Hun Sen. The newly elected National Assembly approved a new constitution that provided for Sihanouk's return to power as King of Cambodia. He was coronated in September 1993. King Sihanouk also ratified the new constitution and named the Crown Prince, Norodom Ranariddh as first prime minister. Hun Sen became second prime minister. This continued the compromise agreement that had been worked out in June.

When UN peacekeepers left, the Khmer Rouge stepped up violence and continued with its civil war. Despite government advances against the guerrillas in 1994, war continued in 5 of 21 provinces. King Sihanouk became ill and had to spend considerable time in China for treatment. At the same time, the coalition government found it difficult to compromise on important issues, so some economic and social advances achieved during the UN mission (lower corruption and crime, greater free speech, better utility services, etc.) were lost. Cambodia thus faces considerable challenges in its bid to stabilize and bring prosperity to its long-suffering people.

THE PEOPLE

Population

Cambodia's population of 10.2 million is growing annually at 2.9 percent. The largest ethnic group is the ethnic Khmer, estimated at over 70 percent of the population. The second largest group (about 10 percent) is the Sino-Khmer (mixed Chinese and Khmer). In the past, the Chinese were powerful traders in Cambodia, and many settled in the country. Because the Khmer and Sino-Khmer dominate the population, their customs and lifestyle are more fully explained here than those of smaller groups. In fact, some people use the terms "Khmer" and "Cambodian" interchangeably.

The Chams (perhaps 5 percent of the population) are descendants of the Champa Kingdom (eighth century A.D.), which was centered in present-day Vietnam and contained people of Malaysian origin. These people converted to Islam and are still Muslim today. There are also many Vietnamese settlers and some Chinese in Cambodia. The ethnic Khmer and ethnic Vietnamese are historical enemies and the Vietnamese minority has increasingly been subjected to violence. Women make up 64 percent of the population (a figure higher than in most countries) because of the large number of men killed in conflict since 1975. As a result of civil war (1978–89), 200,000 people became internal refugees, wandering from area to area because they had to leave their villages during fighting. An additional 370,000 settled in refugee camps on the Thai border. Repatriating these people was one of the UN's most important goals, but continued violence has made the task more difficult for Cambodia's government.

Language

The Khmer language comes from an older language called *paali*, which developed as a successor to Indian Sanskrit. The closest languages to modern Khmer are Thai (Thailand) and Lao (Laos), both of which share several common words (though not necessarily equivalent meanings). Khmer has 26 vowels and 33 consonants. It is often difficult for Westerners to speak and write, even though it is not a tonal language. French is sometimes used to communicate with officials and traders because it was used during the French colonial period. English is understood in a few areas, such as the markets in Phnom Penh, and is becoming more popular in the cities.

Religion

Except for the Cham minority, which practices Islam, Cambodians are Theravada Buddhists. Christianity is often considered synonymous with Catholicism, which is not favored because of its connection to former Vietnamese settlers and past colonial powers. Most Buddhist records, libraries, monasteries, temples, and shrines were destroyed and the monks killed by the Khmer Rouge. Not until 1989 did the government again recognize Buddhism as the state religion. Only memories and a few books from educated survivors remain to restore Buddhist practices. But the people overwhelmingly favor rebuilding the pagodas, and they often take up collections on holy days to accomplish this. Private businesses are making Buddha sculptures and paintings, as well as other ornaments associated with worship, to help people regain their heritage. Traditional practices are being revived with government encouragement. It is a general belief that a man should have a monk's education for at least three months, if not several years, even if this is a drain on family and national resources. Monks generate no income.

General Attitudes

Although Buddhist monasteries were destroyed and religious worship banned during the Pol Pot regime in the 1970s, Buddhism generally shapes the lives and perspectives of Cambodia's people. Many believe that Buddhist teachings have helped the people survive the years of war and grinding poverty. Cambodians are traditionally known as optimists. Optimism was harder to find between 1975 and 1990, but the return of King Sihanouk and the chance for peace encouraged people's hopes for a better life. Although Pol Pot still lives and the Khmer Rouge is still a power to contend with, Cambodians today recognize that they have their greatest opportunity in decades for progress and peace. Unfortunately, the campaign for national renewal and democracy is complicated by remnants of war (specifically, millions of hidden land mines that kill or wound farmers and others on a regular basis), the internal refugee problem, and continued Khmer Rouge violence. Citizens are fighting back by joining mine removal teams, pressing the government for greater reform, and reviving traditions.

The group or community (often defined as the extended family) is more important than the individual, as are ancestors and rulers. The individual generally lacks privacy and rights, and expects to act for the good of the community. Difficult economic times spawned a segment of the population that ignores this principle, but that small group is acting against traditional behavior.

Personal Appearance

Western-style clothing is fairly common in Phnom Penh, although it is simple and not always the most modern. Of traditional clothing, the *sampot* and *sarong* (for women) and the *sarong soet* (for men) are common. Each is a large, rectangular piece of colored cloth that is wrapped around the hips like a skirt or kilt down to the ankles. A *krama* is a large scarf that is used as a hat, a small blanket, or even a baby carrier. Young women may wear small, colored (red, pink, or bright yellow) hats.

CUSTOMS AND COURTESIES

Greetings

Cambodians greet one another by placing both hands together in a prayer position at chest level without touching the body. The higher the hands, the greater the sign of respect, although they should never be held above the level of the nose. This gesture is accompanied by a slight bow to show respect for persons of higher status or age. Persons holding or carrying something may simply bow their heads slightly. Shaking hands is not common in Cambodia; indeed, it embarrasses women if attempted. Although there are many terms used in greeting, one common greeting is *Sok sebai*.

Gestures

Rules governing gestures come from Buddhism. While sitting, one should not point the feet towards a Buddha image or any person. To Buddhists, the head is the most sacred part of the body. One does not touch another person's head (even a child's), and one generally avoids sitting or standing on a level more elevated than that of an older person. Raising the voice is a sign of a bad personality. It is very improper to embarrass another person in public. Waving the hand is a friendly gesture, as is an "open" or friendly face, good eye contact, or a smile. In communication, one must be careful to clearly distinguish between a "yes" that a person is listening, and a "yes" meaning the person understands.

Visiting

Among friends and relatives, visiting is frequent and usually unannounced. People remove their shoes when entering a home or pagoda (place of worship and religious education). A houseguest may be greeted with a bouquet of jasmine flowers placed on their desk or table. Cambodians are extremely hospitable and friendly in general, although they are cautious about inviting strangers into the home. Guests are usually offered something to drink and sometimes other refreshments. If a meal is provided, guests are given the best place to sit and the best portion of food.

Eating

Cambodians eat with chopsticks, spoons, and their fingers—depending on the food and family custom. Cambodians enjoy dishes that have been influenced by Indian, Chinese, and European cuisine. In general, Cambodian food is blander and consists of more fish and gravies than foods in Thailand or other neighboring countries.

LIFESTYLE

Family

The family is important to the Khmer people. The average family has four children and is often willing to adopt orphans or care for foster children on behalf of another family in need. Bonds formed through adoption are just as important as direct lineage. Multiple generations usually live together or near one another. The elderly are cared for by their children. Because so many men died at the hands of the Khmer Rouge, Cambodia has a large number of orphans, widows, and single-parent families. Single mothers try to remarry. Those who do not find another spouse tend to gather in small clans of women and children for mutual aid and companionship. Khmer tradition allows for a man to take more than one wife (including widows), but this is rarely practiced because of the economic burden involved.

Dating and Marriage

Khmer girls are shy and often lack self-assurance. Improved feelings of self-worth often come with marriage. While boys and girls are generally able to choose their spouses, dating is organized such that a girl's exposure is limited to certain choices. Khmer do not intermarry with other ethnic groups, although intermarriage was a common practice in the past. Wedding celebrations last a full day and are occasions for many guests, much food, and plenty of music.

Diet

There are two basic dishes in Cambodia: soup and rice. A bowl of soup may have any combination of fish, eggs, vegetables, meat, and spicy broth. Rice is the staple food of Cambodia. Over 20 years ago, Cambodia was known as "the cradle of rice," and a number of different varieties were grown. Today, that number is much smaller and Cambodia is not as productive. Rice is prepared many ways, and it is eaten at every meal. Bowls of rice may differ in flavor depending on which region the rice is from. In addition to soup and rice, Cambodians enjoy vegetables and a wide variety of fruits throughout the year. Seafood and fish are also common.

Recreation

There is a general lack of theaters and sports facilities because leisure activities were banned by Pol Pot and most facilities were destroyed or fell into decay during the 1980s. Still, the people enjoy soccer, table tennis, volleyball, and badminton. They also dance, play music, and sing. Video machines are becoming more accessible and are used to create small theaters in the villages. Other leisure activities include picnics, card playing, and Sunday rides on bicycles or motorcycles. Religious festivals and weddings are also opportunities for recreation.

Holidays

Cambodia has both national public holidays and Buddhist celebration days. The main national holidays include Liberation Day (7 January), Revolution Day (17 April), and The Front Day (2 December). The Chinese New Year is celebrated in February. The Buddhist New Year in April is celebrated for three days. In the last week of September, an important Buddhist festival, *Chun Ben*, is marked on behalf of the dead and one's own salvation. Before it begins, a person is supposed to accomplish a "seven pagodas" duty. This means one should either worship at seven pagodas or perform seven moral "good turns" (or a combination of both) to please one's ancestors. Six weeks after *Chun Ben*, large or wealthy families raise money to pay for the living expenses of the monks. Also in the fall, the Water Festival provides three days of fireworks, traditional dancing, canoe races, and other events. Funerals are an occasion for gathering. White (not black) is worn, and music is an integral part of the event.

Commerce

Nearly 90 percent of the population is engaged in agriculture, food processing, or forestry (logging and rubber processing). In addition, many people take extra jobs in town or work on roads to help make a living. Wages are low. Business hours are from 8:00 a.m. to 1:00 P.M. and 3:00 to 6:00 P.M. or dusk. During the UN mission, Phnom Penh, the capital, became a boomtown with bustling shops, plentiful food, and a good climate for conducting business. After the UN departure, conditions deteriorated, but the city is still the country's business and financial center.

SOCIETY

Government

Cambodia is a constitutional monarchy. King Sihanouk is head of state, and the two prime ministers are heads of government. The prime ministers see to the daily tasks of government, but the king is involved in matters such as dealing with the Khmer Rouge or speaking out against social abuses. The National Assembly has 120 members. The voting age is 18. Political parties follow traditional lines based on pre-1990 divisions and alliances.

Economy

The economy has not yet been able to recover to its postindependence strength. Food shortages are common in rural areas. The industrial sector is all but nonexistent. Timber is the major industry; mining for precious stones is conducted primarily by individuals. The economy remains tied to agriculture. Rubber is an important export in addition to fish, rice, and pepper. Legalized smuggling has allowed goods from Thailand to be made available on the market. Foreign investment and tourist receipts remain low. Cambodia's Human Development Index (0.307) ranks it 147th out of 173 countries. Real gross domestic product per capita is estimated at $1,250. These figures indicate the majority of Cambodians

either earn no cash income (i.e., they are subsistence farmers) or do not earn an income sufficient for their needs. The currency is the *riel* (CR).

Transportation and Communication

The six national highways that radiate from Phnom Penh would provide a transportation network if in good condition. However, only limited repairs have been made during the past 20 years. Some roads are impassable while others may delay travel. It may take four hours to travel less than one hundred miles. Bikes and motorcycles are often used to traverse short distances. Many rely on buffalo-drawn carts or walking. The communications system is not adequate outside the capital. Recent improvements to the transportation system include the renewed operation of Royal Air Cambodge in 1995, offering limited regional and domestic service, and a massive overhaul of the country's main port at Sihanoukville, which is expected to meet international standards by the end of 1995.

Education

The education system was destroyed under Pol Pot, and the majority of educated people were killed by the Khmer Rouge. Cambodians, however, are slowly regaining their education. Although books and other materials are lacking, especially in rural areas, literacy is rising. It is currently estimated at 35 percent. With the rebuilding of the pagodas, many schools (which are adjacent to the pagodas) are reopening. Currently, Phnom Penh has many private "street schools" with self-proclaimed teachers who offer instruction in English and French to informal students.

Health

Sanitation is poor. Diseases from water and mosquitoes are common. Running water is available only in a few hotels. Otherwise, one must take it from rivers or wells. Intestinal parasites, hepatitis, dengue fever, and malaria are all common ailments. Thousands of people suffer from wounds they received by stepping on hidden mines left over from the years of fighting. Adequate medical care is not available to many people, but the government has tried to establish a basic health care system. International relief organizations work with government hospitals to provide care and improve the current system. The infant mortality rate is 110 per 1,000. Life expectancy is about 50 years.

FOR THE TRAVELER

U.S. citizens need a valid passport and visa to enter Cambodia. The political situation in Cambodia is unsettled and a few Western tourists have been killed. Call the State Department (202) 647–5225 for the latest travel warnings. Be in good physical condition and have updated vaccinations. Prepare to pay cash for most transactions. The Angkor Wat was one of the greatest tourist attractions in the 1960s, and travel opportunities are again being made available to see this symbol of Khmer culture. For travel information, contact the embassy at (202) 726–8076. The Royal Embassy of Cambodia is located at 4500 16th Street NW, Washington, DC 20011; phone (202) 726–7742.

A *Culturgram* is a product of native commentary and original, expert analysis. Statistics are estimates and information is presented as a matter of opinion. While the editors strive for accuracy and detail, this document should not be considered strictly factual. It is a general introduction to culture, an initial step in building bridges of understanding between peoples. It may not apply to all peoples of the nation. You should therefore consult other sources for more information.

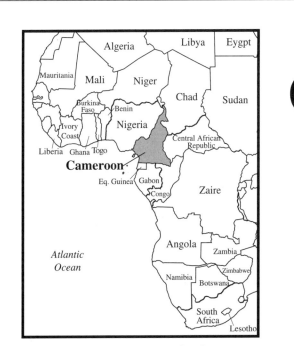

Boundary representations not necessarily authoritative.

Republic of
Cameroon

BACKGROUND

Land and Climate

Located just north of the equator, Cameroon (183,567 square miles or 475,440 square kilometers) is slightly larger than California. The north is dominated from Garoua to Lake Chad by a dry plain where Sahara winds and hot temperatures are standard from October to May. Cooler winds and rain between June and September allow for large irrigated farms and grazing. A plateau of 2,000 to 4,000 feet (610–1220 meters) covers much of central, southern, and eastern Cameroon. Here, dry-season daily heat is relieved at night and by occasional showers, and from May to October rains bring abundant water to the plateau's cities and agricultural regions. In wetter grassfields above 4,000 feet (1220 meters), the November to April dry season is cooler; rains are heavy and cool for several weeks after midyear. Rich volcanic soils provide for agriculture in this area. The Atlantic coastal lowland is between 15 and 50 miles (24–80 kilometers) wide and is hot and humid all year. Douala's average temperature is 78°F (25°C). The region supports large areas of rubber, banana, cocoa, oil palms, and timber.

History

Various complex political structures, from bands and tribes to large kingdoms, were present in the area long before it was discovered by European explorers in the 1500s and named for the prawns (*cameroes* in Portuguese) found along the coast. In the following centuries, southern Cameroon supplied the Atlantic slave and commodity trades, while northern peoples participated in the Muslim culture and economy organized by the Fulanis and Hausas south of the Sahara. Germany united south and north into a colony between 1884 and 1916. Germany's defeat in World War I led to the partitioning of Cameroon; the east was administered by France and the west by Britain. The French area was ruled tightly from the capital, Yaoundé. The smaller British area (on the western fringe) was ruled more loosely from Nigeria. Anticolonialism grew after 1945 and independence was achieved in French Cameroon in 1960. British Cameroon elections in 1961 joined its south in a federation with Cameroon, its north with Nigeria. Former French and British areas kept separate educational, legal, civil service, and legislative structures until a 1972 referendum adopted a national, one-party system.

Cameroon has had only two presidents. Ahmadou Ahidjo, a northern Muslim, governed from 1960 to 1982, when, during a visit to France, he was told he was terminally ill. In a move he later regretted, he turned power over to his prime minister, Paul Biya, a southern Christian. After a 1984 rebellion led by forces loyal to Ahidjo, Biya dismantled the opposition. Under domestic and international pressure, Biya instituted reforms in 1990, but unrest and strikes continued into 1991. Multiparty presidential and parliamentary elections were eventually held in 1992, but were boycotted in large numbers. Still, more than 50 parties contested seats in parliament. Biya retained his office as president.

THE PEOPLE

Population

Cameroon's population is 13.1 million and is growing at 2.9 percent annually. Over half the people live in rural areas, but cities are growing rapidly. Douala, center of commerce and industry, has more than one million residents and the capital, Yaoundé, has more than 700,000. Cameroon is often known as Africa's crossroads because of its many ethnic groups. The largest groups are the Fang, Bamileke (in the west), Fulani (north), and Pahouin (south). The Pahouin are also known as the Beti. No single group comprises more than 20 percent of the population and most comprise fewer than 1 percent. Cameroon's more than 200 ethnic groups have widely different backgrounds—from Fulani kingdoms to tiny bands of Pygmies that hunt in the southern forests. More typical are the farming and trading central and western peoples (half the population) with independent chieftaincies and rich cultural traditions.

Language

Cameroon has some 240 languages, nearly 100 of which have some written form. It is common for Cameroonians to speak several local languages. French and English are the official languages, and most urban residents can speak and read one of them. Rural people are generally not fluent in either. French is primarily used in the eight francophone provinces that were colonized by France. English is only common in the two anglophone provinces once governed by Great Britain. No local language is used widely enough to have official status. Some languages have regional dominance, such as Fulfulde in the north, Ewondo near the capital, and Duala on the coast. Pidgin English, an ever evolving language with roots in English and other European languages, emerged during colonization to facilitate trade and communication between ethnic groups. Use primarily in anglophone provinces for common daily interaction, it is also sometimes used between Francophones and Anglophones who cannot otherwise communicate.

Religion

Over half the population is Christian, with about twice as many Catholics as Protestants. About one-fourth is Muslim (mostly Sunni). Most of the rest follow indigenous beliefs. Even Christians and Muslims often respect and practice these local beliefs. Indigenous practices are especially evident in certain ceremonies, traditional medicine, and family relationships. Merging religions does not create contradictions for the believers; they adopt the elements they feel enhance their religion's overall value.

General Attitudes

Complicated leadership patterns basically revolve around those with title and rank, either inherited or earned through education or wealth. Leaders often maintain a support base by providing favors to family members, village members, and those of the same ethnic group or social class. Cameroon is a group-oriented society; everyone has a place in the group and each group has a clear leader. Individualism is not encouraged. When one person of a group benefits from something (such as a high wage), the group expects to share the benefit.

Family and friendship ties are strong and obligations run deep. For example, even distant relatives or "junior" siblings (a half sibling or someone from the village) can expect a family to house and feed them, regardless of the hardship it might cause. Guests cannot be asked to leave except in rare cases. The practice is accepted because the host family assumes it will someday benefit from the same network. Deep, complex bonds also exist between fellow students or local residents of the same sex and age. These bonds mean that service, respect, and cooperation usually come before personal interest. Social change is disrupting this system, but it remains important.

Personal Appearance

Cameroonians consider a clean, well-groomed appearance and fashionable dress the marks of good character. All but the very poor have formal clothing for special occasions. The tall, Muslim people in the north wear colorful, flowing robes. The shorter southern people also wear robes, but more often wear Western clothing. Western clothing dominates in urban areas throughout the country.

Women often braid their hair and apply rich oils to their skin for a glossy appearance. Embroidery and *appliqué*, beads, shells, feathers, and ivory signify high or royal status for the wearer. Rural women do not wear pants. Muslim women often wear a lot of jewelry. They also cover their heads in public. They like to color their hands and feet with patterns using henna (a plant) dye. More intricate designs are drawn on their legs and arms for special occasions, such as weddings.

CUSTOMS AND COURTESIES

Greetings

Among men, handshakes are taken seriously and are used to greet even friends or coworkers one sees every day. In francophone areas, a brief handshake is used when meeting for the first time. Family or close friends may also brush alternate cheeks while they "kiss the air." In anglophone provinces, a slightly firmer handshake is most common. One's wrist is offered if the hand is dirty. Hugs are reserved for family and close friends. Close male friends might snap the middle finger and thumb while pulling the hands away from a handshake.

An informal anglophone greeting is *How na?* (Pidgin for "How are you?"). "Good morning" (*Bonjour* in francophone areas) and "Good afternoon" (*Bonsoir*) are more formal. Various local greetings are used depending on the ethnic group. Greetings are followed by inquiries about family welfare. People on the street may call to each other from a distance with "pssssst," but some don't consider this polite.

Throughout Cameroon, seniority (defined by gender, age, or prestige) is recognized by the left hand touching the right arm during a handshake or by bowing the head. To show special respect for authority, a man might bow from the waist (women curtsy); in the north, women may kneel. Eye contact with respected individuals is avoided, but one doesn't turn one's back to them. To approach traditional royalty, one speaks through cupped hands, bows, and greets the chief with upturned hands; one never touches the chief, even to shake hands.

Gestures

Using the right hand for greetings, eating, or to pass an object is always preferred. A person who uses the left accidentally or out of necessity apologizes. One points with head gestures or by puckering the lips. Legs may be crossed at the ankles, but not the knees; one does not cross the legs in front of those with higher authority. It is considered indecent for women to cross their legs in front of men in some areas. For all, it is important to keep the soles of the feet from pointing at others. Agreement is shown by a quick head nod. In rural areas, pleasure is often displayed by dancing. Grief may be shown by placing the hand on one's opposite shoulder and bowing the head, or by resting both hands on top of the head (one hand on top of the other). Beckoning is done by waving all fingers with the palm down. A hand extended and cupped upward is a request that something be shared.

Visiting

Visiting is a main form of entertainment in Cameroon. Punctuality is not expected. Social visits are casual and relaxed, except in more conservative homes where rank and gender distinctions are important. In such homes, women and children rarely appear; if they do, they are not introduced. Cameroonians enjoy visiting, especially on Fridays after mosque or Sundays after church. Unannounced visits are common, although strangers are expected to arrange visits in advance. Each individual is greeted at a small gathering.

A host is expected to offer guests something to eat and drink. Guests who drop in during a meal are asked to join in. Invited friends might bring food or drink as a gift. Food is not an acceptable gift from others because it may be interpreted as questioning the host's means or hospitality, but one can present other gifts. Gifts for children are offered through the parents. One removes street shoes before entering a Muslim home. Business matters are not discussed during social visits. Among northern Muslims, people show subordinance by removing shoes 100 meters (about 100 yards) before arriving to see a tribal chief. Foreigners and government officials, considered on the same level as chiefs, do not remove their shoes.

Eating

The largest daily meal is eaten in the afternoon. Evening meals usually consist of leftovers. Food is not taken for granted or treated casually, so formal meals are often blessed, and elders are served first. In rural areas, women do not eat with the men or older boys, but by the cooking fire with younger children; women also serve the meal.

Water is made available before and after meals for washing hands; this is important because many people eat with their right hands from communal bowls. Bottles are opened in the drinker's view; the host leaves the cap loose and the guest pours. If given food, a guest must taste it. Smelling it first is an insult. Even if guests are not hungry, it is polite to eat a small portion and then say they have eaten recently. But in many areas, not being hungry is considered being sick, so guests are generally expected to eat plenty. Cameroonians would rather share a meal and eat less than eat alone. In restaurants, hosts expect to pay for everything.

LIFESTYLE

Family

Large families are common in Cameroon, often with as many as ten children in rural areas. Urban families are smaller. Young children are cared for by their mothers until weaned. At that point, older siblings and other family members share in raising them. Often, a child is raised by grandparents or even a relative's family. By age ten, children are farming, herding, or doing domestic work.

The family structure is patriarchal. Children are raised almost exclusively by women, who may even be responsible for clothing and feeding them if the father does not provide

enough money. Fathers become more involved with their sons regarding career choices, marriage, and property issues. Grandparents remain within family compounds, receiving basic needs and affection. People remember ancestors by drinking in their honor after pouring some of their drink on the ground.

Women spend much time associating with one another, especially in polygamous families. They have civil rights but can be sent back to their families by an unsatisfied husband. They have no property rights, but do most of the farming and other productive work. More women in the south are getting an education and entering the job market, but this is not common in the north.

Dating and Marriage

Although arranged marriages may involve months or years of negotiations that create obligations after marriage for relatives on both sides, many couples meet on their own and have simple court ceremonies. A church wedding and reception might follow sometime (even years) later, depending on finances. Women marry at the average age of 19, men at 27 (younger in rural areas, older in cities).

Men are expected to marry, but may have many girlfriends in addition to one or more wives. Islamic law allows men to have up to four wives if each can be cared for equally. Polygamy is still common in rural areas but is decreasing for economic reasons. Marriage is often viewed more as a social contract than an affectionate relationship. Women are raised to be mothers more than wives. Because women surrender civil rights when they marry, educated women with jobs sometimes choose to have children, but not to marry. Their extended families help raise the children and provide financial support.

Diet

Staple foods include corn, millet, cassava, "peanuts" (groundnuts), yams, and plantain. Grains in the south are often cooked with palm oil, seasoned with hot pepper, and topped with a sauce made from fish, meat, or vegetables. *Fufu*, a common dish, is a stiff paste made of boiled corn, millet, or cassava. *Garri* is grated cassava that is dried over a fire until light and flaky. Meat and rice are luxuries for villagers. An urban breakfast might include tea or coffee, fruit, and bread. Rural breakfasts consist of the same foods that are eaten for the main meal. Energy snacks and street foods include raw sugarcane, boiled cassava, boiled eggs, roasted corn, fresh fruit, and nuts. Muslims usually prefer tea to coffee. Beer is popular on social occasions, but water is the main drink in the home.

Recreation

Team sports and individual athletics are sponsored by companies and urban social clubs. Soccer is the most popular sport. Cameroon's national soccer team competed in the 1994 World Cup. Men and women in schools and cities play team handball, volleyball, and basketball. In January, a marathon is run up and down Mount Cameroon (13,451 feet or 4,100 meters). Traditional board games, played with seeds or pebbles, are popular. Monthly feasts sponsored by savings societies provide recreation for many adults. Culture and Development Weeks bring urban migrants and students on vacation back to their home villages once a year, using feasts, dances, and athletic contests to raise funds for schools and community projects. Movies, videos, and television are popular in cities.

Live music, dance, radios, and portable cassette players are popular everywhere.

Holidays

Cameroon's national holidays include New Year's Day, Youth Day (11 February), Labor Day (1 May), and Unification Day (20 May). Unification Day marks the 1972 union of the French and British zones. Some religious holidays have national recognition, including Easter, Assumption (15 August), and Christmas for Christians. For Muslims, the most important holidays include a three-day feast at the end of *Ramadan* (a month of fasting each day from dawn until dusk), and the *fête de mouton* (lamb feast), held forty days later in honor of Abraham's willingness to sacrifice his son.

Commerce

The cash economy dominates in urban areas, but bartering and payment-in-kind still exist in rural areas. Most retailing is done curbside, from market stalls, in small shops, or out of converted cargo containers. Only Douala and Yaoundé have department stores. Multinational banks dominate trade and finance, but credit unions handle local savings and investments. In addition, people can form or join *tontines* (*njangis* in anglophone provinces)—savings societies of 10 to 12 members (men, women, or both). Members pool their capital, provide loans to each other, and sponsor social activities. Doing business is considered a delicate matter, and taking one's time is essential. Stores are usually open from 7:30 or 8:00 A.M. to 5:00 or 6:00 P.M., often closing for a two-hour lunch break. Street vendors do business late into the evening. Stores commonly close on Saturday afternoon. Sunday is quiet except in the Muslim north.

SOCIETY

Government

Cameroon is a unitary republic. A president and cabinet form a strong executive branch. Several parties are represented in the 180-seat National Assembly, including Biya's Cameroon People's Democratic Movement. Main opposition parties are the National Union for Democracy and Progress and the Social Democratic Font. Local courts for domestic and land law are maintained by hereditary kings in the north and west and appointed chiefs elsewhere. These rulers enjoy strong loyalty among many ethnic groups and are regularly consulted about national politics. The voting age is 20.

Economy

Economic prosperity depends largely on oil, coffee, and cocoa prices. Because oil reserves may run out by the year 2000, Cameroon is looking for ways to expand other industries. Agriculture employs a majority of the labor force in either growing or processing food. Most regions are able to feed themselves; some provide food for other areas; and some export cash crops such as coffee, cocoa, cotton, rubber, and timber. The currency, the *CFA franc*, is tied to the French franc. Cameroon's Human Development Index (0.447) ranks it 124th out of 173 countries. Real gross domestic product per capita is $2,400, which has almost tripled in a generation. These figures indicate more people are able to meet basic needs, even though 37 percent continue to live in poverty. Growth is inhibited by poor management and corruption.

Transportation and Communication

Francophone provinces enjoy better transportation and communication systems than anglophone areas. For example, the Nord-Ouest Province (anglophone) has over one million people, but few paved roads. This makes it difficult for its crops to make it to market, especially during the rainy season. Local travel in vans or sedans is common for public transport throughout the country. Taxis are available in cities. Many people travel by foot, on bicycles, or by motor scooters. Trains connect only three cities. The domestic airline serves four provinces. Most telephones are located in large urban areas. Mail service is not reliable. Radio and television services are owned by the government. A free press is growing. Perhaps the most effective communication is by *radio trattoir* (pavement radio), a system of verbal relays that passes news and information with great speed.

Education

The literacy rate is 55 percent. The education system is still divided between French and English patterns. Rural children enter school knowing neither French nor English, while urban children at least know one of them. Primary school enrollment is higher in the south than the north. Still, most children complete only about two full years of school. More boys than girls actually finish school. Secondary school enrollment is low due to exam failures, space shortages, higher fees, and parental choice. Muslim children memorize the *Qur'an* (Koran) at evening Koranic schools.

There is a full university in Yaoundé and smaller universities in four other cities. Informal education and apprenticeships provide vital vocational skills.

Health

Cameroon lacks an adequate health care system. Hospitals, while able to provide emergency services, often cannot provide basic (especially long-term) care. Patients' families must supply food, medicine, and some care. Still, a low-cost rural health program has helped decrease the infant mortality rate to 77 per 1,000 and increase life expectancy to between 54 and 58 years. Cameroon confronts a full range of tropical and other diseases, including malaria and cholera.

FOR THE TRAVELER

U.S. travelers must have a valid passport and a visa to enter Cameroon. There is a departure tax, payable in *CFA francs* at the airport. Take precautions against malaria. Vaccination against yellow fever is required; it is recommended for cholera. Avoid swimming in freshwater lakes or ponds. Do not drink water unless it has been boiled or otherwise purified. Peel or cook all fresh fruits and vegetables before eating. Eat only well-cooked meat. There are tourist beaches at Kribi and Limbe, and northern attractions like Waza (for wildlife) and Mandara (for volcanic formations). It is common for authorities to expect a "tip" to perform their duties. For more information, contact the Embassy of Cameroon, 2349 Massachusetts Avenue NW Washington, DC 20008; phone (202) 265–8790.

Printed on recycled paper

Republic of
Cape Verde

Boundary representations not necessarily authoritative.

BACKGROUND

Land and Climate

Cape Verde is an archipelago of islands located some 278 miles (445 kilometers) off the West African coast. There are two island groups, consisting of a total of ten principal islands and eight smaller islands. Cape Verde's land area is 1,557 square miles (4,033 square kilometers). This is a bit larger than Rhode Island. The capital is Praia, located on São Tiago. The islands are of volcanic origin and are arid. Sahelian vegetation is prevalent, and the high rate of soil erosion does not favor plant life. The landscape does have variety, however, with tropical valleys and coasts giving way to mountain pine forests. The average temperature is 75°F (25°C). The dry season begins in November and ends in July, while the rainy season spans August to October. Winds blowing off Africa's deserts send dust and dry air to Cape Verde. Rains fall irregularly and sometimes not at all for years.

History

Portuguese explorer Antonio Da Noli is credited with the discovery of Cape Verde in 1455. It is believed some islands were inhabited by such West African groups as the Wolor, Serere, and Lebou prior to his landing. Within ten years Da Noli brought slaves to Cape Verde from the Guinea Coast in order to develop sugar plantations. The plantations proved unproductive given the inhospitable climate. Cape Verde came to be used by Portugal as a crossroads for trading slaves, gold, and other valuables.

More recent history began jointly with Guinea-Bissau. In 1955, the African Party for the Independence of Guinea and Cape Verde (PAIGC) was organized by Amilcar Cabral, Luís Cabral, Aristides Pereira, Pedro Pires, and others. After some 20 years of guerrilla warfare against Portugal, both Cape Verde and Guinea-Bissau gained their independence. Cape Verde became independent 5 July 1975. Cabral, the movement's leader, was assassinated 20 January 1973 in Conakry, Guinea, presumably under orders from Portugal. Pereira was then elected president and Pires became prime minister. They led the government under a single-party system until 1990. In the nation's first multiparty elections in 1991, António Mascarenhas was elected president and Carlos Veiga became prime minister. They represent the Move for Democracy party.

THE PEOPLE

Population

Cape Verde has a population of about 423,000, which is growing at an annual rate of 3 percent. The most populated islands include São Tiago (48 percent of all people), São Vincente (13 percent), Santo Antão (13 percent), and Fogo (10 percent). More than 52 percent of the population is comprised of women. The largest cities are Praia (80,000 inhabitants) and Mindelo (40,000). The population is evenly split between rural and urban areas. Most Cape Verdeans (71 percent) are descendants of a mixture of Black Africans and

Portuguese, while 28 percent is Black African and 1 percent is European.

Language

The official language is Portuguese. However, the national language, Crioulo, is most commonly used on a daily basis. Crioulo is a mixture of Portuguese and African and other languages. A project to publish a Crioulo dictionary is currently underway, but the language remains an unwritten tongue. Since the majority of people do not speak or write Portuguese well, many people have difficulty understanding all the information in newspapers, on television, or on the radio. Realizing this, both television and radio stations have recently added a news program in Crioulo. Many educated people speak English and French, which are offered in secondary school.

Religion

In Cape Verde, freedom of worship is allowed and religious differences are accepted. Nearly all Cape Verdeans are Christian. More than 80 percent of them belong to the Roman Catholic church. About 12 percent is Protestant, with the rest belonging to other groups. People are very religious in Cape Verde, as can be seen by the great attendance at Mass and by the many sayings of a religious nature used in everyday conversation. On Sunday, the churches are always crowded and one must come early to get a seat. The Catholic church also has a great deal of political and social influence. In fact, some people credit it for the Movement of Democracy's electoral win in 1991.

General Attitudes

Compared to the industrialized world, people in Cape Verde do things at a relaxed pace. For example, while going to work a person may stop and greet a friend, even though this may make that person a few minutes late. Another characteristic of Capeverdians is that they are determined and do not give up easily. Farmers, for example, continue to plant crops every year hoping for rain, even if it has not come for many seasons.

In order to avoid confrontation, Capeverdians do not state opinions directly, and they are not at ease with a direct apology. Capeverdians are hospitable, generous, and friendly. They are also open to the outside world, as twice as many Capeverdians live away from the islands (mainly in the United States, Netherlands, France, and Senegal) as on them. In general, individualism is not promoted. One's success is to be used to help the less fortunate in the family and not simply to be enjoyed alone. The primacy of the group over the individual also means that there is a lack of privacy in Cape Verde.

Personal Appearance

Western clothing dominates in urban areas. Most people dress informally. Even highly ranked public officials wear shirts with short sleeves to work. Older people dress more conservatively than the younger generation, wearing longer dresses or darker colors for example. People dress up in their finest clothing when going to church. Teenagers also dress up when they go to the *Praça* (town plaza). Shirts with English inscriptions, such as the names of American sports teams and cities, are popular.

Rural people might mix Western clothing with more traditional styles, but their appearance is always neat and clean. Rural women favor dresses, or blouses with wraparound skirts, and a head scarf. Rural men wear lightweight shirts and pants, and sometimes a wide-brimmed or other kind of hat. Adults do not usually wear shorts.

CUSTOMS AND COURTESIES

Greetings

Greetings generally involve a short handshake and a long greeting. It is always important to greet someone prior to talking. Women often kiss each other on each cheek. If acquainted, urban men and women might also kiss each others' cheeks. Parents or elders may be greeted with a kiss to one cheek. Crioulo is used most of the time for greetings. Dialects vary between islands, but the most standard phrase is *Modi ki bu sta?* (How are you?). The response is *N'sta bom* (I am fine). After initial greetings, it is polite to ask how each other's family is doing. When conducting business, especially with strangers, the Portuguese *Como estas?* (How are you?) is used. In response, one answers *Estou bem* (I am fine).

An older person is respectfully addressed with a title before their name: *Senhor* (Mr.), *Senhora* (Mrs.), *Tio* (Uncle), or *Tia* (Aunt). Also as a sign of respect, parents and relatives are addressed by familial titles: *Pai* (Crioulo for father) or *Papa* (Portuguese for father), *Mae* or *Mama* (mother), *Tio*, or *Tia*. Friends address each other by first name.

Gestures

In Cape Verde, beckoning is done by waving all fingers with the palm facing up. It is not proper to beckon the elderly. When talking, people stand in close proximity and often touch each other during the conversation. This is an important part of communication. Hand gestures are otherwise not used much.

Eye contact during conversation is important among peers. However, it is a sign of respect to look down when talking to older people or to persons who are teaching. Cape Verdeans, who are generally music-oriented people, tend to whistle their favorite tunes in public.

Visiting

Cape Verdeans visit each other often. It is not necessary to call ahead and most informal visits are unannounced. Hosts are hospitable and treat their guests well. Guests are offered a drink and some sweets in most cases. Guests arriving at mealtime are invited to eat. It is not considered rude to decline a drink or a meal, but doing it consistently would probably be offensive. When invited to dinner, guests are not expected to contribute to the meal. Nevertheless, it is common practice that dinner invitations are reciprocated. Sometimes, a guest may bring a small gift to the host.

When invited to an event, guests say they will try to attend, even if they know it will not be possible. Saying "no" directly to an invitation may offend the inviting party, since it is interpreted as not valuing the invitation.

Cape Verdeans are not as conscious of time as people in industrialized nations. They are often late, even by an hour or more. This is especially true for dances. Although scheduled to start at 9:00 P.M., a dance may not begin before 11:00 P.M.

(with guests beginning to arrive at 10:30 P.M.). Being late at a home does not insult a host. It is automatically assumed that the guest had something to do prior to arriving.

People frequently socialize outside of their homes in Cape Verde. In fact, urban people gather daily at the *Praça* between 5:30 and 8:00 P.M. to discuss their day, make plans for the weekend, or talk about issues affecting the country.

Eating

In general, breakfast is eaten between 7:00 and 9:00 A.M. and lunch is between noon and 2:00 P.M. After lunch, many people take a short nap of about 30 minutes. For the wealthiest, coffee or tea with cookies and cakes is served around 5:00 P.M. and supper is around 8:30 P.M. For most people, however, supper is at about 7:00 P.M.

With the influence of Portuguese colonization, Cape Verdeans usually use forks, knives, and spoons during meals. At a restaurant or café, it is not uncommon for the wealthiest person to pay for the entire meal, especially if the others in the party have financial difficulties. Tips are not expected in restaurants, cafés, or taxis, but they are welcomed.

LIFESTYLE

Family

In Cape Verde, the average family has five or six children and is led by the father. The extended family unit is important to each person; group (family) success takes precedence over individual success. Some elderly parents live with their children. Adult children often live in their parents' house until they get married, even if they have a job. Many women work outside the home; they comprise 29 percent of the labor force. Three women have cabinet positions in the current government. Regardless of their responsibilities outside the home, women are generally expected to do all household cleaning and cooking and to care for the children.

Most households are modest. In fact, only about half of all rural homes have access to electricity. Rural homes are made of stone or brick, stone being plentiful in the islands. Urban homes are more commonly made of cement and other materials.

Dating and Marriage

Dating customs are similar to those in Western countries, with young people meeting through school, community events, and work. Couples enjoy going to movies, dancing, going to the beach, and having parties. Young people are free to choose their mates, but families often have input or play an integral role in planning the wedding and other celebrations. Some couples live together instead of getting married, or they do so until they can afford the expensive wedding celebrations. A religious ceremony is typically followed by an evening reception that may accommodate more than two hundred people. Fidelity is important in marriage, but male infidelity is somewhat tolerated.

Diet

The most commonly eaten foods in Cape Verde are rice and corn. Rice, although imported, is relatively inexpensive; corn is grown locally. Rice is often served with fish and beans (black or pinto). Corn is often served with beans, pork, manioc, and sweet potatoes. *Catchupa* is the national dish. It is a stew made of corn and meat with manioc that is cooked slowly in water. Since Cape Verde is an archipelago, fish and fish products are important to the diet.

To complement their diet, people eat fruits and vegetables, such as bananas, papayas, mangos, lettuce, and tomatoes, and others. Cape Verdeans enjoy sweets at any time of day, cakes and marmalades being among the favorites. Two popular sweets include *doce de leite* (made of milk, sugar, and lemon) and *doce de coco* (made of coconut and sugar, it looks like a table tennis ball).

Recreation

In their leisure time, Capeverdians visit each other, go to the beach, read, and play *futebol* (soccer). Soccer is the most popular sport, and people watch or listen to soccer broadcasts with undivided attention. On Sundays, people can be seen on the streets with their ears "glued" to the radio. In recent years, basketball and some other sports have increased in popularity. In urban areas, television is gaining a wider audience.

Cape Verdeans like to spend time at the islands' beautiful beaches. They also enjoy music and dances. Three of Cape Verde's unique music and dance styles include *Morna*, *Coladeira*, and *Funáná*. The first has a slow rhythm and mostly sad lyrics, while the *Coladeira* is more upbeat and joyful. The *Funáná* is even more lively, and has a strong beat. It was actually forbidden before independence and only survived in the countryside. Now enjoyed throughout the country, it is the most popular dance music.

Holidays

Cape Verde's official holidays are New Year's Day (1 January), National Hero's Day (20 January), Women's Day (8 March), Labor Day (1 May), Children's Day (1 June), Independence Day (5 July), All Saints' Day (1 November), and Christmas (25 December). An additional holiday in February is added in some areas where *Carnaval* is important. National Hero's Day commemorates the death of Amilcar Cabral, who led the fight for independence. Other national heroes are also honored on this day. While every 5th of July is a holiday, an official celebration takes place only every five years in order to minimize the financial costs of celebrating Independence Day.

Commerce

Businesses are open from 8:00 A.M. to noon, and from 2:30 to 6:00 P.M., Monday through Friday. A pilot project is currently underway to determine if working hours can be changed using an 8:00 A.M. to 4:00 P.M. schedule, with a shorter (30 minutes) lunch break. A few businesses use this alternate schedule, but it is unclear how popular it is. Cape Verde has both stores where prices are fixed and open-air markets where prices are negotiable. The main open-air market, *Sukupira*, is in Praia. Staple goods are mostly sold in stores and are purchased less frequently, while fresh foods may be purchased several times a week.

SOCIETY

Government

Cape Verde is a republic administered through a parliamentary democracy. The National People's Assembly is the legislative body; it deliberates on, amends, and adopts national laws, plans, and budgets. The legislature has 82 directly elected members. According to the 1992 constitution, six of the legislators are elected by and represent emigrants living abroad. Previously, there were only three such representatives. Cape Verde's president is the head of state, and the prime minister is the head of government. Both serve five-year terms.

In opposition to the Movement for Democracy party stands the African Party for Independence of Cape Verde (the former ruling party). The voting age is 18. There are 14 districts in the country, roughly representing each inhabited island. Because a multiparty democratic system was in place within 16 years of independence, Cape Verdeans point to their society as an example of genuine democracy in Africa.

Economy

Relatively speaking, Cape Verde is a poor country. Its Human Development Index (0.474) ranks it 122d out of 173 nations. Real gross domestic product per capita is $1,360. About two-thirds of the people are considered wage earners, but many do not earn enough to meet basic needs and unemployment is high (25 percent). The country's lack of success is explained by the fact that Cape Verde's resources are limited or underdeveloped. For example, the fishing and lobster harvesting industries are not well developed. In addition, the economy is not growing fast enough to keep up with population growth. Fish, bananas, hides, and skins are the main exports, while much of the country's food and consumer items are imported. Most rural people work on road construction, fish, or are subsistence farmers. Urban residents work mainly for the government, are in the small retail business, or fish.

Without aid from the international community, as well as remittances from Cape Verdeans living abroad, the country's standard of living would be lower than it is. The currency is the Cape Verdean *escudo* (CVEsc).

Transportation and Communication

Most areas in Cape Verde are accessible by roads, but many of them are not paved. Those that are paved are often in disrepair, but the government is trying to address the problem. Interisland transportation by sea is also used for both passengers and freight, but most people do not travel much between islands. Locally, Cape Verdeans use a combination of transportation methods—going by foot, riding bicycles, or traveling by motorcycles and sometimes cars. Some people ride animals, but most have access to the public bus system.

Telephone services are available in urban areas. Having service installed in a private home is expensive, and one is billed for each call, even local ones. The one national television station broadcasts to the entire country. On a clear day, television broadcasts from nearby countries can be received. There are three radio stations and a few newspapers. Postal delivery is slow and not always reliable, especially in rural areas.

Education

Enrollment in primary schools (ages seven to twelve) is compulsory, and 85 percent of the children within this age group attend. About 48 percent of the school-age population attends secondary schools, while less than 1 percent holds a college degree. Given that Cape Verde has no college or university, the country relies on overseas fellowships to provide its people with higher education. The government pays for all educational costs. The official literacy rate is 66 percent.

Cape Verde's dropout rates in primary and secondary schools are high for many reasons. First, classes are taught in Portuguese, creating a learning barrier for the majority of children, who speak Crioulo at home. Also, it is difficult for rural people to appreciate the value of or need for an education. It is not seen as necessary for earning a living. Economic constraints further compound the situation. For instance, the relatively high cost of transportation in rural areas, coupled with the need for children to help with work at home, can lead even eager students to drop out.

Health

Health care is provided by the government, free of direct financial costs to the patient. However, the waiting lines at the hospital are costly in terms of time, and the quality of care is not always adequate. This is due to the lack of equipment and to understaffing. Most people in urban areas, but only half of all rural residents, have access to safe drinking water, which is vital to good health. The country's infant mortality rate is 57 per 1,000; life expectancy ranges from 60 to 64 years.

FOR THE TRAVELER

A passport and visa, as well as an inoculation against yellow fever, are required for U.S. citizens to visit Cape Verde. In addition, vaccinations against typhoid and tetanus are recommended. Vegetables should be washed or cooked before being eaten. Peel fruits prior to eating them. Cape Verde is appreciated by people who enjoy the beach, the sun, a slow pace of life, and dancing. Surfing, scuba diving, and other water sports are available in the islands. There are many historical sites of interest. For more information, contact the Embassy of the Republic of Cape Verde, 3415 Massachusetts Avenue NW, Washington, DC 20007; phone (202) 965–6820, or the Permanent Mission of Cape Verde to the United Nations, 27 East 69th Street, New York, NY 10021; phone (212) 472–0333. Travelers should also contact the Consulate General of Cape Verde, 535 Boylston Street, Seventh Floor, Boston, MA 02116; phone (617) 353–0014.

Central African Republic

Boundary representations not necessarily authoritative.

BACKGROUND

Land and Climate

The Central African Republic covers 240,533 square miles (622,980 square kilometers) and is a little smaller than Texas. The south is very green, with areas of dense rain forest. Farther north, the land becomes drier, but most of the country is covered by savannah. The Central African Republic is landlocked. Only one river, the Oubangui (on the southern border), can be used by large boats during the rainy season. But there are many small rivers.

Generally, daytime temperatures are hot, but nights cool off to 55°F (13°C) during November and December when cold winds blow off the northern desert. There is a rainy season, from May to November, and a second, shorter season in late February or early March. This precipitation is called the "mango rains" because it allows mango trees to produce fruit for the mango season in late March.

The Central African Republic government has been implementing a variety of conservation projects. Elephant hunting is banned, although poaching is a problem. Several preserves in the north and southwest protect wildlife and rain forests.

History

Central Africa has an ancient heritage, but prior to French control of the area in 1887, it was inhabited by the Aka (pygmy) and peoples migrating inland to escape the coastal slave trade. The French established the area as the Ubangi-Shari territory in 1894 and united it with Chad in 1906 as the Ubangi-Shari-Chad colony. In 1910, the colony was united with the Congo and Gabon as the Federation of French Equitorial Africa. Ubangi-Shari became autonomous in 1958 and independent in 1960. At independence, the name was changed to Central African Republic.

David Dacko served as the country's first president, but was overthrown in a coup led by Colonel Jean-Bedel Bokassa in 1966. In 1976, Bokassa created a monarchy and crowned himself Emperor Bokassa I. Dacko staged a coup in 1979 while Bokassa was out of the country and restored the republic. General André Kolingba overthrew Dacko in yet another coup in 1981. The military ran the government until 1985, when Kolingba appointed civilians to his new cabinet. Kolingba created the *Rassemblement Démocratique Centrafricain* (RDC) as the only legal party in 1986. Elections in 1987 were used to approve a new constitution and a six-year term in office for Kolingba. By the 1990s, however, in a climate of bleak economic conditions, other parties became active and posted candidates in 1993 elections. Bokassa ran for president, but lost in the first round of voting. Ange-Félix Patasse was elected president in the second round.

THE PEOPLE

Population

The population is about 3.1 million. Over 500,000 people live in and around the capital, Bangui. Other urban areas can be found, but over half the people live in small towns and villages. Still, urban areas are growing faster (4 percent) than the overall population (2.1 percent).

More than 80 ethnic groups inhabit the Central African Republic, although two account for over half of the total population. In addition to the Gbaya (34 percent) and the Banda (27 percent), there are the Mandjia, Sara, Mboum, M'Baka, Sango, and others. There is a significant Aka (Pygmy) population along the southwest border. The Mbororo, descendants of the Fulbé (or Fulani), are migratory herding people who do not consider themselves Central Africans; others also recognize them as distinctly different. In addition to local peoples, a significant population of Portuguese-, Greek-, and Arabic-speaking merchants live in urban areas.

Language

Sango and French are the two main languages used, but each ethnic group also has its own language. Sango (a Bantu tongue) is the national language. It was spread years ago as a trade language. French is the official language, but it is used mostly in government. Most people are fluent in their own tongue and Sango. French is spoken only by the more educated (about 10 percent).

The government promotes Sango because it reinforces national identity. It recently introduced Sango as the language of instruction in primary school. Many official speeches are made in Sango rather than French, especially if the audience is primarily Central African. The national radio, *Radio Centrafrique*, broadcasts in both Sango and French.

Religion

There are several religions in the Central African Republic. About half of the population is Christian, mainly Catholic and Baptist. About 15 percent of the population is Muslim. The rest practice local religions. In fact, even Christians and Muslims maintain traditional beliefs or combine local practice with Islam or Christianity. For example, funerals may be less Catholic and more African. A belief in magic is widespread. People also seek the services of local charmers for guidance.

General Attitudes

Central Africans are friendly, gentle, and generous. Strangers are greeted with smiles. There is a high sense of community among the people, including a strong commitment to the family and loyalty to one's ethnic group. Young people attending school away from home can expect to live with relatives, no matter how distant the relationship.

Central Africans tend to live in the present. Because there are many immediate daily concerns and limited resources, money is usually spent when obtained. Savings are not common. Those with money left over are expected to share it with family members who need it; saving money is considered a sign of greed. There is a degree of uncertainty about the future, so people are fatalistic about their lives. At the same time, they have a genuine appreciation for and enjoyment of the present.

Ethnic groups have strong internal bonds and often have identifying characteristics like specific trades, customs, or facial features (tattoos, scars, henna leaf designs, etc.).

Personal Appearance

Central Africans take pride in being clean and well dressed. Wealthier urban men may wear a shirt and slacks or a Western-style suit. A *complet*, also popular, consists of pants and a matching shirt jacket that buttons to the collar. A common traditional outfit consists of pants and matching *boubou* made from bright, locally produced fabric. A *boubou* may be cut as a pullover-style shirt, but a *grand boubou* is more like a robe that reaches the man's knees or feet. Embroidery on the front is popular.

Urban women commonly wear traditional styles. One outfit is a tight-fitting, short-sleeved blouse with a matching *pagne* (long, wraparound skirt). Wealthier women might wear a short and a long *pagne* at the same time. The way a woman ties her *pagne* and allows the cloth to drape over her body conveys a number of unspoken messages, such as marital status. Women usually wear some sort of head wrap. A scarf is required to enter a church. Gold jewelry is a status symbol. Hairstyles can be elaborate. Girls learn at an early age to braid and weave hair.

Rural people and the urban poor dress modestly. They often wear secondhand Western clothing or a combination of local styles with Western T-shirts. Villagers often go barefoot to save their shoes for special occasions.

CUSTOMS AND COURTESIES

Greetings

A handshake is used in formal and social settings, along with verbal greetings. If close male friends meet informally, a greeting might begin by slapping the right hands together. Then, each would grasp the other person's middle finger with the thumb and middle finger, and "snap." Women sometimes kiss each other on alternating cheeks. After these physical gestures, inquiries about one's health, family, and crops usually follow. This is true even when meeting by chance; just a passing "hello" to a friend or coworker is not polite.

A common Sango greeting is *Bara ala!* or *Bala mo!* (Greetings to you), followed by *Tonga na nyen?* (How's it going?), or *Ala yeke senge?* or *Mo yeke?* (Are you okay?). French greetings include *Bonjour* (Good day) or *Salut!* (Greetings), followed by *Ça va?* (Everything okay?). French is not used in villages.

How one addresses a person depends on the situation. Formally, titles are used alone or with the last name. Respected older men may be addressed as *baba* (Sango for "father"), and women as *mama* (mother). Informally, first or last names, nicknames, or family affiliation (cousin, brother, sister) may be used. A very close friend may be called *ita* (brother or sister) or *cousin* (cousin). When meeting a small group, one greets each person individually. To greet a larger group, one might raise both hands, palms facing the group, and say, *Bara ala kwé* (Sango for "Greetings, everyone").

Gestures

Beckoning is done by extending the hand, fingers out and palm down, and waving the fingers inward. During conversation, "yes" can be indicated by raising the eyebrows. This gesture is sometimes accompanied by a quick inhalation or a glottal clicking sound. One might ask, "What?" or even "How are you?" by holding the hand out next to the body, palm open and down with the fingers relaxed, and flipping the hand over. Surprise or shock may be expressed by slapping the forehead with an open hand, sometimes saying "Aye!" or "Mama!" A hissing sound may be used to attract attention. Children often cross their arms over their stomachs as a sign of respect when speaking to a person of authority. Pointing with one finger is impolite. Forming a circle with the thumb and index finger means zero. One may show respect when shaking hands by supporting the right wrist with the left hand and bowing slightly. Young friends of the same age and sex often hold hands while walking and talking.

Visiting

Visiting is a popular way to spend free time; it is common to "drop in" uninvited at a friend's home. After greeting those present, the visitor is offered a chair or stool (*barambo*) and something to drink. Visitors may be asked to sit inside the home, but it is more common to sit outside on the porch or in the shade of a nearby tree. The visitor is usually given the nicest place to sit. During the visit, everyone might talk or listen to the radio. Sometimes very little is said and everyone just relaxes. Visitors arriving at mealtime are asked to share the meal. It is impolite to refuse offers of food, drink, or a seat.

Invited guests are not necessarily expected to be prompt. Hosts are patient with late guests and accomodating of those who arrive early. The host will often accompany a departing guest for a short distance.

Eating

The number of meals eaten in a day depends on family income. At mealtime, people (especially children) may sit on the ground or on low stools around the food, which may be on a mat or a low table. Townspeople often have Western-style tables and chairs. While plates and utensils might be used, food is generally eaten with the hands from a common bowl. The right hand is used unless the type of food requires both hands. Before and after the meal, soap and water are passed around to wash the hands. In villages, men and boys eat together. Girls and young boys eat near their mother by the cooking fire. The mother eats last because she is usually still preparing food while others are eating. People generally snack throughout the day. Popular snack foods include peanuts, small pieces of grilled meat, *makala* (fried dough), fried sweet potatoes, hard-boiled eggs, *mangbele* (cassava dough wrapped and boiled in leaves), and *kanda* (meat, fish, fruit, or termites wrapped in a leaf and steamed).

The average person rarely eats at a restaurant, but when one is invited to do so, the host expects to pay for the meal. Friends that decide together to eat out pay for their own meals.

LIFESTYLE

Family

The extended family is the basic social unit; it includes the mother, father, their children, grandparents, aunts, uncles, and cousins. They may live together in one home, and great emphasis is placed on taking care of elderly relatives. Adults often consider nieces and nephews as daughters and sons. Families are relatively large, and can seem larger because men may have more than one wife (or girlfriend). Each wife or girlfriend lives apart from the others. Women are responsible for raising their children and providing the family with food. The man provides money for school, clothing, and the home.

Special pride is taken in introducing someone as, for example, *mon frère, même mère, même père* (my brother, same mother, same father). *Un frère* (a brother) might be a half brother or other relation. *Un cousin* could be a very distant relative. *Ita ti mbi* (Sango) can mean brother, sister, half brother, cousin, or even close friend.

Depending on one's income, a home may be made of mud or cement bricks, a dirt or cement floor, and a thatched or tin roof. The kitchen may be a thatched hut away from the home where women cook over an open fire; outhouses are also located away from the home. The wealthy might have structures for a kitchen and bathroom attached to their homes. People don't spend much time in the home, but are busy with daily activities.

Dating and Marriage

Traditional customs are followed in rural areas. Parents sometimes arrange a marriage, and older men sometimes take young women as wives. In larger urban areas, men and women usually choose their own spouse. Although illegal, the practice of paying a bride-price to the bride's family is common. Depending on the groom's financial status and reputation, the bride-price can be quite high. It consists of money, clothing, animals, jewelry, household items, food for the wedding party, and other items. A wedding party can last for days. Men are allowed, by custom, to have relationships outside of marriage, but women are not. Polygamy is common, but less so than in the past. The poorest can only afford one wife.

Diet

Lunch is the main meal of the day; dinner consists of leftovers or fruit. A traditional meal is *ngunza* with *gozo*. *Ngunza* is a thick sauce made from ground cassava leaves, tomato paste, and peanut butter. A *kpu* (looks like a giant mortar and pestle) is used to grind the leaves and prepare many other foods. *Gozo* is a thick paste made by soaking the cassava root in water, drying it in the sun, grinding it into flour, and mixing it with boiling water. The *gozo* is formed into balls and dipped into *ngunza*. Meals may also include sauces with meat (beef, chicken, goat, gazelle, monkey, snake, even elephant) or fish. There is a variety of fruits and vegetables in the country, including sweet potatoes, tomatoes, avocados, bananas, oranges, grapefruit, guavas, papayas, pineapples, and mangoes. The Central African Republic imports powdered milk, noodles, rice, and other items.

Recreation

Because girls and women do household work, tend the fields, and do the shopping, recreation mostly applies to men and boys. They enjoy playing and watching soccer and basketball. Several amateur teams compete in the capital and in each large town. Some towns sponsor scout troops.

Schools provide all students with some recreation. Basketball, soccer, handball, and track and field are popular. Children also like to sing and play games at recess. Some schools have other extracurricular activities, such as theater. Church groups provide social activities, too.

Music is important. Each ethnic group has a distinct style and ensemble of instruments (skin drums or log drums). Specific drumming rhythms are used for certain events.

Holidays

Central Africans observe "official" and religious holidays. Official days include New Year's Day (1 January), *Fête du*

Travail (Labor Day, 1 May), *Fête des Mères* (Mother's Day, end of May), Independence Day (13 August), and the Declaration of Independence from France (1 December). This last day is the biggest holiday, celebrated country wide with parades and festivities. School children practice for months to perform on this day. For Mother's Day, men stay home to cook and women get together to socialize, play sports, and dance.

Religious holidays include Easter and Christmas for Christians. Muslims celebrate the end of *Ramadan* (the month of fasting during which Muslims go without food or water during the day) with a feast, and *Tabaski* (Feast of the Sacrifice), which commemorates Abraham's willingness to sacrifice his son.

Commerce

Offices are generally open Monday through Friday until early afternoon. Shops are open Monday through Saturday from early to late, with a couple of hours' break in the afternoon. Some outdoor markets are open only in the morning or afternoon. Many open on Sunday, a popular day for shopping and socializing. Prices in open markets are negotiable, but some staple foods are sold at fixed prices. Post offices sell stamps in the morning; those with public telephones stay open later so people can make calls. Business meetings are usually preceded by socializing, which is important for good relations.

SOCIETY

Government

The Central African Republic's president serves as chief of state and head of government. The National Assembly has 85 deputies. That body is advised by an Economic and Regional Council. When the two bodies are in session together, they are called a Congress. There is a separate judicial branch. The country is divided into 16 prefectures, each of which is divided into sub-prefectures. Each town has an elected mayor. In addition, a *makunji*, or village chief, is elected in each village. The responsibilities of the *makunji* depend on the strength and popularity of the mayor. All citizens have the right to vote at age 21. President Patasse's party is the Movement for the Liberation of the Central African People (MLPC). It overtook Kolingba's RDC in the 1993 elections. In addition to those two major parties, more than 20 others are now active.

Economy

The economy is based on agriculture, and most people are subsistence farmers. Coffee, cotton, tobacco, peanut and palm oils, and wood are exported and used locally; food crops and livestock are raised for domestic consumption. Industry usually centers on food processing and textiles. France is an important trade partner. It also provides loans and grants to the country. The currency is the *CFA franc* (Fr).

The Central African Republic's Human Development Index (0.249) ranks it 160th out of 173 countries. Real gross domestic product per capita is $641, which has declined steadily in the last generation. These figures indicate the vast majority of people (e.g., subsistence farmers) do not earn an income or do not earn enough to meet basic needs.

Transportation and Communication

The main form of intercity transportation is the *taxi brousse* (bush taxi); this can be a small pickup or a van. They are crowded and overloaded with luggage, but affordable. People also hitchhike, while some have mopeds or bicycles. Short trips (up to 30 miles) are sometimes made on foot. Very few roads are paved. Post offices handle mail and telephone services. The government runs radio and television facilities. Radio programs are broadcast in French and Sango.

Education

Children begin primary school at age seven. Attendance is mandatory, but only about two-thirds of eligible students are enrolled. School is free, but students may not have enough clothing or food to stay in school. Books are scarce, so teachers write lessons on the board and students copy them in their notebooks. About 10 percent go on to secondary school. Successful graduates (about 2 percent) may go to the university in Bangui or to a technical school. Some study abroad. The literacy rate is 38 percent, although it is lower for women.

Health

The country lacks adequate health care. Health care professionals are often dedicated, but underpaid. Public clinics exist in cities, but equipment is usually outdated and patients are required to provide their own anesthetics and medicine (available at pharmacies). Public facilities are virtually nonexistent in smaller towns and villages. Private clinics are found in the capital and missionaries run rural clinics. Traditional healers in rural areas treat illness with organic medicine and rituals. The infant mortality rate is 137 per 1,000. If a child survives to age six, there is a good chance of living to adulthood. Women often have children in their late teens and many die in childbirth. The average life expectancy is 49 years. Malaria, hepatitis, polio, intestinal parasites, and river blindness are common.

FOR THE TRAVELER

U.S. citizens need a valid passport and visa to travel to the Central African Republic. Professional photographers need special permits. A yellow fever vaccination is required; cholera, rabies, polio, typhoid, and hepatitis vaccinations are recommended. Malaria is endemic. Avoid swimming in rivers or pools of water because of the threat of schistosomiasis. Peel or cook fruits and vegetables before eating them, and purify or boil all drinking water. Eat only meat that is hot and well cooked. Do not take pictures of government installations or military personnel. High fees are charged for exchanging travelers checks and foreign currency. French *francs* might be accepted by some in the capital. Those traveling beyond the capital should expect to go by bush taxi and use cash for all transactions. Don't expect to get by speaking English. Visitors leaving by air must pay an airport tax of 3,000 CFA *francs* (or 60 French *francs*).Tourism is not actively promoted, but there are many interesting sites to visit. For more information, contact the Embassy of the Central African Republic, 1618 22d Street NW, Washington, DC 20008.

People's Republic of
China

Boundary representations not necessarily authoritative.

BACKGROUND

Land and Climate

At 3,705,751 square miles (9,597,905 square kilometers), China is just larger than the United States. But because much of it is covered by mountains or desert, the majority of people live in the fertile east, where rivers and plains allow for good agriculture. While summers are warmer and winters colder, China's climate is much like that in the United States. Monsoons cause frequent summer floods. China experiences several climates and has many geographical features, from the Himalayan mountains to the Qinghai-Tibet Plateau (known as the "roof of the world") to subtropical islands. Some of the world's longest rivers are in China; the Yangtze River is 3,900 miles (6,300 kilometers) long. The Great Wall of China stretches 1,500 miles (2,400 kilometers).

History

The Chinese have one of the world's oldest continuous civilizations, spanning some 5,000 years. From its earliest history, China was ruled by a series of dynasties—some were native (such as the Ming Dynasty) and some were nomadic tribes (Qing Dynasty)—that were eventually absorbed into Chinese culture. A revolution inspired by Sun Yat-sen overthrew the Qing Dynasty in 1911. In the 1920s, with the country fragmented by opposing warlords, Sun Yat-sen established the Kuomintang (KMT) political party in an effort to unify China.

After Sun's death in 1925, Chiang Kai-shek took control (1927) and ousted the once-allied Communist party. The Communists, led by Mao Zedong, are famous for their Long March across China to regroup and fight the KMT for control of China. After the Japanese were defeated in World War II, the civil war ended with Mao's forces in control and Chiang's army fleeing to Taiwan to regroup and return. They never did. Mao ruled from 1949 to 1976.

While the Chinese initially welcomed communism, the periods of the Great Leap Forward (1958–61) and the Cultural Revolution (1966–76) had disastrous effects on the country. More than 40 million people starved or were killed during Mao's rule. Policymakers after him have been more pragmatic, and Mao is not the hero he once was. Deng Xiaoping, a more moderate leader, dictated policy during the 1980s. His policies led to foreign tourism, a more liberal economy, growth, trade, and educational exchanges. Unfortunately, the Tiananmen Square massacre in 1989 and a subsequent government crackdown slowed China's open-door policy.

In 1992, Deng and his moderate supporters won a quiet power struggle to bring China back on track toward economic reform. China quickly became one of the world's fastest growing economies; by the year 2000 it is expected to be the largest economy (the United States currently holds that position). Political liberalization is nevertheless resisted by certain leaders, partly out of the natural tendency of authoritarian societies to conserve power. But even moderate leaders contend that socialism can be maintained in an era of prosperity. Improvements in material welfare, others say, will eventually bring social and political change. For the majority of people, the issue is not who governs but whether the standard of living rises. And the great majority of people desire any change to occur peacefully, rather than through uprisings and distress.

THE PEOPLE
Population
China's population is the largest in the world, with 1.19 billion people. To reduce the 1.1 percent annual growth rate, the government officially sponsors family planning programs and offers incentives (money, housing, and educational advantages) to families that have only one child. This policy applies mainly to the Han Chinese (92 percent) and not necessarily to minorities. Fifty-five minorities make up 8 percent of the population, 15 of which include more than one million people. These are the Zhuang, Mongolian, Hui, Tibetan, Uygur, Miao, Yi, Buyi, Korean, Manchu, Dong, Yao, Bai, Tujia, and Hani nationalities. The population density is 316 persons per square mile (122 per square kilometer), but it is actually much higher (even more than 3,000) in some eastern regions.

Language
Standard Chinese (Putonghua), based on the Mandarin dialect, is the national language and is spoken by more than 70 percent of the population. Other dialects are also spoken, including Wu (in Shanghai), Min, Yue (Cantonese), and Kejia. Each of the 55 minorities speaks its own language or dialect. In some cases, education and all official transactions may be conducted in the local minority language. Chinese does not have a phonetic alphabet; it uses characters to express words, thoughts, or principles. A romanized alphabet *(pinyin)* is used to help teach Chinese in school and for international communication. While up to 50,000 characters exist, only about 8,000 are currently in use. Chinese requires a knowledge of 1,500 to 2,000 characters for basic literacy.

Religion
While the government officially encourages atheism, the people may exercise religious beliefs within certain guidelines. Buddhists, Taoists, Muslims, and Christians all practice their religion. Temples and churches are open to the public, but since public worship is frowned upon people often worship at home. While the government allows domestic religious groups to print materials, hold meetings, and worship, they are carefully monitored. Unauthorized activities can lead to imprisonment or other restrictions. Christianity is growing, and unofficial estimates claim that up to 5 percent of the population is Christian.

General Attitudes
The Chinese are noted for good manners, hospitality, and reserve. Confucianism, the ancient philosophy of social order, still has a great influence on attitudes and actions. The elderly are respected. The Chinese are very proud of their nation's long history and of past Chinese achievements. Foreign visitors should respect this and refrain from negative comments about China. Authority is respected and obedience emphasized; this keeps open political debate to a minimum.

The principle of *guanxi* binds friends and associates in committing a friend to do what he can for another friend when called upon. To violate *guanxi* is to "lose face" (to lose reputation or honor), another important principle in Chinese society. "Keeping face" means avoiding embarrassment, failure, defeat, or contradictions. Children are expected to uphold the family "face" or its sense of social respect. That has meant different things in different eras. For today's urban children, it means to be well-educated, well-dressed, and money-earning, in addition to traditionally valued traits like loyal, polite, and kind.

Society is changing in China as economic opportunities expand. The goal of many families, for which they generally save for many years, is to build or have a nice home. Owning a house is a symbol of a better life. Most people want their children to have greater prosperity than themselves.

Personal Appearance
Chinese attire is traditionally conservative and simple. In the past, most wore the same style pantsuits because of government policy. Reforms and economic modernization have made Western styles the most popular in urban areas. Many women wear dresses. Bright colors, Western suits, jeans, and jackets are increasingly popular. Nevertheless, styles are not always as modern as in other nations and "Mao suits" are still worn by the very conservative. Ethnic minorities wear clothing reflective of their cultural past and the climate in which they live. Throughout China, people strive to keep themselves and their surroundings clean.

CUSTOMS AND COURTESIES
Greetings
The Chinese nod politely or bow slightly when greeting. A handshake is also acceptable, especially in formal situations or to show respect. A greeting common to foreigners is *Ni hao ma?* (How do you do?). While many Chinese accept this term and use it, there are also various, more traditional terms. A common informal greeting is *Chi le ma?* (Did you eat?). The response is either *Chi le* (Yes) or *Mei you* (Not yet).

The Chinese tend to be formal in their introductions; they use the full titles of their guests but are less precise in identifying themselves. Chinese names usually consist of a one-syllable family name, followed by a one or two-syllable given name. A person is either addressed by the full name or by a title and family name. In lieu of professional titles, the Chinese equivalents of Mr. and Mrs. are used. Thus, Wang Jian-Jun can also be called Mr. Wang, but never simply Wang and rarely ever Jian-Jun. In place of titles, the terms *Lao* (old) and *Xiao* (young) might be used between friends to show special respect.

Gestures
Except in crowds when physical contact is unavoidable, Chinese do not like to be touched by people they do not know. A smile is preferred to a pat on the back or a similar gesture. This is very important when dealing with older people or those in important positions. Chinese use their open hand to point rather than one finger. To beckon, all fingers wave with the palm of the hand facing down. In some regions, it is common for people to spit in public after clearing their throat. Government fines have tried to curb this behavior, but because it is necessitated by health conditions, it remains common.

Visiting
Invitations are usually extended for formal events, but otherwise it is common to drop by unannounced. When invited, one is generally prompt; being more than a few minutes late is impolite. Guests conduct themselves with restraint and refrain from loud, boisterous speech and actions. Valuable gifts are usually not accepted from strangers, but small gifts may

be given by friends. Friends often bring gifts such as tea, cigarettes, fruit, chocolates, cakes, or wine when they visit. Hosts rarely open wrapped gifts until visitors leave. Refreshments are usually offered, but it is not impolite to decline them. The host will probably insist several times before accepting the guest's refusal. People enjoy gathering for discussion or playing card and table games. Many ancient and popular games originated in China, including *Majiang*, Chinese chess, and various card games. Conversation topics generally include personal experiences, family, business, or a mutual interest.

Eating

The Chinese use chopsticks for all meals. When finished, a person places the chopsticks neatly on the table; they are not left in the rice bowl. Food is placed at the center of the table and may include more than one type of main dish to be eaten with rice. Some food is taken to be placed in the rice bowl, which is then held close to the mouth for eating. Bones and seeds are placed on the table or a dish, but never back in the rice bowl.

At restaurants, a revolving tray at the center of the table allows guests to sample from several dishes. Toasts are offered to the whole table and sometimes even to a neighboring table. At formal banquets, guests have a short, friendly speech prepared to respond to a host's remarks. Tipping in restaurants is traditionally considered an insult—something a superior does for an inferior—but with economic change, it is now popular in the Guangdong and Fujian provinces and is spreading elsewhere.

LIFESTYLE

Family

Historically, loyalty to the family unit has always been important to the Chinese. During the Cultural Revolution, the state tried to shift loyalty to the government and families were often split by work or study assignments. Family planning policies limited couples to one or two children, imposing fines or sterilization on violators. This practice continues in many areas, but not to the extent of the past. Less than 10 percent of all families have more than two children. Housing is generally poor and in short supply. Small apartments without bathrooms are the norm in cities, while simple, dirt-floor homes are common in rural areas. Most housing is owned by the government or a person's work unit. In an effort to improve housing conditions and availability, the government is encouraging people to buy their own homes or apartments. It is also raising rents gradually to provide companies with the incentive to build more and better houses and apartments.

Dating and Marriage

Chinese customs stress moral purity. Intimate relations and public displays of affection are discouraged. To help the family planning program succeed, young people are encouraged to marry late. In fact, college students are forbidden to marry until after graduation. The sanctioned age for marriage is 22 for men and 20 for women. Those who marry before that age are not eligible for some of the same benefits as those who wait. To marry, a couple first seeks permission from the local governing unit. If granted, a legal contract is recorded without a wedding ceremony. The couple then joins family and friends in a marriage celebration. While simple festivities are common, many urban couples are spending large amounts of money on Western-style receptions/parties, a large feast, and in buying household items. This is a matter of "face," so considerable attention might be paid to the celebration. Wedding rings are traditionally not a part of marriage, but they are becoming more common. The bride retains her maiden name and does not take the family name of her husband.

Diet

Generally, a wide variety of food is not available in China, except where private enterprise is encouraged. What the people eat depends largely on what is produced in the region where they live. Dishes with rice, potatoes, cornmeal, tofu, and other grains are staple meals. Dishes made with pork, beef, chicken, or fish are popular but expensive. Specialties vary from region to region, from duck in Beijing to spicy dishes in the Sichuan province. Fruits and vegetables are eaten in season; few dairy products are available or eaten. Sauces are mixed with vegetables and meats, and eaten with rice. Noodles are also common. *Man tou* (steamed bread) is a staple in northern China.

Recreation

In cities, theaters, operas, ballets, films, and cultural monuments all provide recreation. Imported movies are popular; the average Chinese attends more than 10 each year. Traveling cultural groups perform in rural areas. Many restrictions have been lifted on travel in the country, and the Chinese enjoy visiting other parts of China. Sports are popular and facilities are found in most cities. Favorites include table tennis, swimming, and soccer. Table and board games are played in homes and parks. *Majiang* is the most popular table game in China, and probably 90 percent of the people play it. *Wei qi* (known as *Go* in other countries) is a strategy game played in more educated circles. Chinese chess is another favorite. Parks and courtyards are often filled in the morning by those practicing *taijiquan*, a traditional form of shadowboxing that provides exercise and therapy.

Holidays

Official public holidays are 1 January, Labor Day (1 May), National Day (1–2 October), and Chinese New Year (also called Spring Festival), which is held for three days in January or February, according to the Chinese lunar calendar. As the most important holiday, the Spring Festival is marked by banquets, family gatherings, carnivals, and dragon dances. Extra food provided by the government includes fish (a symbol of abundance), meat, prawns, rice, and Chinese dumplings (*jiaozi*). Festivals are also celebrated around the country, including the Lantern festival (15th of the first lunar month), the Dragon Boat festival (fifth of the fifth lunar month), and Tibet's Fruit-Expecting Festival (August).

Commerce

Office hours are generally from 8:00 a.m. to noon and 2:00 to 6:00 p.m., Monday through Saturday, while shops are open from 9:00 a.m. to 7:00 p.m., every day. State-run restaurants often close by 8:00 p.m. It is improper to be late for business appointments. Until recently, the state determined what career a person would have and where one would work. This is changing with the increase in private ventures, as more people are being allowed to seek their own jobs. Private firms do not operate like assigned work units, which have customarily provided housing, day care, health care, and other benefits.

SOCIETY

Government

The People's Republic of China has a Communist government. National policy is determined by a 20-member Politburo and, more importantly, its seven-member Standing Committee. Jiang Zemin is president and the General Secretary of the Chinese Communist Party (CCP), which is the only legal party in the country. Li Peng is premier. Deng Xiaoping, while no longer officially head of state, is still considered China's most powerful individual and is the *de facto* leader of China's government. The National People's Congress has nearly 3,000 members, indirectly elected at local levels. The last elections for that body were in 1993.

Economy

China's large economy is offset by its large population, meaning the real gross domestic product per capita is just $2,946, a level that reflects China's status as a developing country. And while the figure is rising rapidly, wealth is not equally distributed. In a state accustomed to equal wages for all, this has caused no small amount of contention between average people. Still, a vibrant and growing private sector and government policies designed to liberalize the economy are improving living standards for many people. China's Human Development Index (0.644) ranks it 94th out of 173 countries.

At the 1992 Party Congress, delegates accepted the need for an economic revolution. Officials wish to create a "socialist market economy," noting that socialism (or communism) does not have to be synonymous with poverty. Since then, daily economic life is some cities has become more like that in Hong Kong or other free-market cities. Urban areas are experiencing a growth in the middle class. Private enterprise is encouraged, and Western institutions like the stock market are beginning to thrive. While the economy is growing at more than 10 percent, inflation, corruption, and crime are also on the rise. A large government budget deficit threatens the social security network and other institutions.

A better economy has improved life in villages substantially, so that diets are better, health is better, and people are generally content. The prevalence of absolute poverty has been cut in half since 1980. Once-common shortages for consumer goods are rare in today's economy. Nonetheless, 100 million people are still very poor; many still live in inadequate housing (even caves in some regions) and few have any say over what happens to them in their lives. This contradictory situation is hard for foreigners to understand, and is becoming harder for the Chinese to accept.

China produces manufactured goods, oil, minerals, coal, and steel. While only one-tenth of China's land is arable, the country is a world leader in the production of rice, tobacco, corn, barley, soy beans, peanuts, eggs, and pork. Wheat, fish, and potatoes are also important agricultural products. About 61 percent of the population is employed in agriculture. The currency is called *renminbi* and the standard unit is the *yuan*.

Transportation and Communication

All major transportation facilities are state owned. Individuals travel by train, bicycle, or bus. Domestic air travel is also available, but expensive, and not always reliable. In some areas, people travel by river barge or ferry. Roads between cities are often in poor condition. Very few people have cars. Communication systems, though weak, are getting better. The government controls radio and television broadcasts and there is only one officially sanctioned television station (CCTV). However, an information revolution has brought satellite disks, fax machines, and electronic mail to China, making it nearly impossible for the government to control what people read and hear.

Education

China's goal for the 1990s is to provide an elementary education to every citizen. While 96 percent of the first grade-age children are enrolled, only about 65 percent finish elementary school. The government eventually plans to extend mandatory schooling to nine years in all areas. To increase adult literacy, a TV university was established to give instruction over radio and television. Only a small fraction (5 percent) of all people attend college; these students often receive the best government or management positions after graduation. Tuition fees are being charged at the undergraduate level, and may eventually extend to the graduate level. College students must work at least five years after graduation before they can apply to study abroad. Literacy is 78 percent.

Health

While malaria and cholera are problematic in China, the people are generally healthy. The average life expectancy is 68 to 72 years. Medical care is usually free for urban Chinese and subsidized for rural people. The health care system concentrates on prevention. The extensive network of programs emphasizes immunizations, prenatal care, pediatrics, and sanitation. Facilities are simple, but the system has greatly improved the basic health of the people and significantly lowered infant mortality to 32 per 1,000. It is much lower in some cities. Water is not usually potable, and open sewers are common. Traditional Chinese medicine (use of medicinal herbs and acupuncture, among other things) is combined with Western medical techniques in treating illness and injury.

FOR THE TRAVELER

A visa and valid passport are required of all visitors. While some areas are closed to tourists, one can see most major cities. Visas are easiest to obtain if a tour is booked with a group. Tour groups receive the best accommodations. Individuals traveling without prior arrangements or itinerary may encounter some difficulties. Visas are also often sold at various locations in Hong Kong. Those not traveling in groups should have some understanding of Chinese. Malaria pills are recommended, as are gamma globulin shots. Clean and peel fruits and vegetables before eating, and do not drink unboiled water. Wash-and-wear clothing is best to take, as modern cleaning facilities are not always available. The China National Tourist Office, located at 350 Fifth Avenue, Room 6413, Empire State Building, New York, NY 10108, has more information on travel opportunities. China's embassy is located at 2300 Connecticut Avenue NW, Washington, DC 20008–0163.

Federal Islamic Republic of the
Comoros

Boundary representations not necessarily authoritative.

BACKGROUND

Land and Climate

Comoros is located in the Mozambique Channel of the Indian Ocean. Its three islands, Anjouan, Mohéli, and Grand Comore, together are about the same size as Delaware, covering 838 square miles (2,171 square kilometers). These volcanic islands were formed in succession from east to west, Grand Comore being the youngest. It has less evolved soil than the other islands and so lacks their ability to support agriculture. All the islands are mountainous, with Grand Comore being dominated by Mount Karthala (7,800 feet—2,400 m), which has a large active volcanic crater. Mayotte Island to the southeast is geologically the oldest member of the Comoros archipelago, but it is currently a French territory.

The hot, humid rainy season (*Kashkazi*) runs from November to March, but it varies annually. The pleasant season of *Kusi* (April–September) has warm, clear breezy days and cool nights. Comorian waters are home to the ancient coelacanth fish, thought to be long extinct before one was seen in South Africa in 1938.

History

Africans arriving in the 13th century were thought to be the first inhabitants, but discoveries in 1990 led to theories that Persians may have actually settled the islands in the 800s. Malagasy people from Madagascar came in the 16th century, but the population remained small until the islands were used by Arab slave traders as holding areas.

Arab slavers set up towns and mainland Africans formed their own communities. Over time, the islands became divided into various opposing sultanates. Except for pirates and a few other sailors, Europeans paid the islands little attention until the 19th century "scramble for Africa." The French, having occupied Madagascar, became interested in the Comoros to counter a British presence in East Africa and the Seychelles. A sultan on Grand Comore allied with the French in the 1870s,

and by 1886 the entire four-island archipelago was proclaimed a French protectorate.

In 1958, Comorians voted to remain a French overseas territory while assuming responsibility for internal affairs. Saïd Mohammed Cheik became president of the Council of Government. Though he served as mostly a figurehead, he gave Comorians their first idea of self-determination. Cheik moved the capital from Mayotte to Moroni on Grand Comore (1962–64). As part of the global decolonization effort, a referendum for independence was held in 1974. Of the total population, 94 percent voted for autonomy, but 64 percent of Mayotte's residents voted to remain under French control. Hence, when the Federal Islamic Republic of the Comoros became independent in 1975, France maintained possession of Mayotte. Comoros still has an internationally recognized claim to the island, on which France supports a large naval base, because of the overall popular vote for independence.

Ahmed Abdallah, elected as the first post-independence president, was overthrown after only a few months in office by a socialist visionary named Ali Soilihi. Soilihi was assisted by European mercenaries led by Bob Denard. Soilihi's austere policies managed to boost agricultural production and increase the number of schools. However, his strict approach alienated Comorians, his economic policies were not appreciated by Western donors, and his criticism of many Islamic traditions offended Muslim nations. Having little foreign or domestic support, Soilihi was overthrown in 1978 by Abdallah (with Denard's help).

Abdallah led the country away from the socialist economy, but he faced the challenges of a 1977 volcanic eruption and a 1978 influx of Comorian refugees from Madagascar. He was only able to maintain order with Denard's assistance. Comorian resentment of the mercenaries grew and, by 1989, Abdallah had planned to oust Denard with help from France and South Africa. In November 1989, Abdallah was murdered at home and Denard took control for several weeks until France forced his departure.

The head of the Supreme Court, Saïd Mohammed Djohar, was elected president in 1990. Economic crisis and political unrest soon gripped the country and Djohar was targeted in several coup attempts. Elections in 1993 were marred by violence. In an effort to stabilize the country in 1994, Djohar named Halifa Houmadi as prime minister. Houmadi set out to obtain international aid to pay striking public servants and also addressed the secessionist movements and political rivalries.

PEOPLE
Population
The population of 530,000 is growing annually at 3.5 percent. Nearly half is under age 15, and 74 percent lives in rural areas. The capital, Moroni, and Mutsamudu are the largest cities. Grand Comore has the most residents, followed by Anjouan and Mohéli.

There are no true ethnic divisions, but Comorians are divided by language and other factors. Most Comorians are descendants of both Arab slavers and the African mainlanders they brought as slaves to be shipped north to the Arabian peninsula and the Nile basin. Those with more Arab blood tend to enjoy higher social status than darker-skinned people (such as the Mohélians). A few families have Malagasy or Asian ethnic backgrounds.

Language
French and Arabic are official languages. All official business is conducted in French. Indigenous languages are Bantu tongues derived from Swahili. Shingazidja is spoken on Grand Comore (locally called *Ngazidja*). Shinzduani is Anjouan's (*Nzduani*) language, and Shimwali is spoken on Mohéli (*Mwali*). People understand each other's languages, as well as the Shimaore spoken on Mayotte. Comorians traditionally use the Arabic script, but the Roman alphabet is being promoted.

Arabic is learned by four- and five-year-olds attending *Qur'anic* schools, and while few adults speak it, most read the alphabet. Many Comorians know some French. Since French is the language of instruction in schools, anyone with a secondary education will be fairly fluent. English is offered in school, but usually only workers connected to travel can speak it.

Religion
Nearly all Comorians are Sunni Muslims and Islamic traditions play a key role in daily life. Muslims accept the *Qur'an* (Koran) to be the final word of *Allah* (God) as revealed to the Prophet Muhammad. Muhammad is revered as the last and greatest in a long line of prophets from Adam and Abraham to Moses and others. Devout Muslims pray five times daily; the call to prayer is heard regularly from mosques in even the smallest villages. On Friday, all men (even less devout ones) go to their town's largest mosque for the noon prayer. Comorians have little sympathy for Islamic fundamentalism.

Non-Islamic (mostly African) beliefs are present, but they have largely been incorporated into Islamic practices. Many people maintain a belief in good and evil spirits and use *gris-gris* (charms) to ward off the evil ones. Some attend special ceremonies to bring out spirits. Other religions are tolerated. Most foreigners are Christians; large towns have both Catholic and Protestant churches.

General Attitudes
As Muslims, Comorians believe all events occur according to *Allah's* will. This faith is expressed as fatalism and people often feel they do not control their conditions. Comorians have a wonderful sense of humor. They enjoy a good joke and often exchange humorous light insults with friends.

Individual needs are subordinate to the family. People expect to share in both the successes and failures of family members. Within the larger community, sharing one's wealth is a way to increase a person's social standing and influence, both of which are highly desired. Material possessions are desired, the acquisition of which is seen as the will of *Allah*. Gifts from relatives working in France are particularly prized.

Personal Appearance
Quite conscious of their appearance, Comorians dress well in public. The traditional Islamic emphasis on cleanliness is not taken lightly. Urban men usually wear Western shirts and slacks. They have a nice suit for formal occasions. Elders, rural men, and urban men going to mosque more often wear the traditional white robe (*kandu*). Regardless of their outfit, men usually wear an embroidered cap (*kofia*). Shorts and a sloppy appearance are frowned upon. Most adults wear plastic flip-flops on their feet, although professionals wear shoes to work.

Women rarely wear pants except in cities. They wear Western dresses with colorful patterns and nearly always carry a printed shawl (*leso*) that is often worn as a head covering. Anjouan women often wear a *shiromani* (traditional cloth) over their dresses (or skirt and blouse) and pulled up over their heads. Women on all islands occasionally wear a face mask made of ground sandalwood that is considered a cosmetic and skin lightener.

CUSTOMS AND COURTESIES
Greetings
Comorian men shake hands at every opportunity. They offer a verbal greeting to women, as touching women in public is considered improper. In private, among relatives, men and women may sometimes kiss on the cheek. Women might also greet their female friends with a kiss.

Upon greeting, Comorians exchange several standard phrases, depending on the level of formality. The Shingazidga version of an exchange between social equals is *Edje?* (an informal "Hello") followed by *Ye yapvo?* (What's up?). More formal terms are required for greeting elders, professionals, or strangers. *Bariza husha* (Good morning), *Bariza hazi?* (How's work?), and *Bariza masihu* (Good evening) are all common Shingazidga phrases. In fact, *Bariza* can precede anything to form a greeting.

On Anjouan, *Djedje?* (How how?) is the most common informal greeting, followed by *Habari?* (News?). Mohéli has similar greetings. Comorians also use traditional Muslim Arabic terms like *Asalaam alaikum* (Peace be unto you). A positive response to something is often followed by the Arabic expression *Insha'Allah* (God willing) or *Alhamdul'illah* (Thanks be to God).

When calling out to someone, Grand Comorians often precede the addressee's name with *Bo* (e.g., "Bo Mbaraka!"). Titles are used to address people. Some are *mwana hangu* (my child/brother) for good friends, *coco* for a grandmother, *fundi* for a teacher or craftsman, and *mzé* for an elder man.

Gestures

Comorians beckon by opening and closing a hand, palm facing down or out. One indicates direction with the index finger. Members of the same sex often hold hands while walking, but members of the opposite sex do not touch in public. After a shared joke, it is common to slap each other's hands and laugh. Polite refusal is expressed by placing a hand on the chest while verbally thanking the offerer. Various other hand gestures are used in the course of conversation.

A child respectfully greets an elder with both hands cupped and extended while saying *Kwezi*. In response, the elder clasps the child's hands and says *Mbona*. The exchange is like asking for and receiving a blessing. On Anjouan, the elder raises the cupped hands to the child's forehead before saying *Mbona*.

Visiting

Comorians make informal daily visits to close friends; it is impolite to lose contact with any friend or family member for more than a few days. Extended families are large, so such social obligations are numerous. People enjoy having guests in their homes. It is a special honor to host a foreigner.

Within a village, Comorians visit freely without prior arrangement. Time for visiting is usually set aside from 4:00 to 6:00 P.M. When visiting someone in another town, it is more polite to give advanced notice (*Oulaha*) and thereby allow the hosts time to prepare. Guests are offered food and drink, and it is impolite to refuse. Weekday visits are short (an hour or less) but weekend ones can take the entire afternoon and include at least one meal. Visitors usually only take gifts when returning from foreign travel.

Eating

Comorians eat cold leftovers, if anything, for breakfast along with hot, sweet tea. The afternoon meal includes a sauce-covered starchy food like cassava or green bananas, and some meat. *Putu*, a hot pepper sauce, is served to season all types of food. Dinner features a rice dish and is the main meal.

Affluent urban families eat at a table with Western utensils. Otherwise, families eat on a mat on the floor, everyone sitting cross-legged around several shared plates of food. Rural women usually eat separately from men, especially if guests are present. If a guest eats with the entire family, he or she is considered a very close friend.

Comorians wash hands in a dish of water before and after eating. Utensils (mostly spoons) are not uncommon but the hand (right only) is most often used. For large gatherings, food is served buffet-style and guests stand and eat from many plates. They take a handful of rice from a large common bowl and compress it with sauce before putting it in their mouths. No one eats until a short blessing has been offered.

While some urban men eat at restaurants when they can't get home for lunch, most Comorians (especially in rural areas) consider eating out embarrassing—it implies the person is poorly fed at home, has no family, or has marital problems.

LIFESTYLE

Family

Comorians have little concept of the "nuclear" family. The extended family is large, especially in villages where polygamy is common. Men are in charge of family finances and property, while women control the household. Men do little domestic work; they farm or fish for the family's subsistence. Women seldom leave home except to do chores or for holidays, although some urban women do have outside jobs. Comorian women are not submissive and are proud of their traditional role.

Children use their father's given name as their own surname. At about age 18, sons might build themselves a *paillotte* (thatched hut) near the family home. They still eat at home and take part in family activities, but sleep and entertain guests at their own dwelling. Daughters live at home until they marry. Small children are cared for by older sisters, and elders live with the adult children when they can no longer live alone.

Dating and Marriage

In Comoros, there is very little open dating. A man and woman seen together are assumed to be romantically involved. Wealthy urban youth might go to dance clubs, but most socializing is discreet.

The most conspicuous social "statement" in Comoros is the Grand Marriage. Any man who wishes to be a full-fledged member of the community's group of elders, or *Notables*, must marry off at least his eldest daughter in a Grand Marriage. Maternal uncles can also give a Grand Marriage for nieces. This highly expensive, multi-ceremony event lasts more than a week. Families save for it for years and can expend their life's savings hosting the entire village for dances and meals. Guests offer expensive gifts, which are recorded so the recipients can properly reciprocate in the future. A Grand Marriage that involves much local purchasing benefits the community and so brings greater status to the host. The groom and both families also gain greater status for their roles in the wedding. The bride's father builds the newlyweds a house. If any problems occur, the husband must leave and the woman keeps the house.

The Grand Marriage began simply as a celebratory event, but it has taken on great social importance. On Grand Comore, rising competition between families to host better ceremonies has serious implications. Families save so much for the event that they spend less on basic needs. Some go into debt, which is passed on to future generations. Couples can marry without a Grand Marriage, and many do, but the respective families will not join the highest social class until a Grand Marriage is held.

Diet

Comorians eat mostly imported rice, usually topped by a fish or meat sauce. Plentiful local fish (tuna, barracuda, wahoo, and red snapper) are the main source of protein. Cassava (manioc root) is eaten fried, boiled, or grilled. Tarot, green bananas, breadfruit, and potatoes (both white and sweet) are often served. Chicken, goat, and imported beef are popular meats. Pork is forbidden by Islam. Comorians love to spice their foods with *putu*. Most people have access to bread, and fruit is plentiful. Oranges, bananas, pineapples, papayas, mangos, passion fruit, litchi, and others are eaten seasonally. Coconut is used in some sauces. Urban markets sell tomatoes, onions, cucumbers, and green beans. Cloves, cinnamon, saffron, and cardamom are indigenous spices. Water, tea, and fruit juice are taken with meals.

Recreation

Soccer is the most popular sport and each town has a team to compete at the national level. Young men enjoy basketball and volleyball. There are no real movie theaters, but most villages have a video hut that plays VCR tapes for a small admission price. Television is available in towns with electricity, but only a French overseas broadcast is receivable. Comorian youth like to organize village dances. Musical tastes range from Western pop to reggae to traditional wedding dance music. Men spend free time walking, visiting, and playing games such as cards, dominoes, or *mdraha* (a pebble-and-board game). On weekends, families and friends might take a picnic to the beach.

Holidays

National holidays include New Year's Day (1 January), the Lunar New Year, Labor Day (1 May), and Independence Day (6 July). Islamic holidays are based on the lunar calendar and so vary every year. During *Ramadan*, the holy month of fasting, nothing is eaten between dawn and dusk, but the nights are filled with activity and eating. At the end of the month is the most celebrated and holiest day, *Id-al-Fitr*. Comorians visit, share gifts, and feast all day long. Forty days later, *Id-al-Adha* honors Abraham for his willingness to sacrifice his son. Comorians celebrate Muhammad's birth for a month, with *Maulid*, his actual birthday, being a national holiday.

Commerce

Business hours are 8:00 A.M. to 6:00 P.M., but most offices close at least two hours for lunch. Stores are closed Friday afternoon and Sunday. Asian (Pakistani and Indian) merchants operate on a large commercial scale and have considerable economic influence. Open markets offer produce and meat, and stores have basic supplies; specialty items are only available in larger cities. Store prices are set, but market prices are negotiable. Business is conducted in the home only if the people are well acquainted.

SOCIETY

Government

The country's president is chief of state and head of government. The Federal Assembly has 42 seats. Over 20 parties are represented in the legislature and so none has a majority; this contributes to instability. Each island has an appointed governor and each prefecture has an elected prefect. All citizens may vote at the age of 18. The democratic constitution, last revised in 1992, is based on the French model.

Economy

Comoros is called the "Perfume Islands" because it is the world's leading exporter of ylang-ylang, the oil base of many French perfumes. Comoros also exports vanilla, cinnamon, and cloves. With the once-valuable world market in these commodities rapidly shrinking, the country finds itself in a difficult situation. There are no factories or other productive industries, although some small businesses have emerged since 1991 to generate growth above 3 percent. France's 1994 devaluation of the Comorian *franc* led to panic and instant higher prices. The economy relies on foreign aid and remittances from Comorians who work abroad. Foreign investment in a hotel resort on Grand Comore has opened tourism as a possible source of revenue. The country's Human Development Index (0.331) ranks it 141st out of 173 countries. Real gross domestic product per capita is $700. These figures reflect the fact that most people do not earn a wage; 80 percent are subsistence farmers.

Transportation and Communication

Although Comoros has few roads, most of them are paved. Private, unregulated *bush taxis* connect all villages in each island. Moroni and Mutsamudu have city taxis. Boats ferry passengers and cargo between islands. Air Comoros also connects the islands and flies to Madagascar. Grand Comore's international airport receives traffic from Europe and neighboring countries. Mutsamudu boasts a deepwater port for large ships.

A few private radio stations broadcast in addition to the main government one. The national weekly newspaper, *Al-Watwan*, is found in cities. Private homes rarely have telephones, but each island has public pay phones. All international mail must go through Paris.

Education

The educational system is based on the French model, but it does not function effectively. Schooling is free and every village has an elementary school (*école primaire*), but teachers are poorly trained and often not paid. Teacher strikes shortened the school year in 1994 and led to student unrest as well. Only about 30 percent of all students finish elementary school, and even fewer go on to junior high (*collège*). A small number continue to high school (*lycée*) and sit for the graduation exam. There is a teacher training college, but no universities. Formal education is geared toward academics. Because there are no state-funded technical training schools, many youths take apprenticeships with craftsmen instead of going to school.

Health

Malaria is the greatest health problem in Comoros, but diarrhea and intestinal parasites are also common. Cities and towns have hospitals, but basic supplies and equipment are lacking. Patients provide their own medications and food. A new public hospital in Mitsudjé (south of Moroni) does offer better care. The infant mortality rate is 80 per 1,000; life expectancy averages 58 years.

FOR THE TRAVELER

U.S. citizens may enter Comoros with a passport, but they must purchase a visa on arrival. Various vaccinations and measures to protect against malaria are recommended. Drink only bottled water, although Moroni's water supply is considered safe. Wash and peel fruits and vegetables. Dress modestly in light fabrics. Women should cover their knees and tie loose hair (loose hair=loose woman). Visitors enjoy many fine beaches, recreational diving and fishing, and climbing to the Karthala crater. For more information, contact the Comorian Permanent Mission to the United Nations, 336 East 45th Street, Second Floor, New York, NY 10017; phone (212) 972–8010.

A *Culturgram* is a product of native commentary and original, expert analysis. Statistics are estimates and information is presented as a matter of opinion. While the editors strive for accuracy and detail, this document should not be considered strictly factual. It is a general introduction to culture, an initial step in building bridges of understanding between peoples. It may not apply to all peoples of the nation. You should therefore consult other sources for more information.

CULTURGRAM™ '96

Arab Republic of
Egypt

Boundary representations not necessarily authoritative.

BACKGROUND

Land and Climate

Covering 386,650 square miles (1,007,258 square kilometers), Egypt is just larger than Texas and New Mexico combined. Most of it is dry and arid desert, spotted with small, inhabited oases. Part of the Sahara Desert is in southwestern Egypt. The Nile River, the longest in Africa, runs north through Egypt into the Mediterranean Sea, providing a fertile delta area and the lifeblood for the country. Before the Aswan Dam was built, this area was subject to seasonal flooding. Now the dam regulates water flow and allows for more predictable crop planting, although it has also caused some environmental problems. Summers are hot and humid, with temperatures reaching 100°F (38°C). Winters are moderate, with lows near 40°F (4°C). Annual rainfall ranges from virtually nothing in the desert to about eight inches in the Nile delta. In the spring, the *Khamasiin* (a hot, driving, dusty wind) blows.

History

The earliest recorded Egyptian dynasty united the kingdoms of Upper and Lower Egypt around 3110 B.C. Today's Egyptians are proud of the Pharaonic heritage that followed. In 525 B.C., Egypt came under Persian control. Alexander the Great's conquest in 332 B.C. brought Greek rule and culture to Egypt. As one of the first nations visited by Christian missionaries (the apostle Mark), Egypt was Christianized within three centuries and followed a Coptic patriarch. Because of Byzantine religious persecution, Egyptians welcomed the Muslim invasion that began in A.D. 642. By the eighth century,

Egypt had become largely Muslim. For centuries, Egypt was ruled by successive Islamic dynasties, including the Ottoman Turks in the 16th century. France's Napoleon invaded in 1798, but Egypt was still associated with the Ottoman Empire until World War I.

France and Britain vied for influence over Egypt throughout the 19th century, during which time Viceroy Muhammad Ali successfully governed and reformed Egypt (1805–48). France and Britain exerted increasing control over Egyptian affairs after the completion of the Suez Canal in 1869, and Britain made Egypt a protectorate in 1914. Although given official independence in 1922, the Egyptians regard 1952 as the beginning of real independence. In that year, a revolution overthrew the British-supported monarchy. Gamal Abdel Nasser ousted the first president of Egypt in 1954 and became a popular and influential leader and statesman. Nasser was responsible for a number of reforms, including universal education, land reform, nationalization of major industries and banks, and Egyptian leadership of the Arab world. He governed until his death in 1970.

During Nasser's tenure, Egypt fought two wars that involved Israel (1956 and 1967). The Sinai Peninsula was taken by Israel in the 1967 war, a crushing blow to Egypt's pride. Upon Nasser's death, his vice president, Anwar el-Sadat, succeeded him. His government orchestrated a war (1973) in which Egypt restored its national honor by crossing the Suez Canal and regaining a foothold in the Sinai. Sadat liberalized economic policy, greatly reduced relations with the Soviet

Union, and signed a peace treaty with Israel (1979) that returned the Sinai to Egypt. In 1981, Sadat was assassinated by Muslim fundamentalists who disagreed with his policies. Vice President Hosni Mubarak succeeded him and became an important leader of moderate Arab nations.

Islamic fundamentalists ("Islamists") also oppose Mubarak, since they view an Islamic state as the only viable government for Egypt. The Islamists oppose Western art, music, literature, and values. Their quest to overthrow the secular state has not only included pressing the government to restrict freedom of expression, liberal education, and secular law, but also commiting violent acts against Coptic Christians and Western tourists. Government agencies' responses to the Islamists have been excessive at times, but the general Egyptian public seems to support official efforts. Voters reelected Mubarak to a third presidential term in 1993. His administration vigorously battles the more violent extremists, but has not stood in the way of moderate social change effected by the Islamists' popularity in Cairo.

THE PEOPLE

Population

Egypt's population of 60.7 million is growing annually at 1.9 percent. The majority (90 percent) are descendants of both native Egyptians and Arabs that conquered Egypt in the seventh century. The rest of the population is composed of Nubians (southern Egypt), Bedouin nomads, Greeks, Italians, and Syro-Lebanese. Nearly all Egyptians live on the arable land along the Nile River, because the rest of the country is mostly desert. Cairo, the capital, has between 12 and 14 million inhabitants. An exact count is impossible due to migrants, informal residents (up to 5 million), and other factors. Alexandria claims more than 3 million residents. Over 65 percent of the people are younger than 20 years old.

Language

Arabic is the official language in Egypt, although English and French are used in business and education. Written Arabic differs from the standard Egyptian dialect (Cairene) spoken in daily life. Egyptians are enormously proud of Cairene and its rich expressions. They like to use it for wordplays, jokes, clichés, and riddles. Cairene is therefore an integral part of Egyptian culture.

Religion

Over 90 percent of all Egyptians belong to the Sunni branch of Islam. Islamic philosophy is deeply rooted in the minds, hearts, and behavior of the people. Islamic scripture, the *Qur'an* (Koran), is considered the final, complete word of *Allah*. Muslims accept and revere all major Judeo-Christian prophets from Adam to Jesus, but they proclaim Muhammad to be the last and greatest. Although Egypt is offically a secular state, Islamic principles are very much a part of its laws, business relations, and social customs. The Islamic day of worship is Friday, a day for men to pray at the mosque (as opposed to praying at home or at work on other days) and hear a sermon. Women pray at home or in a separate part of the mosque. Islam is practiced every day through dress and dietary codes, praying, and constant references to *Allah's* will

or blessings. Muslims pray five times daily, always facing Makkah, Saudi Arabia. Other religious groups are also found in Egypt, including a significant minority of Coptic Christians (over seven million), whose religion dates to its separation from Rome in the fifth century.

General Attitudes

Egyptians generally prefer a relaxed and patient life, characterized by the phrase *Ma'alesh*, meaning roughly "Don't worry" or "Never mind." This term is used to dismiss concerns or conflicts that are inevitable or not serious. Both business and leisure activities are governed by the concept of *Insha'allah* (If *Allah* wills), which dominates all aspects of Muslim life. Patience also influences life, as the people view events in an expanded time frame. Egyptians are expressive and emotional, and are well-known for their marvelous sense of humor. This has helped people endure difficult economic and living conditions with great composure. Part of Egyptian humor is a love for riddles (especially during the month of *Ramadan*), jokes, sarcasm, and wordplays. Egyptians often identify with community groups to the point that personal needs become secondary to those of the group. Generosity goes hand in hand with the sense of community and homelessness is fairly rare even in crowded Cairo.

Society is currently engaged in a serious debate over its future course; that is, both secularists and Islamists are battling for the hearts of Egyptians. Secularists desire Egypt to remain a secular state in which multiculturalism, a free press, and diversity can flourish. The Islamists see greater devotion to Islamic principles in schools, government, and the arts as the answer to Egypt's problems with poverty, government corruption, and other social ills. Both sides of the debate have strong followings throughout the country.

Personal Appearance

Dress standards in Egypt follow traditional patterns. In public, most women completely cover their hair and bodies, except their faces and hands. Men wear modest clothing and skullcaps, and sometimes grow a beard. A beard can be a sign of religious faith, but it can also express membership in certain political organizations. In large cities, modest Western-style clothing has been popular, although trends toward fundamental Islamic practices have led many women to return to stricter observance of Islamic dress codes. Business representatives wear business suits.

CUSTOMS AND COURTESIES

Greetings

Warmth in personal relations is important to Egyptians and greetings are often elaborate. Because social classes play a key role in society, phrases used for greetings depend largely on the differences between the individuals' social classes. Generally, however, friends of the same sex shake hands and kiss on the right and left cheeks. If the greeting comes after a long absence, the kisses may be repeated more than once and even end with a kiss on the forehead. Men greet women with a handshake only if the woman extends her hand first. Otherwise, the greeting is verbal. First names are not used unless one is invited to do so. Good friends exchange first names in informal settings, but they may add a title to the first name in formal settings. To thank someone for a compliment, one responds with an equally respectful compliment on the same subject or wishes *Allah's* (God's) blessings.

Gestures

Physical distance between members of the same sex is closer than in the United States, and much farther apart between members of the opposite sex. In fact, good friends of the same sex may walk hand in hand in public. Yet, except for married or engaged couples that walk arm in arm, a man does not touch a woman in public. It is impolite for the bottom of one's foot to point at another person; also, feet should not be propped on a table or chair in the presence of others. Pointing at a person is impolite, as is walking in front of a praying person.

Visiting

Because personal relationships with friends and relatives are so vital, visiting is one of the most important pastimes in Egypt. Not visiting for a long period is a sign of the relationship's insignificance. Married children often visit parents on Fridays and holidays. If a gift is given, it is passed and received with either both hands or only the right hand, not the left. Alcohol is prohibited by the Islamic religion, so it is not given as a gift to a Muslim. Business visits usually begin with light conversation over coffee or tea to establish trust and confidence. Visitors to a mosque remove shoes before entering and wear clothing that covers the entire body.

Eating

Egyptians prepare elaborate and expensive meals when they have guests. Sometimes a person will not eat everything on the plate because leftover food is a symbol of abundance and a compliment to the host for providing so well. Or, in restaurants, food is left as a sign of wealth (one can afford to leave food behind). Finger food is eaten with the right hand. When Western utensils are used (mostly in large, urban areas), the continental style—the fork in the left hand, the knife remaining in the right—is observed.

LIFESTYLE

Family

Families are extremely important in Egypt. In most homes, a young woman is protected by her brothers and may even be accompanied by them in public. Traditionally, a man's honor is based on how well he protects the women in his care. In rural areas, a young woman may discontinue her schooling when she comes of age. It is customary for extended families, including families of brothers and sisters, to live under the same roof. Increased urbanization, however, is changing this tradition toward a home with only a nuclear family. Still, close ties are maintained, and cousins are often as close as siblings. The thought of putting the elderly in a rest home is repulsive to Egyptians; children expect to support their parents in old age. Parents often play a key role in planning the future of their children, with their influence ranging from the choice of profession to the selection of a mate. Egyptians value this support as a source of emotional security.

Dating and Marriage

Although attitudes toward dating are changing in Westernized circles, dating is not widespread. Public displays of affection are frowned upon. Moral purity is highly valued in a woman and is usually a key requirement in the marriage contract. Traditionally, marriages were arranged between heads of families, often with little input from the couple involved. Now, however, individuals have more say as to whom they wish to marry. Because marriages join not just two people but two families, both families are heavily involved in wedding preparations. Housing is expensive and hard to acquire, given the large urban population and number of migrants. Therefore, engagements may last until the couple saves enough money for their own apartment.

Diet

Egyptians eat rice, bread, fish, lamb, chicken, turkey, and stuffed vegetables. *Tahina* (sesame seed paste), tomatoes, yogurt, and cucumbers are also eaten with meals. The *Qur'an* prohibits the consumption of pork and alcohol. Traditional foods include *fava* beans prepared as *foul* or *ta'miyya*, and flat Egyptian bread. Meat is expensive and eaten only occasionally, sometimes just once a month. Bread is eaten with every meal.

Recreation

Soccer is the national sport, but sport clubs also offer tennis, swimming, and horseback riding. Many enjoy going to the movies in urban areas; a wide variety of Egyptian and foreign films are shown. In the Middle East, Egypt is well-known for its dedication to cultural arts—evident in its cinema and television programming. Many enjoy watching television, even in rural areas. While the wealthy have private clubs for socializing, men of all other classes go to coffee shops for recreation. At a coffee shop one can play various table games such as backgammon and dominoes, have refreshments, and relax with friends. Many coffee shops cater to specific groups or professions (barbers, plumbers, etc.). Even the smallest village will have at least one coffee shop. Women socialize in the home.

Holidays

The Western (Gregorian) calendar is used for all business and government purposes, but the lunar calendar is used to calculate the dates of Muslim holidays. The lunar year is about 11 days shorter than the Western calendar year, so holidays vary each year. During the month of *Ramadan*, Muslims go without food or drink from sunrise to sundown and eat only in the evening. *'Aid al Fitr* is a three-day feast held at the end of *Ramadan*. Another major religious holiday is *'Aid al Adha* (Feast of the Sacrifice), which commemorates Abraham's willingness to sacrifice his son. The prophet Muhammad's birthday *(al-Mawlid)* is also celebrated. National holidays include Labor Day (1 May), the Anniversary of the Revolution (23 July), and Armed Forces Day (6 October). *Sham el-Nasseem* is celebrated at the beginning of spring. The lunar New Year is also an official holiday.

Commerce

Business hours are generally from 8:30 A.M. to 1:30 P.M. and from 4:30 to 7:00 P.M., Saturday through Thursday.

Government offices are open from 8:00 A.M. to 3:00 P.M. In the summer, many workers take a longer lunch break because of the heat, then work later in the cool evening. Shops are generally closed on Friday afternoon, but work is not prohibited. Street vendors are common, and people in high-rise apartments will often lower a basket from balconies to purchase something from a passing salesman. Also common are outdoor *souks* (markets), where businesses sell their products. This encourages barter trade. Prices in tourist shops near hotels are fixed. During the month of *Ramadan*, business hours are often cut back by an hour and work slows down in many areas. However, many shops open again in the evening.

SOCIETY

Government

The Arab Republic of Egypt is divided into 26 governorates. The president is chief of state, and a prime minister is head of government. The legislative branch consists of a 454-seat People's Assembly and a 258-seat *Shura* Council. All but ten representatives in the assembly are elected, but more than 80 council members are appointed by the president. The *Shura* Council acts as a consultative body, so the assembly is the main legislature. Elections for that body are set for November 1995. Citizens are required to vote at age 18. Mubarak's party (National Democratic Party) dominates the Assembly, but some opposition parties and independents also hold seats. Religious-based political parties are banned.

Economy

More than one-third of the people are employed in agricultural pursuits, such as growing corn, wheat, cotton, rice, barley, and fruit. Egypt also produces cheese and dairy products. Chief industries include food processing, textiles, chemicals, cement, petroleum, and metals. Egypt exports cotton, petroleum, yarn, and textiles. Important natural resources are oil, natural gas, lead, and other minerals. The Suez Canal is a vital source of income. Tourism is usually a leading industry, but threats of violence have kept travelers away and have crippled the tourist industry. The currency is the *Egyptian pound* (£E).

Egypt's Human Development Index (0.551) ranks it 110th out of 173 countries. Real gross domestic product per capita is $3,600, which has more than tripled in the last generation. These figures reflect Egypt's success with long-term economic reform that has improved the climate for international investment, brought inflation to below 10 percent, and stimulated growth at a rate (4 percent) higher than population growth. However, about one-fourth of all Egyptians remain in poverty and an even larger number struggle to meet basic needs.

Transportation and Communication

In urban areas, people travel by car, bus, and taxi. Cairo has a modern, efficient subway, the first in the Middle East. Unfortunately, with such a large urban population, the transportation system is still overburdened. Between cities, travel is by train, bus, and even taxi. There is also a domestic airline. In rural areas, a few still travel by donkey and camel. Water taxis use the Nile River. Many improvements have been made in the phone system in recent years. While getting a phone takes a long time and is expensive, the system is efficient; people without phones make calls from a central phone office. There are five main television stations and seven radio networks.

Education

The government subsidizes free education through the university level, although not all are able to take advantage of it. Recent programs aimed at building schools in rural areas have succeeded in bringing some educational opportunities to the poor. The overall literacy rate of 48 percent—lower for women and in rural areas, but higher for men and urban youth—will increase significantly in the next generation. Most children who begin primary schooling now also complete it. A significant number go on to secondary school. Universities are located in most urban centers, and nearly half of all students are women. Education is viewed as the key to a better life, and parents will sacrifice much to hire private tutors so their children can excel in school. Parents often measure their personal success by that of their children, and they work their entire lives to provide them with a better life than their own.

Health

Egypt has many excellent doctors, but medical facilities are limited, especially in rural areas. However, the infant mortality rate is falling (currently 59 per 1,000), and life expectancy averages about 60 years. A UN program sends doctors and volunteers into villages for one-week clinics ("medical caravans") to provide hygiene education (such as how to brush teeth), examine children, dispense medicine, give shots, administer first aid, and teach family planning. The government has expanded this program by establishing a hospital in every small city. Private hospitals for the wealthy are equipped with the latest medical technology.

FOR THE TRAVELER

In addition to valid passports, visas are required to visit Egypt, but they can be obtained on arrival or through the consulate. Bottled or boiled water is recommended. Be wary of unprocessed dairy products and avoid all fruits or vegetables that cannot be peeled or cooked. Typhoid, tetanus, and hepatitis vaccinations are recommended. Dress conservatively in respect for cultural norms. Note that tipping, or *Baksheesh*, can be important in Egypt. It is wise to carry plenty of small change to reward personal services. Taxi drivers, beauticians, and waiters should be tipped at least 10 percent. For travel information, contact the Egyptian Tourist Authority, 630 Fifth Avenue, Suite 1706, New York, NY 10111; phone (212) 332–2570. Offices are also located in Los Angeles and Chicago. You may also wish to contact the Egyptian Educational and Cultural Bureau, 1303 New Hampshire Avenue NW, Washington DC 20008; phone (202) 296–3888.

A *Culturgram* is a product of native commentary and original, expert analysis. Statistics are estimates and information is presented as a matter of opinion. While the editors strive for accuracy and detail, this document should not be considered strictly factual. It is a general introduction to culture, an initial step in building bridges of understanding between peoples. It may not apply to all peoples of the nation. You should therefore consult other sources for more information.

Republic of
Equatorial Guinea

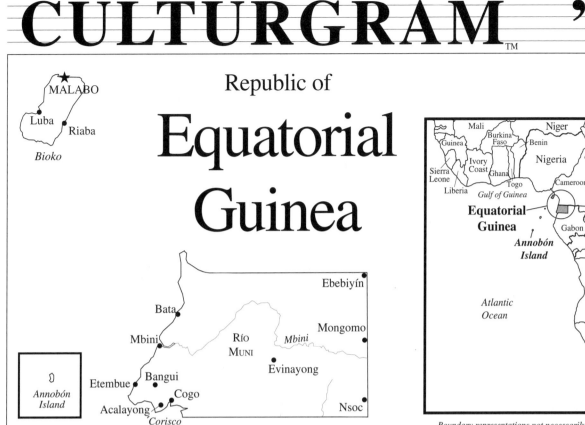

Boundary representations not necessarily authoritative.

BACKGROUND

Land and Climate

About the size of Maryland, Equatorial Guinea consists of a small continental portion and several small islands. It covers 10,830 square miles (28,050 square kilometers). Río Muni, the continental portion, lies between Gabon and Cameroon on Africa's west coast just north of the equator. The country's largest river, Río Mbini, divides it in half. The largest island, Bioko, is the site of the nation's capital, Malabo. The island is about 19 miles (30 kilometers) from the Cameroon coast, far enough north of Río Muni (about 95 miles or 153 kilometers) to make transportation and communication difficult. Bioko enjoys fertile volcanic soil and a 10,000-foot peak (3,008 meters). Annobón Island lies 370 miles (592 kilometers) southwest of Bioko. The entire country is covered by dense rain forest and has a humid climate. The average temperature is 80°F (27°C). Bioko is generally hotter and wetter than Río Muni.

History

The histories of Bioko and Río Muni are strikingly different. Río Muni remained isolated from contact with the West until the twentieth century. The Bubi on Bioko, however, retreated upland as the natural harbor of Malabo changed from Portuguese to Spanish to British and then to Spanish hands again between the late 1400s and early 1900s. During this time, Malabo was primarily a slave trading center, except during the British occupation of 1827 to 1843. During the first half of the 1900s, Spain developed the infrastructure to support cocoa plantations on the island. Because of that system, Bioko has a relatively high per capita income, a high literacy rate, and better health care.

Conflicting claims to the mainland were settled in the Treaty of Paris (1900) that set the borders for Río Muni and gave it to the Spanish. The lives of the indigenous people of Río Muni were not really affected until the 1920s when Europeans established coffee production there. Río Muni and Bioko were artificially joined by the Spanish as Spanish Guinea.

In 1959, Spanish Guinea was made part of Spain, with all indigenous peoples gaining full citizenship. Representatives were sent to the parliament in Madrid. In 1963, a measure of autonomy was granted and a joint legislative body was set up. On 12 October 1968, full independence as Equatorial Guinea was granted peacefully, and Francisco Macías Nguema became the first president in a multiparty election.

An attempted coup and an antiwhite incident in Malabo were among the events that led to tighter political controls. In 1972, Macías assumed complete control over the government and presidency for life. He deteriorated into a brutal ruler and all government functions completely eroded except for internal security. The economy existed only due to Spanish, Cuban, Soviet, and Chinese assistance. Under Macías, about one-third of the population was either exiled or executed. Twenty thousand Nigerians left, which greatly disrupted Bioko's cocoa production, the nation's primary source of income. Churches, banks, and schools ceased to operate.

On 3 August 1979, Teodoro Obiang Nguema Mbasogo, the commander of the national guard and a nephew of Macías, staged a successful coup and Macías was executed after a trial attended by international observers. Obiang Nguema remains president of a country that is still struggling to overcome the years of trouble. A single-candidate election was held in 1989, in which Obiang Nguema was elected to another seven-year term. The country legalized a multiparty system in its new 1992 constitution, but Obiang Nguema still retains control of the political system and independent parties do not yet exist.

THE PEOPLE

Population

The population is about 409,000 and is growing at 2.6 percent annually. The predominant ethnic group is the Fang (80 percent), whose traditional territory is Río Muni. The Fang, a Bantu people, migrated from what is now southern Sudan over a 250-year period and have inhabited Río Muni and surrounding areas for about 150 years. The traditional territory of the Bubi (15 percent) is the island of Bioko. The Bubi came to Bioko from the shores of Cameroon and Río Muni. Annobón Island is inhabited by Angolan people, brought there by the Portuguese. Most Equatoguineans (80 percent) live in rural areas. The country's two largest cities (Malabo and Bata) each have about 40,000 residents.

Language

Because Equatorial Guinea was colonized by Spain, Spanish is the official language and the primary language of business, government, public schools, and urban life. However, it is not usually spoken in the home. French, spoken in surrounding countries, is increasingly influential and Pidgin English is common in the markets. Local languages prevail in villages, none of which are written. If a transaction requires writing, Spanish is used. However, most traditional transactions do not require writing and people have extensive mental skills for keeping track of such dealings. Fang is spoken in Río Muni and Bubi is spoken in rural areas of Bioko. Annonbónese is spoken on Annonbón and Coriscan on the island of Corisco. Ndoe and Kombe are spoken by their respective groups.

Religion

Due to colonization, the population is 83 percent Roman Catholic. While people actively honor the Catholic calendar (celebrating holidays and saints' days), traditional African practices are commonly mixed with Western rites. An example is the Fang *defunción*, a three-day celebration to honor the passing of the dead, which occurs four to six months after the death. Clan members may come from all over the country to take part in the traditional dancing and feasting, and to hear the *nvet* (a traditional stringed rhythm instrument) player create a bridge to the ancestors by means of his song, which assists the soul's passage to the beyond. Traditional healers continue to play a religious role and polygamy is accepted among many who profess Catholicism. Other Christian denominations do exist, with some Muslims and Baha'is in the country as well.

General Attitudes

Equatoguineans are warm, friendly, and generous. Mainlanders are generally known as being more gregarious than islanders. All ethnic groups, however, love a celebration. Village life, in particular, revolves around the celebration of life's passages (birth, marriage, death) and the Catholic calendar.

Generosity is both in the people's nature and part of clan obligation. This provides for a type of social security for the elderly and disabled, but it also makes improvement of an individual's economic situation difficult. One is expected to share gains with the extended family.

Traditional religious beliefs, mixed with Catholicism, focus heavily on the unexplainable and the mysterious. Fate is accepted without question. Equatoguineans highly respect elders, village officials, and political figures. There is pride in the clan, the village, and the nation.

Personal Appearance

The average person commonly wears secondhand Western clothing, sold at low cost by Christian missionaries or in the market. Dress in urban areas is more formal than in villages. Traditional dress is highly valued but too expensive for most people. Rural people reserve their best colors, fashions, and mended clothing for celebrations and church. Women generally wear dresses rather than pants or shorts, even when working their fields in the rain forest.

CUSTOMS AND COURTESIES

Greetings

Greetings are accompanied by enthusiastic handshaking and sometimes a bit of a bow. Each person in a small group is greeted individually. A wrist or forearm is extended if the hand is dirty. In cities, Spanish greetings such as *¡Buenos días!* (Good day!) and *¡Buenas noches!* (Good evening!) are common. A light kiss on each cheek may be used to greet women.

In villages, handshakes with local greetings are more common. For example, *Mbolo* (Hello) is common on the continent. Rural Fang women often greet each other by joining both forearms to the elbow, bowing slightly at the hips and knees, and issuing a long, low, guttural *sah* (Hello). Among the Fang, who consider their ethnic group a family, one also asks where the other is going or has been. This custom of keeping track of family members is such a habit that the Fang often ask the question of non-Fang people.

In cities, the use of titles and the proper honorifics is very important when addressing someone. *Señor* (Mr.), *Señora* (Ms. or Mrs.), or an official title are commonly used with the last name. Respected older people may be addressed as *Don* or *Doña* with their first name. Rural people use first names, which often have a Spanish origin, or African nicknames when addressing one another.

Gestures

People use hand gestures during conversation and for many of life's situations. For example, the hands pressed together in prayer position and opened up as if empty can mean anything from "nothing left" to "such is life." Drawing the fingers closed with the palm facing down indicates "come here."

In Fang, *ka* means "no" and is often accompanied by a finger wagging back and forth close to the face. People stand close to one another, often touching while they talk. Holding hands or locking arms while talking or walking is common for men and children. Such physical contact is not appropriate for members of the opposite sex. Even husbands and wives do not display affection in public.

Visiting

Equatoguineans are very social, and visiting is an important way to establish and maintain social contacts. A visit is itself considered a gift, but people might also take fruit or bread to their hosts. Visits are usually returned. People drop by unannounced in villages, but might make prior arrangements in the cities. Arranged visits rarely begin on time, as the concept of time is more flexible than in the West. Visitors may be offered water, beer (in the city), *tope* (palm wine), *malamba* (cane alcohol), or a meal. Although one may refuse refreshments, it is polite to at least taste some of the food offered. However, since Equatoguineans often have personal taboos concerning a particular food, hosts are not offended by a refusal to eat a certain item.

Upon entering a village, it is polite to visit the *abaa*, a hut made of bamboo and palm leaves, and greet the elderly men who socialize there and work on crafts.

Eating

Urban people tend to follow Spanish eating customs, with a light breakfast of coffee or tea and bread, a main meal at midday, and a light dinner between 8:00 and 10:00 P.M. In rural areas, people often eat only a light mid-morning meal and supper just before dusk. When invited for dinner among the Fang, guests might eat alone in a reception room reserved for the male head of household, or senior male family members may eat with the guests. Women serve the meal and then eat in the kitchen with the children.

Western utensils are used for most meals. Only in very informal settings is food eaten with the hands. Then, even peanut pastes and sauces, bundled in banana leaves and tied with melango fiber, become finger foods. Because it is improper to drink from a common container, an appropriate type of leaf is picked and formed into a leaf cup for each person whenever glasses are not available.

LIFESTYLE

Family

As in much of Africa, polygamous extended family structures still dominate rural life, while nuclear families are more common in cities. "The family" actually refers to the entire clan, which once also implied a village. The power structure revolves around gender, age, and clan status. This system leaves women with limited power, although they do control the production of food. Each wife in an extended family has her own kitchen (used for both sleeping and cooking) or her own cooking fire, in which area she is the authority figure. The kitchen is the center of family life. The husband has his own building and wives take turns spending time with him there. Wives also share child care and household chores.

Cousins are considered siblings; aunts and uncles are considered mothers and fathers. Children must obey their elders, even older siblings, but especially their various mothers and fathers. It is not uncommon for children to be sent to live with other family members. Large families are prized as a sign of wealth, health, and virility; having six or more children is common. Women grow the food, cook, clean, serve, haul water and firewood, and raise the children. Men are responsible for hunting, building and maintaining houses, making tools and baskets, and clearing the *fincas* (agricultural plots in the forest) twice a year.

Dating and Marriage

Young urban people like to date by going to late-night discos. Young rural people more commonly meet at large celebrations that involve other clans, but discos are becoming popular for them as well. Many marriages are still arranged. When two people marry, a three-day wedding celebration of dancing and feasting marks the woman's acceptance into her husband's clan. This celebration is preceded by negotiations between the two families on the *bride price* (paid to the bride's family), which can be extremely high. Because of the expense, young people often enter into a common-law relationship and begin having children before they are actually married. Any children born before the wedding technically belong to the woman's father, but the groom can take the children when he pays the *bride price* and formally gets married. In the rare case of divorce, the *bride price* must be returned to the husband, who retains the children, while the woman returns to her family.

Diet

Cassava and other starchy roots, which adapt well to rain forest agriculture, are the main staple foods. Fermented cassava (*yuca* in Spanish, *mbo* in Fang) sticks are eaten with nearly every meal. Meat is the preferred source of protein when available and may include anything from goats, chickens, rodents, and monkeys to snakes. Fish is also a traditional favorite. Peanuts, another staple, are prepared in many different ways, such as peppery leaf-roasted rolls, peanut brittle, or sauce. A favorite dish is ground squash seeds made into a curd similar to tofu. Papayas, pineapples, bananas, and plantains are abundant. The cities are more influenced by Spanish cuisine and have access to seafood, bread, and pasta.

Recreation

Social visiting is a primary leisure activity. *Voy a pasear* (I'm going visiting) is a common weekend pastime. Drumming, dancing, and singing surround holidays and family events. Soccer is the only group sport, but it is very popular and every village has a soccer field. A traditional strategy board game is played with rocks and seeds. The two cities have cultural centers, sponsored by the French and the Spanish, where art exhibits and occasional music and theater performances occur.

Holidays

National holidays include New Year's Day (1 January), Easter (including Good Friday), Labor Day (1 May), Corpus Christi, the President's birthday (5 June), Armed Forces Day (3 August), Constitution Day (15 August), Independence Day

(12 October), Immaculate Conception Day (8 December), and Christmas (25 December). Easter is the most important holiday, with a week of celebrations from Palm Sunday to Easter Sunday. Independence Day is marked by large gatherings, singing, and food.

Commerce

Generally, hours for businesses, banks, and government offices are 7:30 A.M. to 2:30 P.M. Stores operate from 8:00 A.M. to 1:00 P.M. and from 4:00 to 7:00 P.M. Even in the open-air market, bargaining is uncommon. In rural areas, traditional patterns such as clan obligations have a substantial impact on business negotiations.

SOCIETY

Government

The country is a unitary republic. The constitution provides the president with extensive powers; he is commander in chief of the military and minister of defense. He also appoints all cabinet members and makes laws by decree. The unicameral House of Representatives of the People has 60 representatives. Fifteen are appointed by the president and the rest are elected by district. Parliament is not able to act without the president's agreement and he has the right to dissolve the legislative body. If elections are held in 1996 as planned, a multiparty system could emerge. Each of the seven provinces has a governor appointed by the president. The judicial system is also headed by the president and his judicial advisers. When not in conflict with constitutional law, tribal laws and customs are usually honored.

Economy

Most people (90 percent) are engaged in subsistence agriculture. The main exports are cocoa beans, timber, and coffee. Cocoa production, which dropped in the Macías years, is now beginning to revive, but it is still well below capacity. Conversion in 1985 to the *CFA franc*, which is a hard currency tied to the French *franc*, provided a much needed stepping-stone out of isolation. Timber harvesting is increasingly relied upon to attract foreign capital. Most timber is shipped out as raw logs, however, with very little manufacturing taking place in Equatorial Guinea. Some success has been achieved with petroleum production, and there is potential for increased trade with neighboring countries in local food crops such as cassava, taro, pineapples, and coconuts. Spain is the main trading partner. Equatorial Guinea's Human Development Index (0.276) ranks it 150th out of 173 countries. Real gross domestic product per capita is estimated to be $700. These figures reflect the fact that two-thirds of all people live in poverty. Either they do not earn an income (i.e., they are subsistence farmers) or their income is insufficient for their basic needs.

Transportation and Communication

For common people, the accepted mode of transportation is walking. Few can afford bicycles. *Bush-taxis*, which are privately owned cars for hire, are the only transportation to rural areas. They collect passengers at the market and leave when full; there are no schedules. For many, a ride in a *bush-taxi* is a special event for which to save. There are two or three weekly flights between Bata and Malabo, as well as out of the country. There is also a weekly flight to Spain.

A radio-phone system connects district capitals, but people do not otherwise have access to telephones. There is one government-owned television and radio station. There are no national or private newspapers or magazines.

Education

While the majority of all children attend primary school, only about 11 percent are enrolled in secondary schools. Malabo offers an academically oriented agricultural vocational school. Bata has a post-secondary vocational program that offers courses in agriculture, metalworking, and carpentry, but placement is limited. The Catholic church has made important contributions to primary and secondary education, as well as to health. About half of the population is literate.

Health

The population's primary health problems are malaria, diarrhea (among young children), and intestinal parasites. Availability of Western health resources is generally poor, with very few doctors and clinics. In most parts of the country, traditional tribal medicine is still relied upon to provide effective care for many health problems. The infant mortality rate is about 103 per 1,000; life expectancy averages 52 years.

FOR THE TRAVELER

U.S. visitors need a valid passport and visa to enter Equatorial Guinea. Visas are easiest to obtain at the embassy in Douala, Cameroon. As health care is unavailable, visitors should arrive in good health. Malaria prophylactics are necessary and some vaccinations are required. Contact your county health office for information, or call the U.S. Centers for Disease Control Travel Hotline at (404) 332–4559. Water is not safe to drink, and fruits and vegetables should be peeled or cooked before being eaten. Do not swim in freshwater ponds or lakes due to the presence of bilharzia. Running water and electricity are available daily on a limited basis in Malabo and Bata. Declare any cash in excess of US$40 upon arrival to avoid forfeiting it upon departure. Registration with the U.S. embassy is advised. Embassy personnel can provide information about travel and photography restrictions. For more information, contact the Equatorial Guinea Mission to the United Nations, 57 Magnolia Avenue, Mt. Vernon, NY 10553; phone (914) 667–9664.

State of
Eritrea

Boundary representations not necessarily authoritative.

BACKGROUND

Land and Climate

Eritrea sits on the Horn of Africa bordering the Red Sea. It consists of the mainland and the Dahlak Islands. Covering 46,842 square miles (121,320 square kilometers), it is a bit larger than Pennsylvania. Central highlands rise to an elevation of more than 8,000 feet (2,500 meters) near the east coast, forming an escarpment of the Great Rift Valley. Western elevations are lower. The Koba Sink lies below sea level and is very hot.

The semiarid highland climate is mild and dry; temperatures rarely fall to freezing. The rainy season (June–September) yields six to thirty-seven inches of rain, depending on elevation, but the precipitation is not always dependable. Drought has severely cut crop production in the last few years. Rain falls between October and February on foothills and lowlands east of the northern escarpment. This allows for an extra growing season. During the war for independence, recurrent drought and fighting left thousands dead from famine. Others were forced to flee because food aid could not be distributed and farmers had no replacement seeds or animals. Officials expect sustainable agriculture to be possible only with proper irrigation.

History

Eritrea's original inhabitants were joined successively by people from the Nile River area and by Egyptians, Cushites, and Semites. The region was later influenced by Greeks, Turks, Egyptians, and Persians. The name *Eritrea* comes from the Greek *erythrea* (red).

After 1885, Italy colonized the region, establishing some industries and confiscating arable land. Āsmera, the colonial and current capital, still displays a distinct Italian influence. Italian forces pressed west and eventually conquered Ethiopia in 1935. Ethiopia's Emperor Haile Selassie I requested intervention from the League of Nations. In response, the Allied Powers of World War II eventually halted Italy's advances and forced its surrender at Āsmera in 1941.

Britain then governed Eritrea as a protectorate until 1952, when the UN-recommended federation with Ethiopia took place. Ethiopia moved to assert greater control over Eritrea by annexing it as a province in 1962. The Eritrean Liberation Front organized initial resistance, and the Eritrean People's Liberation Front (EPLF) later led the movement. After Haile Selassie I was deposed in Ethiopia by Marxists in 1974, the liberation movement gained popularity. Over the next two decades, the EPLF steadily captured territory as it received financial support from Eritreans outside the country and as it took arms and vehicles from the Ethiopian army. Over time, the EPLF set up schools, industries, and a hospital. By 1990, it occupied the strategic port of Mits'iwa (Massawa).

Ethiopia's Marxist dictator, Mengistu Haile-Mariam, was opposed by many ethnic groups and, by 1990, had lost support from former Communist countries. When he was about to flee, the EPLF took Āsmera on 24 May 1991, forcing the Ethiopian army to abandon Eritrea. In an April 1993 referendum, 98 percent of all Eritreans voted for independence, which was declared 24 May 1993. Eritrea quickly joined the United Nations and other organizations and established diplomatic ties with many countries. In July 1993, Ethiopia (under a new government) and Eritrea signed an Agreement of Friendship and Cooperation to establish good relations and grant Ethiopia access to the Red Sea.

By 1994, the country was busily working to repair war-damaged institutions, feed the hungry, establish a free-market economy, and draft a new constitution. President Issaias Afwerki, a former EPLF leader, scheduled elections for May 1997.

PEOPLE
Population
Of Eritrea's 3.2 million people, the vast majority (85 percent) live in rural areas. The largest ethnic groups are the highland Tigrinya (50 percent), and the Tigreans (33 percent) of both highland and lowland areas. The remaining population is composed of Saho, Bilen, Afar, Hedareb, Kunama, Nara, and Rashaida minorities.

More than 500,000 Eritreans fled the country during the war. Nearly 200,000 are returning from Sudan. Of thousands living in North America, Europe, East Africa, Saudi Arabia, and Ethiopia, many desire to return and are waiting for housing and jobs.

Language
Eritrea has two primary languages: Tigrinya and Arabic. Tigrinya is spoken by highland Christians and is closely related to Tigre, spoken by Tigreans. Tigrinya and Tigre use an ancient *Ge'ez* script. Like Arabic, they are both Semitic tongues. Arabic, native to the Rashaida, is widely used in commerce. Educated people often speak English, having studied it in school since the British Administration. Most minority groups speak their own languages but have fluency or familiarity with a national language.

Religion
Some Ethiopians follow traditional practices usually classified as animism, but nearly equal portions (roughly 40 percent each) follow Islam and Christianity. Although Roman Catholics and Protestants are found among the more affluent and Westernized Eritreans, most Christians are Coptics who accept the teachings of the Ethiopian Orthodox Church. The Eritrean Orthodox Church now has its own bishop but maintains ties to the church in Ethiopia. The Orthodox Church is conservative, uses the *Ge'ez* language, and incorporates both monks and married priests in its clergy.

Whereas most Christians reside in the highlands, Muslims tend to inhabit the lowlands. They include many Tigreans and Kunamans, as well as nearly all Saho, Nara, and Rashaida people. These Sunni Muslims were integrated into the EPLF and are well represented in government. During the war, fighters (of which 30 percent were women) of different religions often married. Indeed, the war helped unite religious leaders in a common cause, which is a factor in the country's religious freedom and tolerance. By law, neither religion nor ethnicity can be the basis of a political party.

General Attitudes
Eritreans are optimistic, hardworking, committed people who love their country and their independence. They are grateful to the EPLF, whose leaders genuinely want to maintain the respect it worked to establish for cooperative effort, manual labor, equality among ethnic groups, and equal participation by women. People are well disciplined. Whereas crime is often a major problem for societies in transition, it is almost nonexistent in Eritrea. Eritreans believe in self-sufficiency, community cooperation, and friendliness. They are aware of challenges they face in building a nation anew, but despite poverty and other hardships, they are confident they can succeed.

Personal Appearance
Eritreans have dark skin, black curly hair, and narrow facial features. Western-style clothing is popular in urban areas, with even girls and women often wearing trousers. Rural dress is more traditional. Highland Christian women wear white cotton dresses with a woven border at the hem, or embroidery on the bodice and skirt, and a shawl with a matching border. Their hair is customarily braided in tight, narrow rows up front, but is left free and fluffy behind. Highland men wear a long-sleeved, knee-length white shirt over white baggy trousers. They also wear white cotton shawls with colored borders. Work clothing or "daily dress" is less decorated and is made of heavy, off-white cotton.

Muslim men wear *jalabiyas* (long gowns) and embroidered caps with turbans. Women usually cover their dresses with black or colorful cloth called *luiet*. The cloth can be loosely draped or sewn to be more tailored. Some Muslim women wear veils that cover all but their eyes. Throughout Eritrea, women use henna as a skin conditioner, hair tint, or dye to decorate their hands and feet.

CUSTOMS AND COURTESIES
Greetings
Greeting styles vary by region and ethnic group. Highlanders greet with a handshake. Nudging right shoulders at the same time is common between male former fighters and villagers. Urban dwellers (opposite or same sex, relatives, and acquaintances) shake hands and kiss the air while brushing alternate cheeks three times. Verbal greetings depend on the time of day but nearly always involve an inquiry about well-being. S*alaam* (Peace) is a general greeting or leave-taking phrase. Muslims grasp and kiss each other's right hands, ask *Kefelhal?* (How are you?), and answer *Hamdellah* or *Marhaba* (both roughly mean "fine").

Friends call one another by nickname. Older people are addressed by title (equivalents of Mr., Mrs., Miss, Aunt, Uncle, and so forth) and their name. Professional titles are used in formal situations. Second-person plural is used to show respect. A person's given name is followed by the father's name, so that Mhret, the daughter of Tesfai, is called Mhret Tesfai.

Gestures
The right hand is used for eating and making gestures. It is used alone or together with the left hand to pass or receive items. A hand held high is a greeting, whereas a hand waved back and forth indicates a negative response. Snapping fingers shows agreement. To beckon, one waves all fingers with the palm facing out. Pointing with a finger to indicate location is fine, but pointing at people is impolite. In discussion, old men often gesture with their fly whisks to emphasize a point or indicate direction. Seated girls keep their legs uncrossed—knees touching and covered—with elbows on their knees as a sign of respect.

Visiting
Relatives and good friends visit each other often and without invitation. Guests may be offered food or asked to join the family for an upcoming meal, which they may accept or

politely decline. They are always served tea or coffee. The latter involves a prescribed sequence of roasting and pounding the coffee beans. The coffee is then boiled, heavily sweetened, and served in small cups. Three customary rounds might be accompanied by fresh popcorn. People enjoy the prolonged conversation encouraged by this coffee ceremony.

When visiting on special occasions, townspeople often take villagers gifts of coffee or sugar; villagers take urban dwellers local produce or food (such as bread), a chicken, or firewood (which is precious due to soil erosion and deforestation).

Special events require invitation and involve women and men socializing separately. Wedding guests take *ingera* (sour bread) for the feast or they contribute its cost. *Ga'at*, a thick barley porridge, is served at gatherings to welcome new babies. When someone dies, friends and relatives gather for the burial. For at least 12 days, they attend the bereaved family, cook their meals, divert their attention with games and entertainment, help receive many visitors, and collect money for the family.

Eating

Among highlanders, adults and children eat separately. Among other Eritreans, families eat together, although children eat separately when guests are present. In such cases, the hostess serves the guests and eats later with the children.

To begin each meal, the oldest man takes a piece of bread, blesses it, and offers some to each person. Diners eat with the right hand from a large communal tray set on a low table. Each person only eats the portion directly in front of him or her. In Christian homes, mealtime etiquette is stressed because heaven is watching. Restaurants offer traditional and Italian foods. Tipping is only common in hotel restaurants.

LIFESTYLE

Family

The family is more important than any of its individual members, who will sacrifice as necessary for the good of the group or for future generations. A family unit typically consists of parents, four or more children, and frequently grandparents. Respected for their wisdom, the elderly are always cared for by adult children. After marriage, a son and his wife usually live with his parents for at least two years before establishing their own home.

Village men are farmers. Women work on the farm and do all household work. Chores, especially food preparation, can be lengthy. Some urban women work outside the home and employ house servants.

Village homes, usually made of stone, have thatched or metal roofs and concrete or dirt floors. City dwellings, made of stone or brick, have metal roofs, tiled floors, and water and electricity. Nomadic and seminomadic peoples (Afar, Hedareb, Rashaida, and Tigre) have different lifestyles than the settled population. Accordingly, their homes are portable or built with whatever materials they find when they settle temporarily. Regardless of the style, homes are kept clean and neat.

Dating and Marriage

In Eritrea, nearly all marriages are arranged by families. Among the monogamous Tigrinya, parents suggest marriage partners to establish family alliances. The couple involved usually makes the final decision to marry, although some rural couples may not be acquainted before they wed. The bride is often some ten years younger than the groom; in cities she will have completed secondary school before getting married.

The wedding celebration involves at least a week's food preparation and requires a month to brew *suwa*, a beer, and *miyess*, a honey mead. The bride's female relatives provide food for a banquet following the morning church ceremony. After a display of gifts, the couple enters the banquet to share a meal with their attendants. Some urban couples also cut a tiered wedding cake. For two or three weeks, the couple stays at home while relatives provide their meals.

Among Muslims, wedding festivities include the bride's arrival on a camel and a feast where guests sit on floor mats to eat from bowls. Muslim men may have up to four wives if they can provide for each equally. Due to the economic burden, this practice is diminishing.

Diet

Eritreans traditionally enjoy a wide variety of foods, but after years of drought, famine, and war, both culinary skills and food levels have deteriorated. The preferred meal is meat (chicken, goat or sheep mutton, or beef) cooked with onion, garlic, red pepper, spices, and clarified butter. *Shuro*, a typical meal of garbanzo bean flour and spices, is similarly cooked. Lentils or other vegetables are served. Spicy main dishes, eaten for lunch or dinner, are complemented by *ingera* (also called *taitah*), a sour pancake bread made of millet or corn flour fermented in water. Breakfast may be tea served with honey and unleavened *k'itcha* bread, bits of bread (*fit fit*) and yogurt, *ga'at* and yogurt, or leftovers.

Coptics eat no dairy products or meat on Wednesday and Friday. Other Christians often abstain from dairy products during the Catholic Lent. Muslims abstain from pork and alcohol.

Recreation

Whole families participate in annual church festivals, social visits, and helping relatives prepare food for weddings or babies' baptisms. Even urban dwellers often return to their home villages for such celebrations.

In Āsmera, espresso coffee bars are popular meeting spots, especially for men. Villages have tea shops. Women visit mostly in each other's homes. They also get together to weave baskets used to store and serve food.

Boys enjoy soccer, bicycle racing, a game similar to field hockey, and another game that is like horseshoes but uses stones. Boys and girls play *gebetta*, a strategy game played with pebbles on a playing surface they create by making depressions in the ground. Girls enjoy drumming and dancing.

Holidays

Eritrea's holidays include International Women's Day (8 March), Independence Day (24 May), Martyr's Day (20 June), and the Anniversary of the Start of the Armed Struggle (1 September). Christian holidays include Christmas (7 January); *Timket*, the baptism of Jesus, also in January; Easter; and *Meskel*, the finding of the true cross by St. Helena, in late September.

Muslims celebrate *Eid el Fitr* at the end of *Ramadan*, the holy month of fasting in which they go without food and drink each day from dawn to dusk. Forty days later they observe *Eid el Adha* to mark the completion of the annual pilgrimage to Makkah and to honor Abraham for his willingness to sacrifice his son.

Commerce

Government offices and businesses are open weekdays, 8:00 A.M. to 5:00 P.M., with a two-hour closing for lunch. Most are also open Saturday morning. Stores, shops, and markets open daily after 5:00 P.M. Bargaining is officially discouraged in favor of posted prices. Before conducting office business, several minutes of social conversation are expected.

SOCIETY

Government

After independence, the EPLF installed the Provisional Government of Eritrea (PGE), which will govern until 1997. Officials receive a minimal salary and live in modest circumstances to avoid losing public trust.

In 1994, the EPLF became a civilian political party, the People's Front for Democracy and Justice (PFDJ). It will remain the governing party until full multiparty elections are held. The PGE's National Assembly has the highest legal power. It consists of the PFDJ's 75-member Central Committee and 75 members elected at large. The Assembly outlines and regulates policy, approves the government budget and ministerial appointments, and elects a president to be head of government and commander-in-chief of the army. President Issaias Afwerki has 15 cabinet ministers. When the legislature is not in session, the president holds the highest legal authority. The judiciary functions independently.

In 1996, the PGE will introduce a constitution that guarantees basic personal rights and sets forth a multiparty democracy. The constitution is being drafted by an appointed commission that is consulting extensively with Eritreans from villages, cities, and expatriate communities all over the world.

Economy

Eritrea, though poor, has great economic potential. Statistics are not yet available on such measures as gross domestic product, but per capita income is estimated to be less than US$150. Eighty percent of all people depend on subsistence agriculture for their living. Because of drought and war, food production levels are low. The government and aid agencies are filling the gap with short-term food supplies, but long-term solutions are being developed. Such plans have impressed international donors, who are sending funds to help the country rebuild roads, schools, ports, and the telecommunications system. Solar and other technology is being explored as an alternative to wood and charcoal.

Under a liberal investment code, foreign investment is steadily increasing. Private enterprise is beginning to flourish. Industries that were nationalized by Ethiopia are being returned to private ownership and new ones are opening. Eritrea's four potentially most productive economic sectors include tourism, thanks to a long coastline; marine resources, including fishing and petroleum; trade, as Eritrea is situated on the world's busiest shipping lane; and mining for gold, copper, silver, marble, potash, and iron ore. Current exports include sesame seeds, gum arabic, leather shoes, beer, and refined petroleum. The currency is the Ethiopian *birr*, but a national currency is expected in the future.

Transportation and Communication

Major roads crossing the country are under repair; most city streets are paved, while country roads are not. Public buses serve even remote villages and are the most common transport within cities. Taxis are available. Telephones are used mostly by government and business offices. Public phones are found at central urban locations. The government administers the postal system and provides radio and television broadcasts. Weekly English and semiweekly Arabic and Tigrinya newspapers are also printed by the government.

Education

Because of the war's destruction, few children (about 100,000) are presently attending school. Of those who do attend, 23 percent finish grade six and only 6 percent complete all 11 years. The literacy rate is 20 percent. Nevertheless, education is highly valued in Eritrea. The national goal is to have mandatory free education up to seventh grade that will emphasize skills needed to develop rural areas. To that end, schools are under repair or construction, teachers are in training, and instructional materials are in development. For the first several years, students are taught in their native tongue but can study English and Arabic or Tigrinya. From the sixth grade on, instruction is in English. Adult literacy classes are being offered to help those no longer in school.

Health

Maternity and child care are high priorities of the Primary Health Care Programme (PHCP) because more than 21 percent of Eritreans are women of childbearing age, 18 percent are children under age five, and the population is growing at 3.4 percent. The infant mortality rate is 125 per 1,000. Common health problems include malnutrition, malaria, parasitic and upper respiratory infections, diarrhea, and other diseases. The PHCP plans extensive education in preventing disease and malnutrition.

Currently, comprehensive medical services are centralized in a few hospitals. The plan is to have a hospital in each of the eight provinces, with health care centers at the sub-provincial, district, and village levels. By 1993, more than 30 clinics were under construction. Doctors and nurses are in short supply, but by 1994 the PHCP had trained and posted nearly 1,500 health workers to various communities.

FOR THE TRAVELER

U.S. citizens need a passport and visa to visit Eritrea. A yellow fever vaccination certificate may be required. Travelers enjoy the mild climate, people's enthusiasm for building their country, and numerous historical sites. Accommodations range from first-class hotels to small *pensiones* with shared bathrooms. Modest clothing is a must (no shorts or sleeveless dresses). Water is purified, but underground pipes are unreliable, so visitors should treat their drinking water. For more information, contact the Embassy of Eritrea, 910 17th Street NW, Suite 400, Washington DC 20006; phone (202) 429–1991.

Printed on recycled paper

Federal Democratic Republic of

Ethiopia

Boundary representations not necessarily authoritative.

BACKGROUND

Land and Climate

Ethiopia, a landlocked country on the Horn of Africa, covers 435,184 square miles (1,127,127 square kilometers). It has access to the Red Sea through Eritrea's port at Aseb, which is near Djibouti. Sudan, Eritrea, Kenya, Somalia, and Djibouti share borders with Ethiopia. The Great Rift Valley, which is subject to earthquakes, separates the northwest highlands from the southeast mountains. Addis Ababa is 8,000 feet (2,438 meters) above sea level. There are also lowlands to the west, which are often hot; the hottest days average 95°F (35°C), but can rise to as high as 120°F (49°C). Temperatures in the highlands average between 60°F (16°C) and 74°F (23°C). The rainy season is from mid-June to mid-September in the highlands, and the period from October to February is extremely dry. Rainfall varies widely from year to year, a factor that causes extreme problems for agriculture and animal husbandry, the two main sources of work and sustenance for Ethiopians.

History

Ethiopia is one of the oldest countries in the world. It is the oldest independent country in Africa, and was known to the ancient Greeks and Egyptians. For centuries, its coast, which is now part of Eritrea, was important to regional trade. By far the most important period of consolidation was the Kingdom of Aksum (A.D. 100–800), during which the foundation of modern Ethiopia was laid. A strong monarchy, which lasted until a 1974 military coup deposed Emperor Haile Selassie, was established. According to tradition, many of Ethiopia's rulers traced their ancestry through a single line to Solomon and the Queen of Sheba. During the Aksum period, the monarchy and most people embraced Orthodox Christianity. Muslim invaders pressured the people during the seventh century, but they were largely repulsed. In the following centuries, Ethiopia had periodic contact with Western Christian nations, who were intrigued to find Christianity in Africa. Islam did not have much influence until the nomadic Oromo (who were Muslims) moved into the central region in the 17th century.

Around 1885, the Italians began colonizing Eritrea and tried to move inland. They were defeated in 1896 by the Ethiopian army under Emperor Menilek II. That victory spared Ethiopia further aggression until the 1930s. Mussolini's Italian Army invaded and occupied Ethiopia from 1935 to 1941, when the British helped the exiled Selassie regain control. Selassie had been Ras Tafari Makonnen, regent to the Empress Zauditu (daughter of Menilek II) during the 1920s. Ras Tafari gained power and took the throne away from the empress, declaring himself Emperor Haile Selassie. After his return in 1941, he ruled autocratically. General economic and political unrest led to Selassie's fall in 1974; when he died a year later, a socialist state was proclaimed. The country was named the People's Democratic Republic of Ethiopia.

A provisional government took control and began nationalizing industry. Mengistu Haile Mariam led that government beginning in 1977. A 1987 constitution established a national assembly, which elected Mengistu president. Mengistu faced several problems, including a ongoing civil war (that began 1961) with the Eritrean People's Liberation Front (EPLF), which sought Eritrea's independence. Other ethnic groups were also fighting for control of the government. Mengistu was known to rule as a dictator. Famine in the 1980s became all the more difficult to deal with because of the fighting and the Marxist economy.

An attempted 1989 coup led Mengistu to announce economic reforms in 1990, but rebel groups were not satisfied with the lack of political reform. Fighting intensified in 1991, and in May, Mengistu resigned and left the country. An assault on the capital by the Ethiopian People's Revolutionary Democratic Front (EPRDF) led to the government's collapse. At the same time, the EPLF took separate control of Eritrea, and the Eritrean leadership announced plans for independence.

The new Ethiopian leader, Meles Zenawi of EPRDF, established a provisional government that promised to sponsor fair elections with all ethnic groups represented for the first time in history. As a result of negotiations, Ethiopia agreed that Eritrea would become independent if Ethiopia could retain access to the seaport. Eritrea held a referendum in 1993 and it passed almost unanimously. Eritrea therefore declared independence in May 1993, already having made strides in creating a separate economy and political structure. Both Eritrea and Ethiopia realize they can work together for mutual benefit, and there have been no conflicts between them since 1993.

In Ethiopia, a constituent assembly was elected in 1994 to review and revise a draft constitution put forth by President Zenawi. The constitution was ratified and full national multiparty elections were held in May 1995. Several parties posted candidates, although many boycotted the actual polling in protest of EPRDF's domination of the election process. Nevertheless, President Zenawi, who was running for parliament, won his seat in a landslide victory. As leader of the majority EPRDF, he became the new prime minister. Ethiopia became the Ethiopian Federal Democratic Republic and the first meeting of an all-new parliament was set for September 1995.

THE PEOPLE

Population

The population of Ethiopia is about 54.9 million and is growing at 3.4 percent a year. The Amharic people of central Ethiopia account for about 25 percent of the population, and they were politically dominant for many years. The Tigreans in the northwest comprise almost 12 percent of the population. The Oromo (40 percent) and Somali (6 percent) live in the south. Other larger groups include the Sidamo (9 percent), Shankella (6 percent), and Afar (4 percent). Addis Ababa, the capital, has 1.4 million people. Ethiopia's growth rate is often subject to drought conditions, which can kill hundreds of thousands at a time. During famines, it may sink to less than 1 percent. Droughts caused widespread famine in the 1980s, and droughts after 1988 combined with civil war to hinder the population's ability to feed itself. Harvests in the 1990s, however, have been good and peace has allowed for some stability.

Language

Amharic, a Semitic language related to Hebrew and Arabic, is the official national language and is used in commerce and administration. Tigrinya is the most widely spoken daily language and Orominga is also used. The liturgical language (*Ge'ez*) of the Ethiopian Orthodox church has produced a large and vibrant literature of considerable importance. English is taught in most schools, making it the most widely understood foreign language.

Religion

About 40 percent of the population belongs to the Ethiopian Orthodox church (Christian), a leading influence in Ethiopian culture since the fourth century. Indeed, Ethiopian Christians stress that, while Christianity was introduced by European colonizers in other countries on the African continent, it was adopted by Ethiopian rulers in A.D. 332 —before many Western nations were exposed to it. Christianity's legacy can be seen in many ancient structures, including churches in Lalibela carved from stone in the 13th century. The Oromo of the southeast and northwest are mostly Muslim. Much of the remaining population follows traditional religions such as animism, which stresses the reverence of all living things.

General Attitudes

All peoples of Ethiopia, whether Christian or Muslim, tend to be somewhat complacent and passive, enduring adversity with a stoicism unknown in the Western world. They also tend to be quite formal in their dealings, not only with strangers, but with each other. A strong sense of individualism pervades the Ethiopian personality. Individuals are expected to stand up for their rights and desires. At the same time, genuine concern for others and courtesy are noticeable personality traits of Ethiopians.

The people of Ethiopia generally do not consider themselves to be Africans because of their history and Christian heritage. Ethiopians are proud of the fact that they escaped colonization in the 19th century when much of the rest of the continent was held by Europeans.

Personal Appearance

In larger cities, most people wear Western-style clothing under the traditional white *shamma* (toga). Men in some ethnic groups wear turbans. Women generally wear dresses. Full native dress is still worn by many, particularly on holidays. Conservative dress is a must for visitors. Due to poverty, many Ethiopians in rural areas have little to wear, but the people care for their appearance as much as possible.

CUSTOMS AND COURTESIES

Greetings

Like most Semitic peoples, the Amhara place great emphasis on formal but very courteous greetings to both friends and strangers. Shaking hands with one or both hands, though more gently than the Western handshake, is common between members of the same sex. Friends often embrace each other formally but warmly. Members of opposite sex do not greet each other physically.

Gestures

Pointing is generally considered rude. One never uses the left hand to give or receive items; the right hand or both hands are used. It is an insult to refer to a person as *Galla*, a name once used for the Oromo people. Trilling the tongue is an expression of excitement or happiness.

Visiting

The Amharic home is a highly private and personal domain. Visits are not made without an invitation. If one is going to a home for the first time, a small gift is in order. Visitors are expected to accept any refreshments or food offered. Conversation should avoid highly personal topics and is best kept casual. Among other ethnic groups, visiting in the home with relatives and close friends is a vital social function. Relatives visit frequently and do not usually need an invitation.

Eating

Amhara hosts take pride in offering guests the best meal they are capable of providing, whether at a public restaurant or in the home. Visitors are often given more food than they are able to eat. Leaving some food on the plate is polite because it indicates the host's ability to provide more than adequately provide for guests. As is the custom in the Semitic world, food is eaten with the fingers of the right hand (never

the left). Western utensils may be available to international visitors. In restaurants, a tip ranges from 10 to 15 percent, unless it has been included in the bill; if so, only a small amount should be left.

LIFESTYLE

Family

The extended family is strongly patriarchal throughout Ethiopia. Sons usually bring their brides to live with or near their father's family, and three or more generations in the male line frequently live under one roof. The women of the household are responsible for its upkeep and for child care. Indeed, a woman's duties and privileges are well-defined both within the home and elsewhere, and women often lead sheltered lives. Age is highly respected in Ethiopia, and the elderly are cared for by their adult children. Only a small percentage (6 percent) of the population is older than age 60.

Dating and Marriage

Western-style dating is not common in Ethiopia, as traditional norms are still strong in most areas. Because marriage represents the union of two families, the choice of spouse is most often arranged by the families. While the individual has some freedom in the decision, most abide by traditional methods of finding a mate. Marriages tend to last long and divorce is not common.

Diet

The Ethiopian diet includes lamb, goat, and fowl. Ethiopians do not usually eat pork, turkey, or ham. Common foods include *injera*, a fermented bread made of teff flour, and *wat*, a spicy stew made with beef or chicken. Strict religious dietary and fasting customs, especially for Muslims, also affect the menu. For the many people who have limited access to food, a daily diet consists of grains and relief supplies.

Recreation

Leisure time is generally spent in the home. Individual games of skill (board games and races) are the most popular kinds of recreation, and soccer is the most popular sport for men and boys. Women do not usually play sports, but socialize with one another at home.

Holidays

Ethiopia follows the Coptic calendar (similar to the Julian). Because each of the 12 months has 30 days, there is a 13th month with only five or six days. There is a seven-year difference between the Coptic calendar and the Gregorian one used in the West. Therefore, 1996 in Western societies is 1989 in Ethiopia. Also, the 24-hour day begins at sunrise, not midnight, so 7:00 P.M. is popularly called "one o'clock." However, business is conducted using Western time and calendar standards. Easter is by far the most important holiday, but other Christian Holy Days (particularly saints' days) are also marked. Muslims celebrate their religious holidays. May Day (1 May) and National Revolution Day (12 September) are also celebrated. Christmas is 7 January.

Commerce

With most people employed in agriculture, work schedules depend on the season and the crop. In poorer areas, many have to work long hours to provide basic necessities and some 30 percent of all laborers are unemployed. In large cities, businesses are open from 8:30 A.M. to 1:00 P.M. and from 3:00 to 8:00 P.M., Monday through Friday. Saturday hours are 9:00 A.M. to 1:00 P.M. Government offices close at 6:00 P.M. on weekdays.

SOCIETY

Government

The new constitution provides for an executive branch headed by a prime minister with strong executive powers. The 448-seat parliament is dominated by the EPRDF, but opposition parties are also represented. Regional governments are based somewhat on ethnic groups, and Addis Ababa has a 92-seat city council. All citizens may vote at age 18.

Economy

Ethiopia's economy is based almost entirely (85–90 percent) on agricultural and animal husbandry, although only 12 percent of the land is arable. Most crops are used for the Ethiopians' basic subsistence. Coffee is the main cash crop, accounting for 60 percent of all export earnings. Other important crops include *teff* (a native grain), wheat, millet, pulse, and barley. Drought, soil erosion, and civil war have all contributed to the poor economy and periodic famines. Still, the country has the potential for self-sufficiency in grains and the development of vegetable and fruit crops. Improvements are already visible. In addition to coffee, Ethiopia exports animal hides.

The Ethiopia's Human Development Index (0.249) ranks it 161st out of 173 countries. Real gross domestic product per capita is $370, a figure that has only improved slightly in the last generation. These figures reflect the facts that most people do not earn an income (that is, they are subsistence farmers), and those that do earn an income do not have enough to meet their basic needs. The economy is naturally one of the most significant areas of focus for the new government. Ethiopians are skilled and industrious; they are fully capable of rebuilding their nation. The currency is the *birr* (E$).

Transportation and Communication

The general transportation system is not well developed. The cities have buses, which are often overcrowded, but many in the rural areas rely on animals (donkeys and camels) or walking for their transportation. Most roads are not paved. Taxis are available in Addis Ababa, some for fixed rates, some with negotiable rates. There is also a rail system. Ethiopian Airlines operates with relative efficiency. Communication systems are in place, but they are mostly for government use. One television station and four radio stations broadcast in the country.

Education

Education is not compulsory in Ethiopia, and the literacy rate is about 24 percent. It is higher for men than for women. Less than half of all school-aged children are enrolled in school. Until 1991 many children were fighting as soldiers in the civil war. About one-third of all students finish primary schooling, which begins at age seven, and go on for secondary school beginning at age thirteen. The average adult has completed about two full years of formal education.

Health

While some medical facilities are available in Addis Ababa, most Ethiopians do not have access to proper medical care. There is only one physician for approximately every 100,000 people. Life expectancy is between 51 and 54 years, and infant mortality is 106 per 1,000. Malnutrition and diseases such as meningitis, cholera, and yellow fever are common. Water is not potable. The United Nations and several countries have attempted to improve the conditions in Ethiopia through various programs, but long-lasting solutions will take time.

FOR THE TRAVELER

Passports and visas are required of U.S. citizens; a visa should be applied for well in advance. Expect to pay cash for all services and items; traveler's checks and credit cards are not generally accepted. Yellow fever vaccinations are recommended, and one should take precautions against malaria. Tourist information is available through the Ethiopian National Tourist Organization, PO Box 2183, Addis Abbaba, Ethiopia, and Ethiopian Airlines, 405 Lexington Avenue, New York, NY 10174; phone (212) 867–0095. You may also wish to contact the Chancery of Ethiopia, 2134 Kalorama Road NW, Washington, DC 20008; phone (202) 234–2881.

A *Culturgram* is a product of native commentary and original, expert analysis. Statistics are estimates and information is presented as a matter of opinion. While the editors strive for accuracy and detail, this document should not be considered strictly factual. It is a general introduction to culture, an initial step in building bridges of understanding between peoples. It may not apply to all peoples of the nation. You should therefore consult other sources for more information.

CULTURGRAM ™ '96

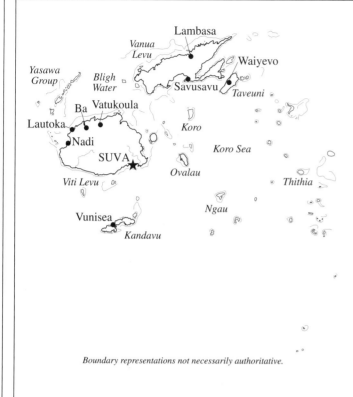

Boundary representations not necessarily authoritative.

Republic of
Fiji

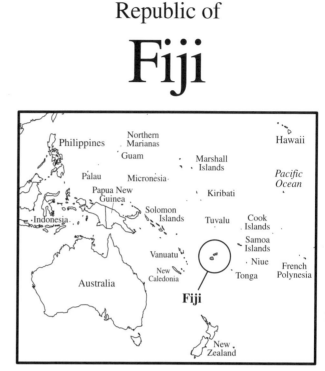

BACKGROUND

Land and Climate

Fiji is located in the southwestern Pacific, north of New Zealand. More than 300 islands make up Fiji but only about 110 are inhabited. Covering 7,054 square miles (18,270 square kilometers), Fiji's total size is about the same as Hawaii or just smaller than New Jersey. Three main islands, Viti Levu, Vanua Levu, and Taveuni, are home to the majority of the population. The larger Fijian islands are volcanic, mountainous, and surrounded by coral reefs. The windward sides are covered with dense tropical forests. The leeward sides consist of grassy plains that receive less rain. The climate is humid and tropical. The rainy season is from November to April, when violent hurricanes are possible. Annual temperatures change little and range from 72°F to 86°F (22–30°C).

History

The islands of Fiji were first settled some 3,500 years ago by what are now known as the Lapita people, perhaps from Asia. Various Pacific peoples migrated to the Fijian islands, which they called *Viti*; Western explorers used the Tongan word *Feejee* to name the islands and the people. Although the Dutch had a brief encounter with Fijians in 1643, it was Captain James Cook of England who spent more time with them in 1774. Later, trade vessels came for sandalwood, which was used in ornamental carving and cabinetmaking. The islands were known by many as the Cannibal Islands because of the Fijians' reputation as fierce warriors and ferocious cannibals.

After years of tribal warfare, Chief Ratu Cakobau converted to Christianity in 1854, united rival tribes under the new religion, ended cannibalism, and became King of Fiji in 1871.

Cakobau was aware of European competition for territory in the Pacific and offered to cede the islands to Great Britain (after the United States refused the same offer) in 1874. Britain brought in laborers from India, whose descendants now make up nearly half the population. Exactly 96 years to the day after cession to Britain, Fiji gained its independence (10 October 1970). Ratu Sir Kamisese Mara became the first prime minister and his Alliance Party (mostly ethnic Fijians) governed until 1987, when a coalition led by the National Federation Party (mostly ethnic Indians) won a majority in parliamentary elections.

Two weeks after the elections, however, General Sitiveni Rabuka led a military coup to restore control to native Fijians. The coup was halted because Britain's governor general (Queen Elizabeth's representative) assumed executive control and negotiated a settlement between the Indians and Fijians. Rabuka then staged a second coup, establishing a civilian government dominated by Fijians. Fiji was subsequently voted out of the Commonwealth by its member nations. Rabuka appointed Mara (the first prime minister in 1970) prime minister. A new constitution was ratified in 1990 that favors indigenous Fijians over Indians. It is a continuing source of tension between these two groups. General elections were held in 1992, and Rabuka was elected prime minister.

THE PEOPLE

Population

There are about 764,000 people in Fiji, a population that is growing at 1 percent annually. Relatively few people live in urban areas. There are only nine towns, and six of them are on the main island, Viti Levu. The two largest towns are Suva and Lautoka. Indigenous Fijians and Fijian Indians have nearly equal numbers, together forming 95 percent of the total population. The Indians are descendants of Asian Indians brought as laborers by the British in the 1800s to work on sugar plantations. They live mostly on Viti Levu. About 5 percent of the total population is made up of other Pacific Islanders, Chinese, and Europeans.

Language

English is the official language. Fijian and Hindustani are widely spoken. Fijian can be written in two different ways, one of which is more phonetic than the other. For instance, the letter "b" is pronounced with an "m" sound before it, as in the case of the town Ba. Its name can be written Ba or Mba, but it is pronounced MBAH. Also, a "q" is usually pronounced NGG. That is, *yaqona* is pronounced YANGGONA. In this text, most words are written in the more standard, less phonetic spelling. Hindustani is an Indian language. However, the Hindustani spoken in Fiji is called *Fiji Bat* or Fiji Talk and differs slightly from the Hindustani spoken in India. English spoken among the people often includes words and phrases from both Fijian and Hindustani and other languages.

Religion

Fijians are mostly Christian, belonging to various churches. Methodists and Roman Catholics predominate. Indians are either Hindu or Muslim and the Chinese are either Christian or Buddhist. There are also some Sikhs and Christian Indians. The people often celebrate festivals of other religions. Freedom of religion is guaranteed by the constitution. Religion plays a major role in the lives of all Fijians.

General Attitudes

Fijians are generous, friendly, and easygoing. Daily life in Fiji is relaxed and casual. Some call it the "Pacific Way." People enjoy life. The community is important, as is evident in community ceremonies, cooperative building projects, and community pride. The custom of *kerekere* dictates that a relative or neighbor can ask for something that is needed, and it must be willingly given without expectation of repayment. An exception is if the requested item was a gift from someone else, in which case the person does not have to give it away.

Although the Fijians have abandoned their tradition as fierce warriors for a more peaceful life, they remain proud of their cultural heritage and traditions. Ethnic tensions exist between Fijians and Indians. The two groups rarely mix and are political opponents. Indians often feel discriminated against by the Fijian government. They point to such inequalities as land ownership to argue their case. More than 80 percent of all land is owned by Fijian clans and Indians do not have access to it. These tensions have increased since 1987,

when Indians gained political power through elections and were then overthrown by the Fijian-dominated military.

Personal Appearance

Light, casual clothing is worn throughout the year, but public attire is fairly conservative (no bathing suits), especially for women. In traditional villages, women do not wear shorts or pants. Daily clothing for Fijian men and women is most often the *sulu*, a medium-to-long wraparound cloth made of colorful cotton. Businessmen, clergy, and civil servants (such as police officers) wear a tailored *sulu* made from suit material. This *sulu*, called a pocket *sulu*, is worn with a short-sleeved shirt and sometimes a tie. Indian men wear long pants and shirts. Indian women wear a *sari* (wraparound dress) or a *salwaar kameez* (pants with a matching, long tunic). Fashions in the larger urban areas are changing due to Western influence.

CUSTOMS AND COURTESIES

Greetings

The most common way to say hello among indigenous Fijians is *Bula!* (pronounced MBOOLA, meaning health). For formal meetings, a handshake and a more formal *Ni Sa Bula!* are used. The Fijian handshake can last a little while, as the greeters continue polite conversation before they let go. Fijian Indians often use shorter handshakes and say *Namaste* when they greet. Fijians are friendly and will go out of their way to greet whomever they meet. When passing a rural Fijian house, a person is greeted with *Mai kana* (Come eat). In this casual society, it is common to address most people by their first names. When people are related or have an established relationship, they may greet by reference to that relationship rather than using their first names. For example, close friends may address each other by *itau* (a traditional friendship), and male cousins might use *tavale* (cousin). Chiefs are addressed by the title *Ratu* before their first names.

Gestures

Among Fijians, tilting the head down and avoiding eye contact while speaking to someone shows respect. Staring is offensive. One indicates agreement by raising the eyebrows, closing the mouth, and making an "mm-mm" sound (similar to a sound that would mean "no" in the United States). A "thumbs up" gesture means "good" or "okay." Pointing directly at someone while speaking to them is considered rude. Standing with hands on hips is thought to be aggressive or brash. Pointing the bottom of one's foot at another person is considered impolite. Among Fijians, it is especially offensive to touch someone's head (except for a child's). Beckoning is done by waving all fingers of the hand with the palm facing down. Physical displays of affection, even between married couples, are frowned upon. A custom called *cobo* (pronounced THOMBO) is used when accepting a gift, presenting *yaqona*, or excusing oneself when reaching above a person's head. It is done by clapping cupped hands three or more times.

Visiting

Visiting is an important part of social relations. Most visiting is done unannounced and guests are welcome.

It is customary to remove one's shoes when entering a home. Sitting cross-legged on a mat-covered floor is common in a Fijian home, but Indian homes have furniture. A chief or guest sits in a place of honor. It is impolite to stand higher than those who are sitting, so one takes care to also be seated or to walk in a stooped position when others are seated. The people of Fiji are hospitable; they enjoy sharing a visitor's company and visits may last a long time. Refreshments are nearly always offered, including tea, juice, or food. It is impolite to refuse them. Instead, one accepts the offering and says *Vinaka* or *Dhananbaad*, the respective Fijian and Hindustani words for "Thank you."

An important symbol of social relations is *yaqona*, which is made from the root and lower stem of a shrub in the pepper family. The powdered root, when combined with water, is Fiji's national drink. It is sometimes called *kava*. It may be offered to guests as a special sign of goodwill. The bitter-tasting drink numbs the tongue and, drunk in large enough amounts, can bring a mild sense of well-being. *Yaqona* is used to mark special occasions and end disputes, and it is drunk at all official ceremonies. Both ethnic Fijians and Indians use the drink socially. *Yaqona* is prepared in a *tanoa* (a special wooden bowl) and drunk from a *bilo* (coconut shell). When a stranger enters a Fijian village, he seeks out the chief or village headman to ask for permission to enter and visit, and is expected to present some unpounded *yaqona* to him.

Eating

Traditionally, neither Fijians nor Indians used eating utensils, but spoons and forks are becoming more common in urban areas. In Fijian villages, breakfast consists of tea drunk from tin bowls and possibly rice or any leftovers from the previous night's dinner. For all meals, Fijians spread a cloth on the mat-covered floor, sit cross-legged, pray, pass a bowl of water around for washing hands, and eat from tin plates and bowls. The water bowl is again passed after the meal. Women and girls usually eat after the men and boys. Food is shared in Fijian villages, due not only to communal obligations, but also to the fact that most homes do not have refrigerators to keep leftovers. For large feasts and special meals, food is still cooked in the traditional manner in a *lovo* (ground oven).

Indian homes generally have a small wash basin in the dining room for washing hands. The right hand is used to eat. Indian meals consist of curries, rice *dhal* (lentil soup), and *roti* (round, flat bread used for scooping up the curry). Tipping is not expected in restaurants.

LIFESTYLE

Family

The Fijian people are family oriented and the father acts as head of the home. Families can be large. The elderly are usually cared for by their children. Villages are composed of families that form clans or *mataqali* (land-holding units). This extended family system has a collective or communal way of living. *Kerekere* plays an important role in family relationships. Subsistence chores are shared between men and women. Men are engaged in spear fishing, gardening and construction, while women do line and small net fishing, as well as the cooking, weaving of *ibe* (pandanus mats) and collecting wild food.

The traditional Fijian home is called a *bure*. It is usually built of local hardwoods, a thatched roof, and woven floor covers. The four doors are usually kept open for circulation and are used by different people. Visitors enter through the front door, except for the village chief, who enters at the side. A *bure* is one large room and is usually built by the entire community. Other than beds and sometimes a dresser, furniture is not considered necessary. Cooking is done in a smaller, separate structure.

Indians usually live in furnished tin, cement, or wood homes. Urban dwellers of any ethnic group often live in Western-style homes. Some rural Fijians have adopted the tin, cement, and wood homes.

Dating and Marriage

Dating is traditionally nonexistent in Fijian culture, but Western influences are changing society so that dating is found in some areas. Affection is not shown in public. The ethnic Fijian man chooses his own wife and a grand wedding ceremony is held, accompanied by a *solevu* (a great feast). In high chiefly Fijian families, the parents must still approve their children's future spouses. Indian parents have customarily arranged their children's marriages, but this practice is also changing with Western influence.

Diet

The mainstays of the Fijian diet are boiled taro and cassava, starchy roots that can be grown in the family garden. There are some leafy vegetables and many tropical fruits (papayas, mangoes, pineapples, bananas). Many dishes are prepared in *lolo* (coconut milk). Seafood, chicken, pork, and beef are all eaten in Fiji. Foods are rarely deep-fried, but are steamed, boiled, or roasted instead. Indian cuisine is often made with curry and is spicy. *Roti* is a daily Indian staple. Hindus do not eat beef; Muslims don't eat pork. Many Indians are vegetarians.

Recreation

Fijians are sports enthusiasts. The most popular team sports are rugby, soccer, and cricket. Fiji's national rugby team is among the best in the world. Visitors enjoy the beaches, golf, many water sports (snorkeling, wind surfing, scuba diving, etc.), and game fishing. Festivals are also a time of recreation for many people. The traditional Fijian game of *veicaqe moli* (kick the orange) is played by women in villages during January to celebrate the new year. The winning team must present the losers with clothes, while the losers are responsible for mixing and serving *yaqona* to the winners that night.

Holidays

Official public holidays include New Year's Day, Easter, the Queen of England's Birthday (13 June), a Bank Holiday (1 August), Fiji Day (or Independence Day, 10 October), the Prophet Muhammad's Birthday (26 October), Prince Charles's Birthday (14 November), Christmas, and Boxing Day (26 December). Boxing Day comes from a British tradition where gifts were presented to tradesmen and service persons. It is now a day for relaxing and visiting friends and family. There are also many festivals throughout the year to celebrate different events. The largest, held in Suva for a full week in August, is the Hibiscus Festival. Also popular is *Diwali*, the Hindu Festival of Lights, held in either October or November.

Commerce

Businesses are open Monday through Friday, usually 8:00 A.M. to 4:30 P.M., with an hour break for lunch. Restaurants and stores remain open during lunch, but are closed Saturday after 1:00 p.m. All stores close on Sunday, with the exception of some restaurants that are permitted to remain open. Nearly all businesses in Fiji are owned by Indians and Chinese.

SOCIETY

Government

Fiji's government is comprised of three branches. The executive branch consists of a prime minister, a cabinet, the Great Council of Chiefs (highest ranking members of the traditional Fijian chief system), and a president. The president serves as chief of state, but the prime minister is head of government. Parliament has two houses, a 34-seat Senate and a 70-seat House of Representatives. Senators are appointed; 24 seats are reserved for Fijians. Representatives are technically elected (the last vote was in 1994), but 37 seats are reserved for Fijians and 27 for Indians. The two main political parties are the Fijian Political Party and the National Federation Party (mostly Indians). A number of smaller parties operate, but have little power. The judicial branch is headed by a Supreme Court. A new constitution is expected by 1997.

Economy

Subsistence farming is the key economic activity for most Fijians. Primary cash crops include bananas, rice, taro, cassava, pineapples, coconuts, and copra (a coconut product). Until recently, sugar was the most important industry and major source of revenue. Tourism is gaining rapidly, however, and now equals sugar in economic importance. Fiji also exports ginger, gold, lumber, and processed fish (mostly tuna); it has started to manufacture clothing and furniture on a small scale.

The economy suffered dramatically following the 1987 coups, but it regained its strength by 1990 and has been growing at 1–3 percent annually. Fiji's Human Development Index (0.787) ranks it 59th out of 173 nations. Real gross domestic product per capita is $4,858, which has more than doubled in the last generation. While poverty still affects up to 30 percent of rural families, these figures indicate the younger generation can expect more economic opportunities than the adult generation. The currency is the Fijian dollar (F$).

Transportation and Communication

Most people travel by bus (open-air) because service is regular and inexpensive. Taxis and private automobiles are also used but are more expensive. Relatively few people own cars. Following the British tradition, traffic travels on the left side of the road. A ferry service and two airlines provide travel between more populated islands. Fiji has a modern communications system, with satellite links to other countries. There are about 60,000 phones in the country. There are eight radio stations, which broadcast in English, Fijian, and Hindustani. Limited television broadcasts, now available in Suva and Nadi, are slowly expanding. There are two daily English newspapers, a weekly Hindustani paper, and two weekly Fijian papers.

Education

For the past 15 years, the government has worked to provide free education for grades one through eight, and it hopes to extend this in the future. Many schools are operated by religious groups such as the Catholics, Hindus, Latter-day Saints (Mormons), Methodists, and Muslims. Each school has its own uniform, and most accept both boys and girls. The University of the South Pacific is a joint effort at higher education by several small Pacific Island nations. It receives substantial funding from Fiji's government, and one of its many campuses is located in Suva, the capital. Fiji also has a medical school, an Institute of Technology, and a College of Agriculture. The literacy rate is 86 percent.

Health

There is usually very little disease in Fiji and the water supply is safe to drink. An influenza epidemic occurred after a cyclone in 1993. The government provides most medical care through local clinics. The infant mortality rate is 18 per 1,000; life expectancy averages between 63 and 67 years. Life expectancy rates are rising steadily and infant mortality rates are falling.

FOR THE TRAVELER

Due to the general lack of disease, no inoculations are required for travel to Fiji. U.S. travelers must present a valid passport and proof of onward passage upon arrival to receive a 30-day visa. There is a F$20 departure tax. To use electrical outlets, dual-voltage small appliances or a voltage converter and a plug adaptor are necessary. Taxi fare is reasonable and fixed, but one should agree on the price before taking longer trips. Water is safe in hotels and urban areas, but precautions should be taken in rural areas. For information on travel opportunities in Fiji, contact the Fiji Visitors Bureau, 5777 West Century Boulevard, Suite 220, Los Angeles, CA 90045. You may also wish to contact the Embassy of Fiji, 2233 Wisconsin Avenue NW, Suite 240, Washington, DC 20007.

A *Culturgram* is a product of native commentary and original, expert analysis. Statistics are estimates and information is presented as a matter of opinion. While the editors strive for accuracy and detail, this document should not be considered strictly factual. It is a general introduction to culture, an initial step in building bridges of understanding between peoples. It may not apply to all peoples of the nation. You should therefore consult other sources for more information.

CULTURGRAM ™ '96

Gabon

(Gabonese Republic)

Boundary representations not necessarily authoritative.

BACKGROUND

Land and Climate

Gabon lies on Africa's west coast and straddles the equator. It is about the same size as Colorado, covering 103,347 square miles (267,670 square kilometers). It comprises the drainage basin of the Ogooué River. About three-fourths of the country is low-lying equatorial rain forest, which is harvested for timber. Forests are dotted with small towns and villages. Although the Gabonese practice a sort of slash-and-burn agriculture, their small population has thus far left the forests mostly intact. It is only the larger-scale logging that can threaten the virgin forests. In 1995, the government implemented controls to ensure logging is conducted only at sustainable levels. The east is slightly higher in elevation and is covered with grasslands. Gabon's climate is moderate in the dry seasons, May to September and December to February, and hot in the rainy seasons, September to December and February to May. Libreville has an average temperature in January of 80°F (27°C) and in July of 75°F (24°C). It receives about 99 inches (251 centimeters) of rain each year.

History

The earliest inhabitants of Gabon were the Pygmies. Migrations of Bantu peoples (A.D. 1000) resulted in Bantu domination of the area. The southern-most part of Gabon was ruled by the powerful Bantu Bakongo empire, centered at the mouth of the Zaire River. When the Portuguese arrived in the 1400s, the rest of Gabon was made up of small migratory villages of hunting and farming Bantus. Soon, the export of slaves and ivory to Europe began. These exports were replaced with timber and rubber by the early 1800s. Trade was dominated by coastal peoples who eventually allied themselves with France. Interior people first resisted French colonization, but Western explorers, traders, and missionaries opened the area in the 1800s to eventual incorporation into French Equatorial Africa (present-day Gabon, Congo, the Central African Republic, Cameroon, and Chad).

Gabon was not developed much during the colonial era because of its small population and dense forests. This minimized contact with colonial rulers. Independence came in 1960. Borders were based on French Equatorial Africa's artificial internal boundaries rather than natural ethnic groupings. The first president of Gabon was Leon M'ba. M'ba died in 1967 and was succeeded by Albert-Bernard Bongo, who has been reelected to several successive seven-year terms.

Bongo instituted a relatively tolerant one-party rule that lasted until 1990. In the 1970s, Gabon joined OPEC and Bongo adopted Islam, changing his first name to El Hadj Omar. Protests and strikes in 1990–91 forced the president to loosen political restrictions and to legalize opposition parties. Gabon's subsequent transition to multiparty democracy has been slow. In the 1991 free elections, over 40 parties ran for seats in the national assembly. Bongo's party won a majority. Multiparty presidential elections were held in 1993, and Bongo was reelected president.

THE PEOPLE

Population

The current population of Gabon is about 1.1 million, but an accurate count is not available. All Gabonese, except Pygmies, belong to one of Africa's many Bantu-speaking groups. Gabon's largest is the Fang, comprising 30 percent of the population. Others include Eshira, Adouma, Mbeda, Bakota, Omyene, Okande, and Bateke. There are more than 40 different ethnic groups, but most are small. The country is also home to many immigrants, especially from other French-speaking African nations, who work as shopkeepers, tailors, dressmakers, teachers, cabdrivers, and laborers. A large number of Western workers manage many of Gabon's export industries. Gabon's largest city and capital, Libreville, is home to about one-third of the total population. Other cities are Port-Gentil (100,000), Franceville (30,000), and Lambaréné (20,000). More than half of the people live in towns and villages.

Language

French is Gabon's official language. Nearly all publishing and broadcasting occurs in French, and it is the most commonly heard language in cities. Taught in schools, it is the only language the Gabonese have in common, and basically the only written language. Local languages are oral. Most Gabonese speak both French and their ethnic group's native tongue. People are usually not fluent in another ethnic group's language, even though many different groups live close to one another. In the north, Fang is more common than French.

Religion

About 60 percent of the population is Roman Catholic, 20 percent is Protestant, and the remaining people practice local animist beliefs or are Muslim. Most Muslims are immigrants from other countries. Going to church is a popular social occasion, especially for women and girls. Most Christian clergy are from the West, but meetings are influenced by African music and are conducted in the local language by village elders. In their daily lives, people mix local beliefs with Christianity, often turning to tradition in times of emergency, rather than to Western religion.

General Attitudes

The Gabonese are generally polite and kind. Although they get loud and angry in disputes, problems are quickly resolved and hard feelings rarely remain. The Gabonese are considered outspoken and even argumentative among some West African neighbors. Certain ethnic groups do not often say "please" and "thank you" because there is no tradition for these words in their languages. Regardless of whether the words are used, kindness and consideration are acknowledged and favors are usually repaid.

The Gabonese tend to be fatalistic—accepting life as it is. They see themselves less as individuals and more as members of a family (including the extended family and, in rural areas, the village), then as part of an ethnic group, and finally as Gabonese and Africans. They are proud of Gabon's accomplishments since independence and of its status as a relatively prosperous African country.

Personal Appearance

The Gabonese wear both Western and African clothing. All people like to be neatly groomed and dressed as well as possible. Modesty and cleanliness are important. The Gabonese borrow their fashions from neighboring countries. Women like elaborate, braided hairstyles—some sticking straight out, others in intricate loops, and others tied in bunches—and they change them often. Women might wear loose-fitting dresses made of colorful, embroidered fabric, or a colorful *pagne* (wraparound skirt) with a blouse.

Urban men might wear Western suits, or more often just shirts and pants. Muslims might also wear a *boubou*, a loose-fitting, long-sleeved, embroidered cotton shirt extending to mid-calf that is worn over loose-fitting pants. Fabrics are colorful and designs often bold. The youth wear shorts or other casual attire.

CUSTOMS AND COURTESIES

Greetings

The Gabonese shake hands and smile each time they meet, even if several times a day. If one's hand is dirty, a closed fist is extended (palm down) so the greeter can "shake" the wrist or forearm. Urban friends might hug and brush alternating cheeks while "kissing" the air. In small groups, each individual is greeted. In larger gatherings, one can raise both hands to the group and say, *Bonjour tout le monde* (Hello, everyone). People of the same sex, especially men, often hold hands while talking or walking. It is improper, especially in rural areas, for members of the opposite sex to do this. Rural women might clasp forearms when greeting. Older rural men often shake another person's hand with both of his hands.

Urban greetings include the French *Bonjour* (Good day) and *Bonsoir* (Good evening). Common throughout Gabon is the Fang *Mbolo* (Hello). Greetings include asking about one's family and health. Older people may be addressed as *mama* or *papa*. People of about the same age may be called by their first name or *mon frére* or *ma soeur* (my brother or my sister). At work, *monsieur* (Mr.), *madame* (Ms. or Mrs.), or a title is used with the last name.

Gestures

A closed fist with the thumb extended up means "good." Rubbing the thumb against the index finger means "money." Hitting a raised, closed left fist with the right palm open means *beaucoup* (many, much). Hooking one's right thumbnail behind a front tooth and snapping it to make a loud clicking sound indicates a statement is true. One may express enthusiasm by shaking the wrist rapidly to make the fingers slap together. A person points by quickly extending puckered lips. "Come here" is indicated by holding the hand vertical, palm facing out, and waving the fingers. A taxi is hailed by waving an extended arm, palm down, from shoulder to waist. Muslims object to contact with one's left hand. It is impolite to touch someone's head.

Visiting

Visiting is common after work or on weekends in urban areas, and anytime one is home in villages. Most rural socializing takes place Sunday after morning church services. Hospitality is important, and guests are often offered food, especially if a meal is in progress. A drink is always offered and an empty glass is quickly refilled. A guest who is not hungry should at least taste offered food. Guests are not usually expected to bring gifts, but friends might bring food or drink. In urban areas, a new acquaintance might make a vague appointment

("I'll drop by next week") before visiting, but most visits are unplanned. Rural people might invite passing friends in for a drink; it is impolite to refuse, even if one has something else to do. Rural women socialize in the *cuisine* (kitchen), where much of daily life usually takes place. Kitchens are generally separate from the living quarters (*salon*), as open cooking fires are often used. The *salon* consists of a living room and bedrooms. Rural men often socialize and work together in open-air structures called *corps de gars*.

When guests are invited, promptness is unimportant and time is a formality. The favor of an invitation is customarily returned at a later date. It is polite to knock before entering a home. If the door is open, the visitor imitates the knocking sound by saying *kokoko*. One does not enter without announcing one's presence.

Eating

An urban breakfast, eaten around 7:00 A.M., may include bread, croissants, butter, marmalade, eggs, yogurt, and coffee. Lunch might be around noon; dinner is after dark, even as late as 9:00 P.M. Most people use utensils, but certain foods are eaten with the hand.

In villages, breakfast may consist of leftovers from the day before, but adults might also have bread and coffee or hot chocolate. Adults are usually working around lunchtime, so children returning from school eat a light meal or leftovers. Adults also eat light; they might harvest fruit for a snack. The main meal is eaten in the evening (usually after 7:00 P.M.) when work is done. Snacks are eaten throughout the day. People often eat with the right hand or a spoon. Rural Gabonese men and older boys usually eat in the *salon*, with women and young children eating in the *cuisine*. The father often has his own bowl. Small families might eat together in the *cuisine*, with adults sharing a bowl and children sharing one. Guests are given a separate bowl.

LIFESTYLE

Family

The Gabonese feel great loyalty toward family members. Family obligations require the Gabonese to extend hospitality (food, lodging, and expenses) to any member of the extended family who asks for it, even for a prolonged period of time. Traditionally, an extended family lives in a large compound of several buildings, usually sharing cooking, child care, and other chores. A man, his wife (or wives), their children, and often cousins or other relatives live in the compound. A man with more than one wife provides each with a separate home and kitchen whenever possible. Since this is expensive, the trend is to have only one wife. Still, an unmarried man may have children by more than one woman, and married men often have mistresses.

A village functions as an extension of the family. Villagers who move to cities have a spirit of unity with fellow villagers they meet there. They make regular visits back home; students might return on weekends or holidays to work and visit.

Dating and Marriage

Western-style dating occurs mostly among the urban educated. Rural courtship involves the boy visiting the girl at her parents' home. An engaged couple may date outside the home. The family often has great influence in the choice of a marriage partner. Girls are sometimes promised at a very young age, although the wedding does not take place (if at all) until after puberty. A groom must often give gifts (*dot*) to the bride's family when they get engaged and when they marry. The Gabonese generally marry within their ethnic group, but outside of their village to avoid marrying relatives. Women are often encouraged to have a child or two before marriage to prove fertility. These children are often raised by the woman's mother and are not taken into marriage. If a marriage fails, the *dot* must be repaid and children born in wedlock remain with the father.

Diet

The most widely grown food is cassava (*manioc*). A typical meal consists of either plantain (boiled and mashed) or *bâton de manioc*, a dough-like paste made from cassava. It is served with meat or fish in urban areas, and with fresh meat among villagers that have had a successful hunt. Imported sardines or locally caught small fish might be eaten when meat is unavailable. The main course is often prepared as a stew in peanut butter or palm oil sauce. Hot peppers (*piment*) are frequently used. A green-leaf vegetable, cut into strips and boiled, is usually served. Water is the most common drink, but beer is also popular.

Yams, taro, peanuts, and corn are grown in Gabon. Coffee, cocoa, sugarcane, and palm oil are produced for commercial purposes. There are many tropical fruits: papayas, bananas, pineapples, mangoes, avocados, and *atangas* (a violet, bitter fruit about the size of a golf ball). *Atangas* are often boiled until soft and then spread on bread or rice. Some non-Gabonese call this fruit "bush butter."

In remote areas, people hunt wild animals (gazelles, anteaters, snakes, crocodiles, boars, etc.) and grow food for themselves. Insects, like termites, are not an uncommon part of the diet.

Recreation

In the capital, Western forms of recreation are common, including movies, dancing, and swimming. Visiting is the most common leisure activity everywhere. Soccer is Gabon's most popular sport. Basketball is also popular. Television is available in much of the country. Dancing to drums and local music is common and usually a part of weddings, religious ceremonies, and other occasions. A traditional strategy game for two players called *songo* (in Fang) is popular. It is played on a wooden board with pebbles or seeds. Tag and tug-of-war are also enjoyed.

Holidays

Official public holidays are given for major Christian holy days, including *Pâques* (Easter), *Pentecôte* (Pentecost), *Toussaint* (All Saints' Day, 1 November), and *Noël* (Christmas). The Islamic holy days of *Fin du Ramadan* (a feast at the end of *Ramadan*, a month of fasting) and *Fête de Mouton* (a feast to honor Abraham's willingness to sacrifice his son) are observed according to their dates on the lunar calendar. *Jour de l'An* (New Year's Day) and *Fête du Travail* (May Day, 1 May) are celebrated. *Fête National* commemorates independence on 17 August.

Commerce

A few minutes of greetings and small talk precede discussions of business. Businesses generally open between 7:00 and

9:00 A.M. and close for lunch at noon. Lunch lasts until 2:00 or 3:00 P.M. to allow for a break from the hot weather. Businesses are then open until sometime between 5:00 and 7:00 P.M. Many offices open on Saturday morning. Small food shops are open through lunch, late in the evening, and on weekends. In these shops, and in open-air markets, prices are negotiable. A majority of small and medium-sized companies and shops are owned by non-Gabonese (usually from other West African countries).

SOCIETY

Government

Gabon is a multiparty presidential democracy with a president, a prime minister, and a 120-seat national assembly (*Assemblé National*). Everyone over age 18 must vote. To limit the president's traditional dominance, his term has been reduced from seven years to five, the national assembly and prime minister have more constitutional authority, and the government is becoming more balanced. Major parties include the Gabonese Democratic Party, two factions of the National Recovery Movement, and the Gabonese Party for Progress.

Economy

During the last century, Gabon's major exports were *okoumé* (a hardwood) and soft woods used to make plywood. Timber exports continue, but they have been exceeded by oil exports since the 1970s. Manganese and uranium are also exported. Export industries are mostly owned by Western companies.

Because of the value of Gabon's exports, the country has one of the highest per-capita incomes in Africa. However, most wealth is in the hands of a small minority and the average person does not necessarily earn a decent income. Real gross domestic product per capita is $3,498, a figure that has almost tripled in the last generation. Gabon's Human Development Index (0.525) ranks it 114th out of 173 nations. These figures indicate the country has the potential to extend economic opportunities to its people.

Progress is hindered by the instability of oil prices, the lower demand for uranium, and a 1994 currency devaluation by France. The currency (*CFA franc*) is tied to the French *franc* and France cut the value of the *CFA franc* in half. Gabon's government is trying to diversify its economy to reduce dependence on oil; diversification would provide more people with jobs, too. Most people (65 percent) are involved in subsistence agriculture. Thirty percent work in industry or commerce.

Transportation and Communication

Roads between major cities are not paved and are difficult to travel during the rainy seasons. A domestic airline provides service to many areas, but flights are expensive. The TransGabonais railway (one of Bongo's major accomplishments) provides daily service between Libreville and Franceville. Only government officials and the wealthy have access to private cars. Animals are not used for transportation, and bicycles and motorcycles are rare, so people walk a lot. They may get from one town to another by way of an *occasion* (bush taxi), which is often crowded. Passengers pay a commonly understood fare and take their luggage, food, and animals with them. Goods are transported by rail to Franceville and by truck or air everywhere else, making imports much more expensive in the interior than in the capital. The post office provides reliable mail and phone service between many locations. Mail moves slowly because it is all sorted at the capital, regardless of its origin or destination.

Education

Gabon follows the French system of education, with students attending school for up to 13 years and ending with a *bac* (baccalaureate) exam. Free education is guaranteed to all, even though the government reduces education spending when oil revenues fall. The system has produced a literacy rate of 61 percent, high by African standards. In the past, many schools were run by churches. But the government, which sets curriculum and appoints teachers, is replacing cleric administrators with government officials.

Nearly all children are enrolled in and finish primary school, which lasts six years (to age 11). Only one-fifth continue on for seven years of secondary school. Students who pass the *bac* may attend one of Gabon's two universities free of charge. Living expenses are paid for those with passing grades. College graduates often work for the government.

Health

Gabon has a relatively good national health care system. Doctors' services are free, but medicine is not. Small towns have clinics, although sometimes not well equipped, and cities have hospitals. People in villages must travel to the nearest town or city for medical care. Traditional methods of healing are popular. Villagers might visit a local "healer" as well as, or instead of, a town doctor. Serious medical problems can only be treated in Libreville. The average life expectancy is between 53 and 58 years. Infant mortality is estimated to be 94 per 1,000. In 1913, French humanitarian Albert Schweitzer built a hospital in Lambaréné and expanded it in 1952. It still functions and is supported by the government.

FOR THE TRAVELER

U.S. citizens need a valid passport and visa to visit Gabon. There are few tourists in Gabon; most foreigners are expatriate workers and their families. Hotels and restaurants are expensive. A vaccination is required for yellow fever and recommended for cholera. Take precautions against malaria. Water is safe to drink in cities, but one should have only bottled drinks elsewhere. Avoid eating unpeeled fruits and vegetables, and eat only well-cooked foods. Plug and voltage adapters are necessary to use North American appliances. For more information, contact the Embassy of the Gabonese Republic, 2034 20th Street NW, Washington, DC 20009; phone (202) 797–1000.

CULTURGRAM '96

Republic of

The Gambia

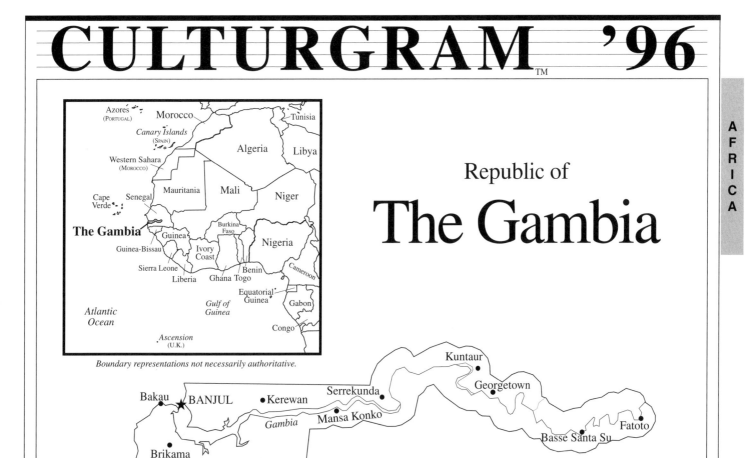

Boundary representations not necessarily authoritative.

BACKGROUND

Land and Climate

The Gambia is located on the coast of West Africa, about 10 degrees latitude north of the equator. It is one of Africa's smallest countries, occupying a narrow strip of land on both sides of the River Gambia, about 400 kilometers (250 miles) in length. Covering 4,363 square miles (11,300 square kilometers), The Gambia is slightly larger than Maryland and is surrounded on three sides by Senegal. The River Gambia provides excellent transport from the Atlantic coast to points inland. The capital, Banjul, is an island that is connected to the mainland by bridge. Surrounding Banjul are various urban areas that collectively make up the *Kombos*.

The Gambia experiences two seasons: a humid, rainy season from June to October, and a dry season from November to mid-June. The average daily high temperature is 88°F (31°C); nights are hotter in the summer than during the rest of the year. Temperatures are somewhat cooler upriver.

History

The Gambia was once part of various large African empires, including the Serrahule and Mandinka empires of the fifth and sixth centuries. The country's modern history is closely linked to the River Gambia. It is believed the Portuguese were the first Europeans to navigate the river in 1455, but it was not recognized as a European possession until 1783 when the British claimed the river and its surrounding territory. The British remained in the country until 1965 when The Gambia became an independent state and a member of the (British) Commonwealth. In 1971, the country became a republic and enjoyed several years of relative peace and multiparty democracy under the leadership of President Dawda K. Jawara.

In July 1981, political turmoil led to an attempted coup while Jawara was in England for Prince Charles's wedding. The coup ended when Senegalese troops intervened at Jawara's request. As a result of Senegal's involvement, the two countries accepted an old idea and joined together in closer union, establishing a Senegambia confederation in September 1981. Close diplomatic relations and the loose confederation continued until 1989 when Senegal withdrew. Jawara, who had been reelected several times and was considered personally popular, faced strong opposition in the 1992 elections, but still won with a majority.

In July 1994, young army officer Lieutenant Yahya Jammeh seized power in a bloodless coup, forcing President Jawara to flee to Senegal. Jammeh suspended the constitution, banned political activity, and detained top military and government officials. Although he promised a swift return to civilian rule—as soon as corruption had been cleaned up—his government quickly settled in for a long tenure. Western nations withdrew aid, business (international trade) suffered from the uncertainty, and Jammeh announced in October 1994 that he would remain in power until 1998. Gambians did not welcome the news, despite Jammeh's promises of a new constitution, a free market economy, a crackdown on crime and corruption, and a return to democracy by December 1998.

THE PEOPLE
Population
The current population is estimated at 959,000. The Gambia is inhabited by five major ethnic groups: the Mandinka (42 percent), Fulani or Fula (18), Wolof (16), Jola (10), and the Serrahule (9). About 5 percent of the population is comprised of a community of Europeans, Americans, Mauritanians, Lebanese, Syrians, and people from neighboring countries.

The Mandinkas are descendants of the Mali Empire, whereas the Fulanis migrated from the Guinea highlands. Larger Mandinka settlements are found upriver (east of the capital), but a few are found in the Banjul area. Wolofs are from the Senegambia area; it is believed that they and the Jolas have always lived in the region. The Serrahules, who are basically traders and live in the Banjul area, migrated from Mali and Mauritania. About 80 percent of Gambians live in rural areas. The largest cities are Serrekunda, Banjul, Brikama, and Bakau, a suburb of Banjul, respectively.

Language
Although English is the official language, most Gambians speak Wolof and/or Mandinka on a daily basis. Official business and school instruction is conducted in English. Most Gambians who have attended school speak English, and Gambians with contacts in Senegal also speak French. French is encouraged in the high school curriculum. Wolof is the commercial language. Informal conversations are conducted in the respective local languages, which include Fula, Creole, Jola, Serere, and Serrehule. None of these languages is written, although members of the religious elite sometimes use Arabic characters to "write" in Wolof or Mandinka.

Religion
About 85 percent of Gambians are Muslim, 13 percent are Christian, and the remaining 2 percent are animist. Religious differences are not emphasized and there is a lot of intermarriage and tolerance between people with different backgrounds. Religious freedom is guaranteed. Most Christians live in Banjul, Bakau, and Serrekunda, whereas Muslims are found throughout the country.

Muslims basically believe in *Allah* as God and Muhammad as his prophet. They accept Jesus as a prophet, but not as the son of God, as Christians believe. Muslims pray five times daily, give alms to the poor, and try to make a pilgrimage to Makkah, Saudi Arabia, at least once in their lifetime. Muslims also fast each year during the month of *Ramadan*, going without food or drink from sunrise to sunset each day. Most entertainment is temporarily suspended during *Ramadan* because of the fast, which commemorates *Allah's* revelation of the *Qur'an* to Muhammad.

General Attitudes
Gambians are generally self-confident, outgoing, and positive about life. They are usually open and hospitable toward strangers because sharing and openness are valued over secrecy and individualism. People eat and spend what they have today, hoping that Allah will provide for tomorrow. Most lead lives of great simplicity.

Gambians are proud of their heritage, but many are also curious about Western civilization. Westerners are often approached by young people interested in going to a Western nation. Most Gambians are pleased to host international guests; this is known as *Tarranga*. The Gambia's social value system includes a belief in strong family bonds, honesty, friendliness, sharing, respect, and communal effort. These values are changing as Western ones are introduced. For example, elders (especially those with gray hair) are traditionally considered wise and irreproachable—one should not speak boldly to elders, but rather listen carefully to their advice. Yet the Western concept of children standing up to their parents has led some Gambians to do the same, and it is now not uncommon to see a child talk back to a parent.

Time is perceived differently in The Gambia than in the West. Gambians prefer to take their time with activities. Appointment times are given in general terms ("around lunchtime"). Further, if something cannot be done today, it will be done tomorrow or the next day. This attitude is not as prevalent in farming communities, since work must be done according to the seasons.

Personal Appearance
Most Gambians value neatness. Shorts are only worn by children up to the high school level. Men usually wear dress pants and shirts. Many people mix Western and African clothing (Western pants with an African shirt, for example). Some men may also wear an "ambassador suit" (also called a safari suit). Suits and ties are common in offices, whereas school children wear uniforms.

While most older women wear a traditional colorful dress called a *Deppeh* or *Grandmbuba*, older men wear *Haftans* (tailored, long robes) or *Warambas* (shorter, more flowing robes). Younger women often wear a *Dagit* (skirt and blouse outfit).

CUSTOMS AND COURTESIES
Greetings
It is important in The Gambia to greet people before starting a conversation. Even formal business is not conducted without greeting the participants. A handshake and the greeting process are usually initiated by the younger person. The initiator follows the handshake with *Salama lay kum* (May peace be upon you), to which a person responds *Wal lay kumma salam* (May it be upon you, too). When greeting an elder, one may start by saying the elder person's first name once and his last name several times. As part of a greeting, inquiries are made about the individuals' health and that of their families. Greetings may last a minute or two. If a girl greets an elder, she might shake hands, but she may also dip her knees toward the ground to show respect. Traditionally, the girl would actually kneel, but the gesture is more of a curtsy today. Boys do not kneel or curtsy when they greet elders.

A person of the same age group as one's parents is greeted as "mother," "aunt," "father," or "uncle," regardless of their relation to the greeter; these titles are combined with the first names (Aunt Marie). This greeting is especially common in and near Banjul, Serrekunda, and other cities. In some other towns, especially in the east, the Mandinka greeting *Summo lay* (How are people at your house?), is common. The customary response is *Ibbi jay* (They are fine; they are there).

The Wolof also use *Na ka nga def* (How are you?) and respond *Ma ngi fi rek* (I am alright; I am here).

Gestures

To beckon, Gambians wave all fingers inward with the palm facing down. The left hand is avoided for most activities (shaking hands, passing items, eating), but it is used to shake hands with someone departing on a long trip as a sign of wishing a safe journey. Direct eye contact with older people is disrespectful. The index finger is a sign of good luck and safety. For instance, a Gambian might dip it in food to taste before eating—it is believed this can prevent food poisoning. Dipping the finger is also a substitute for saying prayers before a meal.

While eating on the streets is uncommon for adults, people might eat peanuts or oranges sold at street stands. Children might eat on the street and elders may chew kola nuts or bitter kola. Kola nuts are round and have a caffeine effect; bitter kola is elongated and bitter, but is not a stimulant. When one yawns, one must cover the mouth and then touch the forehead. Burping after a meal is not rude; it is a positive comment on the food. It is often followed by a word of thanks to the cook or Allah for providing the meal.

Visiting

Visiting friends and relatives is common and is a way to maintain strong relationships. People normally visit friends and relatives without prior notice. Guests are always welcome and should never be turned away. Even if the host is about to leave, he will stay a while to talk with the guest. Visits are most common in the late afternoon or evening when the sun is mild and there is enough shade to be outside. The normal greeting takes place first with both parties standing. The host then offers a drink or food. It is also common for people to visit during mealtime, in which case the guest is expected to at least taste the food.

Gifts are not an obligation when visiting, but it is not unusual for people with a mango or other fruit tree to bring some fruit to the host. Visitors from other towns normally bring gifts, which may range from vegetables to chickens. People chat about local developments: who is marrying whom, who has died, when the next naming ceremony will be, and so on. When a guest leaves, a host may offer a gift in the form of taxi fare. Although most visiting is done at home, some is done at work or in public places.

Eating

Most Gambians eat three meals a day. Breakfast is usually from 7:00 to 9:00 A.M., lunch from 1:00 to 3:00 P.M., and dinner from 7:00 to 9:00 P.M. Many wage earners, however, do not have lunch until after 4:00 P.M. when government offices close. Eating patterns are different in farming communities. Lunch is the most important and largest meal of the day. Most Gambians sit on a floor mat to eat; elders may sit on a low stool or bench. Although some urban Gambians eat with utensils, most prefer to eat with their hands from communal bowls. The left hand steadies the bowl while the right is used to eat. Conversation is limited. Food does not have to be finished. It is impolite for children to reach for meat in a bowl; they must wait to be given a portion. Children also look down while eating and do not engage in conversation with their elders. Leftovers are divided equally among the children. Since

eating and drinking at the same time is not acceptable, drinks are usually only served after a meal. If soft drinks are served, water will be served first.

Few Gambians eat in restaurants because each family usually prepares three meals a day at home. Tourists often eat in restaurants and tips are expected.

LIFESTYLE

Family

The Gambian family structure is not limited to the nuclear family, but is based on the extended family. Three generations may live together in one household. Most Gambians refer to one another by their family title. For example, one is a "brother," "sister," "aunt," "grandfather," and so forth. It is common to call more than one person father or mother, and there are various kinds of "relatives." If one is not related by blood, they may become related by long years of friendship, comingling, or working together.

Families, usually headed by the father, are generally large by Western standards. The family is the nucleus and pillar of the community, as well as the source of individual strength, recognition, and social standing. The concept of marriage goes beyond two people to extend to the community, especially when a son marries and introduces his new wife to the family compound.

Although women of the younger generation often work outside the home, most older women remain in the home as housewives.

Dating and Marriage

Boys and girls do not normally socialize together. "Boys with the boys and girls with the girls" is a popular Gambian phrase. Young boys are not generally welcome to visit a girl's house, and can only court a girl with parental permission. Although dating is not accepted, some dating occurs at night without the knowledge of parents. This may include meeting at parties, soccer games, or on the street. The youth also meet at marriage ceremonies or school. It is not unusual for a boy to tell a girl "I love you" at first sight.

While the practice of arranged marriages is rapidly diminishing in urban areas, it is still common among rural families. Men and women share family responsibilities, but women are responsible for household chores while men provide the family income. Although polygamy still exists, especially in rural areas, only a few men have more than one wife.

Diet

For breakfast, bread with butter or jam and hot tea are popular in urban areas. People might also eat *Rui/monno* (pap), *Chura* (porridge), or *Accara* (fried bean flour). These breakfasts can be purchased from street vendors or prepared at home. Rice is the main staple and most Gambians eat rice and stew for lunch. The stew, which always includes spices and vegetables (eggplant, cabbage, cassava, and/or okra), varies from a fish, chicken, or beef base to a peanut butter base. Pork is forbidden for Muslims but is still sold in some urban markets. Other popular lunch dishes include *Benachin* (jollof rice), *Superkanja* (okra soup), and *Domoda* (peanut butter stew). Dinner may be leftover rice from lunch, *Chereh* (a form of millet couscous), fried fish, beef sauce with bread, or salad with potatoes and chicken or beef. Gambians eat more fish than beef, but couscous with a special beef sauce is popular for certain festivals.

Recreation

Gambians spend their leisure time at festivals or ceremonies, such as weddings, burials, or naming ceremonies. People also visit friends and relatives as a form of recreation. Although The Gambia has beautiful beaches, most Gambians rarely use them, except for young men who may play beach soccer or go swimming. While soccer is the most popular sport, Gambians also wrestle, run track, and play tennis, basketball, and cricket. Family outings are not common. Playing cards or checkers is popular.

Television programming is provided only at night. There are movie theaters in Banjul, Serrekunda, and Bakau, but going to movies is not popular among Gambians. Many prefer to watch videos at home.

Holidays

The Gambia's official public holidays include New Year's Day, Independence Day (18 February), Easter (including Good Friday), Labor Day (1 May), and Christmas. Most holidays, except Labor Day, are celebrated with festivals, which include ethnic dances, house parties, dances, and local wrestling competitions. Muslim holy days that also have official recognition include *Eid-el-Fitre* (three-day feast at the end of *Ramadan*), *Eid-el-Kabir* (Feast of the Sacrifice, held in conjunction with the summer pilgrimage to Makkah), and *Mauloud-el-Nabi* (Muhammad's birthday). Muslim festivals fall on different days each year because they are set by the lunar calendar.

Commerce

Offices are open from 8:00 A.M. to 4:00 P.M., Monday through Thursday. Shops remain open until 6:00 or 7:00 P.M. Businesses close on Friday by 1:00 P.M. for the afternoon (Muslim) prayers. Almost all buying and selling in The Gambia, except in a few large or well-established stores, is subject to barter. Goods are sold in the market, in stores, and on side streets.

SOCIETY

Government

The Gambia has five divisions (Lower River, MacCarthy Island, North Bank, Upper River, and Western) and one major city, Banjul. Until the coup, the democratic system included an elected president and parliament. For now, Lt. Jammeh rules by decree and is advised by a handful of junior military officers.

Economy

The economy depends on agriculture, which employs 75 percent of the labor force. The Gambia exports peanuts, but cotton, rice, millet, maize, and sorghum are also key crops. Trade with neighboring countries, especially Senegal, is vital to economic growth. A growing number of people are involved in the fishing industry. Seafood is exported to Europe. Tourism is an important source of revenue and The Gambia is a favorite destination because of its peaceful government, nice beaches, and pleasant weather. It is uncertain how the new political climate will affect tourism.

The Gambia's Human Development Index (0.215) ranks it 166th out of 173 countries. Real gross domestic product per capita is $763. Forty percent of rural people live in poverty. These figures reflect the fact that most people do not earn a wage and that incomes are not sufficient to meet basic needs. Economic opportunities are limited to the few who are educated or wealthy. The currency is the *dalasi* (D).

Transportation and Communication

The Gambia's main road to major cities and leading upriver is paved, but only major streets in other cities are paved. Public buses run from Banjul to other cities, but they are very crowded. People usually walk in the cities and take the bus from one city to the next. Taxis are usually available.

The Gambia has a modern telephone system, but most Gambians do not own a phone. Public phones are available for use at a fee. There are several newspapers and two radio stations. Radio Gambia is controlled by the government, but the other station (Radio Syd) is private.

Education

Although only about 28 percent of Gambians are literate, there are no tuition fees at the primary education level. Preschools and kindergartens are available. Beginning at age eight, students spend about six years in primary school. About one-fifth proceed to high school for five years, provided they pass the Common Entrance Exam. Those who do not pass may go to secondary technical school for four years. High school graduates may spend two years in Sixth Form as preparation for college. While there is a highly specialized technical institute (Gambia Technical Training Institution) and a college for teachers (Yundum College), The Gambia has no university.

Health

The Gambia's health care system includes some facilities in Banjul and the Kombos and regional health centers at upriver locations. Government doctors and nurses staff these clinics. Private doctors are also available. The Jawara administration failed to invest in health programs in general, and did not build any much needed hospitals. The immunization program is fairly extensive, but infant mortality remains high (123 per 1,000) due to poor hygiene and nutritional deficiencies. Life expectancy ranges from 47 to 51 years.

FOR THE TRAVELER

U.S. citizens need a passport and visa to visit The Gambia. A yellow fever vaccination is no longer required. Malaria precautions are recommended. There are a number of interesting places to visit, including the Stone Circles that date from A.D. 750, James Island, Abuko Nature Reserve, and Tendaba Camp. No violence has been associated with the military coup, and travel appears to be safe. For more information, contact the Embassy of The Gambia, 1155 15th Street NW, Suite 1000, Washington, DC 20005; phone (202) 785–1399.

Republic of
Ghana

Boundary representations not necessarily authoritative.

BACKGROUND

Land and Climate

Ghana lies in the tropic zone on the Guinea Coast of West Africa. Covering 92,100 square miles (238,540 square kilometers), it is about the same size as Oregon. The south is dominated by low-lying plains that alternate between grass cover and mangroves. The west and southern interior are primarily tropical forests. About 5 percent of Ghana is arable. Forests and woodlands cover 37 percent of the total land area. The Volta River country is covered with savannah woodlands and swamps. A dam on the Volta River has created the largest man-made lake in the world: Lake Volta. The north is primarily dry grassland. It has two seasons: rainy from April to October, and hot and dry the rest of the year, with temperatures reaching 100°F (38°C). The Harmattan subseason (two months between late November and early January) brings hot, dry, and dusty winds to the north. In the south, rain is expected between April and June, and again in September and October. Temperatures in the southeast range from 74°F (23°C) in October to 86°F (30°C) in June.

History

Ghana takes its name, though not its modern boundaries, from one of the great inland trading empires that flourished in West Africa from the fourth to the eleventh centuries A.D. The fabled university city of Tombouctou (Timbuktu—now in Mali) was part of ancient Ghana. Because of the diversity of ethnic groups, the history of the country is quite varied.

Modern history began when Portuguese traders arrived in the 16th century. They mined gold and established headquarters for the slave trade. The area became known as the "Gold Coast," and several European powers established forts there. In 1874, Britain took control of the Gold Coast. After several years of battles with the Asante of the interior, the British gained control of present-day Ghana in 1901.

The Convention People's Party (CPP), under the leadership of Kwame Nkrumah, won legislative elections in 1951, and for the first time the black majority controlled the government. On 6 March 1957, Ghana became the first Black African colony to gain independence from Britain. Three years later, the country became a republic and Nkrumah was elected president. Unfortunately, his socialist policies led to a significant drop in the standard of living. While he was on his way to Vietnam in 1966, Nkrumah was deposed by a military coup. General A. A. Afrifa ruled until general elections were again held in 1969. But after three years of civilian rule, the military again took over in 1972, and Prime Minister Kofi Busia was dismissed.

In 1979, Flight Lieutenant Jerry Rawlings, with a group of junior officers and enlisted men, overthrew the government, arrested dozens of government officials, and executed eight of them, including three former heads of state. Rawlings drafted a new constitution, held elections, and just six months after gaining power turned the government over to newly elected Dr. Hilla Limann and the new national assembly.

However, Rawlings was not satisfied with government performance and again seized power in December 1981. He outlawed all political parties, suspended the constitution, and appointed a seven-member Provisional National Defense Council (PNDC).

In 1988, a national assembly was established, but members could not belong to political parties. The assembly was to represent different walks of life rather than political views. It was eventually determined that Ghana would return to democratic rule. A constituent assembly, composed of elected and appointed officials, helped draft a constitution to legalize political parties and provide for elections. National elections were held in November 1992. Rawlings won the presidential race and thus remains leader of the country.

THE PEOPLE

Population

The population of Ghana is more than 17.2 million and is growing rapidly at 3.1 percent a year. While 99.8 percent of the population is Black African, it is divided into more than 100 different ethnic groups, each with its own language and cultural heritage. Some major groups include the Fante in the coastal areas, the Asante in the south-central area, the Ga-Adangme and Ewe in the south, and the Hausa and Moshi-Dagomba in the north. The 0.2 percent nonblack population is mostly European, with some Lebanese merchants and communities of Indians and Chinese. The largest city is the capital of Accra, with more than one million people. Kumasi, a bustling trade center for the entire country, is also home to a large population.

Language

English is the official language of Ghana, partly because of the country's colonial association with Great Britain and partly because there are so many ethnic languages that just one of them could not effectively serve as the official language. English is used in the schools, business, and government. There are movements to make several local languages official as well. Widely spoken as primary languages are Akan (44 percent of the population), Mole-Dagbani (16 percent), Ewe (13 percent), and Ga-Adangme (8 percent). The Twi dialect of Akan is the language most commonly used on a daily basis to communicate between ethnic groups. Most Ghanaians are at least bilingual.

Religion

Traditional African beliefs and practices still play a major role in the lives of the people of Ghana. These are inseparable from the life and culture of Ghanaians and are retained regardless of any other religious affiliation. About 24 percent of Ghanaians belong to various Christian churches, 30 percent are Muslim, and 38 percent completely maintain their traditional beliefs.

This traditional faith is characterized by a belief in a Supreme Being who has created all things and has given various degrees of power to all living (animate) and nonliving (inanimate) things. Out of respect for the Supreme Being, who cannot be approached directly, traditional Ghanaians often communicate with him through intermediaries. Intermediaries can include animate or inanimate objects, as well as the spirits of ancestors. People especially seek guidance through their ancestors. Because of this, ancestor veneration is an important aspect of the culture and worship. These traditional beliefs are often referred to by outsiders as *animism*, because of their emphasis on showing reverence for living things. Many Ghanaians would not accept the term *animism* to describe their worship. Traditional faith also includes a belief in wizards, witches, demons, magic potions and other supernatural phenomena.

General Attitudes

Ghanaians are very warm, friendly, and sociable people. They are polite, open, and trusting—even with strangers. They tend to take life at a more relaxed pace, viewing time as a series of events rather than a matter of hours or minutes. People are more important than schedules. Tolerance and acceptance are typical individual characteristics. The group is valued over personal needs.

Ghanaians are proud of their status as the first sub-Saharan colony to gain independence from a European power. Although greatly influenced by Western civilization, the people are striving to develop a nation and culture that is uniquely African. Western visitors should take care not to act, or give the impression of being, superior just because they come from industrialized nations. This is offensive to Ghanaians.

Personal Appearance

Ghanaian dress is modest, neat, and generally conservative. Casual dress is the rule for most occasions, although a suit and tie or dress are required for more formal occasions. Shorts are not acceptable public attire. Western dress is normal in urban areas, but officials often wear traditional *kente* cloth robes on ceremonial occasions. Non-Western attire for men varies by region and ethnic group. For example, in the south men may wear long, colored cloth wrapped around the body somewhat like a toga. Northern men wear long tunics made of wide strips of rough cotton cloth that are sewn together. Muslim men wear robes similar to Arab Muslims, except that the Ghanaian version is colorful. Regardless of what one wears, the design of the cloth can reflect the person's status. Women usually wear a traditional, long, wraparound skirt, a separate top, and a head scarf. Women prefer bold colors and large prints. Extra cloth is wrapped at the hips or added to sleeves. The head cloth generally matches the dress.

CUSTOMS AND COURTESIES

Greetings

Because of pronounced differences between ethnic groups, greetings vary from area to area. English greetings and handshakes are common. Indeed, a handshake is important when greeting most people. Before beginning a conversation, a general greeting such as "Good morning," "Good afternoon," or "Good evening" is necessary. Most greetings are in the dominant local language and are followed by questions about one's health, family welfare, journey, and so forth. Titles and family names are used to address new acquaintances. Friends and family members often use given names. Children refer to any adult that is well-known to the family as "aunt" or "uncle," even when they are not related. By the same token, adults of the same age might refer to each other as brother or sister, regardless of their relationship, and will use "auntie" and "uncle" for respected older people.

Gestures

Courtesy is important. It is impolite to gesture with the left hand. It may be considered improper by some, especially Muslims, to pass or receive items with the left hand. Either the right hand or both hands should be used. When yawning or using a toothpick, a person covers the mouth. Among Muslims, and some other groups used to sitting on the floor, it is improper to allow the sole of one's foot to point at another person. Generally, feet are not placed on chairs, desks, or tables—especially those being used by another person. It is impolite and an act of defiance for a child to look an adult in the eye. It is common and appropriate for friends of the same sex to hold hands while walking or speaking. It does not signify anything beyond friendship. However, members of the opposite sex (except relatives) do not hold hands or show any affection in public.

Visiting

In a society where friendly social relations are important, visiting plays a key role in everyday life. Friends and relatives visit one another frequently, often unannounced, and appreciate the visits of others. Ghanaians work hard to accommodate their guests. Most visits occur in the home. It is polite to at least take a small gift for the children. Some hosts prefer that their guests remove their shoes when entering the home. Guests are nearly always served drinks and often other refreshments. It is impolite to refuse these offers. Visitors are usually welcome to stay as long as they wish. It is polite to avoid visiting during mealtime, but an unexpected guest would be invited to share the meal. Visiting is most popular on Sunday, and many people like to dress up for the occasion. When a visit is over, guests are accompanied to the bus stop or taxi stand or given a ride home. It is impolite to let them leave on their own.

Eating

Ghanaians usually eat meals with their right hand. A bowl of water is provided at the beginning of the meal, in which each person washes the hands. Food is scooped and formed into a ball with the right hand before being eaten. Water is also passed around at the end of the meal for diners to wash their hands. Foreigners may need to become accustomed to the food, which is often spicy. Most larger restaurants serve Western food as well as native Ghanaian food. While a service charge is often included in the bill, it is customary to leave a small tip.

LIFESTYLE

Family

Family structures vary from one ethnic group to another, but the extended family is strong and vital in most areas. Some groups have a matriarchal family organization, in which inheritance is passed down through the wife's family rather than the husband's. In these groups, the chief responsibilities for the family fall on the women. Others have male-dominated structures. Polygamy (having more than one wife) is also practiced by some Ghanaians. Extended families of three or four generations often share one household. Children are looked after by the entire community and can move about by themselves without direct supervision.

All elderly members of the family are deeply respected and exercise a great deal of influence on family decisions. Ghanaians normally sacrifice their own desires and ambitions for the sake of the family unit. Funerals are very important and last three days. For those people involved, everything else comes to a stop and all attention is directed toward funeral-related activities.

Dating and Marriage

Many marriages are still arranged by families, although the children have the right to reject undesirable arrangements. More Westernized practices of dating are also found among a growing number of urban youth. Marriage in rural areas (and to some extent in urban areas) may also follow tradition, which allows a man to take more than one wife. Still, the Christian marriage with its monogamous restrictions is becoming prevalent. Traditionally, the groom pays the bride's family a *bridal token* to indicate responsibility for the new bride.

Diet

The diet consists mainly of yams, cassava (a starchy root), maize, plantain, and rice. Ghanaians enjoy hot and spicy food, and most of their meals are accompanied by a pepper sauce made with meat, fish, or chicken. Fish is most common due to cost. Popular dishes include *fufu* (a dough-like combination of plantain and cassava), *ampesi* (a green vegetable dish), and palm or peanut oil soups and sauces. Ghana also produces a variety of tropical fruits and vegetables to supplement the diet.

Recreation

Soccer is the national sport to which most people are highly devoted. Ghanaians are also fond of boxing, field hockey, horse racing, and track and field. Where available, people enjoy the theater, movies, cultural presentations, and music and dance festivals. Ghana has its own movie industry. Various ethnic group festivals are celebrated throughout the country.

Holidays

Holidays include Independence Day (6 March), Good Friday (Friday before Easter Sunday), Easter Monday, Republic Day (1 July), Christmas, Boxing Day (26 December), and 31 December (to celebrate the 1981 revolution). Boxing Day comes from the British tradition of giving service personnel and tradesmen small boxed gifts. Today, it is generally marked by visiting friends and relatives.

Commerce

Most businesses are open from 8:00 A.M. to noon and 2:00 to 4:30 P.M., Monday through Friday. Some are open on Saturday morning. Business dress is conservative. *Dash* is a common Ghanaian form of compensation in money, goods, or favors for personal services performed. Except in restaurants and for bellhops in hotels, *dash* is normally paid before the service is given. While the system of *dash* is discouraged by the government, it is widely practiced, and includes anything from watching a car to expediting the movement of goods in and out of the country.

SOCIETY

Government

Ghana is a constitutional democracy, although in practice the country is still in transition from a dictatorship to a multiparty democracy. The president is head of state and head of government, but he must now work with the elected legislature (a national assembly) in establishing laws and policy. The governing National Democratic Congress dominates the assembly, but opposition parties are becoming more organized and stronger. They include the New Patriotic Party and the People's Heritage Party, among others. The voting age is 18. Ghana is divided into 10 regions.

Economy

The Ghanaian economy is based primarily on agriculture, which employs more than 50 percent of the labor force. Cacao (from which cocoa is made) is the most important cash crop, accounting for about 45 percent of all exports. Other crops include corn, root crops, sorghum, millet, and peanuts. With gold, bauxite, aluminum, and diamonds as natural resources, mining is also important to the economy. Fishing, light manufacturing, and timber are key industries. Economic growth is dependent on world prices for Ghana's exports, of which gold is the most important. World price fluctuations can cause great financial strain and economic difficulties at times.

Government policies have successfully reduced inflation to manageable levels. Ghana has been privatizing and modernizing its economy for several years. A stock market has existed since 1990. Ghana remains an essentially poor country, as poverty affects more than 40 percent of all people. The country's Human Development Index (0.382) ranks it 134th out of 173 countries. Real gross domestic product per capita is $930, which is actually lower than it was at independence. The currency is the *cedi* (¢).

Transportation and Communication

While the transportation system is underdeveloped, a rail system connects Accra with Kumasi and Takoradi. A fairly good system of buses connects major cities. There are also some domestic flights available. Most people do not own cars but rely on public transportation or other means of travel. The *tro-tro* is a minibus used for public transport of shorter distances. A *tro-tro* is crowded, but efficient and inexpensive. Taxis are also available. Communications systems are equally underdeveloped, although the government is seeking to upgrade facilities and networks. Mail and phone services are often unreliable, but the informal method of passing information works rapidly and well: letters or messages are passed to a driver or passenger traveling in the intended direction until they reach their destination.

Education

Ghana is striving to increase the availability of primary education, but efforts have so far not improved conditions of overcrowding or underfunding. Schools are organized on three levels: primary (six years), junior secondary (three years), and senior secondary (three years). Today, every administrative district has at least one high school. The literacy rate is 60 percent. For men the figure is 70 percent, but it is only 51 percent for women. About 30,000 students now study above the secondary school level, including students at the four universities in Ghana (at Legon, Kumasi, Cape Coast, and Tamale).

Health

Although the government is working to increase the quality and availability of medical care, standards do not equal those in the West. Medical facilities are limited outside of Accra and other major cities. Malaria and other tropical diseases are still present in Ghana. Ghana lacks a clean water supply and modern sewer system, which presents a serious health hazard to even urban residents. Intestinal disorders are common. Many people rely on various forms of herbal medicine and traditional healing. The infant mortality rate is 83 per 1,000, which is lower than in the past but still very high. The average life expectancy is 53 to 57 years.

FOR THE TRAVELER

A tourist visa is required with a valid passport and can only be obtained with proof of finances, a letter from one's employer, and an onward ticket. Vaccinations against yellow fever are required. Cholera vaccinations and malaria suppressants are recommended. Water is not potable, and bodies of fresh water are not safe for swimming. One should peel all fruits and vegetables before eating. Dual-voltage small appliances or a voltage converter and a plug adaptor are necessary to use electrical outlets.

Visitors should not use the word *tribe* when referring to a Ghanaian's ethnic background. This word has negative connotations and Ghanaians may be offended by its use or question the visitor's intentions. The term *ethnic group* is a suitable substitute, but questions about a person's ethnic background should be reserved until one is well acquainted.

An American traveler should consider contacting the U.S. Embassy on arrival (in Accra, on Ring Road East) for any advisories on Ghanaian law, which can differ substantially from U.S. law. Getting arrested for breaking a law can cause many difficulties. Any visitor staying more than seven days must register with the Ghana Immigration Service within 48 hours of arrival. For more information, contact the Trade and Tourism Department of the Embassy of Ghana, 3512 International Drive NW, Washington, DC 20008; phone (202) 686–4520.

Republic of
Guinea

Boundary representations not necessarily authoritative.

BACKGROUND

Land and Climate

Guinea covers 94,000 square miles (243,460 square kilometers) and is somewhat smaller than Oregon. The nation is divided into four regions: the coast of lower Guinea; the central, mountainous Fouta Djalon; the savanna of upper Guinea; and the forest in the southeast. Numerous major rivers, including the Niger, Bafing, and Gambia, have their sources in Guinea.

Guinea has two distinct seasons: the rainy season, or *hivernage* (May to October), and the dry season (November to April). As much as 170 inches (67 centimeters) of rain may fall on the coast annually, while the savanna region receives only about 60 inches (24 centimeters) each year. Average temperatures range from 80°F to 90°F (26–32°C), but temperatures above 100°F (38°C) are not uncommon. Nighttime temperatures in the Fouta Djalon may fall to as low as 50°F (10°C).

History

For thousands of years, Guinea was populated by various peoples. In the 10th century A.D., Soussou and Malinke groups began to move into the area, pushing the former inhabitants into smaller regions. Upper Guinea was part of the Ghana Empire in the 10th and 11th centuries, then the Mali empire until the 14th century, and the Songhai empire until the 19th century. The Fulani moved into Guinea in the 17th century and brought Islam with them. They pushed the Soussou to coastal areas, where the Soussou established trade with Europeans. While not a major slave trade area, Guinea was affected by that trading as well as by disputes among European groups. In the 19th century, El Hadj Umar came from Senegal to reform the practice of Islam in Guinea. His fundamentalism was accepted by the Fulani and the Malinke, and his influence accounts for Guinean Muslims' devotion to Islam today. Almamy Samory Toure, a follower of Umar, was a great leader in the late 1800s; he was so powerful that it took France until 1904 to capture him and complete their conquest of the region.

French rule, which began in the 19th century, brought private ownership of communal land and the expansion of commercial and service jobs. An urban elite that adopted the French language and culture evolved, but most of the area's people continued to live a subsistence agriculture lifestyle until the 1940s.

After World War II, several labor parties were established, including the *Parti Democratique de Guinee*, led by Ahmed Sekou Toure. In 1958, this party organized support to vote against Charles de Gaulle's proposed French community and then declared independence. Guinea was the only French colony to vote "no" on the issue. Thus, unlike other francophone African states, it was cut off from France's financial aid and other assistance programs. Guinea was also shunned by other Western nations and, in this relative isolation, developed a strong national identity.

Toure, once loved by the people for his leadership, never allowed elections and governed a one-party state. He deteriorated into a dictator and began facing opposition from various groups. Nevertheless, Toure survived several attempted coups and continued to rule Guinea until his death in 1984. Two weeks later, the military took control of the government and established the Second Guinean Republic under Lansana Conte. In 1990, a committee was established to oversee Guinea's transition to a multiparty system. A constitution that provided for a democratic government was drafted and accepted in 1991. Presidential and parliamentary elections were held in late 1993. Lansana Conte was declared president.

THE PEOPLE

Population

Guinea's population of approximately 6.3 million is growing annually at about 2.4 percent. More than one million people live in the capital, Conakry. Another 250,000 live in each of the regional capitals of Labé, Kankan, and Nzérékoré. Almost three-fourths of the population lives in rural areas. The major ethnic groups include the Fulani (35 percent) in the Fouta Djalon, the Malinke (30 percent) in upper Guinea, and the Soussou (20 percent) in the coastal region. There are numerous other ethnic groups, sometimes comprising only one village.

Language

French is the official langugae of Guinea, but most rural people do not understand it. In different regions various African languages are spoken. On the coast, the language is Soussou; in the Fouta Djalon, it's Pular; in upper Guinea, it's Malinke; and in the forest, numerous languages intermingle, including Guerze, Kissi, and Toma. Except for a few religious phrases, Arabic is only spoken by those who have learned to read the *Qur'an* (Koran).

Religion

Guinea's government promotes religious freedom. About 85 percent of the population is Muslim. Most other Guineans are Christian. Animism is still practiced by certain rural groups, as well as among some Muslims and Christians. For example, people remain superstitious and buy *gri gri* (good luck charms) for their children. Animists in the forest do not trust people of other religions or races because these groups have destroyed or otherwise violated sacred forests.

Guinean Muslims are devout and follow the traditional worship practices of praying five times daily, avoiding alcohol, professing the name of and attributing all to *Allah*, and giving alms to the poor. They accept the *Qur'an* as scripture that was revealed to Muhammad, Islam's last and greatest recognized prophet.

General Attitudes

Guineans identify strongly with their families and ethnic groups. Although various groups coexist without serious strife, there is a tendency to reserve help and trust for one's own group. Tensions exist between ethnic groups, religions, and social classes in some areas, but they have not yet seriously threatened stability.

People speak often of religion in discussing how one should act. Most Guineans strongly believe that whatever happens is *Allah's* will, and they accept disappointment or sorrow with this attitude. Such fatalism also means people live more for the present, assuming the future will take care of itself. Daily living and interpersonal relationships are often more important than material goods. The Guinean sense of time is relaxed and people may arrive hours late for an appointment or event with little explanation.

Personal Appearance

Guineans wear Western styles as well as traditional Muslim and West African clothing. To work, men may wear a short-sleeved suit coat and matching pants, or they may wear a Western-style shirt, a tie, and pants. Muslim men may wear long robes called *boubous* over loose pants and a shirt. Women often wear brightly patterned, locally tailored blouses or Muslim-style robes called *petits boubous* with a matching *pagne* (length of cloth wrapped around the waist). Some women also wear Western-style dresses. No matter what style a person wears, it is extremely important in Guinea that clothing be clean, well pressed, and in good repair.

CUSTOMS AND COURTESIES

Greetings

Greetings are an important part of everyday interaction. To fail to greet someone or to skip a greeting in favor of conversation is an insult. Guineans most often use greetings in French, Arabic, or the language of the particular region or individual to whom they are speaking. *Bonjour* (Good day) and *Bonsoir* (Good evening) are the common French greetings. Greetings are usually followed by inquiries about the other person's family.

When walking along the road, a person might call out greetings rather than stopping. Even strangers are greeted, including store clerks, taxi drivers, or anyone with whom one is about to interact. Upon arrival at a gathering, Guineans greet every person with a right-handed handshake. When the right hand is not clean, a closed fist is extended and the other person shakes the wrist. Raising both hands, palms out, is common to greet a larger group or someone who is a bit distant for a handshake. Some older men also use this greeting rather than shaking hands with women. If seated, a person shows respect by standing up to shake hands. Respect is also conveyed by grasping one's own right forearm with the left hand while shaking hands. A left handshake might be used when good friends are parting for a long time.

When addressing others, Guineans use titles, such as *doctor*, *madame* (Mrs.), or *monsieur* (Mr.), instead of names. Familial titles, such as *frere*, *tanti*, and *cousin* (brother, aunt, and cousin), are also used—with strangers as well as within the family.

Gestures

Handing objects to or accepting them from another person is done with the right hand. Beckoning is done by waving all four fingers with the palm down. Hailing a taxi is done by extending the arm, palm down, and waving the hand. To show respect, eye contact is avoided, especially with older people. Men and women do not show affection in public, but friends of the same gender often hold hands or walk arm in arm. People avoid pointing the soles of their feet at others.

Visiting

To visit someone is to honor them, and Guineans are gracious hosts. They frequently invite friends over for a meal, but invitations are not necessary for one to visit. People sometimes visit to simply exchange greetings. To pass by a friend's home without stopping briefly is an insult. Proper greetings are exchanged at every visit, regardless of the purpose. A visitor usually does not bring a gift; rather, a visit is reciprocated with a return visit. The exception is when a person returns or arrives from out of town; then food (fruit, vegetables, or rice), fabric, or a specialty of the region from which the person traveled is an appropriate gift.

Guests may be offered fruit or a beverage if the visit is not during mealtime, but they are otherwise often invited to eat. It is not impolite to say one has just eaten. However, the host usually insists the guest eat something, and it is rude to refuse entirely. So, generally, the guest eats at least a small portion and thanks the host and the person who prepared the meal.

During visits there are often several-minute gaps in conversation, filled only by a repeat of the greetings and inquiries about the family. When guests are ready to leave, they say they must go, shake hands, and thank the host and family for their hospitality.

Eating

Most Guineans eat with the right hand from a common platter that is often placed on the floor or a mat. In some families, people eat separately according to age and gender. Before and after any meal eaten with the hands, a bowl of water is made available for washing hands. It is polite to eat only from the part of the dish that is immediately in front of oneself. The oldest person or the woman who prepared the meal may divide the meat and vegetables among those eating. Most Guineans do not drink during a meal because it implies the food is not good enough to satiate the appetite. Most drink water after the meal. Conversation is minimal, but guests always thank the host at the end of the meal. The host often replies with *Albarka*, an Arabic term used to credit *Allah* (God) for providing the food.

Eating patterns differ for each family. Many Guineans living in nonagricultural settings eat the main meal at midday and another meal or leftovers in the evening. Breakfast may include coffee and bread, as well as any leftovers from the previous day. In agricultural settings, people working in the fields eat a larger breakfast, which may include hot cereal. They then eat their main meal upon returning from the fields in the evening.

LIFESTYLE

Family

The family is the most important social unit in Guinea. Extended families living together—and sharing child care, domestic chores, and meals—are common in rural areas. While extended families are also common in urban areas, the number of nuclear families living in individual homes is increasing. Obligations to one's extended family run deep and can involve giving money, lodging, or other favors to distant relatives. In general, the eldest male presides over the household.

Large families share a common compound with separate homes or rooms for individuals or nuclear family members. Sturdy homes made of thick mud and thatched roofs are common in rural areas, while urban homes may be single or multifamily cement block structures.

Dating and Marriage

Urban youth may date as in Western cultures, but they more often associate in groups. The choice of a mate may be influenced by the family. Women usually marry before they are 20 and men usually wait until they are 25 or older. Traditionally, the man presents ten kola nuts to the woman's family to propose marriage. The head of the woman's family cracks the nuts to signal his approval. The groom offers fabric, jewelry, or cattle to the bride and her family. Muslim men are allowed to marry more than one wife (up to four total), but they must be able to financially support each one.

Diet

The main meal usually consists of rice with a sauce made from palm oil and tomato paste, peanut butter, or ground leaves. Meat or fish and vegetables, such as manioc, sweet potatoes, or squash, may be cooked with the sauce. Millet is a popular grain in the Sahelian region near Mali. The Malinke eat *too* (pronounced TOE), made from cassava or rice powder. Avocados, peanuts, mangoes, papayas, bananas, oranges, pineapples, and sometimes watermelons are eaten in season. Muslims do not drink alcohol or eat pork.

Recreation

Soccer is the most popular sport in Guinea. Basketball and volleyball are also favorites. Sports are mostly for boys, but urban girls participate through school. Many urban areas have facilities and organized sporting competitions. Guineans also love music and dancing. Traditional musical instruments include the *kora*, a lute-harp (made from half of a large calabash) with metal or fiber strings; the *balafon*, a wooden zylophone; and a wide variety of drums and other percussion instruments. Family gatherings, visits, and local festivals provide recreation for many people, especially in rural areas. Dancing is popular at weddings and other celebrations.

Family celebrations held for Christian baptisms and weddings in both Muslim and Christian traditions are important. It is customary at these events for *griots* (traditional singers) to sing about individual guests (their name, appearance, character), and the honored person is expected to give the *griots* a small sum of money in return.

Holidays

Guinean holidays include New Year's Day, Easter, *Tabaski* (a Muslim holiday commemorating Abraham's willingness to sacrifice his son to God); a feast at the end of *Ramadan*, a month in which Muslims do not eat or drink from sunrise to sunset; Labor Day (1 May); *Mawloud* (the Prophet Muhammad's birthday); Independence Day (2 October); All Saints' Day (1 November); and Christmas. Muslim holidays involve people attending a mosque, visiting friends and family, and eating large meals.

Commerce

Government offices and businesses are open 8:00 A.M. to 4:30 P.M., Monday through Thursday. They close by 2:00 P.M.

on Friday. Offices are closed Saturday and Sunday. Urban markets are open all day, every day, but many merchants close Friday afternoon and Sunday. In rural areas, market day may be only one day a week. Business transactions can take some time to complete in Guinea, and patience and persistence are vital.

SOCIETY

Government

Guinea is officially a multiparty democracy consisting of 33 administrative regions. The elected president is head of state and head of government. President Conte began his five-year term in 1994. The 114 members of the new National Assembly also began serving in 1994. The voting age is 18. In opposition to the governing Party for Unity and Progress (PUP) stand a few small parties, including the Rally for the Guinean People (RPG) and Union for a New Republic (UNP).

Economy

Guinea has abundant natural resources, including 25 percent of the world's known reserves of bauxite, along with diamonds, gold, and other metals. The country also has great potential for hydroelectric power. While bauxite and alumina are currently the only major exports, the Guinean government plans to encourage the mining of other resources. Other industries include processing plants for beer, juices, soft drinks, and tobacco. The government encourages a free market economy and is working hard to promote foreign investment. A continued privatization effort is expected to help the economy and encourage more growth.

Agriculture employs 80 percent of the nation's labor force. Under French rule, and at the beginning of independence, Guinea was a major exporter of bananas, pineapples, coffee, coca, peanuts, and palm oil. Unfortunately, insufficient capital and isolation caused these exports to decline under Toure. If democracy brings an infusion of new investment, exports may be revived. The currency is the Guinean *franc* (GF), which is not tied to any international currency and cannot be converted. It is not allowed outside Guinean borders.

Guinea is one of the poorest countries in the world and has the lowest Human Development Index (0.191) ranking out of 173 countries. Real gross domestic product per capita is $500, a figure that has hardly increased in 30 years. This indicates that economic life is not improving in Guinea. Most people do not earn a sufficient income or have no income at all.

Transportation and Communication

Guinea is working to pave roads that link major cities in each of its regions. But most roads, especially in rural areas, are unpaved and not maintained well. Air Guinea flies from Conakry to regional capitals. Guinea also has an intercity bus service (*Sogetrag*) that serves most of the nation's regions. Taxis and trucks are the main means of public transportation for most people, few of whom own cars. Many Guineans travel within their regions by motorcycle or bicycle. Short distance travel is by foot.

The government sponsors a weekly newspaper, *Horoya* (Liberty), which is available in Conakry. National radio and television programs are broadcast from Conakry. In each region, a radio program in the local language is also broadcast. Domestic and international telephone service is available, but most people do not have phones.

Education

Guinean education is based on the French system and includes six years of primary school, four years of middle school, and three years of high school. Students follow one of three tracks: social science, mathematics, or natural sciences. National tests are required for graduation. Enrollment levels are low; only about one-third of all children attend primary school and the number drops to 15 percent for secondary school. Only about 15 to 30 percent of the population is functional in French, partly because school is sometimes taught in local languages rather than French. This is necessary because children begin school without knowing any French. French was not used as the language of instruction under Toure, but it was reintroduced in the Second Republic. Guinea has four universities, and several trade and vocational institutions.

Health

Despite efforts to improve health conditions, the national health care system is weak. Half of all doctors are in Conakry, and they are scarce in the rest of the country. Only the wealthy can afford quality care. However, many *Centres de Sante* (health centers) are being opened in rural areas where people can get low-cost care and essential medications. Traditional healers practice in nearly every village and are often the first source of rural care. Childhood diseases and malaria are widespread. Waterborne diseases are common. The infant mortality rate is 139 per 1,000. Life expectancy ranges from 41 to 46 years.

FOR THE TRAVELER

U.S. visitors need a valid passport and visa to enter Guinea. A yellow fever vaccination is required. Immunizations for hepatitis, tetanus, polio, typhoid, meningitis, and rabies are recommended, as are malarial suppressants. Voltage adaptors and converters are necessary to use electrical outlets, but electricity works only part of the time in villages and towns. Visitors should travel with their own drinking water (either bottled or treated).

Guinea's geographical beauty is a great attraction for visitors. The Fouta Djalon region has several waterfalls, including Kin Kon near Pita and *La voile de la mariee* (Bridal Veil) near Kindia. Accommodations and transportation, especially outside Conakry, are somewhat lacking, but Guinea offers a glimpse of West Africa unspoiled and less commercialized than the region's more popular tourist sites. For more information, contact the Embassy of Guinea, 2112 Leroy Place NW, Washington, DC 20008; phone (202) 483–9420.

A *Culturgram* is a product of native commentary and original, expert analysis. Statistics are estimates and information is presented as a matter of opinion. While the editors strive for accuracy and detail, this document should not be considered strictly factual. It is a general introduction to culture, an initial step in building bridges of understanding between peoples. It may not apply to all peoples of the nation. You should therefore consult other sources for more information.

Republic of
Guinea-Bissau

Boundary representations not necessarily authoritative.

BACKGROUND

Land and Climate

Guinea-Bissau is a small West African country that includes the Bijago archipelago. About the same size as Massachusetts, Rhode Island, and Connecticut combined, it covers 13,946 square miles (36,120 square kilometers). A low-lying coastal plain rises to savanna in the east. Guinea-Bissau is cut by three rivers that flow into the Atlantic Ocean. Mangrove swamps are common along the coast. The climate is tropical and temperatures average near 80°F (27°C). The rainy season is hot and humid; the dry season is hot and dusty. The coolest time of year is December to January. Bissau is the capital city.

History

The Portuguese began exploring the region around present-day Guinea-Bissau in the 15th century, first establishing themselves on the islands of Cape Verde, about 350 miles (560 kilometers) northwest of Guinea-Bissau. They claimed the area around current Guinea-Bissau as Portuguese Guinea. Trading posts were established and, in the 1600s, they began exporting slaves from the territory. As the slave trade diminished in the 1800s, Bissau became an important commercial center. The Portuguese did not begin to conquer inland territory until this time.

Initially helped by the Muslims, the Portuguese subdued animist groups and by 1936 had gained control of the entire area. In 1952, the colony of Portuguese Guinea became a province of Portugal. In 1955, Amilcar Cabral and others formed the African Party for the Independence of Guinea and Cape Verde (PAIGC) and led most ethnic groups in a guerrilla war against the Portuguese, beginning in 1961. By 1972, the PAIGC controlled most of the country (including the Cape Verdean islands) and held national elections. It declared the independence of Guinea-Bissau in September 1973; Portugal officially granted independence one year later. Luis Cabral became president. In 1980, he was overthrown and the union between Cape Verde and Guinea-Bissau was dissolved. João Bernardo Vieira assumed control after the coup. As the new leader of the PAIGC, Vieira was elected president of the Council of State in 1984 and reelected in 1989. In both cases, he was not opposed because the PAIGC was the ruling and only official party.

In 1990, a committee was formed to recommend changes in the constitution and electoral process so a multiparty system could gradually be established. The nation's first free elections were held in July 1994, but opposition parties (which had become active as early as 1991) were not well-organized. The PAIGC retained its dominance by gaining 62 of 100 parliamentary seats. Vieira faced a closer race for president, but won the post in the second round of voting. Manuel Saturnino Costa, national secretary of the PAIGC, was appointed prime minister. In January 1995, he negotiated substantial financial support from international lenders to fund a three-year economic reform program designed to help Guinea-Bissau create sustainable growth.

THE PEOPLE

Population

Guinea-Bissau's population of 1.1 million is growing annually at 2.4 percent. Only 20 percent of the people live in urban areas, as the majority are farmers and fishing families living in small villages. Most of the population is Black African. The country has been described as a melting pot of West African ethnic groups. There are at least 13 major groups with distinct languages, customs, religious beliefs, and forms of social organization. The largest of these groups include the Balanta (27 percent), Fula (23), Mandinga (13), Manjaco (11), Papel (10), Beafada (3), Mancanha (3), and Bijago (2.5). Some Cape Verdeans, Senegalese, and Mauritanians also live in Guinea-Bissau. More than 40 percent of the people are younger than age 15.

Language

Although Portuguese is the official language of Guinea-Bissau, but it is reserved mostly for business and government use. The language of daily interaction is Kriolu, a mixture of Portuguese and various African languages. Nearly everyone in Guinea-Bissau speaks Kriolu either as a native tongue or a second language. Some people speak French because of contact with neighboring, French-speaking countries, and many different African languages are spoken in rural areas.

Religion

While 30 percent of the people are Muslim and 5 percent Christian, the rest follow traditional beliefs—sometimes called "animism." Religious preference is tied to ethnic grouping. The Fula, Mandinga, and Beafada, among others, are Muslims. The Balanta, Manjaco, Papel, Mancanha, Bijago, and others are animists. Many animists believe in a creator-god that can only be contacted through other gods or supernatural beings (*iran*). The *iran* reside in shrines usually built near large trees. Persons considered "spiritual advisors" or intermediaries perform ceremonies to the *iran* and services for people (casting spells, telling fortunes, and treating illness). Animists who convert to Christianity and Islam often mix their old and new beliefs rather than abandon their animist traditions. Seeking advice from spiritualists and using amulets and charms are common throughout the country.

General Attitudes

Guinea-Bissauans are friendly and hospitable. They are peace loving and nonaggressive. They generally try to avoid confrontation and therefore also refrain from making direct or assertive statements. Although some tensions exist between various ethnic groups, most are united because of their struggle for independence against the Portuguese. This feeling of unity has helped Guinea-Bissau avoid major internal conflict.

Guinea-Bissauans are ready to help one another and, although the country is poor, there are relatively few beggars or homeless people. People love to socialize with friends; a desire for privacy may be considered anti-social. Most Guinea-Bissauans believe nature is controlled by gods and spirits, and that people are relatively powerless in regard to nature. They tend to be fatalistic about their individual conditions and may seem less motivated to change them. However, such acceptance of one's conditions helps one cope with the difficulties of life. This is obvious in the fact that patience, perseverance, and even resignation are valued.

Personal Appearance

Western-style clothing is common in urban areas. Clothing is informal, but not immodest. While short-sleeved shirts are more often worn in offices than suits and ties, adults do not wear short pants or other less conservative attire in public. In rural areas many people prefer traditional clothing. For example, Bijago women wear short straw skirts, Muslims wear long robes that cover their bodies (but women do not wear veils), and many women wear long, colorful, wraparound skirts with loose-fitting tops. Intricately braided hairstyles are popular with women.

CUSTOMS AND COURTESIES

Greetings

Greetings are an important way to show respect for others. It is rude to start speaking without first greeting a person. Traditional, ritualized greetings, especially those exchanged among rural Muslims, can last several minutes and involve polite inquiries about the person's health, family members, and work. At a minimum, people ask each other, "How are you?" and respond, "I am fine." The people use either Portuguese or a native language such as Kriolu in their greetings. Portuguese for "How are you?" is *Como esta?* Kriolu is *Kuma di korpu?* (How is your body?) or simply *Kuma?* In Portuguese, "I am fine" is *Estou bem* (esh-TOE BAIN); in Kriolu it is *Sta bon*.

People shake hands when they greet. Some hold on to the hand for a while after the initial handshake. If one's hand is dirty, it is offered closed and a person shakes the wrist instead. In urban areas, the Portuguese tradition of kissing alternate cheeks (first right, then left) is common. Except at large gatherings, it is polite to greet each individual in a group rather than the group as a whole. The same applies when a person leaves; each individual should be addressed. Good friends may call each other *Primo* (cousin) or *Mano* (brother); strangers are often addressed as *Amigo* (friend). In more formal situations, titles, such as *Senhor* (Mr.) or *Senhora* (Mrs.), are appropriate. To address an older person, many Guinea-Bissauans use the term *Tio* (uncle) or *Tia* (aunt).

Elders are highly respected and are not called by their first names. In business and government circles, first names are also avoided, but they are commonly used among friends in rural areas.

Gestures

Beckoning is done by waving all four fingers with the palm facing down. Some rural Guinea-Bissauans may point directions with their tongues. Personal space is smaller than in the West; people stand close together when conversing, and touching is an important part of communication. Friends of the same sex often walk hand in hand, but this does not suggest anything beyond friendship. Stretching in public is rude. A common gesture is associated with the Kriolu word *nega*, which means to refuse, negate, or deny something. When someone says *nega*, the person bends one or both arms and quickly flaps them once against the side of the body (like a bird). By this, the person definitely means "no." As a sign of respect, children are taught not to look elders or superiors in the eye. Muslim elders addressing each other often look sideways. Women are supposed to avoid eye contact with men unless they are romantically involved.

Visiting

Because visiting is considered a generous and thoughtful act, visitors are treated with great hospitality. Most Guinea-Bissauans offer guests something to drink. Unless the drink has been bottled (especially water), foreign visitors should politely decline the offer or let the drink sit; this is not improper. If visitors arrive while the hosts are eating, they are invited to share the meal. It is rude to refuse this offer, even if a person is not hungry. Guests should at least take one bite before saying *N justa* (NG JUICE-ta), Kriolu for "I've had enough."

It is not necessary to make appointments before visiting, although they are sometimes used in urban areas. Invited guests may arrive up to two hours later than a scheduled time without offending the hosts. Guests show appreciation to hosts with gifts of tobacco, kola nuts, bread, sugar, fruit, or *cana* (cane alcohol). Some topics of discussion—poverty (of the hosts), sickness and death, marital status, and one's educational background—are not appropriate. Discussing these topics could lead to embarrassment for the hosts. It is also inappropriate to criticize or joke about the ethnic group of anyone present. Likewise, the use of the word "tribe" is offensive. It is better to use the term "ethnic group" (*etnia* in Portuguese; *rasa* in Kriolu).

Eating

In urban areas, breakfast might be eaten between 7:00 and 9:00 A.M., lunch between noon and 3:00 P.M. (including time for rest or a nap), and supper between 8:00 and 10:00 P.M. Mealtimes in rural areas vary according to ethnic group, season, and personal habits. Some eat only once or twice a day. Among most people, except in urban areas, the main dish is usually served in large bowls placed on mats on the floor or ground. An older person usually divides the food into individual portions. Individuals eat only from the portion that is directly in front of them. It is impolite to move the bowl while others are eating. In many parts of the country, families eat separately according to sex and age. Most ethnic groups use only the right hand for eating; the left is used for personal hygiene. Others, especially in urban areas, eat with utensils in the continental style (fork in the left hand, knife in the right).

LIFESTYLE

Family

The value placed on the extended family has a great impact on society and individuals. Conformity and contribution to the extended family are considered more important than individual interests. In return for conformity, individuals enjoy a sense of belonging and security. Most Guinea-Bissauans desire large families. Most ethnic groups have a male-dominated family and political structure. There are intricate rules governing which tasks belong to men and women. Most rural families engage in agriculture and have rudimentary living conditions; they do not have electricity, running water, or other modern conveniences. Urban families enjoy somewhat higher living standards.

Dating and Marriage

Traditions regarding dating and marriage vary widely. Muslims are generally stricter about moral behavior and interaction between boys and girls, but young women often marry in their teens. Arranged marriages are common in rural areas. Social norms in urban areas are less rigid than in rural villages and some urban youth prefer to live together without legally getting married. Marriage can be very expensive because the bride's family often requires the groom to provide costly gifts or to farm family land for many years. In addition, a communal feast must be furnished at the wedding. Many men marry late because they have to save money for the event. Polygamy is a common practice, especially among Muslims (Islamic law allows a man to have up to four wives). The more wives a man has, the more respected he is.

Diet

Rice is very important to a person's diet. Guinea-Bissauans often say that if they haven't eaten rice at a meal, they haven't eaten at all. In rural areas, a normal meal consists of rice or millet and some type of sauce (made of palm oil or peanut paste, for example) served with fish or meat, if available. Among some groups, cattle are only killed for ceremonial feasts, although their milk is used for food. While fish is plentiful in coastal areas, it is not often eaten by those further inland. Tropical fruits (mangoes, papaya, and bananas), vegetables (manioc, sweet potatoes, corn, and squash), and peanuts are eaten in season. Muslims do not drink alcohol or eat pork. Throughout much of Guinea-Bissau, malnutrition is a serious problem.

Recreation

Soccer is the most popular sport in Guinea-Bissau. People take advantage of the rainy season work schedule to attend local soccer matches or listen to World Cup broadcasts. Some urban dwellers enjoy basketball and tennis, while traditional wrestling (*luta livre*) is popular in rural areas. The people love music and dance, both of which are an integral part of traditional ceremonies. Visiting friends is a common activity. Many urban dwellers socialize late into the night. Discos are popular. Television broadcasts, which began in 1989, are reaching more people each year.

Holidays

Official holidays include New Year's Day (1 January), National Hero's Day (20 January), Women's Day (8 March), International Worker's Day (1 May), Martyrs of Colonialism Day (3 August), Independence Day (24 September), Readjustment Day (14 November), and Christmas. *Carnaval* is usually held in February (before Ash Wednesday). Traditional dancing, parades, and papier-mâché masks are combined in several days of frenzied activity.

Two major Muslim holy days are also national holidays, a feast at the end of the Islamic month of *Ramadan* (a month in which Muslims fast from sunrise to sundown) and *Tabaski* (40 days later). In rural areas, various ethnic groups also maintain their own calendars and holidays.

Commerce

During the rainy season (May to October), government offices are open from 8:00 A.M. to 3:00 P.M., with no lunch break. This is a "short" schedule because of an increased demand for labor in the rice fields and because it is difficult to travel on the muddy roads. During the dry season (October to May), office hours are from 8:00 A.M. to noon and 3:00 to 6:00 P.M. Private merchants use the dry season schedule all year.

SOCIETY

Government

Guinea-Bissau is a democratic republic divided into nine regions. The president is chief of state, and is elected in a national vote. The prime minister (a new office in 1994) is head of government, and is appointed by the president on recommendation of the majority party in parliament. The National Assembly's one hundred members are all elected. All citizens are eligible to vote at age 15.

Economy

Guinea-Bissau is one of the poorest countries in the world. The country's Human Development Index (0.224) ranks it 164th out of 173 countries. Real gross domestic product per capita is $747. Most people do not earn a wage, being subsistence farmers, or their wages are not sufficient to meet basic needs. Guinea-Bissau must import much of its food and fuel, as well as manufactured goods. It exports cashews, fish, peanuts, and palm products. With about 85 percent of the labor force working in agriculture, greater agricultural productivity as well as industrial development are top priorities. Many natural resources are underdeveloped. Before they can be utilized, however, the government must implement structural and fiscal reform. With the three-year (1994–97) economic plan, officials hope to achieve growth at more than 3 percent and inflation as low as 15 percent. To do so, land and property reform, tighter business regulations, and agricultural self-sufficiency will be targeted in addition to fiscal measures. The currency is the Guinea-Bissauan *peso* (PG).

Transportation and Communication

Most roads are not paved. Therefore, travel is difficult during the rainy season. Rivers are used for major transportation. Public transportation is minimal, although *bush taxis* (pickup trucks with seats and a roof for baggage) are used for long-distance travel. Otherwise, people walk. Phone service is adequate in Bissau but underdeveloped elsewhere. Mail service is unreliable. The national radio station broadcasts mostly in Portuguese and Kriolu. There is one national weekly newspaper.

Education

Educational opportunities are limited and the literacy rate is about 36 percent. School facilities are inadequate. The national goal is to provide four years of compulsory education, but attendance is low. Drop-out rates are high because of family needs. The fact that all school instruction is conducted in Portuguese also causes problems. Because children do not learn Portuguese at home, they are essentially being taught in a foreign language. Using Kriolu as the language of instruction is also difficult because its written form has only recently been developed and there are very few printed materials available in Kriolu. The nation has secondary schools, but students must move to Bissau to complete their last year of high school. A few vocational and teacher training schools exist, but there are no universities.

Health

Medical facilities are generally inadequate. Life expectancy is low, averaging between 45 and 49 years. The infant mortality rate is 120 per 1,000. Major causes of death include malaria and gastrointestinal infections. Bilharzia and tuberculosis are widespread. A cholera epidemic in 1994-95 threatened coastal villages. Water is not potable.

FOR THE TRAVELER

A passport and visa are required for U.S. citizens to enter Guinea-Bissau. An exit visa is required to leave. The yellow fever vaccination, although no longer required, is still recommended. Other vaccinations and malarial suppressants are also strongly recommended. Uncooked or unpeeled fruits or vegetables should not be eaten; all food should be well cooked and served hot. Visitors should not swim in freshwater ponds or streams. Tourism is not well developed, but some beach resorts have been and are being built. It is appropriate to stand still when the national flag is raised or lowered; traffic stops and people stand outside their cars when it is lowered in the evening.

For more travel information, contact the Permanent Mission of Guinea-Bissau to the United Nations, 211 East 43d Street, Suite 604, New York, NY 10017; phone (212) 661–3977, or the Embassy of Guinea-Bissau, 918 16th Street NW, Mezzanine Suite, Washington, DC 20006; phone (202) 872–4222.

Commonwealth of
Hong Kong

Boundary representations not necessarily authoritative.

BACKGROUND

Land and Climate

Hong Kong is a British territory located on the south coast of China. Occupying an area about half the size of Rhode Island, Hong Kong covers 402 square miles (1,040 square kilometers). Hong Kong includes the New Territories (adjacent to China's Guangdong Province), the Kowloon Peninsula, two large islands (Hong Kong and Tai Yue Shan), and 200 smaller islands. The peninsula and islands are mountainous. Only a fraction (7 percent) of Hong Kong's land mass is arable, and natural resources are scarce. Hong Kong Island and the tip of the Kowloon peninsula form the natural harbor that has made Hong Kong such an important center for commerce. The climate is tropical with seasonal monsoons. Hong Kong experiences more seasonal change than most tropical areas. From September to March, the weather is generally dry and cool (50–65°F [10–18°C]). Hot, rainy weather prevails the rest of the year, when temperatures range from 80°F to more than 90°F (26–34°C).

History

The British East India Trading Company began using the Hong Kong Harbor for trade with China as early as 1699. The Chinese ceded control over Hong Kong Island to Great Britain in 1842, following the so-called Opium War, in which the Chinese tried to halt opium shipments to China. Kowloon was ceded after the Arrow War in 1860, and the New Territories were acquired on a 99-year lease in 1898, which effectively extended Kowloon to the Chinese border.

Hong Kong's importance as a free port was not established until after World War II, when it became a leading commercial port and tourist center. It also became a point of refuge for Chinese fleeing changes in China. During the 1980s, it was a destination for Vietnamese refugees.

With the lease on the New Territories due to expire in 1997, the British and Chinese governments began meeting in 1982 to determine Hong Kong's future. The resulting 1984 agreement states that Hong Kong will become a Special Administrative Region of China in July 1997. The agreement (called the Basic Law) provides for the continuation of Hong Kong's unique social, economic, legal, and other systems for 50 years after 1997 and for Hong Kong's smooth transition to its new status as part of China. The prospect of an eventual transfer of power raised fears in Hong Kong, as well as some calls for independence. China is increasing its activity in the colony. In 1991, it negotiated the right to have a voice in an important new airport project, as well as other concessions.

The transition process became tense in 1992 when Hong Kong and British officials supported a plan that would increase democratic political participation in the colony before 1997. China strongly opposed any strengthening of democratic institutions and sought to derail the effort by threatening to dismantle any system created outside of the 1984 agreement. But citizens of Hong Kong strongly favored greater democracy and the government, under Governor Christopher Patten, pressed ahead. In 1994, Hong Kong's 60-member Legislative Council passed the reform package that lowered the voting age from 21 to 18, eliminated appointed local council seats (replacing them with elected seats), and introduced other measures. China's reaction to the reforms was to suggest it would not abide by the Basic Law, but may instead install a socialist government after the transition. What actually happens will depend on negotiations and developments in both nations between now and 1997.

THE PEOPLE

Population

Hong Kong's population is about six million, but is not growing. During the Japanese occupation of Hong Kong in World War II, the population was as low as 600,000. After the war, and following political upheaval on the Chinese mainland, large numbers of people began to flow into the colony. Most settled on the peninsula or Hong Kong Island, transforming the two areas into a highly urbanized, densely populated metropolis. There are more than 14,000 people per square mile (5,900 people per square kilometer) on the entire territory, but few people actually live outside the main urban area. Hence, Hong Kong is one of the most densely populated areas in the world. Hong Kong is ethnically homogeneous; nearly 98 percent of the people are Chinese, mostly Cantonese with roots in the nearby Guangdong Province. Only about 57 percent of all residents were actually born in Hong Kong.

Language

Hong Kong maintains two official languages: Chinese and English. Street signs, telephone directories, and government documents are written in both. Although dialects from all provinces of China can be heard in Hong Kong, the Cantonese dialect dominates and is officially recognized. Most students study English, and English-speaking visitors have relatively few communication problems in business circles and tourist areas. The Chinese are delighted with Westerners who speak Chinese, especially the Cantonese dialect, and will praise them for their abilities.

Religion

The Chinese have a heritage of diversity with respect to moral philosophy and formal religion. Strong elements of Taoism and Confucianism, both of which originated in China, and Buddhism, with roots in India, form part of the religious life of many Hong Kong residents. Folk religious practices and ancestor veneration are also widespread. Many homes contain brightly decorated boxes with pictures of deceased relatives, smoldering incense sticks, or symbolic offerings of fruit, which are all part of the Chinese custom of honoring ancestors. Marriages and funerals are special ceremonial events. There is little congregational worship in the Western sense. The faithful observe special occasions with visits to shrines and temples or perform informal rites on the sidewalks near their homes. Nearly all major Christian denominations are also represented in Hong Kong, and about 10 percent of the population is Christian. It is not yet clear how Hong Kong's current climate of religious freedom will be affected in 1997.

General Attitudes

Hong Kong is referred to as the "Pearl of the Orient." The name not only describes its scenic beauty, impressive modern structures, and magnificent natural harbor, but also the energetic, hardworking people that have built Hong Kong into a major trade center. The Confucian ethic of proper social and family relationships forms the foundation of Chinese society. The Chinese are very conscious of their social position in relation to the people with whom they deal. An individual's actions reflect on the entire family. "Saving face" or avoiding embarrassment, shame, or dishonor is very important. In social interaction, the Chinese are careful to allow others to escape from potential embarrassment with dignity; causing someone to "lose face" is improper. The Chinese value modesty and patience over aggressive behavior.

Many social attitudes and traditions are changing as the colony approaches union with China in 1997. Thousands of people emigrated to other countries (66,000 in 1992 alone) to seek citizenship or a new life. This disrupted traditional family structures, employment patterns, and daily culture. Emigration slowed in 1994, and many people began to return. In 1994, 17 percent of those who left returned. Some had gained citizenship elsewhere and were returning to jobs and family, but others were simply returning to remain part of Hong Kong. Still, many people continue to leave, not willing to trust the future to Chinese control of Hong Kong. The initial emigration led to the feeling that the best and the brightest were leaving, but recent trends indicate that many strong leaders and business people are staying to take advantage of the booming economy in southern China. These people feel that they can be as prosperous under the Chinese as they were under the British.

Personal Appearance

All styles of clothing are worn in Hong Kong, from traditional to modern, from European to Asian. Modesty is important in public, as is cleanliness. Western-style suits are worn in business circles.

CUSTOMS AND COURTESIES

Greetings

Both English and Chinese greetings are common in Hong Kong. Handshakes are therefore appropriate. The Chinese practice modesty and reserve in dealing with others; aggressive behavior is offensive. Humility or self-demeaning comments are normal in describing oneself or one's accomplishments. Sincere compliments are given and appreciated, but the Chinese try to deny praise. Upon greeting, polite conversation usually includes inquiries about one's health, business affairs, or school activities.

Gestures

When sitting, it is most proper to place one's hands in the lap and keep one's feet on the floor. Although traditional Chinese will not cross their legs, one may do so without offending. Winking at someone is impolite and can have bad connotations. An open hand is usually used for pointing. Beckoning is done with the palm down and all fingers waving. Talking loudly is inappropriate.

Visiting

During the Chinese New Year or other festivals, it is traditional for a guest at someone's home to take a gift of fruit or candy for the hosts. Gifts are not expected on other occasions or for ordinary visits. However, a first-time guest may wish to present a small gift as a special token of respect. People offer and receive all gifts with both hands. Contrary to customs in other Asian societies, shoes are not usually removed when entering a home. Visitors should sit when invited to do so and maintain good posture. Special effort is made to greet and show respect to older people. When visiting with others, correct social manners include generosity.

Eating

The Chinese usually use chopsticks when eating at home. Dishes of food are typically placed in the center of the table. Everyone helps themselves by taking portions of food with chopsticks from the central plates and placing them in their own personal bowls of rice. It is proper to hold the rice bowl close to one's mouth when eating. The host will refill the guest's bowl with more rice and other food until politely refused. It is considered impolite to make noise or talk too much during the meal. It is traditionally inappropriate to eat food on the street. Because of the cosmopolitan nature of Hong Kong, restaurants offering many types of food are available, including most American foods. Therefore, eating habits follow the custom most associated with that type of food. Service is often included in the bill, but it is still customary to leave a tip.

LIFESTYLE

Family

Chinese family members are bound by a strong tradition of loyalty, obedience, and respect, as reflected by one of the lowest divorce rates in the world. While families have traditionally been large, the trend toward smaller families is clearly seen in Hong Kong. The Chinese do not usually display affection in public, but this is changing among the youth. A source of stress for many families in Hong Kong is the sharp difference between traditional values and more modern, or Western, practices. Also straining the traditionally strong family is the decision of so many to leave Hong Kong before China takes control in 1997. These families must often leave the elderly and disabled behind, sometimes with no one to care for them.

Dating and Marriage

Marriages arranged by the parents of the bride and groom are no longer common. Western-style dating and marriages have become quite normal. Couples tend to marry at an older age than those in Western countries. A large banquet (such as a 12-course meal) is the highlight of the elaborate wedding celebration.

Diet

Most food is imported. Rice is the main staple for Chinese families. Chinese dishes are often prepared with fish, pork, chicken, and vegetables. A large variety of fruits are also available. Business is often conducted over lunch or dinner. Lavish restaurant meals are traditional for weddings and other special events.

Recreation

Movies and television are perhaps the most popular forms of entertainment. Beach outings and picnics are also enjoyed. Favorite sports include table tennis, soccer, skating, squash, tennis, swimming, horse racing, basketball, and boating. The noise of *mahjong* tiles (a game that is a cross between dominoes and cards) being slapped on a board often fills the streets, as people enjoy playing the game in parks.

Holidays

Holidays are based on the lunar calendar and may fall on different days each year. The Chinese New Year is often in February and is the most important holiday. Week-long festivities include parades, visiting relatives, paying one's debts, and displaying messages of prosperity and longevity on doorways. The *Ching Ming* Festival in April is a time for honoring the dead and includes ancestor worship activities. In June, the Dragon Boat Festival is celebrated with dragon boat races. The Mid-Autumn Festival is a harvest holiday celebrated with lanterns and moon cakes. Other holidays include the British Queen's Birthday (June), Liberation Day (August), *Chung Yeung* (in October, also a time to honor the dead), Easter, and Christmas.

Commerce

Hard work is the basic element of life for most. A six-day, 48-hour workweek is common. Business hours are from 9:00 A.M. to 5:00 P.M. five days a week, and from 9:00 A.M. to 1:00 P.M. on Saturdays. However, shops are usually open from early in the morning until late at night, especially if the owner lives in an apartment above the shop. In the evenings, the streets are still very busy with people enjoying the many activities of Hong Kong's nightlife.

SOCIETY

Government

Hong Kong is a British colony. Its external affairs are the responsibility of the United Kingdom, but the Hong Kong government administers local affairs. China currently has a consultative role in policy matters. As a colony, Hong Kong's governor (currently Christopher Patten) represents the British queen and is assisted by an Executive Council. The Legislative Council enacts laws and controls the finances. All those older than age 18 who have lived in Hong Kong for at least seven years are eligible to vote for members of the Legislative Council. The 60-member council elected in the September 1995 elections will be the legislature sitting when China takes control in 1997.

Economy

With very little agriculture, Hong Kong has to rely on shipping, commerce, and manufacturing for its survival and success. *Hong Kong* means "fragrant harbor," and the busy harbor is the key to its business. It is a free port; no tariffs are levied on imports or exports. Duties are placed only on tobacco, liquors, cosmetics, and a few other items. The chief industries are textiles, clothing, toys, electronics, and plastics. Tourism is also a significant source of income.

More than 35 percent of the population is employed in manufacturing. While rice and some vegetables are grown in Hong Kong's rural areas and the New Territories, most food is imported from countries such as China. Hong Kong's economy is very healthy, growing annually at about 10 percent in the 1980s and only slowing for a short time to less than 3 percent. In 1994, the rate was about 5 percent. Joint ventures with Chinese firms, as well as Hong Kong ventures in southern China are adding to a robust economic performance and a strong stock market. Indeed, investments in China's Guangdong Province have already blurred the border between China and Hong Kong. In 1995, investors became cautious due to political issues in China, but few expect major declines in investments. Unemployment is only about 2 percent, but inflation is more than 10 percent.

The nation's Human Development Index (0.875) ranks it 24th out of 173 countries. Real gross domestic product per capita is $18,520, which has increased dramatically in the last generation. These figures reflect Hong Kong's economic prosperity. Although income distribution is somewhat unequal, the majority of people benefit from good wages, modern social services, and economic opportunities available in the open market system. The currency is the Hong Kong dollar (HK$).

Transportation and Communication

A subway system offers rapid transit to major locations on Hong Kong Island and Kowloon. Trains connect Kowloon and the New Territories. There is an extensive bus and minibus system. Taxis are widely available. Following the British tradition, all traffic travels on the left side of the road. A ferry connects the islands and the mainland. Hong Kong has all the modern communication systems necessary for excellent domestic and international service.

Education

Scholarship is a long-standing Chinese tradition, and formal education is valued highly by citizens of Hong Kong. A free, nine-year education program is required of all children. Nearly all children complete the primary level; three-fourths proceed from primary to secondary school. Entrance to the better secondary schools is based on a competitive examination. There are three government-financed, post-secondary institutions and five technical institutes in Hong Kong. The two universities allow entrance to less than 15,000 students, so large numbers seek higher education abroad. Hong Kong's literacy rate is estimated at 90 percent.

Health

Excellent low-cost medical care is available in all hospitals and clinics, although the government facilities are often crowded. The people enjoy one of the highest life expectancy rates in the world, averaging 77 to 84 years. The infant mortality rate is 6 per 1,000.

FOR THE TRAVELER

No visa is required for U.S. visitors staying less than one month, but a valid passport and proof of onward passage are required. English-speaking policemen have red shoulder tabs on their uniforms. Electrical outlets require plug and voltage adaptors for American appliances to work. If traveling to mainland China, unless with a guided tour, one should retain some Hong Kong dollars for transportation back to the hotel from the border. When flying out of Hong Kong, one must arrive earlier than usual for an international flight, since check-in can take longer; there are strict limits on the size and weight of carry-on luggage. The airport tax must be paid in Hong Kong dollars. For information about travel and shopping opportunities in Hong Kong, contact the Hong Kong Tourist Association at 590 Fifth Avenue, Fifth Floor, New York, NY 10036; phone (212) 869–5008, or at 10940 Wilshire Boulevard, Suite 1220, Los Angeles, CA 90024. For visa information contact the Consular Section of the British Embassy at 19 Observatory Circle NW, Washington, DC 20008; phone (202) 986–0205.

Printed on recycled paper

CULTURGRAM ™ '96

Republic of
India

Boundary representations not necessarily authoritative.

BACKGROUND

Land and Climate

Covering 1,269,338 square miles (3,287,590 square kilometers), India is roughly one-third the size of the United States. A small section of the Himalayan mountains lies in the disputed territories of the north. The Ganges plain below is fertile and densely populated. South of the plain is the Deccan plateau. About half of the country is under cultivation and one-fourth is forested. Most of the country experiences three basic seasons: March through May (hot summer), June through September (rainy), and October through February (cool winter). Temperatures rarely go below 40°F (4°C) in January and will reach 100°F (38°C) during the summer. Variations exist according to region and elevation.

History

The Indus Valley civilization dates back more than 5,000 years. Around 1500 B.C., Aryans arrived from Central Asia and gradually pushed the native Dravidians to the south. Buddhism flourished in King Asoka's reign in the third century B.C., but declined afterward. The northern Gupta Kingdom, from the fourth to sixth centuries A.D., was a golden age of science, literature, and the arts. Southern India also experienced several great empires. Arab, Turk, and Afghan Muslims ruled successively from the eighth to eighteenth centuries, providing some basis for the historical animosity between Hindus and Muslims. Then Portuguese and Dutch traders entered India. The English eventually assumed political control of the area.

After World War I, Mahatma Gandhi led a continuing nationalist movement, advocating civil disobedience and passive resistance in a campaign to gain autonomy from Great Britain. Gandhi's goal was realized in 1947, when India was granted independence. Religious rivalry and violence led to the establishment of Pakistan as a Muslim state. India became a republic within the British Commonwealth; Jawaharlal Nehru was the first prime minister. Gandhi was assassinated in 1948. Nehru's daughter (Indira Gandhi) was prime minister twice (1966–77 and 1980–84). She was assassinated by her own Sikh body guards after Indian troops stormed the Sikhs' Golden Temple in a violent clash with separatists. Violence marked the Sikh movement for independence in Punjab Province through the early 1990s. While violence has subsided, the desire for independence remains strong. Muslims also desire secession in the far north area of Jammu and Kashmir, where continued fighting has postponed scheduled local elections until 1996.

Indira Gandhi's son, Rajiv, was elected prime minister in 1984. He lost the 1989 election to V. P. Singh. Two years of economic troubles, tensions between castes, a rise in Hindu fundamentalism, and violence between religious groups caused both Singh and his replacement to resign. During elections in 1991, Rajiv Gandhi was assassinated as he campaigned for the premiership. Congress Party leader P. V. Narasimha Rao then became prime minister. Riots sparked by the 1992 Hindu destruction of a treasured Muslim mosque left hundreds dead and again threatened government stability. Rao remained in office, however, and worked to improve economic and social conditions throughout India. His four-year economic liberalization program attracted large amounts of foreign investment by 1995 and earned international praise, but it angered some political elements in India who did not agree with the program's social cuts. Rao's Congress Party suffered a division, making him vulnerable in scheduled 1996 elections.

THE PEOPLE

Population

India has the second largest population (920 million) in the world behind China. It is growing annually at 1.8 percent. India is one of the most ethnically diverse countries in the world, but factors other than ethnicity are more likely to separate people. These include rural/urban, religious, and socioeconomic differences. The Indo-Aryans make up the largest ethnic group (72 percent), while the Dravidians account for 25 percent of the population. The remaining 3 percent is made of a myriad of other groups, including Mongoloids.

Language

India has at least 300 known languages, 24 of which each have one million or more speakers. Besides Hindi and English, there are 14 other official languages, including Bengali, Urdu, Punjabi, and Sanskrit. At least 30 percent of the population speaks Hindi. English is important for business and government and is the language of national communication. Hindustani, a blend of Hindi and Urdu, is spoken widely in northern India.

Religion

India's constitution proclaims the country to be a secular state, which is particularly important in a society of such religious diversity. India is the birthplace of Hinduism, Buddhism, Jainism, and Sikhism—all of which believe in reincarnation. It is also the adopted home of most followers of Zoroastrianism. Slightly more than 82 percent of the people are Hindu. Hinduism is extremely diverse, polytheistic, rich in ceremony, and associated with the caste system. Although Hinduism lacks an authority structure, it does have clearly defined beliefs regarding the purpose of life. The caste system dictates that individuals must work their way up to the highest caste through reincarnation before they can exit life on earth to a better existence. Below the fourth caste (laborers) are the "Untouchables," with whom other Hindus are to have no contact, and who are usually poor and powerless. The caste system has been constitutionally abolished but continues to be practiced. It limits social and economic mobility for millions of Indians, and maintains the status of the privileged few.

Almost 12 percent of the people are Muslim, who follow scriptures (the *Qur'an*) revealed by *Allah* to the prophet Muhammad. The Sikh religion (2 percent, mostly in Punjab) began around the 16th century, drawing on principles from both Hinduism and Islam. It stresses simple teachings and devotion. The Sikh practice of tolerance is reflected in offers of free food and shelter to anyone who comes to their places of worship. Buddhism, although it began in India and flourished for a time, did not maintain a following in India. Less than 1 percent of the population is Buddhist. Jains, though powerful in India, also make up less than 1 percent. Jains practice a reverence for life (*ahimsa,* literally "nonviolence"), self-denial (especially monks), and follow a vegetarian diet. Less than 3 percent of the population is Christian.

General Attitudes

Indian people are religious, family oriented, and philosophical. They believe strongly in simple material comforts and rich spiritual accomplishments. Abundant expressions of gratitude are typically saved for real favors rather than routine courtesies. Physical purity and spiritual refinement are highly valued. Fatalism is widespread in the country, as it is a component of the major religions of India. This leads one to accept one's course in life as the will of God or fate. The ideals of humility and self-denial, as encouraged by Mahatma Gandhi, are highly respected. Indians are proud of a rich heritage that has produced numerous architectural and artistic masterpieces.

They are equally proud of being the world's most populous democracy—where free elections have determined leadership since 1947. The tolerance and social harmony necessary to maintain democracy has been weakened by violent clashes between Hindus and Muslims. Many Hindus want India to become a Hindu state rather than a secular nation. They resent special Muslim minority rights, and Muslims resent Hindu domination. Tensions also exist between social classes and between rural and urban areas; the clash is not only one of money and power, but also traditional versus modern values. All of these issues reflect the highly complex nature of Indian society, presenting a challenge to India's people to find a future that will continue to accommodate diversity.

Personal Appearance

Women in India generally wear a *saree,* a long length of fabric draped in variations that can represent socioeconomic status and religious affiliation. Or they wear a colorful type of pantsuit with a long shirt that extends to the knee. Women also wear considerable jewelry. Hindu women may wear a *bindi*, or red dot, on their foreheads. Traditionally, this was a sign of femininity, gracefulness, and marital status, but in modern times it has become more often an optional beauty aid, with the color of the *bindi* frequently matching the wearer's outfit. After marriage, the *bindi*, accompanied by white powder on the upper forehead (or vermilion powder in the part of her hair), signifies the woman's husband is alive; widows do not wear a *bindi*. Men may wear Western-style suits or more traditional clothing, such as the *dhoti* (large piece of cloth wrapped around the waist). As with women, this varies with region and religion. Sikhs wear turbans and specific items with religious significance, while Hindus and Muslims may wear a long shirt with pants, sometimes accompanied by a jacket or a vest.

CUSTOMS AND COURTESIES

Greetings

The *namaste* is the traditional greeting used in India. One's palms are pressed together (fingers up) below the chin and the term *namaste* (in the south, *namaskaram*) is spoken. For superiors or to show respect, a slight bow is added. Indians do not usually shake hands with or touch women in formal or informal gatherings. This is a sign of respect for a woman's privacy. Indian men will, however, shake hands with Westerners, and educated women may do so as a courtesy. "Hello" and "Hi" are acceptable greetings among equals, but more formal terms like "Good morning" or its equivalent are necessary for superiors. It is polite to use titles such as *professor*, *doctor*, *Mr.*, *Shri* (for men), *Shreemati* (married women), *Kumari* (single women), or the suffix *ji* with a last name to show respect. The right hand is used for the *salaam* gesture of greeting and farewell with Muslims. Indians usually ask permission before taking leave of others.

Gestures

Whistling is very impolite. Women do not wink or whistle; such behavior is considered unladylike. Public displays of affection are inappropriate. It is impolite to sniff or handle flowers displayed at bazaars. Postage stamps are not licked, but water is provided to moisten them. Grasping one's own ears expresses repentance or sincerity. One's feet or shoes should not touch another person, and if they do, an immediate apology is necessary. Excessive hand gestures or verbal articulation are considered impolite. Beckoning is done with the palm turned down, and pointing is often done with the chin. A person must cover the head when entering a Sikh shrine.

Visiting

Most visiting occurs in the home, and visits between friends or family are often unannounced. The need for prior arrangements is increasing in large cities. At social gatherings, guests are often adorned with a garland of flowers, which should be immediately removed and carried in the hand as an expression of humility. Guests repay the host's hospitality by giving gifts, such as specialty foods (fruits, sweets) from other areas of the country, or something for the children. Guests invited for a meal customarily bring sweets, flowers, or fruit for the hosts.

Many Indians do not wear shoes inside the home. Most at least remove shoes before entering the living room. Hosts offer their guests water, tea or coffee, and fruits or sweets. It is polite for a guest to initially refuse these refreshments, but to eventually accept them. When visitors are ready to leave, they often indicate it by saying *namaste*. In temples, saffron powder, holy water from the Ganges River, and sometimes food are offered to visitors as *prasad*, or blessings from the gods; it is discourteous to refuse these gifts. Women cover their heads when entering sacred places. Among the more traditional elements of society, women may not be involved in social functions. Indians are too polite to say "no" to an invitation; if they cannot attend, they will more likely say "I'll try."

Eating

Eating habits vary sharply between traditional and modern settings. Modern (most often urban) families will eat together and follow many Western customs. Traditional families may use the right hand instead of utensils for eating their food. Also, women may eat after other members of the family and any guests. Diners might drink from a communal cup; if so, the lips never touch it. A gesture of *namaste* can indicate one has had enough to eat. Some Hindus object to having their food handled by members of lower castes.

LIFESTYLE
Family

The basic social unit in India is the family, which takes precedence over the individual. Families are generally large, but the government is actively encouraging family planning to curb rapid population growth. Extended families often live together or near each other. The elderly are respected and cared for by their families. The father is head of the household. A middle or upper-class father expects to financially take care of the children until they have finished an education and taken a job—regardless of how long it takes. Few women work outside the home. However, a growing number of urban woman are part of the workforce, making important professional contributions to Indian society.

Dating and Marriage

Dating practices of Western countries are not common in India, although urban residents are affected by Western standards. Traditional marriages are still arranged by parents, often with the consent of the bride and groom. Marriage is sacred to most Indians and is considered to endure beyond death. Chastity is the most treasured virtue of womanhood. Weddings are times of great celebration, expense, and feasting. Ceremonies are often elaborate and vary widely from region to region. In many, the bride and groom exchange garlands and/or words before they circle around a fire three to seven times to solemnize the marriage. Bright clothing, jewelry, and flowers are part of nearly every type of ceremony. Giving a dowry (money, land, etc.) to the groom is still common for the bride's parents, even though the practice is illegal. Divorce rates are very low.

Diet

Foods vary widely in India, depending on the culture and region. For example, rice is a staple in the south, while wheat bread *(roti)* is the staple in the north. Indian meals are usually very spicy. Different types of curry (eggs, fish, meat, or vegetables in a spicy sauce) are popular. Vegetarianism is widely practiced, often for religious reasons. All castes have different food laws and customs, as does each religion. The Hindus consider cows to be sacred and will not eat beef or even use anything made of leather. Muslims do not eat pork or drink alcohol. Betel leaves and nuts are commonly eaten after meals to aid digestion.

Recreation

Soccer, cricket, and hockey are favorite sports. India's motion picture industry is one of the world's largest. Every major city has more than a hundred modern theaters, some equipped with elevators and restaurants. Musicals and romance films are typical, and are the source of India's pop music. Dance performances and music concerts are also popular. India's classical music has two styles, northern and southern, both of which are played according to rigid rhythm rules. Recreation is often found in the many religious and folk festivals throughout the year.

Holidays

India's national holidays include International New Year's Day (1 January), Republic Day (26 January), Independence Day (15 August), and Mahatma Gandhi's Birthday (2 October). Numerous spring and harvest festivals are common between January and March, celebrated with dancing and many colorful events. One such festival is *Holi*, a celebration to mark the end of the cold season, during which people toss colored water and powder on each other. *Baisakhi* is the Hindu New Year, a time for feasts, fireworks, and dancing; it also marks the beginning of Punjab's harvest season. *Id-ul-Fitr* is celebrated with prayers and greetings by Muslims at the end of *Ramzaan*, the month of fasting. Snakes are venerated during the summer festival of *Naag Panchami* because of their association with Hindu gods. The Hindu Lord Krishna's birth is celebrated in August or September during *Jan mashtami*. *Dussehra* (under different names in various regions) is held around October to celebrate the triumph of good over evil. *Diwali* (Festival of Lights) is a Hindu holiday celebrating the triumph of light over darkness. Thousands of lights decorate stores and homes at this time of goodwill. Christians celebrate Christmas and Easter.

Commerce

Normal business hours generally run from 9:30 A.M. to 1:00 P.M. and 2:00 to 5:00 P.M., Monday through Friday. However, many people must work far more than a 40-hour week to buy basic necessities. Government offices open at 10:00 A.M. These hours are mostly for urban areas; hours in rural areas vary. Bazaars and fairs are popular in India. Rural areas may have a fair every week—some for trading animals, others for selling farm produce and handicrafts, and others as part of a festival.

SOCIETY

Government

A democratic republic, India has 25 states and 7 territories. The president, elected by all members of parliament and the state legislatures, is a head of state with mostly ceremonial duties. The government is led by a prime minister. India's parliament consists of two houses: the *Rajya Sabha* (Council of States) and the *Lok Sabha* (House of the People). Elected by the legislatures of each state, not more than 250 members serve in the *Rajya Sabha*. All but two of the 545 members of the *Lok Sabha* are directly elected by the Indian people. India's president, currently Shankar Dayal Sharma, nominates the others. All citizens may vote at age 18. The major opposition to the Congress Party is the Bharatiya Janata Party, but numerous smaller parties have legislative representation.

Economy

Despite increased industrial development, India remains primarily an agricultural nation. It is self-sufficient in food and agricultural production is expanding. Employing more than 65 percent of the population, Indian agriculture is a leading world producer of peanuts, rice, cheese, tobacco, wheat, cotton, milk, sugarcane, and rubber. Other important crops include cereals, oil seed, jute, tea, and coffee. Export earnings come mainly from tea, coffee, iron ore, fish products, and manufactured items. Textiles are a principal domestic product and also a profitable export. India is rich in natural resources with coal, iron ore, natural gas, diamonds, crude oil, limestone, and important minerals. Industrial production has been increasing over the years, as have high technology industries. The growing middle (consumer) class is consuming new products. Tourism is also increasingly vital for income.

Despite India's booming economy, serious problems remain. About half of the people live in poverty, and income distribution remains rather unequal. The government's most delicate challenge is to balance economic liberalization/modernization with meeting the large population's social needs. The country's Human Development Index (0.382) ranks it 135th out of 173 countries. Real gross domestic product per capita is $1,150. The currency is the *rupee* (Re).

Transportation and Communication

Roads in urban areas are generally well developed, but those in rural regions may be unpaved and impassable in heavy rains. In cities, buses, which are often crowded, serve as the main source of public transportation. Taxis are also plentiful, but meters are not always used and rates change often. Trains connect major cities. Other common forms of transportation include rickshaws (bicycle driven), motor scooters, and horse-drawn *tanga*. Traffic travels on the left side of the road. Televisions are widely owned and very popular, especially in urban areas. Radios are even more widespread, as they are more affordable. Newspapers are also plentiful. Domestic telephone service is not well developed.

Education

Education is a primary concern in India. Although schooling is free and compulsory from ages six to fourteen, facilities are often inadequate and many children do not attend school. Government programs are trying to meet the increasing demand for education. Some progress has been realized because the literacy rate has risen to 52 percent in the past few years. India has more than 100 universities, 3,000 colleges, and at least 15 institutes dedicated to research in the arts and sciences.

Health

The people of India face several health challenges stemming from poverty, malnutrition, poor sanitation, and overpopulation. Religious beliefs (such as Hindu rat worship that allows rats to breed uncontrollably) also pose certain threats. Diseases such as cholera, yellow fever, malaria, typhoid, and hepatitis endanger many, especially rural inhabitants who lack access to medical care. Health care workers seek to improve health standards by teaching hygiene, nutrition, and family planning. The infant mortality rate is 78 per 1,000, while life expectancy is about 58 years.

FOR THE TRAVELER

A visa and a valid passport are required for U.S. travelers. Yellow fever vaccinations are necessary, but others are recommended. Drink only treated or boiled water. Eat only well-cooked meats served hot, and thoroughly washed fresh foods. Because of violence or instability, travel may at times be restricted to certain areas. For more information, contact the Government of India Tourist Office, 30 Rockefeller Plaza, Suite 15, North Mezzanine, New York, NY 10112; phone (212) 586–4901, or the Embassy of India, 2536 Massachusetts Avenue NW, Washington, DC 20008; phone (202) 939–9839.

Republic of
Indonesia

Boundary representations not necessarily authoritative.

BACKGROUND

Land and Climate

Indonesia is made up of 13,670 islands that stretch some 3,200 miles (4,800 kilometers) along the equator, south, east, and west of Malaysia. It shares the island of Borneo with Malaysia and Brunei. Its portion is called Kalimantan. It also shares the island of New Guinea with the independent country of Papua New Guinea. Indonesia's province there is Irian Jaya. The largest non-shared islands include Sumatra, Java, Celebes, and Timor. Only 6,000 islands are actually inhabited. Covering 741,096 square miles (1,919,400 square kilometers), the islands total about one-fifth the size of the United States, or three times the size of Texas. The popular island of Bali is also in Indonesia. The dry season extends from June to November, with temperatures ranging from 80°F to 90°F (26–32°C) or more. The wet monsoon season is from November to March or April. Rainfall is heavy. The climate is hot and humid year-round, although it is somewhat cooler in the mountains of the larger islands.

History

When Christopher Columbus reached the Americas, he was looking for the East Indies to get access to the rich spice trade. Most of the islands he sought but never found are part of present-day Indonesia. Early Indonesian culture was influenced by India in the first century B.C. Islam was introduced through Muslim traders in the 15th century. Western traders were active in the region during the 16th and 17th centuries. In fact, Indonesia became a Dutch colony in 1816 and remained so until the 1940s.

The Japanese occupied the islands during World War II. Upon Japan's defeat, Indonesian nationalists proclaimed independence from the Netherlands in August 1945. A republic was formed under President Sukarno. A Communist coup attempt, supported by China and led by Indonesia's large Communist party, was suppressed in 1965 by General Suharto. Thousands died in the rioting and violence surrounding the coup. Suharto banned the Communist party and became president; he continues to lead Indonesia today.

When Suharto loosened control on the press and opposition groups in the early 1990s, many people demonstrated for greater democracy and a change of leadership with the 1993 elections. These people felt Suharto's government had denied certain civil rights (such as freedom of speech) for too long. Suharto was, however, the only candidate on the 1993 ballot, and was therefore reelected to a five-year term. He is expected to retire in 1998. Although accused of human rights abuses (particularly against rebel groups), giving special treatment to relatives, and being an authoritarian ruler, Suharto is credited for creating Indonesia's vibrant and growing economy. He is appreciated by the people for the better life they now enjoy. As a strong figure, he is also seen as the only man who can hold Indonesia's rich diversity of peoples together.

THE PEOPLE

Population

There are more than 200 million people in Indonesia. The population is growing annually at 1.6 percent and is the fourth largest in the world. Indonesia's ethnic make-up is very diverse, consisting of approximately 350 distinct ethnic groups; many have their own language and most have their own customs and heritage. Of the largest groups, 45 percent are Javanese, 14 percent Sundanese, 7.5 percent Madurese, and 7.5 percent Coastal Malays. The remaining 26 percent belong to various, smaller groups.

Java is the most densely populated island. Although it comprises just 7 percent of Indonesia's land, it holds 60 percent of the country's people. Since the late 1960s, the government has carried out a transmigration program to resettle people (mostly Javanese) to other islands in order to ease population growth problems on Java. Millions of people have been moved; some have had success but others have been sent to isolated or unsuitable areas. Reforms have addressed those problems and the program continues with the intent to make life better for the migrants and for the people on Java.

The farmers of Java and Bali form the largest cultural group. They are predominantly Muslim and have strong social and spiritual values. They are skilled in the arts of native dance, music, and drama. The commercially oriented traders of the coastal region, mostly Muslim, have a high regard for religious learning and law. Some northern areas are strongly Christian. The tribes of Kalimantan (part of Borneo) and Irian Jaya (western half of New Guinea) maintain tight kinship bonds, practice animistic religions, and have a clan-oriented economic and social life. The people on Bali are mostly Hindu and belong to traditional kingdoms. Ancient cultural practices are being lost to Westernization, but some Balinese leaders are working to save them.

Language

The official language is Indonesian (a variety of Malay). However, some 300 other languages are also spoken in the country. Of them, Javanese is the most common with more than 70 million speakers. More than half the population speaks some Indonesian or Malay. Because Dutch was the official language until 1942, some older adults still speak it. English is the leading international language and is taught as a third language in the schools (after the main ethnic language and Indonesian).

Religion

At least 87 percent of the population is Muslim. In fact, Indonesia is home to the world's largest Muslim population. Muslims believe in *Allah* as God, and that Muhammad was *Allah's* last chosen Prophet (following a long line of Biblical prophets). They accept the *Qur'an* (Koran) as scripture, which they believe was revealed by *Allah* to Muhammad through the angel Gabriel. Muslims show their devotion by professing the name of *Allah* and the Prophet, fasting during the holy month of *Ramadan*, donating to the poor, making a pilgrimage to Makkah, Saudi Arabia, following dietary codes such as not drinking alcohol and not eating pork, and praying five times daily.

Nine percent of the population is Christian (mostly Protestant), and 2 percent is Hindu. There are also some Buddhists, mostly among the Chinese population. Regardless of their religion, most Indonesians venerate their ancestors. Freedom of religion is guaranteed and religious tolerance is important, but proselyting has been banned by the government to avoid religious conflict.

General Attitudes

Indonesians value loyalty to family and friends more than their own concerns. They rarely disagree in public, seldom say "No" (they say *Belum,* "Not yet"), and generally have time for others. Punctuality, while important, is not emphasized at the expense of personal relations. Indonesians appreciate a quiet voice, an unassuming attitude, and discretion. To embarrass someone is a terrible insult. Indonesians often view Westerners as too quick to anger, too serious about themselves, and too committed to the idea that "time is money." Patience is the key to interaction.

Personal Appearance

Indonesians prefer modest dress, whether they wear Western styles or more traditional clothing. Businessmen wear a shirt and tie; a suit jacket is not necessary. The traditional dress for a woman is called a *sarong*, a long wraparound dress with an intricate *batik* pattern. *Batik* is the national handicraft and has been part of Indonesian culture for centuries. It is traditionally made by using molten wax to create designs on cloth. When the cloth is dyed, the wax preserves a white pattern. Authentic *batik*, made by hand, is being replaced with mass-production imitations. Authentic *batik* clothing may be worn for formal situations by both men and women.

CUSTOMS AND COURTESIES

Greetings

Indonesian culture is based on honor and respect for the individual. Letters begin with *Dengan hormat* (With respect), and respect is also important in greeting others. Men and women usually shake hands and bow the head slightly when introduced for the first time. In Indonesian, they ask *"Apa kabar?"* (How are you?) and the response is usually positive. After an initial introduction, it is unusual to shake hands in greeting; a nod or slight bow is most appropriate. Indonesians shake hands when congratulating someone or when saying good-bye before a long trip. Muslims follow a handshake by touching their right palm to the heart in a show of friendship.

Older individuals are greeted with a slight bow. They are respectfully addressed as *Ibu* (mother) or *Pak* (father). Unless married or engaged to a woman, a man does not usually touch her in public, except to shake hands, even if he knows her well. If a person has a title, it is used in greeting and general conversation. Many Indonesians, especially the Javanese, have only one name and are therefore addressed both formally and casually by that name. Business representatives often exchange calling cards when greeting each other.

Gestures

One should avoid using gestures to beckon another person, except for children or a *becak* (pedicab) driver. Beckoning is done by waving all fingers with the palm facing down. Approval is sometimes shown by a pat on the shoulder, but one never touches the head of another person. The left hand is not used to shake hands, touch others, point, eat, or give or receive objects. Standing with one's hands in the pockets or on the hips is a sign of defiance or arrogance. Crossing the legs is usually inappropriate, but if crossed, one knee should be over the other (never an ankle on the knee). The bottom of one's foot should never face another person. Yawning in public is avoided, but if a person must yawn, a hand should be placed over the mouth. Laughing at another's mistake is very offensive. People on public transportation should offer their seats to the elderly.

Visiting

Indonesians believe that visits bring honor to the host, and they warmly welcome all guests. Unannounced visits are common between friends and relatives. Visitors sit when invited to, but they will also rise when the host or hostess enters the room. A drink is often served, but a guest does not drink until invited to. Refreshments are also usually served, and it is polite to at least eat a little bit to avoid offending the hosts. If the host or hostess is not wearing footwear, it is polite for visitors to remove theirs. Shoes are removed before entering carpeted rooms, feasting places, places of funeral viewings, or holy places (especially mosques). More Westernized Indonesians appreciate flowers from guests invited to dinner, but gifts are not expected by traditional Indonesians. Any gift given is accepted graciously because it is impolite to refuse anything. Gifts are not opened in the giver's presence.

Eating

Although there are many restaurants along the streets, eating while standing or walking on the street is inappropriate. Finishing a drink implies the desire for the glass to be refilled. Many Westernized Indonesians eat with a spoon and fork, but more traditional families eat with their hands. Generally, the fork is held in the left hand and the spoon in the right. It is impolite to eat or drink until invited to do so by the host. Both hands are kept above the table while eating. Compliments about the food are appreciated by the hostess. At restaurants, a service charge is usually included in the bill. Tipping is not common. Public use of toothpicks is avoided; if toothpicks must be used, one hand should cover the mouth during use.

LIFESTYLE

Family

Traditionally, Indonesians have had large families, but people are stopping at two children. Members of the extended family often live under the same roof or near one another. Loyalty and cooperation among family members are highly valued. The home is traditionally dominated by the father, and the mother is responsible for raising children and caring for the household. The trend today is for many urban women to work outside the home, and they comprise 40 percent of the labor force. Women comprise 12 percent of parliament and generally have equal access to education. Indonesian women also have more rights than women in other predominantly Muslim countries, including rights in property settlements, inheritances, and divorce.

Dating and Marriage

Conventional, Western-style dating is uncommon, except in urban areas. Even in a city, in order to date someone, a boy must visit a girl's home several times to get acquainted with the family. After a while, the two can go on a date. If the girl does not want to go, she may tell the boy to stop coming to the home. Arranged marriages have given way to marriages of individual choice only urban areas. They are still common in rural areas. Rural women are often married by the time they are 20 years old. As in other predominantly Muslim countries, a man may have as many as four wives if he can provide for each equally. Yet it is rare to find a man who has more than one wife; women generally oppose polygamy and men usually cannot afford it.

Diet

Rice is the main staple food, and *nasi dan tempeh* (rice with fermented beans) is a typical daily meal. Now nearly self-sufficient, Indonesia once imported large amounts of rice to feed its growing population. Vegetables, fish, and hot sauces are often served with the rice. Tea and coffee are the most common drinks. Fresh fruits are widely available and are often eaten as dessert. Popular meats include beef and chicken. Muslims do not eat pork. Chilies are often used (sometimes in large quantities) in cooking, as are other spices. Coconut milk is used to cook particularly spicy food known as *padang,* which is named after the city on Sumatra where it originated.

Recreation

Indonesians participate in or watch sports of all types. Soccer is very popular among the youth. Indonesians are consistently among the best in the world in badminton. Volleyball and tennis are also enjoyed. Bicycling serves not only as transportation but also recreation. Watching television is a popular nonathletic recreational activity. Going to movies is also a favorite activity. People prefer films from the United States and Hong Kong, but Indonesia does have its own successful film industry.

Holidays

Indonesians celebrate International New Year's Day (1 January), Easter, Ascension, *Idul-Fitr* (celebrating the end of *Ramadan*), Independence Day (17 August), *Idul-Adha* (11th day of the 12th lunar month, celebrating the end of the Muslim pilgrimage to Makkah), and the Muslim New Year. During the Islamic month of *Ramadan*, Muslims do not eat or drink from sunrise to sundown; a family meal is eaten in the evening. Some Hindu religious festivals are also commemorated. Christians celebrate Christmas. A variety of festivals common to certain islands or ethnic groups are also held throughout the year.

Commerce

Businesses are generally open from 8:00 A.M. to 5:00 P.M., but many close for an hour or two in the afternoon. Some, including government offices, will close at midday on Friday for Muslim worship. Some open on Saturday mornings, but most are closed on Sunday. Restaurants close between 10:00 and 11:00 P.M., except for those serving *padang,* which are often open 24 hours. Except in large stores, where prices are fixed, bartering is often practiced in purchasing goods.

SOCIETY

Government

The republic of Indonesia is composed of 24 provinces, two special regions, and one special capital city district. The president is elected by the People's Consultative Assembly (MPR), which is made up of the unicameral legislature (500 members) and 500 other people chosen through a variety of processes. One hundred members of the *Dewan Perwakilan Rakyat* (House of Representatives) are appointed from the military. For the other 400 seats, free elections occur in theory, but issues and candidates are carefully screened and controlled by Suharto's ruling party: GOLKAR. The president holds most of the power in the country and has been reelected several times without opposition. All those married or over age 17 are eligible to vote.

Economy

Indonesia is rich in natural resources, but much of them remain undeveloped. Agriculture still employs 55 percent of the labor force and accounts for 25 percent of Indonesia's production. Important crops include rice, rubber, soybean, copra, tea, cassava, and peanuts. The government promotes increased natural rubber production by planting new trees. Forestry and fishing are also important. Currently, petroleum and liquid natural gas account for about 30 percent of all export earnings. That is, however, substantially lower than it was only a few years ago. When oil revenues were at their highest, the government invested money in manufacturing and other enterprises. This allowed Indonesia to diversify and be protected against wide fluctuations in the price of oil. It also gave jobs to millions of people, and tens of millions of people have benefitted from antipoverty programs and economic reforms.

The country's Human Development Index (0.586) ranks it 105th out of 173 countries. Real gross domestic product per capita is $2,730, which is certain to show substantial gains as the growing middle class becomes more established. Indonesia's rank is also expected to improve in the next few years. Monthly wages are rising. The gross domestic product is growing strongly at about 7 percent.

Inflation is relatively low, as is unemployment. Underemployment is still a problem to be addressed. One of Indonesia's successes is the type of base on which the economy is built. Many cottage industries produce consumer items such as clothing and shoes for markets in the industrialized world, including the United States. The number of employees per enterprise is relatively small, so market shocks are less painful to large groups of people. Many corporations inhabiting skyscraper offices in Jakarta are domestic firms, not foreign ones. Indonesia is also looking to the future of more advanced industries that will further expand revenues. Economic deregulations announced in 1995 are expected to further boost the country's regional and global competitiveness. The currency is the Indonesian *rupiah* (Rp).

Education

Education is free and compulsory between ages six and twelve, although facilities in rural areas are often unable to allow all students to attend. Still, nearly 80 percent of all students complete the six years of primary schooling. About half of them go on to secondary schools, which are divided between junior and senior levels, each lasting three years. The literacy rate is 77 percent and is steadily improving. Each of Indonesia's 24 provinces has at least one university or academy for higher education.

Transportation and Communication

Indonesia is easily reached by international flights; domestic flights connect major islands. There are rail systems in large urban areas. Taxis and pedicabs are readily available. A passenger agrees with the driver on the fare before getting into the cab, especially in taxis without meters. Buses are crowded and roads outside urban areas are not very good. Ferries connect islands. Many people travel by bicycle and foot. Traffic travels on the left side of the road.

Health

Medical facilities are best in urban areas, but the government is striving to improve conditions in villages as well. Significant improvements have been made to the health care system, especially regarding the accessibility of rural clinics and sanitation. The infant mortality rate has dropped by more than 50 percent since the 1970s. It is now 67 per 1,000. Most infants are immunized. Life expectancy rates have also risen substantially to an average of about 61 years. Family planning programs, promoted under the slogan "two children is enough," have slowed population growth and contributed to the healthier lives of most families. Despite the progress, problems remain. Malnutrition, diseases such as cholera and malaria, the lack of extensive prenatal care, and unsafe drinking water all affect Indonesia's people (especially in rural areas).

FOR THE TRAVELER

Tourists do not need a visa for visits of less than two months, but a valid passport is necessary, along with proof of return ticket or onward passage. Travelers should have a yellow fever vaccination and consider taking precautions against cholera and malaria. One should consult a doctor before travel. Water is not potable. Electrical plug outlets vary and adaptor kits are necessary. Indonesia offers a variety of out-of-the-way vacations as well as luxury hotels. Beautiful beaches, charming villages and people, and fascinating culture draw many tourists each year. For information on travel opportunities in Indonesia, contact the Indonesian Tourist Promotion Office, 3457 Wilshire Boulevard, Los Angeles, CA 90010. You may also wish to contact the Embassy of Indonesia, 2020 Massachusetts NW, Washington, DC 20036; phone (202) 775–5200.

CULTURGRAM™ '96

Islamic Republic of
Iran

Boundary representations not necessarily authoritative.

A
S
I
A

BACKGROUND

Land and Climate

Iran is just larger than Alaska or about one-fifth the size of the continental United States. It covers 636,293 square miles (1,648,000 square kilometers). Most of Iran is a mountainous plateau, 4,000 feet (1,200 meters) above sea level, rimmed with two major mountain chains. The desert to the east is largely uninhabited, as are the mountains. There are narrow coastal plains in the north (along the Caspian Sea) and south (along the Persian Gulf). The highest mountain is Mt. Damavānd at 18,386 feet (5,604 meters) in the northeast. The central plateau is very arid and long, hot, dry summers prevail. Winters are cold in the north except for along the Caspian Sea. Fall and spring are relatively short. The country is subject to earthquakes. A northern quake in 1990 killed 40,000 people and injured many more.

History

The area of present-day Iran was known anciently as Persia and was ruled by such powerful emperors as Darius and Cyrus the Great. The Arabs conquered the area in the seventh century, introducing the people to Islam. Both the Seljuk Turks and the Mongols (Genghis Khan) ruled in Iran at one time. Persian dynastic rule was revived when the Safavid dynasty essentially set up the first national government in the 1500s. The Safavids also established Shi'ism as the state religion, linking it with nationalism. They were interested in preventing further expansion of the Ottoman Empire, whose rulers were Sunni Muslims. The Qajar dynasty took over in the 1800s, followed by the Pahlavi dynasty of the 20th century.

This dynasty was created when a military officer, Reza Khan, seized control of the government in 1921 and reigned (from 1925) as Reza Shah Pahlavi. He did much to modernize the country. His son, Mohammed Reza Pahlavi, continued the modernization when he took power in 1941. Known as the Shah, he sponsored literacy campaigns, voting rights for women, and industrialization. Despite these goals, his neglect of basic social problems and his lack of emphasis on Islam made his reign unpopular.

In 1979, the Shah fled the country in response to popular unrest. The Ayatollah Ruhollah Khomeini, the exiled leader of the movement against the monarchy, returned at that time to establish the Islamic Republic of Iran. Khomeini ordered that all laws and practices follow strict Islamic principles. When the Shah was admitted to the United States for medical treatment, Iran's revolutionaries responded by seizing the U.S. embassy in Tehran and holding its personnel hostage until January 1981. The Shah moved to Panama and then to Egypt, where he died in 1980. The United States severed ties with Iran and still has no diplomatic relations with the government. Many Iranian policies, including the sponsorship of terrorism, alienated most Western nations during the 1980s. A war broke out with Iraq in 1980 over the disputed region of Shatt-al Arab. The war drained the economy and many industries were damaged or destroyed in the fighting. A cease-fire was declared in 1988, and a peace treaty was signed in 1990.

Khomeini died in 1989 and was succeeded as the supreme leader (*Valli-e-faghih*) by the Ayatollah Ali Hoseini-Khamenei, who had been president. The *Hojatolislam* (a religious title)

Hashemi Rafsanjani became the new president. He moved to open some communication links to the West and to moderate policies that some had considered restrictive (such as public dress requirements). Rafsanjani was reelected in June 1993. Hopes for moderation in Iranian policies and relations with the West (and particularly the United States) darkened in 1995 when the United States condemned Iran for seeking to obtain nuclear weapons and for sponsoring terrorism. Iran denies the claims, and also denies that the subsequent strengthening of a U.S. trade embargo would harm its international trade.

THE PEOPLE

Population

The population of Iran is 65.6 million and is growing at a rapid annual rate of 3.5 percent. Tehrān, the capital, is the largest city, with more than six million inhabitants. The rest of the urban population (about 57 percent of the total) is divided among various other large cities, including Mashhad (1.5 million people), and four cities with about one million inhabitants each: Tabrīz, Esfahān, Ābādān, and Shīrāz. While urbanization was the trend during the 1970s, the opposite was encouraged in the 1980s. Nomadic life has always played a role in traditional Iranian society and more than 10 percent of the population is nomadic or seminomadic, including the Lur, Bakhtiari, and Qushqa'i. Most Iranians are ethnic Persians (51 percent). Smaller groups include Azerbaijanis (24), Gilakis and Mazandaranis (8), Kurds (7), Arabs (3), Lurs (2), Balochs (2), and Turkmen (2), among others.

Language

The official language is Persian Farsi, but there are many other languages and Persian dialects spoken because of the different ethnic groups in Iran. Turkic, Kurdish, Luri, and Arabic are among the major languages spoken. Turkic is the most widely spoken language after Farsi, as it is the language of the Azerbaijanis and Turkmen. All school instruction is in Farsi.

Religion

Shi'ite Islam is the state religion and has been since the 1500s. Before that time, most Persians were Sunni Muslims. About 95 percent of the population is *Shī'a* (Shiite) Muslim, with some 4 percent belonging the Sunni branch of Islam. Shi'ism adds a strong nationalist element to the religious principles of Islam. Iran is the most populated Shiite Muslim country. Muslims believe in a monotheistic God (*Allah*), that he chose Muhammad to be his prophet, and that there will be a day of judgment. Shiism reveres Fatima, the daughter of the prophet Muhammad; her husband, Ali; and their two sons, Hassan and Hussein; as well as their descendants (*Imams*). Shiite Muslims, unlike the Sunnis, believe that Ali was selected by Muhammad as his successor. Shiites consider the *Imams* to be holy men who have the right to leadership. The 12th *Imam* disappeared; it is believed he will reappear as a messiah to guide Muslims in the future.

The *Qur'an* (Koran), the scripture of the Muslims, is composed of God's revelations to Muhammad through the angel Gabriel. Revelations to other prophets (Adam, Noah, Abraham, Isaac, Jacob, Joseph, Moses, and Jesus) from the Bible are also acknowledged by Muslims. They accept Jesus as a prophet but not as the son of *Allah*, since they do not believe *Allah* begets children. Since the 1979 revolution, a strong conservative and fundamentalist interpretation of Islam has been carried out by the clergy (*mullahs*). Persons belonging to another religion are allowed to maintain their beliefs, but they are subject to civil law as established on Islamic principles. There are about 350,000 Baha'i in Iran, along with 80,000 Christians, and 30,000 Jews. Zoroastrianism, the religion displaced by Islam in the seventh century, is also officially recognized and has some followers. With the exception of the Baha'i, each minority group has representation in the *Majles* (see Government). The Baha'i faith is outlawed because the Shiites consider it an apostate branch of Islam.

Muslims show their devotion through the "Five Pillars of Islam." These include *shahada*, professing that there is no God but *Allah* and Muhammed is his prophet; *salat*, praying five times daily while facing Makkah, Saudi Arabia; *zakat*, giving money to the poor; *saum*, fasting during the month of *Ramadan*; and *hajj*, making a pilgrimage to Makkah once in a lifetime.

General Attitudes

Iranians have a rich cultural heritage, including the great Persian empire, of which they are proud. Although radicalism prevailed in the politics of the 1980s, the people remained hospitable and open to others. They like foreigners as a whole, even Americans. Official statements condemning Western nations express contempt for foreign policy choices rather than hatred towards other people. Iranians value education, culture, cleverness, and wisdom. Their perception of time is more flexible than in the West. Iranians do not stress punctuality over the needs of individuals, who are more important than schedules.

Personal Appearance

Iranians dress formally and conservatively in public. Men usually wear Western-style clothing, although traditional robes and turbans are also worn, especially by religious leaders. Women must be covered from head to foot in public. During the 1980s, a veil and a black *chador* (long dress) were required as well. However, moderations have allowed women to go without the veil and to wear other clothing if it is loose fitting. Even in this case, only a woman's hands and face may be visible in public. The traditionally legal black head covering (*maghna-eh*) while still worn, is being replaced by more colorful scarves. Although this is still illegal, younger women may even let a little hair show on the forehead. Makeup is also being worn again in private gatherings. Black *chadors* cover stylish, modern clothing. Islam generally requires men to wear long sleeves. Bright colors are not worn. Personal cleanliness is important. Most men have beards. At home, Iranians often dress in comfortable pajamas. They may also receive guests dressed in pajamas, which are not only for sleeping but relaxing as well.

CUSTOMS AND COURTESIES

Greetings

A handshake is the customary greeting in Iran. A slight bow or nod while shaking hands shows respect. A man does not shake a woman's hand unless she offers it first. Iranians of the same sex will often kiss each other on the cheek as a greeting and sign of affection. Proper etiquette is essential when greeting another person and one will often ask about the family and the health of the other. A typical Farsi greeting is *Dorood* (Greetings); an appropriate response is *Dorood-bar-to* (Greetings to you). People often use Arabic greetings such as *Salam* (Peace). A common parting phrase is *Khoda hafiz* (May God protect you). Formal titles and last names are used in greetings to show respect. Iranians generally stand when someone (especially an older or more prominent person) enters the room for the first time and again when someone leaves. To shake hands with a child shows respect for the parents.

Gestures

Objects are passed with the right hand or both hands, but not with the left hand alone. The soles of the feet should not point at any person. Crossing one's legs is generally not acceptable. Slouching or stretching one's legs in a group is offensive. Out of respect and to maintain proper distance between genders, men and women do not always make eye contact during conversation. Men and women do not display affection in public, even if married. However, friendship and affection is often shown between members of the same sex. To beckon someone, all fingers are waved with the palm facing down. To tilt the head up quickly means "no" and to tilt it down means "yes." To twist the head means "what?" To extend the thumb is vulgar.

Visiting

Hospitality is a cherished tradition in Iran. Iranian philosophy claims a guest is a gift from (or friend of) *Allah*. Respecting the guest is a way of respecting *Allah*. Guests are therefore the center of attention in an Iranian home and everything is done to make them feel comfortable. Visitors remove their shoes before entering carpeted areas of a home, although this is not often practiced in larger cities. A polite guest compliments the host generously and accepts compliments in return. However, one should avoid complimenting objects; the host may feel an obligation to offer the object to the guest.

When invited to dinner, it is customary for the guest to take a flowering plant, cut flowers, or candy to the host. Iranians do not open gifts in front of the giver. If offered gifts, refreshments, or invitations from a friend, it is polite to decline a few times before graciously accepting and thanking the host several times. The oldest man present receives the greatest respect. Because visiting is so much a part of the culture, families and friends visit one another often, even several times a month if they live close by. Iranians enjoy getting together for conversation, picnics, or just to enjoy each other's company. The common term for visiting is *did-o-bazdid*.

Eating

The midday meal is the most important meal of the day. Dinner is usually served after 8:00 P.M. Elaborate Persian meals will often be prepared for guests, and a host may insist that several helpings are eaten. Food is eaten with the right hand only. Tea is usually offered to guests. During the entire month of *Ramadan*, Muslims do not eat or drink anything from dawn to dusk; in the evenings, families eat together and visit friends and relatives.

LIFESTYLE

Family

The family unit is strong in Iran and provides its members with identity, security, and social organization. The father is the undisputed head of the household. Large families with many children, especially boys, are preferred. It is legal for a man to have up to four wives if he can provide for each equally and if he has permission from his other wife or wives; permission from the government is also necessary. Most men, however, choose to have only one wife. The elderly are respected and cared for by younger members of the extended family. Relatives remain close. Parents feel a lifelong commitment to children, often providing them with financial support well after marriage. Regardless of their age, unmarried persons live with their parents until they marry. Most families are able to provide for their own basic necessities, and there is a growing upper class that enjoys many modern amenities.

If someone has two family names, the second one is the official surname. It is often based on their hometown.

Dating and Marriage

Dating as practiced in the West is not common because members of the opposite sex are rarely alone with each other unless married, related, or engaged. Daughters are usually protected by their families to the point that they do not speak to strangers until married. More traditional families will limit a daughter's education to keep her home. Marriage is a highly valued institution. Most people expect to marry and have a family. Divorce is very rare. Most marriages are arranged by families. In the past, this meant that many girls married their cousins. But new attitudes have developed in some areas regarding education, work, and freedom in selecting marriage partners.

Girls marry between the ages of 18 and 25. Men marry somewhat later because of military service or because they are not earning enough money to start a family. A couple may choose to have a temporary marriage (*sigheh*) that can last between a few days and 99 years. A woman marrying in this arrangement and any children born in the marriage do not have the same rights and privileges as conventional wives and children, but they are accepted as legitimate. Both a man and woman must consent to a *sigheh*, and women marrying for the first time must have parental consent. Couples might choose the *sigheh* as a trial marriage or because the wedding is much less expensive than a conventional wedding. When a *sigheh* is terminated, or if a regularly married couple divorce, the woman may not marry again for at least 100 days. Weddings are elaborate celebrations.

Diet

The diet varies throughout the country. Muslims do not eat pork or drink alcohol. Under current law, alcohol consumption is forbidden. Rice and wheat bread are the most common staple foods. Rice is often served with a meat and vegetable stew. Yogurt is generally served with rice or other foods. Fresh vegetables are important in the diet, and fresh fruit is a favorite dessert. White cheeses are also popular.

Recreation

Iranians enjoy soccer, wrestling, the martial arts, basketball, volleyball, and ping pong. The urban population enjoys going to the movies. Socializing, however, provides the greatest opportunity for relaxation. Iranians also visit tea houses, shop in bazaars, and stroll through the streets.

Holidays

The lunar calendar is used in Iran to determine religious festivals and the new year; the solar (Gregorian) calendar is used to set official public holidays. The Iranian New Year (*Naw Ruz*) is celebrated around the end of March in connection with the spring equinox. This is the biggest holiday of the year and is marked with visits, gifts, and feasts. Businesses close and the celebrations last four days. National holidays include Revolution Day (11 February), Oil Nationalization Day (20 March), Islamic Republic Day (1 April), National Picnic Day (2 April), Armed Forces Day (18 April), the Anniversary of Khomeini's exile (4 May), and the Anniversary of Khomeini's Death (5 May). Religious holidays occur on different days each year. They include feasts for *Aid-e-fitr* to end the month of *Ramadan*, *Aid-e-adha* to commemorate Abraham's willingness to sacrifice his son, and *Aid-e-ghorban* to mark the end of the *hajj*. Other holidays mark the birth and death of the prophet Muhammad and the *Imams*. Also, *Aid-e-khadir* celebrates Muhammad's choosing of Ali (Fatima's husband) as his successor.

Commerce

Iranians conduct business Saturday through Thursday. Office hours are usually from 8:00 A.M. to noon and 2:00 to 6:00 P.M. Summer hours may differ; businesses often close in the hot afternoon and reopen for a short time in the evening. Many businesses are only open until noon on Thursday and most close on Friday, the Muslim day of worship. Shops and retail stores are often open from 8:00 P.M. to late in the evening, with a break from noon to 3:00 P.M. Bartering, especially in the bazaar, is a way of life. Keeping a client waiting is not an insult; clients are often served refreshments while waiting.

SOCIETY

Government

A Council of Guardians (made up of religious and lay leaders) holds power over the constitution, appoints judicial authorities, and approves candidates for president. Twelve of the members are elected, and twelve are appointed. The Council must approve all legislation passed by the Islamic Consultative Assembly (*Majles*). All laws must be in harmony with the doctrines of Islam, as interpreted by the country's religious authorities. The head of government and official chief of state is President Rafsanjani. The supreme leader, the Ayatollah Ali Hoseini-Khamenei, often functions as head of state. The voting age is 15. Voters receive a stamp on their identity papers verifying they have voted. This makes it easier to get government employment or assistance and to qualify for a passport.

Economy

Oil reserves allowed Iran to prosper in the 1970s and early 1980s. Energy production is still the most important economic activity in Iran; oil exports account for 90 percent of all export earnings. After the 1979 revolution, major industries were nationalized, but these became inefficient at producing enough goods for the country's needs. The Rafsanjani government tried to liberalize the economy, but met with stiff opposition from conservative politicians. Still, some progress was realized, and conditions have improved slightly. There is some foreign investment and trade, but economic growth is generally low.

Iran's Human Development Index (0.672) ranks it 86th out of 173 countries. Real gross domestic product per capita is $4,670, an improvement over a generation ago. These figures indicate that a growing number of people earn an income that provides for basic needs. Still, 30 percent of rural people continue to live in poverty.

Transportation and Communication

Iran has a well-developed transportation system with railroads, highways, ports, and several airports. Buses and minibuses provide most public transportation in the cities. A metro rail service operates in Tehran. The number of private cars is increasing. All parts of the country are accessible by telephone, but only a small number of homes have a private line. About one-fourth of all households have televisions, but most have radios. Communication facilities are government-owned.

Education

Elementary schooling is compulsory for all children beginning at age seven. That lasts for five years, and most (89 percent) complete the primary level. A sizable portion of these pupils (74 percent) go on to secondary schooling, which is divided into three sections. The first three years are called "guidance" and are of a general nature; the next three years are called "high school." Upon completion of high school, students are ready to begin a trade career. If they wish to go to college, they must complete a seventh year, called "pre-university." Islamic studies are often stressed over secular training at most levels, but the sciences and math are popular. The literacy rate is 54 percent, which represents about 64 percent for men and 43 percent for women. The University of Tehran, various provincial universities, and several smaller universities provide higher education.

Elementary schools often run on two shifts, with half of the students attending in the morning and half in the afternoon. This allows the growing population to receive an education despite a lack of buildings and teachers. Boys and girls attend separate classes, although not necessarily separate schools. Segregation of the sexes is a fundamental Islamic principle.

Health

Public health services are run by the government, but curative treatment services are divided between the government and private sector. Government facilities and private doctors accept the government health insurance that covers public employees and their families, but private hospitals demand a cash deposit upon admission. Infectious diseases like typhoid, measles, dysentery, and malaria are prevalent. More than 90 percent of all children are immunized against major childhood diseases. Water is safe in urban areas, but not always in rural regions. The infant mortality rate is 44 per 1,000. Life expectancy averages 65 years.

FOR THE TRAVELER

Currently the United States does not have diplomatic relations with Iran. To obtain a visa for travel, one must contact Pakistan's embassy, which represents Iran in the United States. A U.S. citizen must have special permission to visit the country. Vaccinations should be considered depending on the length of stay and areas to be visited. Visitors are expected to abide by Islamic law while in Iran. For more information, contact the Iranian Interests Section, Embassy of Pakistan, 2315 Massachusetts Avenue NW, Washington, DC 20008.

State of
Israel

Boundary representations not necessarily authoritative.

BACKGROUND

Land and Climate

Covering 8,020 square miles (20,770 square kilometers), Israel is about the same size as New Jersey. This does not include the occupied territory (called the Administered Area) of the West Bank. Despite the country's size, the land and climate vary substantially by region. The terrain ranges from fertile valleys and flower-covered hills to unique deserts to the Dead Sea, which is the lowest point on earth (1,300 feet or 390 meters below sea level). The hot Negev desert is home to the Mahktesh crater, as well as mountains and oases. Eilat, a resort town, borders the Red Sea. On the west coastal plain, summers are humid and winters mild. The hills experience more comfortable summers but colder winters, and the Jordan Rift Valley has a relatively pleasant climate. The rainy season is from October to April. Some snow falls in the mountains, and Mt. Hermon receives enough to support snow skiing. An efficient irrigation system makes agricultural land arable all year.

History

The Holy Land, from which the present state of Israel emerged, claims a long history of rule by different powers. A Hebrew kingdom was established from the 12 tribes of Israel that came out of Egypt with Moses. King David ruled this kingdom some 3,000 years ago. After his son Solomon's reign, it split into two states—Israel and Judah—that were later destroyed by Assyria and Babylonia in the eighth and sixth centuries B.C. The populations were dispersed or taken captive, although many Israelites remained in the area. After the Persian conquest of the Middle East, many Jews were allowed to return to the Holy Land to establish a nation and build a temple. The land later fell to the Greeks and then to the Romans. Heavily persecuted, the Jewish population declined sharply during the Byzantine era (A.D. 313–636). In the 600s, the area (named *Palestine* by the Romans) was conquered by Muslims who ruled for nearly 1,000 years.

The Ottoman Turks controlled Palestine from the 16th century until World War I. In the 1890s, Theodor Herzl founded Zionism as an international movement to restore Palestine to the Jews. After World War I, the area came under British control. Various plans for partitioning the area were put forth but never actually implemented. When the Jewish people suffered so heavily from the Holocaust during World War II, they began to immigrate to Israel in large numbers. The British first tried to halt the process, but were unable to stop Jews from seeking a new life in what they consider to be their land of inheritance. In 1947, the United Nations voted to divide the area into two states—one Arab and one Jewish. In May 1948, Israel proclaimed an independent state and the British withdrew. Neighboring Arab nations, opposed to an independent Jewish state, declared war and attacked. Subsequent wars were fought in 1956, 1967, and 1973. In 1979, Egypt and Israel signed a peace treaty; Egypt was the first Arab nation to recognize Israel's right to exist. Arab terrorism and border wars with Lebanon caused problems throughout the 1980s, the major concern being the status of territories occupied by Israel in the 1967 war.

The Palestine Liberation Organization (PLO) renounced terrorism in 1987 and accepted Israel's right to exist. At the same time, it declared an independent Palestinian state in the occupied territories of the West Bank and Gaza, a declaration rejected by Israel. Violence in the occupied territories persisted, sometimes spilling over into Israel itself.

Plagued by continued violence, pressed by the international community, and recognizing a greater opportunity for cooperation due to the Gulf War, Israel agreed in 1991 to sit down with its Arab neighbors and discuss plans for peace. The ongoing Middle East Peace process has often been interrupted by severe violence on both sides, and has suffered many setbacks. Rival political parties in Israel are divided as to whether Israel should even consider full autonomy in the occupied territories, the return of the Golan Heights to Syria, and compromise on several other fronts.

Yitzhak Rabin, who became prime minister in 1992, supported negotiations and worked to find acceptable areas of compromise. Little progress was made until a 1993 breakthrough during secret talks in Norway. Israel and the Palestine Liberation Organization (which represents the interests of Palestinians living in the occupied territories) agreed to establish limited autonomy in parts of the territories. The agreement was signed in historic meetings between Rabin and his PLO counterpart, Yassir Arafat. By mid-1994, Gaza and one town (Jericho) in the West Bank had achieved autonomy. The plan was scheduled to expand in 1995. One of the greatest and most welcomed events was a peace treaty with Jordan in 1994 that ended hostilities and opened the way for mutual cooperation on regional issues. In 1995, progress towards peace with Syria was also made despite the very sensitive issue of Syria's claim to the Golan Heights. Rabin proposed a popular referendum to decide the matter.

Resistance to the overall peace process among more conservative Israelis and especially among militant Palestinian groups such as *Hamas* have hampered negotiations. Progress is also impacted at times by the Jewish community in the United States, which has considerable financial and religious influence in Israel. Arab terrorist attacks continue to promote an atmosphere of distrust and it is uncertain how this will affect and be affected by national elections in 1996.

THE PEOPLE

Population

Israel's population of 5 million includes about 250,000 Israeli settlers in the West Bank, Gaza, the Golan Heights, and East Jerusalem. Israelis refer to the West Bank as Judea and Samaria, the biblical names for the region. Israelis do not consider East Jerusalem an occupied territory, but an integral part of Jerusalem. Nearly 90 percent of the people live in cities. The average population growth rate (2.2 percent) fluctuates depending on immigration. For 1992, it rose to 4 percent because 350,000 people emigrated from the former Soviet Union. Large numbers have also come from Ethiopia. Such immigration waves challenge Israel's ability to provide housing and jobs, but society has mostly been able to absorb the newcomers.

Seventeen percent of Israel's citizens are Palestinian Arabs and members of the Druze and Circasean ethnic groups.

The rest of the population (83 percent) is Jewish. The word *Jewish* does not describe an ethnic group or population—it is a religion, a culture, and a nation. There are three identities in Israel: religion, citizenship, and nationality. Someone could be Christian by religion, Israeli by citizenship, and Arab by nationality. A Jew is Jewish by religion and nationality, but Israeli by citizenship. Because Jews come from around the world, their ethnic makeup is mixed. However, they are usually divided into two ethnic heritages. Sephardic Jews come mainly from the Middle East and North Africa. Ashkenic Jews are from Europe. The Ashkenazim have generally dominated religion and politics, but the Sephardim are well represented in government and business. Despite intermarriage, equalizing incomes, and other factors, historical tensions between the two groups continue to divide Israelis.

By law, all Jews in the world have the right to emigrate to Israel, as long as they can prove their identity (inherited through the mother) or are recognized converts.

Language

Hebrew is Israel's official language. Arabic has official status, is spoken by the Arab minority, and is taught from the fifth grade on in school. English, frequently used in commerce, is spoken by most Israelis and is also taught from the fifth grade on. Nearly all Israelis speak at least two languages, often because they or their parents emigrated from other countries after 1948. Today's immigrants attend government-sponsored *ulpan* classes to learn Hebrew. They also continue to speak their various languages amongst themselves.

Religion

The city of Jerusalem and the surrounding areas have played an important role in the development of several of the world's major religions, including Judaism, Christianity, and Islam. Jerusalem is therefore holy to all three religions and is a source of conflict between them.

Judaism focuses on a unique relationship and responsibility between the Creator and the Jewish nation, as particularly outlined in the Bible's first five books of Moses. Once expressed primarily through temple rites, worship patterns now concentrate on personal action. Orthodox or observant Jews strictly adhere to certain behavioral imperatives, such as honoring the Jewish Sabbath from sundown Friday to sundown Saturday and following dietary codes. Most Jews are nonobservant (secular), but are sensitive to and accepting of Jewish values. Two other traditions—reform and conservative Judaism—have small followings.

About 13 percent of the population is Muslim (mostly Sunni) and nearly 2 percent is Druze. The remaining 2 to 3 percent is Christian, about half of which is Greek Orthodox. Haifa is also the world center of the Baha'i faith, which emphasizes the unity of religion and the oneness of mankind.

General Attitudes

Israel is a land of informality, as evidenced in people's casual dress habits and custom to address each other by first name. Respect is shown in other ways—through courtesy and neighborly help, for instance. Israelis are civic-minded and involved in the community. In a large apartment complex, every family knows each other by name and knows at least a little about each family member. Israelis are inquisitive; they are avid readers and enjoy travel. They value determination, hard work, openness, frankness, and humor. The group, especially family, is more important than each individual member, and Israelis enjoy sharing life with their family and friends. Most people desire to have a home and comfortable life, but material possessions are less important than a strong family.

Israelis are devoted to their culture and state. Israel's very existence is greatly valued. Part of the people's pride for the nation comes with mandatory military service. Women serve two years and men serve three. Arab-Israeli men may volunteer for military service, but they are not drafted. Jewish immigration is encouraged as part of the Zionist movement, the ongoing effort to establish and maintain a Jewish homeland.

Personal Appearance

Most Israelis wear casual Western-style clothing. Men only wear suits and ties on formal occasions, otherwise preferring open-necked shirts and jeans. Women wear slacks and dresses. Orthodox Jews dress more conservatively (long sleeves for men, longer skirts for women). Men might cover their head with an embroidered *kippah* cap or yarmulka. Israeli youth like European and American fashions. Both men and women wear shorts and sandals in summer. Cotton fabric is preferred.

Among ultra Orthodox Jews, men wear black pants and jackets over white buttoned-up shirts with black hats; women do not wear pants and they cover their heads with a scarf. Muslims wear Western or traditional clothing.

CUSTOMS AND COURTESIES

Greetings

Informality governs most greetings. *Shalom* (Peace) is the usual greeting and parting phrase. It may be followed by *Ma Nishma?* (What's up?), *Ma Inyanim?* (What's happening?), or the more formal *Ma Shlomcha?* (How are you?). For women, this last phrase is *Ma Shlomech?*

Handshakes are most common. Additional touching (hugging, kissing) depends largely on one's ethnic origin and the relationship between the greeters. People from Eastern cultures tend to touch more than Westerners. For instance, women might hug and kiss once or twice on the cheek. Close male friends may pat each other on the back or shoulder. Among the very religious, men and women do not touch in public.

When addressing another person, first names are most often used once the person has been introduced. This custom extends to most facets of life, including the military. Even school children call their teachers by first name.

Gestures

Hands are used often in conversation and make the discussion seem very lively. The most common gesture is to bring thumb and fingertips together, palm facing up, and moving the hand up and down; this means "wait a minute" or "hold on." One expresses exasperation by shrugging the shoulders, sometimes also holding open palms up.

Respect for elders is extremely important. For instance, one always gives up a bus seat to an older person.

Visiting

Israelis love to visit friends and relatives. They might drop by unannounced for a short visit or call ahead to arrange something. Invitations to dinner, especially on Friday evening or Saturday afternoon, are common. Invited guests usually take a gift such as flowers or chocolates.

For any visit, hosts always offer refreshments. These typically include coffee, tea, or a cold drink, as well as cake, cookies or snacks (nuts and sunflower seeds). In addition to visiting in the home, Israelis enjoy meeting at cafés for an evening of conversation.

Eating

On average, Israelis eat three meals a day. Breakfast is light. The main meal is traditionally in the early afternoon (except on Friday evening), and supper is usually light. Families are often too busy to eat all together, but they will at least gather for the Friday evening and Saturday afternoon meals. Conversation and a casual atmosphere accompany most meals. If guests are present, it is most polite to accept offers of additional food.

LIFESTYLE

Family

The family is central to Israeli life, with a great deal of care and attention given to children. Ties remain very strong, even as children become adults. Parents feel a deep responsibility to prepare and provide for a child's future. Married children expect to live near their parents or other relatives. They expect to care for their elderly parents. Families come together on holidays, especially Passover, and for big celebrations.

The father is traditionally the head of the family but women have great influence in all decisions. Many women work outside the home and comprise 35 percent of the labor force. Some families (7–8 percent) live either in a *kibbutz* or a *moshav*. In a *kibbutz,* families share the land, work, food, and dining hall equally. They concentrate on agriculture and technology. A *moshav* is a small village (less than 100 families) where families live separately but cooperate in providing for the needs of the community and in marketing the village's products.

Dating and Marriage

Dating is common and young people enjoy dancing, eating out, and going to movies. Among Muslims and Orthodox Jews, dating may be supervised or restricted. Weddings are a great social event in Israel, often including a large dinner party where singing and dancing last well into the night. Of course, traditions vary depending on cultural background. Parents are usually heavily involved in planning weddings and paying for the festivities.

There are no civil marriages in Israel. All weddings must be performed by a religious authority. Rabbis perform Jewish ceremonies and a *Khadi* handles Muslim weddings. Christians go to their clergymen. Divorce and other family issues are dealt with by religious courts. Each religion has the right to adjudicate family matters according to its own customs.

Diet

Israelis eat foods from a variety of cultures. Some of the more popular dishes include *falafel* (pita bread filled with balls of fried chickpea batter), *kebab* (meat and vegetables on a skewer), *tshulnt* (traditional bean stew), *burékas* (pastry filled with cheese and spinach), chicken soup, and Russian *borscht* (beet soup). *Gefilte* fish, a dish of baked or stewed ground fish brought to Israel by European Jews, is popular as a Sabbath dish because it can be cooked ahead of time and served cold. Vegetable salad, mixed with olive oil, lemon juice, and spices, is a staple and usually eaten every day. Salads usually do not contain lettuce. Chicken and fish are eaten more frequently than beef because they are less expensive. Fish restaurants are common. Fruits and vegetables are plentiful and fruit juices are often part of lunch or dinner. Milk products, such as yogurt and cottage cheese, are popular. Many people observe Jewish dietary laws that prohibit milk and meat being eaten together. However, a kosher diet is not important to the more secular Jews.

Recreation

Israelis like to go to movies and concerts. Musicians are highly regarded, as are poets. Hebrew poetry and folk music focuses on the Jewish experience. Soccer and basketball are the favorite sports, followed by swimming, tennis, gymnastics, hiking, and camping. In their leisure time, people read, watch television, or visit friends. People like to take day trips to various places in Israel.

Holidays

Holidays are important in Israel; businesses close and public transportation stops. The Jewish calendar is based on the lunar standard. The month of *Tishrei* (September/October) begins with *Rosh Hashanah* (New Year), followed by *Yom Kippur* (Day of Atonement) on the tenth. The week-long festival of *Succot* (Tabernacles) begins on the fifteenth. *Hanukkah* (the Festival of Lights) is in December. *Pesach* (Passover) takes place six lunar months and two weeks after New Year's Day, and Holocaust Day is commemorated 13 days after that. Other important days include Memorial Day (20 days after Passover), Independence Day (21 days after Passover), and *Shavu'ot* or Pentecost (50 days after Passover). The Jewish day begins at sunset, not midnight. That is why *Shabbat* (Sabbath) begins on Friday at sundown and ends just after sundown on Saturday.

Commerce

State law requires that all workers have one day of rest each week, which is usually taken on Fridays by Muslims, Saturdays by Jews, and Sundays by Christians. Most workers belong to a labor union. General business hours extend from 8:00 A.M. to 1:00 P.M. and 4:00 to 7:00 P.M., Sunday through Thursday. Many shops are open all day. On Friday, businesses close around 2:00 P.M.

SOCIETY

Government

Israel does not have a written constitution. The president (Ezer Weizman) performs ceremonial duties, but the prime minister is head of government. Beginning in 1996, Israel's prime minister will be directly elected rather than appointed from the *Knesset* (Parliament). Since 1948, all governments have been coalitions because no one party has been able to gain a majority. *Knesset* members (120 total) are elected at least every four years; voters cast ballots for parties, not for individual candidates.

Economy

Israel's economy is well developed and modern despite a lack of natural resources. Agricultural items are important exports, but the sector only employs 5 percent of the population. Chief products include citrus and other fruits, vegetables,

beef, dairy, and poultry products. The industrial sector forms a strong part of the economy and includes high technology, diamonds, and machinery. Tourism is another vital sector of the economy. Growth (currently 3.5 percent), unemployment (10 percent), and inflation (11 percent) fluctuate with immigration and the peace process, as well as global market trends. Taxes in Israel are very high. The country's Human Development Index (0.900) ranks it 19th out of 173 nations. Real gross domestic product per capita is $13,460, which has tripled in the last generation. These figures indicate that most people enjoy a comfortable standard of living. The currency is the new *shekel* (NIS).

Transportation and Communication

Bus, rail, and road systems are all well developed in Israel. *Sherut* taxis are used for convenient travel between cities; they carry up to seven passengers on fixed routes. In all cities except Haifa, buses and trains do not run on the Jewish Sabbath and holy days. Taxis and private cars are plentiful. Israel has a highly developed communications system with good domestic phone service. There are several radio and television stations and daily newspapers.

Education

The government provides both religious and secular school systems, and the people are free to choose either. Citizens can also choose between schools taught in Hebrew or Arabic. School is free and compulsory through the tenth grade. Elementary school runs through sixth grade, junior high through ninth, and high school through twelfth. The high school diploma is necessary for college entrance and important for getting a job. Special private schools admit those who dropped out of school but later decided to finish a diploma. Most schools, including universities, hold classes six days a week. The Open University offers correspondence and radio courses to adults and the *ulpanim* system offers immigrants the chance to learn Hebrew. Literacy among Jews is about 92 percent, while Arabs average somewhat lower.

Health

All Israelis are covered by a state-run health plan financed by salary deduction. It was introduced in 1995 to replace the system in which most care was provided at public facilities. The plan now provides payment for care provided by the private sector. Facilities are modern and the quality of care is high. The infant mortality rate is 9 per 1,000. Life expectancy ranges from 76 to 80 years.

FOR THE TRAVELER

U.S. tourists need a valid passport to enter Israel, but no visa is required for stays of up to three months. Travel to certain occupied areas may require a permit. Travelers should drink plenty of liquids and wear hats in the hotter areas. Visitors enjoy Israel's numerous archaeological, historical, and religious sites, as well as beautiful scenery. For more information, contact Israel's Government Tourist Office, 350 Fifth Avenue, New York, NY 10118; phone (800) 596–1199. You may also wish to contact the Embassy of Israel, 3514 International Drive NW, Washington, DC 20008; phone (202) 364–5500.

CULTURGRAM ™ '96

Japan

Boundary representations not necessarily authoritative.

BACKGROUND

Land and Climate

Japan consists of four main islands: Honshū, Hokkaidō, Shikoku, and Kyūshū. Covering 145,882 square miles (377,835 square kilometers), it is just smaller than Montana. Japan experiences all four seasons. On Hokkaido and in northern Honshu, winters can be bitterly cold. To the south, a more tropical climate prevails. Otherwise, the climate is temperate with warm, humid summers, and mild winters. The western side of the islands is usually colder than the eastern side, which faces the Pacific Ocean. The islands are subject to typhoons in September. Japan also has many dormant and a few active volcanoes. Mild earthquakes are fairly common, and more destructive ones hit every few years. The January 1995 quake in and around Kōbe killed more than 5,000 people, destroyed 100,000 buildings, and left 300,000 homeless. This was the worst quake since 1923 (when 140,000 died in Tōkyō), but not the only one since then to have killed thousands.

History

Japan is known historically as the "Land of the Rising Sun," as symbolized by its flag. Beginning over two thousand years ago (with Emperor Jimmu in 600 B.C., according to legend), Japan has had a line of emperors that continues to the present. From the 12th century until the late 19th century, however, feudal lords or *Shoguns* held political control. These *Shoguns* expelled all foreigners in the 17th century on the suspicion they were spies for European armies. Not until 1853, when Matthew Perry (U.S. Navy) sailed into port, did the Japanese again have contact with the West. The *Shoguns* lost power in the 1860s and the emperor again took control. The current emperor, Akihito, took the throne in 1989. Akihito's father, Hirohito, was emperor from 1926 to 1989. Hirohito's reign was called *Showa*, which means "enlightened peace." The deceased Hirohito is now properly referred to as "Emperor Showa." Akihito's reign is called *Heisei*, meaning "achievement of universal peace."

In 1895, the Japanese defeated China and established its influence in Korea. Japan was also victorious in the Russo-Japanese War (1905), which led to its recognition as a military power. Involvement in World War I brought Japan enhanced global influence, and expanded its land holdings according to the Treaty of Versailles. The post-war years brought prosperity to the rapidly changing nation. It soon began to exercise considerable influence in Asia and subsequently invaded Manchuria and much of China. On 7 December 1941, Japan launched a successful air attack on U.S. naval forces at Pearl Harbor. Its military machine swiftly encircled most of southeast Asia. In 1943, the tide of the war turned against Japan. Two atomic bombs were dropped by the United States on Hiroshima and Nagasaki in the summer of 1945. Complete collapse of the empire and surrender ensued. A military occupation, chiefly by U.S. forces, lasted from 1945 to 1952. In 1947, a new constitution was adopted under American direction. It renounced war, granted basic human rights, and declared Japan a democracy.

Since World War II, Japan has maintained a small defense force, but it also receives military support from the United States. The Liberal Democratic Party (LDP) generally controlled politics after World War II, but political scandals in the late 1980s and early 1990s led to various resignations and a much weaker LDP. While it held onto its legislative majority in 1992 elections, the LDP's leader, who was also Japan's prime minister, lost a no-confidence vote in 1993. The LDP splintered, reflecting a growing generation gap. In July 1993 elections, the LDP lost its majority and a new coalition government was formed. It fell in 1994, and a new prime minister formed a minority government that restored some stability to politics.

THE PEOPLE

Population

The population of Japan is 125.1 million. It is growing at 0.3 percent annually. Although Japan's population is half that of the United States, the people live on less than 5 percent of the total territory of the United States. Japan is therefore one of the most densely populated countries in the world. About 45 percent of the people are concentrated in three major metropolitan areas: Tōkyō, Ōsaka, and Nagoya. Overall, nearly 80 percent of the population lives in urban areas. The population is 99 percent ethnic Japanese, with a small number of Koreans (about 680,000) and Chinese. Native Ainu live mostly on Hokkaidō. All non-Japanese must register annually with the police and do not have full citizenship rights.

Language

Japanese is the official language. Although spoken Japanese is not closely related to spoken Chinese, the written language is related to Chinese ideographs (characters), which were adopted in ancient times. The Japanese also use two phonetic alphabets (*hiragana* and *katakana*) simplified from these characters. A third phonetic alphabet (*romaji*) uses Roman letters. English is taught in all secondary schools and is often used in business. The Japanese also place great worth on nonverbal language or communication. For example, much can be said with a proper bow. In fact, one is often expected to sense another person's feelings on a subject without verbal communication. Some Westerners misinterpret this as a desire to be vague or incomplete. The Japanese may consider a person's inability to interpret feelings as insensitivity.

Religion

Traditionally, most Japanese practiced a combination of Buddhism and Shinto. Shinto is a religion without a recognized founder or central scripture. Based on ancient mythology, it stresses man's relationship to nature. There are many gods. All Japanese emperors are considered literal descendants of the sun goddess, Amaterasu. Shinto was important historically in ordering Japanese social values, as illustrated through the Code of the Warrior (*Bushido*), which stressed honor, courage, politeness, and reserve. Today, many households observe some ceremonies of both Shinto and Buddhism, such as Shinto marriages and Buddhist funerals, and most have small shrines in their homes. Religious celebrations and practices, however, are now a social tradition rather than the result of religious conviction for most. Shinto principles of ancestor veneration, ritual purity, and a respect for nature's beauty are all obvious in Japanese culture. About 1 percent of the population is Christian.

General Attitudes

Japanese society is group oriented. Loyalty to the group (business, club, etc.) and to one's superiors is essential and takes precedence over personal feelings. In business, loyalty, devotion, and cooperation are valued over aggressiveness. Companies traditionally provide lifetime employment to the "salaryman" (full-time male professional), and the salaryman devotes long hours of work to the company. This tradition has been undermined by the recession of the early 1990s, but is still a pillar of society. Devotion to the group reaches all age groups; even members of a youth baseball team will place the team's interests over their own. Politeness is extremely important; a direct "no" is seldom given, but a phrase like "I will think about it" can mean "no." Also out of politeness, a "yes" may be given quickly, even though it only means the person is listening or understands the speaker's request. The Japanese feel a deep obligation to return favors and gifts. Age and tradition are honored. While traditions are strong, the Japanese are also experiencing significant social changes in the way they view economic security, family relations, politics, and male and female roles. Various social strains are leading many people to reevaluate what is most important in life.

Personal Appearance

Conformity, even in appearance, is a characteristic of the Japanese. The general rule is to act similar to, or in harmony with, the crowd. Businessmen wear suits and ties in public. Proper dress is necessary for certain occasions. Conformity takes on a different meaning for the youth, however. They will wear the latest fashions (American and European) and colors, as long as these fashions are popular. Traditional clothing, called a *kimono* or *wafuku*, is a long robe with long sleeves, wrapped with a special sash (*obi*). The designs in the fabric can be simple or elaborate. The *kimono* is worn for social events or special occasions.

CUSTOMS AND COURTESIES

Greetings

A bow is the traditional greeting between Japanese. Persons wishing to show respect or humility bow lower than the other person. The Japanese shake hands with Westerners. While some appreciate it when Westerners bow, others do not, especially when the two people are not acquainted. Therefore, a handshake is most appropriate for foreign visitors. Japanese are formal and titles are important in introductions. The family name is used with the suffix *san*. A Mr. Ogushi in North America is called Ogushi-san in Japan. The use of first names is reserved for family and friends. Between business representatives, the exchange of business cards (offered and accepted with both hands) most often accompanies a greeting.

Greetings used depend on the relationship. A worker might greet a superior with *Ohayogozaimasu* (Good morning), but he or she would greet a customer with *Irasshaimase* (Welcome). When business representatives meet for the first time, *Hajimemashite* (Nice to meet you) may be used. *Konnichiwa*

(Hello) is a standard greeting. *Ohayoh* (an informal "Good morning"), *Yahhoh* (Hey!), or *Genki?* (How are you?) are common casual greetings among the youth.

Gestures

It is impolite to yawn in public. A person should sit up straight with both feet on the floor. Legs may be crossed at the knee or ankles, but it is improper to place an ankle over a knee. Beckoning is done by waving all fingers with the palm down. It is polite to point with the entire hand. Shaking one hand from side to side with the palm forward means "no." A person refers to himself by pointing the index finger at his nose. Laughter does not necessarily signify joy or amusement; it can also be a sign of embarrassment. The mouth should be covered when using a toothpick. Chewing gum in public is considered impolite. Young girls often walk hand in hand.

Visiting

Visits are usually arranged in advance; spontaneous visits between neighbors are uncommon in urban areas. Shoes are removed before stepping into a Japanese home. There is usually a small hallway (*genkan*) between the door and living area where one stands to remove the shoes. After being removed, they are placed together pointing toward the outdoors, or in a closet or on a shelf in the *genkan*. Coats are removed before stepping into the *genkan*. Slippers are often worn inside, but are removed before entering rooms with straw mat floors (*tatami*). Japanese traditionally emphasize modesty and reserve. Guests are usually offered the most comfortable seat. When offered a meal, guests often express slight hesitation before accepting it. Light refreshments are accepted graciously. Compliments are denied out of modesty. Guests should avoid excessive compliments on items in the home because this may embarrass the hosts.

When visiting, it is customary to take a gift (usually fruit or cakes) to the hosts. Gifts are given and accepted with both hands and a slight bow. Some people, especially the elderly, may consider it impolite to open the gift right away. Gift giving is extremely important in Japan because a gift says a great deal about the giver's relationship to, and respect for, the recipient. It is, therefore, especially crucial in business relationships. Food and drink are the most common gifts, because gifts for the house would quickly clutter small homes. Gift giving reaches its peak at the end of each year when giving the right-priced gift (the price is more important than the item) to all the right people (family, friends, officials, and business contacts) sets the tone for the coming year.

Eating

Although many youths eat while walking in public, it is generally considered bad manners for adults to do so. Snack foods sold at street stands are thus eaten at the stand. In a traditional meal, the Japanese typically eat from their bowl while holding it at chest level instead of bending down to the table. Chopsticks (*hashi*) are used to eat most meals, but people generally use Western utensils when eating Western food. American fast food is popular among the youth. The main meal is eaten in the evening. Because many people work late hours, they may eat dinner in office building restaurants or on the way home.

LIFESTYLE

Family

The family is the foundation of Japanese society and is bound together by a strong sense of reputation, obligation, and responsibility. A person's actions reflect on his or her family. While the father is the head of the home, the mother has the responsibility for household affairs. Traditionally, it was considered improper for a woman to have a job, but many women now work outside the home. Although the current trend is away from the traditional, multigenerational families, many aged parents still live with their married children. Families generally have fewer than three children. In cities, families live in high-rise apartments or small homes. Larger homes are found in less crowded areas.

Dating and Marriage

Youth in Japan are much like youth in the United States. They begin dating at around age 15 and enjoy dancing, movies, shopping, or eating out. They like Western music and fashion trends. The average marriage age is 27 for men and 26 for women. Weddings can be elaborate and expensive. Marriage ceremonies usually take place in hotels. The couple may wear traditional *kimonos* for the ceremony, Western wedding outfits for photographs and socializing, and different clothing for an evening party. Wedding guests bring gifts, often cash, and leave with gifts from the couple.

Diet

The Japanese diet consists largely of rice, fresh vegetables, seafood, fruit, and small portions of meat. Rice and tea are part of almost every meal. Western-style food is increasingly popular, especially among the youth. Popular Japanese foods include *miso* (bean paste) soup, noodles (*raman*, *udon*, and *soba*), curried rice, *sashimi* (uncooked fish), *tofu*, and pork. *Sushi* is usually a combination of fish (cooked or raw) and rice, with vinegar. Sometimes a vegetable, such as cucumber, is added to the dish or used instead of fish; then the dish is called *norimaki*. *Sushi* is expensive and reserved for special occasions.

Recreation

Baseball, soccer, volleyball, tennis, skiing, and jogging are all popular in Japan. Traditional sports such as sumo wrestling (a popular spectator sport), judo, *kendo* (fencing with bamboo poles), and karate are also enjoyed. Baseball, brought to Japan in the 1870s by an American, is the national sport. It is highly competitive at all levels. The entire country gets involved in the annual national high school championships. Golf, while expensive, is rapidly becoming popular. For leisure, people enjoy television and movies or nature outings. Puppet theater (*bunraku*) and highly stylized drama (*noh* and *kabuki*) are popular among older adults. The Japanese also enjoy music concerts and theater.

Holidays

At the New Year, Japanese take an extended holiday from the last day or two in December to about the third of January. Businesses and government offices close while people visit shrines and relatives. Other important holidays include Adults' Day (15 January), when all those who will turn 20 during the year are honored as coming of age; National Foundation Day (11 February); Vernal Equinox (in March); *Midori No hi* (29 April), Greenery Day—a day to celebrate nature's beauty; Constitution Day (3 May); Children's Day (5 May); Bon Festival (15 August), a time when people take vacation and return to their ancestral homes to welcome visiting ancestral spirits with bonfires; Respect for the Aged Day (15 September); Autumnal Equinox (in September); Sports Day (10 October); Culture Day (3 November); Labor Thanksgiving Day (23 November); and Emperor Akihito's Birthday (23 December).

Commerce

Businesses are typically open from 8:00 A.M. to 5:00 P.M. or 9:00 A.M. to 6:00 P.M. Small shops and large urban shopping areas may stay open much later and do not close for lunch. Business dealings are conducted formally. Time is often required for decisions and agreements. The Japanese may be more interested in the person or company they are dealing with than the actual details of the deal. Many Japanese work late into the evening; overtime is a common necessity.

SOCIETY

Government

Japan is a constitutional monarchy. The emperor is head of state but has no governing power. The prime minister is head of government. He and his cabinet form the executive branch. Legislative power is vested in the *Diet*, consisting of the 511-seat House of Representatives (Lower House) and the 252-seat House of Councillors (Upper House). Japan has 47 prefectures (provinces), each administered by an elected governor. The voting age is 20. In addition to the LDP, major parties include the Social Democratic Party of Japan, Democratic Socialist Party, and the Clean Government Party, among others.

Economy

Japan is one of the most productive industrialized nations in the world. Inflation and unemployment are below 3 percent, and gross domestic product growth is above 2 percent. Japan's Human Development Index (0.929) ranks it third out of 173 countries. Real gross domestic product per capita is $19,390. Japan's ranking reflects the high level of economic and social organization the country is known for, but does not take into account a high cost of living and the lifestyle that many people must lead: long commutes to work long hours and return to cramped housing. Calls for change in how the economy and society functions are increasingly common.

Because Japan has few natural resources, it depends on imported raw materials for industrial success. Also, because more than 60 percent of the land is mountainous, only about 13 percent is suitable for cultivation. Japan must import nearly half of its food supply, including grains other than rice. Major crops include rice, sugar, vegetables, tea, and various fruits. Japan is a leading producer of fish, accounting for 15 percent of the total world catch.

The economy is manufacturing oriented. More than 95 percent of all exports are manufactured items, including automobiles, electronic equipment, televisions, and various other items. Major industries include machinery, metals, engineering, electronics, textiles, and chemicals. The United States is Japan's biggest trading partner. A large trade imbalance is a continuing source of friction between the two nations. The currency is the *yen* (¥), one of the strongest currencies in the world.

Transportation and Communication

A highly developed, efficient mass-transit system of trains and buses is the principal mode of transportation in urban areas. "Bullet" trains (*Shinkansen*) provide rapid transportation between major cities. Subways are also available. Many people have private cars. Traffic is often very heavy in Tōkyō and other large cities. There are five international airports. Japan's communications system is highly modern and well developed. Newspapers and magazines are read by more than 65 million people.

Education

Japan has a high literacy rate (99 percent), and reading is popular. Education is generally free and compulsory from ages six to fifteen. Tuition must be paid for education thereafter. Math and sciences are stressed in school, and requirements are strict. Students are in school Monday through Saturday, with one Saturday off a month. Many students attend private schools, provided they pass difficult entrance exams. Parents often enroll their children in evening *juku* (cram) schools to help prepare for these tests. University entrance exams are rigorous and competition among students is intense. Students study for years and cram for months to take them. Getting into the best schools is more important than one's ultimate performance. Graduation from the top universities usually guarantees students prestigious jobs.

Health

The Japanese enjoy one of the highest standards of health in the world. The infant mortality rate is only 4 per 1,000. Life expectancy is between 77 and 82 years. Companies are generally responsible for providing insurance benefits to employees, but the government also sponsors some social welfare programs. Medical facilities are very good. Pollution is a problem in Tōkyō.

FOR THE TRAVELER

U.S. visitors need a valid passport, but no visa for stays of fewer than 90 days. No immunizations are required. North American small appliances and plugs will usually work in Japan's electrical outlets, unless one plug blade is wider than the other. Because of the strong *yen*, travel in Japan is expensive for Americans. The Japan National Tourist Office has detailed travel information and is located at 1 Rockefeller Plaza, Suite 1220, New York, NY 10020; phone (212) 757–5640. You may also wish to contact the Embassy of Japan, 2520 Massachusetts Avenue NW, Washington, DC 20008.

CULTURGRAM '96

Hashemite Kingdom of
Jordan

Boundary representations not necessarily authoritative.

BACKGROUND

Land and Climate

Covering 35,475 square miles (91,880 square kilometers), Jordan is about the size of Indiana. Most of it is covered by desert. The population is generally concentrated in the west where water makes cultivation more possible. Jordan's only seaport is located at Al'Aqabah. There are mountains in the west, and the Dead Sea forms part of the border with the West Bank and with Israel. The Dead Sea is the lowest point on earth. The Great Rift Valley, through which the Jordan River flows, forms a flood plain between the West Bank and Jordan. Jordanian territory is often called the "East Bank" because it lies east of the Jordan River. The rainy season in western Jordan is between November and April, when temperatures are cold enough to allow for some snow. The rest of the year it is sunny, dry, and hot. Summer nights, however, are cool.

History

As a sovereign state, Jordan has only existed for a short time. But the area has a rich history as part of the Fertile Crescent that was settled and conquered by many peoples. Amorites, Edomites, Moabites, and Ammonites were among the early settlers of the area. Later, at various times, the land was conquered by the Hittites, Egyptians, Israelites, Assyrians, Babylonians, Persians, Greeks, and Romans. The Arabs invaded in the seventh century and established the Umayyad Caliphate at Damascus (now in Syria). Christian crusaders ruled for a time, but the area has basically been Muslim since the Arab invasion. The Ottoman Turks ruled for many years until the Great Arab Revolt (1916). The Arabs were backed by the British. The British then created (1922) the Emirate of Transjordan as a semiautonomous region ruled by the Hashemite Prince Abdullah. Over the years, the British slowly turned power over to local Arab officials, and in 1946 Transjordan became independent. In 1950, the country was given its current name and included the territory now known as the West Bank.

In 1951, Abdullah was assassinated. His son Talal was proclaimed king, but, because of poor health, he was deposed by government officials. Shortly thereafter, Talal's 17-year-old son, Hussein, became the new Jordanian monarch. Hussein still rules today. During the 1967 War, Jordan lost control of the West Bank to Israel. Many Palestinian refugees fled to Jordan. This and other factors led to internal unrest and violence between the Jordanian government and members of the Palestinian resistance being protected by Jordan. Members of the resistance, known as *fedayeen,* were expelled from Jordan in the 1970s after a 1970 assassination attempt against Hussein.

Until 1988, Jordan considered the people of the West Bank part of its population and provided for Palestinian representatives in the Jordanian parliament. The elected legislature had been dissolved in 1976 but reconvened in 1984. In 1988,

Hussein announced the severance of all ties with the West Bank, meaning Jordan no longer claims the West Bank as its territory. It also eased tensions between Jordan and the Palestinian Liberation Organization (PLO). This change of policy brought the dissolution of parliament again because many of its members represented the West Bank. Election laws were rewritten and elections for the new parliament (East Bank only) were held in 1989, and a new legislature was convened. In 1991, Hussein restored multiparty democracy and lifted many martial law provisions that had existed since 1967.

Full multiparty elections—with 534 candidates vying for 80 seats—were held in 1993. A strong voter turnout brought a centrist-minded group of leaders to power in the new parliament. This demonstrated clear support for King Hussein and his participation in the Middle East peace process. That process began in 1991 and focuses primarily on relations between Israel and the Palestinians in the West Bank and Gaza. However, vital regional issues (water, refugees, secure borders, arms, and the environment) involving several countries are also part of the broader negotiations. Jordan signed an economic accord with the PLO in 1994. More significantly, however, it signed a peace treaty with Israel in October 1994. The historic treaty ended years of a "state of war" and opened opportunities for the two countries to cooperate instead of oppose each other's efforts in the region.

THE PEOPLE

Population

Jordan has a population of more than 3.9 million and is growing rapidly at 3.5 percent annually. The capital, Amman, has more than one million inhabitants. Just over two-thirds of all people live in urban areas. Except for small minorities of Circassians (1 percent) and Armenians (1 percent), all citizens of Jordan are Arabs. While about one-fourth of the Arabs are of Bedouin descent, less than 5 percent are currently nomadic Bedouins. Nomadic Bedouins do not live in the same place year-round; rather, they move about to take advantage of seasonal shifts and to graze their livestock. Bedouins live in tents; even Bedouins who are not nomadic often live in tents (complete with carpeting and nice furnishings). Palestinians comprise about half of the Arab population. They are either refugees from the West Bank (having crossed into Jordan after the 1967 war with Israel) or were born in Jordan. A large number still live in refugee camps, even though they are Jordanian citizens.

Language

Arabic is the official and most commonly used language in Jordan. English is widely spoken among the educated.

Religion

About 90 percent of the people are Sunni Muslims. Islamic values and laws are an integral part of the society. Christianity is represented by a few different denominations in about 8 percent of the population. Each religious community has the right to regulate personal matters such as marriage, divorce, and inheritance according to religious traditions. Muslims believe that *Allah* (God) revealed his will to the Prophet Muhammad through the angel Gabriel. The *Qur'an* (Koran) is the scripture of Islam. Muhammad is considered the last and greatest prophet, but major biblical figures (such as Abraham, Moses, and others) are also accepted as prophets. Muslims demonstrate their faith and devotion to *Allah* by professing his name, praying five times daily, making at least one pilgrimage to Makkah in Saudi Arabia, donating money to the poor, and fasting each day during the month of *Ramadan* (see Holidays).

General Attitudes

Jordanians are good-natured, friendly, and hospitable. They place great worth on the family and traditions but are also very modern. Time is not as important in Jordan as in the West. People are more important than schedules. Patience is valuable. Jordanians are proud of their rich cultural heritage and the country's accomplishments. Certain political topics are sensitive and should be avoided by foreign visitors.

Although many Palestinians in Jordan hold Jordanian citizenship, they consider themselves Palestinians first. Some don't consider themselves Jordanians at all and resent being called Jordanians. These people strongly support the establishment of a Palestinian homeland. Visitors should be aware of their views.

Personal Appearance

Most men wear Western-style clothing, often accompanied with the traditional white or red-checkered headdress. Women also wear Western clothing, but many choose to wear traditional Islamic floor-length dresses, head scarves, and veils. Either way, clothing is always conservative and never revealing. Shorts are not worn by adults or teenagers, except during athletic events. The youth enjoy European fashions. It is important to be well dressed and modest at all times. Jewelry is an important part of a woman's wardrobe. Visitors should dress conservatively; cotton clothing is most comfortable.

CUSTOMS AND COURTESIES

Greetings

Greetings are important in Jordanian culture. Jordanians greet each other and strangers warmly. A handshake is the most common greeting, accompanied by verbal greetings and inquiries about each person's health. Friends of the same sex often exchange a kiss on either cheek. A common term for "Hello" is *Mar-haba*. A term used to welcome someone is *Ahlan wa sahalan. Ahlein mar-haba* might also be used as a welcome greeting. When entering or leaving a room, it is customary to shake hands with each person (except, of course, at large gatherings). First names are not used between strangers when greeting.

Gestures

It is improper to pass or accept objects with the left hand only; the right hand or both hands should be used. It is impolite to point the sole of one's foot or shoe at another person. For this reason, crossing one's legs is generally avoided. Good posture is important, especially at social events. It is improper to be affectionate in public. Hand gestures are used a great deal in conversation and for everyday communication.

Visiting

Visiting (and entertaining in the home) plays a fundamental role in Jordanian society. Guests are greeted by both husband and wife. Invited visitors may bring gifts of flowers or sweets, but never alcohol. Coffee or tea is almost always offered to guests, no matter how short the visit. A person who has had enough to drink shakes the empty cup back and forth. Coffee is also served shortly before guests are expected to leave; a person does not leave before this coffee is served. Guests not originally invited for a meal may be expected to remain. It is polite to initially decline the offer before accepting. However, it is impolite to not accept the offer, although some will refuse the invitation up to three times before accepting it. A person will entertain in the home more often than at restaurants because it is a greater honor to be invited to the home.

Visitors should avoid excessive admiration of any object owned by the hosts because the hosts feel obligated to offer it to them. In most cases, the offer is only to demonstrate generosity, and the hosts expect the admirer to decline the item. If the hosts insist several times, the guest must accept it or risk embarrassing the hosts. In any situation where gifts are given, the recipients should not immediately accept them. Excessive praise for children is considered bad luck for the family.

Eating

It is traditional to eat food with the right hand (not the left). Utensils are usually available at functions involving international guests. When invited to a home for a meal, it is polite to leave a little food on the plate. This tells the host that the guest has eaten well and that the host has been generous. When Jordanians have guests, the host provides a large assortment of food. Coffee is important at all meals. *Qahwah Saadah* (Bedouin coffee) is bitter and drunk slowly from small cups. Arabic or Turkish coffee is sweeter; it is not stirred so as to keep the thick grains at the bottom of the cup.

LIFESTYLE

Family

The family is unquestionably the most important unit in Jordanian society. The extended family shares a close relationship. They often live in the same city or housing area. Cousins are usually as close as brothers or sisters are in the West. Arabs love children and lavish time and attention on them. Likewise, the elderly are greatly respected and cared for by their children. Large families are traditionally desired, but family sizes are declining due to economic pressures. To be able to help another member of the family is considered a great honor as well as a duty. Parents will often help or support their children even after marriage.

Gender roles in the family follow mostly traditional lines. The mother is expected to take care of the children and household. Only about 10 percent of the workforce is comprised of women. The father is head of the family and expects to provide for it financially.

Dating and Marriage

Jordanian society is fairly conservative in dating and marriage practices. In general, families still have a significant role in arranging marriages. Young people often meet at universities or offices and persuade their parents to help them in their courtship and subsequent marriage. One-to-one dating is generally reserved for after the engagement party or until the marriage contract has been signed. A bridal token is given to the bride's family by the groom. Women tend to marry in their early twenties, with men marrying after they have means to support a family (usually by their early thirties). Marriage is the norm and all Jordanians expect to marry and have children. The divorce rate is low.

Diet

Islamic law prohibits the consumption of pork and alcohol, and most Muslims are careful to obey these restrictions. Most meals include meat and bread, along with vegetables and fruits that are in season. There are many types of bread. Most common is flat, round bread. A variation of this bread is known in the West as *pita*. The national dish of Jordan is *mansaf*, a large tray of rice covered with chunks of stewed lamb (including the head) and *jameed* (yoghurt sauce). It is eaten by hand from the serving tray. Other popular dishes include *mahshi* (stuffed vegetables), *musakhan* (chicken with onions, olive oil, pine seeds, and seasonings), and *meshwi* (shish kebab). Lamb and chicken are the most common meats. Tomatoes, onions, eggplant, cabbage, and other vegetables are also common.

Recreation

Soccer is the most popular sport in Jordan. Jordanians participate in water sports in the Gulf of Aqaba. Watching television and movies are common leisure activities. Cultural activities and festivals also provide recreation. Visiting relatives is a major form of relaxation.

Holidays

National holidays follow the Western (Gregorian) calendar and fall on fixed dates. They include Labor Day (1 May), Independence Day (25 May), Arab Revolt and Army Day (10 June), King Hussein's Accession to the Throne (11 August), and King Hussein's Birthday (14 November). Christians celebrate Christmas and Easter, but they are not national holidays. Islamic religious holy days follow the lunar calendar, which is a few days shorter than the Western calendar. One important holiday is *'Eid al-Fitr,* a three-day feast at the end of the month of *Ramadan.* During *Ramadan,* Muslims do not eat or drink from dawn to dusk; in the evenings, they eat with family and visit friends and relatives. *'Eid al-Adha* is known as the Feast of Sacrifice and comes after the pilgrimage to Makkah. The birth of the prophet Muhammad *(Moulid al-Nebi)* is also celebrated.

Commerce

Government offices are usually open from 9:00 A.M. to 2:00 P.M., Saturday through Thursday. Businesses are open from 8:00 A.M. to about 2:00 P.M. and from 4:00 to 7:00 P.M. Most businesses close on Friday, the day of worship for Muslims. Christian businesses also close on Sunday. Employers look after the interests of their employees and are responsible for a wider area of concerns than in the West. In many cases an employer is regarded more like an uncle than a boss.

SOCIETY

Government

King Hussein is the head of the Hashemite Kingdom of Jordan. His government is a constitutional monarchy, but he has wide-ranging powers. He must sign all laws before they become effective. He appoints the Council of Ministers and the prime minister, who together govern the country. Abdul-Salam al-Majali became prime minister in 1993. The legislature has two houses: the House of Deputies and the House of Notables. The 80 members of the House of Deputies are elected by the people. The House of Notables is appointed by the King and is the upper chamber. Citizens may vote at age 20. The elections in November 1993 were the first full multiparty elections since 1956. They were significant in other ways, as well. For example, the first woman to ever be a member of Jordan's parliament was elected. Also, Islamic fundamentalists—who generally oppose a secular government—lost several important seats to more moderate candidates. This helped pave the way for the peace treaty signed with Israel in 1994.

Economy

Unlike many other countries in the Middle East, Jordan is not an oil-producing nation. In fact, Jordan is dependent on the oil-producing Arab states for aid and the employment of many Jordanian workers. When oil prices slumped in the 1980s, Jordan's unemployment rose and aid was curtailed, causing difficulties. Likewise, the 1990 embargo against Iraq, one of Jordan's key trading partners and oil suppliers, caused prices and unemployment to rise.

Jordan's natural resources are limited, but they include phosphate, potash, and limestone. The most important exports are fruits and vegetables, phosphates, and fertilizers. Mining and manufacturing activities employ about 20 percent of the labor force. Agriculture employs 20 percent. Unemployment is around 20 percent. The government is encouraging new industries and exports to stimulate the economy. While economic growth is slow, conditions have improved since 1993. The currency is the Jordanian *dinar* (JD).

Jordan's Human Development Index (0.628) ranks it 98th out of 173 countries. Real gross domestic product per capita is estimated at $2,895, which has doubled in the last generation. These figures indicate that a growing number of people have accesss to an income sufficient to meet basic needs. And while economic prosperity is not yet enjoyed by most, absolute poverty affects less than one-fifth of the total population.

Transportation and Communication

Jordan has a good system of transportation. Roads are in generally good condition and connect all major cities. Camels are still used for travel in the desert, although modern vehicles are also common. In cities, taxis are available but expensive. Service taxis, which travel fixed routes and carry a small number of passengers, are less expensive and widely used. Buses are also common. Communication systems are good and modern. Radio and television stations broadcast in Arabic and English. Most homes have a radio, and many are aquiring television sets.

Education

What Jordan lacks in natural resources it makes up for in human potential. Jordan has one of the most highly educated labor forces among Arab states. Education is a primary concern of the government. Adult literacy is about 82 percent (with the youth averaging 97 percent). Public education is free and compulsory for nine years and is available to qualified students through grade 12. The majority of all school-age children are enrolled in an educational institution. A *Tawjihi* exam must be taken by those wishing to obtain education past the 12th grade. There are 53 community colleges and four universities in Jordan.

Health

While good medical care is available in Jordan, certain diseases still pose problems for many people. Cholera, hepatitis, typhoid, and other diseases are found throughout the population. Still, life expectancy rates are relatively high, ranging from 70 to 74 years. The infant mortality rate is 32 per 1,000, which represents significant progress over the last few years. Government-sponsored immunization programs, as well as free health clinics, are improving health conditions. Nearly all Jordanians have access to these facilities.

FOR THE TRAVELER

A visa and valid passport are required for travel to Jordan. A visa can be obtained in advance or on arrival. No immunizations are required, but those staying for longer periods should consider vaccinations against typhoid, cholera, and other diseases. A doctor should be consulted before travel. Water is not potable. Boiled water must be used for brushing teeth, in ice cubes, and so forth. Dual-voltage small appliances or a voltage adaptor and a plug adaptor kit are necessary to use electrical outlets. Do not take pictures of people praying; ask permission of other people before taking their picture.

Jordan offers a number of tourist attractions, including ancient monuments near Amman, Greek and Roman ruins, Byzantine art, and the Dead Sea. The Jordan Information Bureau, 2319 Wyoming Avenue NW, Washington, DC 20008, has more detailed information. You may also wish to contact the Public Relations Office of the Embassy of Jordan, 3504 International Drive NW, Washington, DC 20008; phone (202) 966–2664.

CULTURGRAM '96

Republic of Kenya

Boundary representations not necessarily authoritative.

BACKGROUND

Land and Climate

Covering 224,961 square miles (582,650 square kilometers), Kenya is about the size of Texas. It is located in East Africa on the equator. The northern plains are hot, arid, and semidesert. The population in that part of the country usually practices nomadic pastoralism, moving from one area to another, taking advantage of seasonal grazing patterns. In the southeast, near the coast, humidity is high and the climate is tropical. The western highlands are bisected by the fertile Rift Valley. The climate is moderate in the rich agricultural highlands. Lake Turkana (Lake Rudolf) lies near the Chalbi Desert in the north and Lake Victoria is on the southwest border. Mt. Kenya rises in the center of the country to 17,058 feet (5,199 meters). From December to March the Harmattan winds keep Kenya dry. There are two rainy seasons: the "long rains" from April to June and the "short rains" from October to November; the long rains are more reliable and heavier. Over the past several years, however, rain has been scarce in both seasons and a severe drought has brought hardship to people, particularly in the north. Kenya's unique topography and climate allow for abundant and diverse wildlife.

History

The first inhabitants of what is now Kenya were hunting groups (Dorobo or Bushmen) who lived on the vast plains of the area. They mixed with groups of the Bantu peoples from western Africa who had migrated east. By the 15th century, it is estimated that the Bantu covered much of eastern Africa. More than 50 percent of Kenya's current ethnic groups have Bantu origins. Other peoples from Arabia and North Africa also settled in this area and mixed with the original inhabitants. The Kiswahili language was developed by these mixed peoples.

In 1498, Portuguese explorers arrived and established trading posts, but they were driven out by the Arabs in 1729. After 1740, Arabs ruled the Kenyan coast from a capital on the island of Zanzibar. In 1887, the British East Africa Company leased the Kenyan coast from the sultan of Zanzibar. Kenya became a British protectorate in 1895 and was organized as a crown colony in 1920. Following a period of violent partisan uprisings (called the Mau-Mau Rebellion) in the 1950s, Great Britain granted Kenya its independence in 1963. It remained in the Commonwealth as a sovereign republic.

Jomo Kenyatta, leader of the independence struggle, served as the first president until his death in 1978. He formed a strong central government under one political party, the Kenya African National Union (KANU). He was followed by Daniel Teroitich arap Moi. In 1982, KANU was proclaimed the only legal political party. This was done to avoid having political parties based on tribes. Free elections were still held; all candidates simply had to register with KANU.

Economic difficulties, charges of human rights violations, and political unrest brought calls for Moi to relinquish authoritarian rule and reopen the country to multiparty democracy.

Democracy protests in July 1990 led to the arrest of several dissidents and a ban of publications that criticized the government. Moi denied all requests for multiparty elections. Pressure from other countries eventually led Moi to change his position. First, in 1991, he rescinded the 1982 constitutional provision that gave KANU its dominance. Then, in January 1992, he allowed antigovernment protests. Dozens of political parties formed in anticipation of national elections, which were held in December 1992. Moi won the presidential election, but opposition parties made strong gains in parliament.

Fighting between Kalenjin and Kikuyu ethnic groups in the western Rift Valley in 1993 left many people dead and over 150,000 homeless. Because the government is implicated in various attacks, Western powers have withheld aid and support for Moi. Still, while the violence was a setback to democratization, most Kenyans continued to work for peace and full democracy.

THE PEOPLE

Population

Kenya's population of 27.3 million is growing rapidly at 3 percent annually. Although 99 percent of the population is African, it is divided among at least 47 distinct ethnic groups that developed largely along linguistic lines. The largest of these groups include the Kikuyu (21 percent), Luo (15 percent), Luhya (14 percent), Kalenjin (11 percent), Kamba (11 percent), Kisii (6 percent), and Meru (6 percent). Smaller groups include the Embu, Maasai, Mijikenda, Samburu, Somali, Taita, Teso, Turkana, and others. About 1 percent of the population consists of Europeans, Asians, and Arabs. Nairobi, the capital, has a population of more than 1.5 million, but less than 25 percent of all Kenyans live in large urban areas. Most of the population is concentrated in the southern two-thirds of the country, with the majority residing in rural towns and villages.

Language

English is an official language and is widely used, especially for business and official purposes. However, Kiswahili (also called Swahili) was proclaimed the national language after independence and is therefore also official. It was chosen over other languages because of its linguistic commonality with other Bantu-based languages in the country. It is promoted to encourage national unity. Each ethnic group speaks its own language as a mother tongue and speaks Kiswahili to communicate with other groups.

Religion

The majority of Kenyans are Christians. About 40 percent belong to various Protestant churches and 30 percent are Roman Catholic. Approximately 6 percent are Muslim. Most Muslims live along the coast and in the northeast. About 10 percent of the people follow indigenous belief systems or nontraditional Christian beliefs.

General Attitudes

Kenyans are proud of their cultural heritage, their nation, and its accomplishments. Patriotism is evident in people's respect for the national flag. When and wherever it is raised or lowered, people stop to observe the short ceremony before moving on. The people are warm and friendly. Social systems are group oriented. The individual is expected to be willing to sacrifice personal interests for the interests of the group. The "group" is usually defined by family, which has the highest value in society. To fail to keep close ties with the extended family is considered rebellious behavior. Individuals are expected to share their wealth with poorer family members. For instance, a man with adequate finances may be expected to pay his less-fortunate brother's children's school fees. Wealthier individuals are also expected to help their community. After family (which may be of mixed tribal origin), Kenyans are loyal to tribal affiliations. Land ownership is valued as an indicator of social status.

Kenyans take pride in preserving African wildlife, an effort that has succeeded with considerable international cooperation. Since 1977, hunting has been banned and Kenya has led the fight to preserve the elephant population against poachers. Thirty percent of all Kenyan wildlife lives on several million acres of national reserves. Kenyan preservation values come from an ancient heritage that emphasized coexistence with animals. People believed the rains would stop if animals were unnecessarily killed. By 1995, the elephant population had made a strong comeback and other animal groups were thriving. But success has become a problem; wildlife are increasingly responsible for crop destruction, human deaths, and other damage. Parliament may consider a proposal to allow limited hunting in 1996.

Personal Appearance

Kenyans dress conservatively and modestly. Western-style clothing, with some African variations, is the norm. Only children and tourists wear shorts. Women usually wear dresses, but many young urban women wear pants. Women often wear a *kanga* around their waist as a skirt, to cover their clothes, or shield themselves from rain and wind. A *kanga* is a long piece of colorful cotton fabric. Mothers use it to carry children on their backs. Rural and some urban women wear scarves. Sleeveless dresses or blouses are considered immodest. Light fabrics and short sleeves are common because of the warm climate. Small groups such as the Maasai, Samburu, and Turkana retain traditional dress.

CUSTOMS AND COURTESIES

Greetings

Greeting customs differ between ethnic groups. However, a handshake is common and important throughout the country. Supporting the right forearm with the left hand while shaking shows special respect for a leader or elder. In coastal areas, a traditional Swahili greeting is *Jambo!* (Greetings). *Habari gani?* (What is the news?) or just *Habari?* is common in non-coastal areas. The usual response is *Nzuri* (Good) or *Salama* (Peaceful). English greetings are also acceptable. Kenyans are friendly and greet others with warmth and politeness. They often ask about each other's family and welfare. Upon departing, Kenyans might say *Tutaonana* (We will see each other) or, if evening, *Lala salama* (Sleep peacefully).

Gestures

The right hand or both hands are used to pass and accept items. The use of the left hand alone is improper. The verbal "tch-tch" or "tss-tss" sound is used to express displeasure. Pointing at someone with the index finger is very rude. One beckons by waving all fingers of the hand. People often point with the lower lip. Approval may be shown with both thumbs extended up. It is improper to touch an elder. It is often considered improper to photograph another person without permission. Public displays of affection are not acceptable in most areas, although they are increasingly common in Nairobi. In all areas it is common for men to hold hands while walking in public, while a man and woman would not do so. Eye contact is important, as people are more willing to trust a person who will look them in the eye.

Visiting

Because of strong family ties and friendships, visiting is a common activity among Kenyans. Sunday is a popular day for making visits. Most visits are unannounced; people often drop by for conversation and a cup of tea. No rules exist about how long a visit lasts, but it is impolite for a host to ask guests to leave. Hosts endeavor to make guests comfortable. Invited guests might bring small gifts. Wine is common among Christians; flowers and tea leaves are popular for all groups. In rural areas, sugar, instant coffee, flour, and cornmeal are given.

Eating

When guests are invited to dinner, they usually have some time for conversation while final preparations are being made. After the meal, they stay for more socializing. Afternoon tea is a daily custom throughout the country. Depending on the type of food, and personal or family tradition, people may eat their meal with the right hand or use utensils. It is more common to use the right hand in rural areas, but this is also practiced in cities. When utensils are used, a knife is held in the right hand and a spoon in the left. Hands are washed before and after eating, often in a bowl at the table. Among some traditional families, children eat separately from adults. Men are often served first. Among the Samburu, warriors avoid eating in the presence of women. European cuisine is prevalent in major cities. Indian restaurants are popular in Nairobi and Kisumu.

LIFESTYLE

Family

The family unit usually includes the extended family. There is much interaction between uncles, aunts, and cousins. In fact, children call their maternal aunts "mother" and their paternal uncles "father." The average Kenyan family is large. In urban areas families are smaller and nuclear families are becoming more common. Aging parents are cared for by the family's youngest adult son. Most Kenyans expect to marry and raise a family, because the family is a great source of pride. A small number of educated women are choosing to avoid their traditional role as wives. Some have children but prefer life as a single parent. Women make up 40 percent of the labor force, one-third of college students, and up to half of all graduate students.

Dating and Marriage

Dating starts at about age 18 in cities, but is still rather uncommon in villages. Men and women usually marry between the ages of 18 and 24. The dowry system, where a payment is made by the groom's family to the bride's family, is still in effect. Money has, however, been substituted for livestock as the medium of exchange for the dowry. Wedding details are largely handled by the families. Usually young people choose their partners, but some marriages are still arranged.

Diet

The most common meats in Kenya are goat, beef, lamb, chicken, and fish. Milk, *ugali* (a stiff dough made from either cornmeal, millet, or sorghum), *uji* (porridge made from *ugali* ingredients), red bean stew, *kitumbua* (fried bread), *githeri* (corn and beans), and *chapati* (a flat bread) are staple foods. Popular fruits include pineapples, mangos, oranges, bananas, and papaya. Also common are sweet potatoes and avocados.

Recreation

Soccer is the most popular team sport. Soccer leagues exist throughout the nation. Highly organized, although poorly equipped, leagues even operate in the poorest areas. They give urban youth a chance to develop discipline, teamwork, and physical skills. Track and field activities join soccer as the national sports. Kenya has produced some world-famous runners and other athletes. Many people enjoy wrestling, tug-of-war, and a traditional pebble or seed board game (sometimes called *bao* or *ajua*). Field hockey, cricket, and croquet are popular among urbanites. The Kenyan National Theater offers drama, concerts, and dance programs. Homemade drums and guitars commonly accompany dancing in rural areas. Story telling, riddles, and proverbs are popular.

Holidays

Kenya celebrates New Year's Day; Easter (Friday through Monday); Labor Day (1 May); Madaraka Day (1 June), marking the birth of the republic; Kenyatta Day (20 October), celebrating the day in 1952 when Jomo Kenyatta was arrested for opposing British authorities; *Jamhuri* or Independence Day (12 December); Christmas; and Boxing Day (26 December). Boxing Day comes from the British tradition of presenting small boxed gifts to service workers, tradesmen, and in the past, servants. It is now primarily a day for visiting family and friends. Official holidays are often marked by special parades, meals, and church services. For the Islamic population, the country also observes the three-day feast at the end of the month of *Ramadan* called *Idul-Fitr.* The first day is an official holiday for Muslims, but celebrations on the next two days occur after working hours. During *Ramadan,* Muslims do not eat or drink from sunrise to dusk. Meals are eaten after the sun goes down, and friends visit during the evening.

Commerce

Business and government hours are generally from 8:00 A.M. to noon or 1:00 P.M. and from 2:00 to 5:00 P.M., Monday through Friday. Some businesses are also open Saturday mornings. While prices are fixed in urban shopping areas, bartering is common in rural markets and at roadside stands. Each town has an open-air market twice a week, and roadside stands are open every day to sell fresh fruits and vegetables.

SOCIETY

Government

The Republic of Kenya has eight provinces. The president is head of government and chief of state. He selects a vice president from among members of the 188-seat National Assembly (*Bunge*). All citizens may vote at age 18. In addition to the governing KANU, major parties include the Democratic Party and two groups called Forum for the Restoration of Democracy (FORD-Kenya and FORD-Asili).

Economy

Kenya's usually stable economy suffered badly in the early 1990s from drought, political turmoil, market reforms, global recession, and other events. Growth was stagnant and inflation 40 percent in 1994. Unemployment rose quickly and remains high. Because the population is expanding so fast, sustained economic growth is essential. Some market reforms have been scaled back, and in 1995 the government managed to lower inflation to below zero with tight fiscal policies.

Kenya's Human Development Index (0.434) ranks it 125th out of 173 countries. Real gross domestic product per capita is estimated at $1,350, which has doubled in the last generation. These figures reflect the fact that, while economic opportunities are increasing, about half of all people continue to live in poverty. A majority of Kenyans do not earn an income sufficient for their needs.

Although one-fourth of the labor force is employed in the public service and manufacturing sectors, the economy is based on agriculture, which provides nearly 65 percent of all export earnings and employs 75 percent of the work force. The chief cash crops are coffee, tea, and horticultural products. Pyrethrum, a flower used to make insecticides, is especially important. Other agricultural products include livestock, corn, wheat, rice, cassava, and sugarcane. Kenya has traditionally been self-sufficient in food production, but it is currently not able to feed its population. Industries focus on small-scale manufactured items, oil refinement, and tourism. The vital tourist industry is well developed and concentrates on safaris and beach resorts. The currency is the Kenyan shilling.

Transportation and Communication

International and domestic air links are well developed. Trains and buses are also available for domestic travel, but they can be slow. Taxis are plentiful in Nairobi. Traffic moves on the left side of the road. Four-wheel drive vehicles are used for safari trips and rural transport. Most rural roads are unpaved. Ports operate at Mombasa and Lamu. Kenya has one of Africa's best telecommunications systems. Most Kenyans listen to radio broadcasts in both Kiswahili and English. Relatively few people own televisions. The Kenya Broadcasting Corporation, once government owned, is now a private corporation indirectly controlled by the government. The newer Kenya Television Network (KTN) operates more freely and has more extensive programming. There are three daily national newspapers.

Education

Due partly to a rapidly increasing population and partly to government efforts, primary school enrollment has increased by over 60 percent since 1978 (15 percent since 1984). Enrollment in secondary schools has also risen substantially. Still, only about half of all pupils complete primary education, and half of these go on to secondary school. All students pay fees, but public schools receive some government assistance (such as paid teachers). In many rural areas, children are taught in Swahili the first three years of school, after which instruction is in English. Urban schools usually begin instruction in English. Teacher training is free, but teachers are required to work for the government at least three years after graduation.

Complete education through the university level is available to competent students and to those who are able to pay tuition. There are both public and private schools. *Harambee* (self-help) schools are common in rural areas, depending more on private donations than on government funding. *Harambee* schools draw on the talents of educators from around the world, as well as parents, to offer hands-on agricultural training, academic subjects, and instruction on practical subjects like health and occupations. The literacy rate is 69 percent.

Health

Diseases are less prevalent in the highlands than in low-lying areas, where the climate is less temperate and services less available. Some progress has been made in providing rural medical facilities, better sanitation, and other social services. Infant mortality rates have dropped and life expectancy has risen since the 1980s. The current infant mortality rate is 74 per 1,000; life expectancy averages between 52 and 60 years. Rural Kenyans continue to rely on traditional healing methods.

FOR THE TRAVELER

U.S. citizens must have a visa, a valid passport, and proof of return passage to travel to Kenya. Malarial suppressants are recommended for travel outside of Nairobi and yellow fever vaccinations are suggested. A $20 departure tax must be paid in hard currency.

Many foreign visitors travel to Kenya for its famous safari areas. There are 23 national parks and 29 game reserves covering more than 7 percent of Kenya's total land area. Leading attractions are the populations of zebras, lions, elephants, leopards, cheetahs, giraffes, gazelles, monkeys, and many other animals. Do not purchase any items made from animals, as these have been outlawed. Hunting and poaching remain serious crimes. Do not travel alone; do not carry valuables in public. For more information, contact the Kenya Tourist Office, 424 Madison Avenue, New York, NY 10017; phone (212) 486–1300. You may also wish to contact the Embassy of Kenya, 2249 R Street NW, Washington, DC 20008; phone (202) 387–6101.

Printed on recycled paper

Republic of
Kiribati

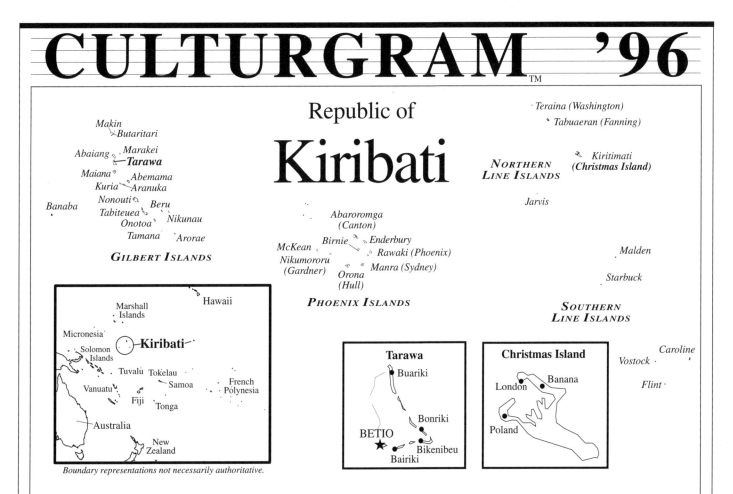

Boundary representations not necessarily authoritative.

BACKGROUND

Land and Climate

The small islands that form Kiribati (kee-re-BAHSS) stretch across hundreds of kilometers in the Central Pacific Ocean. Its 33 atolls form three principal groups: the Gilbert Islands, the Phoenix Islands, and the Line Islands. The Gilbert Islands lie south of the Marshall Islands and north of Tuvalu. To the east lies the Phoenix group (due north of Samoa) and then the Line Islands. Christmas Island is famous for sports fishing and its bird sanctuary.

Kiribati's climate is equatorial, with daytime temperatures usually above 82°F (28°C). The rainy season is from October to March. The dry season is from March to October and droughts occur more frequently on the central and southern islands. There are no rivers, but most islands enclose a lagoon. The most populous island is Tarawa, which is shaped like a triangle; only the southern part is urbanized. All other islands and north Tarawa are without running water and electricity.

History

The first settlers of Kiribati probably came from Southeast Asia and Samoa in the 14th and 15th centuries. Europeans first visited in 1537 when Christmas Island was sighted by Spanish explorers. Commercial activity on the islands began in the early 19th century. The northern Gilberts were a favorite whaling ground and deserting crews began to settle there around 1830. Hiram Bingham, a Protestant who established a mission on Abaiang in 1857, gave the Gilbertese a written form of their language.

During the latter 1800s, thousands of Gilbertese men were recruited to work overseas. They left because of drought and population problems, but they often found their employment conditions harsh. Many later returned to the islands.

In 1886, Britain and Germany signed the Treaty of the Unclaimed Pacific, each taking responsibility for islands in the Pacific that no other imperial power had claimed. Britain took the Gilbert and Ellice islands. At the same time, U.S. and German labor companies were competing for labor recruits. German traders were worried the United States would colonize the islands and Germany would lose out on trade. They asked their government to annex the islands, but it refused because of the 1886 treaty. U.S. traders and Nabureimoa, King of Butaritari, asked the United States to annex the islands. Although Britain did not want another colony, it did not want to lose the islands to the United States, so it made the Gilbert and Ellice Islands a protectorate in 1892.

In 1916, the Gilbert Islands were joined with the Ellice Islands to form the Gilbert and Ellice Islands Colony. The Phoenix and Line Islands, which were never permanently inhabited, became part of the territory during colonial rule. Tarawa was the site of fierce fighting between Japanese and U.S. troops in World War II, as Japan had occupied the area in the early 1940s.

In 1974, the Ellice Islands held a referendum for independence and subsequently became Tuvalu. In 1977, internal self-government was established in the Gilberts and the islands became the independent Republic of Kiribati in 1979. It remains part of the Commonwealth of Nations.

OCEANIA

THE PEOPLE

Population

The population is about 77,800 and is growing at 2 percent. Nearly all inhabitants are Micronesian, and most live on the Gilbert Islands. A small number of Tuvaluans also live in Kiribati. One-third of the total population lives on Tarawa, the capital island.

Life is changing in the rapidly urbanizing South Tarawa area, where migrants from outer islands encounter the Western culture introduced by Christian missionaries and others.

Language

I-Kiribati (EE-kee-re-BAHSS) speak a Micronesian dialect called Gilbertese or Kiribati. The pronunciation of "Kiribati" is derived from the English pronunciation of "Gilberts." English is the official language, but it is rarely heard outside of urban South Tarawa. To speak it in public is considered showing off and is mocked. Even on South Tarawa, people mix English and Gilbertese, using English mostly for words that do not exist in Gilbertese. Older people speak a more difficult and extensive version of Kiribati that younger generations have not retained.

The Kiribati alphabet has thirteen letters. Some words are borrowed from English (and adapted to the Kiribati alphabet and pronunciation) because they were not indigenous to Kiribati, such as *te ka* (the car). Accents differ slightly by location.

Religion

Christianity was first introduced in the 1850s by American Protestant missionaries. The people have since become devout Christians. About 52 percent of people are Catholic, and 40 percent are Protestant (Congregational). Catholicism is more prominent in the north; it was introduced in 1880 by two Gilbertese who had become Catholic while working in Tahiti. Other Christian faiths with a strong presence include the Seventh-Day Adventists, the Church of God, and the Church of Jesus Christ of Latter-Day Saints (Mormons). The Baha'i faith also has followers in Kiribati.

Before Christianity, *te maka* (power or magic) was prevalent as the people's belief system, which included the worship of Nareau (the Creator), the use of charms and spells, and the belief in spirits and ghosts. While no longer practiced on a large scale, it is still followed by some families.

General Attitudes

I-Kiribati laugh readily and easily. They are easy going, practical, and spiritual. People generally accept life as it is; day-to-day concerns necessarily take priority over the future. Work must be done and food gathered, and since fish will still be in the sea and coconuts on the tree tomorrow, the future will take care of itself. I-Kiribati take great pride in their way of life, and many have no desire to adopt the lifestyles of other countries. Respect for *katei ni Kiribati* (the Gilbertese way) is strong. Status is maintained by acknowledging one's equality with others. To elevate oneself or to fall behind the norm is considered bad.

People live modestly and are resourceful. For example, they use every part of the coconut tree: frawns for making mats, midribs to build houses, the sap to make toddy, the nut to dry and sell as copra or use in cooking, and the oil to make soap or refine for a body oil.

The group is more important than the individual. Obligations to extended family come before money, government, one's job, or personal gain. Families will go hungry to make sure their relatives have enough to eat.

Personal Appearance

Both men and women wear a *te bei* (lavalava), several yards of material worn around the waist to below the knee. Men usually wear T-shirts, unless working or fishing. Women wear a *tibutta*, a loose fitting blouse gathered at the neck and a petticoat with hems that are often embroidered in colorful designs or the wearer's name.

Knee-length shorts can be found on South Tarawa and among secondary school students. Almost no women on outer islands wear shorts. Women do not wear long pants or sleeveless dresses.

When I-Kiribati gather in the *maneaba* (meeting house) for a feast, dance costumes include knee-length skirts made from coconut fronds or pandanus leaves. Male performers also wear woven mats wrapped and tied around their waists with belts of woven hair. These braided belts are made from female hair and are highly valued; they may be kept within a family for generations. Brightly colored bands crisscross the dancer's chest from shoulder to waist. Women wear belts of coin-size coconut shell disks or white seashells. Both women and men wear decorations on their fingers, wrists, and arms. Finally, a flower garland or colorful cloth wreath is worn on the head.

CUSTOMS AND COURTESIES

Greetings

I-Kiribati greet each other with *Mauri* (Blessings). A more informal greeting, *Ko na era?* (Where are you going?), reflects people's inherent curiosity. It requires a response, even if vague, such as "to the store" or "to the north." Except at official gatherings, people do not usually shake hands when they greet. Instead, they nod their heads upward when saying *Mauri*. Handshakes are used to send someone off (such as to boarding school or work overseas) or between people who have not seen each other for some time.

To get someone's attention, I-Kiribati call out *neiko* (woman) or *nao* (man), even if the person's name is known. People address each other by their given names in informal situations; even children address their parents by their given names. A person's family name is often their father's or grandfather's given name. In more formal situations, the titles *Nei* (Miss or Mrs.) and *Ten* (Mr.) are used before one's given name to show respect.

Gestures

A raised eyebrow means "yes." A wrinkled nose and nod is used for pointing rather than fingers. Pulling at the lower eyelid with the index finger is a sign that one has seen a person showing off or making a mistake. A quick downward, inward wave of the hand means "come here."

It is improper to touch someone's head, which is considered the most sacred part of the body. If people are conversing, it is rude to walk between them. If it cannot be avoided, the passerby must crouch low or duck.

Members of the opposite sex do not display affection in public, but people of the same sex often hold hands or put their arms around the waist of a friend while walking or talking.

In a *maneaba* people sit cross-legged, and on some islands it is considered rude to show the sole of the foot when doing so. Because modesty is important, people adjust their clothing upon sitting and standing to properly cover themselves.

Visiting

An integral part of socializing is visiting other people's homes. Most people entertain on their *buia*, a raised platform with a thatched roof but no walls. Guests may be invited to play cards or relax. To show respect at one's arrival, the host dusts off a place for the visitor to sit or puts down a clean mat. A drink is offered; if near mealtime, something to eat is also offered. Guests show appreciation by accepting offered food. A cigarette hand-rolled in pandanus leaves is often shared by the group. A host might also call to a passerby to join the group. It is rude not to immediately accept, regardless of what one was planning. The length of stay depends on what the host has prepared. One could sit for only a few minutes or may stay for hours chatting over a pot of tea.

Arriving unannounced for a casual visit is common and part of daily life. On southern islands, custom requires one to call from a distance for the male of the household before approaching the doorway or the *buia*.

Other than casual talk or card playing, the home is not the place for formal entertaining. A *botaki* (feast) requires a written invitation delivered a few days in advance. It is usually held for a special occasion (first birthday, wedding, life's passages) or farewell and welcoming celebrations. *Botaki* are held in the *maneaba*. Every village has a *maneaba* and every church usually has one, too. *Mane* means to collect and/or bring together, and *aba* means the land or people of the land. *Maneabas* are the center of community life, and there are strict traditions regarding their construction, seating arrangements, member duties, and so forth. Some family groups have their own *maneabas*. When visiting one for the first time, it is customary to bring a block of tobacco to be divided among the older men. For some occasions, a cash donation is required upon visiting.

Eating

To eat, I-Kiribati sit cross-legged on mats woven from pandanus leaves. The mats are either on the ground or the *buia*. Bowls of food are passed around; plates and spoons are used, although eating with one's hands is perfectly acceptable and often the easiest way to eat fish. Traditionally, men eat first and women and children eat in a separate area after the men finish. All food on one's plate is eaten. Eating more than one helping compliments the cook. People converse freely during a family meal, but *maneaba* conversation is reserved for after dishes have been cleared and everyone is relaxing.

The morning meal is light and may include bread and a cup of tea or fresh *toddy* (coconut tree sap). Midday and evening meals are larger and include fish, rice, and coconut. Mealtimes may depend on the arrival of fresh fish: regardless of the hour, day or night, fresh fish necessitates a meal. However, on some islands eating fish for breakfast is believed to make one lazy. Fish is served in soup, fried in oil, coated with flour and fried, baked over a fire, or eaten raw.

LIFESTYLE

Family

The family occupies a central role in society. I-Kiribati live in extended families, and adoption among relatives is common. Adoption can be based on a verbal agreement or *bubuti*, a request that cannot be turned down; the word *bubuti* is never used lightly. If a couple cannot have children or desires more, they can *bubuti* one from a relative. Raising children is a serious responsibility in Kiribati culture, but being raised by biological parents with biological siblings is not necessarily the norm. The *bubuti* custom also provides social support for people, since one can request both items and services.

Upon marrying, a woman lives with her husband's family to learn from his relatives how to be a good wife. Large families are highly valued due in part to subsistence agriculture. Families need help fishing, collecting coconuts, and working in the *babai* pits. *Babai* is a taro-like starchy root crop. Women are responsible for housework, cooking, and child care, but some also help men take care of the *babai* pits and collect coconuts. Women harvest shellfish and go net fishing, but usually only men fish from canoes and boats. The father heads the household and the elderly receive great respect.

With land inheritance traditionally divided among one's children, family plots are becoming increasingly small and the government is encouraging people to have fewer children. In many families, children now share the land rather than dividing it.

The average home has a thatched roof, stick walls, and a coral rock floor. Woven coconut-frond mats cover the floor, while pandanus mats are used for sleeping. A home usually has a separate cook house.

Dating and Marriage

The youth interact through school and games; they do not go on dates. Some marriages are arranged in a traditional way, but most people choose their spouses. To make his intentions known, a young man sends a relative (usually an uncle) to tell the young woman's family he wants to propose. This gives her family time to prepare before his parents actually come with their request. A long engagement is preferred by the bride's family so they can weave sleeping mats for their new son-in-law and his family. The groom's family gives bolts of cloth to the bride's family in exchange for these mats.

A young woman's virginity is important and must be proven on the wedding night. To avoid potential disgrace, a couple sometimes chooses elopement, which is accepted as a common-law marriage. For a church wedding, the bride wears her best dress and the groom wears a borrowed suit, since he otherwise has no use for his own. If a man dies, it is common for an unwed brother to assume his place in the marriage. Divorce is handled by the family and not by the courts.

Diet

In addition to eating coconuts with fish, I-Kiribati grate them into tea and use coconut milk to sweeten breadfruit soup or as a marinade with curry for raw fish. Coconut sap is rich in vitamin C and is cut twice daily by young boys. Cutting *toddy* is a skill passed down through generations, and boys take pride in both their yield and quality of *toddy*. Boiled over a slow heat, *toddy* forms a thick, sweet molasses called *kamaimai*. This is used instead of sugar to sweeten drinks, or it can be made into a hard candy. Fermented *toddy* becomes an alcoholic drink known as *kakioki*.

Locally caught fish, breadfruit, pandanus, papaya, and *babai* are eaten regularly. Pork and chicken are usually eaten only at feasts. Imported rice and flour are daily staples. Imported canned food is becoming increasingly important to the urban population. Meals are cooked over an open fire and fried or baked. Without refrigeration, salt is used as a preservative and fish is dried in the sun. Salt and sugar are the only two distinct seasonings, with curry used almost exclusively for raw fish.

Recreation

Nature is seen as a provider, so although children might play on the beach at low tide, people do not swim for pleasure or engage in water sports other than canoe racing. I-Kiribati outrigger canoes are some of the fastest in the world and require precision and balance to skillfully maneuver in changing winds. The most popular sports are soccer and volleyball.

A game unique to Kiribati is called *oreano*. A soccer-sized ball made of a heavy stone wrapped in coconut husk fiber is thrown between two teams of ten players. A team scores if the opposing side drops the ball. The first team to earn ten points wins. Playing bingo and cards are favorite forms of entertainment and videos are gaining popularity. Recreational dancing (called *twisting*) is popular, but it differs from traditional dance. Traditional storytelling dances are important. They are reserved for special *maneaba* occasions. Costumes are as important as the performance itself. Dance techniques passed from one generation to another are often not shared outside the family.

Holidays

Since most of the population is Christian, religious holidays including Christmas and Easter are celebrated. People attend a religious service and then a feast in the *maneaba*, where different families showcase local dances. No gifts are exchanged on holidays and, other than a family's first son's birthday, no birthdays are celebrated. Kiribati independence is celebrated 12 July. The first Monday in August is Youth Day and 10 December is Human Rights Day.

Commerce

Businesses are open weekdays from 8:00 A.M. to 4:30 P.M., with the one bank open between 9:30 A.M. and 3:00 P.M. Stores, especially small family ones, are open as early as 7:00 A.M. and as late at 6:00 P.M. Some are open on weekends, but they do not open until 1:00 P.M. on Sunday because of morning church services. Government offices close for lunch at 12:30 P.M.

Prices are fixed by the government, including those for fish sold on the side of the road. Business is a relatively new concept, so the atmosphere is informal. Most retailing is done through consumer cooperatives. Less than 10 percent of the population earns a cash income; on outer islands, teachers, nurses, and government employees are the only paid workers.

SOCIETY

Government

The Republic of Kiribati has a *beretitenti* (president) as head of state and government. He is elected by the citizens from among a few candidates nominated by the 40-seat *Maneaba ni Maungatabu* (House of Assembly). The current president is Teatao Teannaki. He has a vice president and cabinet, appointed from among the members of the assembly. The next elections are in 1996. All citizens may vote at age 18. Each inhabited island has a council, and the government is represented by an island clerk. Local authority is vested in the *maneaba* council of *unimane* (old men).

Economy

The economy is based on the export of copra (dried coconut) used to make coconut-oil soap and cosmetics. Copra accounts for up to 70 percent of the total cash income for the rural population. Most islanders live by fishing, growing their own food, and raising small livestock. Local industry is confined to small operations, handicrafts, fish salting, and small boat building. Large foreign companies pay Kiribati for the right to fish its waters. A cash economy has only recently emerged on the outer islands, but it prevails on southern Tarawa. The Australian dollar is used as the country's currency.

Transportation and Communication

Buses are only available on South Tarawa. Outer island travel is by foot, bicycle, or motor bike. Interisland air and boat links are available on irregular schedules. Telephones are available in South Tarawa, but other areas depend on radio relays. There are no television stations, but one radio station broadcasts three times daily. A number of monthly newspapers sponsored by churches and a weekly newspaper (*Te Uekera*) are published.

Education

Schooling is compulsory for children between ages six and fifteen. The literacy rate is 80 percent and most children receive a primary education. Because of fees and limited facilities, only about 15 percent of students attend secondary school. Kiribati participates in the University of the South Pacific (based in Fiji), and some students also study in New Zealand and Australia. Tarawa has a Technical Training Institute, a Teacher's College and a Marine Training School.

Health

The government maintains free medical services. Each island has a clinic with at least one nurse. Doctors at the Tungaru Central Hospital on Tarawa provide additional health care. They travel to outer islands to do dental or optometric work when necessary. The infant mortality rate is 62 per 1,000; life expectancy is 60 years.

FOR THE TRAVELER

U.S. citizens need both a passport and visa to enter Kiribati. Visitors should wear modest clothing. Drink only boiled water. There is little tourism in Kiribati because of its remoteness, but hotels and other facilities do exist. For more information, contact the Kiribati Visitor's Bureau, Box 251, Bikenibeu, Tarawa, Kiribati, Central Pacific. You may also contact the Consulate of the Republic of Kiribati, 850 Richards Street, Suite 503, Honolulu, HI 96813; phone (808) 521–7703.

Printed on recycled paper

CULTURGRAM '96

North Korea

(Democratic People's Republic of Korea)

Boundary representations not necessarily authoritative.

ASIA

BACKGROUND

Land and Climate

North Korea is bounded by the Yellow Sea to the west, the Sea of Japan (known in Korea as the East Sea) on the east, China and Russia to the north, and the Republic of Korea in the south. It occupies slightly more than half of the peninsula (55 percent) and covers some 47,250 square miles (120,540 square kilometers). It is just smaller than Mississippi and about 20 percent larger than South Korea. The landscape of North Korea is dominated by mountains and narrow valleys. As a result, the majority of the population resides on only about 20 percent of the land. The mountainous interior is isolated and sparsely populated. The climate is continental, with relatively long, cold winters and hot, humid summers interrupted by a two-week monsoon season. Spring and autumn are more temperate and pleasant. Summer rainfall accounts for more than half the total annual rainfall, which averages about 31 inches (79 centimeters).

History

North Korea was once a part of the kingdom called Koguryo, one of the three kingdoms on the peninsula that were finally united in A.D. 668. A new kingdom called Koryo ruled most of what is now North Korea until 1392, when Yi Song-gye took power and established the Choson (or Yi) dynasty. The Choson dynasty kings controlled the entire peninsula for the next five hundred years, until Korea was annexed by Japan in

1910. At the end of World War II, Korea was liberated from Japan. The United States and the Soviet Union decided to allow Soviet forces to accept the Japanese surrender in the northern part of Korea and U.S. forces to do so in the south. In the north, former anti-Japanese guerrilla Kim Il Sung, with the full support of the Soviet command, took power in 1948. He remained in firm control, carrying out several political purges to eliminate opposition figures, until his death in July 1994. His son, Kim Jong Il took his place as the nation's leader.

On 25 June 1950, the North Korean army invaded South Korea, initiating a war that lasted three years and caused untold suffering to the Korean people. The United States and a military force from the United Nations supported the south and China supported the north. In July 1953, a truce was established along the 38th parallel, the original pre-war boundary. Near the town of P'anmunjom, a demilitarized zone created as part of the truce separates the two Koreas today.

Technically, a peace treaty has never been signed and the two nations are still at war. There have been some minor border incidents and acts of terrorism in the past, but no major fighting since 1953. Tunnels have been discovered that were dug from the North Korean side to South Korea and could have been used for a raid or invasion.

Kim Il Sung placed heavy emphasis on the reunification of the Korean peninsula. In 1990, representatives from both countries held a series of historic meetings designed to promote better relations and encourage eventual unification. Talks continued through 1992, but little progress was made. Only minor treaties, statements, and agreements were signed. Each distrusts the other's military intentions and both wish to determine the peninsula's future course.

In 1993, North Korea threatened to withdraw from the Nuclear Nonproliferation Treaty after international inspectors were refused permission to inspect the country's nuclear program. It was feared that North Korea had the capacity to manufacture nuclear weapons and already possessed a nuclear bomb. Relations with South Korea and other nations quickly soured. Only after various threats and months of intense negotiations with the United States did North Korea decide not to withdraw from the treaty. Some inspections from the International Atomic Energy Agency were granted in 1994, although UN demands were not fully met. Kim's death interrupted negotiations, but they continued under his son, and North Korea signed a nuclear accord. Hopes in both North and South Korea that contact might be allowed or that reunification would soon follow were dashed in 1995 when Kim Jong Il withdrew his country's commitment to the accord. North Korea was to have allowed international experts to help them dismantle old nuclear reactors and replace them with new ones that could create energy but not bombs. North Korea withdrew from the accord when it was told the new reactors were made in South Korea. The future of negotiations, as well as Kim Jong Il's actual authority over military activites, were cast into doubt by his withdrawal.

THE PEOPLE

Population

North Korea's population is about 23 million and is growing at 1.8 percent. Ethnic Koreans comprise almost the entire population. There are no significant numbers of other ethnic or cultural minorities in the country. About 60 percent of all people live in urban areas.

Language

The Korean language plays an important role in the identity of the Korean people. Korean is spoken in both North and South Korea and is written in a phonetic alphabet created and promulgated in the mid-15th century. While the alphabet is called *Hangul* in South Korea, it is known as *Chosongul* in North Korea. Although the Korean language is replete with words adapted from Chinese, the North Koreans, unlike the South Koreans, do not use Chinese characters with *Chosongul* in their newspapers and publications. They prefer to use only *Chosongul*, which is sufficient for most needs. There are also some differences in vocabulary between the North and the South, influenced somewhat by politics and also by the contact each country has had with other nations. Russian, Chinese, and English are taught as second languages in the schools.

Religion

The government of North Korea has constitutionally confirmed freedom of religion. In reality, however, the effectual state religion since the 1950s has been the veneration of Kim Il Sung, the "Great Leader." It is not known whether such veneration will extend to Kim Jong Il. Despite the personality cult that existed under Kim Il Sung, the way of life and philosophy in North Korea echos traditional patterns and is based fundamentally on Confucian thought. Roman Catholic and Protestant beliefs were introduced in the 18th and 19th centuries, respectively. *Ch'ondogyo* (also known as *Tonghak*) is an indigenous religion founded in 1860 as an eclectic combination of Buddhist, Confucian, and Christian beliefs. The present government points to this religion, which has organized a political party, as proof that religious freedom exists in North Korea. The government also permits Christians to meet in small groups under the direction of state-appointed ministers. Shamanism, a native belief in household and natural spirits, gods, and demons, may still have limited influence in rural areas, but it is mostly promoted by the government as an art form.

General Attitudes

The establishment of the Democratic People's Republic of Korea (North Korea's official name) brought about radical changes in the nature of traditional Korean society. The Confucian concept of filial piety and loyalty to one's lineage has been largely supplanted by an intense nationalism that is described as both fiercely proud and excessively paranoid. The interests of the state have taken priority over the interests of the family. Kim Il Sung, through extensive indoctrination, effectively united the North Korean people in the belief that their political system and way of life are superior. Although contemporary North Korean society is structurally and theoretically socialist, the most important and influential concept is Kim's idea of *chuch'e* (self-reliance). *Chuch'e* has a pervasive influence on the North Korean psyche. It colors every aspect of life, from popular music to political speeches and everyday conversation. *Chuch'e* gives people a reason to sacrifice, and it is what has convinced the people that they are better off than other nations.

CUSTOMS AND COURTESIES

Greetings

Confucianism has taught Koreans to behave with decorum and to show respect for propriety. Greetings and introductions, therefore, tend to be rather formal. Handshakes are common among men, but a bow is still most common. A younger or lower-status person always bows until the other offers a handshake or returns the bow. When Korean men do shake hands, the right hand is extended, often supported at the wrist by the left hand to show deference, and the head is slightly bowed. When women meet, they usually extend both hands and grasp each other's hands. Children always bow to adults and wave or bow among themselves.

There are several phrases used in greeting another person, but the most common is *Anyonghaseyo?* (literally, "Are you in peace?"), which is used to ask "How are you?" The Korean language has different levels of formality, so this and any other greeting will differ depending on the people involved. For example, *Anyong?* is used with children, while *Anyonghashimnikka?* is used for superiors. All mean the same thing, but the different endings indicate levels of respect. When greeting a superior, it is common to ask about health and parents. When greeting a subordinate, the questions are about the spouse and children.

Gestures

It is not unusual to see men holding hands in public or walking down the street with an arm slung over a friend's shoulder. This is an expression of friendship. Touching between strangers or casual acquaintances, however, especially between opposite sexes, is considered inappropriate. In most situations, good posture is maintained to show respect for the host or speaker. To sit in a relaxed manner is considered an insult. Care is taken not to expose the bottom of the feet to another person while sitting. Gifts are given and received with both hands. Hands are generally not used too much in conversation. Hats are removed in buildings, as well as in the presence of an elder or superior. One never looks a superior directly in the eye.

Visiting

North Koreans do not commonly visit one another unannounced, and arranged social visits are infrequent. Generally, people visit relatives for the Lunar New Year or Parents' Day, but not so often otherwise. Unless special business calls for it, a superior never visits a subordinate.

Those who are invited are nearly always offered light refreshments, consisting of a drink, fruit, crackers, cookies, or coffee. It is considered polite and a sign of respect for guests to take a gift to the hosts. The value of the gift is far less important than the gesture of giving it. In most cases, a gift will be fruit, a beverage, or something from one's home region. Shoes and hats are removed indoors. In some cases, slippers are provided. Otherwise, people wear only socks in the home. Observing etiquette involves paying particular attention to the host and making sure his feelings are respected. Showing respect for the family and state are of utmost importance for most visits. Koreans are very generous hosts. They view the care of a guest as basic good manners, so visitors are given the best the household has to offer. If there are many guests, then age or status are used to determine who gets the best seat, the best cut of meat, the largest drink, and so forth.

Eating

Families rarely have time to eat daily meals together. Fathers often leave early in the morning and return late at night. They commonly eat their meals at workplace cafeterias. Koreans consider eating while walking on the street ill-mannered and offensive, something only a child is allowed to indulge in. Except during lengthy dinner parties, conversation during meals is quite limited. Eating with the fingers is considered impolite, but slurping soup and noodles is accepted; in fact, it is a practical way to eat hot food at the rapid pace Koreans are used to. Spoons for soup and chopsticks for everything else are the most common utensils.

Restaurants in North Korea are difficult to get into and are very expensive. The average worker would almost never eat in a restaurant. Tipping is not allowed.

LIFESTYLE

Family

The family remains an important part of North Korean life. The population has been constantly exhorted by the government to "love your family, love your state," but obligations have been continually extended outward to embrace the larger society. Beginning in 1948, the government worked to break down the traditional extended family and clan system. Traditional Korean familial devotion was redirected toward the country's ruler, whom young children were taught to refer to as "Father Kim Il Sung." Through his "moral leadership and benevolent instruction" in all aspects of North Korean life, Kim was portrayed by the government-controlled media as a highly paternal figure and a near-god. His picture was everywhere and his will was obeyed before any other. His popularity weakened near the end of his life, as people realized that conditions were not improving.

For most families, the average monthly wage (about US$50) is enough to purchase daily necessities but not enough to pay for any luxury or nonessential goods. Consumerism is discouraged in favor of austerity. However, workers can earn a variety of supplies, benefits, and gifts from either their employers or the government. Both parents usually work and their children go to day care centers, often located at the workplace.

Dating and Marriage

Western-style dating is not allowed, and marriages are either arranged by the parents or carried out with their consent. The government has established minimum marriage ages (27 for men, 25 for women) to allow for the completion of military service and other obligations. Due to a shortage in the labor force, the government provides incentives for married couples to have large families.

Diet

Korean food is generally spicy. *Kimch'i* (a spicy pickled cabbage) and rice are the mainstays of the diet around which most other dishes revolve. Meals usually consist of a number of spicy vegetables, soup, fish, and *kimch'i*. Because of the lower economic level of North Korea, traditional Korean delicacies such as *pulkogi* (marinated beef) and *kalbi* (marinated short ribs) are not as common as in South Korea. A favorite food in North Korea is *naengmyon*, a cold noodle dish. The consumption of soybeans and corn is high, as is that of millet and wheat.

Recreation

Sports are popular and actively encouraged by the government. Sports facilities are plentiful. Soccer is the national sport. Many Koreans also play table tennis. Movies, plays, and operas, usually with strong political messages, are well attended. Family outings and picnics to North Korea's many parks and cultural and historical sites are common Sunday activities. Sunday is the worker's day of rest. Television is also popular and widely available. North Koreans are highly accomplished in all traditional Korean art forms. Performances are highly polished and form is pursued over spontaneity or individuality.

Holidays

In addition to national holidays, there are many commemoration days that can be declared a holiday if local authorities are satisfied production will not be disrupted. The government has discontinued traditional Korean seasonal festivals. Official holidays include New Year's Day, the birthdays of

Kim Il Sung (15 April) and Kim Jong Il (16 February), May Day (1 May), Liberation Day (15 August), Independence Day (9 September), Workers' Party Day (10 October), and Constitution Day (27 December).

Commerce

As with other key aspects of North Korean society, the government is closely involved in the mobilization of labor. Workers are expected to put in at least a 40-hour workweek in addition to attending various political and production meetings. Tightly controlled work teams laboring both on farms and in factories are the norm. By 1958, all farms in North Korea were incorporated into more than 3,000 cooperatives, each comprising about 300 families on about 1,000 acres. Basically self-sufficient in agriculture, North Korea's emphasis has gradually shifted toward mining and manufacturing. The North has about 80 to 90 percent of all known mineral resources on the peninsula, and the extraction of coal, iron ore, and other minerals has fueled North Korea's industrial growth.

SOCIETY

Government

North Korea is a Communist state. The president is head of state. A premier, currently Kang Song San, is technically head of government. The 687-seat Supreme People's Assembly forms the legislature. The last legislative elections were in 1993. In all elections, only a single candidate is chosen to run for each office. The candidates are either from the ruling Korean Workers' Party or a few minor, associated parties. Voters can only vote "yes" or "no" for each person, and they generally vote "yes." The voting age is 17.

Economy

Since the end of World War II, North Korea has changed from an agricultural to a semi-industrialized nation. The means of production are 90 percent socialized. Planning for economic development is centralized and set forth by the government in a series of seven-year plans. Industry's contribution is over 75 percent and continues to grow. Major industries include mining, steel, textiles, chemicals, cement, glass, and ceramics. North Korea exports minerals, metals, and manufactured products. Heavy industry produces much, but there is a shortage of light manufactured items (mostly consumer goods). Agricultural production is maintained through the heavy use of fertilizers and high-yield seeds.

Although the North Korean economy developed at an impressive rate in the 1980s, it lags far behind South Korea's in most areas. Economic output has fallen every year since 1990. This is partly due to the loss of the Soviet Union as a major trading partner. With a weakened economy and no trading partners, North Korea is seeking ways to stimulate growth and production—even proposing free trade zones and other "market oriented" plans. North Korea's Human Development Index (0.609) ranks it 101st out of 173 countries. Real gross domestic product per capita is estimated at $1,750. These figures indicate that basic social institutions exist, but do not provide an opportunity for economic prosperity. Many people do not earn an income sufficient for their needs. The currency is the North Korean *won* (W).

Transportation and Communication

In North Korea, the rail system is the principal means of transportation. The P'yongyang subway is efficient and cheap. Few motor vehicles are available to the general population. The streets, roads, and avenues, at least in the major cities, are broad, tree lined, and well kept. Most Koreans usually walk or ride a bus to their destinations. Factories often provide buses for their workers. Bicycles are generally not available or necessary. Flights are maintained between major cities, and international service connects P'yongyang with Moscow and Beijing. Communications systems are controlled by the government and are adequate.

Education

North Korea has over two hundred universities and colleges, more than four thousand high schools and specialized institutions, and nearly five thousand elementary schools and kindergartens. An 11-year education program is compulsory and free, and illiteracy has been all but eliminated. The estimated literacy rate is 99 percent. Competition is fierce for entry into the prestigious Kim Il Sung University and other institutions of higher learning. The socialist and nationalist focus of the North Korean educational system, while supplying the state with skilled and compliant workers, aims to produce uniformity in thought and action, with little room for individuality and diversity.

Health

Although quality is relatively poor, North Korea's socialist health-care system is extensive. Free health care is provided to the entire population. The average life expectancy ranges between 66 and 72 years. The infant mortality rate is 28 per 1,000.

FOR THE TRAVELER

The United States does not recognize the government of North Korea and does not maintain diplomatic relations with the country. To apply for a visa to travel to North Korea, an individual must apply directly to the North Korean government or through a country that has diplomatic relations with it. Vaccinations are not necessary. Foreign visitors are often assigned an escort who limits access to people and places. Although the U.S. government does not encourage travel to North Korea, it does not prohibit it. Still, groups traveling to North Korea must obtain a license from the Department of Treasury, Licensing Division, Office of Foreign Assets Control, 1500 Pennsylvania Avenue NW, Second Floor NX, Washington, DC 20220; phone (202) 622–2480.

Printed on recycled paper

South Korea
(Republic of Korea)

Boundary representations not necessarily authoritative.

ASIA

BACKGROUND

Land and Climate

Covering 38,023 square miles (98,480 square kilometers), South Korea is slightly larger than Indiana. Its only border is shared with North Korea at the 38th parallel (called the "Truce Line"). Otherwise, as a peninsula, it is surrounded by water. At its closest point, it is 123 miles (196 kilometers) from Japan. Almost 70 percent of the land is forested; just over 20 percent is suitable for cultivation. Hills and mountains dominate the east, while plains are found in the west and south. Korea's climate is temperate, but high humidity makes summers seem hotter and winters colder. Korea experiences all four seasons; spring and fall are the most pleasant times of the year. The monsoon season occurs from mid-July to mid-August. During this time, Korea receives half of its annual rainfall. Korea is traditionally known as the "Land of the Morning Calm."

History

Shilla kings united three warring kingdoms in A.D. 668 and began developing a rich Buddhist culture. By 935, a new kingdom, Koryo, began ruling the peninsula. The name "Korea" comes from Koryo. During the Koryo period, the world's first movable metal-type printer was invented. Koryo fell to the Choson or Yi Dynasty in 1392. The Yi ruled for more than 500 years. In the latter part of the Yi Dynasty, China and Japan sought control of Korea, a struggle that the Japanese eventually won. They annexed Korea in 1910.

At the end of World War II (1945), the Soviet Union entered Korea from the north and the United States entered the south by prearrangement to accept the surrender of Japanese troops. The peninsula was accordingly divided (at the 38th parallel) into two administrative zones. After attempts to hold nationwide elections failed, a pro-Western government was established in the south and Syngman Rhee became president. In June 1950, North Korean troops invaded South Korea, triggering a three-year war. The United States and United Nations sent troops to support South Korea. Concerned that war might spill into Chinese territory, China sent troops to aid North Korea. The war ravaged the peninsula and ended in a stalemate (a peace treaty has still not been signed) with the original border virtually unchanged. Violent border incidents have occurred over the years, and a monthly civil defense drill is still conducted in South Korea.

Rhee resigned in 1960 under charges of political corruption. Although elections were held the following year, General Park Chung Hee seized control of the government and was elected president two years later. He was assassinated in 1979 by the head of the South Korean intelligence agency. A military coup followed and Chun Doo Hwan emerged as president. A 1987 constitution established direct presidential elections and protection of human rights. Roh Tae Woo was elected president. It was not until 1992, however, that full, free elections were held without military involvement. Grassroots democratic movements led authorities to accept elections in order to avoid possible future revolts. Kim Young Sam won the election and became the first civilian to occupy the Blue House (presidential mansion) in over 30 years. He took office in 1993. Kim strove to reform government and continue economic progress, but was also plagued by three major man-made disasters that cost the lives of some 200 citizens.

In 1990, peace talks were held between the prime ministers of North and South Korea—the first such contact since the 1950s. While the two did not reconcile their differences, they did agree to continue meeting in an effort to reduce tensions, open relations, and possibly start unification. Tensions over North Korea's nuclear program and U.S.-South Korean military relations led talks to falter in 1993 and 1994. When North Korea agreed to a nuclear accord in 1994, it was thought that tensions between the two Koreas would ease rapidly. Families split by the war hoped for reunion, and plans were made to speed economic cooperation. However, in 1995 North Korea withdrew its support for the accord and negotiations stalled. As the situation remains, both sides still forbid personal contacts between the two nations. Until relations improve, letters, phone calls, visits, and all other communication are officially impossible.

THE PEOPLE

Population

The population of the Republic of Korea is 45 million and is growing annually at 1 percent. Except for a small Chinese minority, the people are all ethnic Korean, making Korea one of the most homogeneous countries in the world. About 72 percent of the population lives in urban areas.

Language

The Korean language plays an important role in the identity of the Korean people. Korean is spoken in both North and South Korea and is written in *Hangul*, a phonetic alphabet created in 1446 because classical Chinese (the only written language available) was difficult to master. *Hangul* made it possible for the commoner to read and write. It has 24 letters (ten of them vowels), all of which are easy to learn. *Hangul* also instilled national pride in Koreans over time that helped them to resist long periods of foreign occupation. Although not related to Chinese, Korean mixes numerous Chinese words and characters with the *Hangul* script in newspapers and government documents. English is taught in the schools and many people have a good understanding of it.

Religion

Confucianism permeates all aspects of Korean society. It encourages such practices as worshipping at shrines and ancestral tombs. In addition, Confucianism orders social behavior, stressing righteousness and filial piety (family relationships), especially between father and son. Over one-quarter of the people follow the traditions of a folk religion called Shamanism. Important to Shamanism are geomancy, divination, avoiding bad luck or omens, warding off evil spirits, and honoring the dead. Close to 30 percent of the population is Christian. Christianity is growing rapidly and many young people and government officials are Christian. Most Christians belong to a variety of Protestant churches. More than 15 percent of Koreans practice Buddhism.

General Attitudes

The Confucian ethic is evident in the general attitudes of Koreans. There are many rituals of courtesy, formality in behavior, and customs regulating social relations. Hard work and filial piety are valued. Koreans often use extreme modesty when speaking about themselves. Reluctance to accept high honors is the mark of a true Korean. Compliments are graciously denied. Success depends greatly on social contacts. Koreans are quick to make friends and friendships are highly valued. Friends expect to rely on each other for just about anything.

Giving gifts as a means of obtaining favors is common, especially in the workplace, and accepting a gift carries the responsibility of reciprocity. Open criticism and public disagreement are considered very serious because it is not proper to damage another person's reputation. Because of respect for the feelings of others, Koreans may withhold bad news or adverse opinions or express them in an indirect way. South Koreans are proud of their country's accomplishments, including the nation's modern economic success and the influence of its traditional culture.

Personal Appearance

Most Koreans, except for the elderly and some in rural areas, wear Western-style clothing. The youth wear modern fashions, and Korea has an active fashion industry. Clothing often depends on the event. In public, conservative dress is important. Bare feet are inappropriate. In the business world, Western-style suits and dresses are the norm. For special occasions or holidays, however, traditional clothing is often worn. Women wear the *hanbok*, a two-piece, long dress that is often very colorful. Men wear trousers with a loose-fitting jacket or robe.

CUSTOMS AND COURTESIES

Greetings

Confucian principles, although less important in modern Korean society than in the past, are still an integral part of social interactions, including greetings. How one is greeted depends on one's age and social standing relative to the greeter. A bow is the traditional greeting, but it is usually accompanied with a handshake between men. The left hand may support or rest under the right forearm during the handshake to show respect. Women shake hands less often than men. Between professionals meeting for the first time, business cards are exchanged (presented and accepted with both hands after a handshake). A common greeting is *Annyong haseyo?,* which means "Are you at peace?" Young children often greet each other with a simple *Annyong?* To show special respect, an honorific is added to the greeting: *Annyong hashimnikka?* Young children bow or nod in greeting adults.

Gestures

It is not uncommon to see Korean men (usually younger) holding hands or walking with a hand on a friend's shoulder. This is an expression of friendship. Touching older people or members of the opposite sex, however, is usually not appropriate. Feet are not placed on a desk or chair. Both hands (or the right hand, grasped at the wrist or forearm by the left) are used to pass and receive objects. The mouth should be covered when yawning or using a toothpick. Koreans beckon by waving the fingers together with the palm down. To beckon with the index finger is very rude. Facial expressions are often more important than body language in communicating unspoken things. When embarrassed, a person may respond by laughing. Eye contact is important in conversation among peers.

In general, people do not line up for things. In fact, because personal space is limited in Korea, pushing and crowding is common and generally not considered impolite.

Visiting

Guests invited to a home remove their shoes upon entering. While Western furniture is common, in traditional Korean homes, guests are seated on cushions on floors that are heated from below (*ondol* floors). Men sit cross-legged and women tuck their legs to one side behind them. The guest receives the warmest or best position. When visiting relatives, men and women usually separate to socialize. For example, the women gather in the kitchen. Guests invited for a meal or party customarily bring a small gift in appreciation, often something that can be served at the gathering. Wrapped gifts are not opened in front of the giver. Refreshments are usually served and it is impolite to refuse them. A host accompanies a guest to the door or outside at the end of a visit.

Eating

At a dinner party, the meal will usually come before socializing. Items are passed and drinks are poured with the right hand, with the left hand supporting the forearm or wrist. In restaurants, tipping is not expected. A service charge is usually included in the bill. Eating while walking on the street is not appropriate for adults. Chopsticks and spoons are the most commonly used utensils.

LIFESTYLE

Family

The family is the foundation of society and is bound together by a strong sense of duty and obligation among its members. The father is the head of the family; he and the oldest son receive the greatest respect. The oldest son is given the best opportunities for education and success. Although women are active in Korean society (they comprise one-third of the labor force), their status is generally lower than men's, a cultural trait often reflected in the workplace and home. Women retain their maiden names when they marry. A Korean name consists of a one-syllable family name followed by a one- or two-syllable given name. Kim and Park (*Pak*) are the most common family names. In the extended family, the oldest members are paid the greatest honor. On a person's 60th birthday (a date rarely accomplished in the past), extended family members gather for a grand celebration (*hwan'gap*). Families may save money for years just to pay for the event.

Similar lavish attention is afforded to babies. After 100 days of life, a small feast is held in honor of the child's survival to that point (also a date often not reached in the past). A much larger celebration (*tol*) is held at the first birthday. From the many gifts offered, what a child picks up first is thought to signal his or her fortunes in life. Although the nuclear family is now more common, especially in the cities, sons still expect to care for their aging parents. Because of the Confucian emphasis on family hierarchies, detailed genealogies are kept. These records date back many centuries and include a person's birth, relations, achievements, and place of burial. In family clan gatherings, families that rank higher in the genealogy are treated with greater respect by the others.

Dating and Marriage

Dating usually occurs in groups. The youth enjoy going to movies, hiking, taking short trips, and socializing at bakeries and tea houses. While trends are changing, most Korean youth rarely have time for more serious dating before they enter college or the work force. Young people often meet at parties organized for that purpose. In some cases, marriages are still arranged by families for couples who have met but not dated in the Western sense. Traditional wedding ceremonies were rather elaborate, but today they often take place in public wedding halls where couples wear Western-style clothing instead of traditional Korean wedding attire.

Diet

Korean food is generally spicy. Rice and *kimch'i* (a spicy pickled cabbage) are staples at almost every meal. Various soups are common. Rice is often combined with other ingredients, such as red beans or vegetables. *Pibibap* is rice mixed with bits of meat and seasoned vegetables. Chicken and beef are common meats. A favorite delicacy is *pulkogi*, strips of marinated and barbecued beef. Large amounts of fish and *dok* (pounded rice cake) are also eaten. Barley tea is served with most meals. *Soju* and *magulli* are common alcoholic drinks for socializing with guests before meals. Fruit is popular as a dessert.

Recreation

Soccer is popular in Korea. South Korea's national soccer team competed in the 1994 World Cup. Koreans also participate in baseball, boxing, basketball, volleyball, tennis, and swimming. *Taekwondo*, the martial art, comes from and is popular in Korea. Unique to Korea is a form of wrestling called *ssirum*, where contestants are tied together during their match. Mountain climbing and hiking are favorite activities for weekends and vacations. Movies, art exhibits, and theaters also provide entertainment.

Holidays

The New Year is celebrated over three days (1–3 January). Families gather to exchange gifts, honor the dead, and enjoy large meals. Generally, everyone dresses in traditional clothing. After the memorial services, family members bow to each older person in a show of respect. Games are played and fortunes are told. The other important family holiday is *Ch'usok* (Harvest Moon Festival, held in the Fall), where family members visit the ancestral tomb to offer food in honor of the dead. Larger family reunions are common at this time. Other holidays include Independence Movement Day (1 March), Children's Day (5 May), Buddha's Birthday (in May, observed according to the lunar calendar), Memorial Day (6 June), Constitution Day (17 July), Independence Day (15 August), National Foundation Day (3 October), and Christmas. Arbor Day (5 April), Armed Forces Day (1 October), and Korean Language Day (9 October) are marked by various celebrations but are not public holidays.

Commerce

Small, family-owned stores are usually open every day from early in the morning until 10:00 or 11:00 P.M. In many cases, the family lives above or near the store. Larger department stores close by 8:00 P.M. Other businesses are generally open from 9:00 A.M. to 6:00 P.M. Banks and government offices close earlier. The average workweek for a Korean is 50 hours, one of the longest in the world but shorter than it was in the 1980s.

SOCIETY

Government

The Republic of South Korea has an elected president who serves a five-year term. The president appoints a prime minister who is technically, but not in practice, head of government. Members of the 299-seat National Assembly (*Kuk Hoe*) serve four-year terms. The majority party is the Democratic Liberal Party. The main opposition parties are the Democratic Party and the United People's Party. All citizens may vote at age 20. South Korea is divided into nine provinces (*do*) and six special cities (*jikhalsi*).

Economy

Over the past several years, South Korea has experienced rapid economic growth and development. The gross domestic product (GDP) grew at more than 6 percent annually in the late 1980s. The global recession and domestic difficulties caused slower growth in the early 1990s, but Korea is still considered an Asian economic powerhouse. Growth for 1994 was above 7 percent. Since 1987, incomes have risen by 50 percent and the middle class has grown to the point that most families identify themselves as part of it.

South Korea's Human Development Index (0.859) ranks it 32d of 173 countries. Real gross domestic product per capita is $8,320. These figures reflect the economy's vigor and people's access to economic opportunities. Most people earn a decent income and have confidence in their economic future. Korea's success is based on rapid export-oriented industrialization.

The agricultural sector contributes about 11 percent of the GDP. Chief products include rice, barley, vegetables, and fish. About 16 percent of the labor force is employed in agriculture and lives in rural villages, cultivating small plots or collective farms. More than one-third of the labor force works in mining and manufacturing. The rest is involved in service occupations. Korea's industries include textiles and clothing, chemicals, steel, electronics, and automobiles. Shipbuilding is also important. Unemployment and inflation remain relatively low. The currency is the *won* (W).

Transportation and Communication

Air, rail, and bus connections provide a good transportation network between cities. Roads are paved and in good condition. Buses, private cars, and taxis handle public transportation in the cities. Seoul has an efficient subway and a quality express bus system in addition to regular buses. Taxis are plentiful and inexpensive. Drivers will often stop for other passengers during busy hours. Driving habits are aggressive and accidents are common. There are numerous radio and television stations. Many daily newspapers are available. The postal and telephone systems are efficient and modern.

Education

Education is the most valued aspect of Korean culture, a virtue rooted in Confucianism. Education is considered the key to success, respect, and power. The government finances more than 75 percent of Korea's education expenses. Political demonstrations by college students usually occur every spring and are considered part of the students' duty to protect the people against social injustices. Although these activities have often been violent, they have been part of university life for much longer than Korea has been a republic. They decreased substantially after the 1992 elections but still occur when an appropriate cause arises. Schooling is compulsory between the ages of six and twelve and nearly every child completes primary schooling. Most (88 percent of all children) also go on for secondary education. Secondary schools demand long hours and high performance. Extremely competitive and rigorous college entrance exams must be passed to enter a university. Students study intensively for months to pass these exams. Vocational training is also available. The literacy rate is 96 percent.

Health

All segments of the population have access to adequate health care. The best facilities are in Seoul. Most women receive prenatal care and medical attention during delivery. Nearly 80 percent of all infants are immunized. The infant mortality rate is 22 per 1,000. Adults can expect to live between 67 and 74 years.

FOR THE TRAVELER

A valid passport and visa are required of U.S. travelers visiting for more than 15 days. For shorter visits, only a passport is necessary. Water is generally not safe for drinking and should be boiled. No vaccinations are required. Korea has many historical sites and excellent mountain climbing opportunities. The tourist industry is well developed and many people speak English. Although Western hotels are available, Korean-style accommodations (such as the *yogwan*) are inexpensive and provide a cultural experience. For more information contact the Korea National Tourism Corporation, Two Executive Drive, Seventh Floor, Fort Lee, NJ 07024; phone (201) 585–0909. You may also wish to contact the Embassy of the Republic of Korea, 2370 Massachusetts Avenue NW, Washington, DC 20008; phone (202) 797–6343.

CULTURGRAM '96

Laos
(Lao People's Democratic Republic)

Boundary representations not necessarily authoritative.

BACKGROUND

Land and Climate

Laos covers 91,430 square miles (236,800 square kilometers), is slightly larger than Utah, and is one of the few landlocked countries of Southeast Asia. Its major geographical feature is the Mekong River, which defines most of its western borders with Myanmar and Thailand. The Mekong is important for transportation, although rapids make it impassable in some areas. It is also a source of fish and hydroelectric power. Steep mountains cover the north and northeast, which are only sparsely inhabited by ethnic minorities. Most people live in areas such as the Plain of Jars, the Vientiane Plain, and the Bolovens Plateau. Laos has a tropical monsoon climate with a dry season from December to April and rain from May to November. It is always humid. Temperatures can get quite cold, but not freezing, in the northern mountains. In the plateau areas, temperatures range from 57°F to 93°F (14–34°C), with January the coolest month and April the hottest.

History

The first Laotian kingdom (Lan Xang) was established in 1353 by Fa Ngum. It became a major regional trading center. Over the centuries, the kingdom struggled with neighbors for control of trade routes. Lan Xang lasted until 1713, when its three provinces split into separate principalities. These three small kingdoms eventually came under the influence of Siam (now Thailand). The French gained control of parts of Siam in the late 1800s, and the three Laotian principalities of Vientiane, Luang Prabang (Louangphrabang), and Champassak became a French protectorate in 1893.

The Japanese occupied Laos during World War II, but the French returned in 1946. Internal rule over a united Laos was granted to the King of Luang Prabang (King Sisavong Vong) in 1949, but Laos was still part of the French union. With the signing of the Geneva Convention, Laos became independent in 1954. For a short time the nation acted as a buffer between Vietnam and Thailand.

A northern leftist group, Pathet Lao, aided by North Vietnam, gained strength as a rival to the royalty during the 1950s and eventually took control of much of the country. Upon a ceasefire, the Pathet Lao became part of a 1962 coalition government, headed by Prince Souvanna Phouma. The Pathet Lao withdrew from that coalition in 1964. By then, Laos was becoming more and more involved in the war in Vietnam. After the Pathet Lao aligned with the Viet Minh (Communists), they fought against the government until a 1973 ceasefire. The Pathet Lao briefly participated in a new coalition, but then took control of the country in 1975, sending the royalty into exile and declaring the Lao People's Democratic

Republic. Kaysone Phomvihan, leader of the Pathet Lao, became president of the country.

The United States heavily bombed Laotian territory in the early 1970s in an effort to stop the flow of troops and supplies along the Ho Chi Minh Trail that ran from North Vietnam through Laos and into South Vietnam. This bombing left permanent craters in many villages. Since 1989, however, strained relations with the United States have improved. When Phomvihan died in 1992, Nouhak Phoumsavan took the position of president and general secretary of the Communist party. He continues a recent policy of gradually decentralizing economic control of the country.

THE PEOPLE

Population

The population of Laos is 4.7 million and is growing at 2.8 percent annually. About 45 percent of the population is under the age of 15. Less than one-fifth of the population resides in urban areas. The Lao government encourages population growth because it believes more people would help Laos meet labor force needs for development. Laos is an ethnically diverse country. Its 68 known ethnic groups are, however, classified into a few major categories, which vary according to category definition and other factors. The largest group is collectively known as the *Lao Lum* or *Lao-Lu*. These are ethnic lowland Lao related to the Thais of Thailand. They comprise 50 percent of the population. The *Lao Tai* (also called tribal Tai) are distinguished from others in the country by their non-Buddhist beliefs; they make up perhaps 20 percent of the population. The *Phuthung* are the various mountain peoples that are not generally related to other Laotians; some figures indicate they may comprise 15 percent of the total population. Percentages for other groups are difficult to assess. The *Lao Thung* (midland Lao) are considered descendants of the area's earliest settlers. The *Lao Sung* (upland Lao) include the ethnic groups of Meo and Man, and have their origins in southwestern China.

Language

The official language is Lao, the native language of the Lao Lum, which is used in all official communications and taught in schools. Other main languages include Thai, Hmong, and Lao Thung. Some ethnic minority languages have never been codified in written form. A small percentage of older people and those who attended high school prior to 1975 speak French, which has been the language of international commerce in the past. Some English is spoken.

Religion

Nearly all (85 percent) Laotians are Buddhist. The Phuthung practice animism, which emphasizes a reverence for all living things. *Phu* means "spirits," and the Phuthung believe all objects are inhabited by spirits. Buddhism has long been a strong force in Lao culture and remains a major influence in everyday life, despite a Communist government. In Laos, the government sees Buddhism as too important to ban in the name of communism. Even top officials worship in the Buddhist tradition. Each ethnic Lao village has its own *wat* (temple), which is the focal point of village festivities and rituals. Several of the most famous *wats* in Vientiane have been turned into museums. It is common for villagers to take food to monks in a daily ritual where the monks do not look at the donors. Male donors remove their sandals. Women kneel as monks pass by in a procession to collect food offerings. Boys usually spend some portion of their lives living as monks.

General Attitudes

The Lao are a frank, open, and friendly people. They also have a strongly developed sense of courtesy and respect. It is considered very bad taste to publicly criticize a person since it results in a loss of face within the community. Necessary criticisms and suggestions should be made within a general context to avoid placing blame or shame upon any individual. *Bo pen nyang* (Never mind) is a common expression that characterizes Laotians' feelings toward life. Life should be enjoyed at the moment; problems are not taken so seriously as to disrupt this enjoyment. Given the hardships people face in the country, this is an invaluable attitude. Loyalty to family and friends is important. Showing anger or disappointment in public is inappropriate.

Personal Appearance

Lao women wear Western-style blouses with colorful calf-length, sarong-style skirts made of locally handwoven materials in multicolor designs and fastened with a silver link belt. Men wear trousers with casual, open-neck, short-sleeve shirts. Some men wear sarong-type garments rather than trousers. Both men and women usually wear sandals. Some ethnic groups also wear distinct headdresses.

CUSTOMS AND COURTESIES

Greetings

The generally accepted form of greeting among Lao people is the *Nop*, which involves placing one's hands together in a prayer position at chest level but not touching the body. The higher the hands, the greater the sign of respect, although they should never be held above the level of the nose. This is accompanied by a slight bow to show respect for persons of higher status or age. The *Nop* is not only an expression of greeting but also of thanks or regret. It is appropriate to shake hands with Westerners. The Lao address each other by the first name. Children address adults by the first name, prefaced by the equivalent of "Mr." or "Mrs.," or, if well acquainted, "Mr. Uncle" or "Mrs. Aunt," a courtesy title.

Gestures

As in many Asian cultures, the head is considered the most sacred part of the body; the bottoms of the feet are the least sacred. One should not touch a person's head, nor should one use the foot to point at a person or a sacred object. Men and women rarely show affection in public. It is forbidden for a woman to touch a Buddhist monk.

Visiting

It is customary to remove one's shoes or sandals when entering a Buddhist temple or a private home. In Lao homes that are raised off the ground, shoes or sandals are left at the bottom of the stairs. In a traditional home, a person sits on low seats or cushions on the floor. Men may sit with legs crossed or folded to one side. Women sit with legs off to the side. Guests may be served tea or fruit, which should not be refused. One should at least have a taste. It is not customary to bring a gift when visiting.

Eating

The Lao eat with a fork in the left hand and a spoon in the right. However, glutinous rice is eaten with the fingers, which are cleaned with a napkin. Lao food, which is very spicy, is served in communal dishes with meat and vegetables cut into bite-size pieces. In a traditional home, the meal is served while diners sit on a mat on the floor. As a sign of respect to a guest, the host and his family will not raise their heads above the level of that of the guest's. Therefore, they may bring the food in a squat position so as not to offend guests.

LIFESTYLE

Family

The Lao have large, close-knit families, often with three generations living together. The eldest man is the patriarch of the family and represents the household at village meetings. The Lao have great respect for their parents and elders. Among the Hmong, the household is composed of the extended family: parents, unmarried children, and married sons with their families.

Dating and Marriage

Young people are relatively free to choose marriage partners. Young people can meet eligible partners at dances held during festivals, where they are free to sit and talk privately. Marriage is traditionally established by elopement, living together, or a more elaborate marriage ritual among wealthier people. For the first few years of married life, the couple lives with the wife's family, until her first child is about a year old. The couple may then establish their own home or move in with the husband's family.

Diet

Sticky or glutinous rice is the staple of the Lao diet. *Lap* (sautéed buffalo innards mixed with onions, lemon grass, and spices, and served with a rice-flour sauce) is a typical Lao food. Other foods include fish, eggs, chicken, pork, owl, and (rarely) beef. Rice is served with chili sauce or a spicy sauce made with fermented fish. Beverages include coffee and tea. Cultivated foods are supplemented with wild fruits and vegetables from the forest as well as game, such as deer. Hill tribes grow dry rice by slash-and-burn cultivation methods, although the government is attempting to save the forest areas for other uses by resettling some of these tribes to lower elevations near water supplies. This presents a problem for the highland peoples, as they depend on food from the forests for their traditional diet.

Recreation

Popular sports are soccer, volleyball, table tennis, and badminton. *Kato*, played by trying to keep a rattan ball in the air without using the hands, is also a favorite. Entire families often participate in dances at community celebrations. Discos are becoming popular in the cities.

Holidays

Official holidays include International New Year (1 January); *Pi Mai*, the Lao New Year, governed by the lunar calendar and usually in May; Labor Day (1 May); and National Day (2 December), the largest celebration. Religious holidays include *Bun Bang-Fai* in May or June, celebrating the birth, enlightenment, and death of Buddha; *Khao Phansa*, the advent of Buddhist lent in July and *Ok Phansa*, its conclusion in late October; and *Bun That Luang*, a festival at a temple housing a relic of Buddha. All important events are celebrated with a *basi* or *sukhwan*, a celebration involving offerings, food, and rice wine. In a string-tying ceremony, people wish good health and prosperity to friends by tying a string on the wrist.

Commerce

Since 85 to 90 percent of the people work in agriculture, the work schedule is dictated by the requirements of the rice crop. Some periods are full of activity, while others are slower, allowing people to attend to duties at home. Office hours in the city generally run from 9:00 A.M. to noon and from 2:00 to 5:00 P.M. Officially, government offices are also open Saturday mornings. Most shops are small, family-run businesses. In these, and at markets, one is expected to bargain for items. However, gold and silver items are sold by weight regardless of the amount of workmanship involved. Markets stay open until mid-afternoon. Shops are open according to the wishes of the owners, usually until late afternoon.

SOCIETY

Government

The Lao People's Democratic Republic is a Communist state. A new constitution enacted in 1991 provides for an executive branch that consists of a president as head of state and a chairman of the Council of Ministers as head of government. The chairman of the Council of Ministers is General Khamtai Siphandon. The 85-seat Supreme People's Assembly is the elected legislature, for which the last national elections were held in 1992. All Laotians may vote at age 18. There is essentially only one political party, the Lao People's Revolutionary Party, but it claims an alliance to a sister party, the Lao Front for National Construction. There are no opposition parties.

Economy

The Laotian economy is based on agriculture, which employs the majority of the population. The main crop is rice, but corn, vegetables, tobacco, coffee, and other foods are also grown. The government is attempting to expand industrial activities to tap the many resources of Laos, which include timber (58 percent of the land is covered with forests), gypsum, tin, and gold. Some private enterprise is also being encouraged. Laos exports electricity, wood products, coffee, and tin. The economy depends heavily on foreign aid (mostly from Western nations) and must import manufactured goods, medicine, and machinery.

Laos has traditionally been one of the poorest countries in the world. However, economic reforms and better relations with neighbors and the West have allowed for some progress. The country's Human Development Index (0.385) ranks it 133d out of 173 countries. That ranking has improved since 1990. Real gross domestic product per capita has also risen, and is estimated at $1,760. These figures reflect an economy in which most people either do not earn an income (i.e., they are subsistence farmers) or their income is too low to meet basic needs. But a return to family-based farming in some areas, as well as increased economic activity in urban areas, has allowed some families to rise above the subsistence level. Basic social institutions are still not well developed and require investment before futher progress can be made. Inflation is about 10 percent and unemployment is 20 percent. The currency is the *new kip* (NK).

Transportation and Communication

The transportation system in Laos is poorly developed. Most rural roads are unpaved; many are impassable in the rainy season. Public transportation is limited, and there is no rail service. Most people walk, but some have bicycles and motorbikes. Currently, goods are transported over two land routes to seaports in Vietnam and Thailand. The Mekong River is navigable for over two-thirds of its territory. Air travel within Laos is limited, with access dependent on weather conditions and confined to provincial capitals. Communication systems are also poorly developed, with limited electricity, few rural telephones, and few radio stations.

Education

The state provides free education for eleven years (ages six to seventeen), including five years of mandatory primary school and six years of secondary school. The government also emphasizes adult literacy. Although education is free, enrollment in rural areas declines after primary school. While it is estimated that literacy among the youth (under age 15) is above 80 percent, adult literacy is perhaps 55 percent. The average adult has completed fewer than four years of formal education. There are four higher technical institutions: the Electronic Technology and Electricity Institute, the National Building Institute, the School of Transport and Communications, and the National Polytechnic Institute. These and the University of Medical Science are all located in Vientiane. Teacher-training schools are found in Vientiane and other provinces.

Health

Health standards are poor as medical facilities in Laos are inadequate and almost nonexistent in rural areas. Life expectancy averages between 50 and 53 years and the infant mortality rate is 101 per 1,000. Despite these figures, they are at least improving, rather than getting worse. International aid plays an important role in providing modern medical care, but traditional medicine is also important in rural areas.

Malaria, trachoma, typhoid, hepatitis, tuberculosis, and dysentery are problematic in some areas. Water is not safe and must be boiled before drinking.

FOR THE TRAVELER

Travelers need a passport and visa to enter Laos. Visas are granted only on proof of sufficient funds and onward passage. They should be applied for well in advance of one's trip. Prior to 1994, all visitors were accompanied by a government escort, and travel outside of Vientiane was restricted by special permits. This is no longer the case, and travel may be made outside the capital without special permission. There are some exceptions, but most areas where tourists wish to visit are open and safe for travel. It is still advisable to register with the police upon arrival. All items and services must be paid for with cash. Travelers' checks and credit cards are virtually unknown. Facilities outside the capital are underdeveloped. Travelers found distributing any type of religious material may be arrested and deported. Do not take photographs of military installations, property, or equipment; cameras will be confiscated.

Malaria suppressants are recommended outside Vientiane. For additional health advisories, call the U.S. Centers for Disease Control International Travelers' Hotline at (404) 332-4559. Although travel accommodations are often primitive, many say that Laos offers the greatest opportunity to experience traditional Asian culture (especially outside the capital). For more information, contact the Embassy of the Lao People's Democratic Republic, 2222 S Street NW, Washington, DC 20008; phone (202) 332–6416.

CULTURGRAM '96™

Republic of
Lebanon

Boundary representations not necessarily authoritative.

A
S
I
A

BACKGROUND

Land and Climate

Lebanon is slightly smaller than Connecticut. Covering 4,015 square miles (10,400 square kilometers), it shares borders with Syria and Israel. Its western border is the Mediterranean Sea. A low coastal plain dominates the west but gives way to the Lebanon Mountains in the east. Nestled between the Lebanon Mountains and the Anti-Lebanon Mountains on the Syrian border is the fertile Bekaa Valley. The climate is influenced by the Mediterranean. Winters are mild, although wet, and summers are hot and dry. It is cooler in the mountains in the summer. There is some snow at the higher elevations during the winter.

History

A small part of modern Lebanon, known as Mt. Lebanon, was a Maronite enclave in the vast Ottoman Empire, which ruled much of the area from the 16th century to the beginning of the 20th century. Mt. Lebanon and all of Syria became a French protectorate when the French and British drove the Ottomans out of the area during World War I. Lebanon became a republic in 1926, but French troops did not withdraw until 1946. Although Christians were a slight majority of the population, other religions also had significant numbers. Therefore, the government was established to represent the major religious groups. The president was to be a Maronite Christian, the prime minister a Sunni Muslim, and the president of parliament a *Shī'a* (Shiite) Muslim. All religious groups were to receive representation in the National Assembly according to their numbers.

The Christians refused to acknowledge any census after 1932, when they had a majority. This, along with social disparities between Christians and Muslims, led to internal tension and strife. A large number of Palestinian refugees from Israel settled in Lebanon in 1948 and 1967, further complicating internal problems. Civil war erupted in 1975. A 1976 cease-fire maintained a partial peace until 1982, when Israel invaded Lebanon and occupied the area south of Beirut. During a siege of Beirut, a multinational peacekeeping force (MNF) was sent to evacuate members of the Palestine Liberation Organization (PLO) from the city. Except for a brief period, the MNF remained until 1984.

Civil war erupted again in 1983. From 1987 to 1990, fighting was heavy and thousands died. The government could not operate normally or sponsor elections for the parliament, last elected in 1972. Amin Gamayel became president after Bashir Gamayel was assassinated in 1982. He served until 1988, when General Michel Aoun took control of the government. Aoun, a Maronite, ordered the parliament dissolved in 1989. However, parliament did not recognize his authority and elected René Moawad president. He was assassinated a few days later by Aoun loyalists. Elias Hrawi was then elected president of Lebanon. Aoun was dismissed, but he continued to battle rival Christian forces.

Aoun finally surrendered in October 1990 and eventually received asylum in France. Under a peace accord, militias withdrew from Beirut and the Lebanese army established control. The "Green Line" that had divided the city into East and West Beirut was removed and businesses began reopening, despite the devastation. By mid-1991, most militias through-out the country had disarmed and recognized the government's authority. A treaty of mutual friendship was signed with Syria; it provides for joint institutions to govern economic, defense, and foreign policy issues. Syrian troops remained in Leba-non and will stay until Syria determines otherwise. With the 15-year civil war behind them, the people of Lebanon began rebuilding their country. Parliamentary elections were held in 1992 and plans to rebuild the country's infrastructure were announced in 1993 by Prime Minister Rafik al-Hariri. Where government has not been able to move quickly enough, pri-vate enterprise has stepped in to provide water, electricity, and other necessities to wealthy areas. The largest official government rebuilding project began in 1994; it concentrates on Beirut's commercial district. Private firms are also expected to rebuild large areas of the country, eventually benefiting all segments of the population.

THE PEOPLE

Population

The population of Lebanon is 3.6 million and is growing at 2 percent annually. Beirut, the capital, is the largest city and Tripoli is the next largest. About 85 percent of all people live in urban areas. The Bekaa Valley is filled with small, rural villages. About 95 percent of the people are Arabs and 4 percent are Armenians. Armenians live mostly in Beirut.

Language

Arabic is the official language and is spoken by all. French also enjoys official status. It and English are widely spoken by the educated. The Armenian minority also speaks Arme-nian and some of them speak Turkish. It is common for people to speak more than one language, even three or four.

Religion

Lebanese society is based on religion. All citizens carry an identity card on which their religion is listed. While over half of the people were Christian two decades ago, Christians only account for 25 percent of the population today. The largest Christian church is the Maronite Church, an Eastern-rite reli-gion that accepts the Roman Catholic pope. There are ten other legally recognized Christian churches, most of them Catholic or Orthodox-related groups. Most of the rest of the population is Islamic. The largest groups are the Shiite Mus-lims and Sunni Muslims. The Druze, a group that broke away from Islam in the Middle Ages, is another significant faction. Unlike other religions, the Druze do not have an accessible body of scripture; traditions are passed by word of mouth. Little is consequently known about the religion. There is a small Jewish minority.

General Attitudes

Lebanon has had a long association with the West and has been deeply influenced by it. At the same time, traditional values and attitudes that differ from Western culture remain. Therefore, attitudes vary greatly among the people. Compared to life in North America, life in Lebanon is still fairly relaxed and slow paced. People tend to care more about personal re-lationships than time schedules. Most people are involved in local political issues, but personal relationships and family ties are often much more important than political ideologies in determining loyalties.

On a personal level, many tend to have fatalistic attitudes about life. This comes partly from Arabic traditions and partly from the historical difficulty of rising above the educational level or social class of one's parents. But attitudes are chang-ing and many do not accept these limitations. The Lebanese are very proud of their culture, heritage, and country. Before war crippled the economy, Lebanon was a prosperous finan-cial and tourist center. The Lebanese desire to regain that sta-tus, and they have the entrepreneurial spirit and ingenuity to do so. Even during the war, private enterprise thrived. Today, with the focus on peace, people are coming together to re-build and improve their society.

Personal Appearance

Western-style clothing is the standard in Lebanese cities. However, traditional Muslim clothing, such as a woman's *chador* (long dress that covers the entire body and often worn over other clothing) is also worn. It is important to people of all classes to be clean, neat, and stylish. Conservative suits and modest attire are appropriate. Immodest clothing is not worn in rural areas, although it is sometimes seen in cities.

CUSTOMS AND COURTESIES

Greetings

Lebanese people take social amenities seriously. When meeting strangers, acquaintances, or friends, it is important to exchange greetings, to inquire about the person's health and family, and in general to make polite small talk before getting down to business. Handshakes are common for both men and women. Close friends and relatives often appear to kiss each other on both cheeks upon meeting or departing. In urban areas, this custom is used with either gender, although strangers are not greeted this way. The kiss is actually a "kiss of the air" while touching cheeks. In rural areas, only mem-bers of the same sex might greet in this manner—unless the two people are related. Titles such as "Dr." or "Professor" are used consistently where appropriate. In Arabic, these titles are commonly used with a person's first name, but Lebanese are accustomed to hearing titles in English and French. Per-sonal space is more limited than in North America and people may stand closer in conversation. Friends will use each other's titles in meetings and will act more formally than they would in other situations. Common urban greetings include *Bonjour* (Good day), *Salut* (Hello), *Hi*, or the Arabic *Keef halik* (How are you) for women or *Keef halak* for men. In rural areas, only Arabic greetings are common.

Gestures

"Yes" is signified by one downward nod; "no" is expressed by an upward movement of the head or raised eyebrows, some-times accompanied by clicking the tongue. "No" can also be expressed by shaking the index finger from side to side, palm facing out. Pointing or beckoning with the index finger is impolite. To beckon another person, all fingers wave with the palm facing down. Objects are not handed to another person to hold, as this implies servant status. A closed fist should never be waved in the air. For many, it is offensive to pass or receive objects with the left hand. The right hand or both hands should be used. Knees may be crossed, but crossing an ankle over a knee risks offending any person toward whom the bot-tom of the foot is pointed. The soles of the shoes or feet should always face the earth and never another person. Eye contact is important. Men never curse in front of women. Public displays of affection, even between married couples, are not acceptable.

Visiting

Hospitality is a prized tradition in Lebanon. People feel honored to have guests in their homes, and they also love to visit others. Hosts always serve guests something to drink; usually tea or coffee is prepared and served without asking the guests. Hospitality requires that it be accepted, so a word of polite explanation is in order if it is refused. If invited to a meal, guests might bring flowers, a plant, a special dessert, or something for the home. Guests invited for lunch generally do not leave until after 4:00 P.M., and dinner guests are expected to stay the entire evening. It is extremely impolite to leave immediately after eating. If a person has been visiting all evening and is about to leave, but another person comes to visit, it would be an insult to the newly arrived person for the first person to leave. Even if the new guest is visiting only the host, the previous guest stays to talk for a few minutes to show he is not leaving because the new person arrived. Arguments about local and national politics are inappropriate, and the Lebanese would never ask about a person's religion. That would be considered an attempt to categorize or prejudge someone.

Eating

Unspoken rules of hospitality require the host to make guests feel completely welcome. Offering food is one way to do this and Lebanese hosts will be very insistent that their guest eat—even if the guest refuses the food initially. Because it is often customary to refuse an offer a couple of times before accepting it, the host assumes the offer will eventually be accepted. Guests should at least try the food, but they can politely decline a full meal or more refreshments without offending the host.

Western eating utensils are usually used for eating European food or rice dishes. Lebanese tend to eat European foods part of the week and Middle Eastern foods the rest of the week. Except for rice, Middle Eastern foods are either eaten with the right hand, broken pieces of bread, or lettuce. Bread and lettuce serve as scoops. For example, *tabboule*, a popular salad made with parsley, minced onions, diced tomatoes, and other vegetables is eaten with a lettuce scoop. Lettuce is not part of the salad. Meals often consist of many courses and can last several hours. It is not appropriate to discuss business during a meal.

LIFESTYLE

Family

Lebanese families tend to be strong and closely knit. Cousins and other relatives are expected to have close personal relationships. In fact, cousins are generally as close as brothers and sisters. Urban families are usually smaller than rural families. Discipline is strict, and children show respect for their parents and other elders. The father is head of the family. Mothers generally take care of the home and children. Many women who work outside the home do so out of necessity, not choice. Family loyalty is important. Lebanon has a class-based society. The wealthy have access to fine education,

good jobs, and luxuries, while the poor do not. Traditionally, Maronite Christian families have been the wealthiest and most powerful. While the economy is based on the free market, unwritten class distinctions limit many opportunities.

Dating and Marriage

Traditionally, neither Christians nor Muslims dated. All marriages were arranged by the family. Today, Christians and many urban Muslim families follow Western dating habits. Those in rural areas generally continue to follow tradition. Because financial independence is customarily a prerequisite for marriage, men often wait to marry until their late 20s or early 30s. Women usually marry in their early 20s. Christians are generally opposed to divorce, although it is allowed by Islamic law for Muslims. Lebanese law provides for each religion to have a separate court system to handle matters of marriage, divorce, inheritance, and other such concerns, according to the different customs.

Diet

The main meal of the day is eaten between noon and 3:00 P.M. This meal may last two or more hours. Various stews are Lebanese specialties. The cuisine is often spicy and hot. But because of the warm climate, many dishes are also light, that is, they are vegetarian. Such meals are not only better suited to the climate, but are also less expensive. A traditional meal for special occasions is the *meza*. It can be eaten at home or in a restaurant. A large group of people gather for this four- to five-hour event. Several dishes (maybe 20 or more) are all placed on the table; each person takes small portions from the dishes as often as desired. *Arak*, a traditional strong liquor, is served with Middle Eastern (not European) foods, except among devout Muslims. *Kibbeh* is a popular beef dish that can be either baked, fried, or eaten raw.

Recreation

Soccer is the most popular Lebanese sport. Swimming at the beaches is also enjoyed in the summer. Movies are well attended. Skiing is a popular winter sport. One of the most common leisure activities is simply visiting friends and relatives. This is a common practice throughout the Arab world. Neglecting relationships by not visiting regularly constitutes improper social behavior. It is also an insult to the persons not being visited.

The Lebanese enjoy the cultural arts. Before the war, Beirut was a center for cosmopolitan Arabic culture. Music, literature, and other arts and entertainment are again part of the urban lifestyle. Night clubs and restaurants are popular evening destinations.

Holidays

National, Christian, and Muslim holidays are celebrated by the entire country. National holidays include New Year's Day, Labor Day (1 May), and Independence Day (22 November). The Christian holidays include Easter (Friday through Sunday), Assumption (15 August), and Christmas. The Muslim holidays include *Eid ul-Fitr* (the three-day feast at the end of the month of *Ramadan*). During *Ramadan*, Muslims go without food or water from sunrise to dusk. They eat in the evenings. The feast celebrates the end of the long period of fasting; it usually occurs in the spring, according to the Islamic lunar calendar. The Islamic New Year is celebrated in the summer. Also in the summer is *Eid ul-Adha* (Sacrifice

Feast), held at the end of the pilgrimage to Makkah. The prophet Muhammad's birthday is celebrated in the fall.

Commerce

Most people work five days a week, but many work a partial day on Saturday. Business hours are generally from 8:00 A.M. to noon and 3:00 P.M. to 6:00 P.M., Monday through Friday. It is important to socialize before conducting business. When visiting someone's office, a person will likely be offered coffee or another drink (not alcohol), and the two will spend time getting to know each other or catching up on family news. Because Lebanon is a small country, many people know each other, so business is conducted on a personal basis. To establish business contacts, a person is far more successful if he is introduced by a mutual acquaintance. Lebanese business representatives often do not appreciate being approached by strangers.

SOCIETY

Government

Lebanon is a republic divided into five governorates. The Lebanese parliament (a 128-seat National Assembly) has an equal number of seats reserved for Christians and Muslims. In addition, other major religious groups who fought in the war have representation in parliament. The next legislative elections are scheduled for 1996. By law, Lebanon's president must be a Maronite Christian and the prime minister a Sunni Muslim, while the parliamentary speaker must be a *Shī'a* (Shiite) Muslim. This balance is necessary to promote harmony among the country's religions and was part of Lebanon's original constitution. The voting age is 21; men are required to vote.

Economy

Because of the destructive internal conflicts of recent years, accurate information has not been available for the Lebanese economy. However, as statistics emerge, a picture of rapid growth is developing. In 1994, economic growth was estimated to be above 8 percent and the figure for 1995 is estimated at 7 percent. Inflation has been lowered to below 11 percent by Lebanon's aggressive fiscal policies. Strong bond issues have raised considerable amounts of money to finance reconstruction and the resettlement of homeless families. With continued political stability, the outlook for future growth seems bright.

Lebanon's current Human Development Index (0.600) ranks it 103d out of 173 countries. Real gross domestic product per capita is estimated at $2,500. These figures reflect the country's losses during the war, but also indicate the economy's potential to provide access to economic prosperity. The process will take several years, and many people continue to live in poverty. The lowest classes worry about being left behind in the reconstruction period, and it remains to be seen whether a strong middle class can emerge.

Much of Lebanon's industrial capacity was destroyed during the fighting. Formerly important, the banking and tourism industries are striving to again be vital. Foreign investment is becoming more substantial. Agriculture is regaining importance. Key crops include various fruits, grains, potatoes, tobacco, olives, and onions. Agricultural products account for the majority of Lebanon's exports. The currency is the Lebanese pound (L£).

Transportation and Communication

Much of the transportation system was destroyed by the fighting. The railroad system is almost entirely inoperable. Buses and taxis service the cities. Buses are boarded from the back door and exited from either the middle or front doors. Taxis have red license plates. Many families own cars and traffic can be very heavy in urban areas. Similar to transportation systems, communications were disrupted by the fighting, but they are returning to normal.

Education

Low-cost government schools are available but are of low quality. Those who can afford it send their children to higher-quality private schools. The law requires at least five years of compulsory education and most children attend. The civil war disrupted normal educational opportunities in many areas. Because of education's importance, however, schools adapted. If fighting interrupted classes for a week, the school year was extended; if the fighting lasted for months, studies intensified so children could get a proper education. Education is considered the key to a better life. Children are strongly encouraged to go to college; those who go will receive greater family respect than those who don't. Men are encouraged to study science and professional fields, leaving liberal arts more to women. The literacy rate is 80 percent.

Health

Good medical care is generally available to all citizens, even though the health care system was overwhelmed by war. Health care is a private industry and people must have insurance. Houses usually have two water systems: one for the kitchen that is chlorinated and safe to drink, and one for the rest of the house that is not potable. The infant mortality rate is 39 per 1,000. Life expectancy averages between 66 and 72 years.

FOR THE TRAVELER

Despite assurances by Lebanon's government that travel to the country is safe, the U.S. State Department maintains a travel warning and ban for the country. It cites the continued existence of groups that had previously taken Westerners as hostages for its caution in allowing U.S. citizens to travel, even briefly, to Lebanon. Those who do are in violation of U.S. law. An exemption may be granted to such persons as journalists, humanitarian workers, and government officials. To apply, contact the Office of Passport Policy and Advisory Services, U.S. Department of State, 1111 19th Street NW, Suite 260, Washington, DC 20522–1705; phone (202) 955–0231. For additional information, you may also wish to contact the Embassy of Lebanon, 2560 28th Street NW, Washington, DC 20008; phone (202) 939–6300.

Kingdom of
Lesotho

Boundary representations not necessarily authoritative.

BACKGROUND

Land and Climate

Lesotho (pronounced le-SUE-too) is a small, mountainous country slightly larger than Maryland and located in the east-central part of South Africa. Covering 11,718 square miles (30,350 square kilometers), it is completely surrounded by South Africa. Lesotho is divided into three basic geographic regions: the lowlands, which are about 5,000 feet (1,500 meters) above sea level; the foothills; and the highlands, which include peaks of 11,000 feet (3,300 meters). Most of Lesotho's agricultural areas and the largest cities are located in the western lowlands.

Mountains dominate the east. The Drakensberg Mountains in southeastern Lesotho border South Africa and are divided from the Maluti Mountains by the Orange River. The Caledon River forms much of the western border. Because of its elevation, Lesotho does not have a tropical climate like other parts of southern Africa. Lesotho's pleasant climate and sunny skies (averaging three hundred days a year) are increasingly inviting to tourists. Summer extends from November to January and winter is between May and July. Most rain falls from October to April. Temperatures average 90°F (32°C) in the summer and 40°F (4°C) in the winter. The highlands are cooler, and mountains receive snow in winter.

Lesotho's waterways have potential for hydroelectric power and other economic development. A 30-year project (Lesotho Highlands Water Project) began in 1986. Six dams will be constructed to generate electricity, provide irrigation, improve highland access (with new roads), and store water for sale to South Africa.

History

The history of Lesotho, once called Basutoland, began when the Basotho nation was formed from the remnants of tribes scattered by Zulu and Matebele raids in the early 1800s. The people were united by Moshoeshoe (pronounced mo-SHWAY-shway) the Great, who ruled for almost 50 years (1823–70). During a series of wars with South Africa in the mid-1800s, Moshoeshoe lost considerable territory. After an appeal to Queen Victoria for protection against Boer (Dutch-origin farmers/settlers) advances, Britain annexed Basutoland as a territory in 1868.

Basutoland was temporarily annexed (1871) by the Cape Colony (one of the four colonies that later became South Africa), but the people revolted and became a British crown colony in 1884. Even when South Africa formed in 1909, Lesotho remained with the British. South Africa expected to someday annex the region, but was never successful.

Internal self-rule was introduced in 1959 when a new constitution allowed for the first elected legislature. In October 1966, Basutoland was granted full independence from Great Britain as the Kingdom of Lesotho. When independence was granted, a constitutional monarchy was established, with Moshoeshoe II as head of state and Chief Leabua Jonathan as prime minister.

In 1970, when Jonathan's ruling party (Basutoland National Party or BNP) was in danger of losing power to the opposition party, he suspended the constitution and dissolved parliament. Elections in 1985 were designed to favor the BNP and were thus boycotted by other parties. Under internal and external pressure, Jonathan's government was ousted by a bloodless military coup in 1986. A six-man military council took over and technically vested all powers in the hands of the king. In reality, the king had very little power and the military junta ruled the country. After a power struggle, King Moshoeshoe II was forced into exile in 1990 and replaced by his son, King Letsie III, who was given no executive authority. Moshoeshoe returned to Lesotho in 1993, but he was not reinstated to the throne until January 1995.

The junta had promised to restore civilian rule by 1992, but it was not making progress toward the goal. Its leader, General Justin Lekhanya, was forced by a coup to resign in 1991. He was replaced by another member of the six-man council, Colonel Elias Ramaema. Democratic elections were finally held in 1993, in which the BNP was heavily defeated by the Basotholand Congress Party (BCP). BCP leader Ntsu Mokhehle became prime minister. Political stability remained elusive. Soldiers loyal to the BNP rioted in January 1994 and killed the deputy prime minister in April. With military backing, King Letsie dissolved parliament and the BCP government in August 1994. Intense pressure and domestic unrest forced him to reinstate Mokhehle's democratically elected government a few weeks later. Peace was encouraged by South Africa and other countries in the region and a measure of stability was enjoyed in 1995.

THE PEOPLE

Population

Lesotho's population of 1.9 million is growing annually at 2.5 percent. About 20 percent live in urban areas. The largest city, Maseru, has 110,000 inhabitants. The people of Lesotho are called Basotho (or Masotho for a single person). Their language is Sesotho. Between the 16th and 19th centuries, an influx of Sesotho-speaking peoples (refugees from tribal wars in surrounding areas) populated the region. This led to the development of the Basotho (or Sotho) ethnic group, giving Lesotho a fairly homogeneous population (nearly 80 percent Basotho). About 20 percent of the population is of Nguni origin (Xhosa and Baphuti tribes); some are San or Griqua. There are also small numbers of Europeans and Indians. More than 40 percent of the people are younger than age 15.

Language

Both English and Sesotho are official languages. Sesotho (also called "southern Sotho"), a Bantu language, is spoken by nearly all inhabitants. English is used in business. It is also the language of instruction in the schools after the fifth standard (grade). Therefore, most people are able to speak English. Zulu and Xhosa are also spoken by those who work in South Africa's mines or have contact with South Africa's Transkei region.

Religion

The Basotho are fairly religious; nearly 80 percent of the population is Christian. The three largest churches are the Roman Catholic church, the Lesotho Evangelical Church, and the Anglican Church of Lesotho. Christian missions are scattered throughout the country. There is a small Muslim community in the north. About 20 percent follow native belief systems. Some Christians continue to practice some native traditions or rites along with Christianity.

General Attitudes

The Basotho are a courteous, friendly people who are warm and hospitable to others. They laugh when embarrassed. Personal confrontation is to be avoided. Hence, Basotho often say what they think another person wants to hear or what would please the listener, even if reality or intentions might be otherwise.

The elderly are treated with great respect. Lesotho's citizens are proud to have an independent nation, even if it is surrounded by a larger, more powerful country. The Basotho are also proud of their native crafts, including weaving, pottery, and leather works. Shrewdness and independence are highly valued in an individual. Wealth is measured in cattle or sheep. People, especially in rural areas, tend to display a sort of passive optimism, believing that others will help them if they have trouble or that life will take care of itself. People are very proud of their families. Except among the highly educated, one is considered to have reached one's potential upon fathering or bearing a child. The more children a man has, the more respected he is.

Personal Appearance

The Basotho dress in conservative, Western-style clothing but often cover it with a beautifully designed wool blanket, especially in rural areas. The blanket acts as a warm robe for cool evenings. Women tie it at the waist and men fold it on the shoulder when daytime temperatures warm up. Hats are common for men and women. While there are many types of hats, including American baseball caps, most are woven from straw and the *Mokorotlo* or *Molianyeoe* is the traditional hat of Lesotho. It is conical in shape, much like the roof of a rural home, and has an intricately designed knob on top. Women do not generally wear slacks or shorts. The people are clean, neat, and concerned with an orderly appearance.

CUSTOMS AND COURTESIES

Greetings

Greetings tend to be somewhat formal in pattern. Upon shaking hands, two people greet by saying either *Lumela* (Hello) or *Khotso* (Peace be with you). This is followed by *U phela joang?* (How are you?). If acquainted, each makes polite inquiries about the other's family. They also typically ask *U tsoa kae?* (Where have you been?) and *U tsamaea kae?* (Where are you going?); an explanation is expected. The greeting process eventually evolves into a conversation. When two people pass on the street, or do not expect to engage in conversation, only the two basic greetings are used. Greeting habits vary somewhat according to whether men, women, young adults, or children are involved.

In farewells, the person leaving says *Sala hantle* (Stay well). The one staying says *Tsamaea hantle* (Go well). When addressing another person, titles are used for very formal situations, but given names are otherwise used.

Gestures

Pointing with the index finger is impolite. Items are passed with the right hand or both hands. It is common for friends of the same gender to walk down the street holding hands. Or if two people meet on the street and stop to shake hands and greet, they may hold the handshake throughout the conversation, regardless of their respective gender. But otherwise, members of the opposite sex do not touch or display affection in public. Subtle movements of the head and eyes are used to convey positive or negative responses to something.

Visiting

The Basotho are hospitable hosts, and enjoy having guests. Most rural visiting is done without prior arrangement as telephone and mail connections are not extensive. Upon arriving, a visitor knocks on the door and says *Ko ko* (knock knock). The hosts can usually recognize the voice and therefore know a friendly visitor is at the door, and they say *Kena* (Come in). The visitor can then enter the home. It is extremely discourteous to enter without announcing one's presence in this manner, even if the door is open.

When visitors arrive, even if unexpected, it is polite for the hosts to invite them to stay for something to eat. If the visitor is far from home, the hosts offer them shelter for the night. Guests are nearly always served refreshments, such as tea and perhaps cookies or crackers. Tea is also customarily taken in the afternoon. In rural areas, guests at tea will often be served a full meal as well. Guests are not generally expected to bring gifts, although it would not be uncommon for an urban resident to take something to a rural relative.

Socializing among the Basotho not only takes place in the home, but at public places such as the market or *moreneng* (chief compound) during a *pitso* (town meeting). A *pitso* is usually called by the local chief to share important news or to discuss something. If the news is good, an impromptu party may occur.

Eating

The continental style of eating, with the fork in the left hand and the knife remaining in the right, is observed in the capital city, Maseru. In the villages, the people often eat with their right hand or use a spoon, depending on the food. When families are not able to sit down together for a meal, food is left simmering on the stove around the time to eat. When a person is ready to eat, he or she takes what is wanted and eats alone. When the family or group does eat together, the men and/or any important guests of either gender are served first and when they are satisfied, the women and children eat the remainder of the meal. Each person has a separate dish from which to eat. It is proper to finish everything on one's plate, and men might have second helpings.

LIFESTYLE

Family

Lesotho has a strong patriarchal society centered on the family. However, because men often work outside the country during much of the year, the women make many decisions and do most of the farm work. Women also work on the roads and in service occupations. Women make up 44 percent of the labor force. While the nuclear family lives alone in large cities like Maseru, most extended families share a compound. One man is head of the extended family. Their compound includes several buildings, a *kraal* (living space for animals), and a garden. The traditional *rondaval* or *ntlo* (home) is built of stone and sticks held together with cow dung, which dries as hard as concrete and can be painted. Before it dries, people often draw intricate designs in it to beautify the home. Walls are thick, and the circular home is

covered by a thatched roof. Windows are minimal to keep out cold. The diameter of the main home reflects the family's economic status. Its interior is not divided, so families usually have separate buildings for sleeping, cooking, storage, and so forth. Some homes are made of cement block.

Family members are expected to help one another. All those living in a compound contribute to its welfare by doing chores, cooking, minding the cattle, raising chickens, working for a wage and sharing part of it, and so forth. If one person in an extended family falls on hard times, other family members are expected to help if possible. But they are not expected to sacrifice their own needs to offer this help. When a man dies, his possessions are divided among his brothers and sons, who are expected to provide for his wife and any other women in his care.

Dating and Marriage

Young people meet through community activities, but Western dating is not common. Adult children usually remain with their parents until they marry, and often afterwards. Families are heavily involved in marriage/wedding negotiations. A groom's family is expected to pay a bride-price (in cattle or money) to the bride's family. When a woman marries, she moves to her husband's compound, which may be shared with his parents and others.

Diet

The Basotho diet consists of *mealie meal* (cornmeal), rice, potatoes, vegetables (cabbage, peas, etc.), and some fruits. When possible, people eat three meals a day. Modern cold cereals are becoming popular for breakfast, which is often eaten around 10:00 A.M. Lunch is the main meal, and is eaten at midday. It traditionally consists of *Moroho* (cooked vegetables), *Nama* (meat), and *Papa* (corn mush). The evening meal is around 7:00 P.M. and contains the same foods eaten at lunch. *Nama ea Khomo* (beef), *Nama ea Khoho* (chicken), and *Nama ea Kolobe* (pork) are popular meats.

Holidays

Official holidays include New Year's Day, Army Day (20 January), and Moshoeshoe's Day (12 March). Tree Planting Day (21 March) is important because Lesotho is subject to severe soil erosion and has virtually no forests. The government sponsors tree planting projects to provide future building and fuel supplies, and to guard against further erosion. Other national holidays include Family Day (first Monday in July), Independence Day (5 October), and National Sports Day (first Monday in October). Easter (Friday through Monday) and Christmas are the most popular religious holidays. Boxing Day (26 December) comes from the British tradition of giving small boxed gifts to service personnel and tradesmen. It is now usually a day spent visiting friends and relatives.

Recreation

Soccer is the most important sport. Some urban residents play volleyball, netball (girls), and basketball. Visiting and holidays provide leisure and recreational opportunities. The Bosotho like to sing and can harmonize with ease. Most social gatherings involve some sort of singing.

Commerce

Businesses and government offices are open between 8:00 A.M. and 5:00 P.M., Monday through Friday. Some businesses open on Saturday until 1:00 P.M. More than 85 percent of the resident population is engaged in subsistence agriculture, so work schedules vary according to the season. As many as 250,000 men are gone at any one time to work in the mines or factories of South Africa. They may be in South Africa for several months each year or for several years. In Lesotho, the legal working age is 12.

SOCIETY

Government

Lesotho is a constitutional monarchy divided into ten districts. King Moshoeshoe II is head of state, but he has only ceremonial duties. Executive authority is vested in the prime minister. A new constitution went into effect with 1993 elections. Parliament's lower house has 65 elected members; the upper house consists of 22 principal chiefs and 10 appointed members. The voting age is 21. Local authority is vested in the village chief.

Economy

Lesotho lacks natural resources (except water) and relies largely on subsistence agriculture, which includes livestock raising. The economy also depends on wages earned by Basotho workers in South Africa. Their remittances account for between 50 and 75 percent of Lesotho's gross national product (GNP). The country's Human Development Index (0.476) ranks it 120th out of 173 countries. Real GNP per capita is $1,500. These figures reflect higher wages earned in South African mines. But these jobs are not permanent and unemployment can be as high as 50 percent at times. Poverty continues to affect about half of the population, and wealth is highly concentrated.

Grazing rights are communal, but arable land is allocated to individuals and families by local chiefs. Corn, wheat, sorghum, peas, beans, and potatoes are the main crops. Nearly all food is consumed domestically, but asparagus and beans are exported along with wool, mohair, cattle, and hides. Industries include textiles, clothing, and light engineering. Native crafts are also important to the economy. Tourism provides crucial foreign exchange earnings.

Lesotho's geographic location and dependence on South Africa make the economy sensitive to political and economic changes in South Africa. When jobs are lost in South African mines, Lesotho's economy suffers. Commercial ties with South Africa are vital to Lesotho's survival. Both the South African *rand* and the Basotho *loti* (plural is *maloti*) are acceptable currency in Lesotho. The *loti* (L) is backed by the *rand* (R).

Transportation and Communication

Maseru is a small city and it is easy to walk to its farthest points. A number of minibuses operate mostly along Maseru's main street and travel between cities in the lowlands. Other buses travel to eastern points. In keeping with British tradition, traffic moves on the left side of the road. Paved roads are generally in good condition, but most roads are not paved. Domestic air travel links Maseru with some mountain cities; a few flights go to other African countries. Some areas of the country are accessible only by horse or foot. The Basotho pony is famous in southern Africa for its surefootedness. It has been bred over the years specifically for mountain transport. Many people in remote areas have never traveled outside of their area.

The communications system is improving, but interior mountain locations are often accessible only by radio. Telephone service outside Maseru is sporatic. The government sponsors Radio Lesotho and two weekly newspapers. Sevaral private newspapers also function. Television broadcasts are received from South Africa. For an hour each evening, Lesotho preempts the programming to show its own news and some entertainment. Most areas, except remote mountain locations, have access to television.

Education

The overall literacy rate in Lesotho is 60 percent, one of the highest in Africa. Unlike many countries, women have a higher literacy rate (68 percent) than men (45 percent). This is because boys must often tend flocks all day for months at a time when their fathers are working in South Africa. The educational system is largely administered by the three largest churches under the direction of the Ministry of Education. Influenced by the British colonial system, primary education consists of seven levels called *standards*. At their completion, an exam is administered. If the student passes and the family can afford tuition and board, secondary education begins. After another three years and an exam, a Junior Certificate is awarded. Two more years in high school and completion of another exam enable a person to attend the University of Lesotho at Roma. Vocational schools are also available. Basic education is offered through the Distance Teaching Centre to those who do not or did not go to school.

Health

Because of Lesotho's elevation, many diseases common to Africa are not found within the country. Water is generally safe in the capital. Each district has a government hospital in addition to church-sponsored hospitals. The level of health care available varies with location. Services are better in urban areas and near the borders. Those living near the border can seek care in South Africa. Traditional medicine is practiced in remote areas. Life expectancy has risen over the last few years to a range of 60 to 64 years. The infant mortality rate has fallen to 70 per 1,000. Although this is still high, it is lower than in other parts of Africa.

FOR THE TRAVELER

U.S. visitors need a passport and visa to enter Lesotho. Anyone traveling to Lesotho through South Africa must also have a South African visa. No vaccinations are required. Lesotho promotes hiking, fossil hunting, pony trekking, bird watching, and fishing. The tourism industry is developing to handle more visitors. Dual-voltage small appliances or an adaptor and a plug adaptor are necessary to use electrical outlets. For more information, contact the Lesotho Tourist Board, PO Box 1378, Maseru 100, Lesotho. You may also wish to contact the Embassy of Lesotho, 2511 Massachusetts Avenue NW, Washington, DC 20008; phone (202) 797–5533.

Malaysia

Boundary representations not necessarily authoritative.

ASIA

BACKGROUND

Land and Climate

Malaysia has two different and distinct land regions. Peninsular Malaysia is about the size of Alabama and is located south of Thailand and north of Singapore. Heavily forested mountains form the center of the peninsula and are flanked by coastal plains. Major rubber, palm oil, and other agricultural plantations are on the peninsula. East Malaysia is located on the island of Borneo and consists of two states, Sarawak and Sabah. The tiny country of Brunei lies on the coast near the juncture of these two states, which together are about the size of Louisiana. Malaysia's entire landmass covers 127,317 square miles (329,750 square kilometers). Sarawak is a broad coastal plain. Sabah's coastal plain gives way to mountainous jungle. Mount Kinabalu, the highest peak in southeast Asia (13,455 feet [4,101 meters]) is in Sabah.

Malaysia's territory is 63 percent forested. Only 3 percent is arable. The climate is tropical. Humidity is high and temperatures range from 70°F to 90°F (21–32°C). There are two monsoon seasons—June to September in the southwest and October to March in the northeast. Both bring heavy rainfall to the respective coastal areas.

History

Many civilizations prospered on the Malay peninsula long before Portuguese traders arrived in 1511 and captured Melaka, an Islamic religious and trade center. The Dutch took control in 1641, but Melaka was no longer vital and the Dutch did not pursue further development.

Britain became interested in the peninsula in the 18th century and acquired the island of Pulau Pinang (now Pinang) from the Sultan of Kedah in 1786. By the early 1900s, Britain controlled all the Malay states—including those on Borneo—as colonies or protectorates. The British introduced Chinese and Indian labor, as well as the rubber industry, to the region.

The Japanese occupied Malaysia during World War II. Under Japanese occupation, feelings for independence from foreign domination grew stronger. In 1946, the British created the Malayan Union out of Melaka, Pulau Pinang, and the nine Malay states on the peninsula. In 1948, this union became the Federation of Malaya. That same year, Communist insurrections erupted and guerrilla terrorism spread throughout the countryside until it was quelled in 1959. Communist guerrilla warfare continued on a smaller scale against both the Malaysian and Thai governments until a 1989 cease-fire was signed.

In August 1957, Malaysia was granted independence from Great Britain. Six years later the Federation of Malaya and the former British colonies of Singapore, Sarawak, and North Borneo (Sabah) united to become Malaysia in order to avoid a Communist takeover in Singapore. However, tension mounted between the Malay-dominated government in Malaya and the Chinese-dominated government in Singapore. The tension culminated in the creation of an independent Singapore in 1965.

In 1969, racial tension resulted in widespread rioting in Kuala Lumpur, the capital of Malaysia. Ethnic Malays were not satisfied with their share of the country's wealth, their access to business opportunities, and the ethnic Chinese and other groups' domination of other areas of society. The government changed the constitution in 1971 to give Malays more rights. A quota system was established at the same time that required Malay representation (at specified levels) in government, business, and education. The New Economic Policy (NEP) has successfully improved the lives of Malays without damaging the economy. In 1991, the NEP was renewed as the New Development Policy (NDP) and altered to encourage help for poorer peoples of all races. Although the program has discouraged racial integration, it is credited with also discouraging violence between ethnic groups. Mahathir Mohamad, architect of the NEP/NDP, was reelected to his post as prime minister in 1990. He captured a fourth term in elections held in April 1995.

THE PEOPLE

Population

The 19.2 million people that live in Malaysia are racially diverse and have many different cultural backgrounds. Ties between these groups have developed through educational, social, sporting, and cultural organizations, but ethnic groups still remain essentially segregated. The largest ethnic group is the Malays. Together with other indigenous groups, they make up 59 percent of the total population. Some of these other groups include the Sea Dayaks (*Ibans*), Land Dayaks (*Bidayuhs*), Kadazans, Kenyahs, Melanaus, and Muruts. They are mainly farmers, civil servants, or fishermen. The Chinese make up 32 percent of the population and live mostly on the peninsula in the tin- and rubber-producing areas. Most large towns also have significant Chinese communities. The Indians (9 percent) are the third largest group. They also live on the peninsula. Malaysia's population is young, with 48 percent of the population under age 20. The population is growing at 2.3 percent annually. About 45 percent of Malaysians live in urban areas.

Language

Malay *(Bahasa Melayu)* is the official language of Malaysia and is spoken in all areas of the country. The ethnic Chinese also speak one of various Chinese dialects (Cantonese, Hakka, Hokkien, Mandarin, or Min); Tamil is spoken by the Indians. On the island of Borneo, in Sabah and Sarawak, numerous indigenous languages are common. English is taught in the schools and is widely spoken.

Religion

Islam is the official religion of Malaysia, although the constitution guarantees freedom of worship. Ethnic Malays are nearly all Muslim. The Chinese on the peninsula are chiefly Buddhist, with some Taoists and Confucianists. Some practice principles from all three. The Indians are generally Hindu. In the states of Sabah and Sarawak, the denomination percentages are different. In Sabah, about 38 percent are Muslim, 17 percent Christian, and the rest follow indigenous beliefs. In Sarawak, where there are more Chinese, 24 percent are Buddhist and Confucianist, 20 percent Muslim, and 16 percent Christian. The rest follow indigenous or other beliefs. Traditional beliefs and customs are often mixed with a person's formal religion.

General Attitudes

A person's ancestral background is often important to social status and future opportunities. Many Malaysians are fatalistic; they believe successes, failures, opportunities, and misfortunes result from fate or the will of God. Although the people are proud of their country and generally loyal to the Malaysian state, they often identify first with their ethnic group, island, or region. The people are proud of their economic success and beautiful country. Some ethnic tensions exist between the Malays (called *Bramiputras*) and Chinese over preferential quotas designed to improve the economic status of the Malays. The Chinese believe these policies make them second-class citizens, while the majority of Malays believe the policies are the only way *Bramiputras* can overcome traditional Chinese dominance in business.

Personal Appearance

Most people wear Western-style clothing. However, traditional clothing, or a combination of Western and traditional clothing, is also worn. In some areas, Muslim women with head covers, veils, and long dresses are as common as women wearing short skirts or pants. Special headdresses, wraparound skirts, jackets, tunics, and sashes vary between regions and ethnic groups. Many traditional costumes have intricate designs. *Batik* fabric (traditionally hand colored with a hot-wax process) is popular for traditional dress.

CUSTOMS AND COURTESIES

Greetings

A handshake is used between men. A slight bow or nod of the head is common when greeting an older person. Women and elderly persons seldom shake hands, but may offer verbal greetings. When greeting close male friends, men use both hands to grasp the hand of the other. Business cards are often exchanged after an introduction. A common greeting is *Salamat pagi* (Good morning). A casual greeting is *Halo* (Hello).

Gestures

In Malaysia it is not polite to beckon adults, with the exception of close friends. Beckoning is done by waving all fingers with the palm facing down. Individual fingers are not used for gesturing. Giving and receiving gifts with both hands shows respect. Objects should not be moved with the feet. The bottom of a person's foot should not be pointed at another person. Objects are generally not passed with the left hand. When yawning or using a toothpick, the mouth is covered. A slight bow when leaving, entering, or passing by a group of people acts as a nonverbal "excuse me."

Visiting

Visiting one's relatives and friends is an important part of Malaysian life, especially when one does not share a house with the extended family. Dropping by without prior arrangement is common, although more urban dwellers call in advance. Guests are often invited to the home for a meal or socializing. When invited, persons are generally not expected to arrive on time. Punctuality is not as important in Malaysia as in Western nations because Malaysians value people over schedules. Shoes are removed when entering a home. The host will normally serve tea or coffee to guests. Drinks are offered and received with both hands.

Eating

Eating customs differ among ethnic groups. Malays and Indians eat with their hands and with spoons. Chinese eat with chopsticks and spoons. Some cultural groups refrain from eating certain foods. For example, Muslims do not eat pork or drink alcoholic beverages. Hindus and some Buddhists do not eat beef. Tipping is not generally expected in restaurants because service is usually included in the bill. However, some waiters may expect tips from Westerners based on past experience.

LIFESTYLE

Family

Traditionally, the family system is the most important social unit in Malaysia. It is common for two, three, or more generations to live together in the same house. Cooperation, loyalty, and unity are important in the family. Young people respect their elders. Modernization and urbanization have affected the family structure in some areas. In urban areas, nuclear families are common, with members of extended families living in the same city or neighborhood, but not the same house. The younger generations are also moving away from the traditional, large family.

Dating and Marriage

Dating and marriage practices in urban areas are similar to those in other Westernized countries. Attitudes are more liberal. Families stress that dating should wait until after one's education is complete. Despite this, dating usually begins around age 17 or 18. In rural areas, dating habits are conservative. Some marriages there are still arranged by families. The majority of couples, however, make their own choices in consultation with family members. A marriage is seen not only as joining two persons but two families. Customs and ceremonies are also affected by the different religions.

Diet

Due to Malaysia's cultural diversity, a wide variety of foods are eaten. Rice is the dietary staple and fish is the main source of protein. Spiced foods such as hot peppers are also widely eaten. There are a number of different fruits. Durians, large, oval-shaped fruits, are considered king among fruits. Others include pineapples, bananas, and papayas. Malaysians enjoy dining at restaurants.

Recreation

Soccer was introduced to Malaysia in the 19th century and is the country's most popular sport. Other sports include badminton, field hockey, cricket, rugby, and table tennis. There are also facilities for swimming, tennis, cycling, volleyball, and squash. There are three important indigenous activities. The first, *sepaktakraw*, is a competitive team sport played with a rattan ball. *Main gasing* involves spinning tops that weigh several pounds for long periods of time. Martial arts (particularly *silat*) are also performed with great skill. Kite flying is popular on the peninsula. Local festivals, television, movies, and visiting friends also provide recreation for the people.

Holidays

Malaysians celebrate national, religious, and regional holidays. Among the national holidays are International New Year's Day (1 January), Labor Day (1 May), National Day (31 August), and the Birthday of the *Yang di-Pertuan Agong* (first Wednesday in June). The Chinese New Year is a festival spanning several days in January or February.

The three chief Islamic holidays include *Hari Raya Puasa*, the three-day feast at the end of the month of *Ramadan*; *Hari Raya Haji*, the Feast of Sacrifice that comes at the end of the pilgrimage to Makkah; and the birthday of the prophet Muhammad. During *Ramadan*, Muslims do not eat or drink from sunrise to sundown each day; they eat a meal and visit friends in the evening.

Wesak Day (in May) commemorates the birth of Buddha. *Deepavali* is a Hindu festival in October or November that celebrates the triumph of Lord Krishna over a demon king. Christmas is the main Christian holiday. The Dayak ethnic groups also celebrate various festivals that mark the harvest, honor the dead, and honor heroes. In May, the *Kadazan Festivals* celebrate the harvest. In each state, there are also local holidays.

Commerce

While many workers engage in agricultural pursuits that demand variable and long working hours, wage earners usually work a five-and-one-half-day week. Businesses are generally open between 8:30 A.M. and 5:00 P.M., Monday through Friday. Some are open Saturday mornings. In many cases, businesses are closed for one hour at lunch.

SOCIETY

Government

Malaysia, a constitutional monarchy, has 13 states. Sarawak and Sabah are considered self-governing states with foreign policy and other powers delegated from the federal government. In nine of the eleven peninsular states, rulers are hereditary and compose a Council of Rulers. These nine rulers alternate as king of the country for five-year terms. The king is referred to as the Supreme Head of State *(Yang di-Pertuan Agong)*. The current king, Tuanku Ja'afar Ibni Almarhum Tuanku Abdul Rehman, took office in April 1994 and will serve through the end of 1998. He has some executive powers, but the real governing power rests in the hands of the prime minister and parliament. The parliament has two houses: the *Dewan Negara* (Senate) and the *Dewan Rakyat* (House of Representatives). Sarawak and Sabah have 27 and 20 seats, respectively, in the 192-seat House of Representatives. The Senate has 58 members, 32 of whom are appointed by the king, with 16 elected by state legislatures. Prime Minister Mahathir's governing party is the National Front. The main opposition parties include the All-Malaysia Islamic Party, the Democratic Action Party, and the Malay Party Spirit of '46. The voting age is 21. The campaign season prior to national elections in April 1995 was restricted by law to only ten days.

Economy

Despite an economic recession in the mid-1980s, Malaysia's economy is relatively strong. Economic growth has averaged 8 percent in the eight years. Expanding exports account for the strength of the economy. The manufacturing sector has grown in recent years by up to 15 percent, and tourism is developing rapidly. Timber, oil, and palm oil have joined tin and rubber as Malaysia's top exports. About 30 percent of the work force is engaged in agriculture. Besides the major export crops, Malaysians cultivate rice, coconuts, cocoa, fruits, coffee, tea, and pepper. Fishing is also important. Malaysia is the world's largest exporter of natural rubber and palm oil.

Electronics and automobile manufacturing have been successful parts of the manufacturing boom. Foreign investment has played an important role in this sector. The Malaysians produce a car known as the *Proton Saga*. Malaysia's economic success has led to a reduction of poverty and an overall increase in the standard of living. Malaysia's Human Development Index (0.794) ranks it 57th out of 173 countries. Real gross domestic product per capita is $7,400, which has tripled in the last generation. These figures indicate that the rising generation is already living better than the last one. Economic opportunities are available to an increasing number of people, and absolute poverty affects fewer than one-fourth of all people. The international drug trade has affected Malaysia, causing the government to take aim at drug traffickers. Anyone (Malaysian or non-Malaysian) arrested for possessing illegal drugs is subject to the death penalty. The monetary currency is the *ringgit* ($).

Transportation and Communication

Bicycles, motorcycles, and cars are the principal means of transportation; buses, trains, and airplanes are used for longer trips. Following the British tradition, traffic moves on the left side of the road. The majority of Malaysian roads are paved and there is a well-developed national highway system. Taxis are plentiful in the cities. Both domestic and international communications systems are good. There are several television and radio stations. More than 60 newspapers are available in the major languages of the country.

Education

Education is considered the key to social status and success. Six years of primary and three years of secondary education are compulsory. After this, students take an examination to determine whether they may continue school for two more years in a secondary school or in a trade school, both of which require a modest tuition. Most students are instructed in Malay and are required to learn English. Chinese and Indian students, however, may attend special schools where instruction is in the students' native language. These students generally spend an extra year in school because they must also learn Malay.

Secondary-school graduates may take an exam to enter two years of preuniversity education. There are seven universities in Malaysia and more than 30 other institutions of higher learning. Many Malaysians also study abroad; degrees from British, Australian, and American universities are valued. Adult correspondence courses are sponsored by the government. The literacy rate averages 78 percent. This represents about 85 percent for the peninsula and 65 percent for Sarawak and Sabah.

Health

Medical care is partially socialized, with both central and state governments involved. Health care fees are low, and the government has sponsored national immunization, fluoridation, and hygiene campaigns. Problems still exist, of course, and rural health care is not as good as that in the cities. But facilities and care are consistently improving. The infant mortality rate has dropped from more than 25 per 1,000 to only 14 per 1,000; life expectancy ranges from 68 to 71 years.

FOR THE TRAVELER

A passport is necessary for U.S. travelers to enter Malaysia, but a visa is not needed for stays of up to three months. A yellow fever vaccination is required if coming from an infected area and is recommended for travel in Malaysia. Cholera and other vaccinations should also be considered. Malaria suppressants are recommended. Dual-voltage small appliances or an adaptor and a plug adaptor are necessary to use electrical outlets. There are many travel opportunities and interesting tours available in Malaysia. For more information contact the Malaysia Tourist Information Center, 818 West Seventh Street, Suite 804, Los Angeles, CA 90017; phone (213) 689–9702. You may also wish to contact the Embassy of Malaysia, 2401 Massachusetts Avenue NW, Washington, DC 20008; phone (202) 328–2700. Consulates are located in Los Angeles and New York.

Republic of
Mali

Boundary representations not necessarily authoritative.

BACKGROUND

Land and Climate

The seventh largest country in Africa, Mali is about twice the size of Texas. It covers 478,764 square miles (1,240,000 square kilometers). Situated in the middle of West Africa, Mali's north is in the southern Sahara desert. Further south is the semiarid Sahel with limited vegetation, mostly in the form of bushes and a few trees. Together, desert or semi-desert regions cover 70 percent of Mali. Only in the deep south can one find forests and some jungles. The fertile Niger River area is home to most of Mali's economic activity. The river's northern delta is annually submerged. Mali's three seasons are the rainy season, from May to October in the south, but only about a month of irregular rainfall in the north; the fresh or cold season (cool and dry), from November to February; and the hot season, from March to May or June.

History

From the seventh to the nineteenth centuries, parts of Mali were ruled by the kings of the Ghana, Malinke, Songhai, Bambara, and Toucouleur empires. The Songhai empire in the 15th and 16th centuries covered twice the territory of modern Mali. In the 14th century, Mali was one of the most important centers of commerce in Africa. Tombouctou (Timbuktu) was a center of Islamic learning. Malians are proud of their history, retaining it through tale and song.

The French began ruling at the turn of the 20th century, and Mali was a French colony (Western Sudan) until 1960, when it gained independence under a socialist government led by Modibo Keita. In 1968, a group of military officers staged a successful coup and renounced socialism. A military government ruled until 1979 with Moussa Traoré as president. In 1979, civilians were added to the cabinet and a political party was formed called the Democratic Union of the People of Mali (UDPM). Traoré continued as the country's president and general secretary of the UDPM. When popular demonstrations in 1991 were met with Traoré's orders to shoot civilians, key army officers rebelled and staged a coup. Traoré was arrested and put on trial in 1992 and the UDPM was disbanded. Traoré was convicted of ordering the deaths of those who died in the 1991 riots. His death sentence has not yet been carried out.

Since that time, significant steps towards democracy have been taken. A new constitution was drafted and a National Assembly elected. Also elected was President Alpha Oumar Konare. Unfortunately, 1993 student riots forced Konare's prime minister to resign. Rioters set fire to the president's home and the National Assembly building. Konare responded by meeting with student leaders and committing to change the educational system. He also made some changes within his cabinet. Konare also worked early in his tenure to negotiate with Tuareg rebels, who have long struggled to gain independence for their light-skinned ethnic group. The Tuaregs live in Mali, Niger, and Burkina Faso and have fought all three governments. Fighting in Mali decreased significantly after government negotiations began. It is clear that, while many challenges face this fledgling democracy, Malian leaders are ready to address them peacefully.

THE PEOPLE
Population

Mali's population is about 9.1 million, with an annual growth rate of 2.7 percent. Nearly 90 percent of Malians reside in the more fertile southern third of the country, while 10 percent (mostly nomadic people) lives in the arid north that comprises two-thirds of Mali. Eighty percent of all people live in rural areas.

There are about 20 major ethnic groups, several of which comprise less than one percent of the population. The largest group, which makes up approximately one-third of the population, is the Bambara, who generally populate the central and southern regions. The second largest group is the Malinke of the southwest and west. The Sarakole live in the northwest near Mauritania. The Peulh (or Peul), seminomadic herders who traditionally inhabit the northern desert, comprise some 17 percent of the population. Many Peulh have migrated south and settled in the Mopti region due to deteriorating living conditions in the north. The Songhai live in the northeast along the Niger River, as do the Bozo, who earn their living from fishing in the Niger delta. The Dogons live on and around the Bandiagara escarpment (also called the Dogon Cliffs) in the eastern center. The Menianka and Senufo inhabit the southwest, along the Burkina Faso border. The Tuaregs live in the east.

Language

Mali's large number of languages and dialects reflects the ethnic diversity of the country. The official language, French, is spoken by government administrators and in urban areas, and is the primary language of instruction in school. However, the most widely spoken tongue is Bambara. Many Malians speak three or four languages. As is common in Africa, language is mainly oral. Books are published in at least four Malian languages, but history is transmitted by narration from generation to generation, from master to scholar, and from parent to child. A special caste, the Griot, has the responsibility to recount and sing the great past.

Religion

Ninety percent of all Malians are Muslim. Most of the rest, especially in the south and along the Dogon Cliffs, adhere to traditional religions, which usually emphasize animism. About 1 percent is Christian. The Peulh, Sarakole, Moor, Songhai, and Tamashek have been Muslim for a long time. More recent converts to Islam still practice some aspects of their traditional faiths concurrently, including the use of masks or totem animals, and wearing *grigri* charms (amulets used to protect a person from harm or illness). Most Malians are tolerant of other religions, since they mix practices from different belief systems.

General Attitudes

Malians are usually polite and friendly. This helps assure mutual respect among friends and strangers. If they feel slighted, Malians may use a host of unexpected, teasing comments. These are usually humorous and are regarded as attempts to be nice and not offend. Malians often make jokes with other groups about family names or castes. These "joking cousin" remarks help maintain friendly ties and avoid harshness between the many different groups. Malians are rarely confrontational. Malians adapt to nature rather than try to dominate it. Time is oriented more towards tradition and convenience than towards innovation or urgency. Among Muslims, the "will of *Allah*" is seen as affecting all events.

Even though many villages are composed of only one ethnic group, traditional social position and caste membership are often more important than ethnic origin. Between similar ethnic groups, caste membership determines one's relative position. However, between dissimilar groups, such as the light-skinned peoples versus the dark-skinned sub-Saharan Malians, ethnicity is still the main distinguishing factor and cause of long-standing tensions. Traditional roles are often more important than assumed roles. A driver born as a "noble," for instance, may be more respected than a government official from a blacksmith family.

Traditional moral codes remain prevalent. For example, robbery may be a reason to beat a criminal, while embezzlement of public funds (a relatively modern crime) may be pardonable. One must care for one's family and clan, but general civic loyalties are shallow. At the same time, students and student unions are becoming a more vocal and powerful force in society.

Personal Appearance

Western clothing is common in urban areas, although women tend to wear traditional clothing more often than men. Men wear trousers, not shorts, and a shirt. Rural Muslim women wear wraparound skirts, blouses, and sandals; animist women may omit blouses and shoes. Among some ethnic groups, animist boys first wear pants after circumcision (5–12 years old). Neatness and modesty are valued throughout the country.

CUSTOMS AND COURTESIES
Greetings

Men and women either shake right hands when meeting, or (sometimes when greeting the opposite sex) clasp their own hands and bow slightly. A man of power (such as a village chief) will always initiate a handshake. Otherwise, a person joining a group or entering a room initiates a handshake with each adult in the room or area, beginning with the eldest or most senior.

Verbal greetings vary between the ethnic groups. If one's language is not known, a person can use one of the nation's more commonly spoken languages and the other will respond with his or her own language. For example, if one person uses the French *Bonjour* (Good day), the other might respond with the Bambara equivalent, *Nse*. It is impolite not to greet someone when passing them on a path or street. Greetings are usually followed among friends by inquiries about one's family members and their health. Greetings that precede conversation can often last several minutes.

One's family name provides information about the person's ethnic, caste, and geographic origins. Depending on how much trust exists between greeters, Malians may or may not announce their family name to strangers. Rather, a first name will be used in introductions. Often, it is only when people are acquainted that one learns the family name of the other. Friends generally address one another by given names.

Gestures

Because the left hand is considered unclean, it is disrespectful and unhygienic to take a Malian's left hand, offer the left for a handshake, use it to offer food or money, or accept anything with it. The only exception is when a close family member or friend leaves on a long trip, in which case the left hand is used in a handshake as a special gesture to indicate the two people will see each other again. Special respect may be shown during a regular handshake by touching one's own right elbow with the fingertips of the left hand while shaking right hands. Respect may also be shown by touching the forehead with the right hand after a gentle handshake or by touching the chest over the heart with the right hand after shaking. It is impolite to point or gesture with the index finger; the entire hand should be used.

Visiting

Visiting plays an integral part of Malian society, as it is a way to maintain kinship bonds and friendships. Not visiting someone for an extended period of time reflects on the value of the relationship. Visits between rural friends and relatives occur often and usually unannounced, as making prior arrangements is difficult without telephones.

Guests remove their shoes before entering a room or stepping on a mat. Visitors are offered water when entering a compound and may be given the best seating. In villages, guests bring small gifts to their hosts, often including tea, sugar, or kola nuts. Compliments are usually appreciated, but they are denied for modesty's sake. If visitors arrive while hosts are eating, the guest will usually be invited to share the food, but unexpected guests may politely decline the meal. Guests are usually offered refreshments, which they offer to share with the hosts, as it is very impolite to eat in front of others.

If visiting a *dugutigi* (village chief), one takes special care to show respect. In a village meeting, visitors who do not speak the local language (such as government officials or foreigners) will not talk directly to the chief but to one or more persons who pass the communication to the chief and vice versa.

Eating

Urban families usually use a spoon and often other utensils when eating their meals, but it is traditional to eat food with the right hand. Rural people continue to follow this tradition. Family members eat from communal bowls. The male head of the family determines which groups eat from one of several communal bowls. For example, men and boys may share one bowl, with small children and/or women sharing another. Being married or unmarried is also a distinction, as is one's relative age. Adult men and women seldom eat from the same bowl. Each person eats from the portion of the bowl that is directly in front of him.

LIFESTYLE

Family

Traditionally, Malians favor large families, although urban families are becoming smaller. The infant mortality rate is still high and some parents believe they must produce children as "life insurance" to provide a posterity and sufficient hands for agricultural labor. The family or clan chief's authority is incontestable. Babies receive a lot of affection, but children receive family responsibilties as early as age five. Older children care for younger ones. The elderly enjoy great respect. The extended family is cohesive, and members who

can are obligated to help family members in need, no matter how distant the relationship. The average wage earner cares for ten people. Saving money is almost impossible.

For most, life functions at the subsistence level. Crops depend on sufficient rain and surpluses are rare. Houses are made of mud, rocks, and sometimes cement. Few households have electricity or running water. Even for city dwellers, these services are frequently interrupted.

Dating and Marriage

Dating norms vary with the locale. In urban areas, dating begins at about age 15 and promiscuity is widespread. In rural areas, rules differ according to the ethnic or social group. Individuals usually accept the judgment of their families in the choice of a marital partner. Marriage rules are strongly influenced by Islam, but the position of the woman is less dependent than in other Muslim countries since she can, under certain conditions, divorce her husband and rejoin her family. Polygamy is still practiced (as allowed and controlled by Islamic law), but it has been increasingly seen as an economic burden. A Muslim man who wishes to take another wife usually seeks the approval of his first wife and then must provide for all wives (up to four) equally. In urban areas many women no longer accept the status of second, third, or fourth spouse. But some rural women appreciate the extra help that multiple wives can represent.

Diet

The dietary staple is millet. Prepared as a dough-like substance (*To*) or like porridge, it is often dipped in a leaf or vegetable sauce and occasionally a meat sauce (goat, sheep, or chicken). In the north, milk, dates, and wheat are important foods. Urban residents eat rice when possible. Restaurants that serve Western dishes are found in Bamako and in regional capital cities. Malnutrition is widespread in Mali.

Recreation

The most popular sport in Mali is soccer. It is inexpensive, and, as a spectator sport, it provides people with an opportunity to sit together and talk while watching the game. Also, informal peer groups, known as *groupe de "grain,"* often meet together to drink tea and socialize. In Bamako and other urban areas, wealthier people spend considerable time watching television and videos.

Holidays

National holidays include New Year's Day, Army Day (20 January), Labor Day (1 May), and Independence Day (22 September). The most important religious holidays are the feast at the end of *Ramadan* (the Islamic month of fasting, when Muslims go without food and drink during the day and eat in the evenings) and, 40 days later, *Tabaski* (feast of mutton). The dates for these feasts change each year because Islam uses the lunar calendar, which has 28-day months. Christmas and Easter Monday are observed in cities as days off from work. In animist areas, festivals associated with the seasons are celebrated with mask dancing.

Commerce

Most Malians work in agriculture and are not normal wage earners. Wage earners are usually government employees who work 40-hour weeks. The largest such group is Mali's teachers. Because wages are in arrears, many must also work in agriculture to support their families. In urban areas, the number of unemployed people probably exceeds 50 percent. Many of these survive as street vendors. Government offices and larger stores are open from 7:30 A.M. to 2:30 P.M., Monday through Saturday, except Fridays, when they are open from 7:30 A.M. to 12:30 P.M. and from 4:00 to 7:00 P.M. Markets and street vendors are open until late into the evening and on Sundays. Open air markets are open each week, and provide opportunities not only to buy basic goods but also to socialize.

SOCIETY

Government

Mali is a multiparty democracy. President Konare is head of state; he cannot seek reelection after his five-year term. A prime minister (Ibrahima Boubaca Keita) is head of government. Malians directly elect the 116 members of the National Assembly to five-year terms. The voting age is 21. Konare's Association for Democracy (Adema) is the dominant party, but small opposition parties also hold seats in the assembly.

Economy

Mali's few natural resources are limited to small deposits of gold, limestone, uranium, and other minerals. Eighty percent of the labor force is employed in agriculture. Harvests are often poor due to drought or grasshoppers. There is little industry and most enterprises are controlled by the government. Mali's main exports include cotton, cattle, gold, and peanuts. Small enterprises are growing in urban areas, but the purchasing power of the domestic market is limited. Tourism is not significant because Mali lacks the necessary infrastructure (hotels, transport, services, etc.).

Mali's Human Development Index (0.214) ranks it 167th out of 173 countries. Real gross domestic product per capita is $480, which has hardly improved since before independence. Although a small urban middle class has some access to economic opportunities, most people are poor. Joblessness contributed to student riots in 1993. The country depends heavily on aid and development projects from industrialized countries. Aid has increased significantly since the 1991 coup and subsequent elections. The currency is the *Communauté Financière Africaine (CFA) franc*.

Transportation and Communication

Mali is served by international airlines and is linked to Senegal by train. Travel by road is difficult, since most are unpaved and only intermittently passable. However, a recent major effort has extended paved roads from central Bamako to the city's outlying districts. In addition, paved roads link most major cities. From August to December, the Niger River is usually navigable by larger ships. Canoes and small craft can use the river year-round. The availability of public transportation is increasing. Buses link major cities, but outlying areas are usually only accessible by pickup trucks or vans that carry passengers and their cargo.

Radio and television are operated by the government. Television broadcasts can be received in most regions, but access to a television and power source is limited in rural areas. Programs are mostly in French. Radio broadcasts are in local languages. Until just before the 1991 coup, there was only one (government) newspaper. An opposition paper was instrumental in the precoup demonstrations. It and numerous other dailies now prosper as part of a free press. Telephone connections are generally good, but they are not extensive. Most people must go to a post office to make or receive a call. Mail is delivered to postal and government offices, not to homes. Rural people often pass mail from hand to hand in the letter's intended direction.

Education

A low literacy rate (20–35 percent) stems from a primary school enrollment rate of 25 percent and the use of French as the language of instruction. Nearly 40,000 adults read and write in local languages (mostly Bambara). Rural schools are sparse, as villagers must pay for expensive construction materials themselves. Professional training is still relatively rare. Public schools, as well as Catholic, American, and French schools, serve urban areas. Where there is a Catholic or Protestant mission in a rural areas, there is usually also a school. Many people send their children (mostly boys) to Islamic (Koranic) schools and leave them in the care of the teacher. Several colleges offer a bachelor's degree, but Mali's first university is only now being built in Bamako. When completed, the existing colleges will join as departments of the single university.

Health

Medical facilities and services are inadequate or non-existent in much of the country. On average, there is only one doctor for every 17,000 people and one sickbed per 2,000 people. Clinics are often without staff or supplies. Hospitals in the regional capitals have inadequate equipment. The infant mortality rate is 106 per 1,000. Life expectancy is between 44 and 47 years. Widespread epidemics of malaria cause several thousand deaths each year. Influenza, dysentery, venereal disease, Guinea worm, and German measles cause frequent sickness. Yellow fever, cholera, bilharzia, and rabies are also present. Public hygiene is poor in urban areas where sewage collects in open gutters.

FOR THE TRAVELER

A visa and valid passport are required for U.S. citizens to enter Mali. Yellow fever vaccinations are also required if one is coming from an infected area. Other vaccination recommendations depend on the purpose and length of stay. Water is not potable and should be treated or boiled. In areas where the Guinea worm is endemic, water must be strained through cotton cloth. Eat only thoroughly cooked and hot foods; wash and peel fruits and vegetables. Many travel agencies offer programs and interesting travel options. Famous sites are Mopti, Djénné, and the Dogon Cliffs. Overland travel to some areas is not secure. Likewise, crossing the Sahara is unsafe. Check with the U.S. embassy in Mali or call (202) 647–5225 for current travel advisories. You may wish to contact the Ministry of Tourism, located at B.P. 191, Bamako, Mali; phone 223–22–56–73. The Embassy of Mali is located at 2130 R Street NW, Washington, DC 20008; phone (202) 332–2249.

CULTURGRAM™ '96

Republic of the
Marshall Islands

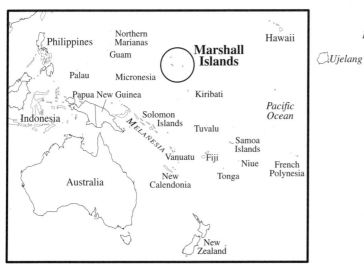

Boundary representations not necessarily authoritative.

BACKGROUND

Land and Climate

The Republic of the Marshall Islands (RMI), located in the north Pacific Ocean, is in the easternmost part of Micronesia. It sits between Hawaii and Papua New Guinea and is north of Fiji. Though difficult to measure, the Marshall Islands include some 700,000 square miles (1.8 million square kilometers) of the Pacific Ocean. The total land area, however, is only 70 square miles (181 square kilometers), which is a bit larger than Washington, D.C. There are two chains of atolls about 130 miles (200 kilometers) apart. The Ratak (eastern or sunrise) chain is made up of 15 atolls while the Ralik (western or sunset) chain has 16 atolls. There are 1,152 islands in these two atoll chains. Atoll islands are coral based and have sandy soil. They are flat and usually narrow.

The climate is hot and humid throughout the year on most islands. The average temperature is 84°F (29°C); the difference between day and night temperatures is about 10°F (5°C). There is more rainfall in the southern atolls. Trade winds blow from December to March and the typhoon season is from August to November.

History

The original Marshallese are believed to have sailed in large canoes from Indonesia and the Philippines through Melanesia. They lived by fishing and cultivating root trees and crops. Neither money nor alcohol were present in the culture. The Marshallese were renowned for their seamanship and for developing an elaborate system of navigation (*meto*) using wave and current patterns represented in stick charts. Unlike Western navigation, these maps emphasize patterns over specific landmarks.

The first Europeans to encounter the islands were Spanish explorers in the early 1500s. However, explorers were fearful of the dangerous reefs that surrounded the Marshalls, so few dared to visit until British Captains Gilbert and Marshall arrived in 1788. Forty years later, Otto von Kotzebue, a Russian explorer, named the islands after the British captain. Soon, whalers began to frequent the islands. Missionaries and traders followed the whalers.

The colonial era started as a number of governments realized the value of the islands for trade and military purposes. The Germans established a coaling station on one atoll in 1878 and later started coconut plantations to produce copra (dried coconut meat) from which coconut oil is extracted. With the end of World War I, the Japanese took control of the undefended Marshall Islands. Under a League of Nations mandate, they became the official ruling power. They too realized the value of the islands and launched several attacks from them in World War II. The Japanese lost control of the islands when U.S. forces moved across the Pacific. The United States, under a mandate from the United Nations, administered the islands after the war as a Trust Territory (including the Marshalls, Mariana Islands, Micronesia, and Belau). The Marshall Islands separated from the Trust Territory in 1979

OCEANIA

and established its own unique relationship with the United States. A constitution was ratified by voters on 1 May 1979.

The United States currently maintains a missile range on Kwajalein Atoll as part of the Strategic Defense Initiative. The United States also conducted 66 atomic tests from 1946 to 1958 on Bikini and Eniwetok Atolls. There is still much controversy over the tests. Some Marshallese receive and continue to press for financial compensation for damages suffered during the testing.

In 1986, the Republic entered into a Compact of Free Association with the United States. Under the compact, the RMI has complete responsibility for its national affairs except in the area of defense. The United States takes responsibility for all security and defense matters relating to the RMI and provides it with substantial financial subsidies. The compact is subject to renewal after fifteen years. In 1991, the RMI became a member of the United Nations.

THE PEOPLE

Population

There are approximately 54,000 people in the Marshall Islands. While there is primarily only one ethnic group (the Marshallese), immigrants from neighboring islands, Germans, Japanese, and Americans have all influenced the ethnic mix. Recently, many Filipino workers have come to the islands to help meet labor needs.

More than half of the people live in the urban centers of Majuro and Ebeye, while the remainder live on outer islands. The population growth rate is extraordinary. At 3.8 percent, it is one of the highest in the world. Reduced infant mortality, infrequent family planning, and improved health care have contributed to rapid growth. More than half of the population is under the age of fifteen. On outer islands, the population of each atoll can usually be traced to one or two family lines.

Language

While English is the official government language and is taught in all schools, few people speak it fluently. Marshallese is the language spoken on a daily basis. It belongs to the Malayo-Polynesian language family and is related to the languages of neighboring countries. There are two dialects of Marshallese, Ratak and Ralik, that are connected to the geography of the two atoll chains. There are also minor differences from atoll to atoll.

Religion

Most Marshallese are Christians, with a majority practicing Protestant faiths. Roman Catholic, Church of Jesus Christ of Latter-day Saints (Mormon), Seventh-Day Adventist, Assembly of God, and Baha'i faiths also have a following. First introduced by the Spanish missionaries in the 1500s, and later reintroduced by New England Congregationalists in the 1850s, Christianity plays an important role in community life. The Marshallese have adapted Christianity to their own culture by making unique feasts, festivals, dancing, and singing part of religious life. Most people honor the Christian Sabbath and are also religious in their homes. Christmas is a time of great celebration. Groups practice dancing and singing months before the holiday. Indigenous religion has all but disappeared, although many still believe in and practice traditional medicine.

General Attitudes

Mantin-Majel, the Marshallese way or manner, is very important. This generally means a casual or carefree way of life. For example, *babu* is a favorite activity (see Visiting). Interactions are particularly nonconfrontational and people are generally reserved in public. A Marshallese will often say what the listener expects to hear. Rudeness is rarely displayed. Time is not as important as interpersonal relations. *Awa in Majel* (Marshallese time) means that meetings and appointments begin when they start and not always at a specific hour. It is more important to wait for all to arrive than to start on time. The family is very important; the group is always more important than the individual. Respect is shown to the elderly, especially to a woman or an *irooj* (land-owning chief). Sharing and borrowing are more common concepts than owning or having. Privacy on the small islands barely exists. People often sit together to be supportive of each other without ever exchanging words.

Personal Appearance

Most men and women wear Western-style clothing. Modesty is important. Men on less traditional islands often wear shorts without shirts, although formal occasions dictate they wear jackets, shirts with ties, and long pants. On some islands, men nearly always wear shirts. Women wear muu-muu-type dresses that cover their legs and shoulders. Traditionally, women never wear pants or shorts. However, the younger generation, being more influenced by Western media and dress, is starting to change its fashion sense, much to the distress of the elders. T-shirts, jeans, skirts and make-up are making their way via the media to the capital (Majuro) and to the outer islands. Women with long hair usually wear it tied in a bun.

CUSTOMS AND COURTESIES

Greetings

Iokwe (pronounced YAH-quay) is the all-purpose greeting appropriate in almost any situation. Like *Aloha* in Hawaiian, it has many meanings based on inflection. It might mean "hello," "good-bye," "love," or "like," and in certain situations it can be an expression of frustration or remorse. While handshaking is not universal, when people do shake hands they might continue shaking for a prolonged period, even for an entire conversation. Another common greeting is *Itok im mona* (Come and eat). It is used both literally and as a general greeting. It is typical for people, particularly on outer islands, to invite passersby in for conversation and a drink of *ni* (coconut water), *jakaro* (coconut sap), coffee, or whatever is on hand. When people address one another, names are not usually used. Instead, a more general reference such as *motta* (friend) might follow *Iokwe*.

Gestures

In Marshallese culture it is improper to point at or touch another person's head because it is considered the most sacred part of the body. The gesture for calling someone to come over is to wave all fingers with the palm facing down.

A person might subtly raise their eyebrows to acknowledge another's presence, to agree, or to say "yes." A quick hissing sound might be used to get one's attention. When coming upon two people in conversation, it is polite not to walk between them. If it is absolutely necessary to pass between them, custom dictates lowering one's head (below the level of conversation, if possible) and saying *Jolok bod* (Excuse me). Prolonged eye contact is not common in conversation. Respect is best shown by looking down rather than into someone's eyes.

Visiting

Visiting is an important aspect of Marshallese society. If people do not visit or accept visitors, others may wonder if something is wrong. From short walks to longer boat trips, the practice of wandering around to visit and chat is a national pastime and is referred to as *jambo*. Individuals and/or families *jambo* at all hours on any given day. Hosts often share drinks and food with their guests. Refreshments range from natural fruits or fish to imported rice, canned meats, and drinks. Visitors are seated on mats (*jaki*) woven from pandanus leaves. New *jaki* are used as sleeping mats, while old ones are used to sit on. It is customary to remove one's sandals before sitting down.

Men sit cross-legged and women tuck their legs to the side. Out of modesty, women are particularly careful to cover their thighs. Many people also lie down (*babu*) to converse, propping their heads with a large stone, coconut, or window sill. Windows in homes are often at ground level to allow the breeze to cool sleepers at night. Pointing one's foot at anyone else is impolite, and one is careful not to step over seated persons but to walk around them. Visits can last from a couple of minutes to a long time. Visitors and hosts often sit without speaking, simply enjoying each other's presence.

Eating

Most Marshallese foods are eaten with the fingers. If food is presented but a visitor is not hungry, custom dictates eating a small amount to show appreciation to the host. The more guests eat, the greater their appreciation. A host is disappointed or confused when a guest refuses an offer of food because hosts enjoy the opportunity to be hospitable. It is better for guests to wrap up offered food and take it with them than to give it back. A common expression, *Kan dikdik kan in iokwe* (Little food with lots of love), speaks to the sharing of food even when there is not enough left for the family. When there is an abundance of food, many meals or small snacks can be eaten in a day. Young children are usually fed first. If a family catches a big fish and cooks it, they are obligated to share part of it with neighbors and members of the extended family. They might, therefore, take a full plate of tuna to a friend or relative. A couple of days later, the recipient would return the plate full of bananas or another food.

LIFESTYLE

Family

The family is the center of Marshallese life. It is the basis of interpersonal and hierarchical relations and land ownership. It is generally much larger than a nuclear family, with many relatives living together as part of an extended family household. Informal adoption is common, and children are often cared for by members of their extended family. This arrangement is very flexible and can extend beyond blood relations. Older parents often care for their grandchildren. Because older people are so respected, they are also taken care of. The society is matrilineal in that land is passed down through women, yet men often act as representatives and wield a great deal of day-to-day power. Women are responsible for child rearing and cooking. They also work outside the home, contributing to copra production, food gathering, and traditional weaving.

Dating and Marriage

Dating starts during adolescence. Because any display of affection between genders is considered socially inappropriate, meeting at night (locally called *nightcrawling*) is the typical method of courtship. Boys approach girls' houses at night, crawling and throwing pebbles to get the attention of their dates. After dating, the next step is to *koba*, equivalent to living in a common-law marriage. A couple makes a commitment to each other, starts living together, and might start raising children. Many people later formalize their relationship and marry in a church.

Diet

Agricultural products in the Marshall Islands include coconuts, bananas, breadfruit, limes, taro, pumpkins, and papayas. Fish, chicken, and pork are also part of the Marshallese diet, especially during feasts (*kemem*). Imported foods include rice, flour, sugar, coffee, tea, and canned meats. They compose an increasingly greater proportion of the diet. There are few customs regarding which foods are appropriate at which times. However, dinner, which usually includes fish, is the main meal of the day. *Kwanjin*, breadfruit baked on coals and scraped, is popular. So are *jaajmi* (raw fish) and *taituuj* (fried banana pancakes). Cooking on outer islands is often done over open fires or in ground ovens.

Recreation

Sports, including volleyball, basketball, baseball, swimming, and canoe racing, are popular. Most schools and towns host local field days. The Marshall Islands send a team to the Micronesian Olympics. Storytelling is also enjoyed.

Holidays

Christian holidays, such as Christmas and Easter, are celebrated. Christmas is a time for singing, dancing, worshiping, and eating. Months of preparation are involved. Constitution Day, the national holiday, is observed 1 May. Many atolls celebrate Liberation Day (various dates) to mark when the Americans liberated them from the Japanese during World War II. Compact Day, celebrating the 1986 agreement with the United States, is 21 October. On New Year's Day, people carol in return for gifts. Other public holidays include Memorial Day (1 March), Fisherman's Day (first Friday in September), Labor Day (last Friday in September), President's Day (17 November), and *Kamoolal* or Thanksgiving Day (first Friday in December).

Commerce

Urban business hours are from 9:00 A.M. to 5:00 P.M. On outer islands, the hours are more informal, as businesses often operate in parts of people's homes. Most stores are closed on Sunday.

SOCIETY

Government

The country has a constitutional government in free association with the United States. The government is divided into three branches. The legislative branch includes 12 traditional chiefs in the council of *Irooj* (upper house), as well as 33 members elected to the *Nitijela* (lower house). President Amata Kabua heads the executive branch and was elected by the *Nitijela*. The judicial branch consists of a Supreme Court, a High Court, and a Traditional Court, which handles land disputes. The country attempts to balance both Western and traditional systems by incorporating into the formal government the influence of the land-based social system of *irooj* (land-owning chiefs), *alaps* (lords), and *rijerbal* (workers). While it is eroding in the cities, the power of the *irooj* and *alaps* and the respect granted by the *rijerbal* remain strong on outer islands. This blend has both positive and negative aspects, with the traditional system sometimes undermining democracy but also providing strong leadership support. The voting age is 18. The next parliamentary elections are scheduled for November 1995.

Economy

There are two economies in the Marshall Islands, the traditional or subsistence economy, and the modern or money-centered economy. The currency is the U.S. dollar ($). The subsistence economy revolves around fishing and farming. It was sustainable for generations because people took only as much as they needed. However, the dramatic increase in population has put pressure on both the land and the sea, forcing people to take more and more. The traditional economy is also undermined by the lure of modernity. The modern economy revolves around copra, or the production of coconut oil, which accounts for 90 percent of all exports. Outside funding, including government and military spending; the service industry, particularly in urban centers; and the production of handicrafts, especially by women on the outer islands, also drive the modern economy. Commercial fishing has also become an important revenue source. National product per capita is about $1,500.

It is difficult to balance the two economies. While the modern economy affords many alternatives, it also brings with it the complications of dependence and rapid, if not unchecked, modernization. While the traditional economy at its best is sustainable, it is inadequate for the growing needs of the Marshallese as skills are lost or forgotten and as the population expands. Agriculture, fishing, and tourism are the development priorities for coming years.

Transportation and Communication

The transportation needs of the Marshall Islands are served by ship and plane. The urban centers host the only major roads suitable for vehicular traffic. Outer islands have cleared paths suitable for bicycles and push carts, and there is usually a major path that can be traveled by pickup truck. The majority of islanders walk. A fleet of ships delivers supplies and passengers to outer islands and collects copra. There is limited domestic air service to each atoll, but the country is connected to international carriers through the Majuro airport. Urban centers have phone service and newspapers, while outer islands communicate through high frequency radios run on solar power. There are a couple of television stations in urban centers; on some outer islands, videos are watched on televisions connected to generators. There is one public radio station.

Education

Universal public schooling is available through grade eight. There is a competitive national exam for admission to the nation's two public high schools. As a result, fewer than half of eligible students attend school beyond the eighth grade. While Marshallese is the language of instruction in school, elementary schools use a bilingual curriculum and greater emphasis is placed on English at the secondary level. There is a College of the Marshall Islands in Majuro. Post-secondary education also occurs in the United States or at off-island schools in the region. The literacy rate is 93 percent.

Health

Hospital facilities and medical care are available in urban areas. The outer islands have trained health assistants who handle less serious cases and preventive care. The health status of the Marshallese is good compared to other developing nations, but there are concerns about diabetes, diarrhea and intestinal diseases, nutritional deficiencies, and influenza and pneumonia. The high infant mortality rate (49 per 1,000) is related to water quality, nutrition, and a lack of medical resources. The average life expectancy is 61 to 64 years.

FOR THE TRAVELER

A passport is recommended for travel to the Marshall Islands. U.S. citizens do not need visas, but must have a round trip ticket with a departure date shown within one month of arrival. There is a departure tax of US$15. Outer island travel is planned most easily from the capital, Majuro. A rental car is unnecessary for touring Majuro as there are many taxis and a bus service. Plans frequently change and delays are to be expected. Drinking water often comes from rain catchments; while it is generally safe, it should be boiled or treated. For cultural information, a visit to the Alele Museum is recommended. Further information can be obtained through the Embassy of the Republic of the Marshall Islands, 2433 Massachusetts Avenue NW, Washington, DC 20008; phone (202) 234–5414.

Printed on recycled paper

Republic of

Mauritius

Boundary representations not necessarily authoritative.

BACKGROUND

Land and Climate

Mauritius is a 718 square-mile (1,860 square kilometers) volcanic island in the Indian Ocean, 690 miles east of Madagascar. The country includes the islands of Mauritius, Rodrigues, and several smaller, uninhabited islands. Lush vegetation covers the island throughout the year. The landscape is marked by impressive mountains that rim a central plateau, deep extinct volcanic craters, rivers, streams, and waterfalls. Surrounded almost entirely by coral reefs, Mauritius has a continuous belt of beaches with lagoons and crystal-clear waters. These waters are always warm (70–80°F or 21–27°C), making swimming possible year-round. About 54 percent of the land is arable. Forests are found in the southwest. The climate is tropical. Winter (May–November) is warm and relatively dry, while summer (November–May) is hot, wet, and humid. Typhoons are possible during much of the summer.

Mauritius is known for its many species of rare birds and plants, some of which exist nowhere else in the world. Three of the world's rarest birds that live on Mauritius are the Mauritian kestrel, the echo parakeet, and the pink pigeon. All are nearly extinct, and scientists and bird watchers come from all over the world to try to see the birds. Mauritius is also known for being the home of the now-extinct (for more than 300 years) dodo bird, a member of the pigeon family. The dodo is a popular theme for tourist souvenirs today.

History

Malay and Arab sailors are thought to have visited the island in the 16th century. It appeared on a map as early as 1502. The Portuguese were the first Europeans to set foot on Mauritius. As a tribute to explorer Pedro Mascarenhas, the islands of Mauritius, Rodrigues, and French-owned Réunion are known as the Mascarene Archipelago. In September 1598, Dutch Admiral van Warwyck arrived on the uninhabited island and named it Mauritius in honor of Prince Maurice of Nassau. The Dutch were the first to settle the island in 1638, but they abandoned it in 1710 when sugarcane cultivation proved a failure. The Dutch are credited with introducing sugar (now a productive industry) and deer to the island, but they are also charged with causing the extinction of the dodo birds.

Guillaume Dufresne d'Arsel claimed Mauritius for France in September 1715 and named it *Isle de France*. From 1735 to 1746, Mauritius flourished and developed under the direction of François Mahé de Labourdonnais. The British won Mauritius from France in 1810.

After the abolition of slavery in 1834, indentured laborers from India were brought to work in the sugarcane fields. While the British officially ruled Mauritius, they allowed French culture, language, and a Napoleonic law code to be maintained by the Franco-Mauritians, who remained the largest European ethnic group on the island. Mauritius gained independence in March 1968 through the leadership of Sir Seewoosager Ramgoolam, who became the nation's first prime minister. As part of the Commonwealth of Nations, Mauritius recognizes Great Britain's Queen Elizabeth II as head of state. She is represented by a governor general, currently Sir Veerasamy Ringadoo. The country has practically no army and has been politically stable since independence.

THE PEOPLE

Population

There are 1.1 million people on Mauritius, a population that is growing annually by 0.9 percent. About 68 percent are Indo-Mauritians, descendants of laborers brought from India to work for the British on sugar plantations. Another 27 percent are Creoles, descendants of Black Africans (from West and East Africa) brought by the French to the island as slaves. Sino-Mauritians (of Chinese origin) account for 3 percent of the population and Franco-Mauritians (of French origin) make up 2 percent. The mixture of these very different ethnic groups has given Mauritius a cosmopolitan and diverse culture. Approximately 40 percent of the population inhabits the urban area that stretches from Port Louis, the capital, to Curepipe.

Language

English is the official language of Mauritius, but it is not spoken much in day-to-day communication. French and English are used in government and business activities. Road signs are in English and most newspapers and media communications are in French. But creole, Hindi, Urdu, Hakka (a Chinese dialect), and Bojpoori are the main spoken languages among the people. Creole (spoken by 90 percent of the population) was developed in the 18th century by early slaves who used a pidgin language to communicate with each other as well as with their French masters, who did not understand the various African languages. The pidgin evolved with later generations to become a useful, casual language. Bojpoori (also written "Bhojpuri") on Mauritius is an amalgamation of that Indian dialect and several other Indian dialects originally spoken by the early Indian settlers. Most Mauritians are at least bilingual.

Religion

All of the world's major religions—Christianity, Islam, Hinduism, and Buddhism—are represented on the small island. Just over half the population is Hindu, although there are two main sects. While they generally share common beliefs, the Sanathan Hindus accept the existence of three primary gods and various secondary gods. The Arya Samajists, however, only recognize the existence of one god. Important

to all Hindus are the principles of reincarnation, *karma* (doing good deeds), and the illusionary state of mortal life. Seventeen percent of Mauritius's population is Muslim, accepting only *Allah* as God. Many of the Chinese are Buddhists. Thirty percent of the people are Christians, belonging to the Roman Catholic church, the Anglican church, or various other denominations.

General Attitudes

The Mauritian people are family oriented and religious. They are also optimistic, outgoing, intelligent, generous, and industrious, with a generally relaxed attitude toward life. This is evident in their more casual approach to time schedules. People are more important than schedules and it is not inappropriate to be late for an appointment. Mauritians have an ability to synthesize and adopt new ideas and cultures, combining orthodox Eastern philosophical values with a Western sense of rationalism, innovation, and achievement.

Personal Appearance

Most urban people wear Western-style clothing and only use traditional attire for special occasions or holidays. However, in rural areas, many men still wear a *langouti* (wraparound cotton garment that extends to the feet and is tied at the waist) on a daily basis. Women also often wear traditional clothing, such as the *saree* (a wraparound skirt, with one end draped over the shoulder). The *saree* is usually worn with a *choli* (tight blouse). Muslim women may wear the *bhajoo* (broad pants that narrow at the ankle that are worn with a long shirt that extends to the knees). Many married Indo-Mauritian women wear a red *tika* on their forehead to signify their husbands are alive. A *tika* is made chiefly from vermilion powder. Casual dress tends to be conservative. Modesty is important.

CUSTOMS AND COURTESIES

Greetings

Mauritians usually shake hands when they meet. The French greeting *Bonjour* (Good day) is a commonly used term. Among the Hindu Indians, the *Namaste* is the traditional greeting, especially in rural areas. A person places the palms together (fingers up) in front of the chest or chin and says *Namaste*, sometimes bowing slightly. English greetings are also acceptable. Among friends and relatives, kissing on both cheeks and hugging is common.

Gestures

It is not proper to pass or receive items with the left hand. Instead, the right hand or both hands are used. The bottom of one's foot or shoe should not point at another person. Beckoning is done by waving all fingers together with the palm down.

Visiting

It is not customary to call before visiting. Guests are always welcome. Tea with sugar and milk is served, often with savories, biscuits, or sweets. The host will usually insist that the guest accept food and drink. It is considered polite for the guest to accept and sample everything served. Guests are not expected to bring gifts, but flowers may be given to the hostess of a formal lunch or dinner.

Eating

Meals are generally eaten with a spoon, fork, and knife, but eating with the fingers of the right hand is often practiced in Indian homes. A guest is usually given the option of using silverware or eating with the hand. An unexpected guest at dinnertime will be invited to share the meal. Hindus do not eat beef. Muslims do not eat pork or drink alcoholic beverages. During the ninth lunar month of *Ramadan*, Muslims go without eating or drinking from sunrise to sundown. Meals are only eaten in the evening or before sunrise during the entire month.

LIFESTYLE

Family

With a strong emphasis on family solidarity, it is common to find extended families with aunts, uncles, and other relatives living together. There is great respect for the elderly; it is the duty of their children to take care of them. Traditionally, families have been large. However, the trend now is to have fewer children (perhaps two or three). The government encourages this trend through family planning programs.

Dating and Marriage

Western-style dating is not common but is increasing among the urban population. Chastity is important, especially among Indo-Mauritian women. Marriage is a strong tradition. Many Indo-Mauritian families arrange marriages for their children, generally with the consent of the bride and groom. Sometimes, grooms in Muslim families follow the practice of giving a dowry to the bride's parents. Divorce is not well accepted and is relatively rare. A wedding is one of the biggest events for all Mauritian families, regardless of the ethnic group or religion. It tends to be a lavish and expensive affair. Wedding ceremonies are conducted along religious lines and vary accordingly. Among Hindus, for example, a bride and groom perform a ritual of walking around a fire during the *Vivaha* (marriage ceremony). As part of a Muslim ceremony, the bride and groom drink from a common cup to signify the beginning of their lives together. Women typically marry in their early 20s, while men marry a few years later.

Diet

Rice is the main staple. *Roti* (Indian flat bread) is also a staple for many. French breads are immensely popular, especially at breakfast. Vegetarian cooking is common because of the religious preferences of Hindus and Muslims. Indian cuisine is most common, but Creole, Chinese, and spicy variations of all three are also available. Fresh seafood is popular.

Some dishes include *faratas* (similar to pancakes), *briani* (rice and vegetables with a mixture of meat, chicken, or fish, and a number of spices), *vanneyen* (chopped fish meatballs in a fish broth), *dohl pouri* (thin bread with mead and curry sauce inside), chicken curry, pickled vegetables, and seasoned squid. Most Mauritians drink tea with milk and sugar after meals. Fruits, Indian sweets, French pastries, and peanuts are popular snacks during the day and especially during afternoon tea.

Recreation

Soccer is the national sport. Horse racing is a popular spectator activity. Movies are the primary entertainment, along with informal social gatherings among friends and family. Listening to music and watching television are also common recreational activities. Playing cards and dancing the *sega* (a Mauritian dance) are especially popular in rural areas. Bar cafés, where men gather to talk and drink, are found in both rural and urban areas. Swimming and water sports are enjoyed. Wealthier Mauritians increasingly go to discos, casinos, and restaurants.

Holidays

In addition to religious holidays for all major religions, there are a few national holidays. They include New Year's Day, Independence Day (12 March), and Labor Day (1 May). With a large population of Christians, the nation celebrates Christmas and Easter. The Spring Festival (in January or February, also called the Chinese New Year) and *Ching Ming* (when the dead are honored) are the two most important holidays for the Chinese. Two holidays significant to the Muslims are *Eid-ul-Fitr*, a three-day feast that commemorates the end of the fasting month of *Ramadan*, and *Eid-ul-Adha*, a feast to mark the end of the pilgrimage to Makkah, Saudi Arabia.

Among Hindus, festivals usually celebrate the victory of a god or principle. For example, *Divali* (Festival of Lights) focuses on the triumph of *dharma* over *adharma*, or light over darkness. The *Cavadee* celebrates the feat of Idoumban, who carried two mountain peaks on his shoulders. *Holi* is a time when people sprinkle each other with colored water in celebration of Prince Bhakta Pralad's defeat of the wicked Holika. During *Maha Shivaratree* it is popular to dress in white and pour sacred water on a representation of Shiva, one of the three primary Hindu gods. The water is drawn from the Grand Bassin, a high-altitude lake that is located in a volcano crater. Special ceremonies take place at the lake on the Great Night of Shiva, which is during the summer festival.

Commerce

Businesses are generally open from 9:00 A.M. to 4:00 P.M., Monday through Friday. Some are open Saturday mornings. Most towns have an open air market that might be open most days (as in the case of Port Louis) or one day each week. Prices in these markets are negotiable.

SOCIETY

Government

Mauritius is a parliamentary democracy. Although Queen Elizabeth is recognized as nominal head of state, the country also has a president, Cassam Uteem, who functions as chief of state. The head of government is the prime minister. The current prime minister is Aneerood Jugnauth, who has served since 1982 and was reelected in 1991. Most governments are coalitions, meaning that several political parties cooperate to form a majority in the 70-seat Legislative Assembly. Cabinet ministers are then drawn from this variety of parties. The current governing coalition is dominated by two parties: Militant Socialist Movement (MSM) and Mauritian Militant Movement (MMM). The main opposition parties include the Mauritian Labor Party (MLP) and Mauritian Social Democratic Party (PMSD). Elections are held every five years; the voting age is 18. Mauritius is divided into nine districts and three dependencies. Local councils govern in urban areas.

Economy

The Mauritian economy has been dominated by the sugarcane crop since the 19th century. The sugar industry accounts for 40 percent of all export earnings and employs more than 20 percent of the labor force. Grown on plantations and small farms, sugarcane covers 90 percent of the arable land. However, it has become less important in recent years due to an increase in earnings from textile exports (44 percent of export earnings) and tourism. Tea, grown in the highlands, is the second most important crop. All but a few staple foods are imported.

Manufacturing industries include textiles, electronics, gemstone cutting, knitted wear, and others. The number of tourists visiting the island has increased dramatically over the last decade, helping Mauritius attain almost full employment. Mauritius has been successful in attracting foreign investment and at diversifying its economy to ensure it will continue to grow. The country's Human Development Index (0.778) ranks it 60th out of 173 nations. Real gross domestic product per capita is $7,178, which has nearly tripled since 1960 and is still rising. These figures reflect the economy's success, and generally indicate a bright future for the country. Both inflation and unemployment are very low. The currency is the Mauritian *rupee* (Re).

Transportation and Communication

All areas of the island are accessible by roads. Buses provide the main form of public transportation. Although crowded, they are reliable and fairly inexpensive. Taxis are available in most areas. Fares are negotiable and usually agreed upon in advance. Following the British tradition, traffic moves on the left side of the road. Mauritius has its own airline, Air Mauritius. Several international airlines fly weekly to Mauritius. The telephone system services most of the island and is quite reliable. Although the telecommunications system is small, it provides good service. There are two radio stations and four television stations, one of which receives broadcasts from neighboring Réunion. The island also has several daily newspapers and other periodicals.

Education

The government has placed great emphasis on education over the last several years. Primary and secondary schooling are free and available to all. Families who can afford the fees send their children to private schools. The literacy rate is 83 percent. Nearly all children are enrolled in primary school and more than half advance to secondary school. The University of Mauritius provides opportunities for higher education, emphasizing agricultural sciences and technology. Many Mauritians go abroad for university studies, mainly to France, the United Kingdom, and India.

Health

The public health care system provides basic services to all citizens free of charge. There are many qualified doctors, both employed by the government and engaged in private practice. Private clinics provide more comprehensive medical care for those who can afford it. Health conditions are steadily improving, as all people have access to safe water, good sanitation facilities, and prenatal care for women. Nearly all infants receive their immunizations. The infant mortality rate is 18 per 1,000. Life expectancy ranges from 66 to 74 years.

FOR THE TRAVELER

Although a visa is not necessary for U.S. visitors staying less than three months, a valid passport and proof of return ticket or onward passage are required. No vaccinations are needed, unless one is coming from an area infected with yellow fever. However, some vaccinations may be advisable, depending on the nature and length of the trip. Consult a physician for more details. Plug and voltage adaptors are necessary to use electrical outlets. Mauritius promotes itself as a scuba diving, snorkeling, swimming, sunbathing, fishing, and exploring paradise. Warm, clear waters and relative isolation from large development draw a growing number of tourists. For details regarding travel opportunities, contact the Mauritius Tourist Information Office, 8 Hafen Avenue, Suite 227, Port Washington, NY 11050; phone (516) 944–3763. You may also wish to contact the Embassy of Mauritius, 4301 Connecticut Avenue NW, Suite 441, Washington, DC 20008; phone (202) 244–1491.

A *Culturgram* is a product of native commentary and original, expert analysis. Statistics are estimates and information is presented as a matter of opinion. While the editors strive for accuracy and detail, this document should not be considered strictly factual. It is a general introduction to culture, an initial step in building bridges of understanding between peoples. It may not apply to all peoples of the nation. You should therefore consult other sources for more information.

Mongolia

Boundary representations not necessarily authoritative.

A S I A

BACKGROUND

Land and Climate

Mongolia is about the same size as Alaska. Covering 604,247 square miles (1,565,000 square kilometers), this land-locked country is sandwiched between Russia and China. Mongolia has three mountain ranges; the highest is the Altai Mountains, located in the far west. Much of southern and eastern Mongolia is occupied by a vast plain. The Gobi region (Mongolia's semi-desert), lies in the south. It can go years without rain, but also has high mountains, oases, and forests. Rivers are mainly in the north. The important Selenge River drains into Lake Baikal, Russia.

Mongolia has an extreme continental climate with long, cold winters and short summers. Little snow falls and annual precipitation is usually less than 15 inches (37 centimeters) per year in the wettest areas. Mongolia is called the "Land of Blue Sky" because it averages 257 cloudless days a year. Winters are very cold (usually below freezing). When blizzards send enough snow to cover the grass, livestock cannot graze and therefore die. This type of weather is called *zud*. Summer (June–August) can be warm, with temperatures reaching above 70°F (21°C). Spring is the rainy season. Less than 1 percent of the land is arable, 8 to 10 percent is forested, and the rest is pasture or desert.

History

Chinggis (Genghis) Khan consolidated the Mongol nation, created the first unified Mongol state, and adopted Buddhism in the 13th century. He and his descendants built an empire that stretched from Korea to Hungary, the largest continuous land empire ever known. His grandson, Khubilai Khan, founded the Yuan dynasty in China in 1279. The Mongol empire began to fragment in the 1300s and Mongols retreated to their homeland. Returning forces clashed, however, with the Oirad Mongolian tribe and civil war ensued. Dayan Kahn's

imperial forces defeated the Oirads around 1500. During the reign of Dayan Khan's grandsons, Buddhism was reintroduced (it had waned with the fall of the empire) and spread rapidly.

Civil war between the loosely confederated Mongolian nobles in the 1600s led the Khalka Mongols to ally themselves with the Manchus of China. The Manchus, who established the Ch'ing dynasty in China, eventually dominated all of Mongolia. During the Ch'ing dynasty, southern Mongolia became Inner Mongolia (now part of China) and present-day Mongolia was Outer Mongolia. The Manchus preserved the nobility and the church and dominated the nation through these institutions. Local fiefs (called *banners*) had a fair amount of autonomy.

By 1911, when the Ch'ing dynasty collapsed, the Mongol-Manchu alliance had already dissolved and the Mongols declared their independence. Because the Eighth Living Buddha (head of Buddhism in Mongolia) was the only unifying political and religious figure in the country, a theocratic monarchy was established under his leadership. It ended in 1919 when the Chinese invaded. They were driven from the capital by the White Russian army in 1921, but the Red (Bolshevik) army allied with Mongolian national hero Sukebaatar to liberate the country in July 1921. When the Living Buddha died in 1924, Mongolia was declared a Communist people's republic. The Communists destroyed the nobility and Buddhist monasteries; thousands died in fighting the changes. A one-party state and a centrally planned economy were established.

With communism's collapse, Mongolia was able to break its economic and political dependence on the Soviet Union. In 1990, the first free elections were held; Mongolians elected their first president and a new parliament. A new constitution was adopted in 1992 and Mongolia's name was changed from the Mongolian People's Republic to Mongolia. New elections in 1992 established a democratic-style government, but not full democracy. Through 1995, the ruling (former Communist) party—People's Revolutionary Party—held on to privileges that kept the opposition weak. Demands for change in election laws, media laws, and legislative rules forced the government to promise change by elections in 1996.

THE PEOPLE

Population

Mongolia's population of 2.4 million is growing annually at 2.6 percent. One-fourth of the people live in the capital, Ulaanbaatar, and another fourth live in other cities. Half of the population is spread throughout rural Mongolia.

Mongolia's population is quite homogeneous. Over 90 percent of the population is made up of subgroups of the Mongol nationality, the largest being the Khalkha (79 percent of the total). They are mostly concentrated in the central and eastern areas of the country. Distinctions between the Khalkhas and other Mongols (including Buryads, Dorwods, Oolds, Bayads, Dzakhchins, Uriyankhais, Uzemchins, and Bargas) are minor. They may be expressed through dialects, certain traditions, and folk costumes. The largest non-Mongol ethnic group is the Kazakhs (5.9 percent). They are a pastoral, Turkic-speaking, Muslim people who live in extreme western Mongolia.

Language

Mongol belongs to the Altaic language family. The Khalkha Mongol dialect is spoken by the majority of people. It is also used in schools and for official business. Other Mongol dialects are used by their respective groups. Mongolia's traditional script was replaced under communism with a Cyrillic alphabet similar to that used for Russian. In 1991, parliament voted to revive the old script. It will eventually be used in all official business and is slowly being introduced in schools. The process is slow due to the lack of printed materials and the fact that few adults can read it. The Mongol alphabet has 26 letters; text is written vertically and individual characters are written differently depending on where they appear in a word. Vowels and consonants are not written separately (as with printed English), but are connected together.

Kazakhs use their own language with a Cyrillic alphabet in schools and local government. Better educated Mongols speak Russian, and many Russian words have been incorporated into the Mongolian language. The use of English is spreading rapidly and many official signs are written only in the traditional script and English.

Religion

Traditionally, Mongols practiced a combination of Tibetan Buddhism (also called Vajrayana Buddhism) and Shamanism. Tibetan Buddhism shares the common Buddhist goals of individual release from suffering and reincarnation. Tibet's Dalai Lama, who lives in India, is the religion's spiritual leader, and is highly respected in Mongolia. As part of their shamanistic heritage, the people practice ritualistic magic, nature worship, exorcism, meditation, and natural healing.

At the beginning of the 20th century, Mongolia had hundreds of monasteries and about 50 percent of all men were monks. The Communist anti-religion campaign in the 1930s destroyed the extensive monastic system. Atheism was promoted and monasteries were closed (shamanistic practices survived). From 1945 to 1990, only one monastery (Gandan in Ulaanbaatar) was in operation.

Reform has allowed freedom of religion and well over 100 monasteries have reopened. Many young people are receiving an education through these traditional centers of learning, and the people are once again able to practice cherished traditions. Boys are increasingly applying to become monks and Buddhism is rapidly regaining its popularity. Kazakh Muslims are free to practice Islam.

General Attitudes

Mongols are proud of their history, especially the era when their empire stretched across much of Asia and Europe. As pastoral nomads, Mongols have always regarded themselves as freer than settled nations. This way of life has given them a love for the environment and wildlife. Cows and sometimes elk wander freely on city streets. Mongols appreciate wide open spaces and feel a oneness with nature. They also value their families. A fast running horse is prized everywhere. Storytelling is a traditional art.

Now that Mongolia is emerging from decades of Communist rule, society is in a state of flux. Because conformity was fostered under communism, people shy away from hard work, personal initiative, and risk taking. This has hindered the rise of entrepreneurship, even though Mongolian egalitarianism also emphasizes shared values and common goals. It has also led to a rise in alcoholism. The nation is searching for ways to help people regain their value for hard work and understand that talent, different opinions, and personal performance are important factors in establishing a democratic society.

Personal Appearance

Western-style clothing is common in urban areas. The youth wear jeans and Western-style jackets. In rural areas, the *deel* (a traditional Mongol gown or tunic) is more popular. A woman's *deel* is made of bright colors, and has silk ornaments and fancy buttons. A man's *deel* is less intricate. Both have a sash, embroidered cuffs, and designs. Urban women often have a silk *deel* for special occasions. A winter *deel* is often lined with sheepskin or fur. In the coldest weather, urban people wear heavy coats, fur hats, and leather boots. Kazakhs have their own traditional dress.

CUSTOMS AND COURTESIES

Greetings

A handshake is the most common greeting in urban areas. A standard greeting in formal situations or among strangers is *Ta sain baina uu?* (How do you do?). Acquaintances prefer more casual greetings like *Sain uu* (Hello) or *Sonin yutai ve?* (What's new?). In rural areas, people exchange their pipes or snuff as a greeting and ask questions such as how fat the livestock are or how favorable the particular season is.

Mongolian names consist of a patronymic and a given name. All people are called by their given names. The patronymic is rarely used in ordinary speech and never alone. Its purpose is to distinguish between people who might have the same name. It is the possessive form of the person's father's name. For example, a person named Hashbatyn Hulan is called Hulan and the father is known as Hashbat. A title often follows the given name in addressing a person. It is used to recognize a person's rank, seniority (in age or status), or profession.

For example, a respected teacher might be addressed as Batbayar *bagsh*, or an honored elder as Sumiya *guai* (Mr.). *Guai* is also used for women. Sometimes a person with a close relationship to an older person will call that person uncle or aunt, even though they are not related.

Gestures

The right hand is preferred for making gestures. Passing items with the left hand is impolite. Rather, both hands or the right hand (supported under the elbow with the left hand) are used. Mongols use their open hand to point. Pointing with the index finger is seen as threatening. To beckon, all fingers wave with the palm facing down. Crossing the legs, yawning, or making eye contact are avoided in the presence of an elder. Women often cover their mouths when they laugh. Mongols do not like to be touched by people they don't know. Unavoidable contact, such as in line or on a crowded bus, is not offensive. However, kicking another person's foot, even accidentally, is offensive if the two people do not immediately shake hands to rectify the insult.

Mongols use gestures to show appreciation and gestures often take the place of a verbal "thank you." Among some, one respectful gesture (*zolgah*) is used when first meeting after the new year: the younger person gently holds the elbows of the older person, whose forearms rest on the younger person's forearms; the older person lightly touches his lips to the younger person's forehead.

Visiting

Mongols enjoy having guests in their homes and are known for their hospitality. Unplanned visits are common among Mongols, but international visitors wait for an invitation. Guests are usually greeted by the host and family members at the door in modern apartment buildings, or outside a *ger* (a circular, domed, tent-like home) in rural areas. The door of a *ger* always faces south. When entering a *ger*, people customarily move around to the left. During formal visits, the host sits opposite the entrance; women sit to the left and men to the right.

Tea with milk is served to guests. *Airag* (fermented mare's milk) might be served instead of tea during summer, and vodka may be served at any time. Guests often give the hosts a small gift. For holidays or birthdays, more valuable gifts are given. On very important occasions, *khadag* (a blue silk band) and a silver bowl filled with *airag* are presented by a younger person to an elder or a person of higher social rank as a sign of deep respect and well-wishing.

Eating

Breakfast in rural areas might include dairy products and tea. In cities, people add bread and sometimes meat. Midday meals in cities are becoming more Westernized, while rural people generally eat dairy products. Dinner is the main meal of the day throughout the country. The whole family sits together for dinner in the evening. Western utensils are common for all meals, but chopsticks are used by some. Most urban dwellers use a knife to cut meat and spoons to eat rice or vegetables. In urban apartment blocks, people have dining tables and chairs. In rural areas, people sit on the floor or on small stools to eat from a low table. In the evening, soup is served in separate bowls. If the main dish is boiled meat, it is eaten from a communal bowl.

At restaurants, meals are served European style. Toasts are commonly made to all seated at the table. A host often insists on paying for the meal. Tipping is not practiced.

LIFESTYLE

Family

Most Mongols live in nuclear families. Elderly parents live with the family of their youngest son (or daughter if there are no sons). That son inherits the family home and what is left of the herd (after older sons have received equal shares). Grandparents are treated with great respect for their wisdom and life experience, which they use to help raise their grandchildren. The father is head of the family, but the mother is responsible for household affairs. In urban areas, both spouses generally work outside the home. Due to a housing shortage, three generations often share a small apartment, with parents sleeping in the living room and children and grandparents in the one or two bedrooms. Urban families have one or two children.

In rural areas, husbands take care of herding and slaughtering, while wives handle milking and food preparation. Older children care for younger siblings. In urban areas, families live either in high-rise apartments or in a *ger*, with its surrounding fence and storage shed. Most rural families live in a *ger*. A *ger* is a tent with a four- or five-piece wooden lattice, a roof frame, and a door. Its average size is 18 feet (5.5 meters) in diameter. The *ger* is covered with one or more layers of sheep-wool felt and a white cloth. It is easy to erect or dismantle and is warm in cold seasons. A *ger* in or near a city will have electricity, but not heat or water. Nomadic extended families often live in a camp of several *gers*.

Dating and Marriage

Traditionally, marriages were arranged between two families. Today, however, individuals make their own decisions. Dating between schoolmates and coworkers commonly leads to marriage. People usually marry between the ages of 18 and 25. Wedding ceremonies usually take place in "wedding palaces." Afterwards, many couples now go to a Buddhist monk to have their future predicted. A large feast treats as many relatives and friends as the new couple's families can afford to feed. In rural areas, the couple then moves into a *ger* provided by the husband's family. In urban areas, they often have trouble finding an apartment. Mongolian families traditionally exchange gifts in conjunction with the wedding. The groom's family usually gives livestock, while the bride's family offers jewelry and clothing.

Diet

The Mongolian diet consists largely of dairy products, meat, millet, barley, and wheat. Mutton or beef is usually eaten at least once a day. Rice is common in urban areas. The variety and availability of vegetables and fruits are limited by the climate. Potatoes, cabbage, carrots, onions, and garlic are generally available. Wild berries and, in a few areas, apples grow in Mongolia. In the summer, people eat milk products (dried milk curds, butter, *airag*, and yogurt) instead of large quantities of meat. A common dinner meal is *guriltai shul* (mutton and noodle soup). Boiled mutton is popular. A favorite meal is *buuz*. It is a steamed dumpling stuffed with diced meat, onion, cabbage, garlic, salt, and pepper. A boiled version of the dumpling is called *bansh*. Salt is widely used as a seasoning.

Recreation

Mongol wrestling, horse racing, and archery are the most popular sports. The entire country gets involved in the annual wrestling championships. Boxing, soccer, volleyball, basketball, and table tennis are also enjoyed. For leisure time, the people enjoy television and movies or nature outings. Visiting friends and family members is also important. In summer, people spend as much time as possible in the countryside. Small cabins in the hills around the capital are popular summer homes for those who own them. Others visit rural relatives. Sunday is a favorite day for picnics. Mongolians enjoy singing. Traditional songs are often sung at weddings or family gatherings. Traditional dance and music performances at a theater in Ulaanbaatar are popular. The youth enjoy rock concerts.

Holidays

Official holidays include New Year's Day (1 January), the Lunar New Year, Children and Women's Day (1 June), and Mongolian People's Revolution (11–13 July), called *Naadam*. The Lunar New Year is called *Tsagaan Sar* (white month). A major traditional holiday marked by family gatherings, *Tsagaan Sar* is preceded by days of house cleaning. People might celebrate a holiday over several days. Between 1969–94, Women's Day was held 8 March, but this day was merged with Children's Day in 1995 to cut back on the number of holidays and thereby curb male drinking.

Commerce

Weekday urban office hours are generally from 9:00 A.M. to 1:00 P.M. and 2:00 to 6:00 P.M., while shops are open from 8:00 A.M. to 8:00 P.M. Offices may open for a half day on Saturday, but shops keep normal hours. Grocery stores have the same hours as shops, but are also often open on Sunday. A large, open market featuring consumer goods, rural crafts, and assorted items operates several days a week on the outskirts of the capital.

SOCIETY

Government

Punsalmaagiin Ochirbat is president and head of state. A prime minister is head of government. Putsagiin Jasray was elected to that post in 1992. Mongolia's 76-seat parliament is called the State Great Hural. All citizens may vote at age 18. The country is divided into 18 provinces and three autonomous cities (Ulaanbaatar, Darhan, and Erdenet).

Economy

Animal husbandry is a key economic pursuit for nearly half of the people. They raise horses, cattle, bactrian camels, sheep, goats, and yaks. Farming is not widespread. A small light industrial base produces animal-skin clothing and building materials. Mongolian goats produce cashmere wool, which has become a valuable export. Mongolia is rich in copper, gold, zinc, tungsten, and silver. In 1994, copper accounted for more than half of all export earnings. In creating a free market, Mongolia must overcome several challenges. For example, while citizens may now own property, people are not sure how to grant land ownership in a traditionally nomadic society. And, while foreign investment is welcomed, many state enterprises continue to operate as if in a socialist market. Still, progress since 1990 has been promising. Inflation has fallen steadily, and is expected to be below 40 percent in 1995. The economy grew by 2.5 percent in 1994. High unemployment remains a serious problem. Mongolia's Human Development Index (0.607) ranks it 102d out of 173 countries. Real gross domestic product per capita is $2,250. Poverty affects one-fourth of all people, and prosperity is still available only to a few. The currency is the Mongolian *tugrik* (Tug).

Transportation and Communication

Paved roads are common in cities, but only about 15 percent of all roads are paved. Cities have buses and trolleys. Cars and trucks are important outside urban areas. Private ownership of cars is limited but increasing. Nearly all international trade and some passenger travel is conducted on the Trans-Mongolian Railway, which connects Ulaanbaatar with Naushki, Russia, and with Erenhot, China. The Mongolian airline provides domestic travel as well as links to Beijing and Moscow.

Telephones are not common. Mail moves slowly. Radio and television stations are government owned, but there are dozens of private newspapers.

Education

The public school system provides free and compulsory education for eight years, beginning at age seven. Two additional years are spent either in general education or vocational training. Mongolia has a literacy rate of over 90 percent because the government takes education to even remote areas. Higher education was once carefully regulated, but it is now being reformed and liberalized.

Health

Free medical care is administered throughout the country by the government. However, doctors tend to concentrate in the capital and other cities. There is a shortage of imported medicines and health care facilities are poorly equipped, especially in rural areas. Maternity and child care are the highest priorities for now. Private insurance and higher quality private clinics (especially dental) are being integrated into the system. The infant mortality rate is 43 per 1,000. Life expectancy averages 64 to 68 years.

FOR THE TRAVELER

A visa and valid passport are required of U.S. citizens. A packaged tour, or hired guide or translator is recommended. Mongolia has many cultural and historical sites of interest, including the "dinosaur graveyard" in the Great Gobi Reserve, the ancient city of Karakorum, the medieval Erdene-Dzuu monastery, and the summer palaces of the Eighth Living Buddha. Boil drinking water. Travelers often pay higher than normal prices. U.S. dollars are often accepted, but only use small bills and coins—no change is given. Personal toiletries and sunscreen may not be available in the country. For more information, contact the Mongolian Society, 322 Goodbody Hall, Indiana University, Bloomington, IN 47045, or the Embassy of Mongolia, 2833 M Street NW, Washington, DC 20007.

A *Culturgram* is a product of native commentary and original, expert analysis. Statistics are estimates and information is presented as a matter of opinion. While the editors strive for accuracy and detail, this document should not be considered strictly factual. It is a general introduction to culture, an initial step in building bridges of understanding between peoples. It may not apply to all peoples of the nation. You should therefore consult other sources for more information.

CULTURGRAM ™ '96

Kingdom of
Morocco

Boundary representations not necessarily authoritative.

BACKGROUND

Land and Climate

Morocco—not including the Western Sahara region, which it claims and administers—is about the size of California. It covers 172,413 square miles (446,550 square kilometers). The Western Sahara has 102,703 square miles (266,000 square kilometers). Spain controls two coastal enclaves (Ceuta and Melilla) in the north. Morocco lies on the northwest corner of Africa and is across the Strait of Gibraltar from Spain. Traversing the middle of the country from north to southwest are two mountain chains: the Middle Atlas and the High Atlas. South of the High Atlas lie the Anti-Atlas mountains, and to the north, along the Mediterranean Sea, runs the Rif Massif range. Most of the country's agriculture is between the mountainous interior and the Atlantic coastal lowlands, into which flow the Oum er Rbia and Tensift rivers. To the south and east of the Atlas chains, the land becomes increasingly arid the closer it gets to the Sahara. The climate varies with the geographic zone and elevation. The coastal north and west have mild winters and pleasant summers, while interior cities experience more extreme temperatures in both seasons. Winters in the mountains are colder and wetter, but summers are cool and nice. Towns closer to the Sahara can be hot in the summer and cool in winter.

History

The earliest known settlers of Morocco were Imazighen (often referred to as the "Berbers"), believed to have come from southwestern Asia. Because of its strategic location, Morocco's history is replete with foreign invasion and rule, beginning with the Phoenicians and continuing with the Romans, Vandals, Visigoths, and Greeks. The Arabs invaded in the seventh century and introduced Islam to Morocco. The Imazighen fought off direct Arab rule and established an independent kingdom in the eighth century. Two powerful Amazigh dynasties prospered until the 13th century, even expanding for a time into other regions. Following other invasions, the Alaouite dynasty, which claims descent from the Prophet Muhammed, took control in the 17th century.

In 1787, Morocco signed a peace and friendship treaty with the United States as one of the first independent nations to recognize the United States as a sovereign nation; the treaty is still in force.

European nations became involved in Morocco in the 19th century, and France made the country a protectorate in 1912. The French ruled until Morocco's independence in 1956, when a constitutional monarchy was established. French and, secondarily, American influence are still strong in Morocco. The current king (in power since 1961) is Hassan II. He is a direct descendant of kings in the Alaouite dynasty that began in 1660.

In 1975, Morocco occupied the Western Sahara following threats of invasion that forced Spain to cede control of their former colony. Morocco began developing the region, but was opposed by its neighbors, particularly Algeria. Some objecting nations supported a rebel group called the Polisario Front. The United States supported Morocco. The ensuing conflict was very expensive and cost many lives. Determined to retain the Western Sahara, Morocco devoted many resources to providing schools, hospitals, roads, and housing to the people of the Sahara.

Negotiations between King Hassan's government and the Polisario guerrillas began in 1989 as part of a UN effort to solve the problem. In 1991, the United Nations agreed to help administer a referendum in the Western Sahara, giving the people a chance to choose annexation by Morocco or independence. A cease-fire went into effect in September 1991, ending 15 years of fighting. The referendum was scheduled for 1992, but was then postponed indefinitely until it could be determined who would be allowed to vote. The Saharan people (Sahrawi) are nomadic, roaming beyond as well as within the borders of Western Sahara; furthermore, many Sahrawi have emigrated to Morocco over the years, clouding issues of eligibility. The United Nations hopes to hold the referendum by early 1996.

THE PEOPLE

Population

The current population is about 28.5 million and is growing annually at 2.3 percent. Morocco's population is composed of three main ethnic groups, the largest being the Imazighen (Berbers) and Arabs. Living throughout the south are the Haratin, descendants of slaves brought up from West Africa. Among the Imazighen are a number of regional groups who call themselves by different names. For instance, people of the Rif refer to themselves as Irifin and people of the High Atlas refer to themselves as Ashilhayn. About half of all people live in urban areas, and urban migration is swelling cities' populations. Casablanca and the metropolitan area of Rabat and Salé account for about 35 percent of Morocco's urban population. More than half the people are younger than age 20. The Western Sahara has an official population of about 206,000, most of whom are ethnic Sahrawis. These are nomadic peoples who live by animal husbandry and subsistence agriculture. Morocco includes them in their official statistics, trade calculations, budgets, and so forth.

Language

The main official language is Arabic, although French also has official status. French is widely used in business, government, and higher education. Moroccan Arabic, called *Derija* (which literally means "dialect"), is the most widely spoken tongue. *Derija* is quite different from the classical Arabic of the *Qur'an* (Koran), the scriptural text of Islam. Amazigh dialects are spoken by the Imazighen peoples, or some 60 percent of the population. Prominent dialects include Tashilhayt (spoken in the High Atlas and Souss valley), Tarifit (spoken in the Rif region), and Tamazight (spoken in the Middle Atlas). Hasaniya, an Arabic dialect, is spoken around Goulmime and south, including in Western Sahara. Spanish can still be heard in the north, which was formerly under Spanish control. English is gaining popularity.

Religion

Islam is the country's official religion. The king is both the political and spiritual leader of his people. All ethnic Moroccans are Muslim. Conversion to another religion is not recognized by the state. Popular religion mixes aspects of various folk beliefs with traditional Islamic practices. Some Christians and Jews live in Morocco, but these peopel generally have European roots. Friday is the Muslim day of worship, when a sermon is spoken at the mosque during the noon prayer. Women are not barred from this activity, but they usually worship at home. Friday is not necessarily a day to close businesses or refrain from work. Muslims believe in a monotheistic God (*Allah*) and a day of judgment. They accept most Biblical prophets, but consider Muhammad to be the last and greatest prophet. Muslims hold that he received *Allah's* revelations through the angel Gabriel and recorded them in the *Qur'an* (Koran). Religion is a matter of daily practice. The five pillars of Islam which Muslims strive to accomplish are to pray five times daily, to profess *Allah* as God and Muhammad as his prophet, to give of their income to help the poor, to fast each day during the month of *Ramadan*, and to make at least one pilgrimage to Makkah, Saudi Arabia.

General Attitudes

Moroccan culture is deeply rooted in Islam. When fortunes turn, people tend to attribute the cause to *Allah*, and the phrase *Insha'allah* (If God wills) is frequently heard. This belief is strongest in rural areas. Urban Moroccans, especially the more educated, do not adhere to it as much. Moroccans value family, honor, dignity, generosity, hospitality, and self-control (particularly of one's temper). A calm attitude gains respect. Women are traditionally restricted to domestic roles, but in urban areas they receive more education and may work outside the home.

Personal Appearance

The national garment is the *djelleba*, a hooded caftan worn by both men and women, except women in rural areas. Although Western-style clothing is becoming more common in Morocco, the *djelleba* is still worn by many. It is important to be neat, well-groomed, and appropriately dressed so one will be treated with respect. When entering a mosque, a Moroccan wears clothing that covers the entire body (except the head and hands); shoes are removed. One does not wear short pants and other recreational attire in public; shorts are reserved for the beach. Visitors should dress conservatively, avoiding low necklines, sleeveless shirts, and short skirts. Women should wear dresses for formal occasions.

CUSTOMS AND COURTESIES

Greetings

Moroccans generally shake hands when greeting each other. One might touch the heart after the handshake to show one's pleasure to see the other person or to show personal warmth. Rural children conventionally kiss the right hand of their parents or elders to show respect when greeting. Westernized people might greet close friends or relatives by brushing or kissing cheeks.

The most common general greeting is *Assalam Oualaikoum* (Peace be upon you), which is used as "hello." *Sbah al Kheir* (Good morning) and *Msa al Kheir* (Good evening) are also used. More formally, one might say *Ahlan Wasahlan* (Pleased to see you). Greetings between friends also include inquiries about each other's well-being and that of their families. Repeated enthusiastic phrases of welcome are often extended to guests. Less fervent greetings might be considered rude. It is polite to greet an acquaintance when passing on an urban street, but people do not greet strangers. In rural areas, most people know one another, so men greet men and women greet women when passing on the street.

Titles are always used in formal situations and to address acquaintances. Friends address each other by first name. Elders might be referred to by a title such as "*hadj*" (an honorable title reserved for those who have completed a pilgrimage to Makkah) or the equivalent of "aunt" or "uncle."

Gestures

Items are passed with the right hand or with both hands, not with the left. It is impolite to point at people and improper to let the bottom of one's foot face a person. Moroccans generally consider it improper to cross their legs. Those that do might cross their legs at the knees, but would not place an ankle over a knee. Raising a hand up is used to hail a taxi.

Visiting

Visiting friends and relatives frequently is considered necessary to maintain relationships. Visiting is most popular on holidays, but may occur at any time. Between family members, it is acceptable to visit unannounced. Whenever possible friends make arrangements in advance. This is less common in rural areas, where telephones are not always available for calling ahead.

Moroccans are warm and gracious hosts. Social visits can last several hours. Guests invited for dinner in urban areas are not expected to take gifts. If they take candy or a small toy for the children, it is appreciated by the hosts. If urban residents visit a relative or friend in a rural area, they are expected to take a gift (staple foods, clothing, household items). Guests invited to a wedding or special event may take gifts for the newlywed couple or person being honored.

Guests are generally offered refreshments, and it is impolite to refuse them. Sometimes, a token refusal is made before accepting the offered item. Milk and dates are served as a sign of hospitality. Guests please their hosts by complimenting them on their home. Men and women do not always socialize together. In rural areas, they more often associate separately, while urban couples will socialize in mixed company. Men also often socialize in public coffee houses, especially on weekends, holidays, or *Ramadan* evenings. At the end of *Ramadan*, heads of households give gifts of money or goods to the poor.

Eating

In most homes, the family eats the main meal of the day together. Before and after eating, each person washes their hands. In rural areas, a basin of water is provided; urban residents just use the sink. Moroccans eat with their fingers from a large communal dish, using the right hand only. Diners eat from the section of the dish directly in front of them.

When guests are present, hosts serve their plates and encourage them to eat as much as they like. If the hosts think the guests have not eaten enough, they will urge them to eat more. In traditional homes, it is impolite for guests to finish eating before the hosts, as this can imply the food did not taste good. Mealtime is an important time for conversation; guests who do not join the discussion embarrass the hosts. In restaurants, service is usually included in the bill, which is usually paid by the host.

LIFESTYLE

Family

Moroccan social life centers around the extended family. One's family is a source of reputation and honor as well as financial and psychological support. It is one's duty to provide financial support to other members of the extended family when it is necessary or requested. The tie between mother and son is the most important relationship. Children are indulged but are also expected to contribute to the family by attaining a respectable position in society. Adult children expect to care for their aging parents when it becomes necessary. Parents do not generally interfere with the domestic or private affairs of their children's families. Polygamy is legal but not frequently practiced. A man may have up to four wives, but he must have permission from any wives he already has and must provide for each equally. Divorce, although frowned upon, is not uncommon.

Dating and Marriage

Dating in the Western sense does not occur in Morocco. In rural areas young men and women often do not meet their mates until they are to be married. Urban couples meet in various situations, ask permission of their parents to marry, and have time to get acquainted before they get married. When a couple is to be married, the man pays the woman's father or eldest brother a sum of money to meet her expenses in the wedding. This sometimes inhibits a man from marrying because he cannot afford to pay the family. Women usually bring a dowry into the marriage. A woman is expected to be a virgin before marriage. Most women are married by their early 20s.

Weddings signify a new union between families and are celebrated as lavishly as possible. A wedding usually lasts two days. The first day is for the bride's female relatives and friends to come together and sing and dance. They decorate the bride's arms and legs with henna dye. On the second day, the groom's family and bride's family meet to celebrate the wedding to show that they are one family.

Diet

Mutton, beef, and chicken are the principal meats eaten in the Moroccan diet. Some sample dishes include *kefta*, ground beef or mutton, seasoned and cooked over charcoal; *tajine*, a meat stew with vegetables; and *harira*, a tomato-based soup with beef or mutton, chickpeas and lentils. Couscous and fish are also common. Coastal Moroccans cook fish in a variety of ways. Mint tea is the national drink. Islam prohibits the consumption of pork and alcohol, and although some men do drink alcohol, it is not entirely socially acceptable.

Recreation

Soccer is by far the most popular sport in Morocco. Morocco's national soccer team competed in the 1994 World Cup. Basketball is also widely enjoyed. Nonathletic forms of recreation include visiting friends, visiting coffee houses (men only), and going to the beach. There are many fine beaches in Morocco, where attire ranges from *djellebas* to bikinis.

Holidays

Each year Muslims observe *Ramadan*, a month of fasting and prayer. During this observance, no eating, drinking, or smoking is permitted from dawn to sunset. In the evenings, families eat together and then visit relatives or friends. Business is slower than usual during this month. Children, pregnant women, travelers, and those with illnesses are exempt from the fast. Foreign visitors are not expected to fast, but they should exercise discretion when eating in public during the day.

Significant holidays include *Aid al Saghir* (the three-day feast at the end of *Ramadan*), *Aid al Kebir* (the feast at the end of the pilgrimage to Makkah), and *Mouloud* (celebrating the birth of Muhammad). Because Muslims use a lunar calendar (28-day months), the dates of these holidays constantly change in relation to the Gregorian calendar. In addition, there are numerous *Moussems* (religious festivals) held throughout the year around the country. Official public holidays include International New Year (1 January), Throne Day (3 March), Youth Day (9 July), Green March Day (6 November), and Independence Day (18 November).

SOCIETY

Government

Morocco is a constitutional monarchy, but King Hassan II has broad powers as head of state. The king names a prime minister and other ministers to run the government, but he retains ultimate executive authority. Members of the *Majlis Nawab* (Chamber of Representatives) are elected partly by direct elections (for 222 seats) and partly by indirect special interest elections (for 111 seats). The special interest groups include political parties, labor unions, and community organizations. There are several parties with relatively equal strength in the legislature. The last elections were in 1993. The voting age is 21.

Economy

Agriculture is the backbone of the economy, employing half the labor force. Most agricultural production is carried out by subsistence farmers, but a small modernized agricultural sector produces food for export. Thirty percent of all export earnings come from agricultural products. Although phosphate, of which Morocco has the world's third largest deposit, has traditionally provided large export earnings, lower world prices have decreased its significance. Still, it accounts for 17 percent of export earnings.

Tourism is growing in importance to the economy. About 15 percent of the labor force works abroad, primarily in Western European countries such as Belgium and France. The money these workers send back to Morocco helps offset the country's foreign debt. A small manufacturing sector is growing and bringing export revenues to the country. The currency is the Moroccan *dirham* (DH).

In an effort to stimulate sluggish economic growth, the government is selling more than 100 state-owned enterprises and encouraging other economic reforms. Unemployment is 16 percent, and low wages prompted strikes and labor unrest in 1995. The country's Human Development Index (0.549) ranks it 111th out of 173 countries. Real gross domestic product per capita is $3,340, which has tripled in the last generation. About 37 percent of the population lives in poverty. These figures indicate that urban residents enjoy an increasingly greater opportunity to earn a decent income but that conditions are not good in rural areas. The upper class holds most of the wealth.

Transportation and Communication

Paved roads connect all major cities and provide access to much of the rest of the country. Public buses and interurban taxis are available throughout the country. Rural people usually walk or ride bicycles or motorcycles to get around. Urban people use the public transit system. Seven airports offer national service. A rail system connects the major cities of the north. The government provides basic telegraph, telephone, and postal services throughout the country. Service is considerably better in urban areas than in rural regions. There are two televisions stations; the government-owned station broadcasts nationwide, while the private station serves major urban areas. Two national radio stations and eight regional stations serve the country as well.

Education

Since the 1980s, the government has devoted considerable resources to improving Morocco's education system. The adult literacy rate, 50 percent, is 15 percent higher than in 1985. Literacy among the youth (ages 15–19) is even higher, reflecting the government's efforts to build schools and train teachers. Still, fewer than two-thirds of all eligible children actually attend school. Girls and rural children are less likely than boys and urban residents to attend school. Of those who begin primary school, about 60 percent go on to secondary school. Preschool offers religious and patriotic instruction. The primary (six years) and secondary (seven years) levels are patterned after the French system; instruction is in Arabic. Students who complete secondary education may seek further education; there are 13 universities and a number of other institutions.

Health

Morocco lacks a comprehensive national health care system, but the Ministry of Health is trying to provide services to every region of the country. Each province has at least one hospital and some clinics, but this does not generally meet the needs of the population. Facilities are severely limited in rural areas. While water in urban areas is usually potable, rural water supplies are not as clean. The infant mortality rate is 49 per 1,000, while life expectancy is between 66 and 70 years.

FOR THE TRAVELER

A valid passport is required, but a visa is not necessary for U.S. travelers staying up to 90 days. No vaccinations are required. Only thoroughly washed and peeled fruits and vegetables should be eaten. Beaches, historical sites, and desert castles are the main attractions in Morocco. For more detailed information on travel opportunities, contact the Moroccan National Tourist Office, 20 East 46th Street, Suite 1201, New York, NY 10017; phone (212) 557–2520. You may also wish to contact the Embassy of Morocco, 1601 21st Street NW, Washington, DC 20009; phone (202) 462–7979.

Kingdom of
Nepal

Boundary representations not necessarily authoritative.

BACKGROUND

Land and Climate

Nepal, a predominantly mountainous and rectangular country, is about the same size as Wisconsin. It covers 54,362 square miles (140,800 square kilometers). The Himalayas in the north contain some of the world's highest peaks; six are higher than 26,000 feet (7,925 meters), including *Sagarmatha* (Mt. Everest). The middle hills comprise the native lands of the famous *Gurkha* foot soldiers and the site of the capital, Kathmandu. To the south lies the Terai, the cultivated fields and subtropical jungles that form the northern rim of the Gangetic Plain. Elevation primarily determines Nepal's climate. While temperatures are fairly moderate around 5,000 feet (1,500 meters), they reach extremes of hot and cold at lower and higher elevations, respectively. Soils and vegetation are also diverse and may vary within a short distance. The cool summers and harsh winters of the north contrast with the subtropical climate of the south. Monsoons from the Indian Ocean bring abundant rainfall to the sub-Himalayan regions between June and September.

History

Various legends surround the ancient history of Nepal. In the sixth century B.C., the *Kirati* (of the *Rai* and *Limbu* tribes) ruled the land. During their reign, Buddha was born in the plains of Nepal. The rule of the *Mallas* (10th–18th centuries) in the Kāthmāndu Valley is known as Nepal's Golden Age of Arts. In 1769, the King of Gorkha, Prithvinarayan Shah, defeated the *Malla* rulers and other principalities to unite the country. An invasion attempt by the British East India Trading Company failed to conquer the infant country in the early 1800s. The British were so impressed with the courage and tenacity of the *Gurkha* soldiers that they accepted Nepal as a sovereign nation; Nepal never became a British colony. In 1846, the first *Rana* took control of the government and became prime minister. The *Ranas* ruled with an iron hand by taking advantage of the young kings.

The Shah monarchs received their sovereignty again when supporters of King Tribhuwan overthrew the *Ranas* in 1951 and brought him to power. Soon after, Nepal was opened to the outside world for the first time. For introducing democratic principles, Tribhuwan is known as the Father of the Nation. There were several unsuccessful experiments with coalition governments and parliaments, but in 1960, King Mahendra inaugurated the *Panchayat Raj* multitiered system of government. This allowed the king to control the government through a partyless system of ministers and a national assembly *(Rastriya Panchayat)*.

Demonstrations for democracy in 1990 led King Birendra, the son of King Mahendra and Nepal's ruler since 1973, to cancel the ban on political parties. He dissolved the *Panchayat* government and allowed an interim one to be formed by representatives of the Congress and Communist parties, along with some nonparty human rights activists. A new constitution was drafted and free elections were held in 1991. The Congress Party received a parliamentary majority in the elections, but the government soon found it difficult to meet high voter expectations. Economic difficulties led to strikes and other unrest in 1993. Elections in 1994 gave the Communists a majority, and Man Mohan Adhikary became prime minister.

THE PEOPLE

Population

Nepal's population is about 21 million and is growing annually at 2.4 percent. To slow the rapid population growth, the government encourages family planning through the mass media. The fertile Kāthmāndu Valley is densely populated. Most people live in rural settlements near water sources; few towns have more than 10,000 inhabitants. Many groups seasonally shift from one elevation to another to take advantage of climatic conditions favorable to cultivation and pasturage. Others, especially in mountainous districts, periodically go to India for temporary employment, to purchase supplies, and to trade goods. Nepal is a very ethnically diverse country. Caste and religion, however, separate the people more fully than race does. About 50 percent of the people are Indo-Aryans. These include the two highest Hindu castes, the *Brahmins* (traditional priests) and *Chetris* (which includes both the ruling Shah dynasty and the untouchable occupational classes). The majority of the Indo-Aryans are of various Tibeto-Burmese groups who have migrated over millennia from the north or east into Nepal; these include the Gurung, Magar, Rai, Limbu, Thakali, and Sherpa, among others. Some other major groups, such as the Newar and Tharu are probably of mixed origin. Indians and Tibetans also live in Nepal.

Language

As many as 20 major languages are spoken with many different dialects. However, Nepali, an Indo-Aryan language related to Hindi, is the official language. The majority of the people speak Nepali to some degree, but more readily use the native tongue of their ethnic group. A growing number of people living in urban areas have some fluency in English. Because many private schools and colleges use English as the medium of instruction, especially at the post-secondary level, the ability to speak English is associated with better education and higher social status.

Religion

Nepal is the only official Hindu state in the world; about 88 percent of the population is Hindu. Except those in the upper castes, Hindus and Buddhists (8 percent of the population) often share the same customs and worship at each other's shrines. Many local animist traditions have also been adopted by the Hindus. Although Muslims (3 percent) do not mix their worship with others, they respect the other religions and are respected by them. There are a few Christians. Proselyting is officially forbidden. Although the Hindu caste system has officially been abolished, it is widely practiced, especially in rural areas.

General Attitudes

Nepalese are religious, family-oriented, and modest people. Physical purity, spiritual refinement, and humility are highly valued. Acceptance of incidents as the will of fate or *karma* (consequences of past deeds) is widespread. The majority of the people believe to some extent that *bhoot* (ghosts), *pret* (evil spirits), *bokshi* (witches), and *graha dasha* (a bad position of the planets) can cause disease in people and livestock. They can also cause crop failures or accidents. Incense, flowers, and foods are offered to pacify the spirits and planets. A rooster or male goat may also be sacrificed. Class consciousness is expressed in the language used to address other persons; class distinctions affect many social relations.

In general, Nepalese believe Westerners are honest, punctual, rational, pragmatic, and fair. At the same time, they have great pride in their own traditions. Westerners are valued as friends because they are good sources of information about the outside world. Until the 1960s, most things from the outside world were called *belayti* (British). After the arrival of U.S. aid programs, however, Westerners and improved crops and livestock generally became known as *amerikane* (American).

Personal Appearance

Although Western-style clothing is most often worn by men, traditional attire is still common for women. Many wear the *sari* (a long, colorful, wraparound dress) and a *cholo* (blouse). Women of Tibetan background wear a wraparound jumper *(bhaku)* and a colorful apron if married. Women in the south and unmarried girls often wear *Punjabi* clothing (colorful pants, tight from the calves down, with a matching tunic that reaches to the knees). Married Hindu women wear a red *tika* (made from vermillion powder) on their foreheads and vermillion powder in the part of their hair to signify that their husbands are alive. Widows do not wear the *tika*, powder, jewelry, or colorful clothing. Proper clothing for a formal situation is important.

CUSTOMS AND COURTESIES

Greetings

Namaste is the traditional greeting. A person places the palms together (fingers up) in front of the chest or chin and says *namaste* (or *namaskar* for superiors). Adults do not *namaste* children. In informal situations, one might raise the right hand in a *salaam* (salute-like) gesture for both greetings and farewells. At formal social gatherings, a guest may be adorned with a *mala* (flower necklace) when greeted. In certain Buddhist communities, a *khada* (white cotton scarf) may be offered instead of a *mala*. The Nepalese do not generally shake hands, although educated men may shake hands with Westerners or each other. In greetings, it is polite to use titles ("Professor," "Doctor," "Director") or the suffix *jee* (or *jye*) with the last name. The Nepalese usually ask permission before taking leave of others.

Gestures

It is rude to touch another person's head or shoulders. Men do not touch women in public. Even physical affection between married couples is reserved for the privacy of the home. However, members of the same sex often express friendship by walking arm in arm or hand in hand. The bottom of one's foot should never point at another person, nor should it be used to move objects. If a person's foot touches another person, immediate apologies are necessary. A person beckons by waving all fingers with the palm down. Other finger gestures, including pointing, are impolite. Parents make a chopping motion with their hand to express anger at their children. If foods or flowers displayed at bazaars are touched, they become impure. A person does not whistle inside a home or at night. Winking at a person of the opposite sex is vulgar. Cows are sacred; a foot may not point at them and they should not be touched. When passing a temple, a *stupa* (Buddhist shrine), or a banyan tree, a person will walk around it (if necessary) to keep it on the right. A person's right side keeps evil spirits at bay and shows veneration for the *stupa*, temple, or tree.

Visiting

Visiting others is an important social custom, and relatives and friends get together as often as possible. Hosts are patient with late-arriving guests because people are more important than schedules. Even if a Nepalese wears a watch, which is common, time is thought of more as a series of events or tied to seasons than as a matter of minutes and hours. Visitors are made welcome in Nepalese homes, even if uninvited or unannounced. Nepalese are warm and hospitable. Some people may be shy about inviting strangers (Nepalese or Westerners) into their homes if the strangers are considered better off than they are. Still, because Hindus believe being kind to strangers can enhance their status in the next life, they will not turn away someone in need.

Tea with sugar and milk is usually offered to guests; it is polite to initially refuse the refreshments before taking them. When entering a home, a Hindu temple, or a Muslim mosque, shoes are always removed. Guests invited to a meal may bring small presents for the children, especially during holidays and for special occasions. Gifts may include food or drinks from guests without a regular income. In general, the right hand is used for eating and for giving or receiving objects. Gifts are not opened at the time they are received. In the southern region, a person stays with his or her own gender group at social gatherings. This is not as prevalent in the north.

Eating

In most homes, men and/or any guests are served first, followed by children; the women eat last. Except in certain northern districts, where chopsticks are used, food is eaten with the hand. Because of the Hindu principle of *jutho* (ritual impurity), food is not shared from the same plate or utensils. When drinking water from a communal container, the lips do not touch the container. Higher caste Hindus are careful that their food is not touched by people outside their caste or religion. Indeed, water cooked or food prepared by any caste lower than one's own is considered *jutho* food, or impure, and it cannot be eaten. At social gatherings involving more than one caste, the Brahmins cook the rice and other food because everyone else is of a lower caste and can eat the meal. Only *roti* (flat bread) can be prepared by a lower caste person. *Jutho* is less important among the Buddhists of the north. When eating out, the person with the higher income insists on paying.

LIFESTYLE

Family

The basic social unit is the family; it takes precedence over the individual. The elderly are respected and cared for by their families. Traditional families are large and include the extended family. In many homes, aunts, uncles, and other relatives with their respective families live together and share the same kitchen. Among the educated, it is increasingly common for sons to set up separate households after marriage rather than live with the extended family. Land is inherited and divided equally between the sons of a family. Women are gaining some property rights. But women, especially among Hindus, generally have few rights or privileges in society. They are responsible for the household and farming (except plowing), and do not socialize in public as much as men. Many

women, mostly those living in urban areas, work outside the home. Rural women are often married before they are 18 years old. They join their husband's extended family at that time and are expected to care for his parents. Some rural men have more than one wife.

Most rural families live in modest two-level houses made of stone and mud with a few small windows. The upper level is used to store food. Houses in the cities are built from bricks, stone, or reinforced concrete. Urban apartment buildings cannot be taller than five stories. Those who live in apartments often share water and bathroom facilities with others. In the south, where the caste system is most dominant, a wide disparity separates the few who live in mansions and the many who live in thatched huts.

Dating and Marriage

Customs regarding marriage vary among the different castes. Traditional marriages are arranged by parents, although sometimes with the consent of the marriage partners. Marriage is sacred, divine, and considered to endure beyond death. Conventional dating and divorce are rare. For the Nepalese, *sat* (chastity) is the most important virtue a woman can bring to a marriage. Sherpas might live together before getting married. Weddings are times of great celebration and feasting. They are expensive and may last up to three days. In Terai, the southern region, a dowry is common.

Diet

Diet varies according to region. Rice with lentil soup and vegetable curry are the main dishes of people living in urban areas or rural upper classes. Many high-caste people are vegetarian or only eat goat meat. Muslims do not eat pork. The middle castes eat goat or chicken when they are available; some eat water buffalo. Hindus do not eat beef; the 1990 constitution makes it a crime to kill a cow. Meat is usually not consumed more than a few times a month and then in small quantities. Larger quantities are eaten only at festivals. Sherpas and Tibetans eat more meat than other groups. Fruits and vegetables are used in season; fruits are considered a snack or dessert.

Millet and corn are staples for most Nepalese, although rice is a staple in the *Terai*. *Roti* may be prepared with different grains. Wheat is preferred as the best, but a Brahmin will also eat a corn *roti*. Millet and buckwheat are more often eaten by poorer people. Hill people eat mush (*dedo*) made of cornmeal, millet, or buckwheat.

Recreation

Several movie theaters in Kāthmāndu show films from India. American movies are not allowed in theaters. Many upper and middle-class families have televisions and VCRs. Video theaters created by families in both large cities and small towns show up to three movies a day to local people. In rural areas, people most often provide their own entertainment. Nepal is a country of many festivals and celebrations. People sing and dance on such occasions, and the men play cards. Popular sports include soccer, volleyball, and badminton. Many adults consider games and sports only for children.

Holidays

Nepal has its own calendar *(Bikram Samvat),* with the new year in mid-April. But dates for religious holidays and festivals are based on the phases of the moon. *Dashain* (two weeks in September–October) celebrates the inevitable triumph of virtue over the forces of evil; it is a time of gift giving, family gatherings, feasts, and rituals performed for the Goddess of Victory. During *Tihar* (three days in October–November), rows of lights are displayed on every building in worship of the Goddess of Wealth. *Tihar* provides married women a time to go home to their parents, receive special treatment, ritually purify themselves, and pray for sons. Sons are special because they stay near the mother (and are not married off into another household, as are women) and can care for her in her old age. *Holi* (February–March) is a lively social event during which people drink heavily, dance in the streets, and throw colorful powders on each other. *Bhoto Jatra* (April–May) is a great festival attended by the king and queen. The birthdays of the King (28 December) and Queen (8 November) are also celebrated. Christmas (25 December) is an official holiday. On the full moon of the month *Baisakh* (April–May), the day Buddha was born, the day he was enlightened, and the day he passed into nirvana are commemorated.

Commerce

Business hours are generally from 10:00 A.M. to 5:00 P.M. Sunday through Friday. Open air markets have different hours and may operate on varying days throughout the country.

SOCIETY

Government

Nepal is a constitutional monarchy. King Birendra is the chief of state, but the prime minister runs the government. Parliament comprises a 60-member upper house (National Council) and 205-seat lower house (House of Representatives); only members of the House are elected by the people. The House appoints 50 members of the Council, and the king appoints 10. The voting age is 18.

Economy

Agriculture is the mainstay of the economy. It provides employment for 93 percent of the labor force. Including forestry, agriculture accounts for a major portion of Nepal's export earnings. Jute and rice are the major export crops. Most rural farmers have virtually no cash income. Due to lack of capital and technology, most people living in urban areas are economically dependent on agrarian enterprises. Existing industrial activity usually focuses on processing agricultural goods. Tourism is the second most important industry.

The incomes of more than four million Nepalese working in India, including the *Gurkha* soldiers, are a major support to the economy. Private trade across the Indian border helps bring needed goods into Nepal. While unemployment is relatively low, underemployment (where workers do not work full-time or where they work at levels below their skills) may be as high as 40 percent. Inflation is around 30 percent.

One of the poorest countries in the world, Nepal's real gross domestic product per capita is $1,130. The country's Human Development Index (0.289) ranks it 149th out of 173 countries. Sixty percent of all people live in poverty, and income distribution is skewed toward higher castes. Most people are not wage earners. The eastern and central regions are more developed and affluent than western regions. The currency is the Nepalese *rupee* (NR).

Transportation and Communication

All major transportation facilities are owned by the state. Roads are better and more numerous in the south. Most people travel by foot or bicycle. Buses are available in some areas. Animals are often used to pull carts. Few people own cars. There is a state domestic airline, as well as a few smaller private airlines. Traffic travels on the left side of the road. Telephones are used only in urban areas; international links are fairly good. Radio Nepal serves most of the country and Nepal Television broadcasts to most of the population. The official newspaper, *The Rising Nepal,* is available in Nepali and English.

Education

Primary school education is free. The government pays teacher salaries at this level but only subsidizes wages (between 50 and 75 percent) at higher levels of education. Even though education is a major concern for the country (more than 85 percent of children are enrolled in primary school), facilities are often inadequate. In rural areas, girls generally leave school by age 12 to care for younger siblings or to help the family farm its land. Secondary school students must pay fees that are often too expensive for villagers. These schools are only located in larger towns, less accessible to villagers. The literacy rate is 26 percent, but for women it is only 13 percent. The government is seeking to reform the system to provide better instruction and better access. Tribhuwan University in Kāthmāndu is the main university; branch campuses operate in other urban centers. Mahendra Sanskrit University is the only other university.

Health

Despite a high infant mortality rate (83 per 1,000) and a relatively low life expectancy (52 years), health conditions have improved in Nepal in recent years. Health services are slowly expanding. Still, water is not potable and diseases such as meningitis, typhoid, and hepatitis are widespread. Hospitals are not well equipped and many people turn to traditional healers rather than go to a hospital.

FOR THE TRAVELER

U.S. citizens need a visa and valid passport to travel to Nepal. A tourist visa is only good for travel in certain areas and permission must be obtained for more extensive travel, especially for mountain climbing. Hiking is a common way to tour Nepal, but the U.S. State Department recommends visitors register with the U.S. Embassy in Kāthmāndu before embarking. Travelers may wish to call (202) 647–5225 for travel advisories. Immunizations are recommended for the diseases mentioned above. For more information, call the U.S. Centers for Disease Control International Travel Hotline at (404) 332–4559. For information regarding travel opportunities, send a self-addressed envelope to the Royal Nepalese Embassy, 2131 Leroy Place NW, Washington, DC 20008; phone (202) 667–4550.

Printed on recycled paper

Commonwealth of

New Zealand

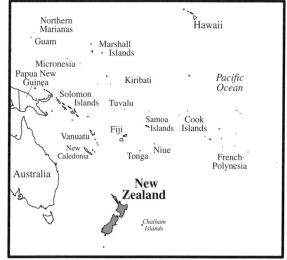

Boundary representations not necessarily authoritative.

BACKGROUND

Land and Climate

New Zealand is about the same size as Colorado. It covers 103,737 square miles (268,680 square kilometers). The mountainous island nation lies in the South Pacific, about 1,000 miles (1,610 kilometers) southeast of Australia. The two principal landforms are North Island and South Island. The smaller Stewart Island is south of South Island. There are also numerous other small islands, mostly uninhabited. The more populous North Island has fertile agricultural land, the largest man-made forest in the southern hemisphere, and a few isolated snowcapped volcanoes. It also boasts hot springs, mud pools, and geysers in its thermal region.

On the South Island, the Southern Alps provide magnificent scenery and opportunities for sports such as snow skiing. There are many glaciers, lakes, and rivers. On the southwest coast are fjords that rival those of Norway. The coastal lowlands are also used for agriculture. Both islands have many sandy beaches. The climate is temperate, with plenty of sunshine, adequate rainfall, and few extremes in weather. In the winter, however, particularly in the south, high humidity makes it seem rather cold, even though average winter temperatures rarely go below 40°F (4°C). Summer highs average about 73°F (23°C). The seasons are the reverse of those in the northern hemisphere. January is in the middle of summer and July is in the middle of winter.

History

Maori migrations from Polynesian islands to New Zealand probably began around A.D. 900. The period of the so-called "Great Migration" of the Maoris is recorded in the 13th and 14th centuries. Dutch explorer Abel Tasman discovered New Zealand in 1642 but did not go ashore; he called the islands *Staten Landt.* The name was later changed by Dutch geographers to the Dutch term for New Zealand *(Nieuw Zeeland)*—named after the Dutch province of Zeeland. The Dutch never returned. The next European to visit (1769) was Captain James Cook of England.

In 1840, the Maoris ceded sovereignty to the British in return for legal protection and rights to perpetual ownership of Maori lands. Only the Crown could buy land from the Maoris; an individual settler could not. Colonization proceeded rapidly. By 1852, Britain granted internal self-government provincial parliaments governed the area. Central administration was established in 1877, and New Zealand became an independent dominion within the British Commonwealth in 1907. New Zealand made valiant contributions in both World Wars. After World War II, New Zealand turned its focus from European ties to Pacific ties, developing trade links with growing Asian economies. By the 1990s, with Europe integrating on its continent, New Zealand began to debate the value of remaining within the Commonwealth. Many government officials argued that retaining the British Queen

OCEANIA

as nominal head of state hindered New Zealand from becoming a fully independent nation. In 1994, the government announced its intention to cut formal ties with Britain within the next several years. Many New Zealanders favor the move in the future, but would not support it today.

When Prime Minister David Lange resigned in 1989 for health and personal reasons, an interim prime minister was named. In 1990, Jim Bolger was elected prime minister. He promised to improve ties with the United States and strengthen the economy. Parliamentary elections were held in 1993 and Bolger narrowly maintained his post.

THE PEOPLE

Population

The population of New Zealand is 3.5 million, growing annually at 0.6 percent. The people are principally of two cultural and ethnic backgrounds: 88 percent are of European (mostly British) descent, and about 9 percent are Maori, the native New Zealanders. The Maoris are Polynesians. Close to 3 percent are other Polynesians, mostly from Tonga, Samoa, and the Cook Islands in New Zealand. Most of these new Polynesians migrated to the country after 1946. Immigration from Pacific islands and Asia is rising and is expected to increase further, especially as people wishing to avoid the Chinese control of Hong Kong, scheduled to take place in 1997, search for a new home.

Language

English and Maori are the official languages of New Zealand. Almost all Maoris speak English. The Maori language is used primarily for Maori ceremonies or other special occasions. Many Maori words have been adopted into English. For example, a *Kiwi* is a New Zealander and a white person is a *Pakeha* (a Maori word meaning fair skinned). There are also English words or phrases used in New Zealand that are not common in the United States. For example, the trunk and hood of a car are called the *boot* and *bonnet*, respectively. Other examples include *come around* (come over), *over the road* (across the street), *pop downtown* (go downtown), and *go to the loo* (go to the bathroom). A *bathroom* is a place to take a bath, *lift* is an elevator, and *petrol* is gasoline.

Religion

Most residents of New Zealand (81 percent) are Christians. There is no state religion, but the Anglican Church has considerable influence (comprising about 25 percent of all Christians). Presbyterians, Roman Catholics, and Methodists are some of the other Christian groups represented in New Zealand. About 1 percent of the people are Hindu or Buddhist. Most of the rest of the population either does not affiliate with a religion or has not specified a particular belief. Church attendance is highest on religious holidays.

General Attitudes

New Zealanders are open, friendly, and hospitable. Their lifestyle is somewhat more relaxed and informal than that in the United States. For example, while a U.S. citizen might discuss occupations, incomes, and career objectives with colleagues, a New Zealander is more apt to discuss leisure activities and family interests. New Zealanders are, on the whole, self-reliant, practical people. They are noted do-it-yourselfers and love to work around their homes and gardens. They are very proud of their country and values.

The Maoris are also proud of their Polynesian heritage and culture, which emphasize humility, truth, and a strong sense of community. While many Maoris have been integrated into Westernized society, they retain roots to their land and ethnic group. Although they are guaranteed the same rights as the *Pakeha*, some Maoris assert that they are often neglected by the government. Indeed, race relations were tense in 1995 as Maoris protested a government plan to limit the scope of a land settlement dispute with the Maoris. In the 1800s, white farmers began confiscating Maori lands. Maoris seek their return or fair compensation, but the government has stated that financial compensation cannot exceed a certain amount and some land rights or access to natural resources may not be restored. The Maoris further seek greater autonomy on their lands, which the government is willing to negotiate. But many people in New Zealand oppose giving the Maoris a sort of separate sovereignty within the country.

Personal Appearance

Western-style clothing is the standard. The Maoris have a variety of traditional costumes worn for ceremonies and cultural events. A neat, clean appearance is important in public.

CUSTOMS AND COURTESIES

Greetings

Greetings in New Zealand range from American-style openness and Maori graciousness to formal British reserve, depending on the person and circumstance. General informal greetings include the New Zealand version of "Good day" (pronounced GID-DAY) or a simple "Hello" or "Hi." After an initial introduction, most people use first names with each other. New Zealanders greet each other with a handshake. Gentlemen usually wait for a woman to offer her hand first in formal situations. Among the Maori, people may also greet each other with a hug or the traditional *hongi*—pressing the noses together with eyes closed and making a low "mm-mm" sound. The *hongi* is not used with non-Maoris except in a *marae* (Maori community center).

Gestures

Waving at a friend is a sign of recognition, but it is more popular to raise both eyebrows in the direction of the person. The mouth is covered if a yawn cannot be suppressed. Chewing gum or using a toothpick in public are considered inappropriate. New Zealanders don't like to stand too close or touch each other during conversation. On a full bus, a man usually gives his seat to an older woman. Children usually give theirs to adults, unless they have paid the full fare.

Visiting

Entertaining in the home is popular and common, even more so than in the United States. New Zealanders enjoy cooking, and therefore like to have friends over for dinner. Summer barbecues in the garden are especially popular and are usually held on weekends. Guests are expected to feel at home. They often remove their shoes unless told otherwise by the hosts. Dinner guests do not arrive empty-handed, but almost always take a gift. Wine (good, but not too expensive) is appropriate if the hosts enjoy it, but flowers, a potted plant, or a box of nice chocolates are also acceptable gifts. House guests should always leave a gift with their host family.

Dropping by unannounced is quite common, although such visits after 8:00 P.M. are not appropriate. Inviting people for afternoon tea (around 3:00 P.M.) is also popular. Hosts take out the best tablecloth, cups, and saucers, and serve fairly substantial refreshments—enough to be considered a meal by some.

Even when not invited for tea or a meal, guests are nearly always offered refreshments. It is rude not to at least offer something to drink. Indeed, even a repairman that is staying more than a few minutes would be offered—and would probably accept—a drink. Common refreshments include coffee, tea, soft drinks, finger sandwiches, cakes, and cookies.

Eating

New Zealanders eat in the continental style, with the fork in the left hand and the knife remaining in the right. When finished with a meal, a person places the utensils parallel on the plate. If they are not parallel, one is not considered finished. Coffee is often served at the end of a meal, especially in restaurants. Hands should be kept above the table. Dinner is the main meal of the day, eaten around 6:00 or 7:00 P.M. Dessert is often included. A light supper is sometimes served in the late evening. When dining out, the dinner hour is closer to 8:00 P.M. In a fine restaurant, the staff consider it their job to let diners take their time. They do not hurry unless requested. At restaurants, people are generally quiet and do not speak too loudly. Ice is not served with drinks, and water is only served on request. New Zealanders do not practice tipping because wages are considered the duty of the employer, not the customers. Waiters and waitresses earn a decent salary and do not expect tips.

LIFESTYLE

Family

Among those of European origin, the average family is a husband, a wife, and two children. However, there is an increasing number of *solo mums*—unmarried or divorced women with children. The state recognizes common-law marriages. An increasing number of women participate in the work force (accounting for nearly 40 percent of all workers), so it is not uncommon for both parents to work.

Home ownership is very important, and most families own their homes. Gardens are a common feature. Among the Polynesians, extended family connections are important. In some cases, three or four generations live together in one house. In Maori villages, the *marae* is important in binding families together. Ceremonies, important meetings, and recreational activities take place at the *marae*.

Dating and Marriage

Although most New Zealand parents restrict one-to-one dating until their children are 16 or 17, group social activities usually begin around age 14. The youth enjoy going to movies, dancing, and having parties. Common for older teenagers is going with a group of friends to the local pub for dancing and drinking. Couples usually marry when they are in their early or mid-twenties. Many choose to live together before or instead of marriage. After a wedding, a sit-down meal and a dance are traditional for wedding guests.

Diet

The New Zealand diet has traditionally been British, with hearty breakfasts and heavy meals of meat and potatoes. While the standard fare is not disappearing, it is being modified to reflect a more heath-conscious population. Seafood and fresh vegetables play a greater role than in the past. Red meat is eaten less often and portions are smaller. Beef, pork, and mutton are still common, as is fish, but poultry (still fairly expensive) is gaining popularity. Fruits are plentiful. Meat pies and sausage rolls (sausage wrapped in pastry) are popular, as are fish and chips. *Vegemite* (yeast extract) is used as a bread spread. New Zealanders believe their cheeses and ice cream are among the best in the world.

A favorite Maori dish is the *hangi*, a combination of meat, potatoes, *kumara* (sweet potatoes), carrots, and other vegetables all cooked in wire racks lined with cabbage leaves. The dish is simmered for hours in the ground.

Recreation

New Zealanders love sports. Rugby is the most popular sport in the winter, followed by soccer. Cricket is the favorite activity during the summer. Girls and women favor netball. Tennis, lawn bowling, and *athletics* (track and field) are also enjoyed in the summer. Since no area is far from the mountains, sea, or rivers, there are many opportunities for mountaineering, *tramping* (hiking), fishing (both deep-sea and freshwater), hunting (on a limited basis), swimming, walking, jogging, and sailing. New Zealanders work hard, but they also enjoy their leisure time. They spend considerable time outdoors, playing sports, gardening, or fixing up their homes. Gardening is one of the most popular leisure activities. People take pride in growing produce that often becomes part of the weekend barbecue.

Holidays

The official public holidays of New Zealand include New Year's (1 and 2 January—an extra day to finish off or continue a summer vacation), Waitangi Day (6 February), Easter (including Friday), Anzac (25 April), Queen Elizabeth II's Birthday (first Monday in June), Labor Day (fourth Monday in October), Christmas, and Boxing Day (26 December). Boxing Day comes from the British tradition where service workers or the poor were given small boxed gifts on the day after Christmas. It is now used to visit and relax. Waitangi Day marks the occasion in 1840 when Great Britain signed the treaty with the Maoris. Anzac honors the armed forces of the nation. In addition, each provincial district has an Anniversary Day, commemorating the founding of the province.

Commerce

Normal shopping and business hours are from 9:00 A.M. to 5:30 P.M., Monday through Thursday and from 9:00 A.M. to 9:00 P.M. on Friday. Many shops are open on Saturday, and corner *dairies* (convenience stores) stay open late seven days a week. Some stores are open on Sunday, but this is a relatively new practice. Government offices are open from

9:00 A.M. to 5:00 P.M., and banks are open until 5:00 P.M. on weekdays.

SOCIETY

Government

New Zealand is a parliamentary democracy within the Commonwealth. As such, it recognizes Britain's Queen Elizabeth II as head of state. She is represented in the country by a governor general (Dame Catherine Tizard). The head of government is the prime minister, who is also the leader of the majority party or majority coalition in parliament. Members of the cabinet are also chosen from Parliament. The 99-seat legislature is technically called the House of Representatives, but is referred to as Parliament. New Zealand is divided into 93 counties, 9 districts, and 3 towns. The two major political parties are the National Party and the New Zealand Labor Party. Prime Minister Bolger leads the National Party. The voting age is 18.

Economy

New Zealand has a modern industrialized economy. But while only about 10 percent of the population is employed in agriculture, New Zealand's international trade depends heavily on the sector. The most important exports include wool, lamb, mutton, beef, fruit, fish, and cheese. New Zealand is the world's largest exporter of wool. Exports to Asia are increasing. Important industries include food processing, textiles, machinery, and wood and paper products.

The country's Human Development Index (0.907) ranks it 18th out of 173 nations. Real gross domestic product per capita is $13,970, which has almost doubled during the last generation. These figures reflect New Zealand's growing prosperity. Most people earn enough to meet basic needs and there is a strong middle class. However, the poorest 40 percent of all households only earn 17 percent of the nation's income, indicating that many people lack access to economic opportunities. Economic growth for 1994 was 3 percent.

Inflation is low, but unemployment (9 percent) remains a problem, especially for the Maori minority. Real unemployment is probably higher, but when one spouse has a job, the other cannot register as unemployed. Prices and wages, once controlled by the government, were deregulated in 1985. A free-trade agreement with Australia, called Closer Economic Relations (CER), took effect in 1990 and has made Australia New Zealand's biggest trade partner. The currency is the New Zealand dollar (NZ$).

Transportation and Communication

A private car is the preferred mode of transportation, although many people in the major cities ride a bus to work. All major cities have good bus systems. Trains and a domestic airline also operate between cities and industrial centers. Many people use bicycles for short-distance transportation. Ferries sail regularly between the two main islands, carrying passengers and cars. The communications system is excellent, providing efficient domestic and international service. There are several television stations in addition to many radio stations.

Education

Education is free and compulsory between ages six and fifteen. Many enter school at age five, but preschools and kindergartens are available for younger children. Secondary education begins at about age 13. Secondary school students wear uniforms. Many high schools are segregated by sex. About half of all students continue two years after the compulsory requirements to finish high school (also called college). Rigorous state exams are given in the third and fifth years of high school. There are six universities administrated and financed by the government. Recent policy changes have led to the requirement that university students pay part of their tuition. There is an excellent system of technical education for those students who want to learn trades for which a university degree is not required. Continuing and vocational education opportunities are also available. The literacy rate is 99 percent.

Health

A comprehensive social security program covers the aged, disabled, sick, and unemployed. A public health care system, maintained through taxes, formerly served all citizens, but it became unable to meet many needs. As a private system emerged to fill the gap (mostly in nonemergency care), government policy changed. Public hospitals serve the poor and needy, while income earners are expected to carry private insurance. Private hospitals receive some government subsidies. Medical facilities are generally good and readily available. The infant mortality rate is 9 per 1,000. Life expectancy ranges between 72 and 80 years.

FOR THE TRAVELER

U.S. citizens do not need a visa for stays of up to three months, but a valid passport and proof of sufficient funds are required. Proof of a return ticket is also necessary. There are no vaccinations required. Water is potable. New Zealand offers beautiful scenery and a variety of vacation ideas. For travel information, contact the New Zealand Tourism Board, 501 Santa Monica Boulevard, Suite 300, Santa Monica, CA 90401; phone (800) 388–5494. You may also wish to contact the Embassy of New Zealand, 37 Observatory Circle NW, Washington, DC 20008; phone (202) 328–4800.

Republic of
Niger

SAHARA DESERT

AÏR MOUNTAINS

TAL DESERT

• Agadez

SAHEL

Niger

• Tahoua
Dogondoutchi
• Maradi • Zinder
★ Birni Diffa
NIAMEY Nkonni
• Dosso

N'guigmi

Lake Chad

Algeria Libya Egypt
Mauritania Mali **Niger** Chad Sudan
Burkina Lake Chad
Faso
Ivory Nigeria
Coast
Liberia Ghana Togo Benin Cameroon Central African Republic
Equatorial Guinea Gabon
Congo Zaire
Atlantic Ocean Angola Zambia
Namibia Botswana
South Africa

Boundary representations not necessarily authoritative.

BACKGROUND
Land and Climate

Niger, a landlocked country three times larger than California, covers 489,189 square miles (1,267,000 square kilometers). Four-fifths of it is part of the Sahara desert, which continues to grow. The Aïr Mountains are located in the Sahara in Niger's northern region. The Tal Desert is in the far east. Desertification and the growing Sahara are causing severe problems in Niger; droughts occur more frequently and last longer than in the past.

Southern Niger is part of Africa's semiarid region called the Sahel. This receives rain and supports scrub brush and baobab trees. All of Niger's farming is done in the Sahel or near desert oases. The Niger river flows near Niamey, making the southwest the most fertile region. Niger is one of the hottest countries in the world, with average daily temperatures above 90°F (32°C) during the hottest months. There are two hot seasons, one before and one after the rainy season (June–September). From November to February, harmattan winds blow sand off the desert and cool temperatures somewhat.

History

Nomads traversed the area of Niger more than 5,000 years ago, but little is known of their history. Tuaregs entered Niger (pronounced nee–ZHARE) from the north in the 11th century and established a sultanate in Agadez by the 15th century, although the area had been inhabited by other people for thousands of years. Niger served as an important trading crossroads for mighty African empires, including the Songhai Empire of Gao in the 16th century. Even today, Tuareg caravans continue to carry salt across the desert. In the 17th century, Djermas settled as farmers near present-day Niamey. Hausaland (southern Niger and northern Nigeria) became the site of a *jihad* (Muslim holy war) by the Fulanis in the early 19th century, which helped ensure Islam's presence in Niger.

Despite strong resistance by all local ethnic groups (especially the Tuaregs) to French military incursions between 1890 and 1900, Niger became a French colony in 1922. The French moved the capital from Zinder to Niamey in 1926, and that small fishing village grew rapidly to hold nearly a half of million people today. In the late 1950s, a fierce political struggle ensued among Nigeriens over independence from France, which was finally granted in 1960. Niger was led by President Hamani Diori until a coup on 15 April 1974, when General Seyni Kountche assumed power as head of the Supreme Military Council. Kountche is generally credited with leading a regime marked by political stability and lack of corruption. A 1984 drought hit Niger hard, and Kountche was forced to negotiate for massive food aid after several years of near self-sufficiency.

After Kountche's death in 1987, the Supreme Military Council continued to govern with General Ali Saibou at its head. Presidential elections were held in 1989, but only Saibou and members of his party were on the ballot. Ethnic and student unrest, as well as general discontent throughout the country, led to increased tension between the government and citizens. In 1991, a national conference appointed an interim prime minister, leaving Saibou with only token powers. A High Council of the Republic was also chosen to run the country until 1993 elections restored civilian rule under a new constitution.

The civilian government, headed by Mahamane Ousmane, proved unstable. A deteriorating economy, ethnic rebellions, and the defection of the prime minister's party (Nigerian Party for Democracy and Socialism) from the governing coalition weighed heavily on the young democracy. Ousmane appointed a new prime minister, but parliament gave him a vote of no-confidence. Parliament was then dissolved in 1994 ahead of elections in January 1995. The National Movement of the Development Society party won a majority, and Ousmane appointed one of its members to be prime minister.

THE PEOPLE

Population

Niger's population of 8.9 million is growing at 3.3 percent annually. About 56 percent of the population is Hausa. Other major groups include the Djerma (22 percent), Fulani (9), Tuareg (8), Kanouri (4), Toubou, and Gourmantche. Djermas live mostly in the southwest around Niamey, the capital and largest city. The Hausa are located mainly around Zinder (88,000 people), although Hausaland actually stretches east nearly to Lake Chad and west nearly to Dosso. The Tuareg and Fulani tend to be semi-nomadic, though many Tuaregs can be found near Agadez and throughout the north. For years, the light-skinned Tuaregs waged a violent rebellion against several African states, claiming repression from black African rule. Although the Tuareg goal of an independent state has not been realized, a peace accord was signed with Niger in April 1995 and all combatants were granted amnesty.

Language

French is the official language, although only about 10 percent of Nigeriens speak it. Most can speak Hausa, which is used for communication between ethnic groups. Ten languages have official recognition in Niger: Arabic, Boudouma, Djerma, Fulfulde, Gourmantchema, Hausa, Kanouri, Tamachek, Tasawak, and Toubou. Many people are multilingual.

Religion

More than 90 percent of Nigeriens are Muslim. They accept major Biblical prophets but believe Muhammad was the last and greatest prophet. The *Qur'an* (Koran) or scripture of Islam, is composed of revelations from *Allah* (God) to Muhammad. Muslims show devotion by praying five times daily while facing Makkah, giving money to the poor, fasting during daylight hours for the month of *Ramadan* (*Azumi* in Hausa), professing there is no God but *Allah*, and trying to make a once-in-a-lifetime pilgrimage (*hajj*) to Makkah. Men visit the mosque on Friday afternoon to pray and worship. Women who go to mosque pray in a different area, but most pray at home or in the fields. Children memorize Arabic verses written with charcoal on wooden boards at local Qur'anic schools. Animist practices exist, primarily in villages, and are often mixed with Islamic rites. A few larger cities have Christian churches.

General Attitudes

Nigeriens patiently accept life as it comes. They often end sentences with *Inshallah* (Arabic for "God willing") to indicate things are out of their control. This allows them to be stoic in the face of frequent hardships. But they laugh often and rarely display real anger in public, especially when it involves personal matters. Time is flexible; waiting is a fact of life. Events and appointments do not necessarily begin on time. People tend to identify with their family, village, ethnic group, and religion before any political party or the nation.

Gender roles are rigidly defined. Women do all the work of the home, such as making flour, collecting firewood, going to the market, drawing each day's water from the well, and caring for the children. Both men and women work in the fields.

Personal Appearance

It is impossible to describe a "typical" Nigerien because of the diverse ethnic and social groups. While an urban professional may wear a suit and carry a briefcase, a village male might wear a long robe and carry a sword. Urban men also wear *boubous* (long robes) or a shirt and pant "suit" of matching material. Most men wear a hat. Tuareg men wear large green or indigo turbans that cover the entire head except the eyes, while Tuareg women reveal the whole face. Fulanis often wear long black robes and plastic shoes. Formal dress for men usually includes *boubous* with extensive embroidery. Men and women of many ethnic groups have distinct facial scars or tattoos; these are often applied to newborns and then discolored over time to make them stand out.

Women often wear a *pagne*, a colorful cloth wrapped as a skirt or made into a blouse. Married women drape an extra *pagne* around their shoulders, and may use it to carry children on their backs. Most women wear some makeup (especially eyeliner), earrings, other jewelry, and head scarves. Women elaborately braid their hair, while men usually keep their hair short. Adults dress as neat, clean, and modest as possible.

CUSTOMS AND COURTESIES

Greetings

Before any conversation, it is important to exchange greetings, which usually include inquiries about a person's health, family, work, and the weather. The greeting depends on the season and time of day. For example, in Hausa, *Ina kwana* (How did you sleep?) is appropriate in the morning, but in the afternoon *Ina oni* (How did you pass the day?) is used. A response to either is *Lahiya lau* (In health). Responses are always positive; only after the greeting is over is it appropriate to admit to illness or bad times.

Nigerien men shake hands upon meeting and saying goodbye. The handshaking may continue for several minutes, until all greetings are exchanged. To show special respect, one might touch the upper chest with his right hand and return to the handshake. It is polite to shake the hand of every adult at a small gathering. For large groups, one raises the hands to chest level, palms out, and gives a verbal greeting. Traditional Muslim men do not shake hands with women. Some urban Nigeriens may greet with a kiss to each cheek. In the east, Kanouris greet by shaking a closed fist at head level and calling *Wooshay! Wooshay!* (Hello! Hello!).

People are generally addressed by title, which is often job related. A taxi driver, for example, would be called *mai mota* (person with the car). It is respectful to address the elderly as *tsohoua* (old woman) or *tsohou* (old man). Any Muslim who makes a pilgrimage to Makkah, Saudi Arabia, earns the title of *el hadj* for men or *hadjera* for women.

Gestures

It is impolite to use the left hand alone for gestures or eating because it is reserved for personal hygiene. Both hands are used together to pass or receive an object. Flicking the five fingers out in an open-handed gesture is insulting. To indicate "five," one brings all the fingertips of the hand together. To beckon, one waves the fingers of the right hand, palm facing down. One can also get a person's attention by snapping the fingers or hissing. Students snap rather than raise their hands to signal the teacher. A loud snap can be produced by shaking the hand so the index finger snaps against the middle finger. One can point by puckering the lips in the indicated direction.

It is improper for men and women to hold hands in public or otherwise display their affection. However, it is common for male friends to hold hands. To indicate approval or agreement, Nigeriens make a clicking sound deep in the throat. Traditionally, only people of equal social standing make extended eye contact. Younger people look down to show respect.

Visiting

Visiting someone's home is a sign of respect. Invitations are rarely issued; people are expected to drop in. Guests are offered the best seat and then something to drink. A large bowl of water for everyone to drink from may be presented. Guests remove shoes when entering a home or sitting on a mat. Gifts are necessary if the visitor stays the night. *Goro* (kola nuts), peanuts, onions, fruit, or soap are common gifts.

Tea is an important visiting custom for Tuaregs, Fulanis, and others. There are at least three rounds of tea. Sugar and mint are added each time to make the strong tea progressively sweeter. To describe the three rounds, Nigeriens use the phrase "Strong like life, subtle like friendship, sweet like love." Made in small, blue teapots over coals, the tea is served in very small cups. It is impolite to leave before all rounds are finished. After a visit, it is polite for the host to accompany guests to the door of the house or compound or even to walk them home.

Eating

Meals are generally served in a communal bowl and eaten with the right hand or a spoon. Nigeriens generally drink after, not during, the meal. The main meal, which may be in the afternoon or evening, often consists of millet paste and a spicy sauce. Rural men and women eat separately, sitting on woven mats. Urban men and women eat together at a table. An urban breakfast may consist of bread and coffee, but a rural breakfast is generally leftovers from the day before. Snacks eaten throughout the day include peanuts, sugarcane, dates, fruit, or candy. People also chew kola nuts.

Restaurants vary from a table on a street corner to expensive outdoor restaurants in large cities. Women usually prepare food sold on the street, but only men eat in public. Men selling cooked meat walk through the cities, balancing a tray on their heads. They also sell bread and coffee on street corners in the morning. Women sit by open fires making *kosai*, a deep-fried bean cake, or doughnut-like *beignets*.

LIFESTYLE

Family

The family structure dominates Nigerien culture. Children must respect their parents. Older people are highly honored and must be obeyed by younger ones. It is common for the elderly to live with their adult children. Children are seen as belonging to the entire community and they may be disciplined by neighbors or friends. Wealthier persons are expected to share with and help the extended family.

The husband is the head of the family. Muslim men may have up to four wives, and animists can take more. Each wife has her own section within a walled family compound. The husband has his own section and spends time with each wife in rotation. Wives take turns cooking for all. The more wives a man has, the more important he is considered to be. Young men are moving away from this tradition, however, because of the financial responsibility and other challenges. Polygamy is less common among the urban educated. Homes are thatched or made of mud bricks. Common family activities often take place under a thatched roof in a corner of the compound.

Dating and Marriage

It is not proper for boys and girls to date without chaperones. Young men and women in cities may meet at arranged social events such as dances or weddings, where the seating is always male-female-male-female. Marriages are typically arranged by the family. An elaborate dowry is paid by the groom's parents to the bride's parents as part of the agreement. Village girls often marry in their teens (around 15) and boys between 18 and 25, while urban people marry later. It is not proper for a woman to be unmarried. The traditional marriage ceremony lasts three days, with a big feast for friends. In some parts of Niger, the bride must identify (in the spirit of fun) one of two hooded men as her husband. She is given hints if necessary.

Diet

Millet, sorghum, rice, beans, and macaroni are the staple foods. They are eaten with sauces often made from okra, Baobab leaves, peanuts, and tomatoes. Goat is the most commonly eaten meat. Yams, potatoes, lettuce, carrots, and tomatoes are available in the cold season (November–February). Fruits like mangoes come in the hot season. Popular foods include *kilshi* (spiced beef jerky), *hura* (fermented milk with millet and hot pepper), and *brochette* (like a shish kebab). *Tuwo,* pounded millet with a tomato or okra sauce, is common in most villages.

Recreation

Traditional dancing, known as *tam-tam*, is popular in the villages where hired drummers play so young women can dance. Members of the audience place coins on the foreheads of the dancers they prefer. The money drops to the ground and is swept up by the drummers' apprentice for their pay.

Women and men do not often spend leisure time together. For all Nigeriens, visiting is the most popular form of recreation. Women socialize when pounding millet, braiding hair, or (on special occasions) painting intricate designs on their hands and feet with henna. Soccer is the favorite sport of boys. Traditional wrestling is popular with men and there is a national competition each year. Men might go to outdoor movie theaters in large cities; karate and Indian romance films are popular. The Tuaregs enjoy camel racing.

Holidays

New Year's Day is 1 January. Independence Day is 3 August, which is celebrated by planting trees to stop increasing desertification. The Proclamation of the Republic (before actual independence) is honored on 18 December. School holidays are at Christmas and Easter.

The Islamic calendar is based on the lunar month, so dates for religious holidays vary from year to year. They include Muhammad's birthday (*Mouloud*), which is the only day married women celebrate outside their family compounds; a feast, called *Karamin sallah* or "little feast," at the end of *Ramadan*, a month in which people do not eat and drink during daylight hours; and *Tabaski* (forty days after the *Ramadan* feast), which commemorates Abraham's willingness to sacrifice his son. On *Tabaski*, also called *Babban sallah* or "big feast," a sheep is slaughtered and shared with friends.

Commerce

Business hours are from 8:00 A.M. to 6:00 P.M., but government and private stores close from noon to 3:00 P.M. for *sièste*, a break to escape the afternoon heat. Markets remain open during *sièste*, and are themselves a social event; people dress up, meet friends, and chat at the market. Roadside tables offer everything from batteries to cookies in the evening. Store prices are fixed, but it is considered an insult not to bargain in the markets. Water is purchased every day from men who pass in the streets balancing large buckets on a pole across their backs. Post offices provide banking services.

SOCIETY

Government

Niger has seven *départements* divided into thirty-eight *arrondissements*, each of which is led by a *préfet*. The president is chief of state. A prime minister is head of government and is chosen from the 83-member National Assembly. Most large cities, including Zinder, Tahoua, and Agadez, still have sultans who hold office based on lineage. Villages often have a chief, a man chosen based on birth and ability. The central government ultimately makes most decisions, but on the local level the word of a sultan or chief carries great weight.

Although the judicial system is based on French civil law, most disputes are solved by traditional methods, such as going to a respected elder or chief. The legal voting age is 18. Men and women stand in separate lines to vote, and a husband may cast his wife's vote if she wishes.

Economy

Niger is one of the world's poorest countries. For several years, it benefitted from uranium exports. But demand for uranium is now very low and the economy is suffering. Uranium still accounts for 60 percent of all exports, but the earnings are minimal. Most people (90 percent) are engaged in subsistence agriculture and herding. Most wage earners work for the government, but the private sector is slowly growing. For many months each year, young village men work for wages in neighboring countries and then return in the rainy season.

Niger's Human Development Index (0.209) ranks it 169th out of 173 countries. Real gross domestic product per capita is $542, which has hardly changed for a generation. These figures indicate most people do not earn an income (i.e., they are subsistence farmers) or their income is insufficient for their needs. Social institutions are unable to provide the rising generation with access to better economic conditions. Niger receives international aid and imports many of its consumer items. The currency is the *Communauté Financière Africaine* (CFA) *franc*.

Transportation and Communication

Only major highways and city roads are paved. Highways connect Niamey to N'guigmi in the east and Agadez in the north. The road between Zinder and Agadez is not yet fully paved. Only wealthy Nigeriens own cars. People often walk long distances to visit relatives and friends or to gather firewood and haul water. They may also use a motorcycle, moped, or bicycle, or ride a donkey or camel.

A national bus line travels major routes, but most people take *bush taxis* (*taxis de brousse*). These are vans that carry anywhere from 17 to 25 passengers; they only leave when full, so no schedules are definite. Every city has an *auto-gare*, a central gathering point for bush taxis, usually near the market. Villagers take *bush taxis* to the weekly market, and the vans often become loaded with livestock, grains, and other goods. During the taxi's frequent stops, vendors sell goods and snacks to passengers through the windows. The taxi also stops for prayer times. Few people have telephones, but post offices usually have a public phone. The government broadcasts on both radio and television. Television is often watched outdoors, where it is cooler, and is powered by car batteries in villages without electricity. Niger's first (1990) independent newspaper, *Haske* (light), competes with a government paper, *Le Sahel,* and other smaller papers.

Education

The school system is modeled on France's, which requires one to pass difficult exams to advance from primary school to junior high and then high school. French is the language of instruction, making learning difficult for primary school children who have never spoken the language before. Enrollment in primary school is mandatory, but only about one-fourth of students actually go. More boys have the opportunity to go to school than girls. The average literacy rate is 13 percent. For many families, Qur'anic schools are a more vital part of education. There is a university in Niamey.

Health

Malnutrition, malaria, and measles are all serious problems. Even "minor" problems like diarrhea may be deadly due to lack of proper medical care. The infant mortality rate is 111 per 1,000. Life expectancy averages 45 years. Only the largest cities have hospitals and there is a shortage of trained health care workers. Larger villages may have a clinic. There is no charge to be seen by a clinic nurse, but patients must buy their own medicines. Traditional herbal medicine is important in rural areas.

FOR THE TRAVELER

U.S. citizens need a valid passport and visa to enter Niger. Yellow fever and cholera immunizations are required, as are malaria prophylactics. Drink only treated or boiled water. Tourism is not well developed, and travel is considered dangerous in the north and southeast. But there is a lot to experience, from Agadez's 16th century mosque to Niamey's giant market. The Tuarag rebellion may prevent travel to Agadez. For more information, contact the Embassy of the Republic of Niger, 2204 R Street NW, Washington, DC 20008.

A *Culturgram* is a product of native commentary and original, expert analysis. Statistics are estimates and information is presented as a matter of opinion. While the editors strive for accuracy and detail, this document should not be considered strictly factual. It is a general introduction to culture, an initial step in building bridges of understanding between peoples. It may not apply to all peoples of the nation. You should therefore consult other sources for more information.

Federal Republic of

Nigeria

Boundary representations not necessarily authoritative.

BACKGROUND

Land and Climate

Covering 356,668 square miles (923,770 square kilometers), Nigeria is about the same size as California, Nevada, and Utah combined. Its geography is as diverse as its people and culture. About 31 percent of the land is suitable for cultivation; 15 percent is covered by forests or woodlands. Desert areas are found in the far north. The country also features the grassy plains of the Jos Plateau in the north central region, sandy beaches and mangrove swamps in the southwest, and tropical rain forests and parklands in the central region. Nigeria is divided into three areas by the Niger and Benue rivers, which meet and flow together to the Gulf of Guinea. These three regions correspond roughly to the boundaries of the three largest ethnic groups. The climate in the north is dry; the rainy season is from April to October. In the south, it is hot and humid year-round.

History

Nigeria, with its many ethnic groups, has a rich and diverse history that stretches back at least to 500 B.C. when the Nok people inhabited the area. Various empires flourished in different regions for centuries. The Hausa, who live in the north, converted to Islam in the 13th century and established a feudal system that was solidified over time. The Fulani built a great empire in the 1800s. In the southwest, the Yoruba established the Kingdom of Oyo and extended its influence as far as modern Togo. The Ibo, located in the southeast, remained isolated. At the end of the 15th century, European explorers and traders made contact with the Yoruba and Benin peoples and began a lucrative slave trade. The British joined the trade in the 1600s, but abolished it in 1807. Although no European power had as yet colonized the area, British influence increased until 1861, when Britain declared the area around the city of Lagos a crown colony. By 1914, the entire area had become the Colony and Protectorate of Nigeria.

When Nigeria became an independent nation in 1960 (and a republic in 1963), tensions began to rise among the various ethnic groups. After two coups and much unrest, the Ibo-dominated eastern region attempted to secede and establish the Republic of Biafra. Two and one-half years of civil war (1967–70) followed, and the Ibos were forced back into the republic after more than one million people died.

In 1979, national elections were held under a new constitution and a representative civilian government was established. This government, however, lasted only until late 1983, when a military coup left General Mohammed Buhari as the leader of the nation. Political parties were banned in 1983. Another coup occurred in the summer of 1985 and Major General Ibrahim Babangida became the nation's new military leader.

A National Electoral Commission was established in 1986 to organize the transition from military to civilian rule by 1992, but elections scheduled for 1989 were not held. Timetables were altered and state elections between two officially approved parties occurred in 1991. In preparation for democracy, the capital was moved from Lagos to Abuja in December 1991. The move was to be completed after the new government took power. Many new buildings and modern infrastructures were built to receive the government. The city only began resembling a capital in 1995, and has yet to see a full transfer of institutions.

National elections set for 1992 were not held until June 1993. Babangida promised to turn over power to whomever won the election to keep his 1985 pledge to restore civilian rule. However, once election results were apparent, Babangida refused to accept them. He annulled the election and announced the military would hold a new vote with new candidates by August. Rioting broke out in the streets, as angry citizens demonstrated against Babangida's move to retain power. In July, he accepted and then rejected a compromise in which the nation's two official parties would form an interim government. Babangida resigned in August and created a civilian government, but it was overthrown by a rival general, Sani Abacha, in November 1993. Abacha quickly dissolved the legislature and all other democratic institutions, declaring himself ruler of Nigeria. He named a politically diverse civilian cabinet, but maintains firm control of the military and country. Strikes and unrest in 1994 failed to force him from power. Abacha promises an eventual return to civilian rule and democracy, but has not provided a timetable for holding elections. In 1995, with the economy progressing and opposition remaining very weak, Abacha still seemed unwilling to relinquish power.

THE PEOPLE

Population

The population of Nigeria is about 93 million and is growing rapidly at 3 percent annually. Nigeria, with one of the largest populations in Africa, is home to more than 250 ethnic groups. The largest groups include the Hausa (21 percent of the population) and Fulani (9 percent) in the north, the Yoruba (20 percent) in the southwest, and the Ibo (17 percent) in the southeast. Other smaller groups make up 9 percent of the population. Each ethnic group has its own distinct cultural heritage.

Language

More than 250 languages are spoken in Nigeria. English is the official language, although fewer than half the population is actually fluent in it. Many consider English a foreign language. Pidgin English is often used in casual conversation. Each ethnic group also has its own distinct language. Hausa, Yoruba, Ibo, and Fulani are widely spoken. Educated Nigerians are often fluent in several languages.

Religion

Nigeria is divided between the predominantly Muslim north (50 percent) and the Christian south (40 percent). Those following traditional African belief sysytems (10 percent) are spread throughout the country. Many Christians and Muslims also incorporate some traditional African worship practices and beliefs into their daily lives.

General Attitudes

Individual Nigerians are proud of the unique cultural heritage of their particular ethnic group. There is some ethnic tension between the Yoruba and Hausa groups, but these tensions are not as high as in the 1960s, and most Nigerians are more united than in the past. They oppose dictatorship, regardless of the ethnicity of the leader, and this previously united striking workers and other citizens of all groups. Nigerians are dismayed that plans for democracy have been unfulfilled. They continue to hope for a more peaceful and democratic future, despite the current situation. Nigerians are sensitive about their past status as a colony and have been striving to create a modern industrial society that is uniquely African and not a "carbon copy" of Western society. Because of the negative connotations attached to the word "tribe," Nigerians avoid its use. It is better to use the term "ethnic group." In keeping with the Nigerian concept of time, life in Nigeria moves at a relaxed pace. Schedules are not as important as the needs of an individual.

Personal Appearance

Dress varies according to the area and culture. In the Muslim north, dress is very conservative for both men and women. Dress is more casual in the non-Muslim east and west. Traditional Nigerian men's dress is loose and comfortable. Although some women and young girls in the cities wear Western clothing, most women wear a traditional, long, wraparound skirt, a short-sleeved top, and a scarf. Nigerian fabrics are known for their bright colors and unique patterns. Shorts are not appropriate attire for adults in some areas.

CUSTOMS AND COURTESIES

Greetings

In Nigeria, greetings are highly valued among the different ethnic groups. Neglecting to greet another is a sign of disrespect. Because of the diversity of customs, cultures, and dialects in Nigeria, English is widely used in exchanging greetings throughout the country. "Hello" is the most common greeting, while "Good Morning," "Good Afternoon," and "Good Evening," are also appropriate. People are courteous and cheerful when exchanging greetings. Nigerians, who treat others with respect, expect to be treated likewise. Personal space between members of the same sex is much closer than in North America. Persons conversing with one another may stand or sit very close.

Gestures

Nigeria is a multicultural nation and gestures differ from one ethnic group to another. Generally, pushing the palm of the hand forward with the fingers spread is vulgar and should be avoided. One should not point the sole of the foot or shoe at another person. Objects are passed with the right hand or both hands, but usually not the left hand alone. Nigerians often wink at their children if they want them to leave the room.

Visiting

Visiting plays an important part in maintaining family and friendship ties. It is common to visit one's relatives frequently. Unannounced guests are welcome, as planning ahead is not possible in many areas where telephones are not widely available. Hosts endeavor to make guests feel comfortable and usually offer them some refreshments. Invited guests are not expected to bring gifts, but small gifts are appreciated. For social engagements or other planned activities, a starting time may be indicated but guests are not expected to be on time. Late guests are anticipated and they do not disrupt the event.

Eating

Eating habits vary between different ethnic groups. Some eat with the hand (right hand only), while others use utensils. Hands are generally kept above the table. At restaurants, a service charge is normally included in the bill, so tipping is not necessary. However, tipping is common for most other personal services.

LIFESTYLE

Family

Although specific details of the family structure vary from one ethnic group to another, Nigerian families are generally male dominated. The practice of polygamy (having more than one wife) is not uncommon since it is allowed by Islamic law. A Muslim male can take additional wives (up to four total) with the consent of the other(s). Islamic law requires him to provide for each wife equally. While the protected status of Muslim women in Nigeria is similar to other Islamic countries, most other Nigerian women enjoy a great degree of freedom both in influencing family decisions and in openly trading at the marketplace. About one-fifth of the labor force is female. Large families traditionally share the work load at home. Nigerians have deep respect for their elders. Children are trained to be quiet, respectful, and unassertive in their relations with adults.

Dating and Marriage

Marriage customs vary, but the payment of a bridal token or dowry is common throughout the country. The groom is expected to give money, property, or service to the family of the bride. Western-style dating is not common in rural areas, but it is practiced by some youth in urban areas. Women usually marry by the time they are twenty and men marry when then are in their mid-twenties. Living together without a formal marriage ceremony is common and socially acceptable. Many couples simply find a wedding to be too expensive.

Diet

The mainstays of the Nigerian diet are yams, cassava (a starchy root), and rice. Nigerians are fond of hot, spicy food. Their meals are normally accompanied by a pepper sauce made with fish, meat, or chicken. Climatic conditions also provide for a wide selection of fruits and vegetables to supplement the diet. Because of the tsetse fly, dairy cattle are scarce in the coastal regions, but canned margarine, cheese, and powdered milk are used as dairy-product substitutes.

Recreation

Nigerians enjoy many different sports, both as participants and spectators. Soccer, wrestling, polo, cricket, and swimming are popular. Nigerians are extremely proud of their national soccer team which represented the country in the 1994 World Cup. Nigerians also enjoy attending movies. English-speaking movies are shown in many cities. Watching television is also a popular leisure activity. Live theater and art exhibits are well attended.

Holidays

National holidays include New Year's Day, Labor Day (1 May), and National Day (1 October). In addition, both Christian and Muslim holy days are celebrated by the entire country. Muslim holidays vary according to the lunar calendar and include *Maulid an-Nabi* (Muhammad's birthday, usually in September or October), *Idul Fitr* (a three-day feast at the end of the month of *Ramadan*), and *Idul Adha* (the Feast of Sacrifice, usually in June or July). During the month of *Ramadan*, Muslims go without food and drink from dawn to dusk. In the evenings of that month, families eat together and visit friends. Christian holidays include Easter (Friday–Monday), Christmas, and Boxing Day (26 December). Boxing Day is a day for visiting. It comes from an old British tradition of giving small boxed gifts to service workers the day after Christmas.

Commerce

Most businesses are open from 8:00 A.M. to 1:00 P.M. and from 2:00 to 4:00 P.M., Monday through Saturday. Shops in the Muslim north close at 1:00 P.M. on Friday, the Muslim day of worship. Government offices usually close by 3:00 P.M. each day. Business is rarely discussed on the phone, and appointments are scheduled in advance. Western business representatives are expected to be prompt, even though they may have to wait after arriving.

SOCIETY

Government

Nigeria is a military dictatorship. Before the June 1993 elections were canceled, the government was to have been modeled after that in the United States, with a president, a two-chamber legislature, and an independent Supreme Court. That would still presumably be the system if democracy is established. General Abacha has ordered a new constitution be drafted by a constitutional conference. For the present time, Abacha rules as head of the Provisional Ruling Council. He is also defense minister in a cabinet with 31 other ministers. The military controls many aspects of the government. There are currently no legal political parties, but pro-democracy pressure groups are as active as possible.

Economy

Nigeria's economy is one of the largest in Africa. It has great potential for high productivity, diversity, and vitality. The political turmoil of 1993 and 1994, as well as fluctuations in the world price for oil and other Nigerian exports, left the economy near collapse. Urban unemployment was above 30 percent and inflation was between 70 and 100 percent in 1994. Aid from Western nations was suspended, and investment dried up. Still, the outlook by 1995 was promising, with a new budget, lower inflation, and economic reforms that were designed to regain international aid. Just the export to Europe of roses and fresh produce produced substantial earnings in a short period of time. Nevertheless, rural poverty, political uncertainty, and corruption continue to hide the economy's true potential.

Nigeria's Human Development Index (0.348) ranks it 139th out of 173 countries. Real gross domestic product per capita is estimated at $1,360, which has hardly changed for a generation. These figures indicate that economic opportunities are limited to a few. Most people earn an income insufficient for their needs; many have no income. Social institutions are not yet developed enough to provide access to better economic conditions.

Agriculture employs about 54 percent of the population and is an important part of the economy. Nigeria is a major producer of peanuts. Other key crops include cotton, cocoa, yams, cassava, sorghum, corn, and rice. Rubber and cocoa are important exports. When petroleum deposits were discovered, oil became the largest export earner for the economy. It now accounts for 95 percent of all export earnings. The Nigerian government used oil earnings to build an industrial base. Now that oil profits are lower, it is trying to develop industry to decrease dependence on earnings from oil. In addition to oil-related and agriculture-processing industries, Nigeria has textiles, cement, steel, chemical, and other industries. The currency is the *naira* (N).

Transportation and Communication

Nigerian cities are linked by roads, railroads, and air routes, but traffic is heavy on the roads, about half of which are not paved. Many people travel by bus in and between cities because few own cars. Fuel is very expensive. Taxis are plentiful in the cities. Nigeria has a modern telephone system, but it is often poorly maintained. The government is expanding the system. The once active press is now somewhat restricted by the government. Most newspapers are printed in English. There are several radio and television stations.

Education

Each of Nigeria's 30 states provides primary and secondary education and some offer higher education. About 70 percent of primary school-age children are enrolled overall. While 85 percent of all pupils complete the primary level, only about 20 percent enroll in secondary school. School instruction is in English, but a new Education Ministry program promotes the use of an area's dominant native tongue in primary schools. The ministry notes that children are being required to grapple with a new language before they can even learn the skills they should acquire. By the time they are 12, most students perform poorly in both English and standard skills. The new program, being tested in a few districts, is designed to give students the basic skills first and introduce English later. Critics claim it will only add to ethnic tensions because not all of Nigeria's 250 languages will be used in schools. The military government may yet choose to suspend the program.

The government supports almost all higher educational institutions. Although education for rural people is limited, previous government programs have doubled enrollment in some areas. Educational emphasis is on applied science and technology, with a goal to introduce more Nigerians into the skilled work force to replace foreign labor. A considerable number of Nigerians attend universities around the world, often on scholarships from the Nigerian government. Nigeria is known for a well-educated work force, even though the adult literacy rate in only 52 percent (63 for men). This figure was only 25 percent in 1970.

Health

Although less than 70 percent of the population has access to health care, conditions are improving. Hospitals offer adequate care in the cities. The best care is available at the medical colleges. Facilities and care are inadequate in rural areas, and infant mortality remains relatively high at 75 per 1,000. About two-thirds of all one-year-olds are immunized. Life expectancy is about 54 years. Tropical diseases present serious challenges for the people.

FOR THE TRAVELER

A visa and valid passport are necessary for U.S. citizens to enter Nigeria. Proof of sufficient funds may also be required. Passports should be carried at all times. Water is not potable and fruits and vegetables should be washed and peeled or cooked before being eaten. Vaccinations for yellow fever, cholera, and typhoid are recommended. Travel to any country after Nigeria will require proof of yellow fever vaccination. Malaria suppressants should be used. Foreign visitors may be charged higher than normal rates for taxis; agree on a fare before departure. Dual-voltage small appliances or appropriate adaptors and plug adaptor kits are necessary to use electrical outlets. Do not expect to use credit cards very much. More information is available from the Federal Ministry of Information and Culture at 15 Awolowo Ikoyi Road in Lagos, Nigeria. Or contact Nigerian Tours, 368 Broadway Room 307, New York, NY 10013; phone (212) 791–0777. You may also wish to contact the Embassy of Nigeria, 2201 M Street NW, Washington, DC 20037; phone (202) 822–1500.

A *Culturgram* is a product of native commentary and original, expert analysis. Statistics are estimates and information is presented as a matter of opinion. While the editors strive for accuracy and detail, this document should not be considered strictly factual. It is a general introduction to culture, an initial step in building bridges of understanding between peoples. It may not apply to all peoples of the nation. You should therefore consult other sources for more information.

Niue

Antiope Reef

Beveridge Reef

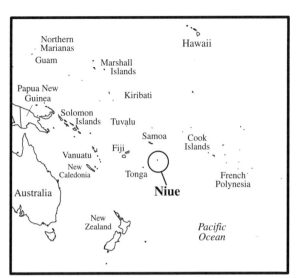

Boundary representations not necessarily authoritative.

BACKGROUND

Land and Climate

The island of Niue is one of the world's smallest self-governing states, covering just 100 square miles (260 square kilometers), which is a bit larger than Washington, D.C. Niue is one of the largest coral islands on earth, formed after volcanic eruption through gradual geological uplift. It now stands about 200 feet (60 meters) above sea level. Niue is rimmed by cliffs and surrounded by coral reefs. Only small vessels can approach the wharf at Alofi, Niue's capital. The perimeter is marked by caverns, chasms, and rugged moonscapes caused by centuries of weathering and shifting. Niue's interior is flat and has a thin soil over the limestone bedrock. There are no lakes or rivers; water is obtained from several deep boreholes that reach the island's underground water table.

The climate is tropical, with summer (December–March) daytime temperatures averaging around 82°F (28°C); in winter (June–September) the average drops to about 72°F (24°C). Droughts are common and a destructive cyclone reaches the island about once every decade. A prevailing trade wind from the southeast makes the seas on the east coast much rougher than on the west.

History

From the people's language it is clear that both Tongan and Samoan immigrants populated the island some one thousand to fifteen hundred years ago, although oral history names five original settlers. Also accounted for in oral histories is the introduction of the coconut, intervillage rivalries, and contacts with other islands. The first *patuiki* (head chief) appeared about four hundred years ago.

Captain James Cook visited Niue in 1774, but the hostile reception he received led him to name the island "Savage Island." Although whalers and missionaries called at Niue several times, it was not until 1846 that a man named Peniamina introduced Christianity on Niue. In 1849, he was joined by a Samoan named Paulo, who spread Christianity to all parts of the island, brought peace among the villages, and prepared the people to accept foreigners.

The British missionary George Lawes arrived in 1861, ushering in the island's transformation by introducing European clothing and goods, writing, and a money economy. Young Niueans gained contact with the outside world by contracting or being indentured to work abroad. Still, society's governing structure remained largely intact, even when Niue asked for protection from the British Crown. In 1901, the first New Zealand colonial administrator arrived.

Change in the form of medical care, radio broadcasting, harbor facilities, and so forth came gradually over the next 50 years. Then, in 1959 and 1960, two destructive cyclones led to an era of rapid change. The reconstruction effort required what was for Niue an enormous influx of materials, vehicles, and organizational support. At about the same time, global efforts to end colonialism led New Zealand to propose a timetable for Niuean independence. Self-government was instituted in 1974. Sir Robert Rex became the premier and served until his death in 1992. He helped form Pacific regional organizations and came to personify his nation in the region. Frank Lui became acting premier in 1992; he was elected to the post in 1993.

PEOPLE

Population

Niue's population of some 2,300 people is growing at 3.5 percent. At its peak, the population reached 6,000, but the relative lack of economic opportunity and resulting emigration decreased the number to present levels. In fact, Niue is

OCEANIA

underpopulated. Certain villages seem almost deserted and there are many vacant houses. Nearly everyone has close ties to someone overseas and overseas visits are common. Some 12,000 Niueans live in New Zealand.

Niueans are Polynesians. Noticeable differences once existed between the *motu* (islanders) in the north and the *tafiti* (foreigners—traders who settled on the island a century ago) in the south. However, this distinction has essentially disappeared due to intermarriage. A small number of Samoans, Tongans, and Europeans live on the island.

Language

The Niuean language can be traced to Samoan and Tongan roots. Dialects, like the people, once differed between north and south, but they have largely disappeared. Most adults speak both Niuean and English fluently.

Niueans value their language and, given the small population and the strength of foreign influence, have done a remarkable job of maintaining its use. Niuean is spoken in the home and at most social events. It is the language of school instruction for five- to eight-year-olds, and is then mixed in decreasing amounts with English until all high school courses except Niuean culture are taught in English. Business and government affairs are conducted mostly in English.

Religion

Only a few vestiges of pre-Christian beliefs remain, such as a *tapu* (taboo) area in Hakupu that is still respected. Almost all Niueans belong to one of five denominations. The two largest are *Ekalesia Niue*, the local offspring of the London Missionary Society that is most closely related to Congregationalism and counts 75 percent of the population as members, and the Church of Jesus Christ of Latter-day Saints (Mormon) with 10 percent. Smaller numbers belong to the Seventh-Day Adventist, Roman Catholic, and Jehovah's Witness faiths. Due to its history and prominence in society, Ekalesia Niue has considerable influence in the political arena. Members of the main denominations mix freely in daily life, but they tend to socialize or work more closely with people of their own faith.

General Attitudes

Since Niue's first contact with Western culture, two main forces have influenced Niuean attitudes: missionary Christianity and the island's relationship with New Zealand. Yet, underlying these factors is the uniqueness of the Niuean culture. The influence of Ekalesia Niue is best exemplified by the fact that boating, fishing, swimming, dancing, sports, business, and broadcasting are either frowned upon or prohibited on Sunday. Also, a good deal of social life is organized by and around churches.

New Zealand's influence comes in the way of clothing styles, food and drink, housing, business practices, and Niue's form of government. And, the majority of Niueans have personal contacts in New Zealand.

Today's society has retained its staple food choices, means of subsistence, and, most importantly, the place of the individual within the *magafaoa* (extended family) from Niue's traditional culture. Political life also still shows traces of the pre-Western era. Unlike other Polynesian societies on islands where food was more abundant and surpluses allowed a hierarchy to be supported, Niuean villages had a loose structure

and authority was widely dispersed. Village councils made most decisions; there were no hereditary ranks or aristocracy. These tendencies persist today.

Niuean life seems to have a weekly rhythm. Religion prevails on Sunday; on weekdays during business hours, Western culture prevails; and the rest of the time is most typically Niuean.

Personal Appearance

With a few exceptions, Western-style clothing is most common. Men often wear a *pareu* (wraparound cloth) for reef activities such as evening fishing, and women wear a *pareu* at home. On special occasions, both sexes of all ages wear leis of fragrant *maile* leaves or of frangipani flowers (in season). Traditional dress is also worn for cultural events.

On weekdays in public, men wear shirts and slacks and women wear modest blouses and skirts. Women do not wear sleeveless tops and often even wear a T-shirt or *pareu* over a bathing suit when swimming. School children wear uniforms through high school. In casual (weekend) settings, most people feel comfortable in shorts, T-shirts, and sandals or bare feet.

CUSTOMS AND COURTESIES

Greetings

Niueans greet each other at work with normal English greetings or in Niuean with *Fakaalofa atu!* (Love be with you!) or the informal *Mafola?* (OK?). Niuean greetings dominate at home or in the village, although people that have spent time overseas might also use English. Men usually shake hands. Women friends meeting after a long absence kiss the cheek.

Niueans might use first names to address one another, but nicknames are more common. In fact, most people have more than one nickname that may be used by different people or on different occasions. Nicknames are most typically the abbreviation of the Niuean and English versions of one's given name.

When parting, people say *Koe kia!* (Good-bye). For two people, the phrase is *Mua kia!* and, for three or more it is *Mutolu kia!* Informal English phrases are also common. If one of the individuals is leaving for a long time, it is most appropriate to say *Monuina [e fenoga]!* (Blessings [on the voyage]!).

Gestures

Niueans, though much inclined to speaking, are more reticent with hand gestures. However, facial gestures are quite important. For example, raising the eyebrows indicates agreement. Directions can be given by a motion of the head or eyebrows rather than pointing. A double shrug of the shoulders conveys negative feelings. Whistling is not common; anciently, it was associated with the sound that approaching spirits made and so was avoided.

Visiting

Informal visits can occur anytime, although Sundays are the favorite time to visit friends and extended family. For casual visits, a flexible and relaxed atmosphere prevails. Customs are more important on special occasions, particularly weddings, funerals, haircuttings, and ear piercings.

These last two events are peculiar to Niue and have become common in this century (although they are in gradual decline). Boys usually do not have their hair cut until they are at least seven years old. At some point after that, but before a boy leaves adolescence, he will have a haircutting ceremony. All the families who in the past have invited the host family to haircuttings are in turn invited to the event. Guests are expected to make a cash contribution in advance; these are opened and tallied.

Before the haircutting day, a temporary shelter (*fale*) from the sun or rain is constructed with coconut leaves. This area, adjoining the host family's home, is then lavishly decorated. Food in large quantities is gathered, including taro, large fish, chickens, pigs, and canned food. Important guests take a turn to cut off a lock of the youth's hair, often making speeches for the occasion. Meanwhile, the food is divided and set aside for guests according to how much they contributed to the event. When the affair is over, the food is distributed and guests take it home with them. Typically, the receipts of the hosts (which can be thousands of dollars) exceed their expenses.

Ear piercing is the corresponding custom for girls, and the event is likewise celebrated with speeches, financial contributions, and food.

After a respected person dies, the family receives visitors for several days. Except for close friends, these visitors arrange to come in groups (such as a family or social organization). They sit while one or a few spokespersons give a brief speech of condolences. The bereaved may pass around refreshments. Each visitor hugs the bereaved person(s) upon leaving.

Eating

Most people eat breakfast and dinner (called *tea*). Wage earners might eat a light lunch at work. Some families use the traditional *umu* (earth oven) for cooking, but many have electric or gas ranges. At special or traditional events, large leaves are used for plates; Western-style dishware is used on a daily basis. Western utensils are common, but so is eating with the fingers of the right hand.

Families gather at a table for all regular meals. Foods may be more traditional staples, such as taro and pork cooked in an *umu*, or they may more closely resemble those eaten in New Zealand, such as bread, potatoes, oven-roasted meat, and so on.

For social events like weddings, eating is a primary activity. Long tables are piled high with taro, roast pig, and other traditional foods; guests help themselves and eat picnic-style. Most Niueans lament the common practice of packing up extra portions to eat at home, but there is usually too much food for those present to finish, so the practice continues.

LIFESTYLE

Family

The *magafaoa* is the center of Niuean life. Children might be raised by an aunt or uncle or grandparent due to family circumstances. In fact, the term for parent, *matua*, is not only used for a biological mother or father, but for whoever is guardian over the child. It is also sometimes used to address elderly family members.

Land is owned by the *magafaoa*, not by an individual, and land courts must keep genealogical records dating several generations back in order to settle ownership disputes. Oral genealogies in various forms extend back to the first settling of the island. *Magafaoa* membership is patrilineal, and the

head of the family is usually a man. Traditional roles are well understood. Men hunt and fish; women cook, care for children, and keep the household. Still, roles are flexible and allow for overlap; paid work is open to both sexes.

Most *magafaoa* land is used for subsistence farming. Bush gardens of taro and other vegetables are owned and worked by the entire family. Similarly, fishing and *uga* (coconut crab) hunting are shared activities where family obligations govern the distribution of the goods. Economic enterprises, ranging from shops to bee keeping to pig raising, that occur outside the *magafaoa* area can be individually owned. Most adults have some source of income outside the family, but the *magafaoa* does cooperate in caring for the elderly or unemployed.

Not only do *magafaoa* members share work and food, they also contribute time and efforts to preparing for special events like the haircutting and ear piercing ceremonies. For certain occasions, friends, business associates, and others are also obligated to help.

Within the *magafaoa*, nuclear units are generally able to set up their own household, usually (but not always) in homes on land belonging to the *magafaoa*. Plenty of housing is available, but a few families will have a home custom-built on leased land. Land cannot be sold, but it can be leased for periods of up to 60 years.

Dating and Marriage

Young people meet and date in many ways: through school, sports, church, social groups, and dances. Openly affectionate behavior in public is rare, but Niueans are quite tolerant of intimacy between unmarried young men and women. Most young people face the problem that there are few eligible partners to whom they are not related.

Weddings are usually prepared by the bride's extended family. They put up the *fale* for the reception, invite a large number of guests, and provide a feast. This is held after the church ceremony. Alcoholic beverages, especially beer, are served by most families. As part of the wedding celebration, members of different families or groups of friends perform songs and dances wearing traditional costumes. In some families, relatives give various outfits to the couple and expect the bride and groom to change clothes several times during the event in order to show off as many elegant outfits as possible. At some point, guests toss small amounts of money at the couple and make wishes (often humorous) for their future.

After the wedding, the couple most often takes up residence with or near the husband's family. They become part of his extended family for all practical purposes, although the bride never entirely loses her obligations to her original family. In some cases, especially when a girl marries a foreigner, the couple might join the wife's extended family.

Diet

While Niueans consume plenty of imported food, their staples are grown locally. Taro is the primary food, but cassava, yams, bananas, breadfruits, coconuts, and papaws are also common. Some families raise pigs; most have chickens (although they tend to eat frozen imported chicken). Since all villages are fairly close to the sea, most families engage in fishing and reef gathering of crustaceans and shellfish.

In addition to chicken, Niueans import beef, canned corned beef, sliced bread, nontropical fruits and vegetables, beer, juices, and soft drinks. Imports arrive only every six weeks and so cannot be relied upon as staples.

A favorite local dish is *faikai*, chunks of fish marinated in coconut cream; another is *takihi*, slices of taro and papaw wrapped in leaves and baked (ideally in an *umu*). Small bakeries produce several varieties of bread, including coconut bread.

Recreation

Cricket (in summer) and rugby (in winter) are the most popular sports. People also enjoy volleyball, soccer, tennis, table tennis, netball, and track events. Alofi has a nine-hole golf course. Cultural events, sometimes competitive, are occasions for traditional song, music, and dance. Some churches have accomplished choirs that devote a good deal of time to their art.

In their leisure time, men like to fish (whether for food or sportfishing for marlin, wahoo, or tuna), hunt (usually for birds), and do woodwork. Some are skilled at making the *vaka* (outrigger canoe), commonly used for fishing. Women gather to make baskets, hats, and other handicrafts. They make many household items from treated pandanus fiber and coconut fronds. Embroidery is also a popular handicraft and tie-dyeing has lately come into fashion. Show days, such as one at Hakupu each June, are occasion for athletics and for displaying handicrafts.

Young people can be found at weekend dances in several halls around the island, and there is usually at least one *fiafia* (party) in progress each weekend.

Holidays

National holidays include New Year's Day, Commission Day (2 January), Easter (Good Friday to Easter Monday), Anzac Day (25 April), Queen Elizabeth II's birthday (first Monday in June), Constitution Day (19 October), Peniamina's Day (a Monday in late October), Christmas, and Boxing Day (26 December). Overseas Niueans often return to the island from around Christmas to early January.

Commerce

Offices and shops are open only on weekdays until 4:00 P.M. Alofi has an open-air market on Friday mornings. Niue has three general stores; all other retail trade is handled by small, family-owned operations. Other businesses, from construction to hospitality, also operate on a very small scale.

Until the early 1990s, most available employment was with the government. Today, the balance is shifting toward private employment (helped by the fact that the government has privatized some state-owned enterprises). Entrepreneurship and the profit motive are recently introduced concepts that contrast with traditional culture.

SOCIETY

Government

Niue is a self-governing territory in free association with New Zealand, which is about 1,000 nautical miles (1,600 kilometers) from Niue. This means New Zealand handles external affairs and defense for Niue. Like New Zealand, Niue recognizes Britain's Queen Elizabeth II as head of state. The legislative body is called the Assembly, which has 20 members (one from each village and six elected at large). The premier, Frank Lui, is head of government. He is elected from and by the Assembly after each general election. The next elections are in 1996.

Economy

Niue relies heavily on aid from New Zealand, Australia, and the United Nations. It also earns income from tourism, the sale of stamps, access fees to fishing waters, remittances from Niueans working overseas, and small amounts of exports to New Zealand. Principal exports include canned coconut cream, honey, passion fruit products, papaws, and handicrafts. The working currency is the New Zealand dollar (NZ$). Niue coinage is sold to coin collectors.

Transportation and Communication

Niue has one perimeter and three cross-island roads. Motor vehicles are common. There is no public transit system, but government workers are provided with transportation to work. Niueans drive on the left side of the road. Links to other countries are limited. A supply ship calls every six weeks, but other vessels stop infrequently at Alofi, the only accessible harbor. Flights to and from Hanan International Airport vary in schedule. Airmail service is routed through Auckland (New Zealand) and depends on flight schedules.

A government-run radio and television station broadcasts six days a week for a few hours each day. Most residents have access to a telephone. There is one weekly newspaper.

Education

Schooling is free and compulsory for ages five to fourteen and conforms to New Zealand standards. Pupils from all villages commute to the nine primary schools and to Niue High School in Alofi. Most students finish primary school (gaining a Fifth Form Certificate), but few finish high school. College courses can be taken through the local branch of the University of the South Pacific (based in Fiji), but full university study must be done abroad.

Health

The government provides most medical and dental services free of charge. New Zealand-trained and expatriate doctors do island rounds, and maternal and child care support are provided at the basic level. Alofi has a hospital that can handle most needs, but patients requiring advanced treatment are evacuated to New Zealand. Infant mortality is low and most tropical diseases are absent. Dengue fever epidemics arise at times, but the illness is rarely fatal. Water is usually safe to drink.

FOR THE TRAVELER

U.S. citizens need a valid passport and proof of onward passage to enter Niue for up to 30 days. Visas are required for longer stays. Niue is a healthful destination with a pleasant climate, a welcoming people, comfortable if simple accommodations, and many scenic wonders. Crime is so rare that for years the prison was closed for lack of prisoners. For more information, contact the Embassy of New Zealand, 37 Observatory Circle NW, Washington, DC 20008; phone (202) 328–4800.

Islamic Republic of
Pakistan

Boundary representations not necessarily authoritative.

BACKGROUND

Land and Climate

Covering 310,401 square miles (803,940 square kilometers), Pakistan is about the same size as Texas and Oklahoma combined. Northern Pakistan has some of the world's highest and most spectacular mountains, including K2 in the Karakoram range. South of Islāmābād, the country is mostly flat. Most people live in the fertile Indus River valley, which runs through the center of the country. The Thar Desert lies to the southeast. There are four provinces (Punjab, Sind, Baluchistan, and the North-West Frontier), the Northern Areas, and Federally Administered Tribal Areas (FATA). Pakistan controls a portion of Jammu and Kashmir, known as Azad Kashmir; India controls the other part. Earthquakes are common in Pakistan and flooding can occur during the rainy season (July–August) along the Indus River. Except in the highlands, the climate is usually hot. In the winter, temperatures average about 50°F (10°C).

History

Pakistan's modern history began with the arrival of Arab traders in the eighth century. The Arabs introduced Islam to the Indian subcontinent. Muslim warriors conquered most of the area in the 900s. By the 16th century, Muslim power reached its peak under the Moghul dynasty. Although many of the inhabitants converted to Islam, the majority of the population (including India) remained Hindu. By the 1800s, the British East India Trading Company had become the dominant power in the area and the last Moghul emperor was deposed in 1858. After World War I, British control of the subcontinent (basically India, Pakistan, and present-day Bangladesh) was contested by various independence movements that united for a time under Mahatma Gandhi. Mohammed Ali Jinnah was leader of the Muslim League and began advocating separate Muslim and Hindu nations in 1940.

In 1947, Britain granted independence to the entire area. Muslim leaders feared the Hindus would control the new country and pressed for independence. A choice was given to each region ruled by a native prince to join either India or Pakistan. The areas that chose Pakistan became East and West Pakistan, separated by 1,000 miles of India. The people of Kashmir (northern India) chose Pakistan, but their Hindu prince chose India, so the area remains in dispute and violence continues today.

East Pakistan (inhabited by Bengalis) declared independence in 1971, which prompted civil war. Indian troops defeated Pakistani troops sent to quell the movement, and the Bengalis formed Bangladesh. In the power vacuum created by the army's defeat, Zulfikar Ali Bhutto was elected leader of Pakistan. During a period of civil unrest in 1977, General Mohammed Zia ul-Haq seized control of the government and jailed Bhutto, who was hanged in 1979. Zia postponed elections indefinitely, suspended civil rights, and established *Shari'a* (Islamic law) as the basis of all civil law. In 1988, Zia was killed in a plane crash. Free elections were held and Bhutto's daughter, Benazir Bhutto, was elected prime minister. She became the first female leader of an Islamic country. Although Bhutto restored civil rights and attempted reforms, poverty remained widespread. She was ousted by the opposition in 1990. Elections in October 1990 brought Nawaz Sharif to power. He began to liberalize the economy and reform the bureaucracy. An attempt by the president to dismiss Sharif in 1993 was overruled by the Supreme Court, and he remained in office. Benazir Bhutto returned to the office of prime minister through elections in 1993. On the basis of her party's parliamentary majority and regained political strength, her choice for president, Farooq Leghari, was elected by both houses of parliament and four provincial legislatures.

THE PEOPLE

Population

Pakistan's population of 128.8 million, growing annually at 2.8 percent, is one of the world's largest. More than 40 percent are younger than age 15. The majority of the people (67 percent) live in rural areas. The two largest cities are Karachi (8 million) and Lahore (4 million). The capital is Islāmābād.

Pakistan's population is divided into five major ethnic groups. The Punjabi is the largest group, comprising about 65 percent. The other four groups are the Sindhi, the Baluchi, the Pashtuns (also called Pakhtuns), and the Muhajir. The Muhajir ethnic group is made up of immigrants from India and their descendants. Pakistan is also home to more than three million Afghan refugees who fled civil war in Afghanistan and live in camps maintained by Pakistan's government. While many refugees are returning to Afghanistan, others continue to arrive because of persistent problems in that country.

Language

Due to the diversity of ethnic groups and the great difference between dialects in a single language, many languages are spoken in Pakistan. English is an official language and is used by the government and educated elite. It is also taught in school. But the other official language, Urdu, is being encouraged as a replacement for English in these cases; it is also the nation's unifying language. While only 7 percent of the people speak Urdu as a native tongue, most people in the country speak it in addition to their own language. Each province is free to use its own regional languages and dialects. Major languages correlate with the ethnic groups: Punjabi, Sindhi, Baluchi, Pashtu, and so forth.

Religion

The force uniting the diverse peoples of Pakistan is Islam. About 97 percent of the people are Muslims. Most of these (77 percent) are Sunni Muslims, while the remainder are *Shi'a* (Shiite) Muslims. Islam pervades every facet of a Pakistani's life from birth to death, and people believe their destiny is subject to the will of *Allah* (God). Muslims accept major Biblical prophets from Adam to Jesus, but they hold Muhammad as the last and greatest of *Allah's* prophets. Muslims believe in a resurrection and a final judgment, but do not accept Jesus as the son of *Allah*. The *Qur'an* (Koran), comprising revelations made to Muhammad, is the chief scripture of Islam. The remainder of the people are either Christian or Hindu, or belong to other religions. Freedom of worship is guaranteed.

General Attitudes

Most Pakistanis are devout Muslims and live according to the philosophy that the will of *Allah* is evident in all things. *Inshallah* (God willing) is a term commonly employed to express hope for success on a project, for one's family, or for a positive outcome to events.

Pakistan is a nation of diversity, and people often identify first with their own group before identifying with the country. Differences also exist between urban and rural populations, the latter being more conservative. They are also evident between the ethnic groups, with Pashtuns and Baluchis being more conservative and traditional than the other major groups.

Today's Pakistan faces important questions about its future, including how much influence *shari'a* should have on society. Most people support the current moderate approach in which *shari'a* is used when practical, but Western legal and business practices also exist. This allows for certain personal freedoms, but some Pakistanis oppose the mixed system because they believe it undermines Islamic values.

Personal Appearance

Although Western-style clothing is worn in Pakistan, the national dress, the *shalwar-qameez*, is more common in both rural and urban areas. Made of cotton, the *shalwar-qameez* differs for men and women. Men wear solid, plain colors, and add a vest or coat for formal occasions. For women, the colors are brighter and patterns bolder, with more tailoring common. Women wear a *dupatta* (scarf) around their heads and sometimes another long scarf around their shoulders. Men usually wear some kind of headdress, and it is often possible to determine a man's ethnic group from his hat. Some wear turbans, others pillbox-type hats, and others *karakuli* (fez-type) hats. There are many variations. It is important to dress conservatively. Despite the heat, Pakistanis cover their legs, arms, and heads in public. Men only wear shorts for athletic events and women never do.

CUSTOMS AND COURTESIES

Greetings

A handshake is the most common greeting, although close friends may embrace if meeting after a long time. Women might greet each other with a handshake or hug. It is not appropriate for a man to shake hands with a woman or to touch her in public, but he may greet a man's wife verbally without looking directly at her. Verbal greetings often include lengthy inquiries about one's health and family; when conversing with each other, men might place the right hand over the heart during this part of the greeting. In Pakistan, the most common greeting is *Assalaam alaikum* (May peace be upon you). The reply is *Waalaikum assalaam* (And peace also upon you). Good-bye is *Khodha haafis*. A title and last name are used when addressing someone in more formal situations. First names are used for friends and relatives.

Gestures

It is not proper for the bottom of one's foot or shoe to point at another person. People may therefore sit with both feet on the ground or squat. If sitting on the floor, or if crossing the legs, feet are positioned so as not to point directly at others. Items are preferably passed with the right hand or both hands. To beckon, all fingers of the hand are waved, with the palm facing down. Using individual fingers to make gestures is very impolite. Male friends may walk hand in hand or with their arms over each other's shoulders, but it is inappropriate for members of the opposite sex to touch in public.

Visiting

As throughout the Islamic world, visiting between friends and relatives is a very important social custom and occurs as often as possible. Hospitality is important and guests are made to feel welcome. In small groups, each person is greeted individually. Personal rapport is important. Visitors are often treated to coffee, tea, or soft drinks and may be invited to eat a meal. Visitors should accept this hospitality, although refusing politely with good reason is appropriate. Guests often bring gifts if well acquainted with the hosts or if the occasion calls for a present. Gifts might include something for the children, a decoration for the home, fruit, or sweets. Above all, gifts should not be too expensive because that could embarrass the hosts. It is customary to socialize before a meal and then to leave soon after the meal is finished. In traditional homes, men and women do not socialize together. Rather, men receive their male guests in a special room to enjoy conversation and refreshments.

Eating

In urban areas, many people have dining tables, in which case they may eat with utensils or the hand. In rural areas, people sit on the floor or ground to eat. Whenever possible, the whole family eats together, usually sharing the same platter and eating from the portion directly in front of them. *Chapati* (bread) is used to scoop up the food. Often fathers feed young children and mothers feed infants. In large groups, men and women eat in separate areas. Extended families often gather for large meals. During the month of *Ramadan*, Muslims do not eat or drink from sunrise to sundown each day. They eat together in the evenings, which are also occasions to visit or offer prayers. During *Ramadan*, it is polite for non-Muslims to not eat or drink in front of Muslims during daylight hours.

LIFESTYLE

Family

The family is the center of social life and support. Although increased modernization has brought many women into public life, men continue to act as head of their homes. It is common for the extended family—a father and mother, their sons, and the sons' families—to live together in the same household. The presiding male of the family has significant influence over the lives of all family members, although women are increasingly taking on active decision-making roles. Islamic law permits a man to have up to four wives if he can care for each equally, but very few actually have more than one. The elderly are highly respected.

Nuclear families are generally large, with the average woman bearing six children in her lifetime. The government stresses family planning to help curb population growth. In the past, large and powerful feudal families had significant power over politics and the economy. As wealthy landowners, they still have considerable influence, although the military and bureaucracy have played equally powerful roles since independence. Today, the feudal families are often turned to by the people when government bureaucracy fails. The average family works hard for a basic living, which does not often include the luxury of modern conveniences.

Dating and Marriage

Boys and girls have little contact with each other; they attend separate schools and are not allowed to date (except among Westernized urban Pakistanis). Individual choice of marriage partners has traditionally played a small role in the marriage process. Arranged marriages are still the norm. Formal engagements may last from a few months to many years, depending on the age of the couple when the arrangements are made. In many cases, the bride and groom meet for the first time on their wedding day. Pakistanis view marriage as a union of two families as much as a union of two people. Both families participate in the wedding preparations. A Muslim holy man, usually called a *Qazi* in Pakistan, completes the marriage contract between the two families. Wedding rituals are elaborate, and men and women celebrate separately. Pakistan has a low divorce rate.

Diet

The mainstay of the Pakistani diet is *chapati* or *roti*, an unleavened bread similar to pita bread. Pakistani food is generally hot and spicy, with curry being one of the most popular spices. Islamic law forbids the consumption of pork and alcohol and there are strict civil laws regarding the sale and consumption of alcoholic beverages. A type of yogurt is a common ingredient in meals. Rice is part of most meals and desserts. Two customary dishes include *pillau* (lightly fried rice with vegetables) and *biryani* (rice with meat and spices). *Kheer* is a type of rice pudding.

The most common meats are lamb, beef, chicken, and fish. Only the more affluent families are able to eat these regularly; the poor eat them on special occasions. For marriage feasts, chicken curry is common. There are significant regional differences in cuisine. For example, while curries and heavy spices prevail in the south, barbecuing is more common in the north. The *kebab,* strips or chunks of meat barbecued over an open grill on a skewer, is cooked with or without spices and is prepared in various ways. Large amounts of vegetables and fruits are enjoyed. Tea is the most popular drink.

Recreation

Introduced during the British colonial period, cricket, field hockey, and squash are among the most popular national sports. Sports developed in Pakistan include a particular type of team wrestling, called *kabaddi*, and polo, which was adopted by the British and exported to England. Pakistanis also enjoy soccer and tennis. Going to movies, watching television (or videos), having picnics, listening to native music, and visiting friends and family members are all popular forms of recreation.

Holidays

Secular holidays include Pakistan Day (23 March); Labor Day (1 May); Independence Day (14 August); Defense of Pakistan Day (6 September); the Anniversary of the Death of Quaid-e-Azam, or Mohammad Ali Jinnah, the nation's founder (11 September); *Allama Iqbal* Day (9 November);

and the Birth of Quaid-e-Azam (25 December). Bank holidays are in December and July.

Islamic holidays are regulated by the lunar calendar and fall on different days each year. The most important ones include *Eid-ul-Fitr*, the three-day feast at the end of the month of *Ramadan*; *Eid-ul-Azha* (Feast of the Sacrifice), which commemorates Abraham's willingness to sacrifice his son, as well as the *haj* (pilgrimage) to Makkah; and *Eid-i-Milad-un-Nabi*, the birth of the Prophet Muhammad. *Eid-ul-Fitr* is the most important holiday because it ends *Ramadan*. During *Ramadan* evenings, many towns sponsor fairs and other celebrations.

Commerce

Because about half of the population is engaged in agriculture, most work schedules are determined by the seasons and the crops. In urban areas, business hours extend from 8:00 A.M. to 4:00 P.M., Sunday through Thursday. In the summer, this is extended by 30 to 40 minutes. Open-air markets and street-side vendors are common; large towns have major bazaars, divided into many tiny shops that are grouped by the product they sell.

SOCIETY

Government

Pakistan is a republic. Its president is head of state and has more constitutional authority than the prime minister, who is head of government. President Leghari supports Prime Minister Bhutto's plans for limiting presidential powers because such constitutional changes would result in fewer conflicts between the two offices. Parliament has two houses, an 87-seat Senate and a 217-seat National Assembly. The prime minister is the leader of parliament's majority party (currently the Pakistan People's Party), and the president is elected by that body and the four provincial legislatures. The main opposition party, the Pakistan Muslim League, is split into at least three different factions, with the Nawaz Sharif faction being the strongest. Numerous small parties hold seats in parliament. The next elections are scheduled for 1997. The voting age is 21.

Economy

Pakistan is primarily an agricultural country; more than half of the people are employed in agricultural pursuits. Pakistan emphasizes high-yield grains to keep pace with a growing population. Agriculture accounts for about 70 percent of all export earnings. Chief products include rice, cotton, wheat, sugarcane, fruits, and vegetables. Clothing and textiles are also important exports. At the time of independence, Pakistan had very little industry. Over the past several years, however, industrialization has grown substantially. Remittances from Pakistani workers in other countries is an important source of revenue. Sharif's economic liberalization program encouraged foreign investment and greater production, and Bhutto's current privatization plan seeks to make industry more efficient. Despite progress, problems remain that hinder growth. Certain resources, natural gas being the most important, could play a role in future development. The country's Human Development Index (0.393) ranks it 132d out of

173 nations. Real gross domestic product per capita is $1,970, which has more than doubled in the last generation. These figures indicate that it is difficult for many families to meet basic needs. Short-term borrowing from landlords and others is not uncommon. While income distribution is becoming more equal, poverty continues to affect 30 percent of the population. The currency is the Pakistani *rupee* (Re).

Transportation and Communication

Local transportation consists of donkeys and horse-drawn carts in rural areas. In cities, buses, minibuses, and motorized rickshaws are available. Although 40 percent of the roads are paved, many are in poor condition. Roads in rural areas are not paved and many areas are not accessible by car. The Grand Trunk Road is a paved highway that begins in India and runs from Lahore to Islāmābād to Peshāwar. Following the British tradition, traffic moves on the left side of the road. There is a domestic airline and a railway. Most people do not own telephones. They are available in hotels, shops, and restaurants. There are several radio stations and newspapers, and one television station.

Education

Characteristic of most developing countries, Pakistan suffers high illiteracy, especially among women. Children either cannot attend school or drop out after only a few years to help the family. Only 35 percent of the people are literate. Still, government efforts have increased the number of primary schools available in rural areas. Primary schooling is free. At secondary levels, efforts are directed at training technicians to aid in expanding the nation's industrial base. Educational facilities, however, are not equipped to meet the needs of the people.

Health

Medical services in Pakistan are limited. Fully equipped hospitals are located in urban areas but are generally understaffed. Outside the cities, medical care is scarce. The government is trying to increase the number of doctors available in the rural areas, but many seek more lucrative employment abroad. Water is not safe for drinking in most areas and malaria is widespread. The infant mortality rate is 102 per 1,000. Life expectancy averages 57 years.

FOR THE TRAVELER

U.S. citizens going to Pakistan must have a visa and a valid passport. Nondiplomatic travelers staying more than 30 days must register with the police. Visitors with a U.S. passport must pay a $20 fee. Permission must be obtained to visit certain areas that are considered hazardous. A traveler may wish to check with the U.S. Embassy in Islamabad upon arrival for any travel warnings. For recorded advisories, call the State Department at (202) 647–5225. Information regarding travel opportunities may be obtained from Pakistan International Airlines, 521 Fifth Avenue, New York, NY 10175; phone (212) 370–9158. You may also wish to contact the Embassy of Pakistan, 2315 Massachusetts Avenue NW, Washington, DC 20008; phone (202) 939–6264.

Printed on recycled paper

CULTURGRAM '96

Independent State of

Papua New Guinea

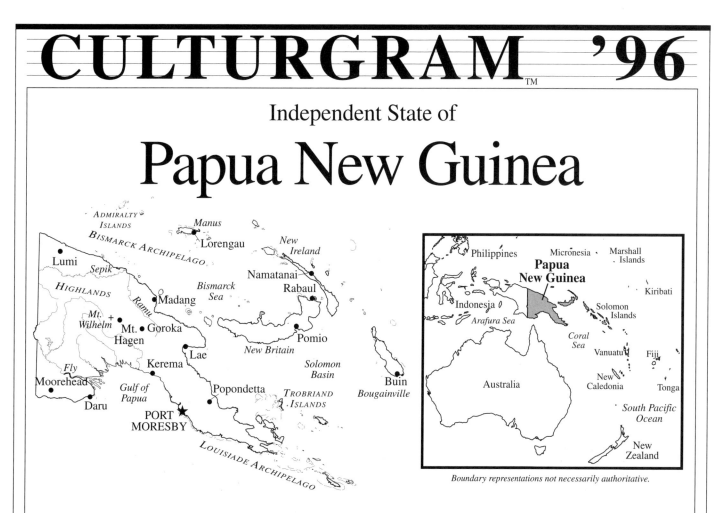

Boundary representations not necessarily authoritative.

BACKGROUND

Land and Climate

Papua New Guinea occupies the eastern half of New Guinea, the second largest island in the world. The country lies just south of the equator and north of Australia. Covering 178,259 square miles (461,690 square kilometers), Papua New Guinea is slightly larger than California and includes a number of smaller islands to the east and north. With rain forests, innumerable waterfalls, winding and powerful rivers, palm trees, white sand beaches, and coral reefs, Papua New Guinea is a rugged and magnificent country. The highest peak, Mt. Wilhelm, stands at 14,793 feet (4,509 meters) in a range that forms a formidable barrier to north-south ground transportation. The Sepik and Fly Rivers are the country's two most famous waterways. Tropical forest covers about 80 percent of Papua New Guinea and swamps cover much of the coastal land. The pristine forests are under severe threat of decimation from foreign loggers who clear-cut pine, mahogany, and walnut trees for huge profits. Plants, animals, and tribal peoples will lose their habitat within 20 years if clear-cutting is not replaced by sustainable-logging enterprises.

The basically tropical climate varies with altitude. The northern wet season lasts from December to March and the dry season from May to October. The south and east are subject to different weather patterns, and their wet season is March to August. Temperatures average around 80°F (27°C) for the lowlands and the high 60s for the Highlands. Some outlying islands get much hotter.

History

Several waves of migration from Asia and the South Pacific islands have taken place for centuries. It is believed the Highlanders were among the first farmers in the world, settling there thousands of years ago. The early Papua New Guineans worked and hunted with wood, stone, or bone tools and weapons. Indirect European contact brought the sweet potato to the island via Asia, radically changing the local diet and culture.

While Europeans made exploratory contact with the island as early as 1512, it wasn't until the 1800s that serious claims were laid to New Guinea and Europeans started to colonize it. Because of territorial disputes, what is now Papua New Guinea was divided into a German territory in the north and a British territory in the south. Even with colonization, New Guinea remained largely unexplored until the 1930s and virtually uninfluenced by the outside world until after World War II.

Australia governed the British area beginning in 1906 and took control of the German area after World War I. The Japanese briefly held the island in World War II, but they were driven out by Allied forces. Australian rule was transformed in 1949 into a trusteeship agreement that was to lead to independence. In 1951 a legislative council, composed mostly of Australians, was formed as the first step toward home rule. A House of Assembly was convened in 1964 that had more indigenous representation, but internal self-government did not come until 1973. Independence was granted in 1975.

OCEANIA

Elections, the latest of which was in 1992, have been held on a regular basis since independence.

THE PEOPLE

Population

The population of Papua New Guinea is about 4.2 million, and is growing at 2.3 percent. The majority (86 percent) live in rural areas. About 98 percent of the people are Melanesian (mostly Papuan). Within this group, there is a wide range of physical types from shorter, muscular people of the Highlands to lighter-skinned people of the coast and very dark-skinned people of Bougainville. Rebels on Bougainville have fought a war of secession since 1988. A peace treaty expected in 1994 did not materialize because rebel leaders refused to attend the document signing. Other groups include those of Polynesian, Micronesian, Chinese, and European descent. Politically, the country is sometimes divided into four groups: Papuans (in the southern Gulf of Papua region), Highlanders (in the central, mountainous region), New Guineans (in the northern Sepik and Ramu river valleys), and Islanders (on outlying islands). The capital, Port Moresby, is the largest city with 193,000 inhabitants.

Language

Linguists have catalogued 836 distinct languages in Papua New Guinea, most of which fall within two basic language stocks: Melanesian and Papuan. The country's rugged terrain accounts for much of the diversity; for centuries, most tribes lived in isolation from one another.

English is the official language and is taught in public schools. The language used at home, however, is almost always that of one's language group. Melanesian Pidgin (*Tok Pisin*) is the most widely used language, allowing different groups within Papua New Guinea to communicate with one another. It was developed by early colonialists and their indigenous laborers. It has roots in English, German, and the local languages of the island of New Britain. *Tok Pisin* contains fewer than 1,800 words, which makes it easy to learn. Motu is the most common indigenous language, used primarily in the Papuan region. In isolated rural areas, many women and older people know only their local language.

Religion

A majority of Papuan New Guineans are Christian, primarily Catholic and Lutheran. The country has been heavily influenced by Western missionaries for the last century, and the result has been a major conversion from animism to Christianity. Strong beliefs in witchcraft and ancestor worship remain and coexist with Christianity. People in remote areas often follow traditional theologies.

General Attitudes

Papua New Guinea is just beginning to feel some national pride and cohesiveness. The people are proud of their diversity and land, which they know is rich in natural resources. Most individuals have a strong sense of belonging to a tribe or language group. They are proud of their families, their ancestors, and the land their families possess. Tribes, not the government, own the land they live on. People value their gardens, and their own physical abilities, endurance, and strength.

There is a desire for material things and a sense of inadequacy in not being able to obtain them. This is not due to the lack of resources, but because people do not save money for personal needs. Family and clan loyalty is strong and there is an obligation to share one's income and possessions. So, while wealth is desired, it is often not possible to accumulate. Reciprocation for sharing is always expected.

People are event oriented. Meetings or gatherings may not take place on time. Things more often begin when everyone arrives rather than according to the clock.

Personal Appearance

Western-style clothing is most common, with traditional attire limited to extremely remote areas. Men wear shorts or pants, but a shirt is optional when one is hot or doing physical labor. Women wear skirts in almost all areas, but pants are sometimes acceptable in urban areas. Both men and women often wear a *laplap* (wraparound sarong). Women usually wear Western tops and brightly colored *meri* blouses. Rural women may go without a top while hot, working, or nursing babies. Rural people seldom own shoes and often have tattered clothing. Traditional wear for special ceremonies might include loincloths, feathered headdresses, facial paint, beads, and shells. *Bilums* (woven string bags) are used by most people. Women hang them from their heads and support them with their backs to carry heavier loads. Men do not carry heavy loads in a *bilum*; they hang it from the shoulder to carry personal items such as tobacco or betel nut.

CUSTOMS AND COURTESIES

Greetings

Papua New Guineans greet by shaking hands. The common question *Yu orait?* (How are you?) is often responded to with *Mi orait. Na yu?* (I'm fine. And you?). Both terms are Melanesian Pidgin. Other greetings vary depending on the area and language group. While Pidgin is used between ethnic groups, people greet members of their own language group with their local language. This is referred to as the *tok ples* (talk place). It is considered rude to use one's *tok ples* if members of other ethnic groups are present.

When passing a stranger, a nod of the head and a smile are adequate gestures. When passing acquaintances, the gestures are accompanied by a short greeting such as *Moning* (Good morning), *Apinun* (Good afternoon), or *Gutnait* (Good evening). When addressing an important official, one uses the appropriate title with a full name. In most other cases, people use first names to address one another. It is common to call an older man *papa* and an older woman *mama*.

Gestures

Gestures with the head, eyes, and eyebrows are important to communication. For example, the question "Where are you going?" might be answered by slightly lifting the head, raising the eyebrows, and moving the eyes in the direction planned. Simply raising the eyebrows can show agreement or acknowledgment. A short hiss and sideways motion of the head indicates disgust or derision. A "tsk-tsk" noise (made by the tongue on the roof of the mouth), accompanied by shaking the head from side to side, can mean surprise, awe, or sympathy. The "thumbs-up" sign is considered offensive to some. Staring at a person of the opposite sex is very offensive. To flag down a public motor vehicle (PMV), one points to the pavement or waves a hand down and toward the road. Men often hold hands in public as a sign of friendship, as do women, but it is not acceptable for members of the opposite sex to do so.

Visiting

Papua New Guineans may spend a large portion of each day visiting, often stopping in at the home of a relative or friend to share some food, smoke tobacco, or chew betel nut and discuss the day's news. Visiting is welcomed, whether impromptu or planned. Visits are usually informal and often lengthy. Gifts of food are often brought, but they are not required. Hosts receiving food as a gift also give a gift when they visit. During an unscheduled visit, hosts do not always stop what they are doing. Visits from relatives can last days or weeks, with the host family providing food and shelter for as long as the guests stay. Hosting long-term guests is becoming especially difficult for urban families because of the high cost of living.

Eating

In general, two large meals are eaten, with snacking throughout the day. Breakfast is called *moning kaikai* (morning food) and dinner is *apinun kaikai*. Some people also eat lunch (*belo*). The most common utensil is the spoon. Hands are used otherwise. Tin plates, bowls, and cups are common throughout the country, but large leaves are still used for plates in rural areas. Food is carefully divided by someone important: a village elder, a guest, or a parent. Guests are not expected to eat everything, but it is important to eat some food and then either take the rest home or give it to others at the gathering. There are rarely second helpings, and asking for them can imply the host has not provided adequately. Most people sit on the ground or floor when eating, although tables might be used in urban areas.

LIFESTYLE

Family

The extended family is the basis of support for most people. While a household is usually occupied by the nuclear family, a child often refers to having more than one mother or father and numerous siblings who, in Western society, would be called aunts, uncles, and cousins. The nuclear family is usually large, with parents raising an average of six children. Couples who are infertile or who have recently lost a child are often given an infant or child by relatives. There is a great deal of obligation and duty associated with family. Extended family members share food, wealth, and work. A family clearing a garden area expects help from relatives and will feed those who provide assistance. Extended families live near one another and often form small village hamlets. The most able family members take care of aging parents.

A majority of family structures are patriarchal, although there are some matriarchal societies in Papua New Guinea. Men usually handle construction activities, such as house or boat building, or clearing land. They also wage relatively frequent tribal fights with bows and arrows and, increasingly, homemade shotguns and other modern weapons. Women usually cook and prepare food, and take care of small children, animals, and the garden. Rural dwellings are usually made of a thatched roof and locally available materials. Urban housing is usually modern and expensive. In cities, both men and women may work outside the home.

Dating and Marriage

Dating traditions and marriage ceremonies vary greatly among the many cultures of Papua New Guinea. A marriage ceremony may take place over a period of days or weeks and involves a great deal of feasting, all-night singing, and exchanging gifts and food. A woman is officially purchased and her family compensated for its loss through a negotiated bride price, which is exchanged in a ceremony before the wedding. A typical price might include several pigs, money, and food. The groom's extended family contributes to the bride price and the bride's extended family shares it.

Diet

The staple food in the Highlands is *kaukau* (sweet potato), while on the coast and in the lowlands *saksak* (a starchy extract from the sago palm) is the main source of calories. Taro is a staple of both regions, as are a myriad of fruits and vegetables from bananas to yams. Along the coast, seafood and coconuts are important. Throughout the country, pigs are raised and butchered for feasts. Small marsupials, wild pigs, birds, and eggs are supplemental sources of protein. Bats, eels, and tree kangaroos are eaten in some areas. Store-bought items, such as rice and tinned fish, are staples in money-rich areas, but they are luxuries elsewhere. Beer is popular as a status drink among men.

The common method of cooking for a family is in a pot or hollow piece of bamboo over an open fire. A *mumu* is traditional for large groups. One type of *mumu* is made by heating rocks over a fire and lining a hole in the ground with them. Food is placed on leaves in the hole and covered with a mound of mud or leaves. Water is poured in to steam cook the food.

Recreation

The national pastime is to sit and talk (*stori*). Men (and occasionally women) enjoy playing cards. The organized sport of choice is rugby, but basketball, volleyball, and soccer (taught in school) are also popular when a ball and field are available. Community tournaments are sometimes held, often in connection with a celebration or political campaign. People also spend leisure time fashioning useful items such as *bilum* bags or weapons. Boys and men hunt birds and wild game with slingshots and bows and arrows. Traditional musical instruments include the *kundu* (hourglass-shaped drum covered with lizard skin) and the *garamut* (log with a small, hollowed out portion where a stick is rhythmically beaten).

Holidays

National holidays include New Year's Day (1 January), Independence Day (16 September), Christmas, and Boxing Day (26 December). Boxing Day, a British tradition of giving small boxed gifts to servants and tradesmen the day after Christmas, is now a day to visit friends and family. Each province also has its own holiday. Some of the local festivals include the Port Moresby Show, featuring traditional and modern events (mid-June); the Yam Harvest Festival of the Trobriand Islands (June–August); the Mt. Hagen (July) and Goroka (early September in even-numbered years) cultural shows; the North Solomons Festival of the Arts (1 September); and the Tolai Warwagira two-week festival in Rabaul (November).

Commerce

Businesses are open from 8:00 A.M. to 5:00 P.M., weekdays, and from 8:00 A.M. to noon on Saturday. Markets and small shops may have extended or irregular hours and are often open on Sunday. Most prices are fixed and bartering is not common, except for crafts or artifacts sold by individuals. Banks are open 9:00 A.M. to 2:00 P.M., Monday through Thursday, and until 5:00 P.M. on Friday. Post offices are open 9:00 A.M. to 5:00 P.M., weekdays, and 9:00 to 11:00 A.M. on Saturday. Only a small percentage of Papua New Guineans earn a regular wage.

SOCIETY

Government

Papua New Guinea is a parliamentary democracy within the Commonwealth, and Britain's Queen Elizabeth II is the ceremonial head of state. She is represented in the country by a governor general, Wiwa Korowi. The prime minister, Paias Wingti, is head of government and is chosen by the majority party in parliament. There are 109 members in the elected national parliament. Each of Papua New Guinea's 20 provinces has a provincial assembly, which elects a premier. At the village level, elected council and committee members settle local disputes. National and provincial elections are preceded by intense and sometimes violent campaigns. The next national elections are in 1997; the voting age is 18.

Economy

Most people (about 86 percent) are subsistence farmers, growing their own food and usually a small cash crop such as coffee. Copra, coffee, palm oil, cocoa, tea, and coconuts are the principal agricultural products. Chief industrial products include coconut oil, plywood, gold, copper, and silver. The Panguna copper mine on Bougainville was a main income source before 1990, when the rebellion shut it down. Several other mines were attacked or shut down by angry landholders wanting a larger share of profits, a situation which led to a crisis of confidence in mining investment. Because of this, the economy suffered negative growth in 1991. The overall crisis passed by 1993 and growth surged. A new gold mine was opened, adding to the advances. Australia is the main trading partner. Papua New Guinea imports most of its manufactured goods. The currency is the *kina* (K).

Papua New Guinea's Human Development Index (0.408) ranks it 129th out of 173 countries. Real gross domestic product per capita is $1,550, which has improved slowly during the last generation. These figures represent the fact that most (73 percent) people live in poverty. Social institutions are unable to create or expand economic opportunities. The rising generation has little expectation of realizing better economic conditions.

Transportation and Communication

Because of Papua New Guinea's ruggedness, travel between cities is often done by air. Except for the Highland Highway, which links the Highland region to the coast at Lae, the road system is limited and often not suitable for travel. Highways and city roads are usually paved, but rural roads are not. Public travel is inexpensive because of a system of privately owned buses and trucks called Public Motor Vehicles (PMVs). Cars are driven on the left side of the road. Travel by boat and ship between coastal and island towns is common. Foot travel on trails and roads is particularly common in rural areas. Most people do not have telephones, except in metropolitan areas. Communication in remote areas is made possible by two-way radios operated by government health centers, by one-way radio, and by word of mouth. Television, newspapers, and postal service are generally confined to major towns.

Education

For Papua New Guineans, schooling is a privilege. The cost of sending a child to a public school is relatively high for many families. This and other factors keep many children from going to school. Students who do attend begin at age seven. About half finish the six grades of primary education and perhaps one-third pass on to high school (grades 7–10) after taking a comprehensive scholastic test. Unfortunately, going to high school is expensive because of tuition and living costs, so even qualified students often don't enroll. High school graduates are encouraged through government scholarships to attend the university in the capital or technical and teacher colleges throughout the country. Literacy is about 52 percent.

Health

Papua New Guineans are covered under a national health care system that usually requires only a small fee for services and medicine. Hospitals are located in provincial government centers, but are often not well equipped. Health aid posts administer vaccinations, perform minor surgery, and dispense medicine in remote areas. People must often walk for hours to reach such a post. Traditional herbal medication is still common. The infant mortality rate is 63 per 1,000, although it is much higher in remote areas where prenatal care is limited. Typhoid and other water-borne diseases and infections are common, along with hepatitis, and respiratory and sexually transmitted diseases. Malaria is common on the coast, in the lowlands, and on islands. Life expectancy is about 56 years.

FOR THE TRAVELER

A visa and valid passport are required of U.S. citizens. A 30-day tourist visa can be obtained on arrival in Port Moresby. Travelers staying longer than 30 days must obtain a visa in advance. Vaccinations are recommended for cholera, tetanus, typhoid, and hepatitis. A malarial prophalactic should be taken. In remote areas, drink rainwater or water that has been treated or boiled. Avoid eating undercooked meat; peel fruits and vegetables before eating. Credit cards are not generally accepted outside resort areas. Some cities, especially Port Moresby, have a *raskol* (thief) or crime problem. Don't go out alone after dark and keep a careful watch on your belongings.

Papua New Guinea has many wonderful sites to see and adventures to experience. For more information or travel brochures, contact the Embassy of Papua New Guinea, 1615 New Hampshire Avenue NW, Suite 300, Washington, DC 20009; phone (202) 745–3680.

Printed on recycled paper

CULTURGRAM ™ '96

Republic of the
Philippines

Boundary representations not necessarily authoritative.

BACKGROUND

Land and Climate

Of the Philippines's 7,107 islands, only about 25 have towns. Most of the population lives on eleven main islands, of which Luzon and Mindanao are the largest. Covering 115,830 square miles (300,000 square kilometers), the Philippines is about the size of Arizona, but the islands are spread over a much larger territory. Many islands are mountainous, and there is a potential for volcanic and earthquake activity throughout the country: a 1990 quake caused death and damage; the 1991 eruption of Mt. Pinatubo buried entire villages and affected global weather patterns through 1993.

The climate is generally tropical and humid. The Luzon highlands, near Baguio, have a very mild climate and low humidity. Philippine soil is very fertile; 26 percent is suitable for cultivation. About one-fourth of the land is covered with forests (down from 40 percent a decade ago). The rainy season extends from June to October. Typhoons are likely from June to November, but they may occur during any season because the Philippines is in the typhoon belt.

History

Malay peoples migrating from Borneo in the 13th century first inhabited Panay Island. Already living on other islands were the Negritos and the Indons (Ifugao and Igorot). Malay fiefdoms spread throughout the islands, including Luzon, and were often at war with one another. Muslim missionaries gained a presence in the 14th and 15th centuries among Malays who had spread south to Mindanao.

When Magellan made the first Western contact in the Philippines in 1521, he found both the warring fiefdoms of the north and the Islamic society of the south. Magellan claimed the entire area for Spain. China, Japan, and other countries tried to conquer the Philippines, but Spain maintained its control for nearly 400 years. José Rizal, writer and patriot, helped inspire a revolt against Spain in 1896. Spain lost a war to the United States and turned the Philippines (not a part of the original conflict) over to U.S. control in 1899. Preferring self-rule, the Filipinos, led by Emilio Aguinaldo, tried to repulse U.S. troops. Internal strife continued until 1901, when U.S. control formally began. Japan invaded the Philippines in 1941 and remained until U.S. forces returned near the end of World War II.

On 4 July 1946, the Philippines became an independent republic, but the United States maintained a military presence. Through the 1960s, unrest over inequality between landowners and tenant farmers threatened government stability and inspired revolutionary movements that are still active. In 1972, President Ferdinand Marcos declared martial law and ruled by decree, effectively controlling all opposition until 1986. During his regime, graft and corruption increased and the standard of living for the peasants did not improve.

In February 1986, Marcos lost presidential elections but declared himself winner anyway. Under the inspiration of his opponent, Corazon Aquino, key government officials and citizens led a peaceful "People's Power Revolution" against Marcos and his army that led to his downfall. After Marcos fled the country, Aquino took office. Marcos died in Hawaii in 1989.

Aquino tried to reform government practices and end corruption, as well as stimulate economic growth. But she faced growing public dissatisfaction, continued corruption, and Communist insurgencies. The military even attempted seven coups against her. With many of her goals unattained, but with democracy restored, Aquino chose not to run for reelection in 1992.

Aquino's successor, Fidel V. Ramos, faced a weak economy, natural disasters, political corruption, and an inefficient bureaucracy. Ramos successfully met many challenges and became popular enough that candidates loyal to him won majorities in both houses of Congress in 1995.

The long official relationship between the United States and the Philippines ended at the latter's request in 1992. Accordingly, the United States pulled out all troops and returned Subic Naval Base and Clark Air Force Base to Philippine control. While many local jobs were initially lost, the government converted the two bases into special economic zones. Domestic and foreign investment quickly filled the gap and created many new private-sector jobs by 1994.

THE PEOPLE

Population

The Philippines's population, 69.8 million, is growing at 1.9 percent per year. About 40 percent is under age 15. More than 9 million people live in metropolitan Manila (including Quezon City and Caloocan City). The people are predominantly of Malay descent: 91.5 percent are Christian Malay and 4 percent are Muslim Malay (Moros). About 1.5 percent are Chinese. The remainder includes a number of indigenous descendants of pre-Malay peoples. Negritos still inhabit the uplands of islands around the Sulu Sea, while the Aetas live around Mt. Pinatubo. The Igorot and Ifugao of the Cordillera mountains in northern Luzon are best known for their stunning 2,000-year-old rice terraces in Banaue.

Language

English and Pilipino are official languages. English is the main language of business, government, and education (fourth grade–college). Efforts in the 1960s and 1970s established Pilipino as official. Most people refer to Pilipino as Tagalog, which is spoken on Luzon. Pilipino is based on Tagalog.

Many ethnic groups who speak any one of more than 80 other languages or dialects were hesitant to adopt Pilipino because it was based on Tagalog, so it failed to replace English as a unifying language. In fact, some groups purposely speak only their original dialect. For instance, in the Visayan region, Visayan dialects (called Cebuano) are used rather than Pilipino. Nevertheless it is considered rude to speak in a dialect that might not be understood by someone present. In this case, English is often used. On Luzon, spoken English is heavily laced with Tagalog words for informal conversation.

Religion

The Philippines is the only predominantly Christian nation in Asia. Approximately 83 percent of the population belongs to the Roman Catholic church. Six percent belongs to the Philippine Independent (or *Aglipayan*) church, and 3 percent belongs to various other Christian churches. Muslim *Moros* live mainly on southern islands, particularly Mindanao. They have tried to secede from the Philippines, engaging in guerrilla warfare over the past several years. Violent clashes between Christians and Muslims occur even as official negotiations continue. In remote areas, people are still heavily influenced by traditional folk beliefs, worshipping a variety of gods. A number of Buddhists also live in the Philippines.

General Attitudes

Filipinos have been influenced by the Chinese, Malayan, Spanish, and U.S. cultures. Consequently, many aspects of these different cultures are evident in Filipino society. Although casual and fun loving, Filipinos are sensitive people; insincerity is easily detected and can ruin a relationship. Individualism is less important than the family. Bringing shame to individuals reflects on their family and is avoided at all costs. Interdependence is more important than independence. Likewise, making social relationships run smoothly is considered more important than expressing personal views or delivering bad/unwanted news. A Filipino may even consider frankness as a sign of a lack of culture. In general, Filipinos have a more relaxed view of time and may not always begin meetings or appointments promptly.

Accepting a favor obliges a Filipino to repay with a greater favor, although never with money. Innovation, change, and even competition are sometimes considered gambles that could bring shame if a person fails. Making changes in social or religious habits may be considered as being ungrateful to parents. Fatalism is a common attitude, characterized by the expression *Bahala na*, which means, roughly, "Accept what comes and bear it with hope and patience." Success may also be attributed to fate rather than ability or effort. The Latin idea of *machismo* is evident in the Philippines; the ideal man is a macho man. Men often make comments about women passing by on the street, but these are ignored.

Personal Appearance

Men working in manual labor wear a pair of shorts and a T-shirt. Other workers wear denim jeans or Western suits. Office workers wear long pants and a shirt. Some men, mostly professionals, may wear the traditional *barong*, a white or pastel-colored embroidered shirt that hangs over the pants. Women generally wear Western-style dresses or skirts with blouses; they may also wear jeans and T-shirts. Rubber sandals are common footwear for casual situations. An active clothing industry produces for export and domestic consumption.

Traditional clothing is worn by some ethnic minorities in highland villages and on outlying islands. In addition, Filipino formal clothing includes an elaborately embroidered *barong* for men, made of finer fabric than the everyday variety. Women wear a *terno,* a full-length dress with a scoop neckline and butterfly sleeves.

CUSTOMS AND COURTESIES

Greetings

Initial greetings are friendly and informal. Handshakes are typical, but verbal greetings are acceptable alone. If people shake hands and wish to show additional respect or enthusiasm, they place the free hand on top of the handshake or use it to pat the other person's shoulder. Common Pilipino greetings include *Kumusta ka na*? (How are you doing?), *Anong balita*? (What's new?), and *Ayos ba tayo 'dyan?* (Is everything alright?). Just as common are the English "Hi!" and "Good morning." Young people are taught to show respect to adults and to address them by a proper title. If a professional title (Doctor, Manager, etc.) is not appropriate, then *Sir*, *Ma'am*, or a familial title is used. The latter depends on the age difference and relationship of the speakers. It is common for young adults to address older adult strangers as *Tita* (Auntie) or *Tito* (Uncle). The elderly might be called *Lola* (Grandmother) or *Lolo* (Grandfather). Numerous other such titles exist in most dialects. Among equals in age and status, first names or nicknames are used in addressing each other. Depending on how close the speakers are, initial greetings may be followed by various questions about one's health, family, and so forth.

Gestures

Hand movement is not excessive in conversation, but Filipinos do use various hand and body gestures to communicate. Raising the eyebrows can mean "hello" or "yes." To beckon, one waves all fingers with the palm facing down. A quick head nod can mean "I don't know." Pointing is often done by puckering the lips. A shoulder shrug with open palms facing up means *bahala na*.

Men offer bus seats to women. Younger people kiss the hand of older relatives or place that hand on their forehead to show respect. Women commonly walk arm in arm or hand in hand, and men may put their arms around each other's shoulder, but displays of affection between men and women are considered inappropriate. Public kissing is for children (who kiss parents or relatives).

Visiting

Filipinos enjoy visiting as often as possible, especially in the *barrios* (small villages or suburbs). Rural visits are often unannounced due to the lack of phones. Among urban residents, visits are less frequent and more planned. Social visits last longer than those with a specific purpose. Guests do not typically take gifts, since the visit itself is considered a gift. However, a guest who has been away for a long time is expected to bring a small, inexpensive gift (*Pasalubong*) to the family. Guests are treated with great hospitality, and are always offered something to drink. Men prefer beer, while women may have soft drinks or coffee. Food is also typically served, except for very short visits. Guests can decline refreshments, but hosts insist until the guests decline three times.

The woman of the house is referred to as *Maybahay* or *Mrs.*, but never *hostess*. If she is unmarried, then *Aling* is used as a prefix to her given name.

Although socializing in the home is most popular, people also enjoy public areas. Urban neighborhoods often have a central park where people can socialize. Villages nearly always have a plaza where political events, dances, meetings, and socializing occur and basketball can be played nearby.

Eating

Filipinos usually eat three meals a day, with at least two snack periods (*merienda*) between meals. Rural families usually eat all meals together, while urban families eat breakfast and dinner together on weekdays and all meals on weekends. The spoon and fork are the most common utensils. Typically, one uses the back of the fork to push food onto the spoon. Hands may be used in large rural gatherings when utensils are in short supply. When guests are present, they are seated nearest the head of the home and are always served first. No one eats until after the guest has had a bite or two. The hosts strive to provide plenty of food for guests. Refusing any offers is impolite, except for health reasons. Guests show their appreciation for the meal by eating heartily. In restaurants, it is customary to leave a 15 percent tip, unless a service charge has been added to the bill, in which case a small tip should still be left.

LIFESTYLE

Family

The extended family is the basic social unit, and more than one generation often lives together in the same household. The average rural family has four children; urban families are smaller. Family ties are very strong; adult children who can do so must support their parents and any needy siblings. Many Filipinos work overseas to earn money for the extended family at home. Recipients of such aid are expected to return help when possible or necessary. Individual family members may sacrifice much to help provide others (especially children) a better life. Or they may work to help find employment or opportunities for relatives within the country.

Filipino women generally enjoy equality with men, holding government, business, and industry positions. Rural women work alongside men in the rice fields. Women also manage the household and family finances and care for the children. A mother's advice to her child is taken very seriously.

Homes built from cement and hardwood are preferred, although bamboo huts are used by the poor. Most homes have one or two bedrooms, a kitchen, and a *comfort room* (bathroom). Rural families may rely on outhouses and outdoor kitchens, but they usually have electricity and a water supply.

Dating and Marriage

In urban areas, dating begins in the early teens. Dancing is popular, as is moviegoing. In rural areas, habits vary according to religion and tradition. Singing karaoke is popular. Most people marry before they are 30 years old. The groom and his family pay for the wedding ceremony and reception. The bride often does not see her bridal gown until the day she is married. Grooms often wear a *barong* made of pineapple fiber. At the reception, during the newlyweds' first dance, relatives may take turns clipping money to the shirt or gown of the couple. Some couples live together instead of or before having a formal wedding. This is generally acceptable, especially if the family cannot afford a wedding.

Diet

Rice, the main staple food, is prepared in a variety of ways and is often included in desserts. Fish, the primary source of protein, is accompanied by vegetables and tropical fruits. A typical meal might consist of boiled rice, fried fish, a vegetable, and fruit for dessert. Fruit is also often eaten for breakfast. Pork is a favorite meat for many people. Garlic is a common spice. *Adobo* is a stew of chicken and pork in garlic, soy sauce, and vinegar. Meats are often roasted and served on skewers. *Kare-kare* is a stew of meats and vegetables served in a peanut sauce. A favorite snack is the *halo-halo*, a drink made from sweetened beans, milk, and fruits served in colorful layers with crushed ice. Seafood is common at restaurants and resorts. For large celebrations, the *lechon*, a stuffed pig roasted over a charcoal fire, is very popular.

Recreation

People spend leisure time socializing or going to movies; the Philippines is a major producer of films. North American films are also available. Video machines and rental stores are found everywhere. Families enjoy picnics at the beach. Sports are generally played on Sunday; basketball is probably the most popular for boys. Girls play sports mostly in school. Volleyball and track are popular. Other recreational activities include gambling, attending horse races or cockfights, and playing *mahjong*, a Chinese table game played with tiles.

Holidays

Filipinos celebrate several national holidays and dozens of local *fiestas*. The latter provide entertainment and recreation, but also encourage former residents to visit family. National holidays include New Year's Day, Easter (Thursday through Sunday), Bataan Day (9 April), Labor Day (1 May), National Heroes Day (6 May), Independence Day (12 June), All Saints' Day (1 November), Bonifacio Day (30 November), Christmas, and Rizal Day (30 December). Christmas is the most celebrated holiday, with decorating beginning as early as September. Children in many areas go door to door singing carols and receiving money and sweets. On Christmas Eve, urban families gather to exchange gifts and enjoy a large feast of special dishes. A large meal is also enjoyed in rural areas, but exchanging gifts is less common. The Christmas season extends through 6 January (Three Kings Day), and is a time of family reunions and great merriment.

Commerce

General business hours extend from 8:00 A.M. to noon or 1:00 P.M. and from 2:00 to 5:00 P.M., Monday through Friday. However, in metro Manila, stores are often open much later and do not close during the day. Hours vary in rural areas. Urban residents shop at supermarkets and open air markets. Rural people rely on their gardens but also shop at small markets where available. *Sari-saris*, small corner convenience stores run out of a home, dot the country. They stock canned items, household supplies, drinks, candy, and other sundry items.

SOCIETY

Government

The Republic of the Philippines has 72 provinces, each of which is divided into municipalities made of *barangays* (barrios). Each *baranguay* is headed by a captain. The central government is led by a president. Congress consists of a 200-seat House of Representatives and a 24-seat Senate. Most government offices are in Quezon City, the former capital named for Manuel Quezon, the first president of the country when it became a U.S. Commonwealth in 1935. The voting age is 15 for local elections and 18 for national elections.

Economy

The Philippines's economy is based on agriculture, which employs 45 percent of the labor force and accounts for about one-third of all exports. The most important crops include rice, corn, coconut, sugarcane, abaca, and tobacco. In addition to agricultural products, the country exports electronics, clothing, minerals, and chemicals. The country's Human Development Index (0.621) ranks it 99th out of 173 countries. Real gross domestic product per capita is $2,440. Income distribution is fairly unequal and poverty affects more than half of the total population. Despite the problems, the economy grew by 5 percent in 1994, and is expected to do even better in 1995. Tax and business reforms are attracting investment. The currency is the Philippine *peso* (P).

Transportation and Communication

Many middle-class Filipinos own cars, but others rely on public transportation. Metro Manila has numerous buses, taxis, and jeepneys. A *jeepney* is a highly decorated type of minibus built on the frame of old U.S. military jeeps. They travel on relatively fixed routes and stop when waved at from the sidewalk. They carry from 10–20 passengers for a low fare; when passengers want to stop, they tap or pound on the roof of the jeepney. Traffic is often heavy and driving habits aggressive. In rural areas, roads and transportation systems are less developed. Local transport often relies on the motorcycle version of the *jeepney*. Travel by foot and on animals is also common. In addition to an efficient domestic airline, ferries and *banca* boats are used for interisland travel. Although the communications system is generally good, service is not extensive in rural regions and between islands. Middle class homes have phones if service is available in the area.

Education

Education is highly valued in the Philippines. Young children can attend kindergarten at age five and preschool before that. Nearly all children begin six years (June–March) of elementary school at age six or seven. A few schools have a seventh year of elementary education. Four years of high school follow for 70 percent of all children. One year of military training is included in the high school curriculum. Graduation is at age 16 or 17. Many go on to college or vocational training. The literacy rate is 90 percent.

Health

Medical service in Manila is generally good. Rural areas usually have a health unit, but it may lack supplies. In 1995, a new law established universal health insurance, paid for mostly on the basis of taxation and other government funds. Before, insurance was difficult to afford and unemployed persons had no insurance. The government sponsors free vaccinations for children. Poor sanitation and poverty are the main reasons for a relatively high infant mortality rate of 50 per 1,000. Life expectancy ranges from 62 to 68 years. Pollution, especially in Manila, is a serious health hazard.

FOR THE TRAVELER

For stays of up to 21 days, U.S. travelers do not need a visa to visit the Philippines, but a valid passport and proof of onward passage are necessary. The country is safe to visit, but guerrilla violence can flare up. Recorded travel advisories are available from the U.S. Department of State at (202) 647–5225. For travel information, contact the Philippine Tourist Office, 556 Fifth Avenue, New York, NY 10036. You may also wish to contact the Embassy of the Philippines, 1600 Massachusetts Avenue NW, Washington, DC 20036.

A Culturgram is a product of native commentary and original, expert analysis. Statistics are estimates and information is presented as a matter of opinion. While the editors strive for accuracy and detail, this document should not be considered strictly factual. It is a general introduction to culture, an initial step in building bridges of understanding between peoples. It may not apply to all peoples of the nation. You should therefore consult other sources for more information.

CULTURGRAM ™ '96

Samoa

(Western Samoa and American Samoa)

WESTERN SAMOA

Asau • Aopo • Tuasivi
Sala'ilua • Satupaitea
Taga • Faleolo • APIA ★
Savai'i • Salani
Upolu

Boundary representations not necessarily authoritative.

AMERICAN SAMOA · Olosega
Ofu ▷ ◁ · Ta'u
Luma ·
Tutuila · ★ PAGO PAGO · *MANU'A ISLANDS*

BACKGROUND

Land and Climate

The Samoan islands are located in the South Pacific Ocean, north of New Zealand and near Fiji and Tonga. Independent Western Samoa, with Apia as its capital, is comprised of two large islands (Savai'i and Upolu) and a few smaller islands. Covering 1,100 square miles (2,850 square kilometers), it is roughly the same size as Rhode Island. About half of the islands are covered with forests. The narrow coastal plains rise to a rugged mountain interior. The islands are still subject to volcanic action.

American Samoa is much smaller than Western Samoa. At 77 square miles (199 square kilometers), it is only a little larger than Washington, D.C. Pago Pago is the capital, located on the island of Tutuila. Ta'u, Ofu, and Olosega form the Manu'a islands. There are a total of seven islands. The climate is tropical and humid, but southeast trade winds often make temperatures pleasantly mild. Temperatures change little, seldom rising above 85°F (29°C) or falling below 75°F (24°C). Most rainfall occurs from December to March. Even during the rainy season, it is sunny for much of each day.

History

What little is known about Samoa's early history comes from oral history. It is generally accepted that Polynesians migrated to Samoa around 600 B.C., coming from the west. Samoa's closest contact was with Fiji and Tonga. In 1772, the Dutch became the first Europeans to visit the islands. Few written records were kept until the 1800s. Not until the 1830s did colonization begin. Missionaries from the London Missionary Society brought Christianity to the people, who quickly accepted it. The Samoan Islands were ruled by chieftains until the 1860s, when they came under the control of the British, Americans, and Germans. Eastern Samoa was later annexed by the United States and Western Samoa by Germany.

After World War I, Western Samoa was given to New Zealand as a UN trusteeship. It finally achieved independence in 1962 as the Independent State of Western Samoa. It maintains a special treaty relationship with New Zealand. Western Samoa became a member of the Commonwealth in 1970 and joined the United Nations in 1976.

American Samoa became important to the United States during World War II, when Pago Pago was a key naval base.

OCEANIA

Although annexation occurred in 1904, the U.S. Congress did not accept the islands until 1929. Because of the base at Pago Pago, American Samoa was administered by the Navy. In 1951, that authority was transferred to the U.S. Department of the Interior. A new constitution was drafted in 1960 and the first elections for governor took place in 1977, when Peter T. Coleman was elected. Coleman was reelected several times after that, and served until he was defeated in November 1992 elections. He remains head of the local Republican Party.

THE PEOPLE

Population

The population of Western Samoa is about 204,000 and is growing at 2.4 percent annually. Most people are ethnic Samoans of Polynesian descent. About 7 percent are Euronesians, or persons of mixed European and Polynesian descent. They come from intermarriages that occurred during the colonial years. Europeans comprise 0.4 percent of the population.

The population of American Samoa is much smaller, with about 55,000 people living there. American Samoa's population is growing at 3.9 percent annually, despite emigration. Eightly-nine percent of the population is Samoan, 2 percent Caucasian, 4 percent Tongan, and 5 percent comes from other groups or is of mixed heritage.

Language

Both nations of Samoa speak Samoan, a language related to Hawaiian and other Polynesian languages. In American Samoa, English is the second official language. English is also spoken by many people in Western Samoa. The Samoans are proud of their language and prefer to speak it over English in daily interaction.

Religion

Almost all Samoans are Christian, and the people are religious. About half are associated with the London Missionary Society, which introduced Christianity to the people in 1831, and belong to the Christian Congregationalist Church. Many other Christian churches are also represented, the largest of which include the Roman Catholic, Methodist, Church of Jesus Christ of Latter-day Saints (Mormon), and Seventh-Day Adventist faiths. In general, the people honor the Christian sabbath and are also religious in their homes. Many families hold evening prayer services (lasting 10 to 15 minutes). Visitors arriving during this service wait until it is over before entering the home.

General Attitudes

Samoans have a strong sense of what is called *fa'a Samoa*, or the "Samoan Way." This generally means a casual way of life that is also careful to preserve tradition. *Fa'a Samoa* allows Samoans to be flexible toward some changes, in understanding the ways of foreigners, and with time schedules. However, it also reminds the people of their heritage and customs. Part of that heritage is a leadership system known as *matai*. In the extended family or kinship group (*aiga*), a *matai* (head) holds authority. The *matai* is selected by members of the group. From birth, Samoans learn and function within this hierarchical order, which forms the basis of the Samoan political system, family life, economic livelihood, and social life. Respect for superiors and adults is important.

Samoans have a speech-centered culture. There are many unique ways of communicating a thought, an expectation, a wish, or a command. Expressed in a certain way, a "yes" may really mean "no." Samoans will often say what they think the listener expects to hear. It is usually considered far worse to disagree with someone in authority or to not give the anticipated reply, than to not do what has been agreed upon. In Samoa, the individual is not as important as the family or group. Sharing and using are more common concepts than owning or having. One is expected to help others within the family, regardless of the cost.

Personal Appearance

Although some men and women wear Western-style clothing, most Samoans wear traditional Samoan attire. Men wear a *lava lava* (a straight, wraparound skirt) with a shirt. Samoan custom forbids women to wear pants, except when participating in athletic events. They usually wear a *puletasi* (a long dress). On Sunday, almost all people wear white. Samoans also feel that a smile is an important part of their personal appearance.

CUSTOMS AND COURTESIES

Greetings

Samoans prize eloquent speech. For this reason, a formal greeting such as *Susu mai* or *Afio mai* (meaning "Listen" or "Come") is offered before beginning a conversation. Use of these terms in greetings indicates special respect. While English greetings are acceptable in American Samoa, Samoan terms are used more often.

Gestures

Beckoning is done by waving all fingers with the palm facing down. Pointing with the index finger is impolite. A person passing a house where village chiefs are gathered must lower any umbrella or other items being carried to at least hip level. Cars do not drive past such gatherings, but people may walk past. These gestures are out of respect for the chiefs. Swaying from side to side indicates contempt or anger.

Visiting

Visitors are not invited to enter a Samoan home until the host has laid out floor mats for the visitors to sit on. In more modern homes, chairs are used instead of mats. Guests are then welcomed by the head of the home. It is customary to leave one's shoes outside and to sit cross-legged on mats. The legs may also be tucked behind a person but never stretched out in front. Legs are also not propped up when sitting on a chair. When a guest enters a home, speeches of welcome are delivered and the guest makes an appropriately formal response. Visitors are expected to sit where the host indicates. It is impolite to speak to someone in a home while standing. Social customs compel the host to make a guest feel as welcome as possible. Samoans believe that anything a person has is at the disposal of others. The attitude of sharing is manifested by the importance of gift giving. After receiving a gift, a person expresses appreciation and often presents a gift in return.

Eating

Most Samoan foods are eaten with the fingers. During a meal, a bowl of water will often be provided for washing hands. A guest may request one before the meal if it is not offered, because hands should be clean before eating. If food is presented but a visitor is not hungry, it is polite to take a small amount to show appreciation to the host. A host will be disappointed if a guest refuses all offers of food or other hospitality. This is avoided because it is improper to make hosts feel they have failed in being hospitable.

If offered *kava* (a bitter drink made from the roots of the yaqona plant), the guest holds the cup out in front, spills a few drops on the floor mat, and says *Manuia* (Good luck) as a sign of respect for the host family. It is impolite to eat while walking on the street.

LIFESTYLE

Family

A typical Samoan village is made up of a series of families. A family member is anyone who is related to the *matai* by birth, marriage, or adoption. The *matai* of a village form the *fono* (council), which governs the affairs of the village. Each *matai* is responsible for the labor, activities, well-being, and housing of his family. Family members are strongly obligated to share their sustenance with the extended family and, to some extent, with the entire village. Land is held in trusteeship in the name of the *matai*. Extended families normally have between 20 and 30 members. Young children are taught not to bother adults and are usually under the supervision of older children. Any adult may freely scold or discipline children when necessary. Discipline within the home is generally strict, and children are taught to respect authority.

Diet

The basic agricultural products in Samoa are bananas, breadfruit, pineapples, papayas, coconuts, copra, yams, and taro (a starchy root). Pork, chicken, and fish are often part of Samoan meals, especially during feasts (*fiafias*). Between 15 and 20 percent of all food is imported.

Recreation

Samoans have their own version of cricket, which they enjoy playing. They also enjoy dancing. In fact, dancing and singing are an important part of life, especially during the *fiafias*. Boating events, volleyball, rugby, and basketball are also popular.

Holidays

Christian holidays, such as Christmas and Easter, are celebrated in both parts of Samoa. In Western Samoa, the national holiday is 1 June. In American Samoa, the national holiday is Flag Day (17 April). The *Swarm of the Palolo* is celebrated each year (usually in late October) when the *palolos* (coral worms) come out to propagate their species. The Samoans consider the worm a delicacy and gather them during this time. White Sunday (second Sunday in October) is a day for children.

Commerce

Business hours generally extend from 8:00 A.M. to noon and from 1:00 to 4:30 P.M., Monday through Friday. The business atmosphere is informal.

SOCIETY

Government

The Independent State of Western Samoa is a constitutional monarchy under a native chief. Chief Susuga Malietoa Tanumafili II has been head of state since 1963. The prime minister (Tofilau Eti Alesana) is head of government. The 47 members of the Legislative Assembly may only be those with *matai* titles. All adults over age 21 may vote. The last legislative elections were in 1994. The country's two political parties are Tofilau's Human Rights Protection Party (HRPP) and the Samoan National Development Party (SNDP).

The Territory of American Samoa is an unincorporated U.S. territory administered by the U.S. Department of the Interior. The U.S. President (William Clinton) is chief of state. The governor is head of government. Governor A.P. Lutali was elected in 1992. The American Samoan legislature is called the *Fono*. Its 21-seat House of Representatives is an elected body whose members serve two-year terms (one seat is reserved for a nonvoting Swains Island delegate). Its last elections were in 1994. The voting age is 18, and the Democratic and Republic parties are the only active political parties.

Members of the 18-seat Senate are chosen by senate districts, according to the *matai* tradition.

Although the people of American Samoa are considered U.S. nationals, they are not U.S. citizens and are not subject to federal taxation. They have one nonvoting representative in the U.S. House of Representatives.

Economy

Agriculture and fishing are the mainstays of both economies. More than half of the population in Western Samoa is employed in agriculture, which is responsible for 90 percent of the country's export earnings. Western Samoans export coconut oil and cream, taro, cocoa, copra, and timber. Tourism is becoming increasingly important as a source of income. The currency is the *tala* (WS$).

In American Samoa, the government is the largest employer, followed by the tuna canning industry. Tuna is the main export, although raw tuna must be imported to be canned. Pet food is also an important export. Tourism is not as important as in Western Samoa, but it is developing. American Samoa conducts 90 percent of its trade with the United States. The currency is the U.S. dollar ($). The standard of living is generally higher in American Samoa than in Western Samoa, due mostly to aid from the United States.

Western Samoa's Human Development Index (0.596) ranks it 104th out of 173 nations. Real gross domestic product per capita is $1,869. This indicates many people can earn an income to support basic needs, but economic prosperity is not available to most. No Human Development Index is available for American Samoa, but its gross national product per capita is $2,600.

Transportation and Communication

Public transportation is fairly widespread throughout Samoa. Most people do not own cars and many have no need for them. Interisland boat transportation is available. Telephones are common in most of American Samoa and in Apia, the capital of Western Samoa, although other areas of Western Samoa lack full service. In Western Samoa, telegrams are the most reliable form of international communication. Television and radio are popular. Local newspapers are available. In American Samoa, the government produces a free daily newsletter. A variety of weekly publications are also available.

Education

In Western Samoa, education is essentially free and compulsory between the ages of seven and fifteen. Inadequate finances and facilities limit educational opportunities for some members of society. The literacy rate is about 95 percent. Many students travel to New Zealand and other countries for higher education. In American Samoa, education is also free and compulsory. It is based on the U.S. system. There is a two-year community college, and many students travel abroad for higher education. The literacy rate is nearly 99 percent.

Health

Hospital facilities and medical care are generally available and of good quality. The quality is somewhat better in American Samoa than in Western Samoa. In Western Samoa, the infant mortality rate is 40 per 1,000 and life expectancy is between 65 and 70 years. In American Samoa, the infant mortality rate is 18 per 1,000 and life expectancy ranges from 69 to 74 years. Water is generally safe and tropical diseases are not a threat.

FOR THE TRAVELER

In both Samoan nations, no visa is required for stays of up to 30 days. A passport is necessary for Western Samoa and proof of citizenship (if a U.S. citizen) is required in American Samoa. Water is safe and no vaccinations are required. The tourism industry is in its infancy, but the islands offer a pleasant climate, many beautiful beaches, and other sites.

For information about Western Samoa, contact the Western Samoa Visitors Bureau, PO Box 882, Apia, Western Samoa. Western Samoa does not maintain an embassy in the United States, but the Western Samoan Mission to the United Nations, located at 820 Second Avenue, Suite 800D, New York, NY 10017; phone (212) 599–6196, may have more information on the country. You may also contact the Royal Western Somoa Consulate 94–537 Waipahu Street, Waipahu, HI 96797; phone (808) 677–7197.

For American Samoa, contact the Office of Tourism, American Samoa Government, PO Box 1147, Pago Pago, American Samoa 96799; phone (684) 633–1091. The Pago Pago address is in the U.S. postal system, but postage for international delivery is required for Western Samoa. For additional information on American Samoa, contact the Pacific Basin Development Council, 711 Kaplolaui Boulevard, Suite 1075, Honolulu, HI 96813–5214; phone (808) 596–7229.

CULTURGRAM '96

Kingdom of
Saudi Arabia

Boundary representations not necessarily authoritative.

BACKGROUND

Land and Climate

Saudi Arabia is the dominant country on the Arabian peninsula. Covering 750,965 square miles (1,945,000 square kilometers), it is about one-fourth the size of the United States and is the world's 12th largest country. The Red Sea borders the west and the Persian Gulf (known as the Arabian Gulf in Saudi Arabia) lies to the east. Most of the country is a vast, arid plain of sand and rock, with rugged mountains to the southwest. There are no major rivers or lakes. Deserts dominate much of the east and south. The largest sand desert in the world is the Rub' al Khali. Some cultivated fields and green oases can be found, and irrigation is making more agriculture possible, but most of the country is dry and barren. Saudi Arabia's greatest natural resource is crude oil, followed by natural gas, iron ore, gold, and copper. The desert climate is subject to great extremes in temperatures, harsh sandstorms, and heat.

History

Arabia has a rich and colorful history that extends for several thousand years. Notable history begins in the seventh century when the Prophet Muhammad began proclaiming the message of Islam from the centers of Makkah and Al Madīnah. Islam soon spread from the peninsula to parts of Asia and northern Africa, as well as other regions of the world. The Arabs had a very advanced society. They invented algebra and excelled in many of today's modern sciences. After several centuries of advancement and power, the Arab empire began to decline after the 13th century.

The peninsula was inhabited by dozens of nomadic tribes, many of which were often at war with one another. In 1902, Abdul Aziz Al-Saud recaptured his ancestral home in Riyadh. After 30 years of fighting, he united the major factions and declared himself king of Saudi Arabia. Four of the king's sons succeeded him in the monarchy, beginning with Saud, then Faisal, Khalid, and now King Fahd bin Abdul Aziz. Another brother, Abdullah, is the crown prince. King Fahd has been a positive influence on peace and stability in the Middle East. When Iraq invaded Kuwait in 1990 and threatened Saudi Arabia, the Saudis hosted the international coalition that liberated Kuwait and protected Saudi Arabia. During and after the 1991 Gulf War, questions of political and social liberalization were raised. While Saudi Arabia determined it would retain its conservative customs, some political changes were announced in 1992.

THE PEOPLE

Population

The rapidly growing (3.2 percent annually) population of Saudi Arabia is about 18.1 million. This figure includes foreign workers (about 4.6 million) who are not citizens. Most foreign workers are from other Islamic countries, but a sizable American community also exists and is associated with the oil industry. Saudi nationals comprise 73 percent of the total population. Of that number, 90 percent are Arabs, and about 10 percent are of Afro-Asian heritage, descendants of settlers from throughout the Islamic world. The Arabs are descendants of many nomadic tribes, some of which, like the Bedouins, still exist.

Language

Arabic is the official language of the kingdom. It is also the language of the *Qur'an* (Koran), the scripture of Islam. English is used in business and educated circles.

Religion

Islam is the only legally and officially recognized religion of Saudi Arabia. Arabia is the birthplace of the revered prophet Muhammad and Saudi Arabia is the home of Islam's two most sacred cities: Makkah and Al Madīnah. Non-Muslims are not permitted to enter these cities. The Arabian peninsula is the center of the Islamic religion, which has spread throughout the world. Each year, hundreds of thousands of Muslims complete a pilgrimage (*Hajj*) to Makkah as part of their religious duties. During the *Hajj*, male pilgrims are expected to wear a white, two-piece, towel-like garment called the *Ihram*. Women can wear traditional clothing but cannot wear a veil. Part of the *Hajj* includes a walk (seven times) around the *Ka'abah* (House of God) at the large Sacred Mosque. It is towards this *Ka'abah* that all Muslims in the world face when they say their daily prayers to *Allah* (God).

Islam accepts all Biblical prophets through Jesus, but Muhammad is the last and greatest of all prophets. Although Muslims believe in a life after death, they do not accept Jesus Christ as God's son. The *Qur'an* (Koran) contains *Allah*'s revelations to Muhammad. Religion is a matter of daily practice and a way of life for Muslims; it is not just a matter of belief and acceptance. In addition to a once-in-a-lifetime pilgrimage and five daily prayers, Muslims also practice their faith through *Shahada* (professing *Allah* as the only god and Muhammad as his messenger), *Zakat* (giving of one's income to help the poor), and fasting during the month of *Ramadan*. Together, these practices are referred to as the "Five Pillars of Islam."

The laws of Saudi Arabia are based on *Shari'a* (Islamic law). All Saudi citizens are Muslims and are restricted from joining any other religion. Foreigners are allowed to practice religion in the home as they wish.

General Attitudes

Life in Saudi Arabia is more relaxed than in fast-paced Western nations. Saudi Arabians prefer to establish trust and confidence before proceeding with business. Saudis are conscious of personal and family honor and can easily be offended by any perceived insult to that honor. The people are generous and hospitable. Privacy is important.

Saudis generally prefer to maintain cultural tradition in the face of modernization. While some may desire more liberal social and political practices, these people are in the minority. Most Saudis are proud that their conservative culture has escaped many of the social problems facing Western nations. While Saudi society may seem closed or repressive, Saudis remind Westerners of the country's strong families, low crime rate, and lack of drug problems.

The people are very religious. Islamic customs therefore play a key role in determining cultural practices. Saudi Arabians are proud of the strength of their modern country and are very patriotic; at the same time, their chief devotions are to family and religion.

Personal Appearance

Saudi Arabian men and women continue to wear traditional Arab dress. The men wear the *ghutra* (headdress) and *thobe* (ankle-length shirt, usually white, that covers long pants). A cloak (*mishlah*) is often worn over the *thobe*. The *ghutra* is not removed in public. Some men have adopted Western dress for some occasions, but the majority retain the customary clothing. A *ghutra* is usually either red checkered or completely white. It is held in place by an *igal* (braided black cord). The white *ghutra* is usually made of lighter fabric and may be seen more often in the summer. Depending on the location, women in public have veiled faces (veiling is not practiced in some areas) and wear an *abaaya* (black robe that covers the entire body). The *abaaya* is often worn over beautifully tailored dresses. Modesty is of utmost importance, even in the heat of the Saudi summers. Visitors are expected to dress conservatively. Tight fitting or revealing clothing is unacceptable.

CUSTOMS AND COURTESIES

Greetings

There are several forms of greeting in Saudi Arabia. The most common is a handshake with the right hand and the phrase *As-Salaamu 'Alaykum* (Peace be upon you). Frequently, males will follow up by extending the left hand to each other's right shoulder and kissing the right and left cheeks. The greeting used depends on the individuals' relationship to each other and their status in society. When accompanied by a woman wearing a veil, a man will not normally introduce her, and one does not expect to shake hands with her. The term for "Good morning" is *Sabah al-Khair*, and for "Good evening" it is *Mesah al-Khair*. A casual hello is *Marhaba*.

Gestures

It is impolite to point with the finger or signal to another person with the hand. A person also avoids the use of the left hand for gesturing. All objects are passed with the right hand or both hands, never with the left alone. It is an insult to point the bottom of one's foot at another person. It is also impolite to cross an ankle over the knee, although crossing one's legs at the knees is acceptable and common.

Visiting

Invitations to a Saudi Arabian home are often given to a man alone. If his wife is invited, she may be sent to eat with the other women in a separate room or quarters. It is inappropriate for a first-time guest to take a gift to the woman of the house. Otherwise, gift giving is common. Dinner guests usually present flowers, sweets, or other small items to the hosts as appreciation for their hospitality.

The Saudis take great care in providing for their visitors. Tea or coffee is served. When a person has had enough to drink, he will cover the cup with the hand or shake it gently from side to side several times and say *bes* (enough). Otherwise, an empty cup is quickly refilled. Alcoholic beverages are never offered in the home and are not presented as gifts. Islamic law prohibits the consumption of alcohol. Coffee is served at the end of a gathering just before it is time for the guests to leave. Toward the end of a business meeting, Saudis may lose interest and direct the conversation to nonbusiness matters.

Eating

Western dining etiquette is only observed in more Westernized circles. In general, food is eaten with the fingers of the right hand only. Bread may be torn with the left hand but is eaten with the right. The Saudis delight in preparing an abundance of food for their guests. Hosts encourage guests to take second helpings and are pleased when they do, but a person can also politely decline further helpings. In restaurants, a service charge is usually included in the bill. The main meal of the day is in the mid-afternoon (usually after 2:00 P.M.), when children are home from school and parents from work. This custom has changed for those whose offices have chosen to remain open in the afternoon. The main meal for these families is in the evening. Conversation is often minimal during the main course of a meal; people prefer to talk before and especially after the meal—while they drink tea or coffee.

LIFESTYLE

Family

Although the Saudi Arabian family is traditionally a strong, male-dominated unit, women exercise considerable influence in the home. Most families live as extended families, but nuclear families are common in urban areas. Even so, sons and their families usually live in a neighborhood close to their father's home. The family is the key to Saudi Arabian society. Infidelity is a crime.

The separation of male and female is a way of life in Saudi Arabia. Rules governing the actions of women are based on Saudi Arabian law and custom and are designed to respect and protect a woman's modesty and honor. A woman's behavior reflects on her family's reputation. Men and women have separate workplaces. Female doctors treat women and children; if they treat men, they are veiled. Women cannot socialize in public with men and are usually accompanied by a male relative in public. Women are not allowed to interact with men outside their family and are forbidden to drive a car or ride a bicycle. Many of these laws also apply to foreigners. Despite the restrictions on public life, men and women can associate freely in the privacy of the home.

Dating and Marriage

Marriages are usually arranged, but a growing minority of young men and women in urban areas are being allowed to choose their mates. Because of the separation of sexes, dating is not practiced. A traditional Saudi Arabian wedding is an Islamic ceremony followed by separate parties for the men and women. Traditionally, men pay a dowry for their brides. Although Islamic law allows a man to have up to four wives, most Saudi men have only one wife. To have more than one, a man must receive the consent of his wife or wives and must

provide equally for each. Chastity is the most important thing a woman can bring to marriage.

Diet

Saudi dishes are composed mainly of rice with lamb or chicken and are mildly spicy. *Kabsah* (rice and lamb) is a favorite dish throughout the country. Rice is also often served with vegetables and a green salad. Desserts are commonly fruits, eaten with Saudi coffee (brewed with cardamom). Seafood is popular on the coasts; there are many varieties of fish. Coffee or tea is served before all meals. Buttermilk and camel's milk are also popular beverages. Muslims do not eat pork or drink alcohol.

Recreation

Soccer is the national sport, but only men are allowed to play or watch at the stadium. Saudi Arabia's national soccer team competed in the 1994 World Cup. Sporting clubs exist throughout the country. Saudi men also enjoy horse and camel races (no betting is allowed, but winners receive prizes), as well as hunting and hawking (falconry). Hawking involves hunting for small game with falcons and requires great skill in training the birds. Young men enjoy volleyball, basketball, swimming, wrestling, and roller skating. Women are generally not involved in sports and do not participate in most other leisure activities, but girls play volleyball and other sports at school. Women enjoy visiting other women; going on family outings to museums, playgrounds, and amusement parks; or doing volunteer work. Videos are popular among all, but there are no movie theaters.

Holidays

The Islamic calendar is based on the lunar month, which makes a year up to 11 days shorter than with the Western calendar. For this reason, with the exception of National Day, celebrated 23 September, holidays vary from year to year. Islam does not use Christ's birth as a reference point for counting years; rather the calendar begins at the year of the *Hegira*, the migration of Muhammad from Makkah to Al Madīnah in the seventh century. The year 1995 roughly corresponds to the Islamic year of 1415. The most important Islamic holidays celebrated in Saudi Arabia include the three-day feast (*Eid al Fitr*) at the end of *Ramadan* and the Feast of the Sacrifice (*Eid al Adha*), which commemorates the willingness of Abraham to sacrifice his son; it also celebrates the annual *Hajj*, during which it occurs. The birth of the prophet Muhammad and the Islamic New Year are also celebrated.

During the Islamic month of *Ramadan*, Muslims do not eat, drink, or smoke from sunrise to sunset each day. Meals are in the evening. No eating is permitted in public (even by foreigners) during the daytime throughout this month. During *Eid al Fitr*, extended families gather for a big feast, visits are made to senior relatives, and children receive gifts and wear new clothes.

Commerce

The workweek runs from Saturday to Wednesday, with Thursday and Friday comprising the weekend. Friday is the Muslim day of worship, when people go to the mosque to pray and hear recitations from the *Qur'an*. Women often stay home to pray. Those who go to the mosque may pray in designated areas, separate from the men. Government offices are open weekdays from 7:30 A.M. to 2:30 P.M. Private business offices are open from around 8:00 A.M. until noon and between 3:00 and 6:00 P.M. General banking hours are from 8:00 A.M. to noon and from 5:00 to 8:00 P.M. Markets, shops, and *souks* (outdoor markets) are open from 9:00 A.M. to noon and from 3:00 to 9:00 P.M. Government offices and banks are closed on Friday, but retail businesses are open in the afternoon and evening. During *Ramadan*, office hours are in the evening and extend past midnight. An increasing number of women work in professional fields and business.

SOCIETY

Government

The kingdom is divided into 14 regions called governorates, each of which is headed by a governor, or *Emir*, who answers directly to the king. The king is chief of state and head of government; he rules with the Council of Ministers. Before 1992, the king, crown prince, and Council of Ministers established all laws. In March 1992, however, the king issued a new "system of governance" (the first written body of law the kingdom has had) that changed the country's political structure and guaranteed citizens a number of basic rights. The *Qur'an* remains the country's official "constitution." The new system provides for a Consultative Council (*Majlis Ashura*), comprised of 60 appointed members, that advises the king and Council of Ministers. The Consultative Council can express its opinion on any matters, can review and initiate laws, and can overrule cabinet decisions if the king agrees. Each governor also has a ten-member Consultative Council, and governorates now have greater autonomy to make certain decisions.

The governance system states that all kings after the current crown prince will be elected by all the princes (there are over 500) and that new crown princes will be appointed and can be dismissed by the king. This change effectively eliminates the hereditary line of rule. The new body of laws does not provide for elections or a representative legislature, but its attention to human rights and public dialogue on policy matters represents a major change for Saudi Arabia.

Economy

Saudi Arabia has a strong economy. It is growing at about 3 percent annually. The country's Human Development Index (0.742) ranks it 67th out of 173 countries. Real gross domestic product per capita is $10,850, a very high level for a developing country. These figures reflect Saudi oil wealth and a significant improvement of living conditions over the past generation. But it is also clear that most wealth is in the hands of the ruling class.

Saudi Arabia enjoys low unemployment and low inflation. Indeed, many workers from other countries form the bulk of the labor force. In the late 1930s, huge oil reserves were discovered. Petroleum and petroleum products form the base of Saudi Arabia's economy, accounting for nearly 90 percent of all export earnings. The Saudi Arabian Oil Company is the world's largest oil company. Because of the harsh climate and terrain, the country imports many foods, but dates, grains, and livestock are produced locally. The country is self-sufficient in wheat and nearly so in poultry and dairy products. The unit of currency is the Saudi *riyal* (R).

Transportation and Communication

The kingdom is continually expanding its infrastructure. Most families own a car. The most convenient way to travel between cities, however, is by airplane. A high-speed train goes from Dammām to Riyadh. Taxis and buses are common in the cities. In desert areas, the camel is still used for transportation (especially among the Bedouin), but automobiles are also common. Saudi Arabia's telecommunications system is modern and extensive.

Education

Kindergarten lasts for two years and is for children ages four through six. Both boys and girls are in classes together. At age six, however, when compulsory education begins, boys and girls attend separate schools. For boys there are six years of primary schooling (*ibtida'i*), followed by three years of intermediate schooling (*mutawassit*) and three years of secondary education (*thanawi*). After one year of secondary school, a student begins to follow either a science track or a literary track. All schooling, including university, is funded by the government. Education for girls did not really begin until the 1960s when the first effort to provide schools for girls began. By the 1980s, the same basic system of education that is available to boys became available to girls. Many women study at universities for their degrees. The literacy rate has increased considerably in the past few years; it is currently 62 percent. The government is committed to increasing accessibility and improving the quality of education.

Health

Although health standards are not equal to those in the West, they are improving rapidly. Free medical treatment is not only available to all citizens of the kingdom, but to pilgrims that come each year to Makkah. There are now several modern hospitals in the major cities, and rural clinics continue to improve care. The infant mortality rate is 52 per 1,000. Life expectancy is between 66 and 69 years.

FOR THE TRAVELER

Saudi Arabia does not issue tourist visas. Only business (or work) and religious visas are available and a person must be sponsored by a Saudi organization to get one. Foreigners who do travel to Saudi Arabia are expected to abide by its social laws and customs, including conservative dress standards and laws regarding the role of women in society. For more information contact the Royal Embassy of Saudi Arabia, 601 New Hampshire Avenue NW, Washington, DC 20037; phone (202) 342–3800.

Republic of
Senegal

Boundary representations not necessarily authoritative.

BACKGROUND

Land and Climate

Senegal lies in the most western part of Africa. The Gambia (a separate country) almost divides Senegal into two parts. Covering 75,749 square miles (196,180 square kilometers), Senegal is about the size of South Dakota. Most of the country north of The Gambia is flat, with rolling plains and few trees. Part of the north, which lies in Africa's semi-arid Sahel region, is subject to desertification. The southeast has plateaus more than 1,600 feet (487 meters) high and the southwest consists of wetlands and forests. Four major rivers flow through the country from east to west. Dakar, the capital, is an important port for West Africa. Senegal has two distinct seasons: the sunny, dry season (November–June), with moderate temperatures, and the hot, humid rainy season (July–October), with temperatures often above 90°F (32°C). Dakar is generally cooler than the rest of the country.

History

Black Africans have historically lived in the area now called Senegal. Great empires and independent kingdoms existed in the area from A.D. 300 to the 19th century. Islamic merchants from North Africa introduced Islam to the animistic peoples of the area in the 10th century. Portuguese sailors first traded with the people in the mid-1400s but were replaced by the French, English, and Dutch in the 1500s. The slave trade was established, and peanuts were introduced as a new crop to supply European demand. Several million West Africans were shipped to the Americas as slaves between the 16th and 19th centuries. Many were sold at an auction house that still stands on Goree Island (near Dakar).

By the 1800s, France began to dominate the area, conquering various kingdoms and establishing Senegal as one of several colonies in its federation of French West Africa. Slavery was abolished in 1848, but French economic, educational, political, and judicial systems remained intact at the administrative level. After World War II, many began to demand independence. On 4 April 1960, the colony gained independence as a sovereign nation, beginning as a member of the Mali Federation. France and Senegal still maintain close political, economic, and social ties. Senegal is also an active member of the United Nations.

After several famines in the 1970s, Senegal moved to create a loose federation (known as Senegambia) with Gambia. The two nations retained full sovereignty but shared military and economic systems. The alliance was dissolved in 1989. In 1981, Senegal's constitution was amended to eliminate restrictions on various political parties. In 1989, hundreds died when violence broke out between Moors of Mauritania and Black Africans of Senegal over a land and grazing dispute. The border between the two countries was closed, but calm was restored through negotiations.

THE PEOPLE

Population

There are approximately 8.7 million people in Senegal, a population that is growing at 3.1 percent annually. More than

40 percent is younger than age 15. Dakar, the capital, has more than 1.5 million inhabitants, but the majority of the people (62 percent) live in rural areas. Most of the people are Black African, including 36 percent Wolof, 17 percent Fulani (Peul), 17 percent Serer, 9 percent Toucouleur, 9 percent Diola, and 9 percent Mandingo. About 1 percent is European and Lebanese and there are other smaller groups. The Lebanese have been in Senegal for many generations and form an influential merchant class.

Language

Although French is the official language of instruction, business, and government, at least 24 languages are spoken in Senegal. Wolof, the native language of the dominant ethnic group, is widely used. In fact, non-Wolofs north of Gambia are bilingual in Wolof and their own ethnic language. Educated Senegalese also speak French. Some speak English, although it is not widely understood throughout the country. Senegalese languages are oral tongues. Although a few attempts have been made to make these tongues written languages, most rural people conduct their lives in their oral languages, for which reading and writing do not exist. Many male Muslims use the Arabic alphabet to write in Wolof or one of the other oral languages.

Religion

About 90 percent of the population is Muslim, 6 percent follows animism and other tribal beliefs, and about 3 percent is Christian (mostly Catholic). The constitution guarantees freedom of religion and separation of church and state. Both Muslim and Catholic holy days are national holidays. In practice, however, Islam dominates social and political activities. The *marabouts* (Muslim religious leaders) influence voting patterns and economic practices. Their power has a strong impact on the country's development. The *marabouts* became powerful during the drive for independence. They were the movement's most vocal and supportive leaders and drew many animists to Islam because of their popularity.

General Attitudes

Senegal has many diverse ethnic groups within its borders, each with its own history, language, and culture. Interactions among these groups and with non-African cultures have produced a multicultural people proud of their origins. Typically, a person's allegiances extend toward the family first, and then, in descending order, to an ethnic group, to a religion, to Senegal, to French West Africa, and finally, to Africa. Personal relations, including doing favors and returning them, are extremely important in daily life.

Concepts of time and distance are defined by a person's background. For example, a Senegalese farmer, whose way of life may not include motor vehicles, will consider a five-hour walk to another village a short trip. But an urban professional might drive rather than walk a short distance. Most other aspects of life are widely different between urban and rural classes. For instance, while wealthy and educated women may hold public office and be employed in important business positions, rural women rarely have any such opportunity. Throughout the country, women are responsible for the daily functions of the household. The Senegalese, urban and rural, are interested in domestic and world politics and appreciate exchanging ideas with foreign visitors.

Personal Appearance

Senegalese place great emphasis on their appearance and personal hygiene. Most bathe more than once a day, and perfumes or colognes are popular. Dressing well is important. Men do not go out in public without a shirt, and few women wear pants or shorts (only urban youths). Only beggars might be barefoot in public. Revealing clothing is not appreciated. Beachwear and athletic clothing are generally only worn on the beach and for athletic activities.

Villagers and some urbanites wear traditional clothing, while most other urban dwellers wear Western fashions. Traditional clothing for men includes loose-fitting cotton robes (*boubous*) worn over bouffant pants and a loose shirt. The amount of embroidery indicates one's level of wealth. Women wear a long robe over a long, wraparound skirt (*sarong*). Muslim women do not wear veils. Muslim women who have made a pilgrimage to Makkah, Saudi Arabia, wear a white scarf, while men who have been to Makkah wear a white turban and scarf; these people are treated with great respect.

CUSTOMS AND COURTESIES

Greetings

Courtesy is extremely important, so greetings should never be neglected. Senegalese greetings vary depending on the circumstances and how well people know each other. Shaking hands and kissing alternate cheeks three times (a French tradition) is common in urban areas. Rural Senegalese only shake hands, and social rules determine who may shake with whom. Traditionally, men would not shake hands with women, but this is changing. When joining or leaving a small group, one must greet each individual separately. Whatever greeting was used between two people is also used when parting. Upon parting, most Senegalese ask each other to extend best wishes to their families and mutual friends.

Gestures

Senegalese receive and give objects with their right hand or with both hands. Use of the left hand is considered unclean. Scratching in public is impolite, as are public displays of affection, although some urban youth hold hands. It is inappropriate to eat while on the street. Senegalese tell street vendors they are not interested in their goods by motioning with a pushing back gesture and avoiding eye contact. Taxis are hailed by raising one arm. In traditional families, children and women curtsy to their elders to show respect. Eye contact is avoided with a person considered to be a superior (in age or status) or of the opposite sex. Men and women keep their distance in public and are expected to be dignified and reserved around members of the opposite sex. More relaxed behavior is acceptable with members of the same gender, age, or status. Between men, sharing a kola nut (which contains a mild caffeine stimulant) is a gesture of friendship.

Visiting

Senegalese enjoy visiting one another often in the home. Because most do not own telephones, dropping in uninvited is acceptable and appreciated. Still, uninvited guests try to visit before mealtimes, either in the late morning or early evening. Work, health, family matters, and mutual friends are briefly discussed before a visitor addresses the purpose of the visit.

Senegalese are hospitable and can make a guest feel comfortable without expecting anything in return. However, friends will often bring gifts such as fruit or some cookies for the children. A drink will be offered (usually nonalcoholic), but foreign visitors should not drink water unless it is bottled. To decline a drink, it is polite to say one has just finished drinking. It is impolite to refuse other refreshments. Although smoking is widespread among males, visitors to traditional Muslim homes avoid cigarette smoking until they leave. It is considered bad manners for women to smoke. Asking personal questions is impolite; it is considered bad luck to ask specific questions about children, such as when a baby is due, how many children one has, or what their ages are.

Eating

Generally, breakfast is between 6:00 and 9:00 A.M., lunch from noon to 1:30 P.M., and dinner from 8:00 to 9:30 P.M. In traditional homes, the sexes and different age groups eat separately. The main dish is usually served in large bowls placed on mats on the floor or ground, or on coffee tables. Several people eat from the same bowl using the fingers or a spoon, depending on personal habit, the occasion, and the dish. Proper etiquette for eating is stressed to children at an early age. Having clean hands, eating only from the portion of the communal dish directly in front of a person, and avoiding eye contact with persons still eating are all important. Only the right hand is used to eat. The left can assist the right when eating difficult foods, such as fruit or meat with bones. Occasionally, particularly when hosting Western visitors, some urban Senegalese follow French customs, eating at tables from individual plates with utensils.

LIFESTYLE

Family

In general, the family and its history are a source of strength and pride for Senegalese. In most rural areas and among traditional urban families, extended families live together in family compounds (with a separate dwelling for each nuclear family). But there is a trend to live only with the nuclear family. Baptisms, circumcisions, marriages, funerals, and other important ceremonies are cause for elaborate celebration. Most families live at subsistence levels as agricultural workers, although there is a growing middle class and a small, wealthy elite. The elderly receive great respect and are cared for by their families.

Dating and Marriage

Western-style dating, where relative strangers go out with one another, is uncommon in Senegal. People tend to go out in groups or in couples with a person they and their families know. In fact, a couple's families tend to be heavily involved in courtship. Traditional families arrange marriages, but more urban residents are marrying according to their choice. Couples are often encouraged to marry young. However, it is

acceptable for college students to wait until after they finish school. Some Muslims practice polygamy. Islamic law permits a man to have up to four wives, but he must have the consent of the other wife (or wives), and, according to the *Qur'an* (Koran), he must divide his resources and time equally among each wife's household.

Diet

Food preparation and presentation are skills that Senegalese females learn at an early age. Each ethnic group has its own traditional dishes, and some urban women also cook French meals. Many believe that wealth is measured by body size, because the wealthier the family, the more oil and rice that can be used in preparing dishes. Meals usually consist of one main dish of rice, millet, or corn, over which is served a sauce composed of vegetables, meat (traditional Muslims do not eat pork), poultry, fish, beans, or milk and sugar. A dessert consisting of fruit and/or yogurt might be served. One popular dish is *yassa*: rice and chicken covered with a sauce made of sliced onions and spices. Another is *thiebou dien*, a meal of fish and rice that is typically eaten for lunch. A traditional Wolof dish is *mbaxal-u-Saloum*: a sauce of ground peanuts, dried fish, meat, tomatoes, and spices served with rice.

Recreation

Traditional wrestling is the national sport and pastime. Soccer, however, is the most popular sport. Other favorites include basketball, track and field, and jogging. Many people in urban areas enjoy movies and books. Concerts, discos, and videos are popular in areas with electricity. After the harvest, rural families visit relatives in urban areas. They also enjoy dancing, as well as family and village celebrations.

Holidays

Senegal celebrates Islamic, Catholic, and national holidays. They include New Year's Day, *Mawloud* (celebrating the prophet Muhammad's birth), Easter, Independence Day (4 April), Labor Day (1 May), Ascension, and Whit Monday. On *Tabaski*, the head of each household sacrifices a lamb in honor of Abraham's willingness to sacrifice his son. *Korite* marks the end of *Ramadan*, the month of fasting when Muslims go without food or drink from sunrise to sundown each day of the month. The *Korite* feast lasts for three days. *Tamkharit*, the Islamic New Year, is also the day on which *Allah* determines people's destinies. Islamic holidays follow the lunar calendar and thus are different dates each year. All Saints' Day (1 November) and Christmas are also celebrated.

Commerce

Muslims do not schedule business meetings during prayer times, which take place five times each day. If a meeting runs into prayer time, it might be stopped so the people can pray, depending on the individuals involved and whether the area is traditional or Westernized. Meetings are formal in most cases, and participants do not remove jackets or roll up sleeves. Government office hours are 9:00 A.M. to 5:00 P.M., Monday through Friday, and from 8:30 A.M. to noon on Saturday. Businesses remain open from 9:00 A.M. to 1:00 P.M. and from 4:00 to 7:00 P.M., Monday through Saturday. They close at midday because of the heat.

SOCIETY

Government

Senegal, a multiparty democracy since 1981, is divided into ten regions. The elected president serves as chief of state, and the prime minister is head of government. Habib Thiam was elected prime minister in 1991 and reelected in 1993. The president, Abdou Diouf, was first elected in 1981 and was reelected in 1988 and again in 1993. His party, the Socialist Party, dominates in the 120-seat *Assemblée Nationale* (National Assembly). The main opposition party is the Senegal Democratic Party. Other parties exist, but do not have much power in parliament. All citizens may vote at age 18.

At the rural level, a system of local chiefs and religious leaders provides local leadership and judicial services. Local authority is often more important to the average person than departments of the central government.

Economy

Senegal has an agriculture-based market economy, and 75 percent of the population works in agriculture. Since being introduced by colonial powers, peanuts have remained the country's main cash crop and occupy about 40 percent of all cropland. Other agricultural products include millet, cassava, cotton, rice, poultry, and vegetables. Farmers depend on rain for their crops, but a few projects are experimenting with irrigation.

After the Ivory Coast, Senegal has the most developed manufacturing sector in French West Africa. The most important industries include peanut oil extraction, tourism, phosphates, and food processing (which accounts for 27 percent of all exports). Fish processing is an important part of Senegal's food processing industry.

The country's Human Development Index (0.322) ranks it 143d out of 173 countries. Real gross domestic product per capita is $1,680, a figure which has improved only slightly since 1960 but is higher than some other African countries. This reflects a higher level of economic development, but it also indicates that the benefits of that development are enjoyed by a minority of (mostly urban) people. Inflation and debt hinder progress on many fronts. France, the World Bank, and the International Monetary Fund help finance development projects. The currency is the *CFA franc*.

Transportation and Communication

Major cities are linked by paved roads, while inland villages are connected by unpaved paths and waterways. An airline services the northern and southern coasts. A railroad system extends from Dakar to the north and to Mali in the east. Most people do not own cars; they travel by public transport (buses, taxis, or a minivan system for longer distances), horse and buggy, bicycle, motorcycle, or on foot. The government sponsors a daily newspaper, other political parties sponsor weekly papers, and foreign papers are available. While most urban residents have access to information through print, radio, or television, villages are often isolated because they lack electricity and postal services. Most rural people travel to nearby towns for postal services. They usually have access to a daily radio news broadcast. Radio stations broadcast in local languages, while oral or written messages passed from person to person are the most effective means of communication among villagers.

Education

Senegal's educational system is based on the French model. Classes are taught in French, which is considered the nation's unifying language. From 15 to 30 percent of the population has learned to read and write in French, but because French is not typically spoken in the home, most children do not speak it when they begin school. Many see school, therefore, as being irrelevant to their daily activities, so they drop out of school early. Still, officials hesitate to drop French as the language of instruction because they fear most ethnic groups would resist an educational system based on a single ethnic language. They also believe dropping French would isolate Senegal from the rest of the world. School attendance is also affected by the need for children at home to work in the fields, by a distrust of secular (versus religious) education, and other factors. About half of all students enter and complete a primary education, and about one-third of those go on to a secondary school.

Health

Although health conditions are improving, diseases and infections continue to affect many Senegalese, particularly those in rural areas who cannot afford or do not have access to medical treatment. There is one doctor for every 16,000 persons, but most physicians (70 percent) practice in Dakar. Dakar doctors have access to modern facilities, but rural health-care facilities often lack equipment and medical supplies. The infant mortality rate, currently at 75 per 1,000, is decreasing. Life expectancy ranges from 55 to 58 years.

FOR THE TRAVELER

U.S. travelers need a valid passport to enter Senegal, but a visa is not required for stays as long as 90 days. Proof of onward passage and yellow fever vaccination is required. Water is not potable, but bottled water is safe to drink. Malaria suppressants, as well as hepatitis, tetanus, polio, and typhoid immunizations are recommended. Dual-voltage small appliances and plug adaptor kits are necessary to use electrical outlets. Visitors should be aware of pickpockets and petty theft, especially in Dakar. Serious crime is rare. Tourism is increasingly important to Senegal's economy and many travel opportunities are available. For more information contact the Senegal Tourist Office, 310 Madison Avenue, Suite 724, New York, NY 10017; phone (212) 286–0977. You may also wish to contact the Embassy of the Republic of Senegal, 2112 Wyoming Avenue NW, Washington, DC 20008; phone (202) 234–0540.

CULTURGRAM™ '96

Republic of
Sierra Leone

Boundary representations not necessarily authoritative.

BACKGROUND

Land and Climate

Sierra Leone, located covers 27,699 square miles (71,740 square kilometers) on the coast of West Africa; it is about the size of South Carolina. The country's land is quite diverse. Near Freetown, beaches rise into 3,000-foot (915 meters) mountains; elsewhere, coasts are flat. The north is mostly forest-savanna; the south is cleared forest used for planting. Pockets of rain forest are scattered throughout the eastern Loma Mountains. The rainy season lasts from May to November. Freetown, the capital, receives up to two hundred inches of rain a year. Humidity and temperatures are high year-round. Daytime temperatures are often above 90°F (32°C). During the harmattan, there is a brief respite from the heat and humidity. In this one-month period that begins in late December, the country is swept by cool, dry, dusty winds out of the northeast.

History

Because Sierra Leone was outside the realms of sub-Saharan West African empires, little is known of its history before the 15th century. After that, the lives of the indigenous people were influenced by two major events: the arrival of European explorers, merchants, and slave traders; and the repatriation of slaves from abroad. In 1462, Portuguese explorers encountered the coast and named the region "Lion Range" (*Serra Lyoa*) because of the thunderous roars heard coming from the steep peninsular mountains.

Great Britain became involved in Sierra Leone because of the lucrative slave trade and in order to compete with the growing French colonization of West Africa. Britain repatriated some slaves when slavery was declared illegal and maintained a presence so missionaries could "civilize" the Africans. The British traded commodities such as timber, palm kernels, ginger, arrow root, gum, ivory, hides, palm oil, and rubber. After diamonds and gold were discovered, Britain proclaimed a protectorate over Sierra Leone in 1896. During colonial rule, the combined influences of trade and missionary education permanently altered traditional tribal society.

Independence was granted in 1961 and the first prime minister was Sir Milton Margai. After Margai's death, his half brother, Albert Margai, became prime minister. When Albert lost the 1967 elections, the military sponsored a coup to keep him in power. After two more coups, the elected prime minister, Siaka Stevens, was able to take office in 1968. Stevens's party, the All People's Congress (APC), gained complete control of parliament by 1973, and Stevens ruled a one-party state until he retired in 1985. He was succeeded by Joseph Momoh. By 1990, opposition to the APC's rule was high and Momoh promised a return to multiparty democracy. When it became clear he was stalling, Momoh was forced from power in 1992. The leader of that coup, Captain Valentine Strasser, took power as chairman of the National Provisional Ruling Council (NPRC). Strasser scheduled and later canceled elections, but he promised a return to civilian rule by the end of 1995.

Strasser organized a commission to help prepare election materials and register voters. The program suffered from numerous delays, including an intensification of a 1991 rebel movement. The Revolutionary United Front, associated with factions in war-torn Liberia, aims to topple the government. Strasser invited Nigerian troops to Sierra Leone in 1995 to help fight the rebels. While target dates for the return to democracy may be postponed, the National Provisional Ruling Council has stressed its intent to hold elections as soon as possible.

THE PEOPLE

Population

Sierra Leone's population, about 4.6 million, usually grows at about 2 percent annually. Due to emigration, however, it did not grow in the early 1990s. Emigration slowed in 1995. Eighteen ethnic groups (referred to as "tribes") make up the population. The Mende (31 percent) and Temne (30 percent) are the two largest groups; the Limba is a distant third (8), and remaining groups follow behind. The Krios, descendants of returned slaves, live mostly in Freetown. Most of the people (70 percent) live in rural areas, although cities are densely populated. Nearly all Sierra Leoneans are Black Africans, but a small number are Lebanese. The Lebanese make up an important segment of the merchant class. Although they have been in Sierra Leone for several generations, the Lebanese are not considered to be Sierra Leonean.

Language

English is the official language and is used in government, but only the educated speak it. Krio, a mixture of primarily English, Yoruba, and African languages, is the common language. Most people speak their tribal language and Krio, although in remote villages only the tribal language is spoken. Mende dominates in the south and Temne in the north. French is taught in secondary schools because of the country's many francophone neighbors.

Religion

Both Christianity and Islam are practiced in Sierra Leone, but neither claims a majority of people. Religious affiliation crosses ethnic and family lines. People of different faiths live in harmony because of their willingness to accept various beliefs as part of their eclectic (rather than exclusive) approach to religion. Most people believe in a supreme being, lesser deities, and a spirit world. Those who convert to a formal religion usually retain traditional animist beliefs as well, especially because animism is tied to daily life. Participation in secret societies, where socioreligious activities take place, is high, even among Christians and Muslims. Christianity was brought to Sierra Leone by returned slaves and gained converts through missionary schools. Islam is the fastest growing religion. Most Sierra Leonean Muslims are Sunnis. Lebanese Muslims are Shiites.

General Attitudes

Sierra Leoneans consider themselves first a member of their ethnic group and secondly a Sierra Leonean. Concerns are more provincial than national. People tend to be realistic and practical about their circumstances, which enables them to bear difficult situations. Two common Krio expressions are *Na so God say* (It is God's will) and *Ow fo do?* (What can you do?), to which the response is *Na fo biah* (You must bear it). Education is valued as the key to a better way of life. Material wealth is strived for, because it is a sign of security; young men often flaunt their possessions. There is no strict social hierarchy, but members of the chief's family are treated with great respect, as are the educated or wealthy. Sierra Leoneans are traditionally nonmilitant and peaceful, although a recent rise in militarism and violence indicates this may be changing for young men.

Personal Appearance

Western-style clothing is nearly universal for men and boys. Women wear *lappas*, two yards of ankle-length cloth tied about the waist and topped with an African or Western blouse. Women's heads are often covered, wrapped with fabric that usually matches the *lappa*. *Lappas* are commonly made of brightly colored cotton cloth imported from Europe and Asia. Trousers are almost unheard of for women, as are shorts for anyone but young boys. Maintaining a good appearance, regardless of the weather or one's wealth, is a priority. Traditional clothing is worn on special occasions. For example, over a *lappa* women wear matching long gowns made from *gara*, locally died cotton brocade. Men wear *gara* shirts with matching trousers. Around the shirt collar and pant cuffs is *planting*, fancy embroidery in a contrasting color.

CUSTOMS AND COURTESIES

Greetings

It is imperative to exchange greetings with a Sierra Leonean before one begins the topic of converstion. Greetings vary depending on the ethnic group. In Krio, "Hello" is *Kushe*. In Mende, it is *Bua*, and in Temne it is *Seke*. Men and women shake with the right hand. If meeting a person of high rank, it is customary to support one's right arm with the left arm—implying that the other's hand is of great weight. The Mende may shake another's hand and then touch the same hand to their heart. When greeting, it is polite to ask *Ow di bodi?* (How are you?) in Krio. In any language the response is typically *A tel God tanki* (I give thanks to God) in Krio. "Goodbye" might be said with *A de go* (I'm going) or *Nain dat* (That's all).

To address people, the title *Mr.* or *Miss* is often used with the first name. Other terms vary according to age relationship. For example, when addressing someone of the same age, *brother* or *sister* is acceptable. One may use *auntie*, *uncle*, *ma*, or *pa* to address those older. To call a stranger *padi* (friend) is common.

Gestures

It is impolite to put one's feet on a chair that is used for sitting. It is a sign of disrespect to direct the soles of one's feet towards another. It is also improper for a woman to whistle. Sierra Leoneans frequently hiss to get someone's attention and use the phrase *Ah sey!* (I say). To express displeasure in a rude way, Sierra Leoneans may "suck teeth" (making a sound by pulling air between pursed lips). Only the right hand is used for passing items. Members of the same sex often hold hands or maintain close body contact while talking, but this is rare between members of the opposite sex.

Visiting

Friends visit or *keep time* with one another frequently. Men enjoy sitting in the evenings and drinking fresh palm wine. Women socialize at the cooking house of the family compound. It is common upon meeting a Sierra Leonean to be told to expect a visit, but it is rare to receive an invitation. Unannounced guests are always welcome. It is not necessary to bring a gift when visiting another's home, but it is important to accept what the host offers—usually water or food. Honored guests are often given food upon departure. Although an event may have a designated starting time, guests might not arrive until up to two hours later. When guests leave, they are escorted at least to the edge of the host's property.

Eating

The traditional meal is usually served on a large platter with a bed of rice and a smaller amount of sauce in the center. The sauce is not mixed with the rice. Bones are left in the food; soft ones are eaten and harder ones are put aside. Eating practices vary according to locale and situation. In many homes, the husband may be served separately while the wife and children eat together. When visitors are present, adults eat from the common platter; children may be given spoonfuls of rice in their hands or a separate bowl. In villages, people eat with the right hand while squatting on the ground. In towns, spoons and chairs are more common. People do not drink during a meal; at the end of the meal a cup of water is passed around to drink from and to wash the face and hands.

Restaurants are uncommon, but urban people can buy a plate of rice at a "*kukri* house." Snacks (street food) such as bread and margarine, fried potatoes, fried plantains, fruit, roasted groundnuts, homemade candies, and cookies are available in towns.

LIFESTYLE

Family

Extended families are important in the lives of Sierra Leoneans. This is manifested by the fact that aunts may be addressed as *mother* and cousins as *brother* or *sister*. Three to five generations may live within a family compound. This allows for care of both the young and old while the able-bodied work in the fields. Where there is more than one wife in the compound, the wives share daily tasks and child rearing. This may not be the case for a paramount chief's wives, who may retain separate residences. Women generally take care of the compound, work in the garden and the market, and raise children, while men hunt, clear land, and do farm work. Men may also help with the upbringing of the children, but to a lesser extent than women. Most women give birth to nine children throughout their life. On average, six survive to maturity. *Fostering* is the custom of loaning a child to a childless woman to raise as one who will care for her in her old age; a child might also be lent to a wealthy person or relative who will educate and provide for him or her.

Dating and Marriage

Due to the coeducational system, relationships form early between boys and girls. Although parents try to discourage it, pregnancy among young girls is common. Dating without intending to marry is accepted in urban areas, but not in villages. A date may be just a walk through the town or a chat on the veranda. Marriage customs differ according to the locale. In villages, a marriage may be arranged at any age, but it does not formally take place until the girl reaches puberty. The prospective husband agrees to pay the bride's parents a marriage payment after a great deal of negotiating and, sometimes, input from the whole village. It is the preparation for marriage, not the wedding itself, that is the event. Upon marriage, the woman goes to live in the husband's family's household. Polygamy is common. Western-oriented Sierra Leoneans choose their spouses.

Diet

Locally grown crops are supplemented by imported items, such as tea, sugar, salt, and canned goods. The staple food is rice, eaten with a *plassas* (sauce), the most common one being made from pounded cassava leaves, palm oil, and chili peppers. The diet also consists of groundnuts, sweet potatoes, beans, fish, chicken, goat, small bush animals such as ground pigs (large rodents), *freetambos* (miniature deer), and an abundance of seasonal tropical fruit (bananas, plantains, pineapples, star fruits, breadfruits, papayas, oranges, grapefruits, mangos, and coconuts). The Fulas herd cattle that are occasionally slaughtered and sold in the market. Meals tend to be unbalanced when the price of fish, beans, or groundnuts is high; then the diet consists mainly of rice and leaf sauces. Malnutrition is widespread among children because they receive the smallest portions of protein-rich foods (eggs and meat). Typically, a midday snack is followed by a large meal in the late afternoon; leftovers are put aside for the following morning's breakfast.

Recreation

Soccer is a popular sport and matches are usually well attended. Lack of resources and lack of leisure time make other organized sports uncommon. However, schoolchildren compete among themselves in a variety of events (mostly track and field) during Sports Week. One event is the *paw paw* race where students run while carrying smaller students on their backs. Urban movie theaters usually show Indian, karate, and action-filled American films. Reggae music is widely popular. Disco dances that last until dawn accompany special events, even in towns without electricity, where a generator and sound system are rented for the occasion. Traditional music, dance, and theater play important, symbolic roles in the lives of people, especially those living *up-country* (outside of the capital). Strangers are not permitted to attend certain events where traditional performances take place. Photography is often prohibited, even in public shows.

Holidays

Sierra Leone's national days are Independence Day (27 April) and Revolution Day (29 April). Western and Christian holidays such as New Year's, Easter, and Christmas are universally celebrated, as is Pray Day, the last day of the

Muslim month of *Ramadan*. The tradition surrounding New Year's and Easter is to have a party, sometimes with a sound system, at a nearby river or beach. In towns with high hills, like Kabala, the New Year's tradition is to climb the mountain, taking along livestock to be slaughtered for a celebratory feast. Masquerades are a popular part of big celebrations: masked "devils," which are often associated with specific secret societies, entertain the people. On any holiday, children often go door-to-door asking for (and sometimes dancing and singing for) money.

Commerce

Government offices and retailers are primarily open from 9:00 A.M. to 5:00 P.M. Open-air markets are active during daylight hours. The evening brings out a different selection of goods, usually freshly cooked food and such items as cigarettes, soap, *mosquito coils*, and aspirin. Towns have a designated "market day" that is an expansion of the everyday market, with merchants from nearby villages selling more varied goods. Prices are fixed only in stores; bargaining is expected in markets.

SOCIETY

Government

Sierra Leone is currently governed by the National Provisional Ruling Council, but the future structure of the government is unknown. The unicameral House of Representatives and the Supreme Court were both suspended by the 1992 coup. A new constitution is being drafted by an independent advisory council. A few months prior to national elections, political parties will be legalized and allowed to post candidates according to the rules of the new constitution.

Economy

Despite such natural resources as diamonds, gold, bauxite, rutile, and ilmenite, Sierra Leone remains a poor country with 75 percent of its people engaged in subsistence agriculture. Much of the diamonds and some crops are smuggled out of the country. Sierra Leone relies on food subsidies from abroad and imports most manufactured goods. Export crops include palm kernels, coffee, cocoa, ginger, kola nuts, and piassava. Freetown benefits from a small amount of tourism. The currency is the *leone* (Le), which is sometimes referred to as the *pound*. One *pound* equals two *leones*.

The country's Human Development Index (0.209) ranks it 170th out of 173 countries. Real gross domestic product per capita is $1,020, but this figure is distorted by a highly unequal distribution of income. The vast majority of people are very poor, earning far less than they need. Two-thirds of all people live in absolute poverty, and only a small wealthy class enjoys the benefits of economic opportunity.

Transportation and Communication

Two paved roads link Northern and Eastern Sierra Leone with the capital. Most roads are unpaved, but the government is working to improve road conditions throughout the country. Neither the national airline nor the railroad function anymore, having been phased out under Siaka Stevens. Common forms of transportation are *poda-poda* (lorries), taxis, mopeds, and bicycles. *Poda-podas* are small pickups fitted with seats and a roof; they carry people, goods, and animals. In rural areas, people generally walk except when traveling extremely long distances or when transporting a large load (such as to or from the market). Freetown has a large natural harbor. Postal service is fairly reliable, but rural delivery is unpredictable. Telephones are most common in Freetown, but also operate in surrounding areas and larger *up-country* cities. The capital has several daily newspapers, which are subject to government censorship. The national radio broadcast can be picked up throughout much of the country, but television is currently limited to the Freetown area.

Education

Formal education is based on the British model. Schools are often run by missions. Classes are taught in English, although in rural primary schools instruction in local languages is common. Children may begin school at age five. The dropout rate is high because of parents' inability to pay fees and other difficulties. About one-fifth of school-aged children attend secondary schools. The curriculum often does not address the needs of rural people. The literacy rate is 20 percent. Indigenous education, bush schools, or secret societies teach children skills and customs perceived as necessary by village elders. Such training prepares children to join society as adults. Sierra Leone has several teacher training colleges and one university.

Health

Government-provided health care is inadequate. Most services, such as vaccinations, are provided by the World Health Organization and by mission hospitals. People generally rely on a combination of traditional and Western medicines. Limited knowledge of nutrition and preventative care results in chronic illnesses such as malaria, anemia, and gastrointestinal diseases. Also prevalent are tuberculosis, schistosomiasis, leprosy, and various skin lesions, attributable to nutritional deficiencies, that are slow to heal because of the climate. Water is not potable. Goiter is endemic in the northeastern highlands, where the iodine content of the water is very low. The infant mortality rate is 141 per 1,000. Adults expect to live an average of 46 years.

FOR THE TRAVELER

A passport, visa, and proof of yellow fever and cholera vaccinations are required of U.S. visitors. Malarial suppressants are essential and other vaccinations may be recommended. Drink only bottled soda, bottled water, or undiluted palm wine. Peel fruits and vegetables before eating. Avoid swimming in fresh water. Beware of pickpockets and petty theft. Also beware of violence in the Eastern Province, where the rebels intimidate entire villages. For more information, contact the Embassy of Sierra Leone, 1701 19th Street NW, Washington, DC 20009; phone (202) 939–9261.

A *Culturgram* is a product of native commentary and original, expert analysis. Statistics are estimates and information is presented as a matter of opinion. While the editors strive for accuracy and detail, this document should not be considered strictly factual. It is a general introduction to culture, an initial step in building bridges of understanding between peoples. It may not apply to all peoples of the nation. You should therefore consult other sources for more information.

CULTURGRAM ™ '96

Republic of
Singapore

A
S
I
A

BACKGROUND

Land and Climate

Singapore is an island about the same size as the city of Chicago (244 square miles [632 square kilometers]) and is located off the tip of the Malaysian peninsula. Several smaller islands also belong to the republic. Part of Singapore occupies land that was reclaimed from the sea through landfill operations. Singapore is actually a city-state, with all areas being part of the capital. There are essentially no rural areas.

Except for the central plateau, most of the island is low-lying and originally consisted of wetlands and jungles. Eighty-five percent of the jungle has been cleared. A nature preserve is located in the central highlands. Singapore's climate is virtually unchanging. Temperatures range between 78°F (25°C) and 82°F (28°C) all year. There are no distinct rainy or dry seasons; it is humid and rainy throughout the year. Cool night breezes are common.

History

Before a Buddhist prince named the island Singa Pura and established a thriving port in the 14th century, there was only a tiny fishing village called Temasek on Singapore Island. For many years the island was a source of conflict between various interests on the mainland. In the 19th century,

Singapore's strategic location and natural deep-water ports attracted the British. In 1819, Sir Stamford Raffles established a British trading post on the island and obtained it as a possession in 1824. The trade city was created out of a mangrove wetland and began to thrive.

Singapore was important to the British during World War II and became a crown colony in 1948. Internal self-rule was granted in 1959. The activities of several radical political organizations (most notably the Communists) caused leaders to accept a merger with the Federation of Malaya in 1963. Singapore's inclusion in Malaysia caused domestic political problems, and the government announced the island's independence in 1965. Lee Kuan Yew, first named prime minister in 1959, led Singapore for 31 years. He is popular among the people for shaping Singapore into a solid economic power and for stressing practicality over ideology.

Lee resigned in 1990 in favor of a younger man, Goh Chok Tong. Lee remains the leader of the People's Action Party and an advisor to the government. Goh has continued Lee's policies, citing the need to encourage strong social values through legislation. In the early 1990s, Singapore was criticized by Western and other nations for its severe punishment of convicted criminals. Singapore defended its actions by pointing out its low crime rates and high degree of social order.

THE PEOPLE

Population

Singapore's population is 2.8 million and is growing at 1.1 percent annually. The population density is more than 11,400 persons per square mile (4,400 per square kilometer), making Singapore one of the most densely populated countries in the world. The entire population lives in urban areas. Singapore is sometimes called "Instant Asia" by outsiders because of its great diversity of cultures and peoples. Three major Asian cultures— the Chinese, Malay, and Indian—are all represented in Singapore. Slightly more than 76 percent of the population is Chinese. Fifteen percent is Malay, and about 6 percent is Indian. Various other groups are also represented, including Caucasians and Japanese.

Language

Singapore's multiplicity of languages reflects its racial diversity. Malay, Chinese, Tamil, and English are all official languages. Malay is the national language, while English is the language of administration. All Singaporeans are expected to learn English, which is most widely used in science, technology, commerce, and tourism. But the government encourages the use of all the languages in order to maintain traditional cultures and values. The Chinese speak a number of different Chinese dialects (Hokkein, Chaozhou, and Cantonese, among others), but the use of Standard Chinese (also called Putonghua or Mandarin) is gradually replacing all other forms of Chinese. Most Singaporeans are bilingual or multilingual.

Religion

Singaporeans enjoy freedom of worship, although some religious groups have not been allowed to organize because they are considered antigovernment. Buddhism, Taoism, Confucianism, Islam, Christianity, Hinduism, and Judaism, as well as a number of smaller religions, are all practiced in Singapore. About half of the population is either Buddhist or Taoist, most of whom are Chinese. Many practice a combination of Buddhism, Taoism, and Confucianism. Nearly all the Malays are Muslim. Ten percent of the population is Christian, and about 5 percent is Hindu. A significant minority, many of them Chinese, are either atheists or agnostics. The Christians are generally either Chinese or European. These religions all operate in harmony, with Buddhist and Hindu temples next to Muslim mosques and Christian churches. There are two Jewish synagogues in the country. In some cases, such as marriages or family matters, the religions are allowed to establish government-recognized laws for their members.

General Attitudes

Singaporeans consider their nation to be different than other modern societies because they hold to traditional Asian values. These include having a strong family unit that is responsible for its members, putting society and the group before the individual, and fostering a sense of nationhood. The work ethic is strongly advocated and Singaporeans have a reputation as an industrious people. Likewise, high moral and ethical values are stressed in government and business.

The nation's attention to a well-ordered society has allowed it, as Singaporeans believe, to build a highly prosperous modern economy without suffering the social drawbacks inherent to liberal democracy. Cultural ideals and traditions are extremely important. The government uses laws to discourage the existence of single-parent families and out-of-wedlock births. For instance, a single and never-married mother cannot purchase low-cost housing from the government or get public health benefits for her children. In addition, children are expected to respect and obey parents, as well as be financially responsible for them in their old age. Financial incentives are given to young people who buy apartments near their parents. The government believes these programs are necessary to avoid the negative aspects of materialism.

Singaporeans value discipline, self-control, education, honesty, and humility. Avoiding public criticism that could shame another person is important. Shaming another person, or causing them to "lose face," also shames the offending individual and is a breach of social courtesy. Likewise, "antisocial" acts shame one's entire family. Hence, conformity is stressed in the name of maintaining a strong society.

In the past, the multicultural makeup of the country has led to some racial conflicts. However, the government has been remarkably successful in promoting racial harmony and national unity. Today, most Singaporean youth identify themselves as Singaporean first and as Chinese, Malay, or Indian second.

Personal Appearance

Due to the different ethnic groups in Singapore, as well as the country's modern character, there are many different styles of attire. Western-style clothing is the most common. Lightweight fabrics are the norm. The Indian *sari* (wraparound skirt worn by women) and traditional Muslim suits and dresses are also worn.

CUSTOMS AND COURTESIES

Greetings

Specific greetings and other customs depend on nationality and age group. However, a handshake is the most common gesture of greeting, with the addition of a slight bow for the Chinese and older people. Among the Malay, people clasp both hands in a handshake, then release and touch both hands to their own hearts. While various languages are used for greetings, English is common and acceptable. Between business representatives and other officials, the exchange of business cards often accompanies a greeting.

Gestures

Touching another person's head is impolite. Persons crossing their legs do not place the ankle of one leg on the knee of the other; rather, one knee rests over the other. It is impolite for the bottom of the foot to point at a person. Also, feet are not used to move objects. Hitting the fist into the cupped hand is inappropriate. Beckoning is done by waving all fingers of the right hand with the palm facing down. Finger gestures, such as pointing or forming the rounded "OK" sign, are considered rude. A slight bow when entering, leaving, or passing a group of people shows courtesy.

Visiting

Visiting among relatives is important in maintaining family relations. Married children regularly visit their elderly parents or join them for a meal. Invited guests are expected to be punctual on all occasions. Hosts serve drinks when the guests first arrive. Other refreshments are also usually offered. It is impolite for a host not to offer something to drink or eat. On special holidays, hosts arrange a number of sweetmeats and other refreshments on the coffee table for all guests to enjoy. Compliments are appreciated by hosts, but will be politely denied for modesty's sake. If a gift is given to a host or guest, it is only opened later when the recipient is not in the presence of the giver. Most families require that shoes be removed before entering the home. Shoes are also removed when visiting certain religious buildings (temples, shrines, or mosques).

Eating

Because Singapore is a cosmopolitan society, etiquette and eating habits vary according to the style of food being eaten and the people eating it. Both Western-style utensils and chopsticks can be easily found. Likewise, some foods are eaten with a spoon, some with the hands. In restaurants, a service charge is included in the bill. Tips, therefore, are not usually necessary and may be discouraged in some cases.

LIFESTYLE

Family

Traditionally, the Chinese, Malay, and Indian peoples have encouraged large families. A family-planning campaign reduced growth to the rate of many Western nations. Families have an average of two to three children. The family system is strong. Cooperation, loyalty, respect for elders, and unity are deeply valued in all Singaporean families.

When both spouses work outside the home, grandparents often provide child care to young children. Otherwise, the father is to be the primary provider and the mother the one who cares for the children at home. The father is the head of the household, but women have equal political and educational rights. Men are encouraged to share household responsibilities, but the burden usually rests on women. Children gain certain benefits only through their fathers, a government policy designed to discourage nontraditional family units.

Elderly parents sometimes live with their married children, but may also live alone near their children. Society considers it the responsibility of children to be financially responsible for their aged parents.

Dating and Marriage

Dating begins around age 17. Parents (especially among the Chinese) often discourage dating until a young person

has completed an education. They believe that dating interferes with one's studies. Young people enjoy going to movies, taking walks, dancing, and other activities. Although many of the ethnic groups traditionally arranged marriages for their children, nearly all youth now make their own decisions regarding marriage. Few people live together before or instead of getting married, as this is seen as improper behavior.

Diet

Rice is the dietary staple of Singapore, and fish or other seafood provide the primary source of protein. A wide variety of foods are available. Spicy Malay foods dipped in peanut sauce, Indian curries, Chinese dishes, and a number of European foods are all found in Singapore. Fish-head curry (a fish head in a curry sauce with tomatoes, pineapple, and green onions) is a favorite dish of many people. Pineapple, papayas, bananas, durians, and mangoes are among the most common fruits.

Recreation

Singaporeans enjoy a number of sports, including soccer, badminton, basketball, tennis, and golf. Water sports of all kinds are popular. Among senior citizens, the Chinese exercise of shadowboxing *(taijiquan)* and the French game of *petanque* are favored. The people have access to a wide variety of cultural arts, as well as movies and television programs. Singaporeans also participate in a variety of martial arts, such as *tae kwon do*.

Holidays

A number of holidays are associated with the various religions of the country. While celebrated by the appropriate parties, they are not considered national holidays. However, the most important religious holidays are considered national holidays along with the government's political holidays. These include International New Year (1 January), Chinese New Year (date varies according to the Chinese lunar calendar, usually in February), Easter (including Friday), Vesak Day (celebrating the birth, enlightenment, and nirvana of Buddha and held during the fifth lunar month), Labor Day (1 May), and Singapore National Day (9 August).

Hari Raya Puasa is a feast at the end of the Islamic month of *Ramadan.* During *Ramadan,* Muslims go without food or drink each day from sunrise to sundown. This feast is unique in Singapore, because other religions are welcome to join in a celebration that expresses tolerance and renewal. *Hari Raya Haji*, another Muslim festival, celebrates the pilgrimage to Makkah, Saudi Arabia. *Deepavali* (Festival of Lights) is important to Hindus and Sikhs and celebrates the triumph of light over darkness. Thousands of lights decorate stores and homes, and the festival is celebrated by all people in Singapore as a time of goodwill. Christmas is also celebrated.

Commerce

While shops are usually open seven days a week for as many as ten hours a day, most businesses are generally open from 8:30 A.M. to 4:30 P.M., Monday through Friday, and until 12:30 P.M. on Saturday. If a business is open on Sunday, it is required by law to close on another day. Shops are not under this restriction. One-third of the labor force is female.

SOCIETY

Government

Singapore is a democratic republic with a very stable government. The president, Ong Teng Cheong, is head of state, but the prime minister (Goh Chok Tong) exercises executive authority and heads the government with his cabinet. There are 81 seats in the unicameral parliament, which is dominated by the ruling People's Action Party. The voting age is 20; all citizens are required to vote in national elections. Small opposition parties exist, but have very little power.

Economy

Although Singapore is the smallest country in Southeast Asia, its entrepreneurial economy is the most prosperous. Its people have one of the highest standards of living in Asia. During the 1980s, the economy grew between 9 and 11 percent each year, generating rapid expansion and development. Even growth in the 1990s, despite global recession, was high. In 1994, it was more than 9 percent. In addition to a high standard of living, inflation is low and a condition of "full employment" exists. That means the unemployment rate is below 3 percent.

The country's Human Development Index (0.836) ranks it 43d out of 173 countries. Real gross domestic product per capita is $15,880, which has increased by nearly seven times since 1960. These figures reflect the economy's phenomenal growth rate. Most people earn a good income, although the overall distribution of income is somewhat unequal. All have access to quality education, education, health care, and employment; a growing number is enjoying luxury consumer items and more spacious housing than was available in years past.

Much of Singapore's trade consists of receiving exports from other countries and then reexporting them. Petroleum refining is the largest industrial activity of Singapore, but the republic has also become an important world financial center and manufacturer. Tourism is very important to the economy and is actively promoted throughout the world. Because of limited space, Singapore's agricultural industry is relatively small, so most of the country's food is imported. The United States and Malaysia are two of Singapore's largest trading partners. The currency is the Singapore dollar (S$).

Transportation and Communication

Singapore is served by international airlines and is linked to Thailand and Malaysia by road and rail. Singapore's roads are paved and well maintained. A subway system (Mass Rapid Transit) serves the urban population. Many people own cars, but public transportation is well developed. The communications system is fully modern and extensive. Radio and television facilities are operated by the government. Newspapers are privately owned, but must be licensed.

Education

Valued because of a traditional emphasis on learning among Asian cultures, education is important in Singapore. The country also needs a steady supply of skilled workers, which encourages Singaporeans to take advantage of the nation's educational opportunities. Schooling is free and compulsory for children ages six to sixteen. Six years of primary education are followed by at least four years of secondary education. Nearly all children complete primary schooling, and 70 percent finish secondary school. After ten years of schooling, many continue in vocational schools or preuniversity programs. Children learn their mother tongue in school as well as English. English is the language of instruction. The National University of Singapore was established in 1980, and there are various other technical schools of higher learning. In addition, many students travel abroad for higher degrees. The adult literacy rate in Singapore is 88 percent, but among the youth (15–19 years old), it approaches 100 percent.

Health

All basic health care needs are subsidized by the government, making them available to all citizens. Medical facilities and services are excellent. A high standard of health is attributed to the development of good housing, modern sanitation, and a general concern for sound hygienic practices. The government promotes extensive tree-planting projects and streets are kept clean (there is a heavy fine for littering). Singapore is often referred to as the cleanest city in Asia, which contributes to the overall good health of the people. The infant mortality rate is 6 per 1,000. Life expectancy ranges from 73 to 78 years.

FOR THE TRAVELER

No visa is necessary for U.S. travelers staying up to two weeks, but a passport is required. No vaccinations are needed to visit Singapore, but the country requires a yellow fever vaccination certificate if a traveler is coming from an infected area. Water is safe to drink. Be aware of strictly enforced laws regarding littering, jaywalking, or other such behavior. Also, because of Singapore's strict enforcement of drug possession laws, it is wise to carry prescriptions for all medications to avoid any difficulties with authorities. For shopping, sports, and a number of other reasons, Singapore is a favorite tourist destination. For more information, contact the Singapore Tourist Promotion Board. In New York, the address is 590 Fifth Avenue, 12th Floor, New York, NY 10036; phone (212) 302–4861. For the West Coast, the address is 8484 Wilshire Boulevard, Suite 510, Beverly Hills, CA 90211; phone (213) 852–1901. You may also wish to contact the Embassy of Singapore, 3501 International Place NW, Washington, DC 20008; phone (202) 537–3100.

Boundary representations not necessarily authoritative.

Republic of
Somalia

BACKGROUND

Land and Climate

Somalia, situated on the Horn of Africa, covers 246,300 square miles (638,000 square kilometers). Somalia's northern Guban, a semiarid plain parallel to the Gulf of Aden, gives way to the Ogo Highlands, where Shimbir Berris, the highest peak, reaches 7,900 feet (2,400 meters). Grazing rangeland south of the mountains and west of the Indian Ocean covers most of the country. Pasture quality depends on the amount of rain received from April to June and September to October. The most fertile land lies between the Juba and Shebelle Rivers, where crops are grown commercially. Lower Juba (south of the Juba River), is covered by thick bush but still supports some farming and livestock production. Much of Somalia has been damaged by drought and overgrazing.

Somalia is a hot, semiarid country. Some cities have average annual temperatures of above 88°F (31°C). The Guban is often 100°F (38°C). The mountains are cooler, experiencing all four seasons. Mogadishu is hot and humid all year.

History

Somalis have inhabited the Horn of Africa for centuries, occupying an area from near the Gulf of Aden, south to the Tana River in Kenya, and west to Harar in Ethiopia. Early long-distance trade routes were established and Somali ivory, ostrich feathers, leopard skins, frankincense, and myrrh were carried as far away as China. While the Somalis remained inland, the coast hosted visitors and settlers from India, Persia, Arabia, and Portugal. Their influence on architecture, clothing, language, and customs is evident today.

Islam was introduced to Somalia in the ninth century by Arab sheiks who married into Somali families. Arabs controlled the southern coast between the ninth and nineteenth centuries, with the Sultan of Oman ruling as far south as Zanzibar until European exploration began in the 1800s. The French, British, and Italians all competed for territory in the region. In the 1880s, British Somaliland was established in the north, Italian Somaliland in the south, and French Somaliland in the area of present-day Djibouti. The British ceded lands it held west of the Juba River to Italy in 1925.

Somalis opposed colonialism and still have bitter feelings about the era. A rebellion launched in 1900 against Britain lasted until 1920; it failed but it intensified Somali nationalism and led to independence. In 1960, British and Italian Somalilands were united to form the Somali Republic.

Undermined by clan rivalries and corruption, the new parliamentary government never stabilized. Military leaders staged a successful 1969 coup. General Mohammed Siad Barre became president and suspended the constitution. He sought to reorder society and end tribal institutions by declaring Somalia a socialist state. The regime received significant military aid, especially from its new ally, the Soviet Union.

With many ethnic Somalis living in neighboring countries, Somali often clashed with Ethiopia, Kenya, and Djibouti. As a result of a 1977–78 war over Ethiopia's Ogaden region, nearly one million Somali refugees poured into Somalia from Ethiopia, and Soviet and American weapons and ammunition were left behind.

Political repression and corruption combined with the factors mentioned above to spark a 1981 civil war between government forces and insurrectionists. The northern Isaak-led Somali National Movement (SNM) joined forces with the United Somali Congress (USC), composed mostly of Hawiye subclans, to fight the Darod-led government. In January 1991, the Siad government collapsed and Somalia's political disintegration followed. The northern groups broke with the USC and declared an independent Somaliland, proclaiming the 1960 union illegal. This northern republic has not been internationally recognized but maintains its sovereignty claim.

Meanwhile, southern alliances dissolved and Mogadishu was split between rival Hawiye subclans. The city plunged into anarchy and the entire country was left without a central government. By 1992, famine, disease, and war threatened much of the population. A U.S.-led United Nations (UN) effort was launched to stop the dying. While the initial goal was largely met, rebuilding a viable government proved elusive, and Somalis began to resent international involvement in their political affairs. Relief workers and troops soon became targets of violence and by 1994, anarchy was again the rule in Mogadishu. U.S. troops left in March 1994, and the UN declared the mission over in March 1995. Negotiations between rival clans and with international mediators have continued, but they have not been very productive.

PEOPLE

Population

About 7.5 million people live in Somalia. Related to the Afar, Oromo, and other Cushitic peoples living on the Horn of Africa, Somalis constitute 95 percent of the population. Minority groups include the Somali-speaking Hamari in Mogadishu and a related Arabic-speaking people living in other coastal cities; the Bajun, farmers and fishermen of Swahili origin; the Barawani, who speak a language related to Swahili; and other Bantu-speaking farmers living mostly along the Shebelle River. Before 1991, urbanization was increasing and about one million people lived in Mogadishu.

Somali society is organized into large, extended clan families, ranging in size from 100,000 to as many as two million. There are six very large clans (Darod, Isaak, Hawiye, Dir, Digil, and Rahanwayn) and a number of medium-to-small groups. Each of the larger families is further divided into lineage units that may range from 10,000 to 100,000 individuals. Additional divisions are made in these groups based on kinship alliances of smaller extended families. Once two people know each other's name and clan membership, it is possible for them to know exactly where they fit into society and what their responsibilities are to each other. In rural areas, one can ask about another's lineage directly, but in an urban area it is more polite to identify it through indirect questions (such as about the person's home region).

Language

Somali belongs to the Cushitic language family. It has three main dialects, each of which is difficult for speakers of the other two to understand. The dialects include *Af-Maymay,* spoken between the Shebelle and Juba Rivers; *Af-Benaadir*, spoken on the coast from Mogadishu south; and standard Somali spoken everywhere else. English, Italian, and Arabic are spoken by various educated Somalis.

Until recently, Somali was an unwritten language; songs and poetry played a significant role in oral communication. In the 20th century, unique local scripts emerged and Latin alphabets were introduced by Westerners. By the late 1960s, more than ten local scripts were being used in Somalia. Each script's usage depended on the clan to which its author belonged, its usefulness, and other factors. In 1972, the government adopted a Latin-based script and began to introduce it in schools and government documents. Literacy increased dramatically, due partly to a campaign to teach reading and writing in rural areas. The script has yet to be fully standardized and uniformly adopted.

Religion

Nearly all Somalis are Sunni Muslims. A small number are Christians. All towns have mosques; many on the coast are hundreds of years old, and some Mogadishu mosques are up to one thousand years old. Muslims believe in a single God (*Allah*) and that Muhammad was his last and greatest prophet. Islamic scripture, the *Qur'an*, is believed to be the word of *Allah* as revealed to Muhammad. Muslims are taught to practice their religion through praying five times daily, giving alms to the poor, making a pilgrimage to Makkah, abstaining from alcohol and pork, and attending to other duties.

General Attitudes

Most Somalis in the interior have had little exposure to anything outside of Somalia; even during the colonial era, European culture did not extend much beyond coastal cities. In the countryside, colonial powers were distrusted and disliked, and today's Somalis view foreign assistance as having political motives. They may accept and be grateful for short-term assistance, but they sense paternalism quickly and may react violently to what they view as the belittling of their culture or character. In addition, each person considers himself or herself to be equal among Somalis, even though larger clans claim higher status. Somalis consider themselves subservient to no one but *Allah*. Unlike some Muslim countries, women own property and manage businesses, even as they occupy a vital position in the extended family.

Somalis cherish self-reliance, autonomy, and tradition. They value friendship based on mutual respect. Verbal thanks is not often expressed, since giving obligates the receiver to reciprocate—unless the gift is charity, which is seen as an offering to *Allah* and requires no thanks.

Personal Appearance

Somalis are generally tall and slender with narrow features. Urban men wear Western pants or a flowing plaid *ma'awiis* (kilt), Western shirts, and shawls. On their heads they may wrap a colorful turban or wear a *koofiyad* (embroidered cap). Rural men wear two five-yard lengths of cloth—one wrapped around the waist to hang below the knees, and the other wrapped around the upper body, or carried on the shoulder. For women, the most fashionable northern dress is the *direh*, a long, billowing dress worn over petticoats. The southern favorite is the *guntino*, a four-yard cloth tied over one shoulder and wrapped around the waist. Rural women wear sturdier varieties of the same clothing. All women wear shawls and head scarves. With the exception of a minority near the southern coast, women do not usually veil their faces. Women like sparkling, colorful touches in their everyday clothing. During religious holidays, children customarily receive new clothes if the family can afford it.

Somalis bathe and wash often. They clean their teeth with sticks from a particular tree and polish them with powdered charcoal. Children wash their feet before bed. Women burn incense to perfume their bodies and homes. Henna gives women's hair and skin a glowing reddish tone.

CUSTOMS AND COURTESIES

Greetings

Somalis greet each other by name or, in the case of relatives, by a word that shows their relationship (uncle, cousin, etc.). General greetings vary according to region and situation, but *Nabad* (Peace) is accepted nearly everywhere. The common southern variation is *Nabad miya?* (Is there peace?). Its equivalent in the north is *Ma nabad baa?* The Islamic greeting *Asalaamu aleikum* (Peace be upon you) is a common formal greeting, to which the response is *Aleikum ma salaam* (And peace be upon you). Such phrases are followed by inquiries as to the general health and welfare of the individual and an exchange of information. *Iska warran?* (What's the news?) and *Maha la shegay?* (What are people saying?) are used as a "How are you?" in some parts of the country.

Men firmly shake hands with each other three times before putting that hand to their hearts. In some southern areas, women shake hands with each other and then kiss the hand they have shaken. Somalis of the opposite sex who are not related usually do not touch when meeting.

Gestures

Somalis use sweeping hand and arm gestures to dramatize speech. The eyes follow the direction of the hands, and the fingers may flutter. Many ideas are expressed through specific hand gestures, such as placing both index fingers parallel to one another to indicate "the same." A swift twist of the open hand and wrist means "nothing" or "no." A thumb under the chin indicates fullness. Snapping fingers may mean "long ago" or "and so on."

Visiting

Somali women socialize by visiting at home or at the market. Visitors need not take gifts or food to their hosts. Before entering a family compound, one announces his or her presence and waits awhile in order not to surprise a family. Sweet, spicy tea with milk is served to visitors in urban settings; other refreshments might also be available. In rural areas, tea or milk is offered. A favorite time for urban visiting is late afternoon, when most work is done and it is not too hot to stroll around. In rural areas, night is a better time, as farm chores are completed and animals have settled down. When families socialize, men and women usually interact separately.

Tea shops, which often have tables outside, are centers for men to socialize and discuss current affairs. *Khat*, a leafy green branch from a tree grown in the Ethiopian highlands and elsewhere, is chewed after lunch by men. Women do not usually chew *khat*. After many hours of chewing, a mild high results; sustained use can lead to addiction.

Eating

When more than the immediate family is eating, men and women usually eat separately. In rural restaurants, women might choose to eat in rooms or areas separate from men. For the family meal, men are usually served first and the women and children eat later. Hands are washed in a bowl of water before and after the meal. On festive occasions, hands are also perfumed after the meal. When eating, people gather around a large common platter set on a table or on a mat on the ground. Diners eat with the right hand from the portion of the food directly in front of them; guests are usually given larger servings. Young children are fed from the hand of the mother or a relative. The left hand does not usually have direct contact with food, as it is reserved for personal hygiene and prayer purification. Overeating is considered unacceptable.

LIFESTYLE

Family

Children assume their father's surname and clan affiliation. A mother's family may be from another clan, but warm relationships exist among cousins who knew each other as children. The mother retains her maiden name and position in her clan. Family loyalty is important and families help one another in times of need. It is assumed that help will be reciprocated if needed in the future. Any good deeds bring honor to the family, clan, and society. The most fortunate members of a family feel especially obligated to help the others. Because resources are scarce, the hierarchy of who should be aided is clear. For instance, the extended family of the father's relatives has first priority. Aid can include such things as food, money, or shelter. Urban families might take in children of rural relatives and put them through school. War and repeated droughts have severely strained this system of mutual aid, and social cohesion has suffered—especially in urban areas.

Dating and Marriage

Dating in the Western sense does not exist in Somalia, although it is common for young men and women to participate jointly in traditional dances. Virginity is valued in women prior to marriage. Divorce is legal and does occur. Arranged marriages are common; brides in these cases are often much younger than the grooms. Marriage to a cousin from the mother's side of the family (that is, of different lineage) has traditionally been favored as a way to strengthen family alliances, but this practice has been somewhat disrupted. Since 1991, Somalis have tended to trust only members of their own clan for marriage. Weddings are celebrated by both families. Special foods, like *muqmad* (dried beef in clarified butter) and dates are served. In some areas, the couple is sequestered for a seven-day honeymoon.

Diet

Urban staple foods consist of locally produced meats and imported rice. In farming areas, sorghum, millet, corn, and sesame are common staples. Among the nomads, milk from camels and goats is the main food available, supplemented with grains bought with money from the sale of animals. The milk is made into several varieties of yogurt.

Most people eat pancakes made from flour or millet for breakfast, rice or millet served with milk and *ghee* (butter) for lunch and/or supper, and a small snack of milk or a bean dish in the evening. Nomads typically do not eat lunch when they are herding animals away from their homes. Vegetables are gradually being added to the diet, but they are still a novelty. Bananas, papayas, and mangos are seasonal and plentiful. In some places limes are always available and grapefruit abound in season. Italian pasta has become popular in the cities as an alternative to rice. Fish is a staple in coastal towns.

Recreation

Soccer is enjoyed by the youth; videos are popular in towns. Organized sports have basically been destroyed by war. Cultural arts, however, remain vital leisure and social activities. Poetry is one of those arts and Somala is viewed as a nation of poets. Today poems and songs, part of the oral culture that still flourishes, are recorded on cassettes and sent wherever Somalis live. Many poems are about love, but others contain political commentary. This political poetry is called *gabay*. Common poetic metaphors known throughout society help unify Somali culture. Plays and music are also performed.

Accompanied by songs, stringed musical instruments (in the south), and drums, Somali dancers perform in two parallel lines of men and women, or in circles.

Holidays

Observed Islamic holy days include *'Eid al Fitr* (three-day feast at the end of *Ramadan*), *'Eid al Adha* (Feast of Sacrifice, honoring Abraham's willingness to sacrifice his son), and *Mawliid*, the Prophet Muhammad's birthday. Fasting from dawn until dusk each day of the holy month of *Ramadan* is observed. Prior to the current crisis, independence from Britain in the north was celebrated 26 June, and from Italy in the south on 1 July. The ancient Persian New Year (*Dab Shiid*, or Starting Fire) is celebrated in many parts of Somalia.

Commerce

Organized commerce has been greatly disrupted. Open markets form the basis of daily commercial activity.

SOCIETY

Government

Various factional leaders have sought to form a central government, but no agreement has been reached, although a Western-style government does control the self-declared Republic of Somaliland. While Somalia does not have a unified government, traditional political structures based on clan affiliation still exist. For example, a Somali man in certain clans is customarily part of a *shir*, an open deliberation forum of extended families or clan groups. *Shir* decisions are made by consensus; through elected chiefs, a *shir* can declare war or peace, make policy for participating clans, and even dissolve itself if the alliance breaks down. Disputes within and between families are often solved through informal arbitration panels set up by a *shir*, through dialogue, or by war. Since alliances change, a *shir* is not a source of permanent authority.

Economy

Animal products accounted for the bulk of Somalia's exports before the civil war. Meat in the form of live animals was shipped to Saudi Arabia and other markets; hides and skins were also exported. Somali sheep are especially prized in the Middle East. Agricultural products such as bananas were exported from the south. The nomads herd camels, cattle, sheep, and goats. Northern economic activity is resuming with some exports to the Middle East.

Political instability, lack of a skilled labor force, poor land utilization, and other factors have inhibited economic growth in the past. However, Somalia could access marine resources and possible oil fields. Agriculture and minerals are also areas of significant future potential. Somalia's Human Development Index (0.217) ranks it 165th out of 173 countries. Real gross domestic product per capita is estimated at $759.

Transportation and Communication

The system of roads in Somalia consists mostly of dirt tracks. It does extend between major cities, however, and large trucks once traveled the routes with passengers and goods. A system of minivans transports passengers between towns in times of peace. An international airport at Mogadishu, smaller airports in other towns, and dirt landing fields all exist in Somalia. The Mogadishu airport has been closed to regular international traffic since 1990, but it allows some chartered flights. Northern cities receive regular flights.

Somalia's telephone system no longer works, but a satellite hookup links Mogadishu to other cities. The postal system has also collapsed. The Hargeisa radio station and Radio Mogadishu have been destroyed. Somalis stay informed about international and some local events by listening to the BBC. Oral communication continues to spread news within Somalia.

Education

Somalia's formal education system, from primary levels through university, has been essentially destroyed by war. Somalis, however, value education and many people have established private schools for the interim. Reestablishing public schools will be a challenge for future governments.

The educational system that existed before the war began in the 1940s. Until 1972 the language of instruction was either Arabic, English, or Italian. Traditional schools, where students learned the *Qur'an* in Arabic, served as kindergartens. The introduction of the written Somali script allowed the language to be used in school and in adult literacy programs. By 1975, 47 percent of all Somalis over age ten could read and write in Somali and/or Arabic. Initial gains did not last, however, as by the 1980s only one in ten children was able to attend school. The current literacy rate is about 27 percent.

Health

Somalia's healthcare system has largely been destroyed; there are no modern hospitals. Primary care clinics are run by or rely on international organizations. Violence has forced many of them to discontinue services. Malaria, tuberculosis, and other infectious diseases are prevalent. Children, women of childbearing age, and the elderly have suffered because of unsafe water, poor nutrition, and a lack of medical services. Some 300,000 people are thought to have died in the famine of the early 1990s. Life expectancy averages 36 to 46 years; the infant mortality rate is 123 per 1,000.

FOR THE TRAVELER

Visas are not available for travel to Somalia, and few people outside of international relief workers are visiting. Travel is not impossible, but it is a challenge that requires one to carry personal rations and take certain health and safety precautions. Armed guards must be hired for travel in the south. The Somali Mission to the United Nations is located at 425 E. 61st Street, Suite 702, New York, NY 10021.

CULTURGRAM™ '96

Republic of
South Africa

Boundary representations not necessarily authoritative.

BACKGROUND

Land and Climate

Covering 471,445 square miles (1,221,043 square kilometers), South Africa is slightly larger than Texas, New Mexico, and Oklahoma combined. The country's large interior plateau averages about 5,000 feet (1,500 meters) above sea level. Primarily savannah and semidesert, the plateau is rimmed by a narrow coastal belt, which is subtropical along the east coast and has a Mediterranean climate along the southwestern cape. The three most important rivers are the Orange, Vaal, and Limpopo. Snow is confined to the Drakensberg and Maluti mountains in the east. The seasons are opposite those in the northern hemisphere. Generally there is little humidity, except in the KwaZulu/Natal province along the east coast. The country of Lesotho is completely surrounded by South Africa and sits on a high plateau in the east. Swaziland (near Mozambique) is nearly engulfed by South Africa. South Africa is noted for its long beaches, green forests, rugged mountains, and great canyons. Diversity among plants and wildlife adds to its scenic beauty.

History

The Khoikhoi, San, and other Africans lived in southern Africa for thousands of years, although little is known of their history. In 1652, the Dutch established a provisions station at Cape Town. It supplied ships with fresh foods as they sailed around the tip of the continent. French Huguenot refugees joined the Dutch colony in 1688 and Germans came later. The colonists became known as *Boers* (farmers). They clashed at times with indigenous groups, but stayed mainly in coastal areas. Britain gained formal possession of the Cape Colony in 1814 as a result of the Napoleonic Wars. Dissatisfaction with British rule led many Boers to migrate to the interior between 1835 and 1848. Their migration, which they call the Great Trek, led to war with the indigenous Zulus, Xhosas, and other Black African tribes. The Boers won most of the battles and gained control of large tracts of land.

After the discovery of gold and diamonds in these Boer territories in the late 19th century, Britain annexed parts of the area. Tension erupted into the Boer War (1899–1902), in which the Boers were defeated. Britain combined its colonies, Cape and Natal, with the Boer republics of Orange Free State and Transvaal to create the Union of South Africa in 1910.

Following its election to power in 1948, South Africa's National Party began building the apartheid system that separated the country's population into racial groups: blacks, Coloureds, Indians, and whites. In 1961, the country gained independence from Great Britain, and subsequently withdrew from the British Commonwealth over criticism of its racial policies. For the next three decades, South Africa became the scene of turmoil and violence. The African National Congress (ANC), formed in 1912 to fight for black rights, was banned in 1960. It then launched, with other groups, a guerrilla campaign against the government. Many ANC leaders, including Nelson Mandela, were jailed.

In the 1970s and 1980s, international sanctions and boycotts damaged the economy and isolated the government. Domestic tension increased in 1986 with a state of emergency that allowed police to deal harshly with black protesters.

Frederik Willem (F. W.) de Klerk took office in 1989, and began to move the country toward true democracy. De Klerk freed such political prisoners as Mandela, desegregated hospitals and other public facilities, lifted the state of emergency, and gave the ANC legal status. Mandela later suspended the ANC's guerrilla war. Violent clashes continued, however, between rival black political groups—especially between Zulu supporters of the Inkhatha Freedom Party, led by Mangosuthu

Buthelezi, and the mostly Xhosa ANC. The two groups had long been at odds over the course of South Africa's future and other issues.

Nearly all apartheid provisions were abolished in 1991, and other countries began lifting trade sanctions to welcome South Africa back into the international community. In 1992, de Klerk sponsored a popular referendum to determine white voters' support for his reforms. Voters gave him a clear victory and the necessary support to continue constitutional talks, which proceeded through 1993. Mandela and de Klerk won the Nobel Peace Prize in 1993 for their efforts.

Despite sporadic violence, at times involving white extremists, and predictions of disaster, multiracial, multiparty elections were peacefully held in April 1994. Mandela was elected president, and de Klerk became one of two vice presidents. The country and the world were amazed at how a nation could make the transition from a minority to a majority government without sending the former rulers into exile or without civil war.

For the next several months, Mandela implemented his *Masakhane* (Nguni for "Let us build each other") campaign. Two national anthems (one Boer, one black nationalist), a new flag, new names for old Apartheid-era places, free school lunches for all, new housing projects, better health care, and the promotion of both white and black values all became part of the campaign and South Africa's transformation. Blacks and whites both expressed relief and positive feelings about their new future together. The challenges of black poverty, land rights, jobs, and housing are formidable, but the country seems ready to address them as fairly and quickly as possible.

THE PEOPLE

Population

South Africa's population of 43.9 million grows annually at 2.6 percent. The majority of the population (75.2 percent) is comprised of Black Africans, mostly coming from nine ethnic groups. The Zulus are the largest (18 percent), followed by the Xhosas, North Sothos, South Sothos, Tswanas, Shangaan-Tsongas, Swazis, South Ndebeles, and Vendas. Each has its own cultural heritage, language, and national identity. Before migration patterns led groups to mix with one another, most lived in distinct areas of southern Africa. This inspired the apartheid concept of "homelands," in which blacks were assigned to live in marginal territories covering just 15 percent of the country. Since 1991, blacks could legally live anywhere and the homelands were abolished in 1992. The government is working to restore confiscated lands to blacks with legitimate claims reaching as far back as 1913.

Whites (13.6 percent) include English-speaking descendants of English, Irish, and Scottish settlers and Afrikaans-speaking descendants of Dutch, German, and French colonials. Afrikaners traditionally had large families, but their population growth has slowed in recent years. Coloureds (8.6 percent) are people of mixed race, which most often includes descendants of early white settlers, native Khoikhoi, and slaves imported from the Dutch East Indies during South Africa's colonial period. Indians (2.6 percent) are generally descendants of indentured laborers brought from India during the 19th century or of Indian immigrants who came between 1860 and 1911.

Language

The languages spoken in South Africa are as diverse as its ethnic groups. Afrikaans (a Dutch derivation) is the native tongue of about two-thirds of all whites and most Coloureds, and English is the original language of most other whites and the Indians. English is commonly used in business circles and between some ethnic groups. Many blacks speak Afrikaans and/or English in addition to native languages.

The blacks' native tongues include a variety of Bantu languages, which are roughly divided into four language families: Nguni, Sotho, Tsonga or Shangana, and Venda. Most blacks speak a Nguni language, with Zulu and Xhosa being most prominent. They are joined in the Nguni group by Transvaal Ndebele, Swazi, and Mbayi. Sotho languages (South Sotho, North Sotho, and SeTswana) dominate central South Africa. In addition to the major Bantu languages, a few mixed languages have developed to facilitate communication between various black ethnic groups. Typical is a mixture of Zulu and Xhosa or of a Sotho tongue mixed with Zulu. The mixed languages are only used between ethnic groups, since people prefer to speak their original languages at home or within their own groups. With the advent of majority rule, many white South Africans are learning one of the major native languages. This is helping them become more aware of their diverse culture and is encouraging greater social integration.

Religion

About 60 percent of blacks, most whites, mixed-race peoples are Christians. Afrikaans-speakers belong primarily to the Dutch Reformed Church. English-speaking whites generally belong to other denominations, including Anglican, Lutheran, Presbyterian, Roman Catholic, and Methodist. Blacks typically belong to African Independent Churches (AIC), such as the Zion Christian Church, that combine Christian and traditional African beliefs in their worship patterns. Between 10 and 20 percent of blacks adhere solely to indigenous belief systems. Most Indians are Hindus, although about 20 percent are Muslims and 10 percent are Christians. South Africa's Jewish community is small compared to other religions, but it has had a significant impact on the country's development.

General Attitudes

Today's South Africa and the attitudes of its people are both changing rapidly. Fear among whites of black majority rule has given way to confidence that a government in which power is shared between competing interests can maintain stability and rights for all. Whites are now moving on with life and trying to learn more about their black countrymen. At the same time, they continue to value their European heritage. Afrikaners consider themselves sturdy and independent.

Feelings among blacks are also changing from anger toward whites to anticipation at being more fully involved in a prosperous economy and equal political system. They are encouraged by the fact that they have a black president, that whites are genuinely interested in them, and that they have equality under the law. They are generally aware that their economic situation will not immediately improve, and are willing to accept their newly acquired measure of respect, equality, and dignity that was denied them before 1994. Blacks do not want to marginalize the whites or take away their wealth; instead, they wish to share in the opportunities that create wealth and prosperity. Blacks generally value education as the key to a better life. They express optimism about the future and are anxious to exercise their rights and obligations in the new system. At the same time, they express frustration with the pace of some reforms and have clearly indicated they will not be patient for too many years without visible improvements in their standard of living.

Mixed-race South Africans also benefit from the multiracial system, as their representation in parliament before 1994 was not significant. What seems to unite all peoples is their common claim to South Africa as home, their willingness to look more to the future instead of the past, and a growing desire to build a nonracial and fully democratic society.

Personal Appearance

Urban South Africans wear Western-style clothing, usually made from lightweight cotton. People tend to be well-dressed in public. Men wear suits or shirts and trousers; some wear shorts and knee socks. Women generally wear comfortable dresses or modest pants. Indian women often wear a *sari*, a wraparound-type dress. Some rural blacks retain traditional clothing habits for special purposes or everyday attire. This may include a variety of headdresses and colorful outfits. They also wear Western-style clothing on a daily basis, but women include a scarf or other headdress and they either wear a dress or a blouse and skirt.

CUSTOMS AND COURTESIES

Greetings

Because of ethnic diversity, various greeting forms are used in South Africa. English-speakers use *Hello* and *Good morning*, phrases that are understood by most South Africans. Young English-speakers say *Howzit* (slang for "How are you?") to friends. Afrikaans-speakers say *Goeie more* (Good morning). The Zulu and Swazis greet each other with *Sawubona* (literally, "I see you;" it means hello) or *Kunjani* (How are you?). An acceptable response to either is *Yebo* (Yes). The Xhosa greeting, *Molo*, and the Sotho-language-group phrase *Dumela* have similar meanings. All South Africans shake hands when they greet, but the types of handshakes differ between groups. Some use firmer, others lighter, shakes with one hand; many rural people use both hands. Sometimes, black friends greet with an intricate triple handshake that involves interlocking the smallest fingers, clasping fists, and interlocking fingers again. In all groups, close friends and relatives may hug.

It is generally impolite to use first names with strangers or older people. Professional titles or the equivalents to "Mr.," "Mrs.," and "Miss" are preferred. It is also polite to call an older black man "father" (*Tata* in Xhosa, *Ntate* in SeSotho, or *Baba* in Zulu) or older woman "mother" (*Mama* in Xhosa and Zulu or *Mme* in SeSotho). First names and nicknames are used between friends.

Gestures

South Africans frequently use hand gestures in conversation. It is impolite to point at someone with the index finger or talk with one's hands in the pockets. The right hand is more often used for handshakes, to pass objects, or to gesture. Receiving an object with cupped hands is polite. Indicating "peace" or "two" by forming a "V" with the index and middle fingers is rude if the palm faces inward. Some people shake a hand with index and little fingers extended (the others folded) to express "Hello" or "Goodbye."

Visiting

Visiting is an important social activity for most groups. When possible, visits are arranged in advance, but unannounced visits among good friends or relatives are common, especially in areas where telephones are not accessible. South Africans are very hospitable. They enjoy conversation and socializing. Gender and age groups tend to socialize amongst themselves, with exchanges between such groups being more formal.

Guests are usually served refreshments. In Indian homes, it is impolite to refuse these, and it is polite to accept second helpings if eating a meal. Among most people, dinner guests are not expected to bring a gift but will often bring something to drink (juice, wine, etc.). Etiquette varies between different ethnic groups. When guests are leaving, they are usually accompanied by their host to the gate, car, or street.

Eating

The continental style of eating, with the fork in the left hand and the knife remaining in the right, is generally observed by urban South Africans. In rural areas, people often eat with spoons or their fingers. It is generally not appropriate for adults to eat on the street, unless eating ice cream or standing at a vendor's stand. In restaurants, tipping is discretionary.

LIFESTYLE

Family

White families are small, live as a nuclear unit, are generally close-knit, and enjoy a good standard of living. Blacks have strong extended family ties, even if nuclear units are not always complete. Children are taught to respect their elders and obey their parents. Relatives play an important role in caring for children and providing aid to those in need. This has been necessary due to years of apartheid when fathers had to work far from home; resettlement in the future may help strengthen black nuclear units.

Diet

One's diet is often determined by economic status. Beef, mutton, a variety of curries, green vegetables, pumpkins, and other foods are eaten. Staples include potatoes and rice. Wine, tea, coffee, beer, and soft drinks are common beverages. Rural South Africans and others eat *mealie meal* (cornmeal porridge, sometimes cooked with vegetables and meat). Dinner, usually eaten after 6:00 P.M., is the main meal. The *braaivleis* (barbecue) is a popular weekend event and usually features *boerewors* (*beef and pork sausage*). Fresh fruit and vegetables are abundant and often sold by farmers from roadside stalls. *Biltong* is a popular jerky-like snack made from various types of meat.

Recreation

Soccer, rugby, boxing, swimming, sailing, and boating are popular. All ethnic groups value competitive sports. Those who can afford equipment or club memberships participate in cricket, squash, lawn bowling, golf, field hockey, and tennis. Horse and car racing draw crowds. South Africans appreciate their many beaches and recreational facilities, including swimming pools, parks, libraries, and movie theaters.

Dancing, playing music, attending festivals, and enjoying cultural events are popular throughout the year.

Holidays

The official holidays in South Africa include New Year's Day, Easter (including Good Friday and Family Day on Monday), Human Rights Day (21 March), Freedom Day (27 April), Workers' Day (1 May), Youth Day (16 June), National Women's Day (9 August), Inheritance Day (24 September), Reconciliation Day (16 December), Christmas, and Day of Goodwill (26 December). Each religion also observes other important holidays.

Commerce

In general, businesses and shops are open from 8:30 A.M. to 5:00 P.M., Monday through Friday, and until 1:00 P.M. on Saturday. Shopping centers and supermarkets stay open into the evenings and on weekends. Banks and government offices are open from 9:00 A.M. to 3:30 P.M., Monday through Friday, and until 11:00 A.M. on Saturday. Few businesses and shops are open on Sunday. Pavement (sidewalk) vendors offer sundry items, and small retail businesses (*Spaza* shops) run from black suburban homes sell a variety of items to neighborhood residents.

SOCIETY

Government

South Africa's president, chosen by an elected parliament on the basis of the majority party's recommendation, is chief of state and head of government. President Mandela has two vice presidents, Thabo Mbeki of the ANC and F. W. de Klerk of the National Party. The constitution calls for one vice president to be from the majority party and one from the strongest opposition party. Any party with at least 5 percent of the seats in parliament has the right to a post in the president's cabinet. In the 1994 elections, only the three main parties (ANC, National, and the Inkatha Freedom Party) met this requirement and hold cabinet posts. The Inkatha leader, Chief Buthelezi, is the Home Minister.

Parliament has two houses, a 90-member Senate and a 400-seat National Assembly. The latter body is elected directly by the people, while Senate members are elected by the country's nine provinces (ten members each). The current parliament is also a constituent assembly that will draft a new constitution to take effect in 1999. All citizens are eligible to vote at age 18, regardless of race. The 1994 elections represented the first time that blacks could vote and participate as full citizens of their country.

Economy

South Africa is the richest country in Africa, and whites generally enjoy a high standard of living. The country's Human Development Index (0.650) ranks it 93d out of 173 nations. Real gross domestic product per capita is $3,885. These figures reflect a wide gap between whites and blacks in terms of income, because whites earn far more and blacks usually earn far less. Manufacturing is the most important sector of the economy, followed by mining. The most important exports include gold, other minerals and metals, food, and chemicals. Nearly two-thirds of all export earnings traditionally come from mining (gold, diamonds, chrome, and coal). South Africa has a relatively large industrial base and diversified economy, and new investment is allowing for strong and steady growth. Unemployment is high among black workers, but the government is moving to address the issue. Given the beauty of the land, tourism is important to the economy; while it dropped off in the 1980s, it is now rebounding. The currency is the *rand* (R).

Transportation and Communication

Railroads carry freight and passengers throughout the country. South African Airways serves all major cities of the republic and some overseas destinations. The road system is good and extensive. Many urban commuters take minibus *taxis* to work. An advanced telecommunications system is the best on the continent. Television is available throughout the country, with four channels broadcasting in English, Afrikaans, and the Nguni and Sotho language groups. One cable channel offers a mix of U.S. and British programming. Several radio stations broadcast in all of South Africa's languages. Radio and television services are provided by the government-regulated South African Broadcasting Corporation, but there is a move toward decentralization.

Education

Apartheid segregated educational systems by race. Schooling was free and compulsory for white children between the ages of seven and sixteen. Where accommodations permitted, attendance was compulsory for Coloureds and Indians between seven and fourteen. For blacks, a separate government agency oversaw education, which was only compulsory for the first four years. As in other areas of South African life, segregation in education has been dismantled. It will, however, take some time before all children receive the same opportunities within a uniform system. Blacks receive instruction in their native language to the seventh grade, and choose between English and Afrikaans after that. There are 19 universities in South Africa. The literacy rates vary between the different ethnic groups and are estimated to be whites, 99 percent; Indians, 85; Coloureds, 60; and blacks, 50.

Health

Medical services are socialized, but some private sector participation is also incorporated. Until 1990, many medical facilities were segregated and blacks had inadequate facilities. Public hospitals and clinics are now open to all races. Free care is given to all pregnant women and to children under age six. Disease and malnutrition remain more common among blacks than whites. The infant mortality rate is 47 per 1,000. Life expectancy ranges from 62 to 68 years. Whites enjoy better rates than other groups.

FOR THE TRAVELER

U.S. visitors need a valid passport to South Africa, but visas are not required for tourist stays. Vaccinations are not necessary, but proof of yellow fever vaccination is required of travelers coming from the yellow fever endemic zone. South Africa's tourism industry is well developed, and it awaits a new flood of post-apartheid visitors to showcase South Africa's beauty, diversity, and culture. For more information, contact the Embassy of South Africa, 3051 Massachusetts Avenue NW, Washington, DC 20008; phone (202) 232–4400.

Democratic Socialist Republic of
Sri Lanka

Boundary representations not necessarily authoritative.

BACKGROUND

Land and Climate

Shaped like a teardrop, the island nation of Sri Lanka sits less than 20 miles off the coast of India. Covering 25,332 square miles (65,610 square kilometers), it is slightly larger than West Virginia. About 25 percent of the land is forested (down from 40 percent due to deforestation). The north and east are flat and require irrigation to cultivate rice. Ancient hydroengineering techniques are still in use and are admired even by the modern engineers expanding the irrigation system. Sri Lanka's south-central region is mountainous. Two peaks (Mt. Pidurutagala and World's End Peak) are located near the center of the island. Tea, rubber, and coconut plantations dominate the central mountains, although terraced rice paddies are not uncommon. Sri Lanka has a tropical climate, with temperatures averaging 80°F (27°C) year-round. Highland areas are cooler, but also receive more rain than lowland regions. Seasonal monsoons affect the island.

History

The first inhabitants of Sri Lanka, the Veddahs, have largely been assimilated into society; little is known of their past. Around 500 B.C., an Indo-Aryan group led by Prince Vijaya migrated to Sri Lanka and formed a small kingdom. The present-day Sinhalese descended from this group. In 307 B.C., the Indian Prince Mahinda, son of the great Buddhist King Asoka, introduced Buddhism to the Sinhalese. While Buddhism later floundered in India, it remained strong in Sri Lanka. Hindu Tamils also came to the island at an early date and have kept some cultural and religious ties with the state of Tamil Nadu in India. A second migration of Tamils occurred in the 19th century when the British brought them from India to work on tea plantations.

Sri Lanka was well-known to other nations throughout history, including the Romans and early Arabs (who called the island "Serendip"). Various European powers came to dominate coastal areas, but inland areas remained autonomous until the 19th century. The Portuguese (16th century) were followed by the Dutch (17th century), who were replaced by the British in 1796. In 1815, the British defeated the last native ruler, King of Kandy, and established the island as the Crown Colony of Ceylon.

In 1948, the island peacefully obtained freedom from British rule. The nation has held successive free elections since that time and has never experienced a dictatorship. In 1971, a Maoist group led an uprising of unemployed, educated young people and caused the government to declare a state of emergency to forcibly quell the violence. In 1972, partly in response to the unrest, a new constitution changed the name of the country from Ceylon to Sri Lanka (meaning "resplendent island") and introduced limited socialist measures such as nationalization of some industries.

Yet another new constitution in 1978 declared the country a democratic socialist republic and created a strong presidency. About the same time, Tamil factions seeking an independent Tamil state (called Tamil Eelam) in northern Sri Lanka became violent and began leading insurgent campaigns against the government. In the 1980s, Tamils clashed with Sinhalese in several confrontations that led to thousands of deaths. At the same time, Sinhalese Maoists again attempted to overthrow the government at the cost of some 60,000 lives.

Violence peaked in 1987. The government granted the Tamil language official status, implemented other reforms, and accepted India's offer to send troops into the Tamil areas to establish peace. Although the separatists had originally agreed to turn their arms over to the Indian forces in exchange for autonomy, they backed out and began fighting the Indian troops. By 1988, the Sinhalese were violently protesting the presence of the Indians and a new government came into office promising to send the Indians home. President Ranasinghe Premadasa negotiated the end of Indian involvement, and the last troops were gone by March 1990.

Premadasa's actions won the cooperation of Tamil guerrillas, who halted their militant activities to participate in the electoral process. They won provincial elections in their strongholds and also captured several seats in the national parliament. However, fighting between the government and guerrillas broke out again in June 1990. Several hundred people were killed in five days of fighting before a cease-fire was declared. It later collapsed and violence continued, with entire villages being massacred by opposing ethnic groups. By the end of 1991, the Liberation Tigers of Tamil Eelam (LTTE) had taken control of many areas north of Vauvuniya, including Jaffna. In May 1993, Tiger terrorists killed Premadasa at a political rally. Premadasa's prime minister, Dingiri Banda Wijetunge, was sworn in as interim president until elections in August 1994.

In those elections, Premadasa's United National Party, which had governed for 17 years, lost to a leftist coalition called the People's Alliance. Chandrika Bandaranaike Kumaratunga of the Sri Lanka Freedom Party was elected president on a platform of bringing peace to the country. A widow of a politician killed during the 1980s, she immediately opened talks with the LTTE. Hopes for peace were very high until May 1995, when talks collapsed and fighting errupted once more.

THE PEOPLE

Population

Sri Lanka's population of 18.1 million is growing annually at 1.2 percent. The Sinhalese constitute 74 percent of the population and are concentrated in the southwest. The Tamils are divided into two groups: the Ceylon Tamils (12 percent), whose ancestors lived on the island for centuries; and the Indian Tamils (6 percent), whose ancestors were imported during the British colonial era. About 400,000 Tamils live outside of Sri Lanka, either in India or the West. Tamils live in the north, east, and south-central areas. Moors (locally called Muslims) comprise 7 percent of the population; Malays, Burghers, and Veddahs make up the other 1 percent. Burghers are descendants of Dutch colonists and Veddahs are a remnant of the island's original inhabitants. Colombo (also called Sri Jayawardhanapura), the capital, is the largest city with 1.5 million people.

Language

Both Sinhala and Tamil are official languages in Sri Lanka, but Sinhala is considered to be primary. It is an Indo-European language with roots in Sanskrit and Pali. Its written form is more formal than the spoken version. Tamil belongs to the Dravidian group of languages. English is the primary language of business and about 10 percent of the population speaks it.

Religion

Since the introduction of Buddhism by the Indian Prince Mahinda, Sri Lanka has been a stronghold of Theravada Buddhism, the more conservative branch of the religion. Nearly 70 percent of the population practices it, primarily among the Sinhalese. Although freedom of worship is guaranteed by the constitution, the government has given special status to Buddhism. About 15 percent of the people (mostly Tamils) practice Hinduism. Many Buddhists also honor various Hindu deities. Tamil worship centers around the Hindu god Shiva. But many gods exist in the hierarchy, each having a specific purpose. For instance, women pray to Paththini for health and fertility; businessmen seek the blessings of Kataragama (or Skanda); and students can get help with learning from Ganesh or Saraswathi. The Moors are mostly Muslims, while 8 percent of the population is Christian.

General Attitudes

Sri Lankans are friendly and have relatively open attitudes. They value loyalty to one's group, respect for others, and their ethnic and religious identity. Ethnic divisions run deep, and few people socialize outside of their respective groups. The two greatest values in society are the family and education. Family members help one another and are very close-knit. Parents will sacrifice or work all their lives to provide their children with as much education as possible. Nearly all young people desire a good education. Teachers and persons with a university degree are highly respected in society. Material wealth is also desired, and people are willing to work hard to obtain it. The wealthy, especially those who have become successful in private business, are respected but in a different way than educated people are. In other words, family and education are still more important than money.

The traditional caste system that once dominated society is fading in public life. Most people do not discuss it, and being from a lower caste does not usually limit one's economic or political mobility. However, since one's surname gives indication of caste, everyone is aware of his or her place within the system and that does play a role in social interaction. That is, people still marry and associate with others of the same caste. For religious ceremonies, certain functions are performed by certain castes.

Personal Appearance

Although the youth and people in cities wear Western-style clothing, traditional forms of dress remain popular. Women may wear a *saree* (a wraparound dress that reaches to the ankles) with a tight blouse. The *saree*, made from a very long piece of fabric, is draped over the shoulder and wrapped at the waist in a way that creates tailoring without being sewn. Women also wear a *redda* (a wraparound skirt that is tucked at the waist) with a blouse (*hatte*) that leaves the midriff bare. Traditional attire for men may include loose-fitting trousers combined with a long shirt that reaches to mid-thigh. The shirt has long, loose sleeves and buttons to the neck. Men might also wear a *sarong* (a piece of cloth wrapped around the waist, sometimes held by a belt or *lunghi*) that reaches to the ankles with a *banian* (a sleeveless shirt that looks like a tank top) and a handkerchief draped over the right shoulder.

CUSTOMS AND COURTESIES

Greetings

Forms of greeting vary between ethnic groups. The traditional greeting of placing one's palms together in front of the chest and bowing the head slightly is widely practiced. This is accompanied by the Sinhalese phrase *Ayubowan* (ah-you-byu-one) or the Tamil *Vannakkam* (one-eh-come). Both terms mean "May you be blessed with the gift of a long life." Men often shake hands with men during the course of their greeting, but they do not touch women in public. Titles are important to Sri Lankans, even among close friends. Acquaintances and strangers use the more formal equivalents of "Mr.," "Mrs.," and "Miss." If speaking in English, the title precedes the surname; otherwise, it follows the name. Colleagues might use the title with a given name. Among close friends and relatives, familial titles replace formal ones. For example, in Sinhala one addresses an older male friend as *aiya* (older brother), a younger female cousin as *nangi* (younger sister), and so on.

Gestures

The right hand is used for eating and passing objects. Both hands are used when giving and receiving gifts; a gift presented with only one hand is not given wholeheartedly. To express sincere or gracious giving of any object, one can touch the right forearm with the left hand while giving with the right. Men often hold hands in public, but it is improper for members of the opposite sex to do so. Women are forbidden to touch a Buddhist monk.

The head is considered the most sacred part of the body; the bottom of the feet is the least sacred. People do not touch another's head, nor use a foot to point at anything. Pointing with the index finger is likewise impolite. Beckoning is done with hand held at head level, palm facing out, and all fingers waving together. It is improper to pass between two people in conversation; if it is unavoidable, the passer ducks slightly and apologizes before passing. Shoes are removed before entering Buddhist temples or Hindu shrines.

Wagging or tilting the head from side to side indicates agreement. Shaking it gently during conversation means one is listening. But shaking it firmly with the mouth closed can mean no.

Visiting

Visiting is a favorite pastime. Sri Lankans are very hospitable and strive to make all guests comfortable. Friends often drop by unannounced and are warmly received. Sri Lankans also enjoy inviting relatives and friends to their homes. In such a case, they may bring a small gift of food or other item. Depending on the hosts, guests might remove shoes before entering. Once seated, guests are offered tea, usually sweetened with milk and sugar. It is very impolite to refuse such an offer, although one can ask for a substitute (such as water). Simple snacks are also usually offered, and guests are obliged to eat a little bit. While most visiting occurs in the home, Sri Lankans also enjoy meeting at parks or restaurants and they often take short sight-seeing excursions together.

Eating

Lunch is the largest of three daily meals. The family eats together and all members eat with their right hand. The mother serves men and any guests before other members of the household. After the meal, most people drink water and wash their hands in a bowl of water.

Sri Lankans of all religions seek to avoid those things that would cause spiritual pollution. Because food enters the body, it is considered a prime source of potential pollution. Those who adhere strictly to Buddhist doctrines do not eat flesh of any kind. Some Buddhists, however, include fish or eggs in their diet. Hindus do not eat beef or pork, and Muslims do not eat pork.

LIFESTYLE

Family

The extended family is very important in society. Even if a nuclear family has its own household, it will often live very close to relatives. The husband dominates the family, but the wife manages the the household and has influence in all family matters. Women have economic and political opportunities outside the home, but are expected to be able to maintain all household responsibilities as well. Women do not go out alone after dark. Parents expect to provide their children with all basic needs even into adulthood. The elderly receive deep respect and younger family members often yield to their advice and counsel. Children expect to care for their elderly parents if necessary.

Dating and Marriage

Dating in the Western sense is not common in Sri Lanka. Boys and girls get to know each other mostly through school, but getting together (even in groups) is not generally done. If a young couple desires to have a boyfriend/girlfriend relationship, they are expected to eventually marry. Such couples do go out to parks and so forth, but not always with the knowledge of their parents. More and more people are choosing their own mates, especially in urban areas, but arranged marriages are still very common. Sexual purity is an essential part of the marriage contract on the part of the woman. Marriage between members of different ethnic groups is socially unacceptable.

The timing of various wedding events—when the parties arrive, have the ceremony, sign papers, leave, arrive at their new home—is governed by astrology. Each event is calculated to the minute so as to give the marriage the best possible start. Weddings are a time for family, friends, and food.

Diet

Rice and curry are staples in Sri Lanka. Each ethnic group has contributed dishes to the overall cuisine. A variety of curries (from the Sinhalese) are very popular. Sri Lankans typically consume little meat, but they do eat large amounts of legumes (from the Tamils) and nuts. A main meal usually begins with rice or bread, followed by a curry or *dahl* (lentils) and a vegetable (cabbage, carrots). One popular food is *Pol Sambol*, scraped and spiced coconut. *Katta Sambol* is a very spicy mixture of fried onions and chilies. The Burghers are known for their cakes and sweetmeats.

Recreation

Cricket is the most popular sport, followed by soccer, table tennis, volleyball, and netball (for girls). Most sports are played by men, although girls do play them in school. Attending Western and Sri Lankan movies are favorite pastimes. Sri Lanka has a long tradition in the dramatic arts and people enjoy both live and puppet theater. During New Year festivities, Sri Lankans participate in a number of activities, from indoor games just for women to outdoor sports such as elephant racing or wrestling. Traditional music played on small drums and sitars is popular throughout the country; the urban youth like electric keyboards and guitars. Sri Lankans cherish their many traditional dances.

Holidays

Every full moon (*Poya* Day) is a holiday. *Wesak Poya* in May is celebrated as Buddha's day of birth, enlightenment, and death. Each major religion has at least one national holiday. For example, the country marks *Idul Fitr* (a feast at the end of *Ramadan*, the Islamic month of fasting) and *Idul Adha* (Feast of the Sacrifice) for Muslims. Easter (including Good Friday) and Christmas are celebrated by Christians. *Deepawali* (Festival of Lights) is a Hindu holiday celebrating the triumph of light over darkness. Thousands of lights decorate stores and homes at this time of goodwill. Many other religious holidays honor Buddha or Hindu deities. The Tamil *Thai-Pongal* Day marks the "return" of the sun after a month of evil days; the sun brings a new period of goodwill. The Sinhala and Tamil New Year is usually celebrated in April with great fanfare and rejoicing. Political holidays include National Day (4 February), May Day (1 May), and National Heroes' Day (22 May).

Commerce

Business and government offices are generally open weekdays from 8:30 A.M. to 12:30 P.M. and from 1:00 to 4:30 P.M. Larger towns have a daily open market; small ones have a weekly *Polla* (market) day. Rural residents must travel to the nearest town on *Polla* day to buy basic goods.

SOCIETY

Government

Sri Lanka's central government is headed by a president and a prime minister. Each of the eight provinces has substantial control over local affairs. Parliament has 225 members. The voting age is 18. Rural villages often have a chief or headman.

Economy

Despite an educated workforce and growth potential, the economy is hampered by continued fighting. It grows well in times of peace because of increased investment, tourism, and productivity. Agriculture employs half of the labor force, but does not contribute as much to export earnings as industry, which is dominated by apparel manufacturing. Tea, rubber, and coconuts account for most agricultural exports. Unemployment, historically a problem, is still high but the number of private sector jobs is steadily increasing. Sri Lanka depends on foreign assistance, as well as remittances from the nearly one million Sri Lankans who work abroad (mostly in the Middle East).

The country's Human Development Index (0.665) ranks it 90th out of 173 countries. Real gross domestic product per capita is $2,650. This indicates that many people earn an income sufficient for basic needs. However, income distribution is somewhat unequal, and poverty affects 40 percent of the population. The currency is the Sri Lankan *rupee* (Re).

Transportation and Communication

Buses and taxis are plentiful in urban areas. Major cities are linked by paved roads and rail service. Other roads are not paved and may be difficult to travel in some areas. Rural residents travel on foot, by bicycle, or by bus. Traffic moves on the left side of the road. Few Sri Lankans own cars. Many newspapers, printed in Sinhala, Tamil, and English, are generally free to print what they please. Radio and television broadcasts are available in the major languages. Private homes generally lack telephones, but public phones are located in post offices.

Education

Schooling, which begins at age five, is free and compulsory at the primary and secondary levels. The literacy rate is one of the highest in Asia (89 percent). For young adults, the rate is 96 percent. Nearly all children (97 percent) complete primary schooling and 86 percent go on to complete the secondary level. The average adult has completed seven years of school, a high achievement for the region. The government stresses the development of vocational skills, but traditional values also help maintain a strong liberal arts track. Young people generally aspire to higher education. Entrance to universities is based on "A-level" exams (based on the British model). The competition for spots is so intense that students often pay to take after-school "private tuition classes" that help prepare them for the exams. Even if a student doesn't get into college, a good "A-level" score will help with getting a better job.

Health

Sri Lanka has both public and private health care facilities, with private hospitals and clinics providing higher quality (but expensive) care. In rural areas, *ayurvedic* medicine is widely practiced; it stresses the use of herbs and natural cures. The infant mortality rate is 22 per 1,000. Life expectancy is between 69 and 74 years.

FOR THE TRAVELER

U.S. citizens need a valid passport to enter Sri Lanka, but no visa is required for stays of fewer than 90 days. Vaccinations may be recommended depending on one's itinerary. Malarial suppressants are advisable outside Colombo. Food should be hot and well-cooked; fruits and vegetables should be peeled or cooked, and water should be treated. Avoid ice and dairy products. From ancient cities to national parks to southern beaches, there are many wonderful things to experience in Sri Lanka, which was once called the "Pearl of the Indian Ocean." For more information, contact the Embassy of the Democratic Socialist Republic of Sri Lanka, 2148 Wyoming Avenue NW, Washington, DC 20008; phone (202) 483–4025.

Printed on recycled paper

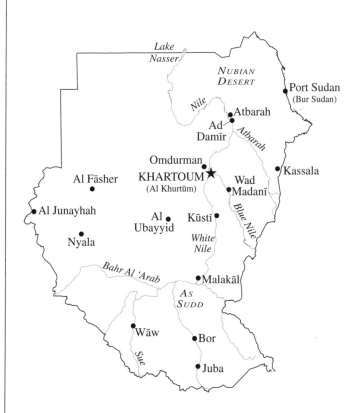

Republic of the
Sudan

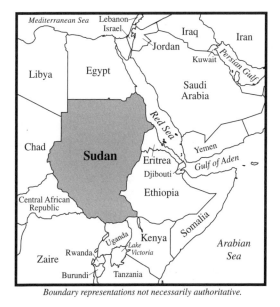

Boundary representations not necessarily authoritative.

BACKGROUND

Land and Climate

At 967,494 square miles (2,505,810 square kilometers), Sudan is the largest country in Africa and is almost one-third the size of the continental United States. Most of Sudan is a large plain. The White and Blue Nile Rivers flow north, eventually converging to form the Nile River, which empties into the Mediterranean Sea. A swampy area (*as Sudd*) dominates a large region in the far south. The Nubian Desert in the north is separated from the Red Sea by low coastal hills. Hills and mountains also run along the border with Chad. The climate varies according to region and altitude, from tropical forests in the south to deserts in the north. In Khartoum, the temperature remains high throughout the year; rain is rare. Dust and sandstorms are common. In the south, however, the rainy season may last up to nine months. Or it may not come at all. The drought of 1991 was Sudan's third drought in six years and its effects were widespread. In 1993, Sudan had a good crop year.

History

Sudan has a long and interesting history. Contacts between Egypt and Nubia, Sudan's northern area, date to several millennia B.C. In Biblical times, the area was known as Cush, named for the Nubian kingdom that ruled northern Sudan between the eleventh and fourth centuries B.C. Cush also briefly ruled Egypt (713–671 B.C.). During the early years of the Christian era, Sudan was part of the Christian Kingdom of Aksum, centered in Ethiopia. When the Arabs successfully invaded Egypt in the seventh century, a treaty with Nubia forbade Nubian settlement in Egypt and Muslim settlement in Sudan.

The area continued to be Christian until the 15th century, when it fell to Egyptian domination. Still, Sudan remained semiautonomous for a number of years. But Egypt began a complete conquest of Sudan in 1821, a process it completed in 1874. Between 1881 and 1885, Muhammad Ahmad Abdullah led a successful revolt against Egypt. But in 1898, Egypt regained control of the region with the help of the British, who became corulers of the region. Two years after Egypt claimed sole ownership of Sudan, an agreement was reached (in 1953) with Britain to grant Sudan self-rule. The Sudanese people had also voted for an independent state, which was proclaimed in 1956. Unfortunately, democracy did not last long.

Since 1958, when a military coup toppled the civilian government, control of Sudan has alternated between civilian and military governments. As each civilian government was unable to solve Sudan's many problems, including the civil war with the south, the military would take power. One such coup in 1969 brought Gaafar Nimeiry to power. In the 1970s, he recognized special autonomy for the south and ended the civil war. He also implemented policies to stimulate the economy. However, his program of Islamization in the 1980s, which sought to impose Islamic law (*shari'a*) on the whole country, rekindled the civil war and eventually led to a coup in 1985. The officers involved sponsored free elections in 1986, but the new government under Sadiq Mahdi was unable to end the civil war and improve economic conditions. In 1988, because of the fighting, relief supplies destined for people affected by drought were not delivered. At least 250,000 people died. Mahdi was overthrown in 1989 by Omar Hassan al-Bashir.

Al-Bashir suspended the Constitution and dissolved parliament and all political parties. Much of his attention was directed toward the war with the Sudan People's Liberation Movement (SPLM). The SPLM's original goal was the establishment of a secular, democratic state, free from control by Islamic law. After years of fighting, however, rival factions formed (chiefly between the Dinkas and Nuers) within the SPLM and southern militias began fighting each other for territory and power. They committed atrocities equal to those claimed by southern residents as having been committed by government forces. These atrocities included wholesale destruction of southern villages and their inhabitants.

With economic conditions at a standstill and drought affecting much of the country, people throughout Sudan faced starvation again in 1992, but relief efforts had to be suspended due to fierce fighting. By 1993, southern forces had weakened significantly and Sudan allowed some relief efforts to proceed. However, they were halted again in early 1994 when the government launched a massive offensive against rebels in the far south, and refugees began to flee towards Uganda. Some shipments were able to get through in 1995.

General al-Bashir declared a unilateral ceasefire in July 1994 and opened negotiations with SPLM representatives. He announced his willingness to create a federal system that would give the southern non-Muslims more control over certain aspects of their lives. Talks collapsed in September, with the SPLM rejecting the proposals as not going far enough. Fighting resumed by November, more refugees were forced to flee, SPLM factions intensified their internal battles, and the southern war continued well into 1995.

THE PEOPLE

Population

Sudan has a population of 29.4 million and is growing annually at 2.3 percent. Nearly 40 percent of the population is Arabic. Up to another 20 percent (from other ethnic groups, such as the Fur, a black African group) follows Arabic customs and lives in the north or central regions. The Nubian minority (about 8 percent) is concentrated around the Nile in northern Sudan. The Dinka, Funj, Nuer, Shilluk, and other Black African peoples of southern Sudan constitute half of the total population. Between 20 and 25 percent of all people live in urban areas. Khartoum has a population of almost two million. Forty-five percent of the population is younger than age 15.

There is a sharp cultural distinction between the people of northern and central Sudan and those in southern Sudan. The cultural information in this *Culturgram* focuses on the Arabic- and Nubian-speaking peoples of the north and center. Historical and statistical information, however, necessarily cover the entire country. The lack of cultural information regarding the southern Sudanese does not reflect a bias against them. Rather, it reflects a lack of reliable information.

Language

While Arabic is the official language of the entire country, it is the primary language only in the northern and central regions. There are over one hundred other languages spoken in the country, including Nubian, Nilo-Saharan languages (Dinka, Nuer, Bari, Lotuko, etc.), Zande, and others. Until 1956, English was an official language in the south, and it is still spoken by some.

Religion

The majority of the Sudanese are Sunni Muslim (70 percent). They live in the north and central areas and dominate politically. The Christian population (5 percent) lives chiefly in the south. The rest of the people follow indigenous beliefs. Religious loyalties play an important role in Sudanese politics. For example, the powerful Ummah party is associated with the Mahdist movement that began in the late 19th century. Mahdists, who are Sunni Muslims, believe that a Muslim teacher named Muhammad Ahmad Abdullah was a guide (*al-Mahdi*) sent to establish God's will on earth. His son created the Ummah party. Abdullah's great-grandson, Sadiq Mahdi, was a prime minister in the late 1980s.

General Attitudes

For all the outward formalities of life, northern Sudanese are surprisingly vocal and expressive. They are an individualistic people given to expressing their opinions openly, although almost always in a polite and considerate manner. They also believe strongly in putting up with the surprises of everyday life. Their view is that whatever happens is the will of God and should be accepted. To Westerners, Sudanese may also appear to be generally disinterested in a given matter. But this habit of quietly appraising a situation does not imply a lack of concern, nor does it rule out future action.

Sudanese society is highly stratified. In addition to an underprivileged lower class, there is also a middle class (in cities) and a small upper class. Government positions are usually filled by members of the upper class. The Islamic institution of *zakat* (tithing to help support the needy) offsets major economic disabilities (in the north) to a surprising extent. Some significant differences—social as well as economic—are apparent between various segments of the population. The vast cultural differences that exist between the Arabic speakers of the north and non-Arabic speakers of the south are a significant social challenge, and a great deal remains to be done before the southern Sudanese will be socially and economically equal with their northern counterparts.

Personal Appearance

In Khartoum, the capital, many men wear Western-style clothing. However, such clothing is less prevalent in rural areas, where flowing robes and turbans are common. Women rarely wear Western dress. In fact, recent (1991) changes in the law require women to follow the Islamic dress code; they must be covered from head to ankle in public. The nomadic people of the desert wear heavy robes to protect them from the heat and blowing sand. In all cases, conservative clothing is the standard. Attire that is not modest is unacceptable in public.

CUSTOMS AND COURTESIES

Greetings

Hospitality is a Sudanese trait shared with the rest of the Arabic world. The northern Sudanese are formal and traditional yet very cordial in their greetings of friends as well as strangers. A firm but gentle handshake with a member of the same sex is always in order, and friends frequently embrace. Men will not touch a woman in public, but they may shake hands if she extends her hand first. The usual verbal greeting is *Salaam'alaykum* (Peace be upon you) or *Ahlan wa-sahlan* (Welcome), followed by *Kayf Haalak?* (How are you?).

Gestures

As in other North African countries, use of the left hand is generally improper. A person will not pass or accept items with the left hand; this is done only with the right hand or both hands. Pointing the finger is considered rude. It is offensive to allow the bottom of one's feet (or shoes) to point at or face another person.

Visiting

The Sudanese home is the owner's private domain, and one does not usually visit without an explicit invitation. Such an invitation may be considered a distinct honor, and it is quite in order for a visitor to take a small gift (but never alcohol) as a token of appreciation. Guests are usually offered coffee, tea, or juice, perhaps with some kind of food. Refreshments should not be refused, since expressing hospitality is very important to the Sudanese. Conversation is kept on a social level, even if one is involved in business dealings with the host. One should not ask about the women of the household nor discuss personal topics. One may ask generally about a person's health, the well-being of his family, and work.

Eating

In a Sudanese home, everyone normally sits on the floor during a meal. Food is eaten with the fingers of the right hand only, never with the left. Most Sudanese have one large meal a day. Western-style restaurants are available in Khartoum.

LIFESTYLE

Family

The Sudanese family is a strongly male-oriented, patriarchal, extended organization. Three generations of males and their spouses and children usually live in the same household. This pattern is the norm throughout Sudan, but it is less dominant in Khartoum, where smaller nuclear families are found. The trend towards nuclear families is also visible in other large cities. The home is a cohesive, private place, to which one can always return for support. Although it is male dominated, the home is managed by the women of the family. Women's roles are quite different from those of men, but women are not necessarily considered subservient.

Dating and Marriage

Western-style dating does not occur in Sudan. Marriages represent the joining of two families, and consequently their arrangement is a matter of concern to all members of both families. Such arrangements, however, are rarely made without approval from potential mates. Marriages tend to endure well.

Diet

Sudanese foods are typically Near Eastern. Lamb, goat, and fowl are the usual meats. Pasta-like dishes are also popular. Other common foods include pancake-like breads made of sorghum or millet flour and spicy soups with meat or eggs. Regional dishes, often highly spiced, are typical in the south.

Drought, civil war, and a poor economy have combined to bring malnourishment and famine to hundreds of thousands of people. More than one million people have no regular access to food and water. Crops have failed. For many, nutrition comes only from relief organizations, and those groups cannot serve the areas where fighting is the worst or where government or rebel forces restrict relief efforts. Malnutrition nationwide among children is more than 25 percent and increasing.

Holidays

While the official calendar is the Western (Gregorian) calendar, daily life is regulated by the Islamic lunar calendar. Muslim holy days (the prophet Muhammad's birthday, Islamic New Year, etc.) are important, particularly the feast at the end of *Ramadan*. During the Islamic month of *Ramadan*, Muslims will go without food or water from dawn to dusk. In the evenings, families eat together and visit friends and relatives. National holidays include Independence Day (1 January), Unity Day (3 March), Labor Day (1 May), and others as determined by the government.

Commerce

The Sudanese government is the country's largest employer. A strong business class controls the commercial sector. Business hours are generally from 8:30 A.M. to 2:00 P.M., Saturday through Thursday. Friday is the main day of worship for Muslims. Business hours may vary slightly in the winter and from region to region.

SOCIETY

Government

Sudan is an Islamic state. Because the military suspended the civilian government in 1989, there is no legislature or elected leaders. A 13-member Revolutionary Command Council (RCC) runs the country and is chaired by General al-Bashir. A 22-member cabinet advises the RCC. Hassan al-Turabi, an Islamic cleric, is said to be the *de facto* leader of the country, even though he is not a member of the RCC. Al-Turabi seeks to spread Islamic fundamentalism and to increase the use of *shari'a* in all aspects of Sudanese life.

Economy

Sudan's economy is based on agriculture, which employs 80 percent of the labor force. Grains (millet, sorghum, wheat, barley), cotton, peanuts, beans, and sesame are the main crops. Cotton is the main export, accounting for 44 percent of total export earnings. Sesame, peanuts, and gum arabic are also exported. Sudan is the world's principal supplier of gum arabic. Industrial activities usually center on processing agricultural items. The development of other industries is hindered by high foreign debt, inadequate transportation systems, and the civil war. Drought has also damaged the economy, but when the country has a successful crop (i.e., rain) year it has the potential to increase economic growth by more than 5 percent. Inflation is more than 120 percent annually. Reforms implemented in 1992 showed some promise of improving long-term economic conditions, but the government cancelled most in 1993 to calm public anger over short-term sacrifices.

The country's Human Development Index (0.276) ranks it 151st out of 173 countries. Real gross domestic product per capita is $1,162, a figure that has risen only slightly since 1960. Eighty-five percent of all rural people live in absolute poverty as subsistence farmers. The currency is the Sudanese pound (£Sd).

Transportation and Communication

More than half of Sudan's roadways are unpaved and often in disrepair. This makes transportation difficult. However, the government is currently investing in infrastructure, including the national railroad and other transportation networks, in the hopes of improving the economy. Relatively few people own private cars. Taxis and buses are available in Khartoum. The communications system is large but poorly maintained and barely adequate. There are five radio and two television stations.

Communications and other systems that rely on electricity suffered in 1995 from frequent and long power outages. Some parts of Khartoum received power only 12 of every 24 hours at times. Since most electricity is generated by hydro-electric dams, the level of available power depends on water levels in rivers (principally the Blue Nile).

Education

Nine years of education is compulsory, but it is often not enforced. Facilities are generally inadequate, especially in rural areas. The literacy rate is 27 percent. About half of school-age children in the northern and central regions are enrolled at the primary level. Three-fourths complete primary schooling, but only about one-fifth go on to the secondary level. The University of Khartoum is a four-year and graduate university.

Health

Parasitic diseases are endemic, particularly in the central and southern parts of the country. Yellow fever, cholera, and malaria are active throughout the country. The health care system is inadequate; there are not enough clinics and doctors to serve the needs of the people. Malnutrition also strains the nation's facilities. The infant mortality rate is 80 per 1,000. Life expectancy averages 54 years.

FOR THE TRAVELER

A visa and valid passport are necessary for entry to Sudan. Visas are issued for visits of seven to ten days. Proof of sufficient funds or a letter from one's employer is also required. The U.S. government suggests that travel is not safe because of the civil war and unstable political conditions. Call the State Department for recorded travel advisories at (202) 647–5225 before departure. Water is not potable, and dairy products should be avoided. Visitors should be sure all food is well cooked and served hot. Fruits and vegetables should be washed and peeled. A traveler should get vaccinations for yellow fever, cholera, typhoid, and possibly other diseases before traveling to Sudan. Malarial suppressants are recommended. Dual-voltage small appliances or adaptors and plug adaptors are necessary to use electrical outlets. For more information, contact the Embassy of Sudan, 2210 Massachusetts Avenue NW, Washington, DC 20008; phone (202) 338–8565.

Syria

(Syrian Arab Republic)

Boundary representations not necessarily authoritative.

BACKGROUND

Land and Climate

Syria is located in the Middle East, bounded by Iraq, Israel, Jordan, Lebanon, and Turkey. It has a small coastline on the Mediterranean Sea. Covering 71,498 square miles (185,180 square kilometers), Syria is about the same size as Indiana and Illinois combined. The country is basically divided into two regions: the coastal region, which includes a narrow range of mountains (the Anti-Lebanon); and a much larger eastern region, which has mountains and large deserts. The disputed Golan Heights are near the Israeli border and are currently occupied by Israel. The proximity of the mountain ranges to the coast guarantees Syria adequate rainfall in the west, but the area around Damascus is primarily desert, which extends to the Euphrates River (the cities of Ar Raqqah and Dayr az Zawr are on the Euphrates). The Syrian desert also covers much of the eastern part of the country. Northern Syria has fertile agricultural land. Syria has very few forests. The climatic range is rather large. Summers (June to August) are hot and dry. Coastal winters (December to February) are mild and rainy. The north is colder and receives some snow.

History

Syria is an ancient land with a rich cultural heritage. Aleppo is one of the world's oldest continuously inhabited cities, and Damascus is one of the oldest continuously inhabited capitals. In its early history, the area was controlled by various peoples, including the Akkadians (2300 B.C.), Amorites (2000 B.C.), Hittites (1500 B.C.), and Assyrians (8th century B.C.). Syria was part of an important commercial and political network. It was conquered by Alexander the Great in 333 B.C., ruled by his successors (the Seleucids), and then brought into the Roman Empire in 64 B.C.

Christianity was strong in Syria until the Muslim conquest in A.D. 634. The first Muslim empire, the Umayyad, ruled the expanding Islamic lands until 750. Egypt controlled the region off and on until the Ottoman Empire conquered it in 1516. Throughout the centuries, Damascus continued to be a vital trade and political center. After World War I, Syria became a French mandate, but an independence movement emerged in the latter 1920s. Independence was not declared until 1941, and elections were held in 1943. Economic and political pressures on the new state led to unrest, and a series of military coups followed. In 1970, the defense minister, Hafez al-Assad, took power.

Assad rules Syria with strict control. His government maintains the martial law declared in 1963 to combat domestic dissent. In 1982, when Muslim fundamentalists rebelled against the government, the military crushed the uprising and thousands were killed. Running unopposed in the 1991 elections, Assad received 99 percent of the vote, giving him his fourth seven-year term as president.

Syria has been a major opponent of Israel. The two countries have fought in three wars (1948, 1967, and 1973). Even after open war between the two nations ended, tensions remained over their respective military involvement in Lebanon (which continues today) and Israel's occupation and virtual annexation of Syria's Golan Heights. However, both nations are participating in the Middle East Peace Conference negotiations and Syria has indicated its willingness to make peace with Israel. Significant progress was made in 1994, which raised hopes in 1995 of an actual peace agreement. High level talks center mostly on the return of the Golan, which Syria insists is a prerequisite to any peace treaty. Israeli leaders are divided as to whether such a move would be possible or desirable, but international efforts are supporting the negotiations.

In general, Assad has tried to increase his country's influence in the Middle East. Syria played a role in winning the release of Western hostages held in Lebanon in the late 1980s and early 1990s. Assad has also attempted to shake the country's image as a terrorist state. In 1986, Syria expelled the terrorist Abu Nidal and claimed it did not sponsor terrorism through other organizations. Assad also cooperated with the international forces deployed in the Gulf War (1990–91).

THE PEOPLE

Population

The population of Syria is about 14.8 million and is growing by 3.7 percent per year, one of the highest growth rates in the world. The majority of the people (90 percent) are Arabs. There are various minorities, the largest of which are Kurds and Armenians. A small number of Turks, Circassians, and Assyrians can also be found, as well as a number of Palestinian refugees. Damascus, the capital, has a population of more than 1.5 million and Aleppo, the focal point of northern trade routes, has 1.2 million people. Almost half of the population is younger than age 15.

Language

Arabic is the official language in Syria. In addition, many of the educated elite speak French and some speak English. Street and business signs are in Arabic, although some are in French. The ethnic minorities also speak their native tongues, including Kurdish, Armenian, Aramaic (Assyrians), and Circassian.

Religion

Although Syria is officially a secular state, religion plays a major role in the country's politics. It is even more important in the daily lives of the people. About 74 percent of the population is Sunni Muslim. Other Islamic groups (16 percent) in Syria include the Alawites, of which the current president is a member, the Druze, and the Shiites. Friday is the Muslim day of worship. Christians account for about 10 percent of the population. The major Christian groups include Greek Orthodox, Armenian Orthodox, Syrian Orthodox, Syrian Catholic, Maronites, and other smaller groups. There are a few thousand Jews in Damascus and Aleppo; their activities are somewhat restricted.

General Attitudes

Educated Syrians are cosmopolitan and well versed in a variety of areas. They are also conservative, dignified, and proud of Syria's national heritage. Many Syrians believe the country should become an Islamic republic (as opposed to a secular state); others think the government should allow more freedoms for political dissent. There are many concerns about the economy and social problems that affect the people of Syria. Thus, although most people are proud of their country, they would like to see some changes take place.

Personal Appearance

Urban Syrians generally dress in Western clothing, although it is not uncommon for a person to wear traditional Arab attire. The way people dress may reflect their religious values. Bedouin women traditionally wear long dresses and the men wear *jalabas* (long robes) and a *keffiyah* (head covering). In the 1980s, veiling became more common among Muslim women, even in the urban areas. This was a result of the resurgence of Islamic fundamentalism. Muslim women, who are generally expected to remain fully covered in public, may wear a Western-style coat or heavy dress, dark stockings, and shoes. They usually cover their hair with a scarf, or use the scarf to cover the entire head (except the face), tucking it into the collar of the coat or dress. Foreign visitors are not expected to conform to the Muslim dress code, but they are expected to dress conservatively. Women may wear pants but not tight pants, and they should cover their upper arms and shoulders.

CUSTOMS AND COURTESIES

Greetings

Syrians are very hospitable. They welcome people by offering an outstretched hand to shake while saying *Marhaba* (Hello). They may also say *Keef haalak?* (How are you?) to inquire about the other person's health. Men may embrace each other in greeting, depending on the degree of their relationship, and female friends exchange kisses on either cheek.

Gestures

It is considered rude to point at other people or direct them with the hand. It is also offensive to rest the ankle of one leg on the knee of the other. This often causes the bottom of the foot to point at another person, which is inappropriate and an insult. One should avoid pointing the bottom of the foot at anyone. Women generally do not cross their legs in public. Men cross their legs at the knee. Items are passed with the right hand or both hands, but not the left hand only.

Visiting

Syrians are more reserved than Westerners in inviting non-family members to their homes. They may invite business and professional acquaintances home for afternoon tea, but they generally meet guests in the early evening or host them at private clubs or restaurants for lunch or dinner. In restaurants, the host pays for the entire group. Visiting hours are in the late afternoon or following supper. Visiting the home is for pleasure or social reasons; business opportunities are not discussed. It is also inappropriate to take bad news to the family at the home.

Eating

Syrian cuisine is famous for its variety and the expertise needed to prepare it. A number of dishes are offered at a formal meal, some to be eaten with the right hand and some to be eaten with Western utensils. Syrians usually decline an offer of food twice out of politeness before accepting it after the third offer. Hosts, therefore, generally offer food or drink three times. If a person truly wishes to decline an offer, which is considered impolite, a refusal must be made at least three times before the host will stop offering.

During the Islamic month of *Ramadan*, Muslims do not eat or drink from sunrise to sundown each day; meals are served in the evening and friends visit one another. During *Ramadan*, special attention is paid to the needs of the poor and business hours are shortened.

LIFESTYLE

Family

The family is the basic unit of society and the center of an individual's life. All activities revolve around family members and family life, and any achievement advances the reputation of the entire family. The father is the undisputed leader of the family. Both paternal and maternal relatives are part of the everyday interactions between all family members. Most social activities are organized by and for the family. Children may socialize with cousins, aunts, and uncles. Although nuclear families are becoming more common, due to contemporary urban housing and work-related migration away from extended families, one still finds extended family households.

Dating and Marriage

While dating is becoming common in more Westernized circles, it is still restricted to cousins and close friends of the family. University students generally have more freedom to organize social events, but most associations follow previous family acquaintance patterns. Although students are sometimes free to choose a spouse, they are careful to choose one the family approves of. Among more traditional people, dating is not common and families play a dominant role in selecting marital partners for their children.

Diet

Syrian cuisine is varied and quite delicious. *Mezza* (a table full of appetizers) is often served at restaurants and clubs. It includes pastes made of chickpeas and eggplant, dishes of meats (raw or grilled) mixed with spices and wheat, pickles, olives, and breads. Syrians also enjoy sweets. According to Islamic law, Muslims do not eat pork or drink alcohol.

Recreation

Soccer is the most important sport in Syria and has an avid following. Basketball has also gained popularity, especially among schoolboys. Water sports are popular in the coastal cities. Visiting family and friends, or socializing with them in a private club, is a common pastime. Many people own video machines and enjoy watching films or television with their families. Syrians seldom attend movies at a theater.

Holidays

In addition to national political holidays, both Islamic and Christian holidays are officially celebrated. The nonreligious holidays include New Year's Day, Revolution Day (8 March), Labor Day (1 May), Martyr's Day (6 May), Egyptian Revolution Day (23 July), and Libyan Revolution Day (1 September). The most important Islamic holidays (based on the Islamic lunar calendar) include *Eid al-Fitr* (the three-day feast at the end of the month of *Ramadan*); *Eid al-Adha* (Feast of the Sacrifice, which is held during the annual pilgrimage to Makkah, Saudi Arabia, and celebrates Abraham's willingness to sacrifice his son); the Birth of the Prophet Muhammad; and *Ashura* (the Shiite Day of Atonement). Easter is celebrated by the Christians, although there are distinctly separate observances by the Eastern orthodox religions and the Western-oriented groups. The Armenian Orthodox Christians celebrate Christmas on 6 January, while other Christians celebrate it on 25 December.

Commerce

Banking and government office hours are from 8:00 A.M. to 2:30 P.M., Saturday through Thursday. Businesses and stores generally open at 9:00 A.M. and close at 2:00 P.M., opening again around 4:00 P.M. for three hours.

SOCIETY

Government

Syria is a republic, but not a democracy. The president is chief of state and has strong executive powers. He has three vice presidents. A prime minister is head of government. He has three deputy prime ministers and heads a Council of Ministers (cabinet). The legislature is called the People's Council (*Majlis al-Chaab*); it has 250 seats. Since the 1960s, when the ruling Ba'ath party (officially the Arab Socialist Resurrectionist party) came to power with an ideology of liberty, unity, and socialism, few other political elements have been able to gain much influence. Other political parties exist, but Ba'ath dominates all forms of political life. The voting age is 18. Laws are generally based on Islamic law (*shari'a*).

Economy

Syria has traditionally been an agricultural nation. Industrialization decreased the importance of agriculture, but it still employs about one-third of the labor force. Because the government is socialist, many key industries are run by the state, except for small private businesses. The government controls oil refineries, utilities, the railway, and various manufacturing plants. Centralized planning and inefficiency led to economic decline in the 1980s, while drought affected agricultural production as well. The economy rebounded in the 1990s, aided by higher oil exports, better harvests, aid dollars from the Gulf War, and increased foreign investment. Growth in 1993 was above 7 percent. Inflation is about 16 percent. Key exports include textiles, petroleum products, phosphates, fruits, and vegetables.

The country's Human Development Index (0.727) ranks it 73d out of 173 countries. Real gross domestic product per capita is $5,220, which has more than tripled in the last generation. These figures reflect the success of the economy but indicate that a significant portion of the population does not yet earn a decent income or have access to the benefits of economic prosperity. The currency is the Syrian pound (£S).

Transportation and Communication

Syria's location has long made it a crossroads for the region. It has two major ports, Tartūs and Latakia, and two international airports, at Damascus and Aleppo. An adequate system of roads and railways serves the country, but public transportation is inefficient. Buses are the most common form of public transport available. Service taxis operate in the larger cities; they run along set routes and pick up passengers until the taxi is full. They also travel between cities. Telephone service is good within Syria, although limited in some areas. The government controls the media.

Education

Syrian schools include public (free), private religious, and private secular schools. The bulk of all students are enrolled in public schools. The literacy rate is around 64 percent. More than 90 percent of all boys and 70 percent of all girls begin primary education. One-fourth of all students drop out after only a few years; in rural areas the percentage is higher. Half of all eligible students are enrolled in secondary schools. There are four universities in Syria, located in Damascus, Aleppo, and Latakia. There is also an Institute of Petroleum and Chemical Engineering at Hims.

Health

Medical care in the cities is available and reasonably good, but facilities in the rural areas are inadequate. Water is not potable and sanitation is often poor. The infant mortality rate is 42 per 1,000. Life expectancy ranges from 65 to 67 years.

FOR THE TRAVELER

A visa and valid passport are necessary for U.S. citizens traveling to Syria. A transit visa for a stay of three days is available on arrival, but longer visas can be obtained through the embassy. Only boiled water should be used for all purposes, including ice cubes and brushing teeth. All food should be hot and well cooked before being eaten. It is best to cook all vegetables and peel all fruits. Malarial suppressants are recommended. Dual-voltage small appliances or a voltage converter and a plug adaptor are necessary to use electrical outlets. Political conditions may mean certain security restrictions; be sure to obey the police in all cases. For tourist information, contact the tourist office located within the Embassy of the Syrian Arab Republic, 2215 Wyoming Avenue NW, Washington, DC 20008; phone (202) 232–6313. For information about travel in the country, you may also write to the Ministry of Tourism, Furat Street, Damascus, Syria.

CULTURGRAM '96

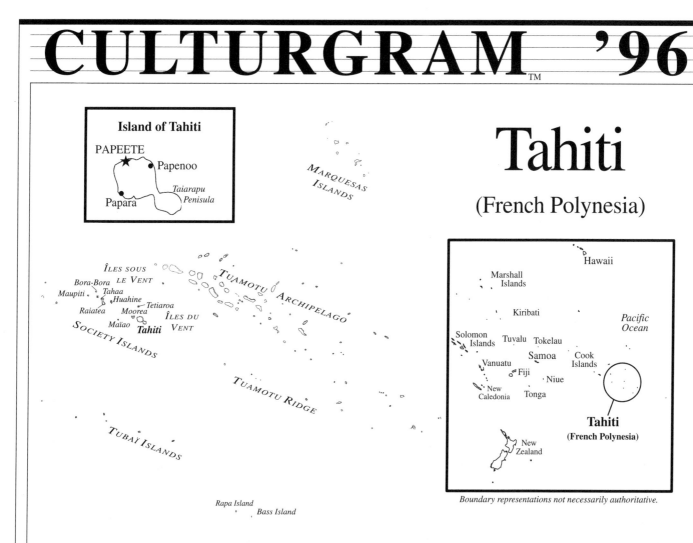

Island of Tahiti

PAPEETE ★
Papenoo ●
Taiarapu Penisula
Papara ●

Tahiti

(French Polynesia)

MARQUESAS ISLANDS

ÎLES SOUS LE VENT
Bora-Bora
Maupiti Tahaa
Huahine Tetiaroa
Raiatea Moorea
Maïao ÎLES DU
Tahiti VENT
SOCIETY ISLANDS

TUAMOTU ARCHIPELAGO

TUAMOTU RIDGE

TUBAÏ ISLANDS

Rapa Island
Bass Island

Hawaii
Marshall Islands
Kiribati
Pacific Ocean
Solomon Islands Tuvalu Tokelau
Vanuatu Samoa Cook Islands
Fiji Niue
New Caledonia Tonga
Tahiti
(French Polynesia)
New Zealand

Boundary representations not necessarily authoritative.

BACKGROUND

Land and Climate

Tahiti is part of the Society Islands, which are part of French Polynesia, a self-governing territory of France. The Society Islands include the groups of *Îles sous le Vent* (Leeward Islands) and *Îles du Vent* (Windward Islands). Tahiti is part of the latter group and is the main inhabited island in the Society Islands. Tahiti is the anchor of the islands, which are also collectively referred to as "Tahiti and her islands." French Polynesia actually stretches across a wide area of the Pacific Ocean, about halfway between California and Australia. The territory includes five archipelagos: the two groups of the Society Islands, the Marquesas Islands, the Tuamotu Archipelago, and the Tubuaï Islands. This *Culturgram* focuses culturally on Tahitian society, but much of the information is applicable for neighboring islands. Statistical information concerns French Polynesia as a whole.

French Polynesia's 130 islands extend over an area as large as Europe, but their combined land area is only slightly larger than Rhode Island (1,413 square miles [3,660 square kilometers]). The Society Islands are a blend of volcanic peaks and lush tropical forests. White, sandy beaches surround each island. Coral reefs provide quiet lagoons of crystal-clear waters in all the groups except the Marquesas. The other Society Islands include Bora-Bora (famous for its lagoons and two volcanic peaks), Huahine, Maïao, Maupiti, Moorea, Raiatea, Tahaa, and Tetiaroa (owned by Marlon Brando). Tahiti's climate is subtropical, tempered by trade winds throughout the year. January and February are the hottest months, with temperatures between 85°F and 90°F (29–32°C). Otherwise, temperatures average between 70°F and 80°F (21–27°C).

History

Tahiti and most of French Polynesia was initially inhabited by Polynesians, although their exact origin is not certain. They began to settle on Pacific islands between 2000 and 1000 B.C. The first Polynesians probably reached the Society Islands in the third century A.D. Before European colonization, the islands were ruled by local chiefs. Englishman Samuel Wallis charted and claimed the islands for Britain in 1767. In 1768, they were claimed by the French, but it was some time before Europeans actually began to settle on Tahiti. In 1769, England's Captain James Cook came to the island. In 1788, the crew of the *Bounty* mutinied against their commander, Captain William Bligh, and escaped to the islands.

OCEANIA

The Pomare Dynasty reigned on Tahiti until Queen Pomare IV signed a treaty with France (1843), making Tahiti a French protectorate in exchange for help in bringing neighboring islands under her control. Her son abdicated in 1880, and the islands became a colony of France. Territorial status was granted in 1957; internal self-rule was obtained in 1977.

THE PEOPLE

Population

Approximately 215,000 people live in French Polynesia. More than half (about 127,000) live on Tahiti. Papeete, the capital of French Polynesia, is by far the largest city, with some 80,000 residents in and around it. The population grows at 2.3 percent annually. Polynesians account for most of the population—78 percent. However, many Polynesians have a mixed heritage that includes either Chinese or European ancestry. About 12 percent of the people are Chinese, forming primarily a merchant class. They are descendants of laborers imported in the 19th century to work in a new cotton industry. The venture failed, but the laborers settled down. Locally born French citizens account for 6 percent of the population, and 4 percent are French or other Europeans.

Language

French is the official language in the territory. It is used exclusively in the schools and is spoken widely on Tahiti. Tahitian, however, is an official regional language for the Society Islands. It remains the language used by the majority of the people and is spoken in the home, especially on the other Society Islands. The Tahitian alphabet has 13 letters. All syllables end with a vowel. The Chinese community speaks the Hakka variety of Chinese or French or Tahitian. One's proficiency in the French language affects one's economic status. English is not widely spoken, although it is understood in tourist areas. Each of the different island groups in French Polynesia has its own language. Some are similar to Tahitian and some are very different.

Religion

Tahitians no longer worship the many gods of nature they once did, but they are still influenced by traditional beliefs. Missionaries from the London Missionary Society arrived just before the end of the 18th century and other Christian missionaries soon followed. The people embraced Christianity and are deeply religious today. Currently, 55 percent of the population is Protestant (converts to the Evangelical Church represented by the London Missionary Society). About 30 percent is Roman Catholic; 6 percent belongs to the Church of Jesus Christ of Latter-day Saints (Mormons); and 2 percent is Seventh-Day Adventist. White is the most common color worn for Sunday services. There are a variety of other Christian religions represented on the island, as well as Judaism and Buddhism.

General Attitudes

Tahitians value personal relations and are warm and receptive, although they may seem shy to strangers before they become better acquainted. They enjoy life and try to live as simply and as happily as possible. Time is more flexible in Tahiti than in most industrialized nations—people are more important than schedules and life is lived at a more casual pace. Still, the West has influenced society and the pace of life is quicker than it once was, especially in Papeete.

Personal Appearance

Lightweight, informal clothing is worn throughout the year. Clothing is always neat and clean. Footwear for both men and women is usually a pair of thongs or sandals without stockings or hose. Dresses of *pareu* cloth are worn at home and at the beach. Women usually wear dresses instead of shorts. Although Tahitians are at home in Western-style clothing, they continue to wear more traditional clothing made from simple cloth wrapped around the waist.

Many visitors know the Tahitians for their traditional dance costumes, which are worn for special occasions or performances. There are many types of these costumes, but some include skirts made of grass *(more)* or cotton fabrics. Local plants and grasses are used for headdresses and belts, as well as necklaces. Dyes are extracted from hibiscus flowers and other plants. *Puroutu* (missionary dresses) more fully clothe a woman and are used to perform the slow hula dances.

CUSTOMS AND COURTESIES

Greetings

Tahitians shake hands when they meet, and use French greetings such as *Bonjour* (Good day) in formal situations. If one's hand is dirty, a wrist, elbow, or even a shoulder is offered instead. It is impolite to not shake hands with every person in a small (fewer than 30 people) gathering. Women might kiss each other on the cheeks when greeting, especially after a long separation. A traditional Tahitian phrase of welcome is *Ia ora!*

Gestures

Beckoning is done by waving all fingers with the palm down. Pointing with the index finger may be considered rude. The most commonly understood gesture in Tahiti is a smile.

Visiting

Tahitians (and French Polynesians in general) emphasize *joie de vivre*, or "joy of life." They are relaxed, natural, and invariably try to make their guests comfortable. A favorite maxim is, "If you act like old friends when you first meet, you will soon feel that you are," and Tahitians try to make that maxim a practice. Guests are free to compliment their hosts on their home or family, but they should avoid singling out any one object or item of decor. Otherwise, the host may be embarrassed. It is customary to remove one's shoes before entering the home.

Eating

Tahiti enjoys a great variety of culinary choices, with excellent French and Chinese cuisine in addition to the traditional native foods. Western dishes are also readily available. Etiquette varies greatly depending on the food and the family. Traditional Tahitian foods are eaten with the fingers, while Chinese food is eaten with chopsticks. Utensils are supplied on request and are used in the continental fashion—with the fork in the left hand and the knife remaining in the right.

It is impolite for guests to refuse food or make excuses for not eating. However, politeness does not require a person to eat everything on the plate. Leaving a little extra will ensure that a second (or third) helping is not served and will satisfy the host that the guest has been well fed. Sometimes, guests are offered a meal and the host family will not join in eating. Guests are expected to accept the invitation and not mind if the family watches. In restaurants, tipping is not customary and is discouraged because it violates the tradition of Tahitian hospitality.

LIFESTYLE

Family

Traditionally, Tahitian families were large, usually with many children and several generations living under the same roof. It is still common for couples to live with the husband's or wife's parents for a time after marriage, but increased contact with Western culture is leading to more nuclear families. Still, family ties are very strong. In Polynesian culture, children are precious and their upbringing is often shared by grandparents or other sets of adoptive parents (*faamu*). This system of informal adoption remains active today, making family relations somewhat complex.

Dating and Marriage

In most Polynesian cultures, the girls are more closely supervised than the boys. Dating, as practiced in Western societies, is generally not found in French Polynesia, except among the French youth and perhaps in Papeete. Tahitians usually get together in groups to dance, sing, talk, or participate in sports. Marriages are traditionally influenced by the families, who used to make decisions based partially on one's social class. However, classes no longer exist and youth have greater freedom in choosing spouses. Marriages are a festive time for feasting and merrymaking.

Diet

Tahitians eat three meals a day. A light breakfast consists of bread and a hot drink. Supper in the evening is also a light meal (except at restaurants and parties). The main meal of the day is at midday. The Tahitian diet consists of fish and other seafood, chicken, pork, sweet potatoes, breadfruit, rice, and local fruits and vegetables. *Poisson cru* is uncooked fish marinated in lime juice, often served as part of salads. Fruits include papayas, mangos, pineapples, and bananas. A type of spinach *(fafa)* is also common. Banana or papaya purées *(poe')* are popular as desserts. They are baked, covered with sugar and coconut milk, and served hot. Coconut milk also covers a popular chicken and pork casserole that includes *fafa*. Fish is often marinated before being baked or grilled. *Tamaaraa* is a Tahitian feast common at parties and in resort areas.

Recreation

Recreation is of prime importance in the life of a French Polynesian. Sports, television, movies, and dances are popular ways to spend leisure time. Soccer is the national sport. Boxing, volleyball, basketball, and cycling are enjoyed. Canoeing, windsurfing, swimming, fishing, and diving top a long list of popular water sports. Because Tahiti is a tourist location, recreation can be a way of life for many who work in the travel industry.

Holidays

National holidays include New Year's Day, Easter Monday, Labor Day (1 May), Ascension, Pentecost Monday, National Bastille Day (14 July), Assumption of Virgin Mary (15 August), *Toussaint* (All Saints' Day on 1 November), Veterans' Day (11 November), and Christmas. Bastille Day, the French national holiday, is celebrated during the middle two weeks of July and is known as the *Tiurai* (meaning July). It is considered the most spectacular celebration of the year. Celebrations include parades, athletic competitions, dancing, pageantry, and cultural events. However, the festivities do not necessarily honor the French but commemorate Polynesian warriors and Tahitian culture. Dance and song competitions are popular, especially during *Heiva Taupiti*, a season of celebrations that begins in May and culminates with *Tiurai*.

Commerce

Government offices are open from 7:30 A.M. to 3:30 P.M. Most stores open from 7:30 to 11:30 A.M. and from 2:00 to 5:30 P.M. Chinese shops are often open from 5:30 A.M. to 10:00 P.M., seven days a week. Other stores are generally closed on Sunday, although Sunday morning is the most important day at the Papeete market, where local merchants sell food, crafts, and flowers.

SOCIETY

Government

French Polynesia is a territory of France, and is governed by French authorities. The chief of state is France's president, Jacques Chirac. He is represented in French Polynesia by a French High Commissioner. The territory has two representatives in France's National Assembly and one in France's Senate. Locally, a Territorial Assembly with 41 elected members chooses a president to be head of government. Gaston Flosse was elected in 1991 as the President of the Territorial Government.

The next local elections are in March 1996, while the next elections for France's legislature are in 1998. The voting age is 18. Two main political parties, the People's Rally for the Republic and the Polynesian Union Party, are joined by a number of smaller parties in the Territorial Assembly. Flosse is a member of the People's Rally for the Republic party, which is a pro-French organization.

Economy

French Polynesia's economy is strongly linked to tourism and the *Centre Experimental du Pacifique* (CEP), France's nuclear testing program. The CEP is coordinated by the French military, which employs a large portion of the labor force. Agriculture is important, producing copra and coconut oil (80 percent of all export earnings), mother-of-pearl (14 percent of exports), vanilla, and various foods for domestic consumption. Tourism is a crucial source of foreign exchange earnings and much of the labor force is employed by the tourist industry. As a result, tourist facilities are nearly always being improved or built. The economy, once reliant on subsistence agriculture, now provides most people with a decent standard of living. The estimated gross national product per capita is US$7,000. The currency is the *Comptoirs Français du Pacifique franc* or CFP *franc*.

Transportation and Communication

Tahiti is linked to other countries by a number of airlines, and small commuter airlines provide efficient domestic service. Motorbikes and cars are the most common form of private, local transportation. Buses are numerous and keep fairly regular schedules. *Le truck* is a popular form of local transportation that carries passengers to various locations on Tahiti. In keeping with the people's tradition of hospitality, tipping is not acceptable for taxi drivers or other service personnel.

Ferry services operate between some islands. Telecommunication systems are adequate for interisland and international communication.

Education

The French government has established primary, secondary, and vocational schools on the islands that comply with French educational standards. School is compulsory and free from ages six to fourteen. Primary education lasts until age 11 and secondary to age 18. At age 14, students enter various tracks depending on their aptitude and choice. Private schools are heavily subsidized by the government and follow a public school curriculum. Adult education programs are popular and free. Many students travel to France or other countries for higher education. Nearly all (98 percent) of Tahiti's young people can read and write.

Health

Medical services are subsidized by the government and are adequate for most needs. Two major hospitals and several private clinics are located on Tahiti, but facilities are limited on other islands. Still, throughout the territory, health conditions are generally good and improving. The infant mortality rate is 15 per 1,000. Life expectancy ranges from 68 to 73 years.

FOR THE TRAVELER

A passport is necessary for U.S. citizens to visit the islands; visas are not required for stays of up to one month. No vaccinations are necessary for Tahiti, which is generally free of tropical diseases, but health certificates may be required of those entering from yellow fever endemic zones. Tahiti has an excellent tourist industry. The islands offer beauty, warmth, and relaxation. The Tahiti Tourist Promotion Board, located at 300 North Continental Boulevard, Suite 180, El Segundo, CA 90245; phone (310) 414–8484, provides more detailed information. You may also wish to contact the Embassy of France, at 4101 Reservoir Road NW, Washington, DC 20007–2186; phone (202) 944–6200, which is responsible for the diplomatic affairs of French Polynesia.

CULTURGRAM™ '96

Taiwan
(Republic of China)

Boundary representations not necessarily authoritative.

ASIA

BACKGROUND

Land and Climate

Covering 13,892 square miles (35,980 square kilometers), Taiwan is about the size of Massachusetts and Connecticut combined. It is located about 100 miles (160 kilometers) east of mainland China. The government on Taiwan also controls the Penghu Islands and other islands near China's coast (Chinmen, Matsu, and Wuchiu). A north-south mountain range forms the backbone of Taiwan. The highest peak, Yushan, rises 13,110 feet (3,996 meters) above sea level. The western half of Taiwan contains the greater population and most of the agricultural activity. Taiwan's climate is subtropical. In the north, the warm, humid summer lasts from May to October. January and February can be cold and rainy; some snow falls at higher elevations. Southern Taiwan is warmer, raining mostly in the summer. Taiwan experiences numerous small earthquakes each year. Typhoons are possible from June to October. The average temperature is 75°F (24°C).

History

Chinese immigration to Taiwan began as early as the T'ang Dynasty (A.D. 618–907). In 1628, the Dutch took control of the island. In 1683, the Manchus of mainland China conquered the island and made it a province of China. The island was ceded to Japan following the Sino-Japanese War (1895) and remained under Japanese control until 1945. During that period, forces on mainland China battled for control of the government. A successful revolution inspired by Sun Yat-sen founded the Republic of China (ROC), but the new government was overshadowed by a period of contending warlords. Sun's *Kuomingtang* (KMT) political movement was led by Chiang Kai-shek after Sun died (1925). Chiang battled the Communist forces of Mao Zedong, and they both fought against a Japanese invasion. After Japan was defeated, civil war continued and Chiang's forces fled from Mao's army, establishing the ROC government on Taiwan.

Chiang's KMT-led government declared itself the legitimate government of all of China and established a policy to eventually reunite with the mainland. Plans by the People's Republic of China (PRC) to invade the island were blocked in 1950 by the United States. In 1954, the United States signed an agreement to protect Taiwan in case of attack from the mainland. The United States and much of the world recognized the ROC claim to legitimacy.

In 1971, however, the PRC was admitted to the United Nations in Taiwan's place. In 1979, the United States also normalized diplomatic relations with the PRC and broke them with the ROC. Relations between the United States and Taiwan continue on an unofficial basis. In fact, many countries have only informal political ties to Taiwan, while they enjoy relatively strong economic relations.

The KMT ruled Taiwan as a one-party state under martial law. After Chiang Kai-shek died in 1975, his son Chiang Ching-kuo replaced him. Taiwan directed its greatest efforts at modernization and developed a thriving economy. Martial law was lifted in 1987 and political reforms allowed a multiparty democracy to begin emerging in 1989. National elections were held for the first time in 1989 and Lee Teng-hui was elected president. Lee is the first native Taiwanese to lead the country. A national assembly was elected in late 1991 to revise the constitution and reform certain government structures. Legislative elections were held in 1992. Lien Chan became premier.

The ROC remains in a state of war with the PRC; two years of military service is required of all young men. For many years, the ROC refused contact with the PRC. However, recent political trends have led to open trade and communication channels. Current debate centers on whether Taiwan should become an independent country (ending its unification bid) or continue its policy of unification under ROC leadership.

THE PEOPLE

Population

The population of Taiwan is 21.3 million. It is growing annually at 1 percent. The original inhabitants of Taiwan make up only 2 percent of the population. They are divided among several ethnic groups, some of which maintain their languages and traditions. The rest of the people are ethnic Chinese. They include Taiwanese (84 percent) and mainland Chinese (14 percent). The latter group migrated to the island after World War II. The Taiwanese are descendants of migrants who left China between the 17th and 19th centuries. As the mainland Chinese who came after 1947 pass away, their children (with no memory of the mainland) feel that Taiwan is their real home.

Language

The official language is Mandarin Chinese. However, the majority of the people also speak Taiwanese, the language of the first Chinese immigrants. Hakka, another Chinese dialect, is also spoken. Some older people speak Japanese and the aborigines speak their own native languages. English is a popular second or third language for students and is widely understood in urban areas. Although the official language of Taiwan and mainland China is the same (Mandarin), vocabulary and idiomatic differences exist. In Taiwan, school children use a simplified character system that helps them "sound out" a word—something impossible to do with standard characters, which must be memorized.

Various systems of romanization (representing Chinese characters and words in Roman letters) have been developed by Westerners and adopted by the government to help Westerners who cannot read Chinese characters sound out names, read signs, and follow maps. The average Chinese would not understand or use romanization. Romanizations differ; for example, the character for "please" can be written *Quing* or *Ching*, depending on the romanization.

Chinese is a tonal language. Each written character can have up to five different meanings, depending on the tone with which it is spoken. For instance, *Ma* can mean "horse" or "mother," and can even function as a question mark, all depending on the specific tone (voice inflection) used.

Religion

Ninety-three percent of the people practice a combination of Buddhism, Confucianism, and Taoism. Confucianism, while emphasizing ancestor veneration, does not proclaim loyalty to any specific deity. It orders social patterns and relationships, forming the Chinese value system. Worship rituals and beliefs come mainly from Buddhism. Christianity, in various forms, is followed by about 5 percent of the people. Some important Chinese figures, such as Sun Yat-sen, have been Christians. Freedom of religion is guaranteed in Taiwan.

General Attitudes

People in Taiwan are generally reserved, quiet, refined, and friendly. Frankness or abruptness, especially in offering criticism of any kind, is avoided. Causing public embarrassment or bringing shame to anyone (a "loss of face") is unacceptable. Loud, tacky, or boisterous behavior is usually regarded as being in poor taste. The Confucian ethic of proper social and family relationships form the foundation of Chinese society. Schools and government foster the tradition of respect for, and obedience to, parents. Moral standards are generally high. Traditionally, men and women do not show affection in public, although this is changing in the larger urban areas. An individual's actions reflect upon the entire family, and people act with this in mind.

Taiwan is a changing society; new social patterns are developing. This causes tension with traditional ideas, but people are adjusting to new concepts. In Taiwan, Westerners are treated with special courtesy and respect; those who return that courtesy are appreciated.

Personal Appearance

Western-style clothing is the norm in Taiwan. The youth, especially in large urban areas, enjoy the latest fashions. Most adults appreciate conservative clothing. Western suits and ties are most common for businessmen. Women wear dresses more often than in the United States. Cleanliness and neatness are the most important factors in appearance.

CUSTOMS AND COURTESIES

Greetings

Asking someone if they have eaten (*Chr bau le meiyou?*) is a common Chinese greeting. The greeting stems from the tradition to never let anyone go hungry; it was always polite to ask if someone had eaten and offer them a meal. Today it is used simply as a "How are you?" Other common greetings are *Ni hau ma?* (Are you at peace?), *Hai hau ma?* (Is everything okay?), and *Ching dzwo* (Please sit), which is spoken to visitors to the home. After initial greetings, polite questions may follow. Adults often ask young people about their schoolwork; the elderly appreciate inquiries about their health.

A nod of one's head and a smile are considered appropriate when meeting someone for the first time, but for acquaintances and close friends, a handshake is most common. A slight bow shows respect. Chinese names are arranged with the family name first, consisting of one or two syllables. A one or two-syllable given name follows. Persons are generally addressed by their full name. Only in rare cases are given names used alone. If speaking to someone in English, a title with the surname is used, such as "Dr. Yu" or "Mr. Lee."

Gestures

One uses the open hand to point; using the index finger is rude. Beckoning is done by waving all fingers with the palm down. People commonly "write" a character in the air when explaining it. It is common for young female friends to hold hands in public. It is often inappropriate to put one's arms around the shoulders of another. Shaking one hand from side to side with the palm forward means "no." People do not use their feet to move objects such as chairs or doors. While sitting, the hands are placed in the lap. Winking is impolite. When handing an object to another person, especially an older person, both hands are used. In conversation, a person referring to himself points to his nose.

Visiting

Shoes are usually removed before entering a home and slippers are worn inside. Guests recognize and greet the elderly first. Visitors are likely to receive tea, candy, fruit, or a soft drink. Dinner conversation often centers on the meal—how it was prepared, what ingredients were used, and where they were obtained. Upon leaving, the host often escorts the guest some distance from the home. To this, the guest offers some token resistance and thanks the host graciously for the hospitality.

When visiting a home for the first time, a small gift, such as fruit, is appropriate. Gifts are also given to hosts during New Year's celebrations. Both hands are used when exchanging gifts or other items. Gifts are not opened in the presence of the giver. Hosts and guests appreciate sincere compliments, but will politely deny them out of modesty. Visitors should not admire an object too much, as the host may feel obligated to present it as a gift. It is polite to stand when a guest, a superior, or an elderly person enters a room.

Eating

Chopsticks and a soup spoon are the common eating utensils in Taiwan. Food is placed in the center of the table. Each person is given a personal bowl of rice. The person is served or serves himself from the dish(es) at the center of the table, placing small amounts of food in the rice bowl. The bowl is held near the mouth and chopsticks are used to eat the food and rice. The person takes from the main dish as often as necessary to complement the rice. Bones and seeds are placed on the table or on a provided plate but never in the bowl of rice or on a plate of food. When the rice bowl is empty, it is refilled. It is impolite to leave rice in the bowl. Children are taught to finish all of their food out of respect for farmers and parents. Chopsticks are placed side by side on the table when a person is finished.

At a restaurant, a host expects to pay. Guests may offer politely to help but should not insist. If toothpicks are used, the mouth is covered with the other hand. It is not proper for adults to eat while walking on the street.

LIFESTYLE

Family

Families in Taiwan have traditionally been large, but a government family-planning program encourages families to have only two children. An education campaign has reduced population growth and the size of today's nuclear family. It is not uncommon for elderly parents to live with their children. In rural areas, larger extended families often share the same home. Although affection is not openly displayed between family members in the Western manner, families have a deep-rooted unity and sense of obligation to each other. Family

members will agree rather than cause disunity in the family. The family as a unit also maintains control over the individual. Children generally yield to the counsel of their parents or to the advice of the oldest member of the extended family.

Dating and Marriage

Except perhaps in urban areas, Western-style dating is not common in Taiwan. Students concentrate on their education and associate with peers but seldom date as couples. Dating generally begins once they are working or pursuing higher education. Those who do date enjoy going to movies or dining at restaurants. People usually only date one person at a time. Men generally marry between the ages of 27 and 30, and women about three years earlier.

Diet

Rice is eaten with nearly every meal. Soup, seafood, pork, chicken, vegetables, and fruit are most commonly eaten. Noodles and breads are also eaten. Sauces are an important part of each meal. Most foods, including vegetables, are stir-fried. Tea is often served with the meal. Mealtime is important in the family and is seldom missed.

Recreation

The most popular forms of recreation are movies, picnics, listening to music, and hiking. Basketball, ping pong, volleyball, baseball, badminton, tennis, and soccer are also enjoyed. Baseball is extremely popular among the youth, and Taiwan's Little League champions consistently do well in the Little League World Series. Taiwan has a professional baseball league. The elderly enjoy shadowboxing as a form of exercise and relaxation.

Holidays

Different calendars are used in Taiwan for different reasons. The Western (Gregorian) monthly calendar is used for official purposes, and political holidays are scheduled accordingly. However, the year in Taiwan does not correspond to the year in the West. Rather than beginning from the birth of Christ (the A.D. system), the Chinese traditionally begin a new year system for each dynasty or republic. The current republic officially began in China under Sun Yat-sen in 1912. Therefore, 1996 is the year 85 in Taiwan. Official holidays include the ROC's Founding Day (1 January), Youth Day (29 March), Chiang Kai-shek's death (5 April), the Birth of Confucius and Teacher's Day (28 September), Double Ten National Day (10 October), Sun Yat-sen's Birthday (12 November), and Constitution Day (25 December).

The Chinese lunar calendar determines Buddhist holidays and the most important celebration of the year, the New Year. It usually falls in February and is celebrated with fireworks, feasts, and worship at various temples. Ancestors are venerated and children receive money from their elders (the money comes in special red envelopes). The summer Dragon Boat Festival is also popular.

Commerce

A five- or six-day, 44-hour workweek is common for wage earners. The traditional break from noon to 1:00 P.M. is being discouraged. Many families own small retail or service shops and have their homes above or near the store. These stores may open as early as 7:00 A.M. and remain open until 10:00 or 11:00 P.M. Family members take turns working in the store. Food and other supplies can be purchased at these stores, but are more likely to be purchased at larger grocery and department stores. Night markets are popular in some areas. Held outdoors, they feature prepared foods, entertainment, and consumer goods.

SOCIETY

Government

Taiwan is a multiparty democratic regime. It is administered through sixteen counties *(hsien),* five municipalities *(shih),* and two special municipalities *(chuan-shih)*: Taipei and Kaohsiung.The president is chief of state and the premier is head of government. The legislature is composed of a Legislative *Yuan* and a National Assembly. The first National Assembly members were elected in 1946 (with a supplementary election in 1986), and included "representatives" of provinces in China. This was part of the Nationalist leadership's claim to authority over China. With political attitudes changing, elections for a second (current) National Assembly were held and limited terms were introduced; representatives are for Taiwan. The voting age is 20. The two largest political parties include the Nationalist Party (KMT) and the Democratic Progressive Party (DPP). Elections for the Legislative *Yuan* are held at different intervals than for the National Assembly. The president faces reelection in 1996.

Economy

Taiwan has maintained dynamic growth for three decades, averaging more than 5 percent every year. Incomes have grown steadily to the point that a strong middle class enjoys a relatively high standard of living. Taiwan is in the top 20 percent of trading nations and is a major exporter of textiles, electronics, machinery, metals, timber products, and high technology items. Taiwan's early growth was fueled by a very efficient agricultural sector and then by adaptable cottage industries. The system created a broad base that could easily adapt to global economic trends, allowing Taiwan to avoid the negative impact of world economic fluctuations. Taiwan's economy remains strong; it has among the largest foreign reserves in the world. Unemployment and inflation are both low, and the average annual gross national product per capita is estimated to be above $10,000.

Since 1987, political reforms have allowed for increased exports and have permitted foreign investment. Taiwan's wealth allowed it to announce, in 1991, a six-year, $300-billion modernization program that will significantly improve everything from schools to sewer systems to roads. Many foreign companies have received major contracts to help complete these projects. Taiwan also invests in the Asian region, and elsewhere. The currency is the New Taiwan dollar (NT$).

Transportation and Communication

In the early 1980s, only the wealthy owned cars, especially given the 100 percent import tax. Most people traveled by motorcycle, motorized bicycles, bicycles, and public transportation. Buses and trains were heavily used. Today, many more people own cars (the import tax was reduced and incomes are higher), and traffic jams are much more prevalent. A rapid transit system is being developed to alleviate congestion. Taxis are readily available and reasonably priced. In rural areas, walking and riding bicycles are still important. Most people in cities have a telephone, while rural inhabitants have access to public phones. Past restrictions on the press have been relaxed in an atmosphere of greater democracy.

Education

Education is very important in Taiwan. Schooling is free and compulsory for nine years (to age fifteen), but plans are being implemented to extend that to twelve years. Most people welcome this change because they believe it will further Taiwan's economic development. Entrance to universities is determined by examinations given each year in July. Students work hard to prepare for these exams, sometimes studying sixteen hours a day, seven days a week, for an entire year. While many students travel abroad for higher education, university and other higher education facilities in Taiwan are good and more students are remaining in Taiwan. The literacy rate is 92 percent. Taiwan's education system has produced a highly skilled labor force.

Health

Taiwan has a modern health care system. Private insurance programs cover the needs of most, and the government provides care for those who cannot afford it. A new regionalization system, designed to create public health facilities and offer basic care to all people, is being established. The infant mortality rate is 6 per 1,000. Life expectancy ranges from 72 to 78 years.

FOR THE TRAVELER

A visa and valid passport are required for U.S. travelers staying more than two weeks. A transit visa is issued on arrival for those staying less than two weeks. No vaccinations are necessary. Boiled or bottled water is recommended. No plug adaptors are needed to use electrical outlets. Many national treasures that would have likely been destroyed during China's Cultural Revolution, had they remained in the PRC, are displayed at the National Palace Museum. The ROC has not only preserved much of the Chinese culture, but it has also developed a culture of its own. Do not take photographs inside Buddhist temples without permission. For more information contact the Taiwan Visitors' Association, located at 166 Geary Street, Suite 1605, San Francisco, CA 94108; phone (415) 989–8677. You may also contact the Taipei Economic and Cultural Representative Office (TECRO), 4201 Wisconsin Avenue NW, Washington, DC 20016-2137; phone (202) 895–1800. TECRO also has offices in several major U.S. cities.

Printed on recycled paper

CULTURGRAM ™ '96

United Republic of
Tanzania

Boundary representations not necessarily authoritative.

BACKGROUND

Land and Climate

The United Republic of Tanzania is located in East Africa, south of Kenya and north of Mozambique. Covering 364,899 square miles (945,090 square kilometers), it consists of mainland Tanganyika and the islands of Mafia, Pemba, and Zanzibar. Tanganyika (about the size of Texas) is a land of great variation. It either shares or borders on three of Africa's greatest lakes (Victoria, Nyasa, and Tanganyika). Most of the country is either low-lying coastal plain, upland plain (the Serengeti), or highland plateau. Tanzania contains the highest point in Africa: Mt. Kilimanjaro rises to 19,340 feet (5,895 meters) above sea level. It also contains the lowest point: the floor of Lake Tanganyika is 1,174 feet (358 meters) below sea level.

Tanzania's equatorial climate—hot, humid, and 90°F (32°C) on the coast—is tempered by inland elevations where temperatures are mild. Rains fall primarily from March to May and October to December, with seasonal variations from north to south. The tsetse fly infests nearly two-thirds of the mainland, making widespread livestock production nearly impossible. The low coral islands of Mafia, Pemba, and Zanzibar lie off the coast of the mainland in the Indian Ocean. Their combined size is about equal to that of Rhode Island. These islands have humid climates.

History

Various peoples inhabited the area now known as Tanzania for thousands of years before traders from southern Arabia began arriving in the eighth century. The Arabs founded the important city of Kilwa as they began settling the coast. Over many generations the Arabs mixed with the local Bantu populations to produce both the Swahili language and the modern peoples of the coastal regions. The Portuguese arrived in the 15th century. The Portuguese and Arabic overlords from Oman and Muscat developed a series of populous and powerful trading cities and sultanates—particularly on the islands of Zanzibar and Pemba. The Sultanate of Zanzibar firmly controlled both the islands and the mainland coast until the mid-1800s. In 1886, Tanganyika became a German protectorate. Zanzibar retained its independence but lost control over Kenya to the British. In 1920, Tanganyika fell under British rule as well.

In 1961, Tanganyika was granted independence, followed in 1963 by a fully independent Zanzibar. In 1964, the two nations merged to form Tanzania. For the most part this union has been very successful, although the Arab majority on Zanzibar would like more control over the economy and politics of the island than they presently hold. The country became a socialist republic under Julius Nyerere. His party (*Chama Cha Mapinduzi* (CCM or Revoluntiary Party) worked to bring unity to a country of many ethnic groups, a goal that he basically achieved. Tanzania enjoyed political stability under Nyerere, who also concentrated on economic development.

Nyerere stepped down as president after constitutional reform in 1985, and chose Ali Hassan Mwinyi to succeed him. Mwinyi was reelected without opposition in 1990, as the ruling

CCM was the only legal political party. Mwinyi was not eligible to run for reelection in the country's first multiparty elections in October 1995.

THE PEOPLE

Population

Tanzania's population of 27.9 million people is growing at 2.5 percent annually. About one-third of the population lives in urban areas. The largest city is Dar es Salaam, with more than 1.5 million people. Dodoma, which replaced Dar es Salaam as Tanzania's capital, is expected to grow when the transition is complete at the end of the century. Over half of all Tanzanians are younger than age 20.

Ninety-nine percent of the population is African, coming from some 130 different ethnic groups. Of these, there are about 30 Bantu-speaking groups. The Nyamwezi-Sukuma (12.6 percent of the population) is the only group with more than one million members. There are three Nilotic ethnic groups, two Khoisan, and two Afro-Asiatic. The merchant/trader class is dominated by people of Lebanese, Palestinian, and Indian origin. Arabs are most numerous on Zanzibar.

Language

Swahili (*Kiswahili*), a Bantu language, originated in the coastal regions of what are today Tanzania and Kenya. It is the primary official language in the country; English is the second official language. Most people speak the language that is associated with their ethnic group (there are more than a hundred languages). But they generally also speak Swahili because it allows them to communicate with people from other ethnic groups. Swahili is also the medium of instruction in the schools. English is used in business, government, and higher education.

Religion

On the mainland, more than one-third of the population is Christian. Another third is Muslim. On Zanzibar, nearly all inhabitants are Muslim. About one-third of the population follows indigenous beliefs, although many of these people have also accepted some Christian or Islamic beliefs. Muslims believe that the Prophet Muhammad was chosen by *Allah* (God), who revealed the words of the *Qur'an* (Koran) to Muhammad through the angel Gabriel. As part of the practice of Islam, Muslims profess the name of *Allah* and proclaim Muhammad's calling. They pray five times daily and expect to make a pilgrimage to Makkah, Saudi Arabia sometime in their life.

It is not unusual for professed Christians to mix their beliefs with local traditions. Thus, the local priest and the traditional healer might carry equal respect in a village where most people are Christian. The two belief systems are not considered contradictory because each has its own place in the daily lives of the people. The government is neutral when it comes to religion and has actively tried to promote religious tolerance throughout the country.

General Attitudes

Regardless of ethnic affiliation, Tanzanian social systems are group oriented. The individual is expected to put himself second to group welfare. Consequently, Tanzanians are extremely polite and generous people, particularly in public. It is considered impolite to pass a person (unless in a large crowd) without showing a sign of recognition, even if only to smile. Tanzanians do not use obscene language of any kind, even mildly. Any kind of verbal abuse or criticism, especially in public, is a major offense reflecting on the person's upbringing and background. Nevertheless, foreigners often perceive Tanzanians (and East Africans in general) as being abrupt and occasionally impolite. This is partly because the word "please" is not native to the Bantu languages spoken by East Africans. The Swahili equivalent, *tafadhali*, has actually been borrowed from Arabic but is still not integral to the culture. As a result, requests are often made without a "please," which is not impolite but simply a cultural habit. *Asante* (Thank you) is also an adopted term, but it seems to be used widely in the culture today. Whether spoken or not, thanks is usually shown with a returned favor or kindness. A deed is considered greater than a verbal "Thank-you."

Personal Appearance

Urban Tanzanians usually wear Western-style clothing, but they dress conservatively. Shorts and other revealing attire are not proper, except in clearly defined work or recreational situations. In rural villages, many people wear traditional clothing associated with their specific ethnic group. Many also wear readily available secondhand clothing from the United States or Europe, and imported clothing from China and India. Muslim men might wear a *kanzu* (long, embroidered cotton gown) with a matching skull cap or they may simply prefer Western-style clothing, with or without a skull cap. Some may wear a *kanzu* only when going to the mosque. Muslim women might cover their hair but almost never their faces. They often wear *kangas* or *kitenge* (several pieces of colorful, cotton wraparound fabric). Women on Zanzibar often wear a large, black shawl called a *buibui*.

CUSTOMS AND COURTESIES

Greetings

The most common Swahili greeting is *Hujambo* (*Hamjambo* for more than one person), usually followed by a handshake. A more casual greeting is simply *Jambo*. A common response to *Hujambo* is *Sijambo* (I'm fine). *Hatujambo* means "We're fine." This exchange is followed by questions about one's home, family, work, or other activities. For example, one might ask *Habari za nymbani?* (How are things at your home?). A common response is *Salama* (In peace, without problems). Each geographic region has a variety of non-Swahili greetings particular to the local ethnic groups, but Swahili is understood by the vast majority of all Tanzanians. Men and women shake hands with each other, although the man may wait for a woman to extend her hand before offering his.

Gestures

The right hand or both hands are used to pass and accept items. The use of the left hand alone, even in gesturing, is improper. The verbal "tch-tch" sound is considered an insult. In many cases, it is impolite to let the bottom of one's foot or shoe point at someone. Therefore, feet are not propped up on chairs or tables and are placed on the ground when sitting. It is impolite to photograph another person without permission. A person will rarely refuse but expects the courtesy of being asked.

Visiting

It is customary to bring a small gift to the home if a person is visiting for the first time. This may include sweets or cookies, but not flowers. Flowers are used to express condolences. Among the Muslim population, visiting is an important social custom; friends and family visit often. Tanzanians enjoy friendly social visits and will enthusiastically welcome all visitors. Hosts do their best to make guests comfortable. Unannounced visits are common and warmly received. Most times of the day are acceptable for a visit except late in the evening (after 8:00 P.M. or so). A host would also not appreciate repeated visits at mealtime. Any guest arriving at mealtime, even if unannounced, will always be offered part of the meal. To not offer a meal would show a lack of hospitality and it is impolite to refuse the offer. If a visit is arranged, a person should do everything possible to keep the appointment. It is rude to not show up for a scheduled visit.

Eating

Throughout the country, a bowl or basin of water is offered for washing hands before each meal. This is especially important because most meals are eaten with the hand. But even if utensils are used, hands are washed before eating. Because the left hand is traditionally used for personal hygiene, only the right is used when eating without utensils. The left might be used when handling difficult foods, such as meat with bones, but it would never be used to take food from a communal bowl. Eating from a communal dish is common, especially when it is *ugali* (see Diet) or rice. Families along the Indian Ocean coast, as well as in villages and towns along the three lakes (Nyasa, Tanganyika, and Victoria) sit on woven mats on the floor to eat meals. Muslims tend to sit crosslegged on these mats, but others sit with one leg tucked and the other stretched out sideways away from the food. Among Muslims, as well as some rural non-Muslims, it is common for men and women to eat separately. When guests are invited, dinner is usually served first and socializing is reserved for afterward. It is therefore impolite to leave a home immediately after a meal. During the Islamic month of *Ramadan*, Muslims do not eat or drink from sunrise to sunset; meals are served in the evening.

LIFESTYLE

Family

Tanzanian socialism is based on *ujamaa*, or "family-hood." The nation's extended families have been encouraged to act as economic as well as family units. Families are traditionally large, usually including either the father's brothers and their families or (less often) the mother's sisters and their families. Urban families are usually smaller and less cohesive than those residing in rural areas.

Dating and Marriage

Western-style dating habits are uncommon among the majority of the people. Traditionally, marriages have been arranged, often within the extended family. Today, while individual preference is permitted, cousin marriages are still encouraged—especially in rural areas. This practice is becoming less common in cities. The husband's family normally gives a dowry to the bride's family. The dowry is generally given for one of two reasons. First, it is a way of showing respect for the bride's parents, of thanking them for raising the woman who will soon join their family. A second reason is the fact that a productive member of the bride's family is soon to be lost. A dowry helps compensate for that. This is important especially in rural areas because extended families share work responsibilities.

Diet

Tanzanian staples include grains, fruits, and vegetables. The most common meats are chicken, goat, and lamb. A popular snack or energy food is *kitumbua*, a fried bread common to much of East Africa. *Ugali*, a stiff porridge made from either cornmeal, millet, sorghum, or cassava is eaten. Cooked bananas are a staple in much of northern Tanzania (particularly around Lake Victoria and in the foothills of Mt. Kilimanjaro) and in the southwest around Mbeya and Lake Nyasa. Bananas are prepared in a variety of ways, including roasted, fried, or made into a paste and mixed with meat and gravy.

Rice is the staple of much of the coastal area and is often cooked with a variety of spices (including cloves, curry, cinnamon, cumin, and hot peppers), which are mixed directly into the rice water as the rice cooks. This is called *pilau*. Dishes that are prepared as a relish to go along with the main starch food (*ugali,* rice, or bananas) are commonly stews of beef, chicken, fish, or goat, green leafy vegetables (cabbage, Swiss chard, spinach), and beans or cowpeas. The Muslims in Tanzania do not eat pork or drink alcohol.

Recreation

Soccer, track and field, and boxing are popular. Tanzania is known for its world-class runners. Big game hunting is permissible under certain restrictions. Tanzania actively fights elephant poaching and ivory smuggling. It has created game parks to protect endangered species. Water sports are popular along the coast. People enjoy socializing at coffee houses or at home.

Holidays

Civic holidays include New Year's Day, Zanzibar Revolution Day (12 January), Union Day (26 April), Labor Day (1 May), *Saba Saba* Day (Farmer's Day, 7 July), and Independence Day (9 December). In addition to the national holidays celebrated in Tanzania, the people honor both Christian and Muslim religious holidays. For Christians, Easter (including Good Friday and Easter Monday) and Christmas are celebrated. The Islamic holidays are based on the lunar calendar and fall on different days from year to year. At the end of the holy month of *Ramadan*, a three-day feast is held to break the fast. The Feast of the Sacrifice, held 40 days later, honors Abraham for his willingness to sacrifice his son. Muslims also mark the birthday of the Prophet Muhammad.

Commerce

General business hours are from 8:30 to 11:30 A.M. and 2:00 to 6:00 P.M., Monday through Friday. Most businesses close by noon on Saturday. Government offices do not re-open in the afternoon; they close at 11:30 A.M. each day. The government regulates certain business dress standards. Most office workers wear Western-style clothing.

SOCIETY

Government

Tanzania is a democratic republic containing 25 regions. The president is chief of state, and a prime minister is head of government. The National Assembly (*Bunge*) has 241 seats. When CCM was the only legal party, all candidates for public office had to be members cleared by a selection board. But the government was not dictatorial, and subjected itself to public scrutiny and criticism. Citizens were generally free to criticize government action. This allowed for the peaceful transition to multiparty democracy. While CCM is expected to dominate politics for some time to come, opposition parties—including National Convention for Construction and Reform (NCCR-Mageuzi) and the Union for Multiparty Democracy (UMD), among others—plan to provide balance and press for bureacratic reforms. All citizens may vote at age 18.

Economy

Agriculture dominates Tanzania's economy, employing 85 percent of the population and accounting for 85 percent of all exports. Key exports include coffee, cotton, sisal, cashew nuts, meat, tobacco, tea, cloves, and coconuts from Zanzibar, and pyrethrum (a pesticide made from chrysanthemums). Tanzania is also a major producer of diamonds.

Economic reforms first initiated in 1986 have encouraged private investment and the creation of new export products. By the early 1990s, the measures had increased ecomic growth to 4 percent and decreased inflation to 20 percent. But corruption, mismanagement and regional problems eventually caused slower growth and the return of high inflation. Western nations that had often granted large amounts of aid to Tanzania withheld funds in 1995 when development programs failed. New trade relations with South Africa, as well as greater democratic reforms, are expected to boost economic performance in years to come.

The country's Human Development Index (0.306) ranks it 148th out of 173 countries. Real gross domestic product per capita is $570. While this figure has doubled in a generation, 60 percent of people live in poverty. Most people either do not earn a wage (i.e., they are subsistence farmers) or they do not earn enough to meet basic needs. Tanzania's currency is the Tanzanian *shilling* (*Sh*).

Transportation and Communication

The transportation system is only partially developed. Most roads are not paved, and the system is not extensive in the rural interior. People often travel by foot or on animals. Buses, trains, and taxis are available in some cities, especially Dar Es Salaam. Trains and buses run between major cities. Few people own cars. Following the British tradition, traffic moves on the left side of the road. The communications system is also not fully developed. Few telephones are available, and the country is served by only two daily newspapers.

Education

Tanzania's literacy rate is 46 percent. Primary school instruction is in Swahili, and English is offered as a second language. English is the main language in secondary schools. A rapidly growing population and a lack of finances make it difficult for the government to increase educational facilities. About 70 percent of all school-aged children begin primary school, but less than 10 percent progress past the seventh grade. Boys are more likely than girls to get an education. The University of Dar es Salaam emphasizes training for community service rather than strictly academic pursuits.

Health

In rural areas, malaria, sleeping sickness, and a wide variety of intestinal parasitic diseases are common. Quality medical care is really only available in the large cities, with the exception of a few remote, well-run mission hospitals. Rural clinics are available, but they often lack trained personnel and sufficient medical supplies. Tanzania has only one doctor for every 24,000 inhabitants. With an infant mortality rate of 110 per 1,000, the need for expanded health care is great. Life expectancy averages 45 to 50 years.

FOR THE TRAVELER

A valid passport and visa are required of U.S. citizens for entry into Tanzania. The embassy charges a fee and can take one month to process a visa application. Travelers should have vaccinations for yellow fever and cholera, as well as other diseases, and should use malarial suppressants.

Water is not safe for drinking, for ice cubes, or for brushing teeth, unless it has been boiled. Eat only food that is hot and has been well cooked. Peel and wash all fruits and cook all vegetables before eating. Photography of certain government installations may be restricted. When taking pictures of people, they may first want to change clothing or pose. Taking pictures of objects rather than people is considered odd, so travelers may want to explain the reason to any Tanzanian companions.

Tanzania would like to improve its tourism industry; the game reserves, mountains, lakes, and islands are all worthy attractions. For more information, contact the Tanzania Permanent Mission to the United Nations, 205 East 42d Street, 13th Floor, New York, NY 10017; phone (212) 972–9160. The Embassy of the United Republic of Tanzania is located at 2139 R Street NW, Washington, DC 20008; phone (202) 939–6125.

CULTURGRAM '96

Kingdom of
Thailand

Boundary representations not necessarily authoritative.

BACKGROUND

Land and Climate

Thailand is located in the heart of Southeast Asia, bordered by Myanmar (Burma), Laos, and Cambodia. It extends down the Malaysian peninsula and shares its southern border with Malaysia. Some have compared its shape to the head and trunk of an elephant or the shape of an ax. Covering 198,455 square miles (514,000 square kilometers), Thailand is about the size of Arizona and Utah combined. The central region is dominated by fertile agricultural land and Bangkok (with eight million inhabitants). The northeast (covering one-third of the country) consists of the Khorat plateau. Forested mountains and steep, fertile valleys form the northern quarter of the nation, an area once rich in timber (primarily teak). The southern, peninsular part of Thailand is comprised of rain forests and rubber and coconut plantations. Thailand's climate is mostly tropical. Cooler temperatures prevail between November and February, but the rest of the year is fairly hot. Rains fall mostly from June to October.

History

Thailand's early history, which may have begun four thousand years ago, is linked with that of southern China. Studies show migration occurred both from Thailand to south China and later from China to Thailand. Between the ninth and thirteenth centuries, present-day Thailand was part of a vast Khmer empire that covered much of southeast Asia. Upon overthrowing the Khmer, the Thai established a kingdom at Sukhothai in 1238. A Thai ruler, Ramathibodi, introduced Theravada Buddhism in the 14th century.

After a struggle against the Burmese in the 18th century, Rama I founded the Chakri dynasty and established Bangkok as the capital in 1782. At that time, the Thai kingdom was known as Siam. The Thais successfully kept European colonialists from their soil. The wise rule of King Mongkut and the reforms of Rama V (Chulalongkorn) kept the kingdom independent. The government became a constitutional monarchy in 1932, and Siam changed its name to Thailand in 1939.

Japan occupied Thailand for a short time during World War II. After the war, Thailand increased its ties with the United States and became an important base for U.S.-led efforts against communism during the 1960s and 1970s. Since 1975, Thailand has been the home to many Indochinese refugees. The present king has ruled since 1946. He is known as Rama IX, but his name is Bhumibol Adulyadej. Despite several military coups, terrorist violence, drug trafficking, crime, and problems with neighboring nations, Thailand's king has always been a symbol of national unity and stability.

Thailand's military has long been politically active. In 1991, it overthrew the elected government and appointed an interim prime minister until elections in April 1992. When no party gained a majority, the coup leader, General Suchinda Kraprayoon, assumed the post. Angry street demonstrations, a violent military response, and eventual royal intervention led Suchinda to resign. In September 1992 elections, pro-democracy parties combined to win a narrow parliamentary majority, a victory against the military that strengthened civilian institutions. A July 1995 election brought the *Chart Thai* (Thai Nation) party to power.

THE PEOPLE
Population
Thailand's population of 59.5 million is growing annually at 1.3 percent. Less than one-fourth of the population lives in cities. Bangkok is the largest city; its population varies between 5 and 9 million depending on the time of year and the constant movement of migrant workers. About 75 percent of the population is comprised of Central Thai, Northeastern Thai, Northern Thai, and Southern Thai. The largest minority is the Chinese, who compose about 14 percent of the people. However, intermarriage with the Thais over many generations makes it difficult to distinguish between the Chinese and the Thais. There are also many Thais of Malay, Khmer, Vietnamese, and Lao ancestry. In addition, ethnic Khmer, Vietnamese, and other refugees also inhabit Thailand, mostly in border regions. About 500,000 mountain people form a number of distinct ethnic groups.

Language
Central Thai is the official language and is used in schools, with other Thai dialects being spoken in various regions of the country. Lao is spoken in some northern areas, and Khmer is spoken along the Cambodian border. Thai is a tonal language, meaning that a given syllable can have different meanings depending on the inflection with which it is pronounced. Central Thai has five tones. Chinese and Malay are spoken by many people. Those with advanced education often speak English. Some minority groups, such as the Mon and Hmong, have their own languages.

Religion
Although Thailand guarantees freedom of religion, and many religions are represented in the country, 95 percent of the population is Theravada Buddhist. Muslims compose about 4 percent of the population. There is also a small number of Christians in Thailand.

Buddhism deeply affects the people's daily lives. Buddhist *wats* (temples) dominate Thai communities. Traditionally, all young men were expected to become Buddhist monks for at least three months of their lives, during which time they studied Buddhist principles. While the practice is not strictly enforced today, it is still important to the people and large ordination ceremonies are often held for young boys entering their training. Ancestor veneration is practiced as part of Buddhist worship. Food is offered in memory of deceased relatives and special ceremonies serve to remind the living to honor the dead. Buddhism in Thailand also incorporates rites and principles from other Eastern religions such as Hinduism, as well as animism, which espouses a special reverence for life based on a belief that all living things possess spirits.

General Attitudes
Thailand means "Land of the Free," and the Thais are proud of the fact that their country has avoided foreign rule (except during Japan's occupation in World War II) throughout its long history. The King and Queen are the most respected and honored persons in Thailand. A Thai would be offended by any joke or ill reference to them. Even images of the King are treated with respect. For example, one does not lick a postage stamp with the King's picture, but wets it with a damp sponge. It is illegal to say or write anything offensive about royalty. Traditionally, success was measured by a person's religious and nationalistic attitudes. The trend is now toward wealth and education. Wealth is generally looked on as a reflection of virtue. The Thais have much respect for those who unselfishly help others and who lead virtuous lives.

The Thai expression, *Mai Pen Rai* (Never mind), characterizes their general feeling toward life, that it is to be enjoyed; problems and setbacks should not be taken too seriously. While Thais are by no means lazy or unproductive, they are generally happy with what they have and who they are. Another name for Thailand is "The Land of Smiles." Thais are a reserved people and usually consider criticism of others to be in poor taste. A sense of humor, laughter, and a pleasant, smiling attitude are highly regarded. On the other hand, showing a lack of reserve by speaking loudly or showing anger in public is offensive and may cause one to lose another's respect.

Thais are proud of their cultural heritage and are often offended by those who see "development" as a need to Westernize and change people's religious and cultural habits. What may seem poor to a Westerner may be a fine lifestyle to a Thai, especially in rural regions where life has not changed for many centuries.

Personal Appearance
While Western clothing is common in most areas, especially Bangkok, traditional clothing is also often worn. There are, of course, the highly stylized costumes of Thai dancers, but most clothing is simpler. Men and women frequently wear straw hats because of the heat. Simple blouses and *sarongs* (tube skirts) are common for women. Men might wear pants and a shirt in public, but change into a long *sarong* or short wraparound at home. Men and women of Chinese descent wear calf-length loose pants and jackets. Intricate headdresses may accompany the traditional clothing of the mountain people. Sandals are popular, but shoes are worn in formal situations. Rural people may wear rubber thongs or go barefoot. Children are required to wear shoes to school.

CUSTOMS AND COURTESIES
Greetings
The traditional and most common greeting in Thailand is called the *wai*. How the gesture is performed depends entirely on the relationship between the people, and there are many variations. Generally, however, a person places the palms of the hands together, with fingers extended at chest level, and bows slightly; women curtsy. The younger person greets first, and the more senior person responds with a *wai* in a lower position. The higher one's hands are placed, the more respect is shown. Bows and curtsies are also more pronounced to show greater respect. The fingertips only go above the level of the eyebrows to reverence Buddha or to greet royalty. For other honored persons, the fingertips may reach to between the eyebrows, with the thumb tip touching the tip of the nose. It is an insult to not return a *wai*, unless there is great social or age distance between the two people, in which case the senior does not return the *wai*. Buddhist monks never return a *wai*. For example, an adult does not exchange a *wai* with a small child. The gesture can mean not only "Hello" but also "Thank you," "Good-bye," and "I am sorry."

Very close friends do not use the *wai*, but greet informally and address one another by nickname. Thais otherwise address each other by their first names, preceded by *Khun* (for example, Khun Sariya), and reserve surnames for formal occasions. In formal situations, visitors may address Thais by using *Mr.*, *Mrs.*, or *Miss* with the first or last names.

Gestures

A person's head is considered sacred and one should neither touch another's head nor pass an object over it. Parents pat their children's heads, but this is the only exception. People try to keep the level of their heads below that of social superiors. The bottoms of the feet are the least sacred part of the body and should never be pointed in the direction of another person. Thais avoid stamping their feet, touching people with them, or using them to move or point at objects.

Body posture and physical gestures are extremely important in polite company and will speak volumes about one's character and regard for others. It is usually offensive to cross the legs while sitting in a chair, especially in the presence of an older person. Placing one's arm over the back of the chair in which another person is sitting is offensive. Men and women generally do not touch or show affection in public. Good friends of the same sex, however, sometimes hold hands. Among the youth, it is becoming more common for members of the opposite sex to hold hands. Women must never touch images of Buddha or a Buddhist monk or offer to shake hands. All religious monuments and shrines are sacred and should not be defiled or treated disrespectfully. Items, especially gifts, are passed and received with the right hand only, never the left. For heavy items, one uses two hands.

Visiting

Thais are very hospitable hosts and enjoy having visitors. The person of highest social rank or age is treated with the greatest respect. In all cases, how one sits, walks, or otherwise interacts with others depends on the status of each person present. It is customary to remove one's shoes when entering a Buddhist temple or private home. Because Thai tradition says a soul resides in the doorsill of a temple *(wat),* visitors avoid stepping on the doorsill.

It is not necessary to take gifts when visiting, but it is not uncommon for guests on extended stays to present their hosts with a gift of appreciation. In the home, people commonly sit on the floor. One does not stretch out their feet in front of them. Women generally tuck their legs to the side and behind them and men sit cross-legged. Men might also sit with their legs tucked to the side to show special respect to the hosts. Guests may offer compliments on the home or children but should avoid admiring any specific object excessively because the host may be embarrassed.

Eating

Thais use forks and spoons at the dining table. They hold the spoon in the right hand and the fork in the left, pushing food onto the spoon with the fork. Knives are usually not necessary because foods are served in bite-size pieces. Rural families may eat around a straw mat on the floor. In northern areas, people eat a steamed, sticky (glutinous) rice with their fingers. Chopsticks are used with noodle dishes and in Chinese homes. Guests usually receive a second helping of food and are encouraged to eat as much as they can. Diners choose small portions from various dishes at the center of the table to eat with rice. Bones and other such items are placed on the plate. Water, the standard mealtime drink, is drunk at the end of (not during) the meal. When one is finished, utensils are placed together on the plate. In restaurants, tips are not usually necessary, but some people give a small amount (5 percent) to the waiter or waitress for special service.

LIFESTYLE

Family

Thai families are close, and several generations may live in the same household. The oldest male is customarily the patriarch of the family. Members of the family (even adults) are usually expected to abide by the advice of their elders, although this is becoming less true with time and modernization. Still, Thais have great respect for their parents and the elderly. Families usually have two or three children. On a farm, all members of the household share the work. When the elderly live with their married children, they often tend the grandchildren. Polygamy was legal until 1935, and to have many wives was a sign of wealth. Because traditions change slowly, many men openly keep mistresses in addition to their legal wife. However, Thai women are becoming less accepting of the practice, and the younger male generation is becoming increasingly willing to commit to one woman.

A family's youngest daughter inherits the parents' home. In return, she and her husband care for the parents in their old age.

Dating and Marriage

In Thailand, girls have traditionally led a more sheltered life than boys, but this is no longer the case. Boys and girls generally have equal access to society. Although Western-style dating is popular in Bangkok, it is not as common in rural areas. According to tradition, if a boy wishes to marry a girl, he must first become well acquainted with the entire family and make himself agreeable to them. He then sends his parents to the girl's family to make his wishes known. If both families agree on the marriage, a wedding date is set. The groom traditionally pays a bride-price to the bride's parents as "compensation" for raising her. Some parents later return the items or cash to the couple as a wedding gift. Pink is the traditional color for bridal gowns. Grooms wear either a Western-style suit or pants and a high-necked jacket *(sua phrarachathan).* Rural newlyweds often live with the bride's parents until they have a child.

Diet

Rice (plain in southern and central regions; glutinous in the north) is the staple food of Thailand. It is usually served with spicy dishes that consist of meat, vegetables, fish, eggs, and fruits. Curries and pepper sauces are popular. Typical meats include beef, chicken, and pork. Thailand boasts a wide variety of tropical fruit year-round.

Recreation

The most popular sports in Thailand are soccer, table tennis, badminton, volleyball, and basketball. *Takro* (a traditional sport played by trying to keep a wicker ball in the air without using hands) and kite flying are favorite activities. The youth enjoy various martial arts. Movies and television provide leisure entertainment. Thai chess, played without a queen and under unique rules, is a popular urban spectator sport.

Holidays

Although the government uses the Western (Gregorian) calendar, Buddhist holidays are set by the lunar calendar and vary from year to year. Official holidays include New Year's Day; Chinese New Year, Chakri Day (6 April); Labor Day (1 May); Coronation Day (5 May); Royal Ploughing Ceremony (11 May); the Queen's Birthday (12 August); Chulalongkorn Day (23 October), honoring the "beloved monarch" (1868–1910), who abolished slavery and introduced many reforms; the King's Birthday (5 December); Constitution Day (10 December); and New Year's Eve. Some important religious holidays include *Makha Bucha*, *Asalaha Bucha*, and *Visakha Bucha*, which mark important events in Buddhism's history. For *Songkhran*, the Thai New Year, people throw buckets of water on each other. *Loy Krathong* honors the water goddess for providing water throughout the year; people float small "boats" with candles, coins, or flowers on waterways.

Commerce

Most businesses are open Monday through Friday from 8:30 A.M. to 4:30 P.M., although some are open until 6:00 P.M. Retail shops are often open seven days a week, especially small, family-owned stores, and many stay open until 10:00 P.M. each day. When prices in small shops are not fixed, bargaining is expected but should be done in good taste because the people make very little profit. Thais buy fresh food in open markets.

SOCIETY

Government

In Thailand's constitutional monarchy, the king is head of state but has few executive responsibilities. The prime minister (Banharn Silpa-archa) heads the government. The National Assembly has two houses: a 270-member Senate, whose members are appointed by the king, and a 360-seat House of Representatives, whose members are directly elected. All adults older than age 20 are eligible to vote. In villages, local chiefs are elected by the people.

Economy

Agriculture has traditionally been the backbone of the nation's economy, employing more than 70 percent of the labor force. But industry, which employs 11 percent, provides the bulk of Thailand's export earnings. This gives the country the reputation of being one of the most advanced nations in Southeast Asia.

Tin (Thailand is the world's third largest tin producer), textiles, fish products, rice, tapioca, and jewelry are among the most important exports. Thailand's manufacturing base also includes electric appliances, furniture, integrated circuits, and plastics. Tourism is an important source of foreign-exchange currency and helps many local economies. Inflation is generally low. While official unemployment is low (4 percent), underemployment is a significant problem. The currency is the *baht* (B).

The country's Human Development Index (0.798) ranks it 54th out of 173 countries. Real gross domestic product per capita ($5,270) has dramatically increased in the last decade. Urban poverty is decreasing, but poverty still affects a third of rural people. These figures reflect Thailand's remarkable economic success in recent years but indicate that success is unbalanced. Income distribution is highly unequal and economic prosperity is only slowly extending to rural areas. Still, more people than ever before can meet basic needs and have access to economic opportunities.

Transportation and Communication

Most large cities are connected by rail, highways, and air service. Local transportation is by bus, taxi, *samlor* (three-wheeled motorized taxi), and *silor* (mini-cab). In rural areas, pedicabs are most common. While most people still do not have cars, greater ownership has significantly increased urban traffic problems. Traffic moves on the left side of the road. Canals (*klongs*) are often used for transportation in rural and some urban areas. The Chao Phraya River serves as the most important waterway for Bangkok. Merchant and commuter traffic on this river is common. The government communications system is well developed, and the public telephone system is adequate for most needs.

Education

Education has been a priority of the government, and literacy and enrollment rates have increased dramatically over the last generation. The literacy rate is 93 percent. Universal, free, and compulsory education lasts for six years (seven in some areas). Nearly all primary-aged children are enrolled, although the figure drops to less than half for secondary education. Entrance to universities is by examination and there is stiff competition for a limited number of places. Sometimes boys, if they come from distant provinces, have greater opportunities than girls to study at universities. This is because boys can live in one of the many *wats* while girls must live in boarding schools and hostels, which can be expensive. Marriage is discouraged until one's education is complete.

Health

Health services have expanded greatly in the last decade, but they are still limited in remote rural areas. Tropical diseases are common outside the cities. The infant mortality rate is 37 per 1,000. Life expectancy ranges from 65 to 72 years.

FOR THE TRAVELER

A visa and a passport are necessary for U.S. travelers. No vaccinations are needed; however, visitors to rural areas should consider vaccinations against typhoid, cholera, and rabies, among others. Malarial suppressants are also advised for rural areas. Bottled or boiled water is the safest. Eat only thoroughly cooked meats; peel and wash all vegetables and fruits before eating. Shorts are not appropriate for most public places. Thailand has long been a favorite tourist destination because of its unique architecture, rural villages, and ancient temples. For information about travel opportunities, contact the Tourism Authority of Thailand, 5 World Trade Center, Suite 3443, New York, NY 10048; phone (212) 432–0433, or 3660 Wilshire Boulevard, Room 230, Los Angeles, CA 90010; phone (213) 380–5943. You may also wish to contact the Royal Embassy of Thailand, 1024 Wisconsin Avenue NW, Washington, DC 20007; phone (202) 944–3608.

A *Culturgram* is a product of native commentary and original, expert analysis. Statistics are estimates and information is presented as a matter of opinion. While the editors strive for accuracy and detail, this document should not be considered strictly factual. It is a general introduction to culture, an initial step in building bridges of understanding between peoples. It may not apply to all peoples of the nation. You should therefore consult other sources for more information.

CULTURGRAM '96

Kingdom of
Tonga

Boundary representations not necessarily authoritative.

BACKGROUND

Land and Climate

Tonga is composed of 170 islands, of which only 36 are inhabited. They stretch north to south across 500 miles (800 kilometers) of the Pacific Ocean. The total land area is less than 300 square miles (750 square kilometers). About half of the land is under cultivation and the soil is very fertile. Surrounding waters provide an abundance of fish and other seafood. The Tongan islands are composed of coral or volcanic formations. Togatapu is mostly flat, with high cliffs in the southwest. Niuafo'ou, located about 210 miles (338 kilometers) northwest of the Vava'u Group, is the world's only home to the *Malau* bird (a flightless bird), which lays large eggs in the sand that are incubated by heat from an active volcano. The volcano has a freshwater lake in the crater. 'Eua has several endemic plants and will eventually be home to a national park. Its rolling hills give way to high eastern cliffs, but the island is surrounded by many beaches. Other islands have similar features.

Tonga is divided into three island groups: Ha'apai, Tongatapu, and Vava'u. The largest individual islands are Tongatapu and 'Eua. The capital is Nuku'alofa. Although located in the tropics, Tonga experiences few extremes in heat, rain, or humidity. Nuku'alofa's average temperature is about 76°F (24°C); humidity averages 76 percent. Northern islands are somewhat warmer and more humid. Cyclones are possible from October to April, and the dry season is from June to November.

History

Written histories do not exist for Tonga before the 17th century, but experts believe the islands were settled by at least 500 B.C. According to tradition, the Tongan ruler was known as the Tui Tonga and was descended from the Creator, Tangaloa 'Eitumatupu'a. The heriditary monarchy reached its zenith in the 13th century, when it ruled not only over Tonga, but also other Pacific Islands (Samoa, Niue, Fiji, and others). The empire eventually declined, even as the population grew. Society became unstable and several Tui Tonga were assasinated. In 1470, a new office was created by the Tui Tonga called the *hau*, or Temporal Ruler. The Tui Tonga became Sacred Ruler, more distant from daily government. The first *hau* created the Tu'i Ha'atakalaua dynasty. In the 17th century, another dynasty was formed by a descendant of the first *hau*. The monarchy was stable and generally presided over a prosperous people. The Tui Tonga tradition continued into the 19th century. Tongatapu, the main island group, was called the Land of Chiefs and the other islands were called the Land of Servants, referring to the arrangement that the high chiefs lived on Tongatapu and the royal subjects lived on other islands. Great honor was paid to the Tui Tonga and other chiefs.

The Dutch were the first Europeans to visit Tonga in 1616. Britain's Captain James Cook visited in 1773 and returned in 1777. He named Tonga "the Friendly Islands" for the way he was treated by the inhabitants. British missionaries from the Wesleyan Methodist Church arrived in 1797. Civil war erupted in the 1790s and continued through the 1820s. An important struggle between Taufa'ahau, the chief of Ha'apai, and the Tui Tonga was impacted by the spread of Christianity. A Wesleyan Mission was established in 1826. Taufa'ahau

OCEANIA

converted to Christianity in 1831, chose the name George (after the current English king), and was victorious in his struggle against the Tui Tonga. He founded the present royal dynasty in 1845, proclaiming himself King George Tupou I. The Wesleyans helped develop a written code of Tonga's laws. When the king fully united all Tongan islands in 1850, the Code of Laws was in effect for all subjects. Serfdom was abolished in 1862 and a constitution was promulgated in 1875.

Facing economic troubles, King George Tupou II asked for and received British aid. The two nations signed a treaty of friendship in 1900. In 1905, Britain made Tonga a protectorate, which was not dissolved until 1970. Tongans point out that Britain never colonized the island, and the Tongans remained essentially sovereign. They look to 1970 as a year in which they rejoined equality with other countries rather than as any kind of independence. Queen Salote Tupou III ruled from 1918 to 1965. She was followed by her son, King Taufa'ahau Tupou IV, who currently reigns.

THE PEOPLE
Population
Tonga's population of about 104,000 is growing annually at 0.8 percent. About two-thirds of the people live on Tongatapu, and Nuku'alofa has some 35,000 inhabitants. Tongans of Polynesian descent make up the bulk of the population. Small minorities of other Pacific Islanders and a few hundred Europeans also reside in Tonga.

Language
Tongan and English are both official languages. Government documents are in both languages, but Tongan is the language of daily communication. English is used in business correspondence and is taught as a second language in school. Tongan was an oral language prior to the 20th century, but received a written form in the Latin alphabet in 1897. The alphabet includes 13 letters: a, e, i, k, l, m, n, o, p, s, t, u, and v. Tongan spelling is phonemic: words are spelled the way they are pronounced. For instance, the traditional greeting *Malo e lelei* is pronounced "MAH-low eh leh-LEH-ee." All consonants are separated by a vowel, all vowels are prounounced, and all words end in a vowel.

Religion
Nearly all Tongans are Christians. The royal family, nobles, and about 30 percent of the population belong to the Free Wesleyan Church, which is the official state church. The king is the head of the church. The Church of Jesus Christ of Latter-day Saints (Mormon) is the second largest church, followed by the Roman Catholic church, the Independence Church of Tonga, and the Church of Tonga. According to royal edict, rules of the Sabbath are quite strict and widely upheld in Tonga. Virtually everything is closed on Sunday, except for emergency facilities.

General Attitudes
Tongans are very proud of their independent nation, their royal heritage, and their Polynesian culture. The "Tongan way" of life (*FakaTonga*) is easygoing and relaxed. Whatever does not get done today can be done tomorrow. This attitude is not one of laziness, but an expression of a relatively worry free approach to life. Tongans are generous, devoted to family and religion, gentle, and friendly. They value cleanliness, good manners, a good education, and respectful behavior, especially toward elders. Men and women who drink alcohol or smoke are not considered good role models.

The youth are becoming more interested in pursuing a Western lifestyle, and pressures to emigrate abroad are increasing. Young people more often associate their agricultural heritage with a hard lifestyle and low income, and see getting a good education and seeking urban or foreign employment as a way to rise above those roots. And while they retain their devotion to core Tongan values, their pursuits cannot help but change Tongan society in the future.

Personal Appearance
Because modesty is valued, most females do not wear short skirts or low-necked dresses. Pants are inappropriate for women. By law, males older than age 16 must wear shirts in public places. Long hair is not appropriate for men. The Tongan word for clothes is *valas*. For many generations, men wore *tupenus* (calf-length pieces of material wrapped around the waist) with a *ta'ovala* (a piece of fine material, made from the leaves of the pandanus tree, that is wrapped around the waist and tied with a coconut-fiber rope). Open-necked shirts were also worn as a sign of respect. Today, Western clothing, including ties, suit jackets, and trousers, is common for everyday use. Still, *tupenus* and the *ta'ovala* are required attire (along with a tie) for formal occasions such as associating with royalty. Tongan women traditionally wore a *kiekie* (an ankle-length skirt), often accompanied with a *ta'ovala*. Today, blouses are worn with the *kiekie*, and women also commonly wear Western clothing.

CUSTOMS AND COURTESIES
Greetings
It is appropriate to greet people either with a handshake or a verbal greeting. Men often hold the handshake for several seconds during a brief conversation. *Malo e lelei* (Hello) is a common daytime greeting, in addition to several different phrases that can be used to say "Good morning." Two such phrases are *Malo e lelei ki he pongipongi* and *Malo e tau mo eni*. "Good evening" is expressed as *Malo e lelei ki he efiafi ni*. Visitors might be greeted with *Talitali fiefia* (Welcome). Upon being introduced, one might say *Fefe hake?* (How do you do?). The polite response is *Sai pe, Malo* (Fine, thank you). When parting, one says *'Alu a* to which the other replies, *Nofa a* (both of which mean "Good-bye"). Tongans customarily call acquaintances by their given names. People meeting for the first time often use titles and family names, since doing so shows respect. If professional titles are not used, *Tangata'eiki* (Mr.), *Fine'eiki* (Mrs.), and *Ta'ahine* (Miss) are appropriate.

Gestures
The use of body gestures is important in communication. Raising the eyebrows means "Yes" or "I agree." It is not appropriate to call anyone other than children by using hand motions. A downward wave of the arm is a gesture meaning "Come here." A forward and upward wave means "Go" or "Good-bye." Young men and boys often walk holding hands as an expression of friendship, but physical displays of affection between members of the opposite sex (or even kissing between parents and children) are considered inappropriate.

When sitting on a chair, it is proper to cross one's legs at the knee.

Visiting

The Tongan society is closely knit and socializing is an integral part of daily life. Women seldom go anywhere without being accompanied by another woman. Tongans passing each other while walking always greet each other, even if not personally acquainted. And relatives (who are often neighbors) frequently visit each other—especially on Sunday afternoon.

Most visits during the week are spontaneous. Unexpected guests are usually welcomed in. However, if a family feels their house is not adequately furnished or cleaned, they may be reluctant to invite a visitor in. Visitors remove their shoes upon entering, and are often directed to the best seats in the house. In a traditional home, men sit cross-legged on the floor and women sit with both legs tucked behind them to one side. Children are kept out of the way as much as possible. Hosts usually offer refreshments such as water, coconut, *otai* (a mixture of cut fruit), or soda. The family always tries to accommodate the guests' needs. If guests arrive unexpectedly at mealtime, the hosts will invite them to stay and eat. A complimentary speech from departing guests is a high honor to the family.

Tongans generally enjoy giving and receiving personal compliments. Guests often compliment the home or family but should avoid admiring any one object too specifically. This may cause the host to feel obligated to offer the item as a gift. Tongans welcome but do not expect gifts from guests. Gifts are not opened in front of the person giving the gift. Flowers are considered gifts on special occasions (weddings, funerals, etc.), but other items may be more appropriate when visiting the home socially. Honored or new guests may be given a gift by hosts when they leave. It is a terrible insult to decline such offers, which may include fruit, tapa cloth, or handicrafts.

Eating

Families eat their meals together whenever possible. On outer islands, they sit on woven mats to eat, but urban households more often have dining tables and other Western furniture. Although the hands were traditionally used to eat with, standard utensils are now most common. A prayer is offered before eating. Conversation is kept to a minimum. When guests are present, they usually eat with a few selected members of the family. Children are sent away or they eat in a different place. Guests are served first and the person who prepared the meal usually eats last.

Standing while eating and drinking is not appropriate, even though others may do it. In restaurants, Tongans do not tip and servers do not accept tips from foreigners.

LIFESTYLE

Family

Families are close-knit and care for each other in almost every situation. In addition to parents and siblings, one's family unit includes grandparents, uncles, aunts, and cousins. In many cases, all family members work together to plant, harvest, cook, and fish. When young married couples live with the woman's parents, the man takes responsibility to provide food for that family. Although families are getting smaller, they remain fairly large by Western standards, averaging three or four children.

In a traditional Tongan family, the father is the head of the family and the mother is his subordinate. However, brothers are subordinate to their sisters (when close in age). That means that the oldest daughter (rather than the oldest son, as in many societies) receives the best of the family's resources. A father's eldest sister (*mehekitanga*) is the leader (*fahu*) over that nuclear family in the highly organized extended-family system.

Homes in modern Tonga vary from the traditional coconut leaf and timber *fale* in rural areas to the frame, tin, or cinder block *fale* in wealthier areas. All families own their homes, but sometimes two families (often two generations of one family) will live within the same house. Technically, all land is leased by heirship allotment from the nobles and is owned by the king. In practice, though, the people "own" the land they live on.

Dating and Marriage

Boys and girls are kept separate from a fairly early age, so interaction is limited until they get older. Teenagers meet at supervised school, church, or village activities. The traditional practice of "dating" only inside the girl's home allows a boy to get acquainted with the girl, her parents, and her family. To date at other locations, a girl is often accompanied by her mother or another member of the family. Marriages are times of great celebration. Ceremonies follow the traditions of the people's religious affiliation. Festivities after the ceremony can include hymn singing, a large feast, and many speeches. Young couples generally have their own home, but may choose to move in with the bride's parents.

Diet

Tongans traditionally eat two meals each day, which may consist of yams, taro leaves, sweet potatoes, cassava, fish, or pork. European-style meals, including a light, early breakfast, a meal at noon, and one in the evening, are becoming popular.

A popular dish is cooked taro leaves with coconut cream and corned beef (*Lu pulu*). Pork and chicken are the primary meats, and fish (tuna, shark, grouper, and parrot fish) is a typical main dish. Roast pig is a favorite. Tongans enjoy abundant mangos, guavas, citrus fruits (oranges, mandarins, lemons, limes, and grapefruits), papayas, watermelon, squash pumpkin, passion fruit, bananas, plantains, avocados, and coconuts. Local vegetables include tomatoes, carrots, onions, green peppers, and cabbage. Tongans produce most of their own food, but an increasing amount is being imported.

Recreation

Tongans are sports enthusiasts. Rugby is the national sport. Most villages compete in rugby, cricket, volleyball, basketball, and tennis. Girls play *netball*, a court (grass, wood, or blacktop) sport very similar to basketball. Movies and dances are also major forms of recreation in larger villages. Dances are usually restricted to traditional Polynesian music, so boys and girls do not dance together. Younger boys play with marbles and slingshots. Picnics on the beach celebrate special occasions. People often drink *kava* root juice and converse late into the night. Men enjoy building boats, canoes, and houses; wood carving is a popular hobby. Women weave mats and baskets, make dolls, and string special flower *leis*.

Holidays

The official holidays in Tonga include New Year's Day, Easter (Friday through Monday), Anzac Day (25 April), The Crown Prince's Birthday (4 May), Emancipation Day (4 June), the Birthday of King Taufa'ahau Tupou IV (4 July), Constitution Day (4 November), King George Tupou I Day (4 December), Christmas Day, and Boxing Day (26 December). Boxing Day comes from the British tradition of giving small boxed gifts to servants and tradesmen. It is now a day for visiting friends and relatives. Anzac Day is a New Zealand and Australian holiday honoring the armed forces; it is marked in Tonga because of the kindgom's close ties with the two larger nations. There are also various local celebrations and festivals throughout the year.

Commerce

Generally, business hours extend from 8:00 A.M. to 5:00 P.M., Monday through Friday, and until noon on Saturday. All businesses close on Sunday. Many women may weave baskets for much of the day to sell locally. Except for produce in the market, merchandise is sold at fixed prices. Purchased items are often wrapped in newspapers. Some supermarkets operate in Nuku'alofa, but most shopping occurs at open markets. People on outer islands without refrigeration must acquire and prepare perishable items daily.

SOCIETY

Government

Tonga is a hereditary, constitutional monarchy. Tongans hold their royalty in high esteem. King Taufa'ahau Tupou IV is the head of state. A prime minister (currently Baron Vaea) is head of government. The king and his cabinet form the Privy Council, which is part of the executive branch with the prime minister and his cabinet. Cabinet ministers are appointed by the king and hold their posts until retirement. The Legislative Assembly (*Fale Alea*) includes the executive branch members, seven members of Tongan nobility (elected by the nobility), and nine directly elected representatives. Legislators are elected as independents; political parties are a relatively new concept. All literate, tax-paying males are allowed to vote, as are literate females older than age 21. The last legislative elections were held in 1993.

Economy

Agriculture and fishing are the mainstays of the economy and provide for nearly all of Tonga's export earnings. Important products include coconuts (coconut oil and copra), bananas, taro, vanilla beans, fruits, and vegetables, and a variety of fish. New export opportunities, such as squash pumpkin to Japan, have provided a recent boost to agricultural expansion. A growing manufacturing industry accounts for about 10 percent of all economic activity. Agricultural activities employ 70 percent of the labor force. Tonga must import consumer items and machinery. It is somewhat dependent on Western aid. Tourism has grown to become an important source of income and jobs. Tongans are not wealthy, but they generally have enough to meet basic needs. The currency is the *pa'anga*.

Transportation and Communication

Many Tongans own and use private cars for local transportation. Public buses and taxis serve the entire island of Tongatapu but are limited on other islands. Ferries travel between the islands and air service is available to the main island groups. Most Tongans listen to the daily broadcasts of the one radio station or watch the broadcasts of the one television station. Television reception from New Zealand and Australia is also possible. There are few telephones and international links are limited. Two weekly newspapers serve the population.

Education

The government provides free and compulsory education for children ages six to fourteen. One year of kindergarten at age five is optional. Tonga has a high level of school enrollment. About two-thirds of the secondary school students attend church-sponsored schools. A trade school offers technical skills to post-secondary students. 'Atenisi University offers a college education, and the University of the South Pacific also has a campus in Tonga. The literacy rate is nearly 100 percent.

Health

Tonga enjoys a generally healthy environment and freedom from most tropical diseases. The government provides free health care to all citizens; private clinics also exist. While each island group has a hospital, the most modern one is in Nuku'alofa; it is the only one that can offer advanced care. Most doctors are trained abroad. Traditional healers play an important role in primary health care; they often prescribe traditional remedies for illness. The infant mortality rate is 21 per 1,000. Life expectancy averages between 65 and 70 years.

FOR THE TRAVELER

U.S. travelers do not need a visa for stays of up to 30 days, although a valid passport and proof of onward passages are required. Travelers are issued a visitor's permit at the airport. Valid yellow fever and cholera vaccination certificates are required of all travelers (except infants) who have been in an infected area prior to arrival. Other vaccinations are not required and water is potable in the capital and resort areas.

Tonga is a lesser known tourist destination in the South Pacific, but its beauty, friendly people, and improving facilities are enticing to many travelers. For information, contact the Tonga Visitors Bureau, PO Box 37, Nuku'alofa, Tonga. Tonga does not maintain an embassy in Washington, D.C., but the Consulate General in San Francisco, located at 360 Post Street, Suite 604, San Francisco, CA 94108; phone (415) 781–0365, may have more information.

Printed on recycled paper

Republic of
Tunisia

Boundary representations not necessarily authoritative.

BACKGROUND

Land and Climate

Tunisia is located on the northern coast of Africa, sandwiched between Algeria and Libya. Covering 63,170 square miles (163,610 square kilometers), it is a bit larger than the state of Georgia. Hundreds of miles of sandy beaches line the northern and eastern Mediterranean coasts. There are mountains along the Algerian border and oases in the southern desert. Orange orchards are found in the Cap Bon (northeastern peninsula) and olive farms in the Sahel (southern semidesert). The climate is mostly mild, with average temperatures ranging from 52°F (13°C) in winter to 80°F (26°C) in summer. Towards the desert, temperatures are much hotter, especially when the south wind (*sirocco* or *sh'hili*) blows. Sea breezes moderate the coastal climate. Winter nights can be cold throughout the country.

History

Throughout its history, Tunisia was a crossroads of many civilizations. Tunisia's indigenous inhabitants are known collectively as Berbers, but they actually call themselves by other names such as the Imazighen. A movement originating in North Africa is trying to establish the use of indigenous names for these peoples. Phoenicians founded Carthage in 814 B.C. and fought the Romans in the Punic Wars. Carthage was captured and eventually destroyed by the Romans. Tunisia's ancient heritage is evident in well-preserved archeological sites and excellent museums.

The two major influences shaping modern Tunisian society are Islam and French colonialism. Islam was introduced by Arabs in the seventh century. Indigenous groups gradually adopted Arabic customs along with Islam, and Tunisia became a center of Islamic culture. The Turkish Ottoman Empire ruled the area between 1574 and 1881. Economic difficulties and French colonial interests led to the Treaty of Bardo (1881), which made Tunisia a French protectorate. French culture soon became very influential and continues to a lesser extent today. Because of its relation to France, Tunisia was a major battleground during World War II.

Before the war, many Tunisians had pressed for independence, and the movement picked up again after 1945. Independence was finally secured relatively peacefully in 1956. Habib Bourguiba, who had led the movement since the 1930s, became Tunisia's first president in 1957. Bourguiba was reelected every five years, always running unopposed, until he was named president for life in 1974. When he became too old to govern (1987), his prime minister, Zine El Abidine Ben Ali legally removed him from power and took over as president. Bourguiba's greatest achievements were in education, women's emancipation, and in adapting Muslim traditions to modern life. His 31 years in power left a strong imprint on the country's political and social systems.

Ben Ali was reelected in 1989 and in 1993. Other political parties have always been legal in Tunisia, but they do not have the power to challenge the governing party. The Islamic

Fundamentalist Movement (*Ennahdha*) is banned because political parties of a religious or linguistic nature are illegal. Islamic fundamentalism has caused social unrest in the past few years and is therefore subject to government controls.

THE PEOPLE

Population

Tunisia's population of 8.7 million is growing at 1.8 percent annually. About 37 percent of the population is under age 15. Most people (98 percent) are of Arab descent. Others, mostly of European descent, live mainly in and around Tūnis or on the island of Djerba. More than half of all Tunisians live in urban areas. Greatly influenced by the French, who ruled the country for more than 75 years, Tunisians consider themselves the most Westernized people in the Arab world. Despite this, most Tunisians identify more with their "Arabness" than with "Westernness." People in small towns and villages tend to be more conservative than those in cities.

Language

Although Arabic is the official language, French is also widely spoken, especially in business and official circles. Tunisians easily switch from one language to the other in the same sentence. Most Tunisians are bilingual, and many speak some English. *Derija* is the Arabic dialect spoken in Tunisia. It is also spoken, with variations, in Algeria and Morocco. *Derija* is a variation of the classical Arabic found in the *Qur'an* (Koran), but it is so different that a speaker of classical Arabic might not understand spoken *Derija*—although he himself would be understood. Tunisians are especially pleased to hear non-Arabs speak Arabic.

Religion

Islam is Tunisia's official religion, and 98 percent of the people are Muslim. The majority are Sunni Muslims of the Malikite tradition, as founded by Malik ibn Anas. He codified Islamic traditions and stressed the importance of community consensus (as opposed to Shiites, who emphasize the authority of Muhammad's descendents). Islam plays an important role in daily life, especially during family events such as births, circumcision ceremonies, weddings, and burials. Friday is Islam's holy day; government offices and many businesses close at 1:00 P.M. In addition to Friday prayer services at the mosque, Muslims pray five times daily. They accept the *Qur'an* as scripture, believing it was revealed by *Allah* (God) to the Prophet Muhammad. While Muhammad is considered the last and greatest prophet, Muslims also accept Biblical prophets as important. In villages without mosques, *zaouia* (small mausoleums built in memory of especially holy men) are the main centers for religious activity. One percent of the population is Christian and a smaller number is Jewish.

General Attitudes

Tunisians are a traditional, yet adaptable, friendly, and open people. They tend to act more formally with international visitors in order to give them the best impression of Tunisian culture. Tunisians are generally eager to share their culture with others. This might include taking a person from another country to their homes for a meal or to a museum, café, or archeological site. They may even invite an international guest to a wedding. Tunisians enjoy learning about guests' families, food, and politics. Hospitality, warmth, and generosity are valued, and cultural arts are important.

While Tunisians are often relaxed and informal with each other, they also emphasize showing respect for one another—especially their elders. Conformity to a group (family or community) and concern for its well-being are usually more important than individual desires. Tunisians tend to use phrases such as *Inshallah* (God willing) and *Allah ghalib* (God is stronger) for expressing hopes or intentions. Difficult times are explained as *maktoub* (fate), an attitude that provides comfort and perseverance. A Tunisian's concept of time is loose; most people do not keep to a rigid schedule and some things can take a long time to get done. "Three days" can easily mean three weeks.

Personal Appearance

Western clothing is common in both urban and rural areas. In Tūnis and other large cities, fashion is influenced by Western Europe, particularly Italy and France. Many rural Tunisians, however, still wear traditional North African clothing. Older women, both in the city and countryside, might wear a white *safsari* (rectangular piece of cloth that completely covers the clothing) while in public. Once worn mainly out of modesty, the *safsari* today also protects clothing from dust and rain. The variety of everyday clothing reflects the diversity of Tunisia's cultural history. Shorts and immodest attire are not worn in public, except in resort areas.

CUSTOMS AND COURTESIES

Greetings

Greetings in Tunisia are an important and expressive part of personal interaction. Friends and family members often greet each other by "kissing the air" while brushing cheeks. Among strangers, both men and women, a handshake is the most common form of greeting. Standard greetings include *Ass'lama* (Hello), *Bisslama* (Good-bye), *Sabah El-Kheer* (Good morning), and *Tass'bah Ala Kheer* (Good night). Asking about the other person's health and family is expected before further conversation. When entering a store or office, a person greets the owner or staff. Neglecting to greet someone upon meeting is a serious oversight. Personal warmth is characteristic of all greetings.

Gestures

Hand gestures are an integral part of communication between Tunisians in everyday discussions and price negotiations. For example, the thumb and all fingertips pulled together and pointing up, while waving toward the body, can either mean "Good!" or "Wait!" depending on the context. Beckoning is done by waving all fingers toward the body while the palm faces down. Using the index finger to point at objects or people is considered rude. Winking at someone in public is inappropriate.

Tunisians generally do not have customs for what is appropriate for the right and left hands. Both are used freely. Like other Mediterranean peoples, Tunisians are spirited in conversational gestures and appreciate the same from visitors. Touching between members of the same sex is common to emphasize speech and communicate warmth. Friends of the same sex often walk hand in hand, but this does not suggest anything beyond friendship. Men and women, however, don't usually hold hands in public because public displays of affection are not appropriate.

Visiting

Family and friends visit each other frequently and unannounced—often in the late evening. Visits can last several hours and guests are usually invited for a meal. Because hospitality is important, a host usually offers food and drink to his guests. Such an offer should be accepted, even if only for a taste. Invited guests might bring gifts of fruit or chocolate (never alcohol) to the host. It is common for first-time visitors to be given a tour of the host's home, especially if a new room or new furniture has been added. On such an occasion, the host may be congratulated with the word *mabrouk*, which is used to congratulate people at weddings or graduations, or on getting a new job or buying a house. Visitors should dress conservatively (covering knees and upper arms).

Eating

Tunisians do not like to eat alone. Eating from a common plate is customary. One uses the fingers of either hand to eat or uses bread as a utensil. Western-style eating from separate plates with silverware is equally common. People wash their hands before and after meals. In some traditional homes, people sit on the floor around a low, round, wooden table at mealtime. A host will often insist that guests have second or third helpings, and it is polite for guests to accept. When a person has eaten enough, he can say *Hamdullah* (Thanks to God) to express he's had a good meal. Burping after a meal is considered rude. In restaurants, the tip is usually included in the bill.

LIFESTYLE

Family

Although many women work outside the home in important positions, society is male dominated. Still, women comprise one-fourth of the labor force. Tunisia is the most progressive among Muslim countries in its laws concerning women's rights at work and in matters of divorce and inheritance. Polygamy has been outlawed since Tunisia's independence in 1956, even though Islamic tradition allows a man to have up to four wives. Generally, men and women have equal authority in the home. In more traditional households, however, men dominate and a woman's role is clearly defined. The extended family is the most important social unit. Honor, reputation, and mutual support are important family values.

Dating and Marriage

Marriage is not only a union between individuals but a link between two families. Traditional weddings, particularly in rural areas, are celebrated over several days, even weeks, through ritualized ceremonies and parties. One activity is called *henna*. On the night before the wedding, women invited to the bride's home apply patterns to her hands and feet using a paste made from henna leaves (the dried paste is removed after several hours, leaving patterns behind). The bride also has her hair and makeup done. During the course of a wedding celebration, a bride may wear one or two traditional dresses as well as a Western gown. Traditionally, marriages were arranged by the parents, but young people now have increasing opportunities for meeting and getting to know one another independently. Since dating in its Western form is generally not accepted, weddings and social gatherings provide a chance for young people to meet.

Diet

Couscous is Tunisia's national dish; it is made of steamed and spiced semolina, and topped with vegetables and meats. Appreciated for its delicacy and lightness, *couscous* is prepared in many ways. *Breek*, another favorite dish, is made of a thin, fried dough stuffed with an egg, cooked vegetables, and tuna. *Tajine* is a crustless quiche of vegetables and meats. Fish, lamb, and chicken are eaten frequently. Tomatoes, potatoes, onions, olives, oil, and peppers are common to Tunisian cooking. A large variety of fruits are sold in the markets, including dates, oranges, apricots, watermelons, and nectarines. Cactus fruit (*hindi*), called the "sultan of all fruits," is widely available in the summer. Alcohol and pork are forbidden by Islam, but alcohol is available in large towns.

Recreation

Listening to music, watching movies (increasingly on VCRs), going to the beach, playing soccer and beach volleyball (mostly men), and simply visiting friends and relatives are among the most popular leisure activities. Most people enjoy *shkubbah*, a traditional card game. Summer art festivals are organized throughout the country and attract large crowds. Coffee houses are popular among men, who go there to play cards, discuss sports and politics, conduct business, and drink coffee. Women do not usually go to coffee houses unless in the company of male relatives.

Holidays

Although Tunisia's secular holidays follow the Western calendar, religious holidays follow the Muslim (lunar) calendar, so they fall on different days each year. The most important holiday period is *Ramadan*, a month of fasting and prayer. While Muslims do not eat, drink, or smoke from sunrise to sundown each day during *Ramadan*, they participate in lively evenings that involve special foods, carnivals, shopping, and festivals. Non-Muslims, while not expected to fast, should exercise good judgement about eating in public and taking part in the evening celebrations. *Aid Esseghir*, a two-day holiday, marks the end of *Ramadan*. People wear their best clothes to visit friends and relatives, and they trade presents of pastry. Other holidays include *Ras El Am El Hejri* (Islamic New Year), *El Mouled* (Prophet Muhammad's birthday), and *Aid El Kebir* (commemorating Abraham's willingness to sacrifice his son).

Secular holidays include: New Year's Day (1 January), Independence Day (20 March), Martyr's Day (9 April), Labor Day (1 May), Republic Day (25 July), Women's Day (13 August), and Evacuation Day (15 October, the day in 1963 when the last of the French troops returned to France).

Commerce

From September to June, business hours are Monday through Thursday, from 8:00 A.M. to 12:30 P.M. and from 2:00 to 6:00 P.M.; on Friday and Saturday, the hours are from

8:00 A.M. to 1:00 P.M. Businesses are closed on Sunday. Many private companies, including banks, have slightly longer working hours during the week and are closed all day Saturday and Sunday. Tunisia has a shortened work schedule for July and August, when most businesses operate Monday through Saturday 7:00 A.M. to 1:00 P.M. Business appointments made well in advance should be confirmed a day, or even hours, beforehand. Tunisian business people usually have tea or engage in small talk before discussing business, but this practice is disappearing among more Westernized Tunisians, especially as time pressures and business contacts with the West increase. Many details in business arrangements are not written down because the business environment does not always guarantee that such things as deadlines will be met.

SOCIETY

Government

Tunisia is a republic, divided into 23 governorates. The central government is headed by a president who appoints a prime minister and a Council of Ministers. Members of the unicameral legislature, the 141-seat Chamber of Deputies (*Majlis al-Nuwaab*), are elected by the people. All citizens may vote at age 20. The ruling party is Ben Ali's Constitutional Democratic Rally Party (RCD), although a number of independents and Islamists are represented in the legislature and smaller political parties do function.

Economy

Tunisia has a diversified economy with agriculture, light industry, and services all playing key roles. Agriculture is especially important in the interior and along the Sahel coast. The textile industry (mostly for export) provides jobs for thousands of laborers, as does tourism—Tunisia's main source of hard currency. Remittances from Tunisian workers in France and income from oil and phosphates are also important sources of income. Most exports go to Europe. The currency is the Tunisian *dinar* (D).

Tunisia's economy is shifting toward a free market and economic growth is about 3 percent. In 1995, export earning rose an impressive 19.6 percent. The work force is educated and productive. The country's Human Development Index (0.690) ranks it 81st out of 173 countries. Real gross domestic product per capita is $4,690, a figure that has more than doubled in the last generation and improved significantly in the 1990s. Those figures and the fact that the distribution of income is not highly unequal reflect increasing economic progress. Absolute poverty is less than 20 percent, and most people have access to economic opportunities. Inflation is low, but unemployment (16 percent) remains a significant problem with serious social implications. The higher the unemployment rate, the more radical the fundamentalist movement can be.

Transportation and Communication

A good network of paved roads and highways links all cities and towns. Major railroads serve northern and coastal areas. Tūnis, the capital, has an efficient light-rail system (*Métro Leger*). Buses are the most common form of public transportation. *Louages* (group taxis) run between cities and are faster than buses. Most families do not own cars. Motorcycles and bicycles are common. In rural areas, people may use donkey carts to transport goods and vegetables. There are airports in major cities. Phone service is good, but it may be slow in summer because the shorter work schedule strains the system. Most people do not have telephones in their homes, but they access them at post offices. The press is regulated by the government. There are four television stations. Postal delivery is efficient.

Education

Education has been an important element in Tunisia's development since independence. One-fourth of the government's budget is spent on education. This allows even the most remote regions to have free schooling. *École de Base* (Basic Education, grades 1–6) is compulsory and nearly all children are enrolled. Advancement depends on passing tests. About half of all students go on to the *Lycée* (grades 7–13). In 10th grade, students choose between two tracks: *Lettres* (Humanities and Social Sciences) or *Sciences* (Math and Science). The rigorous Baccalaureate Exam is taken at the end of the 13th grade; successful students may go on to a university. Passing the test is a great source of pride for parents. While classes are taught in French and Arabic, there is a trend to promote Arabic. Tunisia's literacy rate is 65 percent.

Health

The government provides free medical care to all citizens. There are also several private clinics in major cities. Rural health care may be limited to clinics for child immunizations, family planning, and other basic services. The infant mortality rate is 34 per 1,000. Life expectancy averages 70 to 75 years.

FOR THE TRAVELER

A valid passport is required for U.S. citizens to enter Tunisia, but no visa is required for visits of up to four months. There are no required vaccinations. Water is generally safe to drink, but bottled water is usually preferred. It is recommended to wash fruits and vegetables thoroughly before eating. As tourism is important to the economy, there are many well-run resorts and sites of interest. For more information, you may wish to contact the Embassy of Tunisia, 1515 Massachusetts Avenue NW, Washington, DC 20005; phone (202) 862–1850. You may also contact consulate offices located in San Francisco; phone (415) 922–9222, and in New York; phone (212) 272–6962.

A *Culturgram* is a product of native commentary and original, expert analysis. Statistics are estimates and information is presented as a matter of opinion. While the editors strive for accuracy and detail, this document should not be considered strictly factual. It is a general introduction to culture, an initial step in building bridges of understanding between peoples. It may not apply to all peoples of the nation. You should therefore consult other sources for more information.

Republic of
Turkey

Boundary representations not necessarily authoritative.

BACKGROUND

Land and Climate

Turkey is located at the juncture where Europe meets Asia, forming a bridge and a link to each continent. Covering 301,382 square miles (780,580 square kilometers), Turkey is about the size of Texas. The western portion is called Thrace, while the eastern portion is known as Anatolia or Asia Minor. In addition to several countries, the Aegean Sea, Mediterranean Sea, and Black Sea all border the country. Anatolia is a plateau that becomes more mountainous to the east. Mountains are also found along the Black Sea. Both the Euphrates and Tigris rivers flow through Turkey. The coastal regions are generally low. Winters can be very cold in some portions of the country, although they are mild along the coasts. Summers are pleasant, but can be hot in some areas.

History

Modern Turkey is the most recent in a series of important states and empires that have inhabited the Anatolian peninsula since the beginning of history. The oldest known site of human urban habitation is located in central Turkey at Chatalhuyuk (6500 B.C.). The great Hittite Empire (3000–2000 B.C.), which dominated much of the Middle East, was centered east of Ankara. Ancient Troy, the scene of much of Homer's *Iliad*, was located near the Dardanelles. Alexander the Great captured Anatolia in the fourth century B.C., and the Romans followed three centuries later, establishing important cities, such as Ephesus and Antioch, as major provincial capitals.

In A.D. 330, the Roman Emperor Constantine founded the city of Constantinople, which later became the center of the Byzantine Empire. This great state dominated eastern Europe for one thousand years. The Muslim Seljuk Turks entered Asia Minor in the 11th century and began the long process of Islamization and Turkization. In 1453, the successors of the Seljuks, the Ottoman Turks, captured Constantinople and went on to create a vast empire, stretching beyond the bounds of the Byzantine Empire into the Balkans, the Middle East, and North Africa. The Ottoman Empire survived until World War I when it allied itself with the Central Powers. With the defeat of the Central Powers, the empire was dismembered.

In 1923, out of the ruins of the Ottoman Empire, Mustafa Kemal, a general in the Turkish army, fashioned the Republic of Turkey. Under Kemal, the nation was reformed from an Islamic empire to a secular state with an Islamic majority. Although most of Turkey is in Asia, it has always had important European ties. In 1952, Turkey joined the European security structure called the North Atlantic Treaty Organization (NATO) and provided land for a U.S. military base.

Over the next three decades, the country went through various cycles of political turmoil. In the late 1970s, serious economic problems and political upheaval, which nurtured widespread domestic terrorism, so paralyzed the government that the military seized control in 1980. The military restored stability, called for elections in 1983, and withdrew from power after the elections. The military commander responsible for these actions, Kenan Evran, was elected president. His prime minister, Turgut Özal, became the dominant political figure in the 1980s.

In 1989, Özal was elected by the parliament to the office of president for a seven-year term. Parliamentary elections in 1991 brought Özal's rival to power as prime minister.

Suleyman Demirel had been prime minister before and was twice (1971 and 1980) ousted in coups. When Özal suddenly died in 1993, Demirel was elected by parliament as the new president. Tansu Ciller was chosen to replace Demirel as prime minister until 1996 elections. She is Turkey's first female prime minister. Ciller's government was immediately faced with economic challenges and the ongoing insurgency by Kurdish rebels. A cease-fire declared in 1993 did not hold and violence only worsened in 1994 and 1995. In 1995, Turkish troops swept into Northern Iraq to wipe out rebel bases from which Kurds had staged terrorist attacks. Some Kurdish leaders have offered to end the fighting in exchange for more rights for the Kurdish minority. The Kurds technically have equal political rights, but seek the right to fully use their language and promote their culture. Both sides prefer a peaceful end to the conflict, but they have not as yet been able to agree on any solutions.

THE PEOPLE

Population

Turkey has 62.1 million inhabitants, a population that is growing at 2 percent annually. Ankara, the capital, has more than 3.5 million people. Istanbul boasts a population of 10 million. Istanbul was once called Constantinople and was the center of the Byzantine empire. It is still the industrial, commercial, and intellectual center of the country. About 80 percent of the people in Turkey are Turkish, 17 percent are Kurdish, and 3 percent belong to a variety of smaller groups. Kurds live mostly in the southeast. As in most cultures, urbanization has increased over the years, and 61 percent of Turkey's population now lives in urban areas.

Language

Turkish is the official language of the country. It is related to the Uralic-Altaic languages spoken across Asia (from Finland to Manchuria). Arabic script was used during the Ottoman Empire period, but a Latin-based alphabet has been used since 1928. Most of the Kurdish minority speaks Kurdish. However, Kurdish was banned for many years and some people forgot how to use it. Now legal, Kurdish is expected to revive. Bans on its use in education and domestic broadcasting are still in effect, but Kurdish can be used in some publications and public speaking. Arabic is also spoken. English is an increasingly popular second or third language.

Religion

Although 98 percent of Turkey's population is Sunni Muslim, the government makes it clear that Turkey is a secular state with complete freedom of religion. Islam's status as state religion was abolished in 1923. Still, Islam maintains an important influence on society. In the latter 1980s, corresponding to a rise in Islamic fundamentalism throughout the world, fundamentalist Muslims in Turkey began pressing for greater government use of Islamic principles. However, few people expect Turkey to become a religious state.

Muslims believe in one God, *Allah*, and that his will was revealed to the Prophet Muhammad through the angel Gabriel. These revelations were recorded in the *Qur'an* (Koran), the holy book of Islam. Muslims accept many Judeo-Christian prophets, but proclaim that Muhammed was the last and greatest. Throughout life, they strive to live the five pillars of Islam: professing Allah's name and Muhammad's role as prophet, fasting during the holy month of *Ramazan*, giving aid to the poor, making a pilgrimmage to Makkah, and praying daily at five specific times.

General Attitudes

Turkey is often described as a bridge between East and West. Due to centuries of interaction with Europe and Asia, Turks have incorporated features from both areas into their lifestyle and thinking. At the same time, they are patriotic and have developed a unique society. The people are proud of the achievements of their modern state as well as the accomplishments of their ancestors, who ruled great empires. Turks consider their society to be progressive, Europe-leaning, and a strong influence in the region. They often feel misunderstood by European and other Western nations because of the often publicized Kurdish rebellion. Turkey is known in the United States, Turks believe, mostly for its past and the terrorist violence; Turks emphasize another side of the country, one that is modern and ethnically diverse but tolerant and democratic.

Individually, Turks prize a good sense of humor; it is considered a sign of intelligence. Group orientation is valued over personal assertiveness or aggression, and honesty and cleverness are admirable qualities. People value a good education, secure employment, social status, and an honorable heritage.

Personal Appearance

Western-style clothing is most common. European fashions are especially popular among the youth. Some traditional clothing is still worn in rural areas or for special occasions. Costumes differ according to region. The design of the costume's headdress and the type of material used signify a person's social status.

CUSTOMS AND COURTESIES

Greetings

When greeting friends or strangers, one shakes hands and says *Nasilsiniz* (How are you?) or *Merhaba* (Hello). A typical response to *Nasilsiniz* is *Iyiyim, teshekur ederim* (Fine, thank you). Greetings are followed among friends by polite inquiries about one's health, family, and work. Among close friends of the same (or sometimes those of opposite) gender, Turks clasp hands and kiss on both cheeks when greeting. To show respect to an older person, their hands may be kissed and touched to the greeter's forehead. The youth often greet each other with *Selam* (Salute). Someone entering a room, office, or teahouse might say *Günaydin* (Good morning) or *Iyi günler* (Have a nice day). When parting, it is customary to wish for blessings from Allah (*Allahaısmarladık*) and respond agreeably (*Güle güle*).

Upon joining a small group, one greets each person in the group individually. When addressing others formally, professional titles are used. Otherwise, the title *Hanım* is used for women and *Bey* for men among peers or with younger persons. These follow the given name: Leyla Hanım or Ismail Bey. With older people, one uses *Abla* for women (Fatma Abla) or *Aabey* (Ahmet Aabey) for men. These terms mean "sister" and "brother." If there is a great difference of age, the terms *Teyze* (aunt) and *Amca* (uncle) are used after the first name.

In urban areas, strangers passing on the street are not generally greeted, but rural people are more likely to greet the person.

Gestures

Turks generally use their hands a great deal during conversation, forming gestures that add meaning and emphasis.

Social courtesies are valued in Turkey. One does not put feet on a desk or table, point the sole of the foot toward another person, smoke without asking permission, or cross the legs while in the presence of an older or superior person. It is not proper for adults to eat or smoke on the street. Public displays of affection are not acceptable. For some more traditional people, it is an insult to pass an item with the left hand. The word "no" can be expressed by either shaking the head or lifting it up once quickly.

Visiting

Turks enjoy visiting one another in their homes, and hospitality is an integral part of the culture. Friends, relatives, and neighbors visit often. In large cities, people call ahead, but this is not practical in smaller villages, where unexpected visits occur more frequently. As hospitality is customary, guests are always invited in and offered refreshments. This usually involves something to drink (tea, coffee, soda) and sometimes to eat (crackers and cookies). It is impolite to decline these refreshments. Many Turks remove their shoes when entering a home and replace them with slippers. Guests are expected to do the same at homes where this custom is followed. Visitors are expected to bring a pleasant presence to the home; bad news or accounts of problems are saved for other occasions and locations. It is not polite to ask personal questions of hosts. First-time visitors to a home may bring a small gift, such as candy, fruit, or flowers. Turks work hard to make their guests feel comfortable. For example, even if the hosts do not think smoking is appropriate, they may allow visitors to smoke in their homes.

Eating

Breakfast is usually eaten around 7:00 A.M., or earlier in rural areas. Lunch is at midday and dinner is around 7:00 P.M. Dinner is the main meal and the family generally expects to sit down together for this meal.

Eating habits vary with the region and the food being eaten. The continental style of eating is followed, with the fork in the left hand and the knife remaining in the right. Some foods are eaten with the hand. To begin or end a meal, one might say *Afiyet Olsun* (May what you eat bring you well-being). One may compliment the cook on the meal by saying *Elinize saglik* (roughly, Bless your hand). Meals can be lavish, and Turks are quite proud of their rich cuisine. Types of restaurants range from those offering fast food to international cuisine, but the most common is the Turkish kebab restaurant. Some restaurants include a service charge in the bill (about 10 percent), in which case a 5 percent tip is customary. If no service charge is included, a 15 percent tip should be given.

LIFESTYLE

Family

The primary social unit in Turkey is the family. In rural areas, traditional, patriarchal values prevail. An individual is loyal to and dependent upon the family. The Turkish household often consists of an extended family: a mother and father, their unmarried children, and, in some cases, married sons with their families. The married sons remain until they are financially independent. In urban areas, nuclear families are the standard and traditional authority structures are less pronounced. It is uncommon for a person to live alone, mostly for economic reasons. Polygamy, as permitted by Islamic law, was abolished in 1930. Women gained the right to vote in 1927 and the right to divorce in 1934 when civil marriage contracts were introduced. Urban women frequently work outside the home. Thirty-three percent of the labor force is female.

Dating and Marriage

Except perhaps at universities or in large urban areas, dating in the Western sense is not common. Young people associate more in groups. In the cities, this association is generally open and casual. In rural areas, chaperones are common. Rural families are heavily involved in deciding who a person will marry, but the choice is generally the couple's in urban areas. It is against the law for women to marry before age 15, and men before age 17. In the cities, many wait until their education and sometimes military service have been completed before getting married. Hence, the average age for marriage is 22 for women and 25 for men. Most Turks expect to marry and have children.

Traditional wedding celebrations last three days, and this is still practiced by some in rural areas. Urban couples often follow more European traditions when marrying. Traditional festivities begin with the *Kına Gecesi* (henna evening), an event only for women. They decorate the hands and fingers of the bride with henna leaf dye and dance and sing. On the second day, both sets of parents serve lunch and dinner to their guests. On the third day, the bride is taken to the groom's home on a horse after folk dances are performed. This tradition is increasingly rare because of the time and expense involved.

Diet

Turkish cuisine is among the finest in the world. Lamb and rice are served with many meals. Seafood is more abundant along the coast. The famous *kahve* (Turkish coffee), a thick brew served in very small cups, is served with nearly every meal. Breakfast is usually light, consisting of tea, white cheese, bread, butter, marmalade or honey, and olives. The main meal of the day is eaten in the evening and may consist of several courses. Turkish cuisine is famous for many things, among them the *meze*, a tray or table of hors d'oeuvres, including stuffed grape leaves, salads, shrimp, and a variety of other items. There are also many unique Turkish soups. Shish kebabs (chunks of lamb on a skewer) are a favorite, as are vegetables prepared in olive oil. Rice *pilav* is common. Turkish desserts are famously sweet, including *baklava* (syrup-dipped pastry), *muhallebi* (milk pudding), and others. The most popular drink next to coffee is *raki*, a drink made of fermented grapes (not a wine).

Recreation

The most popular sport for both spectators and participants is soccer, which was introduced by the British in the 19th century. Volleyball, basketball, cycling, grease wrestling, traditional wrestling, swimming, and a variety of other sports are also enjoyed. Picnics are common family activities. August is the month for most vacations. For their leisure time, urban residents may watch television, eat out, visit others, or attend movies. Women often do volunteer work. Rural women visit one another in their homes or watch television. Men throughout the country gather at tea houses (like cafés) to socialize. When at home, they also watch television. Folk dancing and other cultural arts are popular.

Holidays

The ninth month of the Muslim lunar calendar is *Ramazan*, during which practicing Muslims fast from dawn to dusk. At the end of *Ramazan* is a three-day holiday called *Seker Bayrami* (sugar holiday), during which sweets are eaten to celebrate the end of the fast. A second Muslim holiday is *Kurban Bayrami* (sacrifice holiday), which marks the season of pilgrimage to Makkah, Saudi Arabia. It also commemorates Abraham's willingness to sacrifice his son. An animal is usually sacrificed and the meat distributed to the poor. Other official holidays include New Year's Day, National Sovereignty Day (23 April, also Children's Day), Atatürk's Memorial Day and Youth Day (19 May), Victory Day (30 August), and Republic Day (29 October).

Commerce

Businesses are generally open from 9:00 A.M. to 5:00 P.M., Monday through Friday. Some are open for a half day on Saturday. Most people buy fresh produce at open air markets, but get other goods from supermarkets (in large cities) or neighborhood shops.

SOCIETY

Government

Turkey is a parliamentary democracy composed of 73 provinces. The president is head of state, and the prime minister is head of government. The Grand National Assembly (parliament) has 450 members. The voting age is 21. The three largest political parties include the Correct Way Party, Motherland Party, and Social Democratic Populist Party.

Economy

Turkey's economy has enjoyed solid growth over the last several years, due largely to market-oriented reforms introduced after the military coup. Unfortunately, poor management in 1993 damaged economic performance and caused inflation to rise above 100 percent. Industrial production slipped, and many factories laid off workers or cut output. The government is trying to address the problem, but growth for 1994 was less than 2 percent. Turkey's Human Development Index (0.739) ranks it 68th out of 173 countries. Real gross domestic product per capita is $4,840, which has tripled since 1960. Income distribution is unequal: urban residents enjoy far higher incomes than rural people or migrants. A high number of migrants, especially in Istanbul, has increased unemployment and strained urban infrastructure.

Agriculture is the traditional backbone of the economy, once providing the bulk of all exports. Today, it still employs half of the labor force and accounts for one-fifth of all exports. Chief agricultural products include cotton, tobacco, fruit, cereals, nuts, and opium for medicine. Manufacturing employs 15 percent of the labor force but accounts for nearly 60 percent of all exports.

Its success is therefore vital to the economy. Mining and tourism are also important The currency is the Turkish *lira* (£T).

Transportation and Communication

Around major urban areas, the roads are paved and in good condition. In rural areas, infrastructure is generally adequate but not always well maintained. Taxis, buses, streetcars, and *dolmus* (shared taxis) provide public transportation. The railroad is used for travel between cities, as are the airways. Turkey is connected with other countries by international air links. The overall communications system is fairly good, with several television and radio stations broadcasting throughout the country. The press is free and active. Telephone service is best in urban areas.

Education

The government is concerned with meeting the educational needs of its population. Disparities between rural and urban facilities are being addressed by building more rural schools and other reforms. Primary and secondary education is free and coeducational. Primary schooling lasts five years, and secondary education three. Additional years are possible to about age 17. Nearly all children complete the primary level, and about half go on to the secondary level. A foreign language is required. Once a student completes high school, an exam is given to determine the possibility of studying at a university. Universities require modest tuition. There are more than 25 universities in Turkey, the oldest of which was founded at Istanbul in 1453. There are more than 250 specialized colleges and institutions offering vocational and other training. Literacy is 81 percent.

Health

The government provides basic health care to the public, but it is not sufficient to meet the country's needs. Urban facilities are generally modern and adequate, but rural facilities are not as well equipped. Besides public health care, institutions such as the military, state-owned enterprises, etc., provide care to their personnel. Reform measures have been introduced to address the most serious problems, including a relatively high infant mortality rate (48 per 1,000) attributed to poor education about child care and the lack of family planning. The government seeks to reduce the figure to below 30 by the year 2000 through improved child immunizations, prenatal care, education, and other programs. Life expectancy ranges between 68 and 73 years.

FOR THE TRAVELER

A visa is not necessary for U.S. travelers visiting for up to three months, but a valid passport is required. Bottled water is recommended. Fruits and vegetables should be cleaned and peeled before eating. Air pollution in the winter, particularly in Ankara, can be hazardous to those suffering from respiratory ailments. Turkey has a number of interesting sites worth visiting. For information regarding travel opportunities, contact the Turkish Tourist Office, 821 United Nations Plaza, New York, NY 10017. You may also wish to contact the Turkish Embassy's Tourist Office, 1717 Massachusetts Avenue NW, Suite 306, Washington, DC 20036; phone (202) 429–9844.

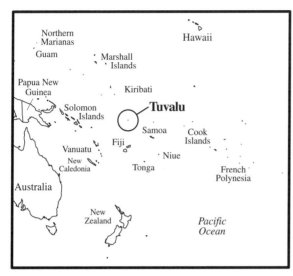

Boundary representations not necessarily authoritative.

Nanumea

Niutao

Nanumanga

Tuvalu

Nui

Vaitupu

Nukufetau

FUNAFUTI
★

Funafuti

Nukulaelae

Niulakita

BACKGROUND

Land and Climate

Tuvalu (too-VAH-loo) is a group of nine small atolls scattered 350 miles north to south in the south-central Pacific Ocean. Named for the eight inhabited atolls, *Tuvalu* means "eight standing together." Niula Kita is a bird sanctuary and was not inhabited until recently. Tuvalu is one of the world's smallest countries, with a total land area of about 10 square miles (26 square kilometers). Six atolls enclose large lagoons; the land portion consists of sand-covered coral rock. Tuvalu also claims an exclusive economic zone (for fishing) of two hundred nautical miles.

Tuvalu's tropical climate is pleasant, with high humidity being moderated from March to November by easterly trade winds. The average annual temperature of 84°F (29°C) changes little during the year. Westerly gales and heavy rains come between November and March. Severe tropical storms have been rare, but cyclones and tidal waves can threaten this country whose highest point is less than 17 feet (5 meters) above sea level.

History

The original inhabitants were probably Polynesian and Southeast Asian travelers who came to the islands at various times from six hundred to two thousand years ago. Each Tuvalu island developed its own political and social system before European contact. Ceremonial and social visits took place between islands.

In 1568, Spanish explorer Alvaro de Mendana sited Nui (and in 1595, Nuilakita), but the islands remained largely unknown by outsiders until a passing ship captain named one atoll Ellice Island in 1819. By 1825, the atolls were on European maps and by 1830 all had been visited and charted (and

given various names by the explorers). In 1841, the entire group was named the Ellice Islands.

Whalers from New England were the most frequent foreign visitors. The London Missionary Society (LMS) of Samoa began founding churches and schools in the 1830s at about the same time the copra (dried coconut meat) trade spread throughout the Pacific. The islands were considered of low economic value and so remained mostly unexploited by outsiders.

By the 1860s, however, peaceful visits were replaced by the establishment of permanent trading posts, missions, and disastrous encounters with slave trader ships. In 1863, Peruvian slavers raided the southern atolls of Funafuti and Nukulaelae, carrying away forever two-thirds of their population to work in Peruvian guano mines.

The Ellice Islands were claimed by the British in 1886, receiving protectorate status in 1892. The colonial administration left most local government in the hands of island councils. The LMS handled education until the 20th century, when the British established a boys' primary school under the direction of Donald Gilbert Kennedy. Kennedy left a legacy in administration, land tenure, cooperative and resettlement efforts, language, and technical skills.

In 1916, the Gilbert Islands (now Kiribati) and Ellice Islands were joined to form the Gilbert and Ellice Islands Colony (GEIC). World War II brought airstrips, U.S. soldiers, and money. During GEIC's independence movement in the 1960s, Ellice Islanders demanded separation from the Gilberts, being heavily outnumbered and culturally different. A referendum was held under UN auspices, and the Ellice Islands became a separate British colony in 1975. A subsequent vote changed the name to Tuvalu, and three years later Tuvalu became an independent nation within the Commonwealth.

OCEANIA

PEOPLE

Population

About ten thousand people inhabit Tuvalu, with one-third living on Funafuti, the capital island. Population growth is about 1.7 percent. All nine atolls are inhabited, with a single village on each outer island (islands other than Funafuti). The majority (96 percent) of Tuvaluans are ethnic Polynesians, while the remainder include mixed descendants of Polynesians and Europeans.

About fifteen hundred Tuvalu citizens are either studying, living, or employed overseas. More than seven hundred work in the phosphate mines on Nauru and Ocean Island. Nauru is set to close in the near future. The government is seeking alternate job opportunities to help keep the workers abroad. Short-term work is available in Tuvalu when projects are in development, but the economy is otherwise not large enough to accommodate all of Tuvalu's workers.

Language

English is Tuvalu's official language and is taught in all schools. On a daily basis, though, most people speak Tuvaluan. It is related to several languages in the region (especially Samoan). Its written form uses the Latin alphabet. Each island has its own dialect. The differences are mostly in sound and vocabulary, and most Tuvaluans understand all the dialects. The Vaitupu dialect is most often used between islands.

The language spoken on Nui is related to Kiribati (Gilbertese). According to legend, I-Kiribati warriors once conquered the island and remained after their victory. They effected a radical change in the language, such that people say it is three-fourths Kiribati and one-fourth Tuvaluan.

Religion

Prior to the introduction of Christianity, Tuvaluans worshipped a number of island gods, placating them with offers of food and possessions. Powerful priests (*Vaka Atua*) acted as intermediaries between the people and the gods, and they presided over special ceremonies.

Today, 97 percent of Tuvaluans are members of the Christian Church of Tuvalu (*Ekalesia Tuvalu*), derived from the Congregationalist foundation of the LMS. Other faiths include the Roman Catholic church, the Church of Jesus Christ of Latter-day Saints (Mormon), Seventh-day Adventist, and Baha'i.

The flow of community life, especially on outer islands, centers around religion. A typical day in a village begins with family prayer at 5:30 A.M. and ends with another at 7:00 P.M. Sunday church services are held at various times and are well attended. Virtually no work is performed on Sunday. The pastor is one of the most important men on the island. Villagers provide him with food and money, and build and maintain his home. They also take great pride in crafting beautiful churches for their meetings.

General Attitudes

Tuvaluan behavioral codes are concerned more with "how things seem" than with what actually occurs. Social offenses that do not become public knowledge are not treated, essentially, as offenses and little guilt is felt by those involved. This non-absolute social code suits the small population because society is based on kinship and devotion to the group.

Tuvaluans admire and expect of each other generosity, a willingness to help, sharing, caring for those who are alone, a sense of humor, and an ability to work hard. Tuvaluans are toughened by living in a close-to-nature existence. They easily adapt to the whims of nature, and they can fix just about anything. Tuvaluans are reserved but friendly and social. As the population aspires to a better education as a means of gaining access to paid employment, basic life skills are becoming less valued. On outer islands, there is a desire for such Western goods as flashlights, fishing gear, guitars, and radios.

Personal Appearance

Funafuti men and women with wage jobs wear light, casual Western-style clothing to work. At home, they wear a blouse or shirt with a *sulu*, a colorful medium-to-long cotton wraparound cloth. Some businessmen, clergy, and civil servants wear tailored *sulus* with pockets and a short-sleeved shirt. Outer islanders also wear a colorful *sulu*, but when they work they substitute a sturdier and less colorful *sulu* and T-shirt.

School children wear uniforms: shorts and shirts for boys, skirts and blouses for girls. Scanty dress is offensive; women do not wear pants or shorts (except some younger women on Funafuti). Many people wear flower garlands (*fou*) in their hair on festive occasions. Shoes are rare, but plastic flip-flops or sandals are worn for such activities as reef fishing or office work.

CUSTOMS AND COURTESIES

Greetings

Welcoming people is an important ritual in Tuvalu. When people first meet or when they arrive from another island or abroad, they shake hands and say, or are welcomed with, *Taalofa!* (Greetings!). Relatives use a *sogi* (sniffing) gesture, in which they press their face to the other's cheek and sniff deeply. They may use this when one leaves or arrives at the island, or as an affectionate way to greet children. If meeting after a long absence, old friends may slap one another on the back as they exchange several phrases that show how close they are and how pleased they are to see each other.

Since most Tuvaluans see the same people often each day, *Taalofa!* is not a casual greeting. Instead, people say *E fano koe ki fea?* (Where are you going?) or *E aa koe na?* (What are you doing/How are you?). Greetings may continue with inquiries about one's family and friends.

Titles and last names are not often used when addressing others. First names are known and used by most all Tuvaluans. Even the pastor is called by his first name. When speaking English, Tuvaluans adapt to the English custom of using titles when appropriate.

Very special occasions call for a feast (*fakaala*) in the *maneapa* (community hall; *ahiga* on northern islands), with food served on a tray woven from coconut fronds. The meal ends when the main chief is finished. It is followed by formal speeches, dances, and more speeches as hosts and recipients thank each other.

Gestures

It is improper to touch another person's head, the most sacred part of the body. In a *maneapa*, one keeps the head low, stooping to walk through a group. Pointing directly at someone or using one finger to beckon is rude. Beckoning is done by waving all fingers with the palm facing down. To look down while conversing shows respect to the other person. Staring is impolite. Raising the eyebrows indicates agreement.

Visiting

Unannounced visiting is an important aspect of Tuvaluan society and guests are always welcome. Sunday is a popular day for such visits, but anytime will do (especially if it is raining hard and no one is working). One wouldn't normally visit early in the morning or when people usually prepare meals or work. Friends do drop by, but mostly relatives visit one another; daughters frequently visit their mothers.

The traditional house has no permanent walls, so visitors need not knock to announce their presence. It is customary to remove any footwear, enter, and sit down on the pandanus mat (*papa*). If the mat is not down, the visitor waits for it to be spread out. If walking past a sitting or lying person when entering, one says *Tulou* (Excuse me) to apologize for being above the level of the person's head. One also says *Tulou* when reaching for something above another person's head.

On the *papa*, one sits cross-legged (or women may extend one leg laterally and tuck the other under it). Except during formal *maneapa* speeches, one might also stretch the legs out straight. Hosts normally offer guests some fresh toddy (coconut tree blossom sap), or share green drinking coconuts or tea. If it happens to be mealtime, guests are invited to eat. If a friend or relative passes by the house during mealtime, someone in the house might call out *Vau o kai!* (Stop and eat with us). The passerby will stop and chat briefly but does not normally stay to eat.

Eating

Tuvaluans eat three meals a day. Breakfast (*kaiga i taeao, inuti*) often includes a cup of warm, freshly cut toddy (*ssali kaleve*). Toddy is cut twice daily by older boys/young men who have responsibility for a few trees each. Toddy is a primary source of vitamin C, especially when fresh. It can also be made into a syrup for cooking or fermented as an alcoholic beverage.

Meals are prepared in an *umu* (cooking house), a separate structure that contains an open fire. Meals may be eaten at home or sometimes away, such as when food is taken by women to a returning fishing party. All meals begin with a blessing. Most food is eaten with the hand. The midday meal (*kaiga i ttuutonu*) is a major occasion on Sundays with families eating together, sitting cross-legged on the mat-covered floor. A water bowl is passed for washing before and after the meal. Neighbors share food, especially after a successful fishing trip or harvest.

LIFESTYLE

Family

Most Tuvaluans are in some way related to each other. Each person knows everyone's general kinship ties and uses the information as a behavioral guide. For example, boys are protective of but do not closely interact with sisters or female first cousins. Since one shares character and reputation with one's relatives, one is also bound to share material goods. To be stingy (*kaiu*) is to be despised, and one can ask for goods from relatives without shame.

Households are shared by the extended family. The elderly are cared for by their children and often help raise their grandchildren. Indeed, grandparents are considered the most qualified to raise children and teach them how to behave in culturally required ways. Mothers, however, are the main disciplinarians and fathers take action in cases of severe punishment.

All family decisions are finalized by the elders. Parents are responsible for providing for the family unit. Women cook, feed the livestock, make household items (mats, thatched roof panels, etc.), see to the needs of the family, and work in the *pulaka* (swamp taro) pits. Men fish, help in the *pulaka* pits, and are responsible for agriculture. Older men become more involved in community discussions, and elderly men make *kolokolo* (coconut fiber string) for use around the home.

The typical house (*fale*) is a rectangular structure made of timber posts (from matured coconut stumps), which support a pandanus thatch roof that covers a loose coral stone floor (concrete in some homes). The floor is elevated above a coral rock foundation and is made comfortable by rough coconut-frond mats under fine pandanus mats. The home is fitted with coconut-frond shutters that are lowered when it rains.

Dating and Marriage

Young people meet at community activities, but dating in the Western sense is not common. It is improper for members of the opposite sex to show affection in public, so young couples often meet secretly at night. Mothers are very protective of daughters. Virginity is highly prized in a bride. Some weddings are quietly arranged several years in advance by the families involved; otherwise, couples make their own choice.

Traditional competition between the bride's and groom's families to provide the best and most food at a wedding feast is discouraged on some islands, either by prior agreement between the families about their respective responsibilities, or by a pastor sponsoring a group wedding of several couples and a combined feast afterwards. Celebrations can last for days. The newlyweds spend their first night at the groom's family home and their second at the bride's family home.

Diet

The Tuvalu diet is comprised of *pulaka*, breadfruit (*fuaga mei*), plantains or cooking bananas (*futi*), cooked or raw fish, crayfish, pork, chicken, and such local vegetables as spinach (*laulu*). Many dishes are prepared in coconut cream (*lolo*). Tropical fruits like papaya (*oolesi*) and bananas are eaten. Foods are normally steamed, boiled, or roasted in a ground oven. Tuvaluans quench their thirst with drinking coconuts (*pi*). Imported items have also made their way into the diet, including flour, sugar, rice, salt beef and corned beef, and tea. They are expensive and less nutritious but accorded higher respect than locally available food.

Recreation

Sports popular in Tuvalu include soccer, basketball, cricket, and volleyball. Young people also play a traditional sort of elongated volleyball (*te ano*). Movies are shown in *maneapas* with generators or electricity.

Tuvaluans love dancing. Special occasions nearly always include the traditional *faatele* or more modern *siva* dance. Young people enjoy the more casual *tuisi* (twist) dances, which are popular fund-raising events. The *faatele* is a line dance performed by men or women (most commonly young women) dressed in pandanus leaf skirts and wearing greenery and flower garlands. Dancers tell stories by their body actions, and are accompanied by others who sing, clap, and beat wooden "drums" made from boxes or biscuit tins covered with mats. The *siva* is performed by young women who dance and sing as young men play the guitar and sing.

Holidays

Public holidays include New Year's Day; Easter; Queen Elizabeth's birthday (in June); National Children's Day (4 August), which features children's sports and crafts; Independence Day (1 October), marked by a parade on Funafuti airstrip and dancing; Hurricane Day (21 October), recalling Hurricane Bebe of 1972; Prince Charles's Birthday (14 November); and Christmas. On Funafuti, Bomb Day (23 April) commemorates the day in 1946 when a Japanese bomb fell through the church roof and destroyed the interior. A U.S. corporal had directed 680 villagers out of the building just moments before.

Commerce

Office hours are 7:30 A.M. to 4:15 P.M., Monday through Thursday, with an hour break for lunch, and 7:30 A.M. to 12:45 P.M. on Friday. All stores and offices close on Sunday. Each island has a *Fusi* (co-op) store that carries staples and sundry items. Funafuti's is the largest; outer island stores often run out of supplies. Prices are set by the government. Other small businesses sell clothes, handicrafts, and nonfood household items.

SOCIETY

Government

Tuvalu is a democracy whose head of state, Britain's Queen Elizabeth II, is represented by a local governor general (currently Tomu Malaefono Sione). The twelve members of the unicameral Parliament (*Palamene*) are elected. Each island has representation. All adults may vote at age 18. There are no political parties. Parliament's members choose a prime minister to lead the government. Kamuta Latasi was elected prime minister in 1993. Local government is managed through elected Island Councils (*Fonopule*). The next elections are in 1997.

Traditional chiefs (*Aliki*) still play a significant role in influencing island events. A long-held distinction between chiefly families and commoners is slowly changing, with chiefs now more often selected on the basis of social standing rather than birth. One's behavior, ability to participate in ceremonies and communal gatherings, and public support figure most prominently in establishing one's social status.

Economy

Lacking industry and minerals, and with exports limited to small amounts of copra and coins, Tuvalu's self-sufficiency at a Western level is impossible. Subsistence farming and fishing are the primary economic activities. The islands are too small and too remote to support a large tourist industry. Many women own small businesses that sell handicrafts. A major source of income is remittances sent to relatives from Tuvaluans working abroad. The country earns some licensing fees from offshore Asian fishing boats that harvest skip-jack tuna. An international trust fund established in 1987 by Australia, New Zealand, and the United Kingdom (also supported by Japan and South Korea) gives the government annual revenues. Foreign assistance provides funds for development projects. Employment opportunities are limited chiefly to the civil service. The currency used is a combination of the Australian dollar ($A) paper money and Tuvalu dollar ($T) coins.

Transportation and Communication

Local transport needs are met primarily by bicycles, motorbikes, and walking. Only a small number of trucks, tractors, and emergency vehicles travel the mostly gravel roads. A minibus and a taxi do run between the government center at Vaiaku and the wharf on Funafuti. One passenger/cargo vessel based at Funafuti provides interisland transport, delivering supplies to and collecting copra from outer islands every one or two months. Flights from the Funafuti airport go to Kiribati and Fiji for connection with international carriers.

Radio Tuvalu, a public AM station, broadcasts forty hours per week, including local programming in English and Tuvaluan and twice-daily world news from Radio Australia. The government news sheet (*Sikuleo o Tuvalu*) is published in Tuvaluan, while another paper, *Tuvalu Echoes*, is in English. Funafuti has extensive phone service, while the outer islands communicate via radiophones.

Education

Each island has a public primary school and Vaitupu has a secondary school. The bilingual curriculum places greater emphasis on English at the secondary level. Private kindergartens and primary schools are available. Primary school graduates may go to one of eight community training centers. A maritime school trains merchant seamen. The University of the South Pacific (based in Fiji) has an extension center on Funafuti. The literacy rate is 96 percent.

Health

Dispensaries staffed by first aid *dressers* are located on all outer islands, and Funafuti has a hospital. Care is provided free. The population is generally healthy, due to a reasonable climate, a good basic diet, and a strong tradition in medicinal skills and natural remedies. With population growth, greater contact with overseas lifestyles, and increasing consumption of imported foods (higher in sugar and starch), the rates of obesity, diabetes, tooth decay, and hypertension are rising. The infant mortality rate is 27 per 1,000; life expectancy is 61 to 64 years.

FOR THE TRAVELER

U.S. citizens require a passport and proof of onward travel to visit Tuvalu. No visa is required for stays of up to four months. Travelers pay a $T5 departure tax. Water is usually treated and safe for drinking. No film is sold locally. Be sensitive to local dress standards and do not abuse the many privileges granted to visitors. For trips to outer islands, it is customary to take small gifts (sticks of tobacco, matches, chewing gum, sporting gear, T-shirts, or cloth). Travel information can be obtained from the Tuvalu Embassy, PO Box 449, Suva, Fiji.

A *Culturgram* is a product of native commentary and original, expert analysis. Statistics are estimates and information is presented as a matter of opinion. While the editors strive for accuracy and detail, this document should not be considered strictly factual. It is a general introduction to culture, an initial step in building bridges of understanding between peoples. It may not apply to all peoples of the nation. You should therefore consult other sources for more information.

Printed on recycled paper

Socialist Republic of
Vietnam

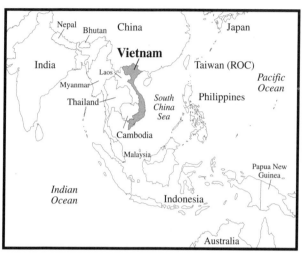

Boundary representations not necessarily authoritative.

A
S
I
A

BACKGROUND

Land and Climate

Covering 127,243 square miles (329,560 square kilometers), Vietnam is just larger than New Mexico and stretches from north to south for nearly 1,000 miles (1,600 kilometers). Flat deltas in the north and south are separated by central highlands that are generally covered by forest and jungle. Hills and mountains are found in the far north. Summer rainfall is heavy in the deltas and highlands. While the south experiences a mostly tropical climate, the north has four seasons (two are short). In the north, the winter months are chilly, but temperatures do not reach freezing. In the south, May to September is hot and rainy, while October to March is warm, humid, and dry. Temperatures are often above 84°F (29°C). Average annual rainfall is 60 to 80 inches (150–200 centimeters). Approximately 22 percent of the land is arable; 40 percent is covered by tropical and upland forests.

History

Vietnam's long history, dating back four thousand years, was partially spent under Chinese domination, which ended in the 1400s. A succession of Vietnamese dynasties followed until French colonial rule took over in the latter 1800s. The French divided Vietnam into three areas: the colony of Cochinchina (south), and the protectorates of Annam (central) and Tonkin (north).

French rule was interrupted by the Japanese occupation in World War II. Following Japan's defeat in 1945, the Allies divided Vietnam into two zones for the purpose of disarming the Japanese. In the south, the British completed the task and restored French rule. In the north, China also completed the task, but ceded power to Vietnam's emperor, Boa Dai, who abdicated in favor of Ho Chi Minh. Even before 1945, the north had resisted colonial rule and Ho was very powerful. He declared Vietnam's independence in 1946 and subsequently led an insurgency against the French and their southern allies. The war culminated in France's defeat in 1954 at Dien Bien Phu.

With the intent of establishing peace, Geneva Accords temporarily divided Vietnam into north and south in preparation for national elections in 1956. The southern regime, led by President Ngo Dinh Diem, was opposed to the Accords and refused to recognize them as binding. Diem did not hold elections as required by the agreement, and a civil war between north and south ensued. The United States, alarmed at the possibility of a Communist takeover in the country, gave substantial support to South Vietnam. This support involved sending American troops and supplies to fight the Viet Cong guerrillas (southern Communists fighting the South Vietnamese government) and North Vietnamese troops (Viet Minh). The war spread to Laos and Cambodia. American activity included extensive bombing in Laos, Cambodia, North Vietnam, and areas of South Vietnam held by the Viet Cong. When South Vietnam's government could no longer maintain popular support and security on its own territory, it became clear that it would not defeat the north. The war ended with the withdrawal of American troops and the fall of Saigon in April 1975. Saigon's name was officially changed to Ho Chi Minh City, but most Vietnamese still call it Saigon. All three Indochinese countries—Vietnam, Laos, and Cambodia—came under Communist governments. Thousands of families fled, and those who remained faced difficult years of poverty, isolation, and repression.

In 1976, Vietnam's north and south were officially reunited as the Socialist Republic of Vietnam. The United States refused to recognize the new government and did not establish diplomatic relations with it. Until recently, this kept Vietnam isolated from most Western nations. After the end of the "American War" (as the Vietnam War is known in Vietnam), troops under Cambodia's Pol Pot regime repeatedly attacked provinces of southern Vietnam. In December 1978, Vietnam invaded Cambodia, deposing the genocidal Pol Pot regime and installing a government loyal to Hanoi. In a related conflict during this period, Vietnam fought off a Chinese invasion. In 1989, the Vietnamese withdrew from Cambodia.

Since then, Vietnam has concentrated on internal development. In 1986, Vietnamese Communist Party General Secretary, Nguyen Van Linh, introduced *doi moi* (renovation), which includes private enterprise and trade, openness to overseas Vietnamese, an interest in tourism, and greater individual freedoms. Since 1989, *doi moi* has been more meaningful and the government is committed to it.

The 1989 peace treaty with Cambodia allowed Vietnam to seek renewed relations with the United States. Washington opened a diplomatic office in Hanoi in 1991 to coordinate the search for Americans missing in action and to pave the way to better relations. Some economic sanctions were lifted in 1992 and 1993, and the U.S. trade embargo was lifted in February 1994. This allowed U.S. businesses to fully participate in Vietnam's economy and trade with Vietnam. The Vietnamese greeted the end of the embargo as the final end of the American War. American investment quickly began pouring into the country, joining many other countries that did not honor the U.S. embargo.

In January 1995, both nations settled long-standing war-era property claims and opened low-level liaison offices in their respective capitals. This was widely seen as the last step before reestablishing full diplomatic relations. Then in July 1995, citing Vietnam's recent efforts to help search for the remains of American service personnel still considered missing in action, U.S. President Bill Clinton granted Vietnam formal diplomatic recognition. The Vietnamese welcomed the long-awaited gesture with expressions of friendship and promises of future cooperation.

THE PEOPLE

Population

Vietnam's population of 73.1 million is growing at 1.8 percent annually. More than 40 percent of the population is younger than age 15. The majority of the people live in rural regions, mainly in the Red and Mekong River deltas and along the coastal plain. The largest cities are Saigon (5 million) and Hanoi (3 million). About 88 percent of the population is ethnic Vietnamese. Two percent is Chinese, an important merchant group. The rest of the population consists of more than 40 minority groups, each with its own language and culture. The government is currently resettling ethnic Vietnamese from high population density areas to less populated highland areas.

Over the years, many Vietnamese fled their country, often in difficult circumstances, in search of better conditions. There are large immigrant and refugee communities in the United States and other countries (some remain in refugee camps). If Vietnam would change its political system, some Vietnamese would return, but others prefer to remain abroad.

Language

Vietnamese is the official language, although there are distinct northern, central, and southern accents. Many ethnic minorities still speak their own languages, but Vietnamese is the language of instruction in school. The most popular foreign languages to study are English, Russian, and French. Most officials understand English.

Religion

Vietnam's constitution has always guaranteed freedom of religion, but only now are people really able and willing to take advantage of it. Buddhism is the most commonly practiced religion (55 percent). Temples and pagodas are visited by large numbers of people offering prayers for success and health to various gods and goddesses. About 12 percent of the population is Taoist and 7 percent is Roman Catholic. Christianity is becoming more popular in cities. Some ethnic minorities remain animists; they practice a reverence for all living things, claiming all life has a soul or spirit.

Regardless of one's religion, nearly everyone participates in ancestor veneration. The Vietnamese believe the deceased go to a place nearby and are therefore accessible to help or hinder the living. Almost every Vietnamese family has an altar for ancestor worship. Family members place fruit and/or flowers on the altar on the first and middle days of the lunar month. Incense is also burned and prayers are made to ancestors for support in overcoming misfortune and achieving good luck.

General Attitudes

The Vietnamese lived under Chinese domination for a thousand years, followed by almost a hundred years of French colonialism (1858–1954). Then came 30 years of civil war that included the war against the United States. This long struggle for independence has given the Vietnamese a deep sense of national pride. People focus on the future rather than the past. They are often baffled by the fixation many Americans still have with the American War, which they see as past history. Because it was very short compared to other struggles, and because two wars have been fought since then (with China and in Cambodia), the American War is not a source of enmity or anger. In fact, rather than being anti-American, most of the people have an interest in all things American. They look forward to doing more business with Americans. Hundreds attend evening English classes just to prepare for friendlier relations with the United States.

As Vietnam faces the future, people are both happy and unhappy. Urban areas are enjoying better basic services, a more open political and cultural atmosphere, and a booming economy. Unfortunately, the countryside—where three-fourths of the population lives—continues to be neglected.

Peasants are still dominated by party officials, still lack access to cultural opportunities and basic services (like electricity), and still live in grinding poverty. The inequality between urban and rural areas must be resolved if all of Vietnam is going to enjoy future prosperity. Better rural conditions are also necessary to avoid rapid, unsustainable urbanization that accompanies mass migrations of rural workers to cities.

Personal Appearance

Everyday dress for both men and women generally consists of slacks worn with a casual cotton or knit blouse or sport shirt. Some women cover their heads in public. For special occasions, the women wear the graceful, traditional *ao dai*, a long dress with front and back panels worn over satin trousers. The Vietnamese do not wear shorts in public except at the beach or work site.

CUSTOMS AND COURTESIES

Greetings

The Vietnamese generally shake hands when greeting and saying good-bye. One uses both hands to show respect for the individual. Bowing the head slightly while shaking hands also indicates respect. In rural areas, elderly people who do not extend their hand first for a handshake are greeted with a slight bow. Women are more inclined to bow their head slightly than to shake hands.

The Vietnamese address one another by full name or by their given names, in which case they add a title that signals their perceived relationship to the other person. These titles are family related rather than professional. Among colleagues, for example, the younger of the two might combine the given name with the title of "older brother" *(ahn)*. A basic greeting combined with the given name and title is *xin chao* (seen-chow). Because Vietnamese is a tonal language, *xin chao* could have six different meanings, only one of which is "Hello." Classifiers for gender and familiarity are also combined with the greeting. The Vietnamese are delighted if an international guest can properly say *xin chao*. In formal meetings, people might exchange business cards while greeting.

Gestures

One should not touch the head of a young child, as it is considered a sensitive spiritual point. The Vietnamese consider it rude to summon a person with the index finger. Instead, one waves all four fingers with the palm down. Men and women do not generally show affection in public, but it is common for members of the same sex to hold hands while walking. The Vietnamese use both hands to pass an object to another person.

Visiting

The Vietnamese have a very strong sense of hospitality and feel embarrassed if they cannot show their guests full respect by preparing for their arrival. Therefore, except between close friends and relatives, it is inappropriate to visit a home without having been invited. Gifts are not required but are appreciated. Flowers, incense, or tea may be appropriate for the hosts. Hosts also appreciate a small gift for their children or elderly parent.

Eating

The Vietnamese use chopsticks and rice bowls for most meals. They hold the rice bowl in the hand; it is considered lazy to eat from a rice bowl that is on the table. Spoons are provided when soup is served. Food is placed on dishes in the center of the table from which each person helps himself. The host might serve guests but usually just invites them to help themselves. If beverages are served, hot tea, coffee, or beer are most common. Often, beverages are not served until after the meal. Tips are not expected in restaurants.

LIFESTYLE

Family

The family unit is traditionally extended, with parents, their unmarried children, and married sons and their families all living in the same household. This is still very much the pattern in the rural regions. In urban areas, there is a tendency for single-family homes. Families maintain strong ties and provide each other with assistance and support as needed. The average nuclear family has six members.

Dating and Marriage

Youth begin dating in their late teens. In urban areas, young people generally go as couples to coffee houses or movies. In rural Vietnam, they tend to socialize in groups. Marriages were traditionally arranged by parents, but this practice is now nonexistent. Young people are free to choose their mates; they are encouraged to marry after the man is at least 25 and the woman 23.

Diet

Rice is the staple food of Vietnam. A fermented fish sauce called *nuoc mam* is the main seasoning used to flavor dishes; special foods are also dipped in it. Vietnamese cuisine is famous for a wide variety of dishes and features excellent seafood. Regional specialties, including vegetables and meats, are often served to guests. Abundant local fruits include watermelon, papaya, bananas, citrus fruits, and others.

Commerce

The average workweek is six days. Most offices are open Monday through Saturday from 8:00 A.M. to 4:30 P.M., closing at noon for one hour. Shops often close for two hours at noon but stay open until about 7:00 P.M. Some larger government stores remain open until 8:00 P.M. Museums and cultural centers keep regular business hours. An initial business meeting may begin with informal conversation over tea or coffee and fruit or sweets. Business attire is conservative but casual. Promptness is important to the Vietnamese; the time stated is the time meant.

Recreation

The Vietnamese enjoy team sports such as volleyball and soccer. Badminton, table tennis, swimming, and tennis are also popular in cities. In urban areas, it is common to see people of all ages out early in the morning for such exercise as jogging, *tai chi* (a form of shadowboxing), yoga, or group calisthenics. Rural people have less leisure time, but spend it in the company of friends and relatives.

Holidays

By far, the most important Vietnamese holiday is *Tet*, the Lunar New Year, which comes in late January or early February. On this day, everyone becomes a year older. *Tet* runs three days during which the Vietnamese spend their time feasting and visiting family and friends. Before *Tet*, houses are cleaned, ancestral graves are refurbished, debts are settled, and strained relationships are mended. *Vu Lan*, a Buddhist holiday emphasizing compassion and forgiveness, falls on the fifteenth day of the seventh lunar month.

Besides *Tet*, Vietnamese public holidays include International New Year's Day (1 January); a day (30 April) to commemorate the 1975 defeat of the South Vietnamese government; Labor Day (1 May); National Day (2 September); and the Anniversary of Ho Chi Minh's Death (3 September). Christians celebrate Christmas and Easter.

SOCIETY

Government

Vietnam is a Communist state, led by a president (Le Duc Anh), a prime minister (Vo Van Kiet), his deputy, and a Council of Ministers. Also powerful is the Communist Party's chairman, Do Muoi. The Vietnamese Communist Party is the only legal political party. All citizens may vote at age 18. The national assembly (*Quoc-Hoi*) has 395 seats. The last legislative elections were in 1992, and the next are scheduled for 1997.

Economy

Although Vietnam's economy was damaged by the war and subsequent embargo, it benefited in the 1980s from *doi moi* and investment from countries not participating in the embargo. For the last several years, private enterprise has been encouraged, and state-owned firms have had to be profitable to remain in business (six thousand were shut down or merged between 1990 and 1995). With U.S., Japanese, and other Asian investment, new plants are opening, previously underdeveloped industries (such as manufacturing, textiles, mining, and oil) are experiencing growth, and entrepreneurs have turned Saigon into a bustling city of commerce. Even Hanoi is becoming more cosmopolitan and business oriented. In 1995, the government worked to streamline management in public firms, set terms for foreign companies exploiting mineral resources, revised other business procedures, and strove to keep inflation under 15 percent. It set a goal for 10 percent growth (in 1994, it was nearly 8 percent).

The dream of the average urban Vietnamese is to become a trader or business person to make money, and many small shops are opening throughout the country. Despite these economic advances, the rural farmers remain locked in poverty. Many men migrate to cities to work temporarily between harvests or at night. Vietnam's great potential for economic progress faces challenges from a growing population, poor infrastructure (i.e., adequate laws, transportation links, skilled managers, and the government institutions necessary to run a market economy), very low salaries, corruption, and a rapidly growing gap between rich and poor. In addition, skilled Vietnamese do not want to work for the government, which desperately needs talented people to improve Vietnam's education, health, and bureaucracy. Agriculture remains the primary activity, employing two-thirds of the labor force. The country's Human Development Index (0.514) ranks it 116th out of 173 countries. Real gross domestic product per capita is $1,250. The currency is the new *dong* (D).

Transportation and Communication

The Vietnamese highway system, built during the period of French colonialism, is extensive, although road quality is variable and rural roads often need repair. Many roads were badly damaged during the war and are still in need of repair. A rail service runs from Hanoi to Saigon through the coastal lowlands. Large cities are connected by air service. Few individuals own cars, but most urban families have at least one motorbike. Bicycles are also used for private transportation. Rickshaws (pedicabs) are commonly used as taxis in cities. Most people depend on local public transportation, which includes bus service to district towns. The communication system is not well developed, but is being updated. The press is controlled by the government, but opportunities for freedom of expression are increasing. The global internet is active in Vietnam.

Education

In support of a traditional emphasis on learning, primary education is free to all, beginning at age five. In some areas, school facilities do not adequately handle all children, so students attend on a half-day basis. The school week is Monday through Saturday. All children are encouraged to finish high school. The dropout rate is increasing as young people leave to look for work. The literacy rate has been estimated at between 78 and 88 percent. University education is also free, but there is stiff competition through examination for limited space. Vietnam has begun experimenting with the idea of allowing students who can afford the tuition, but do not qualify for a government subsidy, to enter a university as paying students. Three private universities have recently opened.

Health

Vietnam's health care system offers free or low cost medical care to all people, but facilities are often inadequate, especially in rural areas. The lack of medicine and proper equipment is also a major problem. Malnutrition affects a large proportion of rural children. Vietnam's infant mortality rate is 45 per 1,000; life expectancy ranges from 63 to 67 years.

FOR THE TRAVELER

U.S. citizens need a passport and visa to enter Vietnam. No vaccinations are required, but travelers may wish to call the U.S. Centers for Disease Control International Travel Hotline, phone (404) 332–4559, for recommendations. The travel industry is growing, but facility quality is not always high. Water should be treated or boiled, and fruits and vegetables should be peeled and washed. Eat well-cooked meat served hot. Avoid using pedicabs that are not associated with hotels or restaurants. Travelers without experience in Vietnam will have the best success with traveling in a group with a Vietnamese-speaking guide. Major credit cards are accepted at most tourist destinations. For information on travel opportunities or visas, contact the Vietnam Liaison Office, 1233 20th Street NW, Suite 501, Washington, DC 20036; phone (202) 861–0737. This office will soon function as Vietnam's embassy. A new location may be chosen in the future.

Printed on recycled paper

CULTURGRAM ™ '96

West Bank and Gaza Strip

Boundary representations not necessarily authoritative.

ASIA

BACKGROUND

Land and Climate

The West Bank is situated between the State of Israel and Jordan, while Gaza is further south, near the Sinai Peninsula. Covering 2,263 square miles (5,860 square kilometers), the West Bank is about the size of Delaware. Except for the city of Jericho, it is an occupied territory of Israel. It has a generally rugged terrain; vegetation is scarce in the east but there is some to the west. There are few natural resources. The West Bank borders the Dead Sea, which, at nearly 1,300 feet (396 meters) below sea level, has the lowest elevation on earth. In the highlands, the climate is cooler and moderate. Overall, the West Bank experiences a temperate climate. About 27 percent of the area is suitable for cultivation.

The Gaza Strip borders the Mediterranean Sea and is only about twice the size of Washington, D.C. It covers 147 square miles (380 square kilometers). Gaza is an autonomous region under self-rule. The climate is also temperate, with mild winters and dry summers. As a coastal plain, much of the Gaza Strip is covered with sand dunes. Only 13 percent of the land is suitable for cultivation.

History

The area known to Christians as the Holy Land was named *Palestine* by the Romans. The history of the West Bank and Gaza is naturally linked to the history of the entire area. Because of its central location between Asia and Africa, Palestine was conquered by many nations. Some 3,000 years ago,

a Hebrew kingdom was established by the descendants of the 12 tribes of Israel under King David. After the rule of his son, Solomon, the kingdom was split into two states—Israel and Judah. Both were later destroyed by Assyria and Babylonia in the eighth and sixth centuries B.C.

After the Persian conquest of the Middle East, Jews dispersed by previous invasions returned to establish a state and build a temple. But the area later fell to the Greeks and then the Romans. In the 600s, Palestine was conquered by the Arabs, who subsequently settled the region. In the 1500s, the Ottoman Turks began to rule and remained in power until after World War I, when Palestine was declared a British mandate. The Balfour Declaration of 1917 pledged British support for the establishment of a national home for the Jews in Palestine, but it also insisted that nothing be done to prejudice the civil and religious rights of the existing non-Jewish communities in Palestine. These two goals conflicted and resulted in problems throughout the mandate.

The United Nations voted in 1947 to partition the area into two states—one Arab and one Jewish, with Jerusalem having a separate status (because of its significance to both). The Jewish State became the independent nation of Israel in 1948. Arab states who had opposed the UN partition immediately declared war. Israel withstood initial advances, but hostilities erupted again into open war in 1956, 1967, and 1973. During the 1967 war, Israel occupied the West Bank, Syria's Golan Heights, the Gaza Strip, and the Sinai Peninsula. East

Jerusalem was also occupied and came under Israeli jurisdiction. As a result of the 1979 Camp David Accords, the Sinai was returned to Egypt and the final status of the West Bank and the Gaza Strip became subject to negotiation.

Peace negotiations during the 1980s broke down several times, even despite the Palestinian Liberation Organization's (PLO) acceptance of Israel as a state. Out of frustration for their situation, the Palestinian Arabs rebelled in 1987 and declared an independent Palestinian state. Their uprising is known as the *intifada*. This led to violent clashes between residents of the occupied territories and Israeli military forces, but it also resulted in peaceful demonstrations, civil disobedience, and other forms of resistance.

A peace conference between Israel, its Arab neighbors, and Palestinians convened in 1991. It marked the first time the Palestinians were able to hold direct talks with the Israeli government. The talks continued into 1993, with little progress due to continuing violence and political conflicts. Only when secret talks in Norway occurred did a breakthrough allow the two sides to sign, in 1993, an initial peace agreement. An actual framework for peace took several more months to construct and the full agreement was signed in May 1994. The agreement ended 27 years of occupation and provided for self-rule in the Gaza Strip and in the West Bank city of Jericho. The self-rule arrangement is to precede possibly greater autonomy in the West Bank. A five-year transition period has been established for negotiations on the final fate of the West Bank. In May 1994, Israeli troops withdrew from Gaza and Jericho and were replaced by a Palestinian police force. Some Israeli soldiers remain to protect Jewish settlements. Yasir Arafat, PLO chairman, was sworn in as head of the Palestine National Authority in June 1994. Israel released many political prisoners and many exiles returned to Gaza.

A wave of enthusiasm for self-rule, as well as diligent work by Palestinian officials to establish the new government, characterized the first weeks of the new arrangement. Even Israelis welcomed the peace and greatly reduced tensions that immediately followed the accord. Conditions soon soured, however, as the Islamic Resistance Movement *Hamas* rejected the agreement and vowed to fight both Israel and the Palestinian Authority. In 1994 and 1995, violent terrorist attacks took the lives of several Israeli citizens, restoring a climate of distrust. Right-wing Jewish groups pressured Israeli officials to slow talks on further self-rule and to crack down on the violence. Still, leaders on both sides of the peace are committed to making it work. In 1995, they announced plans to expand self-rule in the West Bank. Future negotiations may be affected by Israel's elections in 1996, but they are expected to continue.

THE PEOPLE

Population

There are some 1.4 million people in the West Bank and an estimated 730,000 in Gaza. These figures do not include the Palestinian Arabs who live in the State of Israel as Israeli citizens. The Palestinian Arabs of the occupied territories, Jericho, and the Gaza Strip are not Israeli citizens. The figures also do not include about 250,000 Jewish settlers who live in the occupied territories and East Jerusalem through an Israeli government program. Gaza is nearly 100 percent Palestinian. There are also many Palestinians living abroad, either as citizens of other countries (such as Jordan) or in refugee camps. All together, there are about 5.8 million Palestinians in the world. Several Bedouin groups also reside in the area; they retain some traditions but are no longer nomadic.

Language

The language of the Palestinian Arabs is Arabic. A high percentage also speak English or French. English is required as a second language in schools, and French is a popular third language in many (especially private) schools. Because of the Israeli occupation, a large number of Palestinians have also learned Hebrew, although it is an optional language in public schools (except in East Jerusalem).

Religion

Of the Palestinian Arabs, between 92 and 97 percent are Muslims (mostly Sunni). Most of the rest are Christian—generally Greek Orthodox or Roman Catholic, although some are Protestant. Most Christians live in the West Bank. Most Muslims say they are religiously observant, with only about 22 percent being secular. Likewise, only about 18 percent of all Muslims characterize themselves as politically militant because of their religion. Muslims accept major biblical figures as prophets, but do not accept Jesus Christ as the son of *Allah* (God). They believe Muhammad to be the last and greatest prophet of *Allah*, and to have received the *Qur'an* (Koran) by revelation. Devout Muslims pray five times daily while facing Makkah, Saudi Arabia; fast during the holy month of *Ramadan*; try to make at least one pilgrimage to Makkah; donate money to the poor; and follow certain dietary codes. They confess *Allah* to be God and Muhammad to be his prophet. Regardless of religion, being Palestinian unites the people as a group. Christians and Muslims respect each other's religions and honor the respective holidays. Schools are out on Friday and Sunday. Shops close according to the owner's religion.

General Attitudes

Palestinian Arabs value courage, hospitality, and generosity. They generally believe the establishment of the State of Israel in 1948 was illegal and assert they have the right to a sovereign state that provides them with basic human rights, such as the right to vote, freedom of speech, and freedom of demonstration. Even self-rule in Gaza and Jericho does not go far enough to satisfy those who seek full independence. However, the average person living in Gaza is delighted by the new freedom of autonomy. Gazans realize that the future will not be easy, as they must build an economy and a peaceful society, but they are hopeful that a better future will now be possible with the end of the occupation. Residents of the West Bank who still live under the occupation are somewhat less hopeful of acquiring greater autonomy and peace. But, while violent acts against Israeli authority continue to occur, and while many express disappointment with the current situation, people are generally willing to wait for the peace process to work.

Most Palestinians say they respect Judaism, and even Israel's right to exist as a state, but they oppose Zionism as a movement to establish the entire region as only a Jewish homeland. They point to the fact that they, too, have lived in the area for centuries. Palestinians are therefore sensitive to references to the Holy Land as "Israel" because they consider the Holy Land to be Palestine.

Personal Appearance

Western clothing is most common in urban areas and more common in the West Bank than Gaza. Elderly men, or those following traditional Muslim practices, wear long, white, loose-fitting robes and sometimes a turban. Women usually cover their heads with a scarf, although less traditional women wear it loosely and a few choose to go without. During the *intifada*, urban women (more so in Gaza) began to wear tightly drawn scarves, long, loose-fitting dresses, and sometimes even a veil. This switch from Western dress was partly in response to greater religious devotion and partly in response to pressure from religious fundamentalists. With the end of the *intifada*, some urban women are again choosing to wear Western attire or at least loosen or remove their scarves. In small villages, the Muslim dress code remains standard practice.

CUSTOMS AND COURTESIES

Greetings

Al-Salaam 'Alaykum (Peace be upon you) is the usual greeting among the Palestinian Arabs of the West Bank and Gaza Strip. A kiss on the cheek is frequent among close friends of the same sex. A pat on the back or shoulder is a sign of affection. Handshakes are also common. Important to the greeting are various expressions of goodwill and welcome. Friends call each other by their first names. The elderly and other respected individuals are called *Abu*, meaning "Father of." For example, Abu Ahmed refers to the father of Ahmed (the oldest son), whose own personal name might be Ibrahim.

Gestures

It is impolite for the bottom of one's foot to point at another person; also, feet are never propped on a table or chair in the presence of others. Burping in public is inappropriate. It is important to show respect to all elderly individuals, no matter their social status or level of education. Objects are passed and received with the right hand or both hands, especially among Muslims.

Visiting

Except for close friends and relatives, a person will not visit another without an invitation. Relatives and friends may drop by at any time and often do. Visiting is an important part of Arab culture and is a social obligation. When visiting acquaintances, it is polite to ask about a person's family, health, and work. Men also enjoy visiting one another in coffee houses, an activity that is restricted to pre-curfew hours under the occupation but that can occur at any time in the autonomous areas. Women more commonly socialize in the home.

Eating

Eating habits vary between families according to lifestyle. For example, in traditional homes people may eat food with the right hand, often taking their portions from a common plate. More Westernized families eat with utensils from separate plates. In some cases, men will eat separate from women, but families generally enjoy eating at least their main meal together. When guests are present, it is polite for them to accept additional helpings.

LIFESTYLE

Family

Families are often large and play an important role in the life of the individual. The father is the head of the family and the mother takes care of the housework and children. Although few women work outside the home, the number is increasing. Children are encouraged to cherish their heritage as Palestinians. Parents take great pride in their children and find personal success in their accomplishments. Because of this, they will do all they can to help their children succeed and will even support married children if necessary. In turn, children expect to care for their parents in their old age. It is not proper for a family member to die in anger or anguish, so every effort is made to keep the elderly happy. Most homes are equipped with the basic necessities of running water, refrigeration, and electricity. But luxury items are only found in the homes of wealthier families.

Dating and Marriage

Dating is not common. In traditional families, it is forbidden. Girls marry at about age 18 and boys at age 22 or older. Those who do date enjoy going to the beach, seeing movies, or having parties in private homes. At such parties, excessive behavior (drinking, immorality, etc.) is not tolerated. Individuals engaging in such behavior are not accepted by their peers. Cousin marriage is common among the Muslims. Marriages between Christians and Muslims occur, but are fairly rare. A marriage is a time for great family celebration.

Diet

The main meal is eaten at midday or in the afternoon, rather than in the evening. Spicy food is typical. *Falafel* (filled pocket bread) is popular. Other well-liked foods are stuffed grape leaves and spiced rice with nuts. Turkish coffee, tea, and fruit juice are common. Observant Muslims do not eat pork or drink alcohol.

Recreation

Soccer and basketball are the most popular sports among Palestinian Arabs. Playing cards, attending movies, and visiting friends are common activities. Camping is becoming a favorite way to spend leisure time. Gazan families enjoy having a barbecue on the beach. Adults love to socialize at coffee houses or cafés and many people attend performances of the cultural arts when possible.

Holidays

Palestinian Arabs observe both Muslim and Christian holidays. Christmas celebrations in Bethlehem and Easter commemorations in East Jerusalem are known throughout the world. *Ramadan* is the month of fasting for Muslims, who go without food or drink during the daylight hours. In the evenings they eat a meal and visit friends or relatives. At the end of *Ramadan*, a three-day feast called *'Aid al Fitr* is held.

Muslims also celebrate 'Aid al Adha, which comes after the pilgrimage to Makkah and celebrates the willingness of Abraham to sacrifice his son.

Commerce

In the West Bank, commerce is regulated by Israel. Business hours vary according to personal choice, religion, and the current political climate. Under the *intifada,* leaders often called for strikes and other shop closures. These measures are seldom necessary today, but are still possible in the West Bank. More than one-third of all Palestinians work in Israel, as there is yet very little commerce or industry in the West Bank and Gaza. When militant groups commit violent acts, Israel often seals its borders, making it impossible for workers to get to their jobs. During extended periods of such shutdowns, workers may lose their jobs altogether. The Palestine National Authority is seeking ways to create more commerce and jobs in Gaza and Jericho.

SOCIETY

Government

Yasir Arafat is the head of government for Gaza and Jericho and will lead negotiations for Palestinian authority to expand to other areas. There are 24 ministers in the government who have legislative and executive authority; they were appointed by Arafat. According to the Israeli-PLO agreement, the Palestinians have authority in the autonomous areas over specific internal matters, including education, health, taxation, tourism, and social welfare. They also have some control over commerce, and are responsible for day-to-day order. Israel continues to maintain foreign borders and runs joint patrols with Palestinian police officers along key roads. Jewish settlements in the area remain under Israeli jurisdiction.

The West Bank is still administered by Israeli authorities, either directly (in some cases) or through officials chosen by Israel. Elections are not currently allowed.

Economy

Because of the occupation, the economies of both the West Bank and the Gaza Strip are poor and growth has been hampered. Unemployment and inflation fluctuate according to political relations with Israel. On average, though, Gazans suffer from a 50 percent unemployment rate. People in the West Bank generally have higher incomes than those in Gaza. Gazans have a per capita gross national product of about $1,300 and residents of the West Bank average more than $2,000. Both regions are considered poor and in need of substantial foreign investment. The work force is capable of building a solid economy if the necessary infrastructure can be established. Development of substantial or high technology industry had previously been discouraged by Israel, although Israel began issuing permits for a greater number of new Palestinian businesses in 1991. Private enterprise is slowly beginning to expand, especially as wealthy exiles return to invest in promising ventures.

Most industries are small-scale and operated by families. They include cement, textiles, and souvenirs. Agricultural crops include fruits, olives, vegetables, beef, and dairy products. Both new Israeli *shekels* (NIS) and the Jordanian *dinar* (JD) are acceptable legal tender.

Transportation and Communication

Buses are the primary mode of mass transit. Taxis and private cars are also common. Roads are generally in poor condition. Travel between Gaza and Jericho can be made only by specified routes. About half of all families have televisions, but only about 10 percent have telephones in their homes. This inhibits communication and is an area of focus for future development. Newspapers are popular.

Education

Despite a general lack of facilities, Palestinian Arabs have a high literacy rate of about 80 percent. Unfortunately, this translates into about 89 percent for men and only 72 percent for women. Education is valued by society, such that even when schools were closed during periods of the *intifada,* parents organized classes and continued the educational process in their homes. West Bank schools are operated by the Israeli government but Gaza schools are run by Palestinian authorities. There are some private schools supported by international Christian and Muslim organizations. Public schools lack space, materials, and teachers, so Palestinian authorities are seeking aid from donor nations. Nine percent of all Palestinians have had at least some college education.

Health

Health conditions are better in the West Bank than in the Gaza Strip. However, hospital and medical care are difficult to obtain in either region. If found, facilities are often inadequate. Health care is therefore another priority of the new Palestinian government. The United Nations sponsors some medical care programs for Palestinians. The infant mortality rate is much higher in these areas than in the State of Israel. In Gaza it is 37 per 1,000, while in the West Bank it is 34 per 1,000. Life expectancy ranges from 66 to 71 years, depending on gender and the territory.

FOR THE TRAVELER

U.S. travelers need a valid passport, but no visa, to enter Israel. A U.S. passport is also valid for entry to Gaza and Jericho. Travel to some parts of the West Bank may be restricted by the Israeli government. Care should be exercised when traveling because of potential violence. For a recorded message on current travel advisories, call the U.S. Department of State at (202) 647–5225. Contact U.S. embassy authorities in Israel for further information. In the United States, the Israeli Embassy, 3514 International Drive NW, Washington, DC 10118; phone (202) 364–5500, may also have information.

Printed on recycled paper

Republic of
Zaire

Boundary representations not necessarily authoritative.

BACKGROUND

Land and Climate

With 905,563 square miles (2,345,410 square kilometers), Zaire's land area is about the size of the area of United States east of the Mississippi River. It is situated in central Africa, almost entirely within the equatorial zone. The Mitumba Mountains are part of Africa's Great Rift system, running north to south along Zaire's eastern border and separating most of the country from Lake Tanganyika on the border. This range is also prominent in the extreme south. Other important mountain ranges include the Ruwenzori and Virunga, both located in the northeast. Most of the country lies within the vast lowlands of the Zaire River (Congo River) basin. The Zaire River is the world's fifth largest.

Much of Zaire (47 percent), especially in the west, is covered with tropical rainforest. To the north and south of the central rainforest are grasslands, and then north and south of those areas are savannah. Only 3 percent of the land is under cultivation. Temperatures in the eastern mountains and the southeast savannah are cool from May to September, and they occasionally drop below freezing.

The rain forests experience high humidity and warm temperatures throughout the year. Rainfall varies from 40 inches (101 centimeters) in the south to 80 inches (203 centimeters) in the central Zaire River basin. The dry season is generally from April to October, although these months comprise the wet season above the equator, which runs through northern Zaire. The country has many natural resources, a few of which are copper, oil, diamonds, gold, silver, zinc, tin, uranium, bauxite, iron ore, and coal.

History

Long ago, Bantu peoples from western Africa moved into the Congo basin. Several kingdoms existed in the centuries before Europeans arrived. For instance, the Kongo kingdom controlled southwestern Zaire when the Portuguese arrived in the late 1400s. Little European intervention took place until the late 1800s, when Leopold II of Belgium formed an international trading company to exploit the Congo region. The so-called Congo Free State, recognized by the Conference of Berlin in 1884, became, in effect, a feudal estate. Leopold enslaved the people and plundered the land. His harsh treatment of the region inspired Joseph Conrad's novella, *Heart of Darkness*, Mark Twain's *King Leopold's Soliloquy*, and other publications. These eventually aroused an international outcry, and the Belgian parliament was moved to seize the private royal domain from King Leopold in 1908. The area then became known as the Belgian Congo.

After World War II and following the trend in much of Africa, the people negotiated with Belgium for their independence. This was granted in 1960, although the new leaders were not fully prepared to govern such a large country, which they named the Democratic Republic of the Congo.

Soon after the first elections, the province of Katanga seceded. Katanga's separation was followed by general upheaval, the prime minister's assassination, and unrest throughout the region. UN troops were called in to help keep peace in the area. After years of bloody fighting, the revolts subsided in 1965. Mobutu Sese Seko seized power that year with help from Western nations. In 1971, he began an Africanization campaign and renamed the country the Republic of Zaire, after the Portuguese name for the Congo River. Zairians were told to reject foreign models and to draw upon their own heritage in shaping their nation's future. As part of this national campaign, cities as well as individuals were required to replace their Christian or other foreign names with African names, Western-style clothing was banned, and other changes were implemented.

Mobutu ruled a one-party dictatorship through the Popular Movement of the Revolution (MPR). He robbed the national treasury, living in luxury while ignoring the needs of his people. Under pressure in 1990, he lifted the ban on political parties and granted other freedoms that people thought might open the door for democracy. Mobutu allowed a national political conference to open in 1991 with the purpose of establishing a framework for a transitional government and free elections. Unfortunately, Mobutu refused to accept as binding many of the conference's decisions, including one to abandon the name Zaire for Congo and one to dissolve Mobutu's parliament. He did initially agree to the appointment of his chief rival, Étienne Tshisekedi, as prime minister. But when Tshisekedi began challenging Mobutu's authority, the two became locked in a power struggle and Mobutu attempted to replace Tshisekedi, who refused to leave office. Western governments demanded that Mobutu relinquish power, but he refused. In 1993, Mobutu had Tshisekedi ejected from his office building and the country had, for a few months, two governments and two constitutions.

Outside of Kinshasa, the capital, the power struggle resulted in the deterioration of services, schools, transportation networks, and other institutions. Rampaging underpaid soldiers, corruption, and a collapsed economy plunged the country into chaos. Most Westerners left. People in interior towns were cut off because their only means of long distance travel is by boat on the Zaire River. The passenger boats operated by the government had stopped working.

Total collapse was averted in 1994 when a new constitution was adopted and Mobutu agreed to share power over the military. The parliament nominated Kengo wa Dondo as prime minister, and he was accepted by Mobutu. Kengo moved to reduce the size of the unruly military, repair roads and other infrastructure, and reform state enterprises. By 1995, the economy and social structures remained in serious condition, particularly in light of the strain Rwandan refugees placed on eastern Zaire, but the government was at least able to function and begin to address the country's many problems.

THE PEOPLE

Population

The population of Zaire is approximately 42.6 million and is growing at 3.2 percent annually. About 45 percent of the population is younger than age 15. During the last decade, migration to cities has caused the urban population to grow from 25 percent to 40 percent. The rapid shift has hurt both rural and urban areas: cities cannot provide for their expanding populations and villages are losing their labor force.

There are more than 200 distinct African ethnic groups in Zaire, with Bantu peoples accounting for the majority (80 percent). The three largest Bantu groups (Mongo, Luba, Kongo), together with the Mangbetu-Azande, make up 45 percent of the total population. Some minority groups include the Pygmy, Nilo-Saharan, and Afro-Asiatic peoples who mainly inhabit the northeastern part of the country. Although most groups increasingly identify themselves as Zairians, ethnic affiliations remain strong. There are fewer than one million Europeans and Asians concentrated in urban areas. Kinshasa, the capital, has some four million inhabitants and Lubumbashi has more than 800,000.

Language

With more than two hundred different languages, Zaire has had to adopt a special language policy. Although French is the official language and is used in larger businesses, education, and government administration, it is spoken by only about 10 percent of the population. Lingala is increasingly used as the national language of government (military and bureaucracy). Broadcasting, local business, daily communication, and primary school instruction occurs in one of the four national or regional languages, all of which are Bantu. They are Lingala (in the west and in Kinshasa), Kikongo (in the west and southwest), Tshiluba (in central and southern Zaire), and Swahili (in the east). Most people speak their own ethnic language as well as one or more of the official national languages. It is increasingly common for urban people to speak a mixture of local languages and French.

Religion

Eighty percent of the population is Christian. Fifty percent is Roman Catholic and 20 percent belongs to various Protestant organizations. Another 10 percent of the people participate in the indigenous Christian sect known as Kimbanguism, a Protestant offshoot. It was established in the 20th century by Simon Kimbangu. Many Christians also mix traditional animist beliefs with Christianity. About 10 percent of the people are Muslim, residing mainly in the east, but also in Kinshasa. The remaining 10 percent follow traditional beliefs.

General Attitudes

The majority of Zairians are members of one of the many Bantu ethnic groups. Most Bantu peoples share a common cultural heritage. Most distinctive, perhaps, is the general politeness and genuine concern for the welfare of others. This politeness sometimes manifests itself as a gentle disposition and shyness with strangers, which outsiders occasionally interpret as reticence. Although they may seem shy, Zairians reciprocate open and sincere friendliness.

One characteristic of Lingala-speaking Zairians seems to contradict their politeness. Their speech is often abrupt; requests may be made without a "Please" and help accepted without a "Thank you." This is not impolite, but is simply a cultural habit. Lingala was specifically promoted by Belgian colonialists for use by official institutions (such as the police force) because of its directness. Even if a person does not say "Please" (*Bolimbisi* in Lingala or *Tafadhali* in Swahili) or "Thank you" (*Botondi* or *Aksanti*), he or she will show gratitude or politeness through actions.

In general, Zairians are careful not to offend. The desires of friends, family, and colleagues, as well as one's responsibility to maintain the status quo, are paramount forces controlling personal actions. Individualism is acceptable only if it does not conflict with a group's needs. Time is very elastic in Zaire and does not have the importance it does in Western society; Lingala has only one word for both "yesterday" and "tomorrow." Which day a person is actually referring to must be learned from context. Because schedules are not as important as people, appointments may run 30 to 60 minutes late.

Personal Appearance

Western-style clothing is common in most urban areas. A locally styled, two-piece suit (*Abacost*) is also worn by some men. It was introduced by the Mobutu regime in the 1970s as part of an "Africanization" campaign. Until 1990, it was technically a crime to wear Western clothing. Zairian women wear a *pagne*, a long dress made of a five-yard length of fabric, more tailored than an Indian *saree*. Shorts and immodest attire are rarely worn by adults. Children wear shorts.

CUSTOMS AND COURTESIES

Greetings

In urban areas, men and women generally shake hands, smile, and greet each other verbally. The French term *Bonjour* (Good day) is used among the urban elite. But *Mbote* (Hello) is more common. It is followed by *Sango nini?* (What's new?) among Lingala speakers. Outside urban areas, men do not usually shake hands with women but will shake other men's hands. Some rural women greet men by clapping their hands a few times and bowing slightly. In the eastern and southeastern parts of the country, the Swahili greeting *Jambo* (Hello) is common. Other greetings vary by ethnic group.

Gestures

Pointing directly at a person with the index finger is impolite. Beckoning is done by waving all fingers. Objects are passed with the right hand or both hands.

Visiting

Visiting is important in Zaire and hospitality is traditional. Most visiting occurs in the home. Family and close friends often drop by unannounced, but strangers are expected to make arrangements in advance. When a person first visits a Zairian home, a gift is not appropriate. Small gifts, such as food or an item for the house, may be given after a relationship is established. First-time visitors are directed where to sit by the hosts and they generally remain seated. Good friends and extended family members have greater liberty to make themselves at home. If children are present, they are expected to greet each adult with a handshake and perhaps a kiss on the cheek. They are then usually dismissed while the adults socialize.

If a Zairian offers to share a meal, the guest is first expected to show reluctance to join the host's table. But the guest should ultimately accept the offer. Not doing so is impolite. Even if the guest is unable to eat the meal, some of the food should be tried as a gesture of goodwill. Zairians often judge the sincerity of their guests by the way they eat. Even if a meal is not offered, drinks or refreshments are usually served.

Eating

Meals are usually eaten with the fingers of the right hand only. When utensils are used, the continental style of eating is observed, with the fork in the left hand and the knife remaining in the right. Men and women eat from separate communal bowls. When sharing a bowl, people eat only from the space directly in front of them. Only the eldest can distribute meat with both hands to those eating the meal. Hands are washed before and after each meal.

LIFESTYLE

Family

The family is the most important focus in a Zairian's life. Although family structure varies greatly between the different ethnic groups, emphasis is placed on group goals and overall family welfare. Large extended families are the norm in Zaire. They usually live under the same roof or in a group of closely joined homes. In western Zaire, families are mostly matriarchal, with the mother's brother as the male with the greatest authority in the family, rather than the husband. In other areas of the country, patriarchal and polygamous (with multiple wives) families, as well as combinations of these, are common. Urban families, particularly among the more affluent, tend to be more patriarchal and include fewer relatives in the extended family.

Dating and Marriage

Casual dating only occurs among the wealthy in large urban areas. Otherwise, if two young people meet and desire to date, the boy and his family seek permission of the girl's family for him to see her. Subsequent dating usually leads to marriage. Traditionally, marriage is a family affair and is at least partly arranged by parents. Among matrilineal families, the preferred marriage partner is a cousin (one of the mother's brothers' children). However, that pattern is slowly changing, especially in urban areas.

Diet

Staple foods include cassava, rice, potatoes, bananas, yams, beans, corn, fish, peanuts, and various fruits and vegetables. Common fruits include mangoes, oranges, pawpaws, and coconuts. Sugarcane is grown in Zaire. Some foods must be purchased on a daily basis because people do not have ways to keep them fresh. Adequate supplies of food are becoming harder to find in some areas, and malnutrition and starvation are affecting between 4 and 10 percent of the nation's children.

Recreation

Soccer is the most popular sport. Rural Zairians enjoy gatherings that consist of dancing and drum music. Many urban people spend their leisure time socializing, dancing, or listening to Zairian jazz.

Holidays

Zairian holidays include New Year's Day; the Commemoration of the Martyrs of Independence (4 January);

Easter; Labor Day (1 May); MPR Day (20 May), which honors the national political party; Independence Day (30 June); Parents' Day (1 August); the President's Birthday (14 October); Three "Z" Day (27 October), which is the anniversary of the 1971 name change from Congo to Zaire—Mobutu changed the name of the country, currency, and river; Veterans' Day (17 November); the Anniversary of the Second Republic (24 November), which began in 1965; and Christmas.

Commerce

Most people live in small villages and farm small plots of land or catch fish. In the cities, business hours vary. Businesses may open anywhere from 7:00 to 9:00 A.M. and close between 4:00 and 5:00 P.M. Government offices close by 4:00 P.M. In the current situation, both government and business offices may be closed for extended periods of time.

SOCIETY

Government

Zaire is a republic, but Mobutu has ruled more as a dictator than president for many years. Still, his power is decreasing and parliament is hoping to strengthen democractic institutions. Parliament is equally divided between presidential supporters and opponents, and is to be a transitional parliament until elections can be declared. The main political parties include the MPR and the Union for Democracy and Social Progress (Tshisekedi's party). Zaire has ten regions or provinces. Some regions have only limited contact to or relations with the central government.

Economy

Vast mineral deposits and other resources make Zaire potentially one of the richest nations in Africa, but this potential remains largely untapped. The country's Human Development Index (0.341) ranks it 140th out of 173 countries. Real gross domestic product per capita is $469, a figure that is lower than before independence. Zaire's ranking may drop if living standards slide further. Inflation has been so high (10,000 percent in 1993) that a new currency has had to be reintroduced three times in the past few years. The *New Zaire* (Z) was introduced in October 1993 and it immediately began losing value. The devaluation continued into 1995. Urban unemployment is at 80 percent and many government workers have not been paid for months. An informal economy exists for most transactions.

The bulk of the labor force (75 percent) is involved in agriculture. Main products include cassava, corn, palm oil, bananas, rice, rubber, and timber. Coffee is the most important cash crop. Zaire is the world's largest producer of diamonds. It was a principal supplier of cobalt and a major exporter of copper. Mining and mineral processing were the most important industries, but productivity has slipped by 90 percent and many mines are now closed. The most important state-owned mining company, Gecamines, in Lubumbashi (Shaba province), remains open but barely functioning. It was reorganized in 1995 to attempt to save its future.

Vast inland waterways give Zaire great potential for hydroelectric energy. It has one of the largest dams in Africa, the Inga Dam near the mouth of the Zaire River on the Atlantic Ocean. Power is transmitted more than 1,000 miles from the Inga to the southern copper-mining region—one of the world's longest direct-current hydroelectric transmission lines.

Transportation and Communication

While several thousand miles of roadways exist, few are paved and most are unimproved dirt roads. A number of paved roads are crumbling and difficult to travel. Many roads are impassable in the rainy season. Public transportation in cities is all but nonexistent. Private trucks provide transportation, along with taxis in larger cities. The communications system is barely adequate for domestic use. There are no pay phones. The press is generally free to operate, and many new publications have emerged since 1990.

Education

Like the economy, the education system has faltered. Facilities and staff are lacking, and enrollment levels are very low. Few viable institutions exist in interior rural areas. Literacy is much lower than the official estimate of 72 percent. A severe "brain drain" of the skilled and educated is undermining the country's ability to provide adequate education.

Health

There are few physicians in Zaire. Medical help is available in Kinshasa, but adequate health care is a serious problem in rural areas. Medical supplies are lacking throughout the country. International relief organizations or traditional healers are often the only sources to turn to for care. Zaire's infant mortality rate is 110 per 1,000. Life expectancy ranges from 52 to 56 years. Malaria, yellow fever, AIDS, and cholera are widespread. Disease epidemics are common. In 1995, an outbreak of the Ebola virus was discovered in Kikwit, a city of 500,000. Through widespread education and precautionary measures, health officials tried to keep the virus from spreading to Kinshasa and elsewhere. There is no cure for the disease, which causes one to bleed to death internally.

FOR THE TRAVELER

A visa and valid passport are required of U.S. travelers entering Zaire. Fees vary according to the length of stay, and a person must prove return passage before a visa will be issued. Travel to Zaire at this time may not be wise. Crime and instability make travel in some areas hazardous. For recorded travel warnings from the U.S. State Department, call (202) 647–5225. Vaccinations for yellow fever and cholera are required. Malarial suppressants are recommended. Water must be boiled before use, even for brushing teeth. Only eat foods that are well cooked and hot. All fruits and vegetables should be washed and peeled or cooked before being eaten. Do not remove Zairian currency from the country. Be aware of restrictions on photography. For more information, contact the Embassy of Zaire, 1800 New Hampshire Avenue NW, Washington, DC 20009; phone (202) 234–7690.

A *Culturgram* is a product of native commentary and original, expert analysis. Statistics are estimates and information is presented as a matter of opinion. While the editors strive for accuracy and detail, this document should not be considered strictly factual. It is a general introduction to culture, an initial step in building bridges of understanding between peoples. It may not apply to all peoples of the nation. You should therefore consult other sources for more information.

Printed on recycled paper

CULTURGRAM ™ '96

Republic of
Zambia

Boundary representations not necessarily authoritative.

BACKGROUND

Land and Climate

Zambia is a landlocked country sharing borders with Zaire, Tanzania, Malawi, Mozambique, Zimbabwe, Botswana, Namibia, and Angola. It covers 290,583 square miles (752,610 square kilometers). The plateau on which the country lies rises from 3,000 to 5,000 feet (900–1,500 meters) above sea level. Except for the capital, the most populous cities congregate in a region known as the Copperbelt. The Copperbelt lies on Zambia's border where Zaire nearly bisects Zambia. The famous Victoria Falls are near Livingstone on the southern border. In the north stand the Muchinga Mountains. The country shares lakes with Zaire, Tanzania, and Zimbabwe. Three large rivers, the Zambezi, the Luangwa, and the Kafue, flow through the country. The cool, dry season is from April to August; the hot, dry season runs from August to October or November; the warm, rainy season is from November to April. The northwest gets the longest and heaviest rainfall. Average temperatures in the capital of Lusaka are 70°F (21°C) in January, 60°F (15°C) in July, and 75°F (24°C) in October.

History

Between 300 and 1500, Bantu peoples replaced Zambia's original inhabitants and introduced their languages, culture, and institutions, including that of chieftainship, to the area.

The 1800s brought Western missionaries and explorers, among them the Scottish missionary, David Livingstone. The British South Africa Company took control of Zambia in the 1890s and Zambia became a British protectorate in 1924. The discovery of copper deposits led to the establishment of the Copperbelt and precipitated urbanization in that area.

In 1953, the area's European settlers formed the Central African Federation of Rhodesia and Nyasaland from Northern Rhodesia (now Zambia), Southern Rhodesia (now Zimbabwe), and Nyasaland (now Malawi). Northern Rhodesia gained independence when the federation was dissolved in 1963 and became known as Zambia in October 1964. Former African National Congress (ANC) official Kenneth Kaunda became president and head of the ruling United National Independence Party (UNIP). A one-party state was declared and all other political parties were banned in 1972. Kaunda united the country's many ethnic groups, built schools, and attempted to develop a health care system. However, his socialist policies and autocratic style prevented the realization of his goals.

In 1990, after severe food riots, Kaunda agreed to allow multiparty elections, which took place in October 1991 without violence or fraud. Kaunda lost the presidency to union leader Frederick Chiluba. Unlike other long-ruling African leaders, Kaunda peacefully accepted the election results and retired to a modest home in Lusaka.

Chiluba won the election with 84 percent of the vote, and people were very enthusiastic for change. He inherited a poor country, however, and could not meet people's high expectations. While he allowed a free press and promised basic human rights, his government was soon accused of being corrupt and unable to provide the nation with strong leadership. In 1993, Chiluba temporarily declared a state of emergency due to the threat of a coup from his opponents. That threat passed, but a number of his cabinet ministers were forced to resign over allegations of corruption. Chiluba worked to privatize state industries, ended food shortages, and encouraged foreign investment, but transition to full democracy has been difficult.

In 1995 Kaunda came out of retirement to declare his candidacy for president in 1996, citing people's disillusionment with Chiluba.

THE PEOPLE

Population

Zambia has a population of more than 9.1 million. The annual growth rate is about 2.8 percent. With half of its people living in cities, Zambia is one of the most urbanized countries in Africa. Half of the population is under age 15; less than 1 percent is over age 65. Close to 99 percent of the population is African, with only 1 percent being European. The Africans are divided into 73 different ethnic groups, including various Bantu peoples.

Language

English is the official and administrative language spoken by literate people. It is more common in urban areas than in rural areas. Additionally, seven major Zambian languages are spoken: Ichibemba is used in the Copperbelt, Luapula, Northern, and Central provinces; Chinyanja in the Lusaka and Eastern provinces; Chitonga in the Southern province and Kabwe rural areas; Silozi in the Western province and Livingstone urban areas; and Kikaonde, Lunda, and Lovale in the North-Western province. Swahili is spoken to a limited extent in Copperbelt and northern Zambia. There are as many languages as there are ethnic groups. Most Zambians speak their ethnic language in addition to one of the seven national languages.

Religion

It is difficult to determine how many people practice any one religion in Zambia. Many people adhere to a combination of two or more religions or belief systems. Estimates as to how many people practice Christianity vary between 50 and 90 percent, depending on the source of the estimate and whether it considers the combination of Christian principles with indigenous beliefs as practicing Christianity. Likewise, estimates as to how many people practice Islam, Hinduism, and other religions vary. Only a small number of people actually practice indigenous beliefs exclusive of the world religions.

General Attitudes

Zambians are warm and welcoming people, although they may be wary of suspicious-looking strangers. Most Zambians, especially those in the rural areas, are very patient and take life as it comes. In urban areas, where the pace of activities is faster, people are more time conscious. The elderly, chiefs, and persons of high status are shown great respect. The care of the elderly is considered a privilege rather than a burden. Homes for the aged are discouraged, as care is the responsibility of the family. Funerals of near and extended relatives and neighbors are considered extremely important and must be attended as a sign of solidarity and of respect for the dead.

Personal Appearance

Western-style clothing is common throughout Zambia. Men wear trousers or shorts and a shirt in rural and urban areas. Some elderly rural men may wear a short wraparound skirt-like cloth with a shirt. Women wear wraparound skirts with blouses. Rural women often sew their own clothing. Cloth matching the skirt or blouse is often used to wrap a woman's hair.

CUSTOMS AND COURTESIES

Greetings

Greetings vary according to the region and situation. For example, in the Copperbelt region, a common phrase is *Mwapoleni* (Welcome); in and around Lusaka, *Mulibwanji* (How are you?) is common; and, in the south, the preferred term is *Mwabonwa* (Welcome). Adults respectfully address each other on formal occasions as "Mr.," "Mrs.," or "Miss" with their last names, rather than their given names. All local languages have equivalent forms of these terms. Handshaking is generally used to greet in most areas, with the left hand supporting the right to show respect. Kneeling down before the elderly or social superiors is common. Greetings that incorporate clapping and the gentle art of thumb squeezing are also practiced, especially by ethnic groups in the Western, North-Western, and Luapula provinces. Bodily contact while greeting a member of the opposite sex is not traditionally acceptable. Contact between parents-in-law and their children's spouses is also kept distant by most ethnic groups.

Gestures

Handshaking is widely used as a gesture of thanks and friendship. Women commonly clap hands while conversing with others. Girls and women often kneel when addressing elders; men and boys curtsy slightly. Direct eye contact and embracing, as well as public displays of affection, are avoided. Spitting in front of people is a sign of disrespect. Finger pointing is not acceptable.

Visiting

Official and business matters call for making appointments, especially in urban areas. In rural areas or traditional situations, however, people tend to be flexible about time, so allowance is made for delays. An important exception is a visit with the local chief, when scheduling is always taken seriously. Having a visitor in a home at any time is considered an honor to the family. In many Zambian cultures, an unannounced visitor at mealtime is expected to share the food with the hosts. It is considered inappropriate for the host to have to invite the guest to partake of the food. It is also discourteous for the visitor to not join the hosts in eating the meal. Among friends, gift giving is an accepted practice. Both hands are extended when presenting and receiving a gift, and kneeling when giving a gift is also customary in many parts of Zambia.

Eating

In many homes, meals are eaten from communal dishes. Zambians normally eat using the fingers of their right hand. Hands are washed before and after eating. Utensils are used in some homes, mainly with food such as rice or potatoes, but also with *nsima* (see Diet). Water is served with meals. In some areas, especially in villages, the men eat in a place separate from the women and children.

LIFESTYLE

Family

Extended families are important in Zambia, and they are often large. The family structure is somewhat different than in Western societies. For example, in the extended family, a father's brothers are also considered "fathers" in the family and a mother's sisters are also considered "mothers." Cousins are basically considered brothers and sisters. Other members of the same clan who are not actually blood relations may also be considered siblings. Some families are matriarchal, but most are patriarchal. In patriarchal families, the father is the head of the family. In matriarchal families, the mother's brother has the greatest authority.

Dating and Marriage

Traditional marriages take place soon after a girl matures and, in most cases, without dating. Modern marriages are preceded by some dating. In both approaches, elders are consulted and negotiations for the *lobola* (*bride price* or dowry) take place. Church weddings are common, although some couples choose to only register at a district office. The influence of Christianity has decreased the traditional practice of polygamy. Marriages are expected to be fruitful and families

are large. On average, a woman bears seven children, although not all live to maturity. Marital infidelity is common for men and is culturally acceptable.

Diet

Nsima, made from cornmeal, is the national food. It can also be made from cassava (common in the north) or millet (common near the Zambezi River). *Nsima* is prepared as a dough or thick porridge. It might be eaten with a relish made of fish or meat stew and vegetables. Breakfast consists of bread or *nsima* and tea. Rural Zambians often eat sweet potatoes and groundnuts (peanuts) as well. Fresh fruits and vegetables are fairly abundant during and following the rainy season. Two hot meals, lunch and supper, plus breakfast, are the rule for financially secure families. Other families must make do with one hot meal and breakfast. Consumption of beer is heavy. Although bottled beer is available, many rural inhabitants brew their own alcohol.

Recreation

Drinking and traditional dancing are the main forms of entertainment in rural areas. Urban life offers soccer, tennis, basketball, golf, discos, *ifisela* (drama), church activities, volunteer organizations, and social clubs.

Holidays

The holidays celebrated in Zambia include New Year's Day, Easter (Friday through Sunday), Labor Day (1 May), Youth Day (19 March), African Freedom Day (25 May), Heroes' and Unity Day (first Monday and Tuesday in July), Farmers' Day (first Monday in August), Independence Day (24 October), and Christmas.

Commerce

Business hours usually extend from 8:00 A.M. to 5:00 P.M., Monday through Friday. A one-hour lunch break is usually observed. Banks close for a half day on Thursday, but are open from 8:00 to 11:00 A.M. on Saturday. Shops are open 8:00 A.M. to 6:00 P.M., Monday through Friday. They close on Saturday at 4:00 P.M. Rural life revolves around small-scale farming, the main source of income. With the exception of public-sector jobs, rural work schedules are not fixed. Most people are not wage earners.

SOCIETY

Government

The Republic of Zambia has nine provinces. The central government is headed by a president and his cabinet. The cabinet is drawn from the National Assembly. Members of the 150-seat National Assembly are elected by the general population to serve a five-year term. The voting age is 18. The next elections are in 1996. The main political parties include Chiluba's Movement for Multiparty Democracy (MMD) and Kaunda's UNIP.

Economy

Over the past decade, Zambia's economic performance has declined along with the world price of copper. This, combined with high oil prices, high inflation (up to 60 percent), and a growing foreign debt, caused severe economic problems for the country.

Rather than growing, the economy declined by 2 percent per year in the 1980s. Economic problems led to a lower standard of living for most people and are one reason why people demonstrated for change in 1990. The government introduced some fundamental changes in its economic policy in 1990 and some growth was recorded. Under the new administration, free-market principles (such as the end of subsidized food prices) and private enterprise were emphasized, but little progress has been realized.

Zambia's Human Development Index (0.352) ranks it 138th out 173 countries. Real gross domestic product per capita is estimated at $1,010, which is actually lower than the last generation. These figures indicate that economic conditions are not improving enough for people to earn a decent income. Many have no income, but rely on subsistence agriculture. About 64 percent live in poverty (80 percent in rural areas). Still, the existence of an educated labor force indicates that the economic situation for many people could improve with long-term stability, government commitment, and effective social change.

Zambia relies on imports for most of its essential commodities. Mining is the most important industry and copper is still the most important export. Zinc, cobalt, lead, and tobacco are other important exports. There is a fairly large and diverse manufacturing sector. The currency is the *kwacha* (K).

Transportation and Communication

A rail line connects Livingstone in the south with Mufulira in Copperbelt province. The Tazara (Tanzania-Zambia) Railway links Zambia to the Tanzanian port of Dar es Salaam. Buses are the main means of transportation in rural areas, although they are not often punctual. Some Zambians own cars, but they are found almost solely in urban areas. Taxis are available in the cities. Breakdowns are a major problem due to the lack of spare parts for vehicles. Following the British tradition, traffic moves on the left side of the road. A national air carrier, Zambia Airways, operates international and domestic flights. The telephone system is one of the best in sub-Saharan Africa. It, several radio stations, and a number of daily newspapers (two in English) serve all areas of the country down to the district level. Television is available in urban areas and larger towns.

Education

The average literacy rate in Zambia is 73 percent, but it is higher for males and lower for females. Education is free, but the requirement that students provide their own paper is a barrier to many prospective pupils. About 80 percent of Zambian children attend primary school. Because of insufficient facilities and financial constraints, only 20 percent are educated in secondary schools, and only 2 percent in institutions of higher education. There are two universities, fourteen teacher-training colleges, and fourteen vocational and technical institutions.

Health

There are 12 large hospitals and over 60 smaller medical centers in Zambia, but they are concentrated in the urban areas. Health facilities are beginning to operate on a fee-paying basis for such services as medical reports and vaccinations. Medical treatment is free for those who cannot pay, but non-Zambians are required to pay for all medical services. Treatments used range from traditional to modern medicine.

Common childhood diseases such as measles, malnutrition, and diarrhea contribute to an infant mortality rate of 85 per 1,000. Malaria, pneumonia, bilharzia, and AIDS are major health problems among adults. In addition, economic difficulties have led to the breakdown of social services such as treated water and garbage collection. Cholera outbreaks in 1989 and 1990 caused scores of deaths and hundreds of illnesses in urban areas. Shallow latrines, open garbage pits, and polluted water create hygiene problems that allow for epidemics. Life expectancy averages 45 years.

FOR THE TRAVELER

A visa and valid passport are required for U.S. citizens to enter Zambia. Zambia is in the yellow fever endemic zone and a vaccination is strongly recommended. It will be required by any country visited after Zambia. Other vaccinations, such as for cholera, are also advised, as are malarial suppressants. Water is not potable, except in Lusaka. Do not swim in freshwater lakes or rivers. They can be contaminated with a parasitic worm that enters through the skin and causes schistosomiasis. Wash and peel fruits and vegetables before eating, and be sure food is well cooked. To use electrical outlets, voltage and plug adaptors may be necessary. Victoria Falls and national wildlife reserves are popular tourist attractions. For more information, contact the Zambian National Tourist Board, 237 East 52d Street, New York, NY 10022; phone (212) 308–2155. You may also wish to contact the Embassy of Zambia, 2419 Massachusetts Avenue NW, Washington, DC 20008; phone (202) 265–9717.

CULTURGRAM '96

Republic of
Zimbabwe

AFRICA

Boundary representations not necessarily authoritative.

BACKGROUND

Land and Climate

Zimbabwe is a landlocked country in southern Africa. Covering 150,803 square miles (390,580 square kilometers), it is slightly larger than Montana. The country is divided into three regions. The Highveld, where the major cities are located, is the central plateau with altitudes over 5,000 feet (1,500 meters). On both sides of the Highveld lies the Middleveld, which sends water from the Highveld into the Zambezi River (north) and the Limpopo River (south). Near each of these rivers, altitudes drop below 1,000 feet (300 meters); these areas are called the Lowveld. Despite its location in the tropics, Zimbabwe has a pleasant and mild climate because of its elevation. Days are sunny, but not extremely hot; nights are clear and cool. The winter months of June and July are somewhat cooler, but still pleasant. Severe weather is rare.

History

Between the ninth and thirteenth centuries, the area of Zimbabwe was populated by a people that had established trading contacts with commercial centers on Africa's southeastern coast. In the 15th century, the Karanga people (ancestors of the Shona) established a major trading empire at Great Zimbabwe (near present-day Masvingo). The empire lasted until the end of the 17th century, when it came under Portuguese domination. In 1830, the Ndebele people entered the area and conquered the Karanga.

In the 1890s, whites, hoping to discover new gold fields, began to trek north from South Africa. The regions of Matabeland (home of the Ndebele) and Mashonaland (home of the Shona) were claimed for England in 1897 by the imperialist Cecil John Rhodes under the terms of a Royal Charter from Queen Victoria. Rhodes ran the British South Africa Company (BSAC) that colonized much of the region. In 1922, the white voters chose to become a British colony (rather than just a possession of the BSAC) as Southern Rhodesia. In 1953, Southern Rhodesia joined with Nyasaland (now Malawi) and Northern Rhodesia (now Zambia) in a federation, but it dissolved in 1963. Southern Rhodesia, however, was a British colony for two more years.

In 1965, the white-minority government led by Ian Smith issued a declaration of independence from Great Britain. His rule led to ethnic unrest, sanctions from UN members, and several years of civil war. In 1979, an agreement was reached that allowed power sharing with blacks and paved the way to elections in 1980. At that time, Zimbabwe's independence was recognized by the world. Originally, the constitution called for a ceremonial president and a prime minister to form the executive branch of a multiparty parliamentary democracy. The elected prime minister was Robert G. Mugabe.

Mugabe was reelected in 1985. In 1987, his Zimbabwe African National Union (ZANU) political party merged with the other large party in Zimbabwe, Zimbabwe African People's

Union (ZAPU), to form a strong ruling party called ZANU-PF. The constitution was amended to eliminate the office of prime minister and to create a strong executive president. Mugabe was named to the new post. In 1990, he won presidential elections and his party earned a majority in the national parliament. Opposition to ZANU-PF grew in the early 1990s, but was disorganized and divided. Hence, 1995 elections returned Mugabe to office and left his party dominant in parliament.

THE PEOPLE

Population

About 10.9 million people inhabit Zimbabwe. The population is growing at 1.2 percent annually. All but 2 percent of the population is Black African. Individuals of European descent (mostly British) account for 1 percent, and those of mixed descent or with Asian heritage make up the remaining 1 percent. A variety of ethnic groups comprise the Black African population. The largest of these are the Shona (71 percent) and Ndebele (16 percent). While urbanization has increased over the years, 72 percent of the people continue to live in rural settings.

Relations between the races were harmonious after blacks gained political power in 1980. Even though whites held most of the wealth and land, the majority blacks accepted their important role in Zimbabwe's future. And while whites lacked political power, they welcomed the peace that came with full democracy. Unfortunately, when economic hardships hit in the early 1990s, blacks began resenting white wealth and the government began seizing land from whites to give to landless blacks. By 1994, tolerance between the two groups was low and cooperation on many fronts ended.

Language

English is the official language of the republic and is spoken by most educated people. It does not predominate in rural areas, however, where people converse in the tongue of their native ethnic group. Shona and Ndebele are commonly spoken. People often speak more than one language and many mix parts of several languages in daily speech. Both Shona and Ndebele are written languages and are taught in school.

Religion

Zimbabwe has many established Christian churches and missions and a few minority religions (Judaism, Hinduism, and Islam). About one-fourth of the people are Christian. Half practice a mixture of Christian values and traditional beliefs. Traditional beliefs vary and often emphasize ancestor veneration and the belief in spirits and magic. About 24 percent of the people continue to practice traditional beliefs.

General Attitudes

Zimbabwe has an interesting variety of customs. It is, in many ways, a very modern and developed country. In urban environments, one can expect to find the cosmopolitan habits that prevail in Western cities. In remote rural districts, customs are more traditional. Zimbabweans are generally friendly, cheerful, optimistic, and courteous. While very open and enthusiastic among friends, they are more cautious and reserved with strangers. Humility is esteemed. Individually, Zimbabweans are sensitive to racism and discrimination because of the years of colonial subjugation.

Personal Appearance

Generally speaking, Zimbabweans wear Western-style clothing. Traditional African dress is reserved for performing or for special occasions, but fashions from other African countries are becoming more popular. Dressing neatly in clean clothes is important. People do not purposely dress in worn or tattered clothing. Men prefer a suit for conducting business. Young girls sometimes wear shorts, but women generally wear long or short cotton dresses in both modern and traditional styles. It is not uncommon for a woman to wear a scarf on her head.

CUSTOMS AND COURTESIES

Greetings

A handshake is commonly used in greeting. "Good morning, how are you?" is the usual greeting understood by all language groups. "Hello" is also popular. Common Shona greetings include *Manguanani* (Good morning), *Masikati* (Good day), and *Maneru* (Good evening). Greetings among friends may include lengthy inquiries about one's family. A person claps hands when asking how things are. Traditionally, to pass a stranger without any word of greeting is considered bad manners, but this is no longer true in cities. Titles are not commonly used, except in urban areas where English customs are often used.

Gestures

Traditionally, an item is given and accepted with both hands. This is still practiced, particularly in rural areas. A person may clap the hands as a gesture of gratitude or politeness. Women and girls, especially in rural areas, often curtsy as a gesture of politeness. Direct eye contact during conversation is considered rude, principally in rural areas, because it shows a lack of respect.

Visiting

People in rural villages live a slower-paced life than those in the cities. The concept of time is much more flexible in the village than in the city, where people expect invited guests to arrive on time. Unannounced visits are common, especially in villages. While visiting in rural areas, a person may sit or stand without waiting for an invitation. In Westernized urban areas, visitors wait for an invitation from the host before being seated. Small practical gifts for both urban and rural families are appreciated but not customarily expected. Zimbabweans are hospitable and try to make their guests comfortable. Refreshments are always offered, including soft drinks or tea and sometimes a snack. Inviting friends or relatives for afternoon tea is quite popular, and people also enjoy having guests for dinner. It is impolite to refuse refreshments or offers of food. Patience and politeness are important in conversation.

Eating

While many people use Western utensils, it is also common to eat with the fingers in rural areas. Regardless of what is used, water is first provided for washing hands. Depending on the food, rural families may eat from a communal dish. In rural families, parents eat together but children eat in a separate location. When guests are invited, the hostess usually serves each plate, and it is polite to leave a little food behind to show one is not greedy. When finished eating, a person asks permission of the others to leave the table.

Breakfast is eaten before one goes to or begins daily work, and the main meal is eaten after work. Lunch is usually light.

LIFESTYLE

Family

The father is usually the leader of the family, but the mother also exercises influence in the home. The father expects to make all final decisions and to support his family (including children, wives, and any mistresses). Polygamy is still common among some groups. The traditional, extended family unit is strongly evident in rural areas, with more than one generation living together. Urban families, however, tend to be more nuclear. Still, family ties are strong and important. A child is an investment; parents take care of their children and expect to be taken care of in their old age. The concept of nursing homes is highly offensive. The elderly are considered a family treasure and there is always room for them. While urban families often have electricity and running water, some rural families continue to live a more traditional life in thatched-roof homes without such conveniences.

Dating and Marriage

In the past, marriages were most often arranged by families and affection was never shown in public. However, Westernized social patterns are replacing these traditions. Public affection, while not widespread, is not unknown. Young people usually choose their marriage partner. When a couple is ready to marry, customary visits and gifts are exchanged between the groom's representative and the bride's family. The parents plan the wedding. A bridal token, known as a *roora* (or *lobola*), is paid to the bride's parents. Over time, this practice has become more difficult to afford because the bride's family demands more and more. Some segments of society are trying to abolish the tradition, which was once only a small token or gesture. A church wedding ceremony for a Christian couple is often just one of many ceremonies that mark the marriage. It is not uncommon for men to engage in extramarital affairs with the knowledge of their wives. This culturally accepted practice is considered necessary by men to prove virility.

Diet

Sadza, a stiff porridge made from maize (cornmeal), is the staple food of most Zimbabweans and is served at nearly every meal. Various local vegetables serve as a garnish, and meat is eaten when available. In the cities, people tend to eat a more Western diet, including meat and potatoes or rice instead of *sadza*. Locally grown fruits, such as mangoes, bananas, melons, guavas, and papayas *(pawpaws),* are enjoyed at various times of the year. Tea is popular with meals and in the office. Zimbabwe's rich agricultural land usually produces enough food to feed the nation adequately, although the recent drought caused widespread hunger and suffering.

Recreation

Soccer is the favorite sport, but tennis, boxing, rugby, cricket, polo, bowling, field hockey, squash, golf, and horse racing are enthusiastically pursued by various segments of the population. Naturally, income and location have a lot to do with determining one's recreational activities. Swimming in open-air pools is a favorite pastime, but swimming in rivers and lakes is dangerous due to bilharzia (a parasite that has been carried in African rivers for centuries and which infects the liver). People also enjoy watching television and going to movies.

Holidays

The national holidays in Zimbabwe include New Year's Day, Easter (including Good Friday and Easter Monday), Independence Day (18 April), Worker's Day (1 May), Africa Day (25 May), Heroes' Days (11–12 August), and Christmas. Heroes' Days honor the dead. Local religious celebrations are also held throughout the country each year.

Commerce

In cities, businesses, government offices, and shops are open Monday through Friday from 8:00 or 8:30 A.M. to 5:00 or 5:30 P.M. Retail shops remain open until noon on Saturday. Small shops, where necessities and perishables are sold, are open longer each day and also on Sundays. Shops in rural areas keep flexible hours. Banks close at 2:00 P.M. most days, and at noon on Wednesday. Because the majority of the people are engaged in agriculture, work schedules vary and can be long. Women form an important part of the agricultural labor force, often carrying small children on their backs as they work.

SOCIETY

Government

Zimbabwe is a parliamentary democracy. Mugabe is chief of state and head of government. He has two vice presidents and a cabinet. Parliament has 150 members, 120 of whom are directly elected. Twenty members are appointed by the president and ten are reserved for traditional chiefs. The voting age is 18. The country is divided into eight provinces: Manicaland, Mashonaland Central, Mashonaland East, Mashonaland West, Mavingo, Matabeleland North, Matabeleland South, and Midlands.

Economy

Before the 1965 declaration of independence, Southern Rhodesia was one of the most economically developed countries in sub-Saharan Africa. Between 1965 and 1980, civil war, economic sanctions, and other problems damaged the economy and slowed development. Zimbabwe is struggling to recover from its worst drought in this century, forcing it to import food and causing a strain on economic growth. The country is trying to improve its economic situation, basing reforms on a market-oriented economy. The plan to acquire 20 million acres of land held by white farmers and give it to poor black farmers worries some who fear that if the land is given to unproven farmers, the country's food production will decrease. But Mugabe says it is time to allow more people access to fertile land.

Agriculture employs about three-fourths of the labor force. Agricultural products such as tobacco and cotton account for 40 percent of all export earnings. Corn, tea, and sugar are other important products. Manufactured items, including footwear, furniture, and equipment, are very important to the export economy. The mining industry engages in the exploitation of coal, copper, gold, tin, and other mineral resources. The country also promotes its potential as a tourist destination. Unemployment is above 30 percent and inflation is above 20 percent. The currency is the Zimbabwean dollar (Z$).

The country's Human Development Index (0.474) ranks it 121st out of 173 countries. Real gross domestic product per capita is estimated at $2,160, which has more than doubled in the last generation. These figures indicate that the majority of people do not earn an income sufficient for their needs, but that economic opportunities are available to a growing number of urban residents. Up to 60 percent of rural Zimbabweans live in absolute poverty.

Transportation and Communication

Private cars in the cities are relatively common but are not generally used in rural areas. Those who do have cars often use them to provide taxi service (illegally). Buses are the principal means of motorized transportation in rural areas. Bicycles are common, especially among schoolchildren. A railway connects key cities. Zimbabwe is dependent on ports in South Africa and Mozambique for its exports because it has no outlet to the sea. The telecommunications system is extensive but often poorly maintained and therefore not always reliable. Freedom of the press is generally allowed, and newspapers are readily available in the cities. Televisions and radios are likewise common in cities, but limited in rural areas to villages that have electricity.

Education

The literacy rate in Zimbabwe is about 67 percent. The government has been working toward free, compulsory education for all and has built many rural schools to help achieve that goal. While less than half of all school-aged children attended school in 1980, nearly all are enrolled today. Half of all children go on to secondary school, an excellent rate for Africa. There are many primary and secondary schools owned by the government or by church-sponsored missions. Some private schools requiring tuition also exist in the cities. Several teacher-training colleges operate in addition to the University of Zimbabwe in Harare. Commercial and technical training are offered at the polytechnic schools in Harare and Bulawayo.

Health

Towns and cities usually have good plumbing and sanitation systems. Rural areas often lack these, although improvements during the 1980s were substantial. The malarial mosquito has been eradicated in some areas but is still very active in others. Yellow fever and other diseases are also widespread. All basic health services are free to the poor. Traditional healers are often turned to for certain types of illnesses. The quality and availability of medical facilities varies between the cities and rural areas. However, government efforts have brought the infant mortality rate of 1979 (124 per 1,000) down to 57 per 1,000. Life expectancy ranges from 41 to 45 years.

FOR THE TRAVELER

A visa is not required for U.S. travelers to visit Zimbabwe, but a valid passport is mandatory. Officials will also ask for proof of sufficient funds, a travel itinerary, and proof of return passage to the United States. Without these, one may be required to leave on the next flight. Vaccinations are recommended for widespread diseases such as yellow fever. Malarial suppressants are strongly advised.

Zimbabwe has invested many resources into creating an attractive and affordable tourist destination. Wildlife parks, steam engine trains, safaris, a pleasant climate, Victoria Falls, and much more make the country worth visiting. The government encourages travelers not to feed wild animals because they will often need to be destroyed (they begin expecting food and may harm people). Hotel bills must be paid in foreign currency or by credit card; Zimbabwean dollars will not be accepted. Be aware of photography restrictions, especially regarding government property. Information on travel opportunities is available through the Zimbabwean Tourist Office, 1270 Avenue of the Americas, Suite 412, New York, NY 10020; phone (212) 332–1090. You may also wish to contact the Embassy of Zimbabwe, 1608 New Hampshire Avenue NW, Washington, DC 20009; phone (202) 332–7100.

Order Form

Mail to: Garrett Park Press
            PO Box 190B
            Garrett Park, MD 20896

Please send me _____ copies of *Culturgrams: The Nations Around Us*, Volume I: The Americas and Europe.

Please send me _____ copies of *Culturgrams: The Nations Around Us*, Volume II: Africa, Asia, and Oceania.

         ☐ Check for $35.00 enclosed for each book ordered. ($52.50 retail for profit-making organizations).

         ☐ Please bill our organization at $_____ per copy.

Ship to:

_____

_____

_____

_____

Bill to (if different):

_____

_____

_____

_____

Order Form

Mail to: Garrett Park Press
            PO Box 190B
            Garrett Park, MD 20896

Please send me _____ copies of *Culturgrams: The Nations Around Us*, Volume I: The Americas and Europe.

Please send me _____ copies of *Culturgrams: The Nations Around Us*, Volume II: Africa, Asia, and Oceania.

         ☐ Check for $35.00 enclosed for each book ordered. ($52.50 retail for profit-making organizations).

         ☐ Please bill our organization at $_____ per copy.

Ship to:

_____

_____

_____

_____

Bill to (if different):

_____

_____

_____

_____